THE POPULAR & THE CANONICAL

Edited by David Johnson

Debating Twentieth-Century Literature
1940–2000

Routledge
Taylor & Francis Group

in association with

This publication forms part of an Open University course A300, *Twentieth-Century Literature: Texts and Debates*. The complete list of texts which make up this course can be found in the Preface. Details of this and other Open University courses can be obtained from the Student Registration and Enquiry Service, The Open University, PO Box 625, Milton Keynes MK7 6YG, United Kingdom: tel. +44 (0)1908 653231; email general-enquiries@open.ac.uk

Alternatively, you may visit the Open University website at http://www.open.ac.uk where you can learn more about the wide range of courses and packs offered at all levels by The Open University.

To purchase a selection of Open University course materials visit the webshop at www.ouw.co.uk, or contact Open University Worldwide, Michael Young Building, Walton Hall, Milton Keynes MK7 6AA, United Kingdom for a brochure. tel. +44 (0)1908 858785; fax +44 (0)1908 858787; e-mail ouwenq@open.ac.uk

Published by Routledge; written and produced by The Open University

Routledge
2 Park Square
Milton Park
Abingdon
Oxfordshire
OX14 4RN

The Open University
Walton Hall
Milton Keynes
MK7 6AA

First published 2005.

Edited, designed and typeset by The Open University.

Printed and bound in the United Kingdom by The Alden Group, Oxford.

British Library Cataloguing in Publication Data: applied for

Library of Congress Cataloging in Publication Data: applied for

ISBN 0 415 35169 3

1.1

235900B/a300b1introi1.1

CONTENTS

Preface v

PART 1 Varieties of the popular

Introduction to Part 1 3
DAVID JOHNSON

Chapter 1 Daphne du Maurier, *Rebecca* 13
NICOLA J. WATSON

Chapter 2 The poetry of Frank O'Hara and Allen Ginsberg 57
SUE ASBEE

Chapter 3 Philip K. Dick, *Do Androids Dream of Electric Sheep?* . . . 108
ANDREW M. BUTLER

Chapter 4 Manuel Puig, *Kiss of the Spider Woman* 153
KATIE GRAMICH

PART 2 Judging literature

Introduction to Part 2 199
DAVID JOHNSON

Chapter 5 Samuel Beckett, *Waiting for Godot* 210
SUMAN GUPTA

Chapter 6 The poetry of Seamus Heaney 262
RICHARD DANSON BROWN

Chapter 7 Abdulrazak Gurnah, *Paradise* 294
SUSHEILA NASTA

Chapter 8 Pat Barker, *The Ghost Road* 344
LYNDA PRESCOTT

Reader references 400

Appendix 403

Acknowledgements 428

Index 429

PREFACE

The Popular and the Canonical: Debating Twentieth-Century Literature 1940–2000 is the second book in the three-volume series for the third-level Open University course A300 *Twentieth-Century Literature: Texts and Debates*. The other books in the series are *Aestheticism and Modernism: Debating Twentieth-Century Literature 1900–1960* (edited by Richard Danson Brown and Suman Gupta) and *A Twentieth-Century Literature Reader: Texts and Debates* (edited by Suman Gupta and David Johnson).

The three books should ideally be read together as a series of linked studies and debates. However, *The Popular and the Canonical* also stands on its own as an innovative way of reading the literature of the second half of the twentieth century. Following a loosely chronological sequence, *The Popular and the Canonical* is organized around two major debates about twentieth-century literature: What are the major varieties of popular literature? How are we to judge literature? After introductions to each of the two debates, the chapters that follow focus on key literary texts that illuminate these debates. By means of direct exposition and question-and-answer exercises, each chapter provides exemplary close textual analysis, historical contextualization and discussion of the literary texts' reception histories. Avoiding definitive readings of the selected literary texts, the chapters simultaneously develop critical reading skills and convey a vivid sense of the contested nature of critical interpretation.

In Part 1, 'Varieties of the popular', competing definitions of 'the popular' are considered, and a number of on-going debates about popular literature introduced: What is the relation between popular literature and elite/high/classic literature? Can literary texts defined as 'popular' in one context subsequently be defined as 'elite' in another context? Are certain genres of popular literature axiomatically feminine or masculine? How is popular literature related to other cultural forms such as film or television? What political significance can be attributed to popular literature? These debates are developed in relation to the following literary texts: Daphne du Maurier's popular bestseller *Rebecca*, the poetry of Frank O'Hara and Allan Ginsberg, Philip K. Dick's science-fiction novel *Do Androids Dream of Electric Sheep?* and Manuel Puig's postmodern novel *Kiss of the Spider Woman*.

In Part 2, 'Judging literature', working definitions of key terms of literary judgement – 'taste', 'aesthetic' and 'canon' – are provided, and the views of different philosophers and critics on the practice of judging literature are surveyed. Debates about how literature should be judged are introduced: Can literature be judged according to exclusively literary criteria? What influence do extra-literary factors (class bias, masculine bias, Eurocentric bias) exert in the judging of literature? What is the relationship between judging literature and commercial publishing, the education system and the wider political culture? To focus these questions, case studies of two major literary prizes – the Nobel Prize for Literature and the Booker Prize for Fiction – are undertaken. For each prize, there are separate chapters on two literary works: for the Nobel Prize, 1969 winner Samuel Beckett's *Waiting for Godot* and the poetry of 1995 winner Seamus Heaney; for the Booker Prize, Abdulrazak Gurnah's *Paradise* (runner-up in 1994) and Pat Barker's *The Ghost Road* (winner in 1995).

Open University courses are collaborative ventures that involve the labour of many people. Sincere thanks are due to members of the A300 course team who did not write for this volume but contributed generously to discussions that shaped and developed it – Delia De Sousa Correa, Sara Haslam, Lynda Morgan, Steve Padley, Clare Spencer and Dennis Walder; the course manager, Martyn Field; the course editors, Julie Bennett, Hazel Coleman and Alan Finch; and the external assessor, Susan Bassnett.

D.J.

PART 1

Varieties of the popular

Introduction to Part 1

DAVID JOHNSON

Popular literature in the twentieth century has been the focus of much energetic debate. The four chapters in Part 1 of this book look at literary texts that either exemplify popular literature or the appropriation of popular literature into more elite literary forms.

Part 1 commences with Nicola J. Watson's chapter on Daphne du Maurier's popular bestseller *Rebecca*. The second chapter, by Sue Asbee, focuses on two 1950s US poets who engaged with the popular in different ways: Frank O'Hara and Allen Ginsberg. The third chapter, by Andrew M. Butler, shifts to Philip K. Dick's popular science-fiction novel *Do Androids Dream of Electric Sheep?* Part 1 concludes with Katie Gramich's chapter on Manuel Puig's *Kiss of the Spider Woman*, a novel from Argentina that celebrates and extends popular forms. In the course of analysing the distinctive textual and contextual qualities of these selected literary works, a number of interrelated debates are addressed – these are outlined below.

What is popular literature?

The answer to this question is rather less self-evident than you might expect. Both terms – 'popular' and 'literature' – appear in Raymond Williams's *Keywords: A Vocabulary of Culture and Society* (1983). **Read the extracts from Williams's definitions of the two words given below. List the meanings of 'popular', then those of 'literature'. On this basis, write down a preliminary definition of 'popular literature'.**

> **Popular** was originally a legal and political term, from *popularis*, L[atin] – belonging to the people ... **Popular** ... referred to a political system constituted or carried on by the whole people, but there was also the sense (cf. common) of 'low' or 'base'. The transition to the dominant modern meaning of 'widely favoured' or 'well-liked' is interesting in that it contains a strong element of setting out to gain favour ... [From the nineteenth century] **popular** was being seen from the point of view of the people rather than from those seeking favour or power from them. Yet the earlier sense has not died. **Popular culture** was not identified by *the people* but by others, and it still carries two older senses: inferior kinds of work (cf. **popular literature, popular press** as distinguished from *quality press*); and work deliberately setting out to win favour (**popular journalism** ... or **popular entertainment**); as well as the modern sense of well-liked by

many people, with which, of course, in many cases, the earlier senses overlap. The sense of popular culture as the culture actually made by people for themselves is different from all these.

(Williams, 1983, pp.236–7)

Literature came into English, from C14 [the fourteenth century], in the sense of polite learning through reading ... Thus a man of **literature**, or of *letters*, meant what we would now describe as a man of wide reading ... **English literature** appears [at the end of the eighteenth century] ... the sense of a 'nation' having 'a literature' is a crucial social and cultural, probably also political, development ... But there has been a steady distinction and separation of other kinds of writing – philosophy, essays, history, and so on – which may or may not possess **literary merit** or be of **literary interest** ... but which are not now normally described as **literature**, which may be understood as well-written books but which is even more clearly understood as well-written books of an *imaginative* or *creative* kind ... many, even most poems and plays and novels are not seen as **literature**; they fall below its level, in a sense related to the old distinction of *polite learning*; they are not 'substantial' or 'important' enough to be called **works of literature**. A new category of **popular literature** or the **sub-literary** has then to be instituted, to describe works which may be *fiction* but which are not *imaginative* or *creative*, which are therefore devoid of *aesthetic* interest, and which are not *art*.

(Williams, 1983, pp.184–6)

According to Williams, the meanings that have been associated with the term 'popular' include: (1) belonging to the people; (2) low or base; (3) well-liked by many people; (4) deliberately seeking favour or wide approval; (5) inferior (as opposed to quality); (6) past and contemporary literature/culture/art made by the people. Some of these meanings overlap and supplement each other, but the mix of negative (low or base, inferior) and positive (belonging to the people, well-liked) connotations of 'popular' alert us to the need to interrogate precisely what the term means in every context it is used.

What about 'literature'? According to Williams, the meaning of 'literature', like the meaning of 'popular', is unstable, and has shifted considerably since its first appearance in the English language. The meanings of 'literature' have included: (1) the writings that constitute polite learning; (2) a body of writing produced by a particular nation ('English' literature); (3) creative or imaginative writing; (4) substantial or important writing; and (5) writing with aesthetic interest that can be classed as art. These criteria for identifying particular writings as 'literature' function efficiently enough with obvious cases like William Shakespeare or John Milton, but in the final quarter of the twentieth century, much critical energy has been expended in disputing which additional writings – writings by women, writings from beyond England, popular fiction and children's literature, for example – should be admitted to the canon of English literature. Williams's awkward final sentence on 'popular literature' or the 'sub-literary' in the second extract attests to these controversies, and to the entrenched nature of the inherited oppositions, as the former term is cast as an oxymoron, and the latter as a patronizing concession.

It is over twenty years since Williams produced these definitions, and in the intervening years the term 'popular literature' has achieved a much wider academic acceptance. This has happened principally through the expansion of the definition of literature to incorporate previously excluded varieties of writing. In her part-autobiographical study of popular fiction *A Feeling for Books* (1997), Janice Radway explains the changing status of the popular within the study of English literature as follows:

> [The change is] the product of a cataclysmic upheaval in the world of literary studies, an upheaval whose effects had only just begun to emerge in 1985 ... That upheaval has produced profound challenges to older ways of conceiving literature as an honorific category and to related ways of justifying its professional study. I suspect, in fact, that the disputatious, stringent, recalcitrant voices behind movements such as feminist criticism, reader response theory, psychoanalysis, a revivified Marxist criticism, and cultural studies solicited my identification in part because they duplicated the sense of distance I already felt from high culture in spite of all my efforts to seek access to its mysteries.
>
> (Radway, 1997, p.8)

Radway's doubts about what she terms 'the secular religion of high culture' (1997, p.9) were widely shared, and by 2000 popular literature was no longer an embarrassing contradiction in terms, but a substantial and expanding branch of the academic industry. Accompanying this change has been the widespread incorporation of literary studies into cultural studies, with popular literature increasingly studied alongside other popular forms, such as film and television.

We might accordingly draw together at this stage a minimum definition of popular literature: *imaginative writing with wide appeal*. However, this definition is no more than a point of departure for considering the many debates over how a wide variety of writings have been understood in relation to popular culture. In the chapters that follow on du Maurier, O'Hara and Ginsberg, Dick, and Puig, you will encounter a number of different definitions and explore the on-going debates about popular literature that proceed from such differences. Among other things, the following debates are discussed.

- What are the defining characteristics of the different genres of popular literature? In particular, what is the importance of gender in defining popular genres? This debate is given particular prominence in the discussions of the popular forms conventionally regarded as feminine (romances like *Rebecca*) and as masculine (science-fiction novels like *Do Androids Dream of Electric Sheep?*).

- How do definitions of popular literature change in different contexts? Such changes in definition might occur over time (as in the re-classification of nineteenth-century popular novels by Charles Dickens or the Brontës as literary classics in the twentieth century), or over space (as in the different meaning that attaches to popular Hollywood culture in postcolonial contexts such as the Argentine police state of Puig's *Kiss of the Spider Woman*).

- How is popular literature defined in relation to certain overlapping or closely related categories of literature or culture? For example, the relationship between popular music (Bob Dylan) and Ginsberg's poetry is discussed in Chapter 2, and the relationship between Dick's *Androids* and different forms of science-fiction writing, and indeed science-fiction film, is discussed in Chapter 3.

- What is the place of the audience in defining popular literature? One literary historian has pointed out that 'writers of an earlier period who were considered avant-garde now often sell in numbers which give their work a real purchase in contemporary cultural life. Just take one example – Virginia Woolf's *Mrs Dalloway*. In her lifetime this never sold more than 1,500 copies a year. Today it sells 30,000 a year in paperback: more than some Mills and Boon titles' (Worpole, 1984, p.11). Does this mean that Woolf's novels – or indeed 'classics' like *Pride and Prejudice* that entered the bestseller lists following successful television or film adaptations – are now 'popular literature'?

What is the opposite of popular literature?

In the nineteenth century, Matthew Arnold set up a fundamental opposition between 'the popular' and 'culture'. In *Culture and Anarchy* (1869), Arnold divided English society into three great classes: Barbarians (the aristocracy), Philistines (the middle class) and Populace (the working class). Although part of the Populace was law-abiding, 'the vast portion', Arnold complains, 'is beginning to perplex us by marching where it likes, meeting where it likes, bawling what it likes, breaking what it likes' (1993, p.107). In other words, the Populace is threatening anarchy. Arnold's proposed antidote was the energetic propagation of culture, understood as 'the best that has been thought and known in the world current everywhere ... the best knowledge, the best ideas of their time' (*ibid.*, p.79). Culture was to act as a buffer against the anarchy of the Populace that was menacing the world, and a fundamental element of Arnold's idea of culture was literature, understood as canonical writers such as Shakespeare, Milton and Byron. By contrast, popular fiction – described as repetitive, formulaic and exploitative works written for mass consumption – was substantially to blame for England's social crisis.

Arnold's diagnosis was elaborated in the first part of the twentieth century by F.R. Leavis, Q.D. Leavis and Denys Thompson. In *Mass Civilisation and Minority Culture* (1930), F.R. Leavis insisted on the imperative to value the great literary tradition of Dante, Shakespeare, Charles Baudelaire and Thomas Hardy. In collaboration with Denys Thompson in *Culture and Environment* (1933), he confronted the dangers of popular culture: 'films, newspapers, publicity in all forms, commercially-catered fiction – all offer satisfaction of the lowest level' (p.3). The most extended study of popular fiction in this period was Q.D. Leavis's *Fiction and the Reading Public* (1939), which noted that 'the bulk of the public does not buy many books but borrows or hires them', and that the public libraries reveal (for Q.D. Leavis) depressing borrowing patterns: 'A librarian who has made the experiment of putting "good" fiction into his library [the novels of D.H. Lawrence, Virginia Woolf, James Joyce, T.F. Powys and E. M. Forster are Q.D. Leavis's examples] will report that no one would take it out, whereas if he were to put two hundred copies of Edgar Wallace's [popular] detective stories on the shelves, they would all be gone the same day' (pp.4–5). Leavis concludes that despite her gloomy prognosis, teachers and researchers 'fired by a missionary spirit' (*ibid.*, p.271) have the capacity to educate taste, and thus undo at least some of the harm done by popular literature.

One US variant of the Arnold/Leavis position is provided by Dwight Macdonald in his essay 'A Theory of Mass Culture' (1953). Macdonald believes mass culture to be a more accurate term than popular culture, 'since its distinctive mark is that it is solely and directly an article for mass consumption, like chewing gum' (in Rosenberg and White, 1957, p.59). He objects that mass culture, unlike folk art, which was the culture of the common people, growing 'from below' in times before the Industrial Revolution, is 'imposed from above. It is fabricated by technicians hired by businessmen; its audiences are passive consumers, their participation limited to the choice between buying and not buying' (in *ibid.*, p.60). Further, he argues that in the past, folk art and 'high' culture were separated, the 'watertight compartments corresponded to the sharp line once drawn between the common people and the aristocracy' (in *ibid.*, p.61); in twentieth-century US society, however, mass culture has been 'a dynamic, revolutionary force, breaking down the old barriers of class, tradition, taste, and dissolving all cultural distinctions' (in *ibid.*, p.62). While many might embrace such democratic developments, Macdonald fears them and seeks rigorously to conserve the opposition between high and mass culture.

Another way of conceiving the relation between popular literature and its more elevated opposites is the one invented by the modernists, who insisted that 'serious' literature should always administer the shock of the new, and should reinvent from scratch its readers' perceptions of everything. Furthermore, serious literature is for them produced by an 'avant-garde', writers 'ahead of their time', who for reasons attributed to their exceptional ability are never taken up by a mass readership, and are read only by a small discerning audience. By contrast, popular literature is produced by journeyman writers following rigid formulae, who make immediately 'readable' texts derived from serious/high literary classics. Critics who, like F.R. Leavis, were sympathetic to T.S. Eliot's conservative modernism, dismissed this mass audience for popular literature as 'middlebrow'. However, Eliot's was but one of many competing modernisms, and certain left-wing modernist avant-garde writers (such as Bertolt Brecht) viewed 'the popular' rather more sympathetically, seeking to turn popular forms to radical uses.

Let us sum up then. First, let us add to our preliminary definition of popular literature: it is written for middle-class philistines and the working-class mob (Arnold); it is made up of inferior, formulaic, trivial, mass-produced cultural products (Leavises, Macdonald); it is to be distinguished from worthy folk literature of the past (Macdonald); and it is consumed by a middlebrow readership (Eliot). Popular literature contrasts with the tradition of great literature, exemplified by Dante, Shakespeare and Tolstoy, the classics appreciated by an intellectual elite, who are distinguished from aristocrat, philistine and mob alike (Arnold/Leavises). This literature is produced by a self-conscious avant-garde, and aspires to and attains levels of seriousness absent in popular literature. In two lines:

> Popular, low, mass, philistine and mob, formulaic, trivial
>
> Minority, high, elite, avant-garde, classic, serious.

What is the relation between the popular and the minority/high/elite/avant-garde?

These categorical differences between popular and minority literature imposed by literary critics are frequently flouted both in literary works and in the reading patterns of actual audiences. The four chapters that make up Part 1 of this book highlight many instances where borrowings across high and popular divisions have occurred: in the first chapter, Watson considers the borrowings from the classic *Jane Eyre* (high) in the romance *Rebecca* (popular); in the second chapter, Asbee analyses O'Hara's borrowings from jazz and Hollywood (popular) to lyric poetry (high); in the third chapter, Butler analyses Dick's integration of philosophy (high) into a science-fiction novel (popular); and in the final chapter, Gramich examines Puig's extensive reworkings of Hollywood films (popular) in the work of a serious novel (high). In each instance, the precarious authority of the conventional high–popular divisions is underlined. It is important to note that these borrowings occur not only from one form of literature to another (as in *Rebecca* and *Jane Eyre*), but also across different forms of cultural production (from music and film to literature – as in the cases of O'Hara and Puig), and across different academic disciplines (from philosophy to literature – as in the case of *Do Androids Dream of Electric Sheep?*).

The interrogation of the high–popular opposition is developed in a different direction in Part 1 of this book through the extended consideration of the relation between the popular and postmodernism. The defining characteristic of postmodernism is 'incredulity toward metanarratives' (Lyotard, 1984, p.47). Lyotard's term 'metanarrative' can be glossed as 'the general stories that frame many smaller stories'; examples of metanarratives include political stories (for example, that all societies ultimately progress towards the western nation state), economic stories (capitalism is the most efficient form of production and distribution) and cultural stories. Lyotard's version of postmodernism disputes the authority of these metanarratives, and insists that all minority narratives subject to them be given at least equal credence. In the context of cultural stories, arguably the most powerful metanarrative in literary criticism is the one that scripts the hierarchy of high and popular categories of literature. Accordingly, postmodernism relishes disrupting the high–popular hierarchy, and in the chapters on Dick's and Puig's novels two vivid literary articulations of the popular and the postmodern are examined in some detail.

What value – cultural, aesthetic, social, political – is attached to popular literature?

It is a truism to observe that twentieth-century critics have interpreted popular literature in a variety of ways. The contrast between critics in the 1930s, such as the Leavises, who despised popular literature, and critics in the 1990s, such as Janice Radway, who embraced popular literature, are vivid enough, and might be explained as a consequence of political and generational differences. However, these shifts, which have been explored by cultural historians such as John Carey (1992), are complex, and cannot be reduced to simplistic narratives of progress. For example, even critics of the same generation and with common political commitments have disagreed sharply over popular literature. The following two passages, both written by influential Marxist critics, are informed by very different views of Walt Disney's popular cartoon characters. The first was written by Walter Benjamin in 1937 and the second by Theodor Adorno and Max Horkheimer in 1944. **Read the two passages and summarize the views of first Benjamin, then Adorno and Horkheimer.**

> The existence of Mickey Mouse is such a dream for contemporary man. His life is full of miracles – miracles that not only surpass the wonders of technology, but make fun of them ... And to people who have grown weary of the endless complications of everyday living and to whom the purpose of existence seems to have been reduced to the most distant vanishing point on an endless horizon, it must come as a tremendous relief to find a way of life in which everything is solved in the simplest and most comfortable way, in which a car is no heavier than a straw hat and the fruit on the tree becomes round as quickly as a hot-air balloon.
>
> (in Benjamin, 1999, pp.734–5)

> In so far as cartoons do any more than accustom the senses to the new tempo, they hammer into every brain the old lesson that continuous friction, the breaking down of all individual resistance, is the condition of life in this society. Donald Duck in the cartoons and the unfortunate in real life get their thrashing so that the audience can learn to take their own punishment.
>
> (Adorno and Horkheimer, [1944] 1979, p.138)

Benjamin recognizes the pleasure Mickey Mouse affords 'contemporary man', and argues that the impossible miracles and sheer fun in the Disney cartoons provide a welcome relief to 'people grown weary of the endless complications of everyday life'. By contrast, Adorno and Horkheimer argue that the repeated lesson of Disney's cartoons is that 'the breaking down of individual resistance is the condition of life in this society'. Donald Duck's thrashings in the cartoons teach audiences to accept their own punishments in life. Benjamin suggests that the pleasure afforded by Mickey Mouse must be acknowledged in order to understand its success, whereas Adorno and Horkheimer see nothing more than crude thought control by the culture industry when they watch Donald Duck. Of course, Benjamin and Adorno and Horkheimer qualify and develop these quite simple points in sophisticated ways, but nonetheless their differences here do convey a sense of the range of arguments that have been made about popular literature. Not that they exhaust the range of critical opinion: Ginsberg, for example, rejects Adorno and Horkheimer's pessimistic views, and writes much of his poetry on the assumption that popular forms can be used to protest against power.

Without seeking at the outset to prejudice the force of Adorno and Horkheimer's views of popular culture – which, despite fundamental political differences, he shares with the Leavises and Macdonald – the chapters of Part 1 approach popular literature more in the spirit of Benjamin when in 1929 he defended the nineteenth-century genre of chambermaid's romances as follows: 'a start should be made with cheap fiction ... if indeed literary history is ever going to explore the geological structure of the book alps, rather than confining itself to a view of the peaks' (in Benjamin, 1999, p.224). Unlike Lyotard, Benjamin retains a sense of literary peaks and valleys with his geological metaphor, but he rejects confining study to literary classics, and argues that acclaimed cultural achievements and cheap fiction share a common literary history, and that serious consideration of both is therefore necessary. Part 1 turns now to explore the varieties of the popular that constitute an essential part of twentieth-century literature's geological structure.

Works cited

Adorno, T. and Horkheimer, M. ([1944] 1979) *Dialectic of Enlightenment*, trans. by J. Cumming, London: New Left Books.

Arnold, M. ([1869] 1993) *Culture and Anarchy and Other Writings*, ed. by S. Collini, Cambridge: Cambridge University Press.

Benjamin, W. (1999) *Walter Benjamin: Selected Writings*, vol.2: *1927–1934*, trans. by R. Livingstone, ed. by M.W. Jennings, H. Eiland and G. Smith, Cambridge, MA: The Belknap Press of Harvard University Press.

Carey, J. (1992) *Intellectuals and the Masses: Pride and Prejudice among the Literary Intelligentsia, 1880–1939*, London: Faber.

Leavis, F.R. (1930) *Mass Civilisation and Minority Culture*, Cambridge: Minority Press.

Leavis, F.R. and Thompson, D. (1933) *Culture and Environment*, London: Chatto & Windus.

Leavis, Q.D. (1939) *Fiction and the Reading Public*, London: Chatto & Windus.

Lyotard, J.-F. (1984) *The Postmodern Condition: A Report on Knowledge*, trans. by G. Bennington and B. Massumi, Manchester: Manchester University Press.

Radway, J.A. (1997) *A Feeling for Books: The Book-of-the-Month Club, Literary Taste, and Middle-Class Desire*, Chapel Hill: University of North Carolina Press.

Rosenberg, D. and White, D.M. (1957) *Mass Culture: The Popular Arts in America*, Glencoe, IL: The Free Press.

Williams, R. (1983) *Keywords: A Vocabulary of Culture and Society*, London: Fontana.

Worpole, K. (1984) *Reading by Numbers: Contemporary Publishing and Popular Fiction*, London: Comedia.

CHAPTER 1

Daphne du Maurier, *Rebecca*

NICOLA J. WATSON

Overview

This chapter begins by considering *Rebecca* in the context of Daphne du Maurier's life and literary career and in the light of her own account of its composition. This introductory section is followed by a guided tour through the novel, reading it as primarily addressing questions of female identity, before broadening out to consider competing psychoanalytical and historicist readings. The chapter continues by contextualizing the novel within the tradition of women's romance and Gothic romance, relating it especially to its most important and canonical precursor, Charlotte Brontë's *Jane Eyre* (1847). In so doing, it considers the nature of *Rebecca* as a 'popular' classic, and the extent to which such popularity really is opposed to 'high' or 'elite' culture. The last sections deal with some of the responses *Rebecca* has elicited, including Alfred Hitchcock's film, Susan Hill's sequel, Sally Beauman's companion-piece, the 2003 'Big Read' and, more generally, the increasing prominence of literary tourism centred on 'Daphne du Maurier country', in order to explore the processes by which a 'popular' classic may be so identified by its ability to expand beyond its original incarnation in print.

Introduction

'Last night I dreamt I went to Manderley again.' The opening sentence of Daphne du Maurier's fifth novel, *Rebecca* (1938), is these days probably one of the best-known opening sentences in all of fiction. Within its deceptively simple structure (metrically speaking, it is in fact a perfect alexandrine – six successive iambic feet, the stress falling on every second syllable), this sentence holds all that makes *Rebecca* an enduring classic of popular fiction, and so recommends it to our attention as students of the popular. The first-person narration calls the reader to identify with the narrator, and in this way the reader is invited to 'dream' with the narrator; the 'again' sets up the repetition of dreamlike experience that will characterize the narrator's experience, and that equally characterizes many readers' accounts of their own experiences of reading – and rereading – the novel. The dream is clearly driven by desire, longing and, perhaps, denial – and desire, longing and denial are what typically drive popular narrative.

Du Maurier's novel as a whole is about dreams and nightmares, about desire and the repression of desire, about memory and forgetting, about compulsive repetition, about love of place and homesickness. It feels especially appropriate, therefore, that I should be thinking and writing about the dream-landscape that du Maurier's novel conjures up (the back of the 1992 Arrow edition I have in front of me remarks that it 'weaves a special magic that no-one who reads it will ever forget'), full of regret at being confined to my back garden in Oxford by an injury, instead of enjoying my customary annual summer holiday, which I had planned to spend at Fowey (pronounced 'Foy') and Tywardreath in Cornwall, homes of du Maurier throughout her writing life, and now home to the Daphne du Maurier museum and the Daphne du Maurier literary festival. As a child, I walked the cliffs that run from Fowey to Par sands, or sailed round to bathe at Pridmouth beach (Polridmouth on the map), and to play on the old wreck's hooped iron ribs, revealed, rotting on the black rocks, only at low tide. These days, I generally take my children every year, and we do pretty much the same things. I savour the added pleasure of the deliberate repetition of my own childhood pleasures, sophisticated by my definite (but difficult to specify) pleasure in knowing that this is the cove in which du Maurier's Rebecca was lost in her sailing boat. Up there among the trees and beyond the boathouse, unseen and unsuspected even from the heights of the lighthouse-like Gribben tower on the headland, which commands a view in all directions across the country and along the coastline, lies Menabilly, home of the Rashleighs for many centuries, and, for an interregnum of twenty years, home too to du Maurier.

It is possible that you are now feeling faintly startled, embarrassed or even ruffled at this rush of gratuitously inserted autobiographical information. After all, academic text is traditionally studiedly impersonal; students are not usually solicited to take any interest in the academic writer as a person, let alone as a sentimental mother on a beach with her children. However, it is not self-importance that prompts me to start a reading of *Rebecca* from personal reminiscence, but a sense that we cannot study popular literature without admitting within the magic circle of academic discourse some of those things that we as readers all know, even though they are generally rigorously repressed in our essays. Pretending that I am not reading *Rebecca* in a particular place, at a particular time, in a particular state of mind, as someone from a particular social background and as a middle-aged mother, and, equally, that you as students are not just as particularized in similar ways, threatens to downgrade or even render invisible that which in my view makes the popular popular, the reader him- or herself and the sorts of pleasure or comfort he or she derives from reading popular literature. Though *Rebecca* is certainly available to full-on academic reading, and there will be plenty of that over the next few pages, it would be downright dishonest not also to take seriously the processes and practices of popular reading, which, as I hope you will come to agree, include even summer picnics at Pridmouth – real, remembered and imagined.

Daphne du Maurier only came to live at Menabilly as a tenant of the then half-ruined house some years after the publication of *Rebecca*; before that she lived in the Ferryhouse at Bodinnick (still in the possession of the du Mauriers), dropping out from the glittering swirl of writers, artists, journalists and actors that made up her family's social milieu. For two generations the family had been London-based writers: du Maurier's father was the actor–manager Gerald du Maurier, and her grandfather, George du Maurier, had achieved fame as the author of *Trilby* (1894). (In case you are curious, yes, this was the novel that, as one side effect of its immense fame and success, gave its name to a hat.) Fowey was then (in the early 1930s) much more remote from London than now (there was no possibility of commuting every week like modern downshifters), but it was not an unliterary bohemia, being the hideout of, among others, the eminent Cambridge academic and novelist Sir Arthur Quiller-Couch, or 'Q', whose daughter Foy was close friends with du Maurier. Here in Fowey, the young du Maurier began to write in earnest, starting with a historical novel that followed the generations of a boatbuilding family, and was stuffed to the gunwales with sentiment and local colour. This novel, *The Loving Spirit* (1931), would make her name as a local colourist in a mode distantly related to that of Scottish novelist Lewis Grassic Gibbon. However, *Rebecca* was mostly not written in Cornwall, or even in England; it was drafted in large part in Alexandria, where du Maurier found herself unhappily and rebelliously stranded courtesy of her husband's military career. But although du Maurier was not writing *Rebecca* as a tenant of Menabilly, she was writing out of a long past as an obsessive trespasser there.

In 1946, eight years after the publication of *Rebecca*, du Maurier wrote an essay entitled 'The House of Secrets', in which she described her first trespass (frustrated in the event by the encroaching night and her sister's anxieties) and another attempt a year later. This trespass continued for the next fifteen years, extending eventually to the interior, until du Maurier's 'dream' of a house was abandoned to ruin, 'left to die' (in du Maurier, 1981, pp.138). Though abandoned, Menabilly was not for sale because it was entailed in the male line, but after much negotiation du Maurier managed to rent it on a long-term lease. Du Maurier moved into the house in 1943, set about extensive renovations, and lived there until 1969, when the new heir refused to extend the lease, wishing to use the house for his own family (Figures 1.1, 1.2 and 1.3).

Now read the extract from 'The House of Secrets' (Reader, Item 30) and the first chapter of *Rebecca*. What similarities of detail and feeling does the account of visits to Menabilly share with the

Figure 1.1 Menabilly, seat of the Rashleigh family, near Fowey, Cornwall, 1945. Home of Daphne du Maurier and her family from 1943 to 1969. (Courtesy Fowey History Group. Photo: Fowey Public Library, Cornwall.)

Figure 1.2 Daphne du Maurier (Lady Frederick A.M. Browning) on the staircase at Menabilly; photograph by Edward Malindine. A portrait of her actor father hangs on the wall above. To the right is a portrait of herself as a child. (Photo: Popperfoto.com)

Figure 1.3 Daphne du Maurier and her children, Christina, Tessa and Flavia, walking up to Menabilly House from Pridmouth Cove; photograph by Edward Malindine. (Photo: Popperfoto.com)

description of Manderley? What does the account in *Rebecca* add by way of imagery, and what might this suggest about the mode and preoccupations of the novel as a whole?

Rooting her account of the genesis of her novel within an obsession with Menabilly suggests the importance of the house to du Maurier's conception of the piece. So too does *Rebecca*'s bravura opening chapter, the account of the dreaming narrator's 'return' to Manderley. (The importance of Menabilly is as a source for the exterior, grounds and setting of the house, a trespasser's-eye view; the interiors were based on a childhood visit to Milton Manor, near Peterborough; Figure 1.4.) Let us start our reading of the novel as du Maurier does, with the house.

In both accounts, the bare topographical details are recognizably the same – the lodge, the gate, the long, winding, tree-lined drive, the rhododendrons, the secretive and empty house viewed by night. The accounts share a mood of dream, mystery, enchantment, and sexual aggression and anxiety. Crucially, both narrators are outsiders who wish to be inside, a wish that makes them trespassers. There is the same sense of repetition – repeated visits, repeated dreams. Both visitors breathe domestic life into the ghostly house by an act of imagination, seeing the thing that cannot be seen, signalled by du Maurier's trademark subjunctive: 'the door

Figure 1.4   Milton Hall, Peterborough. North front. (Photo: Peterborough Central Library.)

would stand half open as we had left it ... The room would bear witness to our presence' (du Maurier [1938] 2003, Chapter 1, p.1; unless otherwise stated, all subsequent references are to this edition). Both conjure it into life: 'As I stood there, hushed and still, I could swear that the house was not an empty shell but lived and breathed as it had lived before' (*ibid.*). Both accounts are significantly inflected by the fairytale – the way through the dark woods, the mysterious house and the youthful trespasser are familiar motifs from Goldilocks, Hansel and Gretel, and the Sleeping Beauty, the last of which is specifically mentioned in 'The House of Secrets'.

However, the anxiety of the autobiographical essay is both heightened and significantly inflected in *Rebecca* by a series of images that preview some of the novel's preoccupations. While the essay is full of sexual excitement – the narrator identifies herself as the prince in Sleeping Beauty, on a chivalric quest for a lover and taking pleasure in the act of penetrating her seclusion – the passage in *Rebecca* is altogether less optimistic about love, lovers and marriage. The sense of lover-like recognition in the essay is displaced by a sense in *Rebecca* that the woods are full of trees 'that I did not recognize' (1; p.1), with oppressively human-like limbs – 'white' and 'naked' and skeletal, if they are not actually monstrous. Indeed, the wood is full of 'strange' 'unnatural' juxtapositions, 'embraces', 'marriages', and 'bastard' 'half-breed' and 'spurious' outgrowths. Plants strangle one another, parasites kill hosts. There is something overwritten, slightly hysterical, matching the narrator's own over-febrile relation with the house. Taken all in all, the language presents the ruined house and grounds as a nightmare perversion of orderly domesticity. From this opening, we might well guess that this will be a novel in which the domestic, marital and legitimate will be threatened by the incursions and encroachments of 'nature'.

As this change of inflection suggests, there is a real danger in suggesting that the later essay 'grounds' or is the origin for the earlier text, just because the autobiographical experience described predated the writing of *Rebecca*. The later text may, indeed probably does, take as its source *Rebecca* itself, to some large degree. To that extent, the accounts of the genesis of *Rebecca* that du Maurier offered many years after the event in *The Rebecca Notebook and Other Memories*, including 'The House of Secrets', though possibly drawn from her diaries of the time, are really 'intertexts' with *Rebecca*. By 'intertexts' I mean here the texts that have come to cluster around *Rebecca* and that universally endeavour to 'explain' and expand the novel itself. I will come back in much more detail to the question of *Rebecca*'s intertexts, both in this sense and, more generally, in terms of the tradition upon which the novel draws and the texts that it inspires, but for the moment we should note that the accounts taken together make it apparent that du Maurier was very preoccupied with the peculiar relation of middle-class women to country houses. Like Vita Sackville-West's Knole, the great house that partly inspired Virginia Woolf's *Orlando* (1928), and as its name irresistibly insists, Menabilly/Man-derley automatically excluded women from inheriting or possessing it in any way other than purely imaginatively. The problem of female dispossession will turn out to be critical to the structures of *Rebecca*. Such dispossession is dramatized in the novel within the precariousness of the narrator's female identity, which is symbolized by her name.

The nameless heroine

As it happens, the opening chapter that you have just read does not make it clear whether the narrator is a man or a woman, let alone give him/her a name. And although the next chapter does begin to suggest forcibly that the narrator is a woman, and half of an established heterosexual couple, it takes time to discover their names. **Read through Chapter 2, paying especial attention to the names of people and places mentioned. What might their relative frequency suggest? Who remains anonymous?**

The first name on my list is 'Manderley', which occurs no fewer than seven times. Its frequency underscores the importance accorded to it. After that, the names include 'Jasper', to whom we have already been introduced, the Oval, 'England' (repeated twice), 'Mrs Danvers', 'Mrs de Winter', 'Favell', 'Rebecca' (twice), 'Mrs Van Hopper', 'Monte Carlo' and, finally, Max de Winter. In fact, it takes the entire second chapter to turn the 'he' of its first lines into 'Max de Winter', and this is only done by conjoining his name with that of Manderley (2; p.11). Apart from admiring the skill with which du Maurier sketches in the contrast between three or even four locations – Manderley then and now, Monte Carlo and some unspecified continental restaurant – and introduces nearly every character who appears in the rest of the novel, you might also have noticed that the narrator herself remains anonymous. Moreover, although the novel takes as its title a name, *Rebecca*, traditionally the name of its heroine, and often therefore the name of the first-person narrator as well (think of *Pamela*, *Jane Eyre* or *Moll Flanders*), it is clear that the narrator is *not* Rebecca. In fact, we are destined never to discover the narrator's name, even though we learn in Chapter 4 that it is 'lovely and unusual' (4; p.26).

This is perhaps slightly to overstate her namelessness, because, as you will have discovered by now (since I suspect that my prose is less compelling than du Maurier's and you have read on regardless), she does have a title: the narrator becomes the second 'Mrs de Winter', wife to 'Maxim'. It is hard to remember nowadays that not very long ago women abandoned not just their fathers' surnames on marriage, but also their own first name. For society and servants, if not their intimates, they took their husbands' first names as well as their surnames – becoming, for example, Mrs Jonathan Watson. If there were several Mrs Watsons in the family, the junior married women would be known as Mrs James, Mrs Michael and so on, a practice still obtaining in wedding etiquette and the like. *Rebecca* plays with this fluctuating relation between women's names and titles – while the first Mrs de Winter retains her first name (Rebecca) as well as acquiring a new title (Mrs de Winter), the second Mrs de Winter's first name is comprehensively erased under her new title, which inevitably replicates that of the first Mrs de Winter. We might guess that du Maurier's strategy of leaving the narrator nameless (which she herself explained as simply inspired by the technical challenge of doing so) may be a way of exploring the female condition in modern bourgeois marriage.

If you have not already done so, read on from Chapter 3 to the end of Chapter 8. As you read, consider the novel's use of names and titles as an index of status and intimacy. Why do you think that the question of names/titles is persistently conjoined with images of writing?

Names and the writing of names are peculiarly resonant in this novel in surprisingly small details. The note de Winter sends to the narrator is described as having 'No signature, and no beginning. But my name was on the envelope, and spelt correctly, an unusual thing' (3; p.20). This apparently promising opening communication nonetheless underscores the extent to which the narrator will be named by de Winter, and the subsequent continued invisibility of the narrator's name emphasizes her absorption from one anonymity into another, into the ideology and actuality of this unequal marriage, with all its implausible and indeed initially inexplicable disparities of age, experience, wealth and class. It signals, too, her belatedness. As the second wife, she fills a function that has already been shaped by her predecessor. Even before the couple leave Monte Carlo, de Winter has experimented with repeating the honeymoon drive he took with his first wife up to the precipice (5; pp.31–2). The narrator cannot take over Manderley in the same way that one notable predecessor in the woman's novel, the equally trespassing and parvenu Elizabeth Bennet, takes over Pemberley (the similarity in the name of the house is unlikely to be fortuitous) in the last paragraph of Jane Austen's *Pride and Prejudice* (1813). For though the narrator's place and power is enfolded in her imagination in her future title as mistress of the house, which she imagines significantly in terms of the act of writing ('Mrs de Winter. I would be Mrs de Winter. I considered my name, and the signature on cheques, to tradesmen, and in letters asking people to dinner'; 6; p.60), this title and position has been pre-empted by the dead Rebecca, who has already shaped house, social situation and domestic routine. Indeed, we hardly ever see the narrator writing anything, and especially never signing or 'naming' anything, whereas Rebecca's pre-empting pre-eminence is expressed in the physical prevalence of her writing, especially her monogram and signature.

In her attempts to fill the position of Maxim's wife and mistress of Manderley, the narrator is slowly consumed by the effort not to displace the previous wife but to 'become' her. Little by little, as the novel's first half charts, the narrator is actually 'possessed' by a phantom Rebecca with whom she has a stronger, more libidinous relationship than she has as yet with her husband. Even before de Winter has proposed, the narrator is secretly brooding on the lost physicality of Rebecca, bringing her to life, and identifying with her:

> Somewhere her voice still lingered, and the memory of her words. There were places she had visited, and things that she had touched. Perhaps in cupboards there were clothes that she had worn, with the scent about them still. In my bedroom, under my pillow, I had a book that she had taken in her hands, and I could see her turning to that first white page, smiling as she wrote ... Max from Rebecca ... Max was her choice, the word was her possession; she had written it with so great a confidence on the fly-leaf of that book. That bold, slanting hand, stabbing the white paper, the symbol of herself.
>
> (5; p.47)

Rebecca, unlike the narrator, names her husband by right of possession (the narrator, by contrast, has to be given permission to use the name his family uses, Maxim) and retains her own first name. More, she signs herself, rather than being named by her husband. That dashing, aggressive 'R' thus functions as a symbol of apparently forbidden self-definition and self-assertion. Its stabbing violence further suggests that writing is seen as masculine in affect. In the little scene in which the narrator destroys the flyleaf by burning it (6; pp.63–4), the novel provides a premonition of just what it will take to 'unwrite' Rebecca's deviance out of the fabric of Manderley.

The narrator's sense of already being 'pre-scripted' by Rebecca comes to a head in the morning-room in Manderley. So overpowering here is the sense of Rebecca's prior claim to the title Mrs de Winter that the narrator feels as though she is in 'somebody else's house' (8; p.95), loses her head when addressed as Mrs de Winter by Mrs Danvers through the house telephone and denies that she is any such person. In comparison to Rebecca's signature, 'how cramped and unformed was [her] own handwriting, without individuality, without style, uneducated even' (8; p.98). The narrator's identity is situational, and relative; it is made variously by her father, her 'situation' or job as companion to Mrs Van Hopper and, for the bulk of the novel, by her marriage to Maxim and through him to the house and its secrets. By comparison, at any rate through the narrator's anxious eyes, Rebecca is self-making and self-authenticating. Where the narrator is 'unentitled', Rebecca gives the novel its title. She provides an alternative, much more aggressive and transgressive model of female identity.

'R'

Rebecca herself is everything that the narrator is not. Where the narrator feels herself young, ignorant, gauche, confused, powerless and insignificant, she experiences Rebecca (through the material traces preserved by Mrs Danvers) as older, more knowing, more sophisticated, confident, managerial and significant. The little morning-room sums her up in its competence, its conscious taste, its predatory collection of all the best things in the house, the cupid presiding over the writing-desk inside and the invading blood-red rhododendrons enclosing the dancing faun outside, elsewhere revealingly described as a satyr (27; p.423). The dancing figure of untrammelled sexuality associated with the blood-red of the flowers inside and out hints at Rebecca's refusal of the boundaries of marital domesticity. It is not accidental that the sexually unawakened narrator breaks the cupid figurine: there is too much sex, too much red, too much scent around in this room to be quite virtuously marital. Elsewhere in the novel, too, Rebecca is associated with the extra-domestic: with the beach, the sea and London.

In short, Rebecca, like any stepmother figure, for here we verge upon the territory of fairytales, knows much more about sex than her childish successor. Like a child, the narrator comes into a house that is already mysteriously functioning in its own patterns and routines, and she persistently describes herself as a child in relation to the secrets of the house. When Mrs Danvers, surrogate for Rebecca, offers to show the narrator the rooms in the west wing, she feels acute discomfort: 'Her insistence struck a chord in my memory, reminding me of a visit to a friend's house, as a child, when the daughter of the house, older than me, took my arm and whispered in my ear, "I know where there is a book, locked in a cupboard, in my mother's bedroom. Shall we go and look at it?" ' (9; p.102). Keykeeper to Manderley's many rooms, Mrs Danvers lets the narrator into the first secret of Manderley, the secret of Rebecca's sexiness. She instigates curiosity about forbidden things, rendering the hitherto innocent narrator as guilty and furtive as Eve.

Now read on from Chapter 9 to the end of Chapter 19. As you read, make a note of the ways in which the narrator relates to the figure of Rebecca. Pay especial attention to the episode of the costume ball and its aftermath. To what extent does the narrator desire to be Rebecca? And at what point does she cease to desire this?

For the rest of the first half of the book the narrator unconsciously doubles Rebecca: she sits and walks with her dogs; she finds herself wearing her mac and using her handkerchief; she follows her routines; she finally all but brings her to life by wearing her costume at the ball. Her overt dismay at the ways she uncannily replicates Rebecca's life is nevertheless shot through with the desire to become beautiful, powerful and significant, like Rebecca. Her effort in the costume ball demonstrates this desire; it is so powerful that she does clearly become, in her mirror-reflection, the image of Rebecca: 'I did not recognize the face that stared at me in the glass. The eyes were larger surely, the mouth narrower, the skin white and clear? The curls stood away from the head in a little cloud. I watched this self that was not me at all and then smiled; a new, slow smile' (16; pp.237–8). She has her wish; she becomes Rebecca so successfully, not least in Rebecca's delight in deceit, masquerade and multiplicity, that in a cruel reversal of the Cinderella myth, Maxim does finally see her as Rebecca, and to her astonishment violently repudiates her. Her double effort to legitimize herself, both by becoming Rebecca and by reiterating Rebecca's own gesture of inserting herself into the de Winter line in the form of his ancestress Caroline de Winter, fails utterly. Instead of gaining legitimacy, she has erased her identity in becoming a living simulacrum of Rebecca. (Jean Baudrillard's definition of a 'simulacrum' as a 'copy with no original' is especially pertinent, as we shall see, since this 'Rebecca' is a figment of the narrator's imagination.) This erasure is so devastating, so close to death, that Mrs Danvers almost persuades her to commit suicide so that Maxim can reunite with a resurrected Rebecca, brought to life like a vampire at the cost of the narrator's death: ' "He can't forget her. He wants to be alone in the house, with her. It's you that ought to be lying there in the church crypt, not her. It's you who ought to be dead, not Mrs de Winter" ' (18; p.276).

The combination of Mrs Danvers's desire and that of the narrator finally does seem to bring Rebecca back again. Dredged up from the seabed in the coffin of her little boat, *Je Reviens*, Rebecca's body brings with it the fatal knowledge that makes the de Winters' marriage into an equal partnership for the first time, awakening the narrator's sexuality and destroying her innocence: ' "It's gone forever, that funny, young, lost look that I loved ... I killed that too, when I told you about Rebecca" ' (21; p.336). The secret of Maxim and Manderley is the physical presence of the previous, murdered, wife within the house and grounds. The secret is that of Bluebeard's chamber.

The turning-point of the novel is Maxim's confession. At this point, from desiring the absent Rebecca, the narrator allows herself to desire, in fact to be complicit in, the murder of Rebecca. Instead of doubling Rebecca's actions, whether consciously or unconsciously, she now doubles Maxim's in a willed act of imagination:

> I had listened to his story, and part of me went with him like a shadow in his tracks. I too had killed Rebecca, I too had sunk the boat there in the bay. I had listened beside him to the wind and water ... All this I had suffered with him, all this and more beside ... something new had come upon me that had not been before. My heart, for all its anxiety and doubt, was light and free. I knew then that I was no longer afraid of Rebecca ... Rebecca's power had dissolved into the air, like the mist had done. She would never haunt me again.
>
> (21; p.319)

Now read (or reread) from Chapter 20 to the end.

Murder and marriage

The narrator is apparently released from her need to be Rebecca by Maxim's revelations. It is a tribute to the way in which du Maurier has engaged the reader's sympathy for the narrator that the reader does not find her reaction deeply shocking. Far from falling into a well-justified fear for herself, as her fatally inquisitive predecessor does in the tale of Bluebeard on discovering her husband's secret, the second Mrs de Winter is empowered and energized by the knowledge of Maxim's hatred for and murder of Rebecca, and by his love for her, which seems from this point onwards to become more fully sexualized. Newly secure and mature, the narrator can now even deal with Mrs Danvers: ' "I'm afraid it does not concern me very much what Mrs de Winter used to do ... I am Mrs de Winter now, you know" ' (21; p.326). Cinderella finally gets to kick her stepmother in the teeth, though not exactly as a function of her superior virtue. From now on, Mrs Danvers mostly retreats into the background.

What makes the narrator's transformation possible is Maxim's certification of the hitherto envied Rebecca's deviancy from proper womanhood. According to Maxim, Rebecca was ' "incapable of love, of tenderness, of decency. She was not even normal" ' (20; p.304). Though she produced a formidably successful masquerade of domestic femininity, she was in truth the antithesis of virtuous marital domesticity: promiscuous, vicious, ' "rotten through and through" ' (*ibid.*). Though to all appearances she nurtured Maxim and Manderley, she was prepared to transgress the fundamental logic of the house – the logic of primogeniture – by installing within it a bastard heir (remember the imagery of the opening dream-sequence) as a sort of taunt to Maxim's aristocratic, patriarchal and even fetishistic relationship with the house. Along with the narrator's own failure to fall pregnant, this threat also suggests that de Winter is impotent. Later, however, it is revealed that it is Rebecca who is infertile. The discovery that ultimately gets de Winter off the hook – that his first wife was not pregnant but breeding a cancer and therefore had a motive for suicide – is backed up by the apparently casual revelation that Rebecca could never have children, having a malformed uterus (26; p.413). We need to remember here that until very recently cancer had peculiarly horrible and sexist connotations – 'according to popular myth, [it] preys on spinster and nymphomaniac alike' (Modleski, 1988, p.53). Rebecca's 'malformed uterus' confirms that proper womanhood is married, monogamous and childbearing. The Rebecca revealed by Maxim in this scene is thus the dysphoric version of Mrs Danvers's celebration of her previous mistress's glamour, 'spirit', cruelty, cleverness, promiscuity and emotional invulnerability. The murder of Rebecca, confessed, is the equivalent of staking the female vampire in Bram Stoker's *Dracula* (1897). Indeed, Rebecca's white skin and cloud of black hair, along with her regular and dismaying resurrection from the dead, are classically vampiric (Horner and Zlosnik, 1998, pp.111–12).

'Once this version of uncontrolled and unreproductive female sexuality is exorcized,' there should be room at Manderley for a regenerate, conventional domesticity, or so the narrator daydreams: 'I might ... have one or two things altered. That little square lawn outside the morning-room with the statue of the satyr. I did not like it. We would give the satyr away ... We would have children. Surely we would have children' (27; p.423). Yet ultimately the exorcism proves imperfect; the narrator's last dream of many in the car travelling down from London reveals her continued identification with Rebecca – and reveals that she both shares and repudiates Rebecca's imputed desire to punish Maxim:

> I was writing letters in the morning-room. I was sending out invitations. I wrote them all myself with a thick black pen. But when I looked down to see what I had written it was not my small square handwriting at all, it was long, and slanting, with curious

> pointed strokes. I pushed the cards away from the blotter and hid them. I got up and went to the looking-glass. A face stared back at me that was not my own. It was very pale, very lovely, framed in a cloud of black hair. The eyes narrowed and smiled. The lips parted. The face in the glass stared back at me and laughed. And I saw then that she was sitting on a chair before the dressing-table in her bedroom, and Maxim was brushing her hair. He held her hair in his hands, and as he brushed it he wound it slowly into a thick rope. It twisted like a snake, and he took hold of it with both hands and smiled at Rebecca and put it round his neck.
>
> (27; p.426)

The narrator's fantasies of domesticity are less powerful than Rebecca's vengeful anti-domesticity; not only is the house destroyed by Mrs Danvers in vengeance for her dead mistress, but the narrator is punished for her complicity in Rebecca's murder by exile from England and childlessness. In this sense, the narrator ends up doubling Rebecca in a figurative death.

The punishment meted out to the couple is made even more explicit in du Maurier's first draft of the epilogue, which is reprinted in *The Rebecca Notebook and Other Memories*. This contains much of the material that du Maurier later inserted towards the beginning of the book, so as to preserve her finale, the fire at Manderley. But though the portrait of dull, routine exile is already there in this draft, de Winter is a crippled and scarred invalid, and the narrator is childless and facially disfigured herself, in an echo of the appalling imaginary violence meted out to Rebecca's body throughout the text – the arms battered off, the face eaten by fishes.

What this consideration of the dénouement of *Rebecca* might suggest is that the novel is profoundly ambivalent about 'normal' marital sexuality. The de Winters' marriage turns out to have always been founded on murder. Maxim's 'natural' feelings spur him to murder his promiscuous wife. The narrator's jealousy of Rebecca turns out itself to be murderous; to service her own identity and sexuality she is prepared to be complicit in the murder. The crime committed against the free-spirited Rebecca nonetheless is avenged on the supposedly virtuous wife, who dwindles into the companion of an exiled invalid. She seems to pay a price for inhabiting something identified as ? 'normal' heterosexuality.

Freud and femininity

One possible reading of the allure of *Rebecca* is that it both elicits and manages women's anxieties about their own precariously balanced (hetero-) sexuality within patriarchy. To explore this further, we need to turn to Sigmund Freud, the founder of psychoanalysis and theorist of female sexuality. He provided narratives of the development of child and adult sexuality within the nuclear family that remain in their essentials in place today, although much of the detail has been elaborated and contested since. Attending to Freud's story of the development of female sexuality may give us a clue as to the enduring popularity of *Rebecca*, given the perhaps dubious but generally held assumption that *Rebecca* is primarily consumed by women. **Now turn to the extract from Freud's essay 'Female Sexuality' (1931, trans. 1932) (Reader, Item 31). Make sure you read the headnote, because this explains a concept of Freud's that you will need to understand the essay itself – the Oedipus complex. Then read the essay. You may find it both a difficult and an annoying experience, but persevere! Make some notes summarizing Freud's accounts of the development of male and female sexuality, highlighting the differences between them.**

In Freud's schema, the development of infantile male sexuality is relatively straightforward. The baby boy's first love is his mother, and this is unproblematic in earliest infancy, because he is unaware of his father. Once he realizes his father's prior claim upon his mother, he enters the Oedipal phase, so-called because it reprises the ancient Greek myth of Oedipus. (Oedipus, just to remind you, murdered his father without realizing it, went on to marry his mother, and when he discovered the truth of the murder and incest, blinded himself and wandered the world pursued by the Furies.) Consumed by intense jealousy of his father as his principal rival, the child conceives the wish to kill him so as to possess his mother entirely, but is eventually persuaded of the inadvisability of doing away with his father by his fear that his father will castrate him for his presumption. This fear of castration derives from the boy's misunderstanding of girls' bodies; he thinks that castration has been visited upon other 'boys' who have now become girls, and infers that they have been punished in this fashion for their desire for the mother. With this crisis, the child exits the Oedipal phase and, after a period of suppressing his desire for his mother ('latency' – from about five or six through early adolescence), transfers his affections to a permissible substitute for her, another woman. (This is an account of the development of male heterosexuality; Freud offers an alternative narrative for the development of male homosexuality.)

For the baby girl, however, things are more complicated and run roughly like this. Just like her brother, the baby girl at first loves her mother intensely and longs to possess her sexually and to impregnate her. She too regards her father as her rival. Only on discovering her own 'castration', and subsequently her beloved mother's, does she repudiate and denigrate her mother and turn to her father. She replaces her hopes for the penis ('penis-envy'), which would entitle her to compete for her mother, with love for the father, and ultimately with the desire for a child (preferably a boy) by a substitute man. To achieve adult sexuality, she therefore not only has to repress her pre-Oedipal same-sex love for her mother, but her love for her father into the bargain. In short, Freud makes it quite clear that arriving at adult female heterosexuality is a pretty tortuous and problematic business, having at least three outcomes, only one of which is 'normal' heterosexuality (the other two, in his account, are frigidity and lesbianism).

Freud's story of the development of female sexuality is of interest to students of popular literature because of its claims to universality. If *Rebecca* reiterates or reconsiders the framework that Freud lays out, perhaps this would account for the hold on women readers that du Maurier's novel has had throughout its life. **Go back now to 'Female Sexuality', and consider to what extent Freud's story of female sexuality might find echoes in *Rebecca*.**

One puzzling thing about *Rebecca* that Freud's essay might explain is the way in which the most intense relationship in the novel is between the narrator-heroine and the shade of Rebecca. In fact, *Rebecca* might be described as all about a woman's problems of 'over-identification' with another woman. On the face of it, this is a relationship between two wives, one alive, one dead. But read in the context of Freud's theories of the development of female sexuality, the relationship between the younger woman and the older woman, and their rivalry for the affection of the older man, looks more like the repressed early love of the female child for her mother. Freud's remark about the girl's primary relation with her mother is suggestive when put alongside Rebecca's ghostliness: 'Everything in the sphere of this first attachment to the mother seemed to me so difficult to grasp in analysis – so grey with age and shadowy and almost impossible to revivify – that it was as if it had succumbed to an especially inexorable repression.' This notion of repression seems especially pertinent to the secret of *Rebecca*'s appeal.

For Freud, the repressed is what has been known, then has been strategically forgotten and stored in the unconscious, the lumber-room of 'primaeval experiences', but which continually threatens to surface as neurosis ([1920] 1991, p.308). The process of psychoanalysis is designed to uncover the repressed, to free the patient from the need unconsciously 'to repeat the events of his childhood' in adult relations, but it involves resurrecting the supposedly dead past: 'people unfamiliar with analysis feel an obscure fear – a dread of rousing something that, so they feel, is better left sleeping – what they are afraid of at bottom is the emergence of this compulsion with its hint of possession by some "daemonic" power' (*ibid.*). As buried secret and as revenant who returns time and again until the boat *Je Reviens* (its name means 'I Return' or 'I'll be right back') breaks the surface of the water, Rebecca seems to literalize this idea of 'the return of the repressed' in the shape of the disgraced mother.

According to Freud, the female child's chief problem is that in being 'castrated' she is too like her mother – lacking the penis, she is not entitled to rival her father for her mother's affections. On the other hand, the child perceives that she is not sufficiently like her mother to inspire her father's interest. Hence on both counts her bid for the affections of her father, which are more properly turned to her mother, is doomed. This might equally serve as an account of the narrator's predicament once she arrives at Manderley. She must come to terms with a powerful and remote father-figure in the shape of the older Maxim, and she must also deal with her combined desire for and hatred of a mother substitute, Rebecca, who she feels still commands the affections of her husband. Rebecca's surrogate, Mrs Danvers, also fills a maternal role, entrenched as she is in a position of apparently effortless and unassailable power over the household. A Freudian lens might aid too in reading the important scene in which Mrs Danvers shows the narrator the master bedroom. Effectively she displays to the girl what Freud called 'the primal scene' – the forbidden sight/site of parents copulating that initiates the Oedipal phase. It is in this theoretical context also that the narrator's willingness to go along with Mrs Danvers's suggestion for the costume for the ball has plausibility – the narrator's principal desire is to be desired as she assumes Rebecca was and is by de Winter, to take Rebecca's place, to be Rebecca. The subsequent revelation that Rebecca was murdered by de Winter can be read as the fulfilment of the child's wish (following on from her discovery of her 'castration') to murder the mother and possess the father wholly. Such a reading begins to account for the way in which this revelation marks the full sexual awakening of the narrator.

You will, I daresay, have a good many objections to this reading. **Pause now and try to formulate them on paper. You might find it helpful to consider what this reading ignores about the novel.**

One objection frequently made to a psychoanalytic reading such as the one I have just sketched out here is that it suggests two things: first, that most or much literature is managing the same anxieties, so that psychoanalytic criticism reduces all texts to the same small set of stories, which seems both depressing and not obviously true; the second objection, which is related, is that such readings do not seem to leave much room for historical specificity and, therefore, for historical change. If Freud's account of the development of individual selfhood fits all historical periods (which many commentators would now dispute, pointing to the specifically late nineteenth-century version of child-rearing that Freud posits as a norm), and if all works of art about the individual more or less reveal or echo that account, then where can there be any significant differences between a novel written in the 1930s and a novel written in the early eighteenth century? Critics who are especially passionate about this latter point tend to be those who believe in historical change as a force for good (loosely speaking, liberal and radical critics), as opposed to those who are altogether more sceptical about the desirability of historical change (again, loosely speaking, a conservative mode of thought, to which du Maurier herself was attuned – not surprisingly, as a member of the generation that would experience not one but two world wars, with all the massive social change that they brought to her class).

Class warfare

What might come into focus about *Rebecca* were we to consider it as a text with historical specificity? Is *Rebecca*, a text produced during the Depression, in the shadow of oncoming war and in the context of the urgent political debates of the 1930s, simply uninterested in these things? And, even if it is apparently uninterested, can it really escape its own historical specificity? Would thinking about *Rebecca* as a text produced within a historical period and engaging with or smoothing over its anxieties help to account for its popularity?

One of the many things about *Rebecca* that a historicist reading might usefully focus on is the question of class. Certainly, *Rebecca* is a minutely class-conscious book. **Pause here and consider the ways in which class inflects the heroine's situation in relation to Rebecca, Maxim and Manderley.**

From one perspective, class is the foundation of the heroine's predicament at Manderley – it is not just that she is young, timid and dowdy, it is that she is not the sort of girl that persons of Maxim's class marry, as Mrs Van Hopper, however monstrous she may be, understands perfectly well. As a daughter of the professional middle classes, she has not been trained up to the semi-aristocratic set-up that is Manderley, with its routines and retinues of servants, and its social obligations to a wide range of social classes; moreover, she must move from the uneasy position of 'companion' (not quite a servant but certainly an employee) to that of mistress and employer. That shift in class is thoroughly precarious. She is never upper class enough for Manderley, and she feels it acutely. Jack Favell's loucheness makes her feel 'like a barmaid' (13; p.181), Maxim laughs at her for behaving like a 'between-maid' in the matter of the broken cupid (12; p.159), the very kitchen-maid sniggers behind her back in the corridor, she is afraid of the uppity Mrs Danvers and cowed by the judgemental Frith. Above all, she is repudiated by Maxim's grandmother in favour of the first wife who boasted that enviable trio of ' "breeding, brains, and beauty" ' (20; p.304). As an upper-middle-class woman, the narrator finds herself locked in a very small area of virtuous respectability. Over the course of the book she must come to repudiate her initial envy of Rebecca's quasi-aristocratic sexuality, both in its respectable form – 'breeding, brains, and beauty' – and in its raffish, rakish form – the philandering with workmen and artists in London of which we learn later. If the narrator is made restless by Rebecca's enviable freedom, she is also made extremely uneasy by lower-class female sexuality; the barmaid, the programme-seller and the shop-girl, it is implied, operate in a sexual economy outside bourgeois marriage. Her sexuality is therefore not merely circumscribed by the childishness that Maxim endeavours to preserve and enforce on her, but by middle-class views of marriage, which are characterized by loyalty, ordinariness, reticence and a tendency to female renunciation that would be unforgettably epitomized a few years later by the film *Brief Encounter* (1945).

It is certainly possible to focus on the question of the heroine's social status to suggest that the novel is largely about renegotiating perceived power relations between classes. Roger Bromley, for example, has suggested that, in common with most romantic fiction with its conventional story of a bourgeois girl marrying a man of higher class, *Rebecca* is largely designed to repair the decayed 'façade' of aristocratic power. This façade of aristocratic values and ideology 'acts as both an alibi and a disguise for the bourgeois forms, values and perceptions which the texts consecrate and naturalise' (Bromley, 1986, p.153). 'The basic motor of the text is *reformation* and the emergence of a new set of reciprocal social alliances' (*ibid.*, p.156). The agent of reform is the virtuously submissive bourgeois woman. She will exorcize the decadently aristocratic Rebecca, reform the land-owning gentleman Maxim and so shore up the remaining power of the ruling class: 'Maxim is able to survive and adapt, to be reborn through a fusion with his second wife who represents the margins of possibility left to him as, in many ways, a peripheral social figure' (*ibid.*, p.163). The love of a good (middle-class) woman will save both house and man. **Take a moment to consider the following statement made by Bromley and test it against your own experience of the text. To what extent do you find it convincing?**

> In bourgeois ideology, women's sexuality and reproduction have to be incorporated in the sphere of the family which, in turn, becomes the repository of emotions, of sexuality, physical well-being, and the space for situating the free choice of a unique beloved ... In *Rebecca*'s extensive crisis of self and family, Maxim's emotional distress, physical ill-health, absence of affection, and his 'possession' by Rebecca all thwart the fulfilment of bourgeois ideals. The terror and neurosis experienced by the heroine at Manderley reproduce his experience of crisis, which can only be resolved in mutuality and exile from Manderley.
>
> (Bromley, 1986, p.158)

You will have your own views, but, though I believe that thinking about class in this novel is fruitful, I have three major problems with Bromley's reading.

First, it ignores the real investment of the book in Rebecca's forbidden glamour, which I have already discussed extensively above. Second, it does not take into account the thoroughgoing lack of enthusiasm that the novel as a whole shows for the reformed rootless existence to which the couple are doomed by the beginning of the narrative. Third, it is rather judgemental, awarding the novel gold stars for supposedly challenging the existing order. To me, the novel seems altogether more ambiguous in its emotional and political charge than Bromley suggests.

In part, this ambiguity is located in the meaning of Manderley itself. In one light it locates perfect domesticity, and focuses a longing for it. In the interwar period, women were strongly encouraged back into the home, and were subjected to a good deal of pressure to give up the jobs that they had held down during the war to the returning soldiers. Yet, in practice, domesticity must have been both hard to come by for women (after the carnage of the First World War, two-thirds of the population were female), and hard to reinvent (the First World War had also shaken up many of the social structures, including the classes from which those in service had traditionally come); accordingly, it was at once prized and despised. Though du Maurier's novel is dubious about the aristocratic model of domesticity that the narrator inherits, it exhibits a strong undertow of desire and approval for a more middle-class, countrified version of that domesticity – for dogs, shabby sofas, mackintoshes, walking, gardens and families of boys (see, generally, Light, 1991). Yet such domesticity is unattainably lost, placed by the narrative irrevocably in the past. The domestic is passionately remembered in the faint yet powerful charges of small domestic things and rituals – flowers, dogs, food – with an ache of desire and loss so powerful as to constitute one of the most recognizable affects and effects of the novel as a whole: 'Robert would lay the table for breakfast, bring in those piping scones, the clutch of eggs, the glass dishes of honey, jam, and marmalade, the bowl of peaches, the cluster of purple grapes with the bloom upon them still, hot from the greenhouses' (26; pp.400–1). We would be right, I think, to identify this discourse of memory and regret as essentially conservative.

Seen from another angle, however, Manderley epitomizes the entrapping nature of the domestic. The second Mrs de Winter never feels happier than when she has escaped both the house and Maxim and run away to the Happy Valley and the beach: 'I was aware of a sense of freedom, as though I had no responsibilities at all. It was rather like a Saturday when one was a child. No lessons, and no prep. One could do as one liked. One put on an old skirt and a pair of sand shoes and played Hares and Hounds on the common with the children who lived next door' (13; p.169). The narrator here redoubles Rebecca's own regular escapes from the constrictions of house and marriage (it is not coincidental that the narrator almost immediately finds herself in Rebecca's cottage on the beach), albeit in an 'innocent' childlike mode. As the wistfulness about playing on the common with 'the children who lived next door' suggests too, this escape is also class-inflected – there is no 'next door' to houses like Manderley. The conservative qualities of the novel – its pervasive melancholy and nostalgia – are also counterpointed with a real violence directed against the domestic. The struggle between the middle-class second Mrs de Winter and the aristocratic house which she loves but which inflicts humiliation after humiliation upon her as an interloper only resolves with the house's destruction in the name of Mrs de Winter's predecessor and double, Rebecca. This discourse of female violence against marriage and domesticity could almost be described as feminist in temper. It suggests to my mind that a reading of the novel in terms of a class-inflected struggle of ideologies needs to be modified by a sense of how gender identity crosses with class identity.

This ambiguity around the political meaning of domesticity – whether it confines and entraps the heroine or whether it is home to a regenerate moral ideology sponsored by her – is entirely characteristic of the genres to which *Rebecca* is affiliated: romance and Gothic romance. In the next section I will be considering the ways in which *Rebecca* works with this inherited tradition in the hope of further decoding the political charge of du Maurier's novel.

(Gothic) romance

It has often been rather carelessly assumed that *Rebecca* is romance fiction. 'Romance' is a much contested and difficult word with many different technical meanings, but in this context John Cawelti's definition will serve us: 'The crucial defining characteristic of romance is ... that its organizing action is the development of a love relationship, usually between a man and a woman' (1976, p.41). Such fiction tends to have a female protagonist with whom the reader is supposed to identify, and its action usually leads tortuously but inevitably to the 'right true end' of marriage and 'happily ever after'. To quote Cawelti again, 'the moral fantasy of the romance is that of love triumphant and permanent, overcoming all obstacles and difficulties' (*ibid.*, p.42) – usually some combination of social and psychological barriers. Cawelti goes on to speculate that 'most modern romance formulas are essentially affirmations of the ideals of monogamous marriage and feminine domesticity' (*ibid.*). 'Gothic' romance is a variant on romance: 'the gothic romance uses mystery as an occasion for bringing two potential lovers together, for placing temporary obstacles in the path of their relationship, and ultimately for making its solution a means of clearing up the separation between the two lovers' (*ibid.*, p.41). From a more feminist angle, Tania Modleski has pointed out that the Gothic romance – a genre to which *Rebecca*, perhaps the greatest haunted-house story of modern times, is so obviously related – deals 'with women's fears of and confusion about masculine behaviour in a world where men tend to devalue women', 'giving expression to women's hostility towards men while simultaneously allowing them to repudiate it' (1982, pp.60, 66). Gothics 'in part serve to convince women that they will not be victims the ways their mothers were' (*ibid.*, p.83). Joanna Russ helpfully describes the ingredients of a Gothic romance as 'the House, the Heroine, the Super-Male, the Other Woman, the Ominous Dialogue, the Secret, and the Untangling' (quoted in Stoneman, 1996, p.144).

These definitions of romance and Gothic romance apply equally to *Rebecca* and to *Rebecca*'s principal source, Charlotte Brontë's *Jane Eyre* (1847). It has been said by many, including Angela Carter, who herself rewrote *Rebecca* within her retelling of the tale of Bluebeard in *The Bloody Chamber* (1979), that du Maurier simply stole the plot of *Jane Eyre* outright (Carter, 1993, p.163). Du Maurier certainly acknowledged its influence on her (1989, p.21). A comparison of *Jane Eyre* and *Rebecca*, a 'classic' and a 'popular classic', may anatomize the genres within which both are working, reveal to what extent *Rebecca* rethinks *Jane Eyre*, and raise some thoroughly provocative questions about the relative status of 'high' and 'popular' literature.

If you have not read *Jane Eyre*, the following short plot-summary may be useful; but I should say that it is one of those novels that, if you are interested either in the history of the novel or in the history of women's writing, you absolutely must read at some point. Jane Eyre – who narrates her own story – is an orphan, brought up initially in her uncongenial aunt's family, and then sent to Lowood school, where she survives initial injustice, unhappiness and a typhoid epidemic to gain an education suitable for a career as a governess. She takes a position at Thornfield Hall, full of mysterious rooms, noises and events, and falls in love with its owner, the saturnine Mr Rochester. Although he seems for a while to be more interested in the beautiful Blanche Ingram, he reciprocates Jane's affection, but at the altar an objection is raised to their marriage, and it transpires that Mr Rochester's mad wife, Bertha, née Mason, is incarcerated on the top floor of the house. Jane flees the house, nearly dying on the moors, and finds asylum with another family, whose son and heir, St John Rivers, eventually also proposes a marriage, this time not of passion but of convenience, and with it a career as a missionary in India. Now financially independent courtesy of an inheritance, Jane refuses and, after a quasi-supernatural summons, goes back to Thornfield, which she finds a deserted, blackened shell. She searches out Rochester, whom she finds blind and maimed after his unsuccessful effort to save his lunatic wife from the fire that she set herself. They marry, have a son, and in time Rochester regains partial sight.

This summary necessarily leaves out much that is of interest about the novel, but it is sufficient, I think, to make clear what *Rebecca* has in common with its predecessor. Both narrating heroines are dispossessed, orphaned and dependent. They find themselves in a socially ambiguous position, one a governess, ladylike without being a lady, in service without being a servant, the other a 'companion' without being a 'friend'. Both are small, plain, dowdy and middle class. Both come to a quasi-aristocratic house full of mysteries, haunted by some powerful presence, which turns out to be a previous wife. Both are in love with the master of the house, who is gloomy, withdrawn, full of secrets and passions himself, who exploits them shamefully, and who by his crimes threatens them with some form of spiritual destruction. Both are doubled with raven-haired beauties; indeed, Jane Eyre is rivalled and doubled by two, Blanche Ingram and Bertha Mason, opposite sides of the same coin before and after marriage, and these women bear a striking physical and moral resemblance to Rebecca – tall, black-haired, white-skinned and essentially vicious. (In fact, Blanche Ingram, in a scene involving a game of charades, actually impersonates the biblical Rebecca, which may suggest one source for du Maurier's choice of name for her siren.) In both novels the secret of the house, the repression of the previous wife, is the cause of its destruction. So much for the bare bones of the family resemblance; if we take a closer look at a section of *Jane Eyre* it is possible to see the structural similarities in detail. **Now turn to the extract from *Jane Eyre* (Appendix). Read the explanatory note, which sites the chapter within the novel as a whole, and then read the chapter through, noting as you do so any preoccupations, tropes or structures that it has in common with *Rebecca*.**

The first similarity that strikes me has to do with names and titles. As in *Rebecca*, identity is changed and conferred by the pouring of the 'I' into the marital title:

> *I*, at least, had nothing more to do: there were my trunks ... ; tomorrow, at this time, they would be far on their road to London: and so should I (D.V.) [*Deo volente*: God willing], – or rather, not I, but one Jane Rochester, a person whom as yet I knew not ... Mrs Rochester! She did not exist: she would not be born till tomorrow ... and I would wait to be assured she had come in to the world alive, before I assigned her all that property.

If titles are formative of identity, so too are clothes, as present and ominously transformative as the fancy-dress in *Rebecca*: 'garments said to be hers had already displaced my black stuff Lowood frock and straw bonnet'. Jane is offered a moral choice between her future identity as Mrs Rochester and her current morally independent identity in the allegorical choice between the two veils, the 'costly' embroidered veil (which will be torn in two by the first Mrs Rochester) and the 'square of unembroidered blonde' (which Jane will wear to her aborted wedding). The stress on names and clothes points up the way that female identity is threatened and transformed by marriage. Such projected identity is 'wraith-like', 'ghostly', a 'dream' of adulthood from a child's perspective.

Jane's encounter with the mysterious woman (who proves eventually to have been Bertha) doubles the wife and the would-be wife in much the same way as the second Mrs de Winter doubles the first. Both pairs share their clothes: Bertha tries on Jane's wedding veil, a gift from her fiancé, and tears it in two as it is essentially a fraud. Du Maurier reverses the trying-on. The second Mrs de Winter, in her efforts to live up to Rebecca, is betrayed into actually 'being' Rebecca in the costume of Caroline de Winter, and that bridal-white costume is similarly torn. Like Rebecca, Bertha Mason is 'tall ... with thick and dark hair hanging long down her back', and is explicitly compared to the vampire, with which figure Rebecca is implicitly associated.

The problem of maintaining female identity within marriage, which preoccupies both *Jane Eyre* and *Rebecca*, is projected through the geography of the landscape and the house in much the same fashion. Like the pathways through the Happy Valley and down to the beach, the landscape of *Jane Eyre* is emblematic, as in the ominous presence of 'the wreck of the chestnut tree' riven into two as an image of a blasted marriage. The previous wives' bedrooms assume an equal importance as repositories of sexual guilt. Both Jane Eyre and the second Mrs de Winter have the same vexed relation to their husband's house. Like du Maurier's protagonist, Jane Eyre dreams of Thornfield as 'a dreary ruin, the retreat of bats and owls ... of all the stately front nothing remained but a shell-like wall, very high, and very fragile looking'. Jane Eyre eventually sees her premonitory dream fulfilled:

> The lawn, the grounds were trodden and waste: the portal yawned void. The front was, as I had once seen it in a dream, but a shell-like wall, very high and very fragile-looking, perforated with paneless windows: no roof, no battlements, no chimneys – all had crashed in.
>
> And there was the solitude of death about it: the solitude of a lonesome wild.
>
> (Brontë, [1847] 1975, pp.429–30)

This brief account of the similarities between *Jane Eyre* and *Rebecca* forcibly suggests *Rebecca*'s debt to its predecessor in plot, structure and preoccupations. To some extent, however, this is an effect of reading literary history backwards – that is to say, that in trying to find sources for *Rebecca* I have emphasized some elements of *Jane Eyre* at the expense of others. Equally, it is an effect of an inheritance common to both, of woman's Gothic romance, which stretches back to the late eighteenth century and Ann Radcliffe's *The Mysteries of Udolpho* (1794), and before that, as I have already suggested, to the old story of Bluebeard's chamber. Looking across supermarket bookshelves you can see their common successors, books with covers that typically feature an old house with a light in the upper stories (indicating Mystery), and in the foreground a frightened-looking woman. Finally, it is an effect too of du Maurier's conscious craftsmanship. An admirer of the work of the Brontës, du Maurier pays homage to *Jane Eyre*. So close is the relationship between the two texts that you might wonder why there is such a disparity in status between the 'high' text and the 'popular classic', between *Jane Eyre* (academically respectable throughout the twentieth century) and *Rebecca* (pretty much on the edge of that respectability). Indeed, the Arrow edition's claim that *Rebecca* is a 'popular classic' (meaning that it is a 'classic' of popular fiction) strikes the ear strangely. The 'popular' is usually thought of as anything but 'classic'. **Pause here and jot down your thoughts as to how the two texts might be distinguished so as to justify their difference in status.**

There are, I think, a number of possible established ways of thinking about this question.

The first is simply to point out that there may be no permanent difference between *Jane Eyre* and *Rebecca*; one was a popular classic of the nineteenth century, the other a popular classic of the twentieth. (*Jane Eyre*, 1847, was also in its time a bestseller, going through five editions before Mrs Gaskell's life of the author, published in 1857 after Brontë's tragically young death in early pregnancy, stimulated such interest that this partially autobiographical novel sold 35,000 copies over the next two years.) All that differentiates the two is the passage of time, which has elevated *Jane Eyre* into a text 'that has stood the test of time' and whose range of increasingly obsolete reference means that it has become more 'difficult'. In the course of time, *Rebecca* may be elevated in exactly the same fashion. This argument holds that the difference between 'high' and 'popular' is that between the enduring and the ephemeral.

The second is to claim that *Jane Eyre* is simply 'better written' than *Rebecca* – this (questionable) claim might perhaps adduce as evidence variety and elegance of style at the level of the sentence, intensity and originality of imagery, a sensitive use of cadence and rhythm, or a wider range of intellectual allusion and preoccupations evident throughout Brontë's novel. Inversely, and by implication, du Maurier's style might be said to be clunky, cliché-ridden and unenterprising in its vocabulary. This argument holds that the difference between 'high' and 'popular' is simply one of quality.

The third is to ask more generally whether *Rebecca* as a rewrite of its 'mother' *Jane Eyre* is secondary, derivative and thus somehow degenerate, or whether it is original and radical, twisting its inheritance to new ends. This line of attack assigns 'high' status on the basis of originality. For example, while Jean Rhys's later rewriting of *Jane Eyre*, *Wide Sargasso Sea* (1966), is regarded as rethinking Brontë's plot in challenging and radical ways with an original and difficult style to correspond, *Rebecca* has been described by hostile critics as simply a pale and truncated copy of a literary classic, suitable for slavish imitation by a host of future Mills and Boon housewife authoresses – and for consumption by supposedly equally slavish housewives, self-indulgently swigging back the chilled Baileys between chapters. (In case anyone's hackles are rising at this point, perhaps as a housewife I should confess to being rather fond of Baileys myself on occasion.)

Finally, an alternative (more politically pointed) way of putting that question is to ask whether *Rebecca* somehow panders to its readership, functioning as a source of comfort rather than of the intellectual, moral and political challenge attributed to *Jane Eyre* (here you might want to remind yourself of the discussion of Janice Radway's argument in the Introduction to Part 1). Instead of strong-arming the tradition into new, powerfully radical writing, du Maurier's work, it is alleged, is merely degenerate. By implication, it is also formulaic and therefore conservative, providing by its very familiarity 'satisfaction and a basic emotional security', and thus escape and entertainment (Cawelti, 1976, pp.9, 13). This assumes that 'high' literature's cultural function is to change society for the better, and that 'popular' literature is by comparison a mass moral and political analgesic.

You may find it useful to test whether you agree with any of these hypotheses by close attention to the text. Try comparing the description of the garden from the extract from *Jane Eyre* (Appendix) with du Maurier's description of the 'Happy Valley' in Chapter 10 (pp.121–3).

I am not proposing to resolve the question of whether or in what ways one novel is somehow 'better' than the other, but simply to note that the propositions above provide different answers to the question of what might be at stake in maintaining the hierarchy of high and popular. The first answer is actually very similar to the second, in that it suggests that texts count as 'high' or 'elite' when they require a more highly trained aesthetic sensibility, or a broader range of historically aware intellectual reference; the difference is that the first regards this sort of textual difficulty simply as a by-product of historical change. The implied priorities of the third recognizably derive from those of T.S. Eliot and Virginia Woolf as expressed in 'Tradition and the Individual Talent' (1919) and *A Room of One's Own* (1929). The assumption that lies behind it is that the truly literary, the 'high', is on a perpetual mission to modernize. The last also assumes that the function of literature is to be a source of change and enlightenment rather than, say, to confirm and stabilize the status quo. The invocation of the supposedly middle-class female readership of *Rebecca* in the third and fourth propositions tends to assume that such a readership is inherently timid, conservative and uninteresting; strangely, despite the long history of middle-class feminism (and indeed of middle-class female activism in most of the great political causes of the last two centuries), it does not take the view that such a readership might be seething with political dissatisfactions of all sorts. As Harriett Hawkins has observed,

> although it has long been considered respectable in academic circles to take seriously as well as to enjoy popular 'folk' art, proletariat art and non-bourgeois art-forms such as jazz, folk songs and soul music, comparably popular, commercially successful, bourgeois, middle-class, middlebrow art of the kind attracting audiences of twenty-five million people in fifteen different countries has traditionally been ignored if not deplored.
>
> (Hawkins, 1990, pp.xiv–xv)

One might amplify this by saying that the art enjoyed by middle-class middlebrow women has been especially ignored and deplored. Could it be that taking *Rebecca* seriously comes too close to leaving us at home with Mummy? And come to that, too close to Mummy's privately explosive fears and pleasures?

The assumption that *Rebecca* is formula romance fiction is surely a stumbling-block in the way of a proper appreciation of the novel, whether as popular classic or future classic. In fact, *Rebecca* is only 'romance' if the reader confines him- or herself to the narrator's viewpoint. From her point of view, her story *is* ultimately romance, a love-story, with a reasonably happy ending. She achieves that 'happy ending' by rigorous self-discipline: here she is, for example, refusing to notice that she is unhappy with Maxim:

> I did not want anyone with me. Not even Maxim. If Maxim had been there I should not be lying as I was now, chewing a piece of grass, my eyes shut. I should have been watching him, watching his eyes, his expression. Wondering if he liked it, if he was bored ... How lovely it was to be alone again. No, I did not mean that. It was disloyal, wicked. It was not what I meant. Maxim was my life and my world.
>
> (13; p.170)

Her 'happy' ending is foregrounded by being put at the beginning of the book, it is the basis of the story that frames and founds its conscious assumptions. But from the reader's point of view, this love-story and its ending look a good deal less euphoric than the narrator tries to make out, and considerably less euphoric than those of *Jane Eyre*. *Jane Eyre* just about qualifies as romance by preserving marriage as a happy ending. Jane, narrowly saved from bigamy, abandons Rochester rather than become his mistress, and Rochester is so comprehensively punished for his would-be sexual exploitation in body, spirit and purse that Jane can be seen to be doing him a moral favour by marrying him after Bertha's death. The second Mrs de

Winter, however, is married early in the novel, apparently legitimately, before she discovers that she too is living in the grave of an only intermittently dead wife. If Maxim is punished for the murder of his wife by the destruction of his aristocratic house and lineage, she is comprehensively punished for her complicity as accessory after the fact (a hanging offence at the time, it should be remembered) by childlessness and homelessness.

My own view of the novel chimes with that of Nina Auerbach, who writes of *Rebecca* and a couple of other du Maurier novels:

> These brutal tales are not, in the common sense, romances. Technically, they are scarcely romances at all if, as its most articulate readers claim, romances seduce their female readers into 'good feelings' about the dominion of men and the primacy of marriage ... Romance is inherently a soothing and tender genre that aims to reconcile women to traditional lives whose common denominator is home ... Home in *Rebecca* is an *unheimlich* [uncanny] monstrosity whose only alternative is exile. If Daphne du Maurier writes romances at all, their achievement is to infuse with menace the lives women are supposed to want ... For [Mrs de Winter] wifehood is an excruciating ordeal with or without a homicidal husband ... *Rebecca* ... is indelible ... as a study of menacing domesticity.
>
> (Auerbach, 2000, pp.102–3, 104)

Auerbach concludes that, for all du Maurier's undoubted debt to the Brontës, she does not share their sense of female liberation through feeling; instead, her romances have a 'cold heart':

> du Maurier did at times sound like a Brontë, but her heroines scarcely find power and meaning through love. Far from fuelling their individualism, romance breaks them down. The Brontës' novels are a surge toward freedom; for du Maurier's women, such elation is too remote to dream about.
>
> (Auerbach, 2000, p.113)

In this view, du Maurier was in the business of rewriting *Jane Eyre* and she meant to be understood as so doing; furthermore, she was critical, even censorious, about the legacy of romance as a story that lures women to their own destruction. If this is so, then dismissing *Rebecca* as formula fiction is not so easy. It is dubious whether *Rebecca* provides in any uncomplicated way emotional security. Yet *Rebecca*'s debt to romance and Gothic formulas, inherently conservative genres in their investment in monogamous marriage, certainly makes it hard to think in any simple way of the novel as conservative or radical. Is it conservatively complicit with the patriarchal repression of libertarian female sexuality embodied in the murder of Rebecca, and with which the second Mrs de Winter colludes? Or is it post-romantic, radically critical of romance's investment in marriage, carefully rejecting the sort of optimistic marital solution exemplified by Jane Austen's *Pride and Prejudice*, which successfully marries a spirited but impoverished heroine to a haughty and improbably rich and virtuous hero?

This argument tends to come down to what sort of relationship the text sets up with its readers. How much does it command readers to identify unproblematically with the heroine via first-person narration? Like them, the heroine is an eager reader of clues, which are often presented explicitly as text – handwriting, pictures and so on. To some extent, this construction of the woman reader on the model of the heroine is essential to the workings of a fiction about one woman fantasizing about being another (more glamorous, powerful and beautiful) woman. Or is it possible, as I have suggested above, that the text simultaneously solicits the alert reader to stand slightly awry to the narrator's point of view, so achieving a double vision of the text? I think these ambiguities are unresolvable, but they may be the key to *Rebecca*'s enduring fascination, and to subsequent writers' desires to rewrite it. To its ability to inspire a continuing stream of would-be explanatory spin-offs *Rebecca* owes its elevation from mere bestseller to popular classic; the history of this rewriting is the subject of the next section.

Rebecca revenants

Alfred Hitchcock, *Rebecca* (1940)

The sales figures of *Rebecca* (an initial print run of 20,000, followed by twenty-eight printings in Britain alone, becoming a bestseller in the USA and never going out of print since) speak strongly of the immediate success of the novel. Almost straightaway it established itself as the sort of fiction that translated rapidly across different media: this is one of the major factors that enabled it to become a 'popular classic', and, indeed, that identifies it as 'popular'. Du Maurier herself dramatized it for the London stage in 1939, and it was also adapted by Orson Welles for radio broadcast. In future years, it would be made into an opera, and at least two television series, but the film that Alfred Hitchcock directed in 1940, in the shadow of war – with Laurence Olivier as Maxim de Winter, Joan Fontaine as the second Mrs de Winter and Judith Anderson as Mrs Danvers – was to become a classic in its own right. Olivier had just had a signal success as Heathcliff in Hollywood's version of *Wuthering Heights* (1939), and his lover Vivien Leigh hoped to play the first Mrs de Winter (another plum role, to add to her Scarlett O'Hara in *Gone with the Wind* just a year earlier). She would be disappointed, for in the event Hitchcock agreed that Rebecca herself should never appear, underscoring something remarkable that is not immediately apparent in the discussion of the novel above, that the narrator never actually sees so much as a photograph of Rebecca. 'Rebecca' is in fact a composite ghost conjured up by the narrator's incessant jealous speculation, fuelled by the probably untrustworthy and certainly conflicting accounts of Mrs Danvers, Maxim, Frank Crawley and others. The opening scene of the film – de Winter standing on the cliff at Monte Carlo – is remarkable for its insistence on Rebecca's paradoxical invisibility/visibility. Hitchcock carefully does not provide the flashback sequence that comparable films would have inserted. Instead, in this scene, 'the camera pointedly dynamizes Rebecca's absence' (Modleski, 1988, p.53). Never seen by the viewer, intuited only as the object of Maxim's gaze, Rebecca hovers beyond the camera's eye as something that eludes the camera's surveillance and control: she 'lurks in the blind space of the film, with the result that ... unlike the second Mrs de Winter, she never becomes "domesticated"' (*ibid.*). Similarly, as Modleski points out, 'when Maxim tells the heroine about what happened on the night of Rebecca's death ... the camera follows Rebecca's [supposed] movements in a lengthy tracking shot' and consequently 'not only is Rebecca's absence stressed, but we are made to experience it as an active force' (*ibid.*).

In general, Hitchcock's *Rebecca* is at first glance strikingly faithful to its parent text, allowing for the necessary condensation of the novel to make it film-length. This faithfulness, in fact, was not at Hitchcock's instigation, but at that of the producer Harry O. Selznick, who discarded Hitchcock's initial screenplay in favour of something much closer to the book. The opening sequence, for example, is quoted verbatim from the novel, and frames the whole film as first-person narrative (an unusual technical decision) by using a voice-over and a virtuoso dream sequence. Hitchcock's reading of the relation between Mrs Danvers, the dead Rebecca and the second Mrs de Winter elaborates much of the emotional structure that we have been tracing in the parent text. In the scene in which Mrs Danvers shows the narrator Rebecca's bedroom, Mrs Danvers appears as the keykeeper to the master bedroom, the place where, presumably, the narrator's husband had sex with her predecessor. The huge doors, with shoulder-high doorknobs that both forbid and tempt, suggest by their scale the childlike status of the heroine, and insist on the central importance of this forbidden space within Manderley and within the emotional life of the heroine. Mrs Danvers forces the girl into the position of a voyeur, both of the relation between Maxim and his first wife and of Rebecca's imagined body itself – the climax of this scene is the moment when Mrs Danvers encourages the heroine to imagine Rebecca's body, which would have been hardly veiled at all behind the flimsiness of her nightwear laid out on the marital bed. At the same time, Mrs Danvers tries to insert the second Mrs de Winter into the place of the first, much as the narrator has herself been trying to do, pressing the young girl into Rebecca's seat at the dressing-table and pretending to brush her hair as she had brushed Rebecca's. The circulation of quasi-lesbian desire (of Mrs

Danvers for Rebecca, but also of Mrs Danvers for the heroine, and of the heroine for Rebecca) is very powerful. This reading of the womens' relationships as quasi-lesbian was highly controversial and risky at the time. However, Hitchcock qualifies this eroticism by introducing a detail notably absent from du Maurier's novel, a photograph of Maxim set on the dressing-table, central to the shot. The effect of this photograph is remarkable, importing the master of the house into the bedroom as supposedly the object of desire for both women. For Hitchcock, what is at stake in this negotiation between three women is, ultimately, the man.

As in this instance, Hitchcock's alterations to the original generally tend towards making Maxim more important and more sympathetic. His rewriting of Maxim's murder of Rebecca as an unfortunate and practically self-inflicted accident for which he feels irrationally guilty was necessitated by the censors. The murder in *Rebecca* had proved tricky for Hollywood because of the Motion Picture Code and the restrictions of the Hays Office, which declared that no murderer should go unpunished in a film. The unease felt by the censors over the unpunished murder throws up the way in which the narrator herself persistently persuades herself that she is neither frightened nor critical of her murderous husband. The need to exonerate de Winter from murder also entails the rewriting of the early scene on the cliffs near Monte Carlo from a remembered scene of considered murder to a moment of projected suicide. Hitchcock's realization of the end of *Rebecca* also makes certain alterations. Most notable of these is the way that the heroine stays at home in Manderley instead of travelling up to London with her husband, Julyan and Favell to interview the doctor. In some ways this could be said to be against the spirit of the original text, otherwise rather fully realized in the film – the sense that the new marriage works only when it is on the run in a car, and is entirely dysfunctional within the house. This point is made in a brilliantly interpolated sequence in Hitchcock's film in which Maxim and his new wife view a home-movie of the honeymoon at home in Manderley, by which device the car and house are efficiently counterpoised. What Hitchcock gains by leaving the heroine within the house is a rerun of the scene in *Jane Eyre* that we considered earlier, where the madwoman (here played by Mrs Danvers) comes upon the heroine sleeping. In fact, he conflates that scene with yet another scene from *Jane Eyre*: Jane's rescue of her master from his bed set alight by his mad and vengeful wife. Mrs Danvers has a bigger, more unequivocal role as villainous double to the dead wife, and Hitchcock improves on both *Jane Eyre* and *Rebecca* by making the heroine present as the house finally falls to ruins in flames, immolating the guilty housekeeper. Hitchcock also makes the novel more unambiguously romantic. For du Maurier, the death of the house is in many ways the death of everything the second marriage might have restored – the de Winter blood-line and the virtue and respectability of the family. However appropriate its destruction (as the last vengeance of the ghostly Rebecca), the house's end is also a terrible death, infused with a conservative longing for a lost England. It is a cause for mourning. In contrast, Hitchcock picks up the alternative ending provided by *Jane Eyre*. The frame of the husband and wife (and Rebecca's dog, finally won over) embracing in front of the flames of Manderley insists that the marriage is made and saved with the final extinction of Rebecca's double, Mrs Danvers, and with the extinction of Rebecca's troublesome and wandering sexuality, symbolized by the initials curling into flame on the burning bed. For Hitchcock, the destruction of the house seems almost desirable, suggesting strongly his expatriate and ambivalent relation to embattled England. Crucially, there is no suggestion in the film that the couple will be punished by exile and childlessness.

With these alterations, Alison Light argues, Hitchcock realigns the film from the feminine point of view set up in the initial voice-over to something more mainstream and masculine. In this context, we might return to Hitchcock's use of de Winter's photograph in the otherwise exclusively feminine bedroom. The narrator's central function in conjuring Rebecca is sidelined as the men depart for London without her to find out Rebecca's secret. Mrs Danvers is unproblematically demonized as the wicked stepmother (think of the Queen in *Snow White*, forced as punishment to dance to her death in red-hot iron shoes). Light suggests on this evidence that the film as a whole is unable to deal with 'female hostility toward men and marriage' (1996, p.30), the undercurrent of women's Gothic fiction. In this sense, she argues, we are looking at a masculine rereading of the woman's novel: 'what seems like a woman's film turns out to be a man's after all' (*ibid.*, p.31). In the next section, therefore, I turn to a woman's reading of *Rebecca*. Would a woman writer better preserve the 'female hostility' that Light identifies in the text?

Susan Hill's *Mrs de Winter* (1993)

In 1993, Susan Hill, a considerable and well-respected novelist in her own right and with a reputation made in the field of Gothic by *The Woman in Black* (1988), yielded to the temptation and challenge of writing a sequel to *Rebecca*. It became 'the publishing event of the year' and shot to the top of the bestseller list. The copy I have in front of me embosses the author's name in shiny gold and the title in shiny, curly red, and explicitly advertises the novel on its cover as 'the sequel to Daphne du Maurier's *REBECCA*'. What is interesting about this novel, and about Sally Beauman's similarly successful *Rebecca's Tale* (2001), is exactly this status as sequel, or intertext. *Rebecca* has, as I have already mentioned, often been adapted, and, additionally, it has inspired a vast range of modern Gothic fictions, frequently advertising themselves as 'in the du Maurier tradition'. But it is one thing to inspire a desire in readers to repeat the experience by rereading the novel, and by reading derivatives from it, and another to inspire not one sequel, but two, if we count *Rebecca's Tale*, despite Beauman's insistence that it is conceived as a parallel companion piece rather than a sequel pure and simple. Such a phenomenon is very unusual, almost unique, speaking to the importance of the novel itself and to the commercial acumen of its sequels' publishers, but also perhaps to something more. Perhaps it can tell us something about what readers make of *Rebecca*. **What do you think it is about *Rebecca* that makes it possible, or desirable, to provide a sequel? Jot down a few notes before you read on. How would you tackle the writing of a sequel yourself?**

My own view is that *Rebecca* solicits a sequel in three main ways. The first is the most obvious. *Rebecca* disappointingly refuses to provide the expected romance ending. Think about it – usually the heroine is torn between a dark sexy man and a fair reliable man. She either will then choose the fair reliable man like a sensible girl or will be allowed to choose the dark sexy man because the fair reliable man turns out to be a baddie after all. (In case you are smiling slightly here at this cliché, you might want to remember that the second plot is shared by *Pride and Prejudice* and *Jane Eyre*.) Either way, though, she escapes death (actual or moral) and then gets married and lives happily ever after. Even Charlotte Brontë relents a little to the extent of allowing Rochester partially to recover his sight. In common with the other blockbuster of its decade, Margaret Mitchell's *Gone with the Wind* (1936), however, *Rebecca* signally fails to deliver happy heterosexual romance with its conventional promise of domesticity and procreation. In this sense, it leaves readers frustrated of what are supposed to be comforting certainties. A sequel, then, you might think, would try for a more satisfactory conclusion. Second, *Rebecca* is based, as we have already noted, on substitution and repetition. There is no real reason – given that Maxim de Winter is not hanged and his wife is not imprisoned for being an accessory after the fact – that the narrator should not give way again to her obsession about Rebecca, since it is clear that her marriage remains fundamentally unsatisfactory. Such repetition could carry on in *Rebecca*'s obsessive fashion – indeed, at the opening of Chapter 2 the narrator seems to acknowledge a fear that if the couple returned from exile, the process would resume:

> We can never go back again, that much is certain. The past is still too close to us. The things we have tried to forget and put behind us would stir again, and that sense of fear, of furtive unrest, struggling at length to blind unreasoning panic – now mercifully stilled, thank God – might in some manner unforeseen become a living companion, as it had been before.
>
> (2; p.8)

Third, the novel as a whole is organized as an investigation into the mystery of Rebecca herself; structurally, the reader – along with the narrator – is drip-fed revelations about the dead woman. This information remains fragmentary and imperfect; although the narrator, like the wife who stumbles out of Bluebeard's chamber, may desire no further enlightenment, this is not necessarily so for the incurably inquisitive reader peering through the partial (in both senses) account of the narrator. As is the case with a modern celebrity, there must always be something more to know about the 'real' Rebecca, and the deader she is the more tantalizing she remains.

Writing a sequel would require intensive reading of the original to identify the basic logic of the text, and thus its pleasures, and to find a point of entry. Hill solved the problem of constructing a sequel by taking up the beginning of Chapter 2, and experimenting with what happens when the de Winters do try to go back ten years later. She reiterates the essential structures of *Rebecca*, including the first-person retrospective narration. Initially, Rebecca reappears to the haunted second Mrs de Winter as 'text' – in the shape of a handwritten initial on a wreath, in an old photograph printed in a magazine, in newspaper cuttings. This is followed by the reappearance of Rebecca's surrogate, Mrs Danvers, who haunts the heroine, rendering her childless through stress, and ultimately destroys the couple's new sanctuary at yet another awful party. The de Winters' marriage eventually founders because the narrator, in her effort to protect Maxim from his own guilt and remorse, finds herself becoming guilty of keeping secrets from him. Confidence between the two breaks down, and Maxim finally commits suicide down near the ruins of Manderley.

Hill thus chooses to highlight two features of the original – the narrator's unacknowledged fear of and anger at her husband, and Maxim's guilt as a murderer. Only his death will expiate the crime against his first wife and exonerate his second. *Mrs de Winter* perhaps registers the increasing ability of women to express scepticism about the condition of modern marriage.

Sally Beauman's *Rebecca's Tale* (2001)

You might think that one sequel would have saturated the *Rebecca* market, but not so. **Take a moment to consider what you might have concocted if you had been contracted to write a further sequel – what opportunities can you identify? What problems might you foresee?**

Of course, I do not know what you have come up with, but you may find it interesting to compare your ideas with those of the novelist Sally Beauman. There is little space here for a detailed discussion of Beauman's bestselling *Rebecca's Tale*, a long and elaborately constructed novel told by four characters in turn, a detective fiction laced with Gothic and romance, which aspires to have the same effects on the reader as its parent text – to be 'evocative', 'compulsive', 'compelling', 'absorbing', 'captivating' and 'haunting', as the blurb and reviews quoted on the cover have it. There are, however, two remarkable things about this book, viewed as an example of the after-life of *Rebecca* in popular culture. The first is that Beauman took careful account of her audience's previous reading: cannily assuming that buyers of *Rebecca's Tale* would not only be familiar with du Maurier's text and perhaps with *The Rebecca Notebook* but also with Hitchcock's film, and more especially with Hill's *Mrs de Winter*, she scrupulously incorporated these intertexts into her story as part of the parent text. Thus, Maxim's death in the mysterious but deliberate car accident at Manderley, which Hill elaborates from a hint in du Maurier's original epilogue republished in *The Rebecca Notebook*, is built in as recorded history. This is true of many other small details, too. What this suggests is that the story has got loose from its original text and is breeding in the culture at large. The second thing of interest about this rewriting in 2001 is that the main thrust of the novel is to 'discover' the truth not so much about Rebecca's murder as about Rebecca herself, and in so doing to revalue her multiplicity and her perversity. In this sense, Beauman's novel is both a radical revision of du Maurier's novel and entirely true to its spirit of anti-romance. Where du Maurier's novel suggests that every marriage is built upon a crime, though she herself suggests no alternative to a sort of melancholy stoicism on the part of the respectable middle-class woman, Beauman's novel does its best to reject marriage altogether, under the sign of Rebecca.

Across the novel as a whole hovers the desire of Colonel Julyan to see his only surviving and all-too-nearly-on-the-shelf daughter, Ellie, settled in life with a husband. Two candidates present themselves, the first a mysterious man to whom Ellie becomes attached before it is revealed that he has a prior attachment – to a man. Revealed as Rebecca's half-brother, this candidate shares her ability to obsess Ellie. The alternative, a local doctor, suitable in every way, and also sponsored by the father, is turned down by her after the death of her father in favour of taking a degree in Cambridge and living with her lesbian academic aunt. Ellie thus gives up domesticity, marriage and the desire for motherhood, all of which are associated with the widowed second Mrs de Winter, to whom she pays a troubling visit:

> I drove fast: I wanted to leave Mrs de Winter behind as swiftly as I could – and I think I know why. I'd suddenly seen the possibility that I could turn into her. It was one of the options that could lie ahead of me after all; I'd hoped for love, like most people – but if this was what wifeliness meant, I wanted to escape it as fast as possible ... If this was where love led a woman, I feared it. I no longer wanted to listen to the second wife, it was the first wife's voice I needed now.
>
> (Beauman, 2001, pp.595–6)

Ellie gives up her chance of marriage for a freedom that she feels is sponsored by the ghost of Rebecca; her dream is of escaping from the constrictions of marriage to a room of her own in a university city, a room modelled fairly explicitly on Rebecca's boathouse. But where Rebecca escaped to a lover on the boathouse sofa, Beauman's heroine escapes to a neat desk with pink blotting-paper and notebooks filled with her own autobiography. Stopping off on her way to London at the gates of Manderley, Ellie has a final confirmatory vision:

> Beside me, [the dog] made a low whining sound; I felt the soft fur rise on his neck. I bent to reassure him, and then, as I straightened up, I saw – I'm almost certain I saw – someone moving through the trees towards me. She was very swift; I glimpsed only a passing brightness, a quick glitter of movement – but I felt the burn of her glance and it gave me courage.
>
> I think a final salutation passed between us – I certainly felt it did, though I might have imagined it. I waited. When the air was ordinary again, I returned to the car, and told the driver to take me to the station.

> (Beauman, 2001, p.627)

Radio 4 Book Club (recorded at the Daphne du Maurier Festival, May 2003, broadcast June 2003)

Ten years after the publication of Hill's sequel and two after the publication of Beauman's, the BBC ran an event called the Big Read. The turn-of-the-century craze for reading groups and book clubs was becoming mainstream, and Radio 4 was running its own Book Club on air. In conjunction with its weekly broadcasts, a major internet platform was launched, which included its own census of the 'top 100 best-loved books of all time': both *Rebecca* and *Jane Eyre* appeared in the list. Both eventually made the top 21. Tellingly, the BBC was also holding a vote-off between *Rebecca* and *Jane Eyre*: which of the two, visitors to the website were asked, would you rather read? As part of Book Club, Radio 4 went down to the Daphne du Maurier Festival in Fowey, Cornwall, and recorded Beauman in conversation with a group of women speaking about their varied experiences of reading *Rebecca*.

Those who discussed both *Rebecca* and *Rebecca's Tale* with Beauman in 2003 were very much in tune with Beauman's shifting of the meaning of Rebecca. They shared her sense of impatience with the 'needy' and 'dependent' second Mrs de Winter, who was perceived variously as her husband's third victim (if you count Rebecca's hypothetical unborn baby) and as punished for her guilty collusion. The tone of the discussion suggested that any sense of Mrs de Winter as a good wife seemed to have decayed long ago. Instead, both author and audience were clearly identifying with the glamorous Rebecca as a woman who transgressed the norms of male-dominated society, and whose murder was a crime against female sexual freedom. For them Rebecca was the 'real' heroine, definitively supplanting the narrator, whose reasonable enough aspirations to being the heroine of her own romance were hampered not only in her own eyes but apparently also in the eyes of the twenty-first-century reader by her lack of sexual experience, black satin and pearls. If the child heroine finds herself out of favour, so too does the excitingly reticent Maxim. In this milieu, Maxim – played typically in the 1940s on stage and screen by the reigning matinée idol and clearly felt at the time to be a type of the romantic hero, embodying a form of irresistible masculinity – was stigmatized as 'cold' and 'strange'. What the conversation as a whole registered, therefore, was a shift in mainstream ideas about what was appropriately 'feminine' and what was appropriately 'masculine'.

In line with the shift of interest in Beauman's fiction from the victimized second wife to the glamorous and threatening Rebecca, most of these women readers identified very strongly with Rebecca herself, and exhibited marked impatience with the narrator's stupidity over, for example, the costume ball. This does not mean that they are not reading the same book that we have been discussing – after all, the narrator would have preferred to be Rebecca too. But whereas earlier readers seem to have *identified* with the insignificant second Mrs de Winter while *desiring* (like her) to be Rebecca, the Book Club readers not only desire to be Rebecca, they also identify with her. Rebecca's wayward viciousness has always looked like self-determination, but in du Maurier's novel such a form of self-determination deserves murder. In contrast, these women readers concentrated on celebrating Rebecca's murder as brought about by herself. There is warrant for this in the novel, of course: de Winter himself argues this, saying that she won, she made him do it, that he was finally her puppet. Nonetheless, there is a wide gulf between this statement, which tends to exonerate de Winter, and these modern women readers' sense that the guilty murderer should not be allowed to take the credit for the murder.

This range of feeling about the narrator and Rebecca is already built into the novel; the wholly desirable phantom of the first half of the text is only imperfectly erased by the terminally ill vampire of the second. This is hardly surprising; reading the book in conjunction with du Maurier's biography is to reach the inescapable conclusion that she identified herself both with the narrator (as outsider, trespasser and bad manager of servants) and with Rebecca (boyish clothes, hair, manner and gait, strikingly beautiful, passionate about sailing). Like her heroine, du Maurier was given to nude bathing in coves, and ultimately expressed her own bisexuality in a lesbian affair. This massive shift of readerly identification from the narrator to Rebecca, however, may in time lead to *Rebecca* ceasing to be a popular classic

– perhaps, once no-one can imagine sharing the inhibitions and aspirations of the second Mrs de Winter, the story of her tormented relationship with the first will come to seem merely silly.

The Book Club discussion raised this issue of identification both implicitly and explicitly when two lonely male voices rose up from the welter of largely middle-class white women's conversation. One man confessed himself frankly bewildered by the book; the other identified with Maxim as justified in the murder of his unfaithful wife. This unscientific sample of two raises a variety of important critical questions, which you might want to pause to consider here. **Does the text itself 'imply' or 'construct' an imaginary reader in the ways in which the narrator assumes sympathetic knowledge of attitudes, customs, priorities and conventional feelings? If so, who is this reader? Is it a white, middle-class, heterosexual woman? If this is the case, then what of those who are not such readers? Is the text available to them – does it offer points of entry and identification – or does it simply become 'unreadable' from such a stance?**

My own view is that the text is so efficient at constructing its reader that we do not ourselves need to fit neatly into the mould of the text's original 'implied reader' – a white, middle-class, heterosexual woman – or actually to share her supposed preoccupations. If Stephen King is right in saying that in this novel 'Du Maurier created a scale by which modern women can measure their feelings' (quoted in du Maurier, 2003, back cover), or in other words that the novel is a sort of machine that women can use to reflect upon their own socially constructed femininity, then that is going to leave approximately half the population out in the cold for starters. But even those of us who fit into that category a little more neatly than the two male readers I mentioned above cannot possibly share the position of the reader du Maurier originally envisaged, since none of us inhabits the world as it existed in 1938. Moreover, to be a student of the text, it is not necessary to 'be' the implied reader, only to recognize and take account of the contours and reactions of that implied reader. However, the beauty of being able to study a popular classic such as *Rebecca* is that we can bring the readerly reactions (ours or others') that sometimes seem 'prohibited' by academic discourse to energize our studies. Far from being distractions from the task of literary and cultural analysis, the feelings inspired by the text are part of what we need to put under the critical microscope.

In the preceding sections I have been describing how the story of Rebecca has come to be released from the confines of its parent text, and implying that this ability to free-float is itself a description, consequence and condition of its popularity. I have been trying to persuade you that a popular text can be studied not merely through close reading of the text itself, but in terms of its interrelationships with other texts and with social life more largely: through these *Rebecca* has become cultural myth, part of the apparatus by which our society thinks and feels. The Book Club discussion in particular points up the way that *Rebecca*'s enduring popularity is fed by activities around the text as much as by the text itself. These practices broadly derive from two impulses: one, the 'fan-club' impulse to found a community of readers around the common experience of the text; the other, to 'ground' the text within a variety of contexts, often provided by the life-history of its author. The reading practice that is the focus of the next and final section is arguably inspired by both impulses: it is a practice in which I and probably many of you have indulged – namely, the practice of literary tourism. There is a sort of guilt that I as an academic am meant to feel in confessing to literary tourism of this kind – it is faintly disreputable because it seeks to 'explain' the text by recourse to extra-textual experience or context. As I hope to show in the next section, however, it is the structure of desire within *Rebecca* that generates this longing to visit Manderley.

A desirable location: du Maurier's Cornwall

Along with *Rebecca*, du Maurier set many of her most popular novels in Cornwall, her home from her mid-twenties until her death. For me, Cornwall represents longed-for escape, based on many childhood experiences of holiday there; for du Maurier, too, it seems to have represented escape, though this was not rooted in childhood memory. Rather, she seems to have elected it as a founding landscape for her writing, fleeing London and her family's literary heritage there, and locating herself instead in the liminal space that Cornwall has seemed to be from a metropolitan perspective since at least the eighteenth century. Du Maurier found in Cornwall an enabling sense of opportunity and of danger. Historically unruly and ungovernable, far from the centres of national power, Cornwall offered a sublime and transgressive space that du Maurier seems to have felt was as hospitable to her writing as a woman as the Yorkshire moors had been to the Brontë sisters (see du Maurier, 1967).

For good or ill, du Maurier's sense of Cornwall has been remarkably coherent with the Cornwall that continues to serve as a middle-class holiday destination. Fowey's many-coloured cottages, for example, stacked picturesquely up along the edge of the harbour, are now almost universally owned by Londoners. Who knows what fantasies of escape from respectability they house? Fowey and its environs are now called 'Daphne du Maurier country', traced over by literary tourists plotting her texts of melancholy and nostalgia onto the grid of the Ordnance Survey map. **What do you think literary tourists who visit 'Daphne du Maurier country' are looking for? In what ways might *Rebecca* and its intertexts solicit or frustrate such literary tourism?**

Rebecca's instant and continuing success fuelled the characteristically modern demand, both in du Maurier's lifetime and after her death, to know more about the author. By no means all texts have this effect on the modern reader, it should be noted; what makes *Rebecca* so potent in this respect (along with one or two other du Maurier novels) is her use of a first-person narrator. The reader typically identifies, if not necessarily with the narrator herself, with her desire for the house, and for Rebecca. Indeed, *Rebecca*'s protagonist is in some sense herself merely a tourist in Manderley, as the poignant moment when she remembers her childhood trip to the local shop and the purchase of the postcard of the house should remind us from the very earliest pages of the novel (4; p.24; 6; p.59). As the narrator traverses house, garden and shoreline, picking up the traces of Rebecca in her domestic landscape, she begins to construct for us as readers a similar itinerary of desire and investigation. Her obsession with the traces of the dead past, coupled with her efforts to 'see' the inevitably elusive Rebecca, model the seductive and nonsensical trip of the tourist. Like the tourist, she is hopelessly belated, in the sense that she appears after most of the real story has been played out. Like the typical tourist, she is a middle-class interloper in an aristocratic social system, obsessed with a lost, invisible and enigmatic past embodied in an infinitely desirable and ultimately unattainable piece of property. Alert with febrile attentiveness to every clue and trace in the present-day landscape of what once was, condemned to (and desiring to) repeat the past, determined actually to insert her body into the imaginary past (as the Caroline de Winter episode amongst others shows), the narrator efficiently and inevitably both prefigures and constructs the present-day literary tourist. Without the right of occupancy, without rights of birth or family connection or wealth, the narrator tries to make Manderley and its surroundings her own through the sheer force of her own love and desire for it. Given this emotional structure, it is hardly surprising that tourists have subsequently tried to repeat this (failed) act of imaginative possession.

Although *Rebecca* in this sense invents a figure of the tourist, the place names and some of the geography of *Rebecca* are fictitious (as you will know if you have succumbed to the temptation to consult a map). The novel did not aspire to be topographically realistic. It was instead its many intertexts that elected to provide a comprehensive and verifiable map of the terrain of romance. In the first instance, it was du Maurier's autobiographical essays, commissioned to 'explain' the vast popular success of *Rebecca* (she herself was baffled by it), that first began to root the novel in an identifiable and visitable landscape. The identification of Manderley with Menabilly, and du Maurier with the trespassing heroine (in the passages discussed at the beginning of this chapter) began this process. It was accelerated after the author's death, when more details about du Maurier's doings and character became available through the publication of biographies, which made it clear that she had poured a good deal of her own life-experience into the novel. As I have already remarked, the narrator's gaucheness, shyness and anxiety around servants were just as much hers as were her love of the sea, her boyish clothes and her lesbian adventures, attributes conferred upon Rebecca. The central situation, marriage to a moody older man with a previous more glamorous lover, directly shadowed du Maurier's own troubled relationship with her soldier husband 'Boy' Browning and her anxieties concerning his ex-fiancée, Jan Ricardo. The narrator's homesickness in exile paralleled the situation in which du Maurier found herself as she began the novel, beguiling the time and her depression while stationed along with her husband in North Africa. If you return to 'The House of Secrets', you will notice that the trespassing du Maurier explicitly casts herself as an urban tourist: 'We were not yet rooted. We were new folk from London. We walked as tourists walked, seeing what should be seen. So my sister and I, poring over an old guidebook, first came upon the name of Menabilly' (Reader, Item 30). Du Maurier's own later publications, including and especially *Vanishing Cornwall* (1967), conspired to bind her image ever more firmly to the region and also to construct her sensibility as touristic in its melancholic searching out of 'vanishing' pleasures within the mappable landscape. This pleasure of the real location is, accordingly, very visible in Beauman's companion piece, which, without possessing a particle of du Maurier's feeling for place, is commercially careful to be accurate and verifiable in its Cornish geography, while reusing du Maurier's fictional place names. The result has been that it is increasingly possible to tour the area with du Maurier in hand – to view her house at Bodinnick Ferry, to attend the Daphne du Maurier literary festival, to visit the museum and bookshop in Fowey, and even to see some of her locations, most notably Jamaica Inn at Bodmin. In doing so, the tourist proposes, as it were, to check the real experience of the landscape against the experience derived only second-hand from the text (curious as the assumptions this implies about the relation of fiction to reality may be: surely, the fact that novels are not tied to documentary fact is half their point and they are *supposed* to be complete in themselves). But, perhaps above all, the tourist hereby sets out to repeat the narrator's bitter-sweet experience of simultaneous attachment and exclusion, in company with other ardent seekers of this sensation. Viewing Menabilly/Manderley itself, for example, remains impossible without a private invitation or a willingness to commit barefaced trespass. Perhaps in itself that impossibility is particularly true to the readerly experience of *Rebecca*.

Last year I also went to Pridmouth beach again. Picnic over, the children and I climbed up the sloping cliff and then again up, up the many steps of the stripy Gribben tower. We looked out far across the tinsel-flecked sea, and then back inland into the deep green woods within which Menabilly is said to be buried, though it remains, as ever, invisible. It is, surely, its very invisibility and inaccessibility that provoke the dream and desire so characteristic of du Maurier's protagonist within each reader – as the other middle-class women on the top of the tower with me, companionably training their binoculars on the woods and eagerly asking the custodian where, exactly, Menabilly *was*, proved.

Conclusion

I leave you with an exercise that will allow you to calibrate your own sense of what constitutes *Rebecca*'s 'popularity'. Thinking about this should sharpen up your understanding of the debates over the nature of the 'popular', in readiness for the remaining chapters of Part 1.

Here is a selection of theoretical propositions to test against the ideas raised in this chapter. They variously extend and restate the remarks made in the Introduction to Part 1 (which you may wish to revisit at this point). Try to make the argument for each proposition, then debunk it. Finally, give some thought to the interests each proposition might serve.

1   The 'popular' is simply that which is widely favoured or well liked by many people.

2   The 'popular' is what is left over after we have decided what is 'high', based on criteria such as formal complexity, difficulty more generally and, often, moral worth. In short, it is inferior artistic work.

3   The 'popular' is what appeals to the masses, and is thus corruptly commercial, produced for undiscriminating consumption. It acts as a political opiate. (A variant of this argument with regard to popular romance is that it appeals to women and is thus less worthy of consideration because, the implication runs, women are inherently a less discriminating audience.) The more benign version of this is to say that such popular literature acts to facilitate a productive collective dreaming, either in the form of a safety-valve for anxiety and unrest or as a space for the indulgence of utopian hopes and wishes.

4   The 'popular' is a site of ideological struggle between resistant subordinate groups/cultures in society and the dominant groups/cultures in society who perpetually endeavour to incorporate them. Thus, a popular text might be made up of a contradictory mix of different cultural forces; a popular text might also be 'made' out of the struggle between the original text and its readers (here you might want to revisit the preceding two sections).

5   There is no empirical way of distinguishing the 'popular' from the 'high'. This holds both for approaches that examine the text itself *and* for approaches more interested in the history of a text's reception. Nor is making such a distinction of importance.

Works cited

Auerbach, N. (2000) *Daphne du Maurier: Haunted Heiress*, Philadelphia: University of Pennsylvania Press.

Beauman, S. (2001) *Rebecca's Tale*, London: Time/Warner.

Bromley, R. (1986) 'The Gentry, Bourgeois Hegemony and Popular Fiction: *Rebecca* and *Rogue Male*', in P. Humm, P. Stigant and P. Widdowson (eds), *Popular Fictions: Essays in Literature and History*, London: Methuen, pp.166–83.

Brontë, C. ([1847] 1975) *Jane Eyre*, ed. and intro. by M. Smith, Oxford Classics, Oxford: Oxford University Press.

Carter, A. (1993) *Expletives Deleted*, London: Vintage.

Cawelti, J.G. (1976) *Adventure, Mystery, and Romance: Formula Stories as Art and Popular Culture*, Chicago: University of Chicago Press.

du Maurier, D. (1967) *Vanishing Cornwall*, photographs by C. Browning, London: Gollancz.

du Maurier, D. (1981) *The Rebecca Notebook and Other Memories*, London: Gollancz.

du Maurier, D. (1989) *Enchanted Cornwall*, ed. by P. Dudgeon, London: Michael Joseph/Pilot.

du Maurier, D. ([1938] 1992) *Rebecca*, London: Arrow.

du Maurier, D. ([1938] 2003) *Rebecca*, intro. by S. Beauman, Virago Modern Classics, London: Virago.

Freud, S. ([1920] 1991) 'Beyond the Pleasure Principle', in *On Metapsychology: The Theory of Psychoanalysis*, trans. by J. Strachey, ed. by A. Richards, Penguin Freud Library, vol.11, Harmondsworth: Penguin, pp.269–338.

Hawkins, H. (1990) *Classics and Trash: Tradition and Taboos in High Literature and Popular Modern Genres*, New York: Harvester Wheatsheaf.

Hill, S. (1993) *Mrs de Winter*, London: Mandarin.

Horner, A. and Zlosnik, S. (1998) *Daphne du Maurier: Writing, Identity, and the Gothic Imagination*, Basingstoke: Macmillan.

Light, A. (1991) *Forever England: Femininity and Conservatism between the Wars*, London: Routledge.

Light, A. (1996) '*Rebecca*', *Sight and Sound*, 6.5, May, pp.28–31.

Modleski, T. (1982) *Loving with a Vengeance: Mass-produced Fantasies for Women*, Connecticut: Archon.

Modleski, T. (1988) *Women Who Know Too Much: Hitchcock and Feminist Theory*, New York: Methuen.

Stoneman, P. (1996) *Brontë Transformations: The Cultural Dissemination of 'Jane Eyre' and 'Wuthering Heights'*, London: Prentice/Harvester Wheatsheaf.

Further reading

The Daphne du Maurier website (www.dumaurier.org) contains a comprehensive bibliography, links to tourist advice for du Maurier pilgrims to Cornwall, including information on the Daphne du Maurier Festival and associated guided walks, and a revealing 'Guest Book', in which readers are encouraged to share their reactions to *Rebecca*. The material on this site addresses a phenomenon that there has not been space to touch on in this chapter: the formation of virtual reading communities of (usually) women constellated around du Maurier's text.

Caughie, J. (1986) 'Popular Culture: Notes and Revisions', in C. MacCabe (ed.), *High Culture/Low Culture*, Manchester: Manchester University Press. A helpful discussion of definitions of 'popular culture'.

du Maurier, D. (1978) *Growing Pains: The Shaping of a Writer*, Bath: Firecrest. Du Maurier's autobiographical account of her youth.

Forster, M. (1993) *Daphne du Maurier*, London: Chatto & Windus. The essential biography.

Shallcross, M. (1991) *The Private World of Daphne du Maurier*, London: Robson Books. Biographical work with illuminating illustrations.

Storey, J. (1993) *An Introductory Guide to Cultural Theory and Popular Culture*, New York: Harvester Wheatsheaf. A usefully impartial overview and analysis of theories of the 'popular' for those intrigued by the subject.

CHAPTER 2

The poetry of Frank O'Hara and Allen Ginsberg

SUE ASBEE

Overview

After a brief introduction to Frank O'Hara and Allen Ginsberg, I compare a poem by each of them before moving on to study O'Hara's poetry in some detail. The range of reference in his poems, from 'high' to popular (or 'mass') culture, is linked to critical debates that were current in the USA in the 1950s, and O'Hara's innovative voice is considered against more conservative expectations of poetry at the time. A section on gay New York in the 1950s, with particular reference to the cinema, takes us back to the mass-culture debate raised towards the beginning of the chapter. The same debate is significant in the next section, where Ginsberg's work is explored. Acknowledgement of literary tradition and convention is discussed with reference to his poem 'Howl', counterbalancing the view that his 'Beat' writing was completely spontaneous. Reception of *Howl and Other Poems* is discussed with particular reference to the obscenity trial that followed its publication, leading to a section on Ginsberg as a proponent of a counter-culture and as a fierce opponent of capitalism against the backdrop of the cold war. The chapter ends with a discussion of Ginsberg's 'America', and a brief comparison of the two poets.

The poems discussed in this chapter are: by Frank O'Hara, 'Music', 'Personal Poem', 'The Day Lady Died', 'Getting Up Ahead of Someone (Sun)', 'Steps', 'Fantasy', 'Poem' ('Lana Turner Has Collapsed'); by Allen Ginsberg, 'In the Baggage Room at Greyhound', 'Howl', 'America'.

Introduction

In this chapter, I consider two US poets who were publishing their work in the 1950s. They offer quite different ways of thinking about 'the popular': while Frank O'Hara made poetry out of the raw material of popular culture, Allen Ginsberg was widely read and heard, and became a popular poet in his own right. O'Hara lived, worked in and wrote about New York; Ginsberg gave his first readings on the opposite coast of the USA, in San Francisco. They did meet and become friends – O'Hara's poem 'Fantasy' is dedicated 'to the health of Allen Ginsberg' – and occasionally they read at the same event, but even though the poems examined in this chapter are almost exclusively autobiographical lyrics, their work could hardly be more different. O'Hara is part of what is often referred to as the 'New York School'; Ginsberg was at this period of his long career known as one of the 'Beats'. The latter 'were inclined to think the New Yorkers silly and effete', while the New York poets felt the Beats were 'too provincial, unsophisticated, narcissistic, self-mythologizing' and perhaps 'a little too vulgar' (Lehman, 1999, p.335). Ginsberg protests against capitalism, consumerism and social inequalities, using autobiography to serve a public purpose. In contrast, O'Hara's voice is more intimate: he is not unaware of injustice, but exposing it in his verse is not his first concern.

Because anything that interested O'Hara became part of his verse, and because his interests were so diverse, he recognized no distinctions between mass culture and high culture. Ginsberg, on the other hand, made claims for poetry as a new and revolutionary force, sought a new audience within the counter-culture, and became a bestseller.

Before you have any more background to these poets, read O'Hara's 'Music' (Appendix) and Ginsberg's 'In the Baggage Room at Greyhound' (Ginsberg, [1956] 2002, pp.44–8; unless otherwise stated, all references to Ginsberg's poetry are to this edition). Try not to be put off by details you do not understand, but aim instead to arrive at some general points of description and comparison.

Neither poem has a regular rhythm or rhyme. Each deals with a particular moment in the speaker's life, using surroundings as a starting point for meditation: the baggage handling department of the Greyhound bus depot where Ginsberg is working, and the New York City street where O'Hara stops for a sandwich. Each – at least at first – gives an impression of a conversational voice, but the voices are very different and the more one reads/listens to them, the less conversational they seem. Ginsberg's repeated 'nor' in part I imposes a declamatory pattern on his speech and the 'horrible dream' he describes; O'Hara's 'lavender lips under the leaves of the world' lends a surreal aspect that intensifies as the poem progresses.

Ginsberg, 'worrying about eternity' (p.44), sees the baggage room as a kind of 'limbo', until the poem takes the shape of a journey-of-life metaphor: everyone is 'looking for a bus ride back home to Eternity' (p.47). The travellers and workers described are poor, multiracial and of varying degrees of robustness: Spade, the black clerk, dispatches parcels with 'his marvellous long hand' (p.44), whereas 'fairy Sam' limps and Joe, 'with his nervous breakdown', smiles 'cowardly' at the customers (p.45). All the baggage is damaged – 'hundreds of suitcases full of tragedy' – and yet in part II, Spade, reminding the speaker of 'Angel', takes on a religious significance as the pole he uses for grabbing out-of-reach luggage becomes 'an iron shepherd's crook'. A series of short statements towards the end of the poem makes Ginsberg's social concerns quite clear: 'The wage they pay us is too low to live on', and he declares himself a communist (p.47).

O'Hara's 'Music', beginning with a prosaic liver sausage sandwich near 'The Equestrian' (a gilded statue of General Sherman at the southern end of Central Park; see Figure 2.1), soon takes off into a realm of a different order, the speaker describing himself as 'naked as a table cloth'. It is a foggy autumn afternoon, the season is described as one of 'distress and clarity', perhaps suggesting 'charity'(?) and anticipating Christmas, for they are putting up trees on Park Avenue. How can a season be 'like a locomotive on the march'? And anyway, do locomotives march? The more closely O'Hara's lines are examined, the more bizarre they appear, until even the apparent straightforwardness of the last line is in doubt: the word 'terribly' in 'and the stores stay open terribly late' may acquire a sinister resonance, above and beyond any idiomatic exaggeration common in ordinary speech.

'Music' is dated '1953', and 'In the Baggage Room at Greyhound', 'May 9, 1956'. Both poets belong to the USA's cold war years, which gives an added edge to Ginsberg's plain statement that he is a communist, and may make us look back at O'Hara's 'Close to the fear of war and the stars which have disappeared' with new interest. 'Music' may not be as divorced from historical context as it first appears, something worth bearing in mind as you read other poems by O'Hara.

Figure 2.1 Equestrian statue of General Sherman, Central Park, New York. (Photo: Sue Asbee.)

Frank O'Hara: 'unlike anything previous in American poetry'

Frank O'Hara has never been considered 'popular' as such, and he certainly never commanded the kind of audiences that Allen Ginsberg did, but his poems are accessible, recreating and detailing his daily life in New York in the 1950s and early 1960s. O'Hara was prolific, though much of his poetry was not published until after his death. Writing mattered more to him than publishing, and by all accounts he lost interest once he had finished a poem – many survive only in letters to friends. This attitude is significant in any consideration of popular culture at the time and suggests a paradox: O'Hara is uninterested in the possibilities of preservation that poetry (and art in general) offers, and had little thought of a lasting reputation. Nevertheless, the act of communication – not only in poems in letters to friends, but as a daily activity – was paramount. The title of an essay he wrote on his own poetic practice, 'Personism: A Manifesto' (1959), emphasizes the personal element. I will consider this essay in some detail later, but for now it is enough to say that although it has the tone of an irreverent spoof, the serious intent was to do away with the kind of abstraction that modernist writers aimed for. 'Personism' works in direct opposition to the depersonalization of T.S. Eliot and James Joyce. In Joyce's *Portrait of the Artist as a Young Man* (1916), Stephen Dedalus maintains that the artist, 'like the God of creation, remains within or behind or beyond or above his handiwork, invisible, refined out of existence, indifferent, paring his fingernails' (Joyce, 1977, pp.194–5). There is no question of O'Hara standing apart from his work; although he does occasionally create personas, most of his poems insist on authorial presence and many describe his daily life.

Compiling *The Collected Poems* from verse written in letters scattered among friends and acquaintances was a major task for the editor Donald Allen, a fellow-poet and friend of O'Hara. The collection came out in 1971 and was widely reviewed. Harriet Zinnes wrote that, at the time of his death in 1966, O'Hara was 'not unknown as a poet, but his influence was hardly extensive' (in Elledge, 1993, p.58). By 1973, his reputation was growing: in her review, Marjorie Perloff was 'especially struck by the growing cult of Frank O'Hara' (in *ibid.*, p.59). Even O'Hara's followers (Perloff calls them his 'disciples'), whose work had previously appeared only in coterie publications, had 'begun to take over the literary scene' (*ibid.*). His friends were artists and writers, as Bill Berkson and Joe LeSeur's *Homage to Frank O'Hara* (1978) testifies: Jasper Johns, Willem de Kooning and Alex Katz, among many others, contributed to the volume after his death. He lived in and wrote about New York, working as a curator at the Museum of Modern Art. Through his work, and because they moved in similar social circles, he knew Andy Warhol and other Pop Art artists. His poems record his love of and enthusiasm for the city, his friends, cinema, poetry, painting and music, whether classical or jazz. Because of its subject matter and style, O'Hara's poetry allows us to make significant contributions to debates about popular culture.

Terrell Scott Herring argues that there is 'no distinction' between the language of O'Hara's poems and 'the language of everyday life' (2002, p.417). **Read 'Personal Poem' now (Appendix). Try to decide if Herring's statement is true for this particular work.**

The fact that there is no rhyme certainly contributes to a sense of ordinary speech, although the lack of punctuation leaves readers in some doubt about where emphasis should fall. The rhythm of the poem is irregular too: although the lines are about the same length, they do not follow any regular scheme. There is no overtly 'poetic' language in evidence, with the exception perhaps of the phrase 'luminous humidity'; even there, 'humidity' offers a straightforward description of the climatic conditions. There is none of the complex imagery found in 'Music' either. The language may not be my everyday language – or yours – but it is conversational, carrying conviction that it belongs to the everyday of the speaker; it is relaxed and informal. The desire for a silver hard hat and implied admiration for construction workers makes an interesting juxtaposition with the names of novelists and critics in the third part of the poem, but these highbrow names do not generate critical debate: 'we don't like' and 'we like' simply focuses on the speaker's and LeRoi's agreement, working like a refrain to create a sense of 'us'. The poem begins with the first-person singular pronoun and moves to 'we' in the middle; the speaker, alone again by the end of the poem, is 'happy at the thought' that possibly 'one person out of the 8,000,000' is thinking of him. As Stephen Burt argues in an article in the *London Review of Books*, if you concentrate 'on O'Hara's "I" for too long ... it threatens to – no, it very much wants to – dissolve into a network of encounters with others' (2000, p.27). **If the 'I' of the poem is not the main subject, what is?**

I would suggest that the point of the poem is the importance of personal relationships in the overcrowded metropolis of New York. The overall impression is light-hearted, amusing and possibly even inconsequential, but more disturbing aspects of life are registered: LeRoi brings news of police brutality against the black jazz musician Miles Davis and a lady collects nickels for 'a terrible disease'. While the response to the latter is flippant ('we don't give her one we / don't like terrible diseases'), reaction to the news about Miles Davis is not expressed. LeRoi Jones, a black poet (now known as Amiri Baraka), would certainly have had views that O'Hara was likely to share, but these are no more debated than the relative merits of Henry James or Herman Melville. The poem records surface detail, acknowledging an imperfect world, but one that remains subject to the speaker's mood: he is 'happy' at the end of the first section and the word is repeated in the last line.

In the Introduction to O'Hara's *Collected Poems* (1971), his friend John Ashbery describes the frenetic energy of O'Hara's life in New York and the diversity of his interests, all of which 'provided him with a sort of reservoir of inspiration: words and colours that could be borrowed freely from everywhere to build up big airy structures unlike anything previous in American poetry and indeed unlike poetry, more like the inspired ramblings of a mind open to the point of distraction' (1971, p.ix). In a passage in 'Burnt Norton' (1935), T.S. Eliot describes 'strained time-ridden faces / Distracted from distraction by distraction' in a 'place of disaffection' (1974, p.192), which can be read variously as referring to the London Underground, limbo and Dante's *Inferno*. There is a link between Eliot's diagnosis of alienation in modern society and Ashbery's use of the word 'distraction', which was a key term in the debates about popular culture at the time. Dwight Macdonald, a critic of popular culture, started writing on the subject in the 1940s; his concern that high culture was under threat is eloquently voiced in 'A Theory of Mass Culture', first published in 1953 and reprinted in Bernard Rosenberg and David White's collection of essays *Mass Culture: The Popular Arts in America* (1957).

The terms 'popular culture' and 'mass culture' were synonymous in the USA in the 1950s. Macdonald believes mass culture to be a more accurate term, 'since its distinctive mark is that it is solely and directly an article for mass consumption, like chewing gum' (in Rosenberg and White, 1957, p.59). His objections are that, unlike folk art, which was the culture of the common people, growing 'from below' in times before the Industrial Revolution, mass culture is 'imposed from above. It is fabricated by technicians hired by businessmen; its audiences are passive consumers, their participation limited to the choice between buying and not buying' (in *ibid.*, p.60). He goes on to say that in the past, folk art and high culture were separated, the 'watertight compartments corresponded to the sharp line once drawn between the common people and the aristocracy' (in *ibid.*, p.61).

Read the passage below. What concerns underlie Macdonald's account?

> If there were a clearly defined cultural *elite*, then the masses could have their *kitsch* and the *elite* could have its High Culture, with everybody happy. But the boundary line is blurred. A statistically significant part of the population, I venture to guess, is chronically confronted with a choice between going to the movies or to a concert, between reading Tolstoy or a detective story, between looking at old masters or at a TV show; i.e., the pattern of their cultural lives is 'open' to the point of being porous. Good art competes with *kitsch*, serious ideas compete with commercialized formulae – and the advantage lies all on one side.
>
> (in Rosenberg and White, 1957, p.61)

Macdonald is anxious about the blurring of boundaries and lack of distinction between high and mass culture. He is in no doubt about what constitutes 'good' art, and fears that this is under threat. It is partly a condition of his rhetorical strategy, but also significant that the choice is between television or *old masters*, rather than any other kind of art: in New York, presumably he would choose to visit the Metropolitan Museum rather than the Museum of Modern Art, where O'Hara worked on the exhibitions of Jackson Pollock, Franz Kline and Willem de Kooning, the 'Action Painters' later known as Abstract Expressionists. Macdonald's phrase ' "open" to the point of being porous' reminds us of Ashbery's description of O'Hara's mind 'open to the point of distraction', but whereas Ashbery uses the qualifying adjective 'inspired', Macdonald is condemnatory.

Like nineteenth-century capitalism, Macdonald goes on to argue, mass culture is 'a dynamic, revolutionary force, breaking down the old barriers of class, tradition, taste, and dissolving all cultural distinctions' (in Rosenberg and White, 1957, p.62). Instead of seeing this as a positive force, it is something to be deplored. He continues:

> It mixes and scrambles everything together, producing what might be called homogenized culture, after another American achievement, the homogenization process that distributes the globules of cream evenly throughout the milk instead of allowing them to float separately on top. It thus destroys all values, since value judgments imply discrimination. Mass Culture is very, very democratic: it absolutely refuses to discriminate against, or between, anything or anybody. All is grist to its mill, and all comes out finely ground indeed.
>
> (in Rosenberg and White, 1957, p.62)

One of his many examples includes *Life* magazine irresponsibly publishing 'nine color pages of Renoirs plus a memoir by his son, followed by a full-page picture of a roller-skating horse' (in Rosenberg and White, 1957, p.62). (I would dearly love to see that horse.) The imaginative possibilities prompted by such juxtapositions – in *Life*'s case almost certainly unintentional – were part of dynamic change in music, the visual arts and literature at the time. For example, going to John Cage's 'Music of Changes' concert on 1 January 1952 made Ashbery and O'Hara realize that 'chance could be a determining element in a work of art' (Lehman, 1999, p.339). The apparently inconsequential could be incorporated into a poem: a telephone call, a newspaper headline or a scrap of conversation overheard in the street could all be included. Poetry was not a criticism of life nor even a record of experience, 'but the experience itself' (*ibid.*). Composers such as Cage and, earlier, Erik Satie used 'found' materials – sounds not necessarily produced by conventional musical instruments. In the visual arts, there are parallels in the techniques of collage and montage, where, for example, arrangements of newspaper clippings are used. The artist no longer needs to be a craftsman in the sense that the old masters Macdonald admires were.

Although many would cheer the notion of a 'dynamic, revolutionary force' breaking down old barriers, Macdonald is fearful of a future where his value judgements are not recognized. It does not take much imagination to see those barriers applying to class, as well as taste: after all, the point about mass culture and its 'commercialized formulae' is that it is cheap and readily available. Mass culture is for the poor, high culture for the wealthy. Followed through, Macdonald's beliefs suggest a longing for the security of a stratified society where everyone knows their place, something that the USA always prided itself in opposing.

I will return later to Ashbery's assessment of O'Hara's as a mind 'open to the point of distraction'. Meanwhile, his comment that O'Hara's work was 'unlike anything previous in American poetry' raises questions about exactly what expectations there were of poetry in the USA in the mid-twentieth century. **Now read the extract from David Lehman's *The Last Avant-Garde* (Reader, Item 32) to help you decide exactly what O'Hara was doing that was so new.**

Lehman's summary explains what he sees as the orthodoxy of US poetry at the time, and the way in which it was supported and verified by the work of academics like William Empson and Cleanth Brookes. Lehman is not dismissive of New Criticism, made central to the study of poetry since the 1920s, but he points out that it helped to make both writing and reading poetry the preserve of academics, a cultural elite. He identifies a 'conflict between academic and antiacademic poetry', citing anthologies that were compiled in the 1950s as if in support of each side. He sums up by saying later in the essay that the 'orthodox poem of the 1950s had heightened diction, tight logic, and a sense of moral earnestness' (Lehman, 1999, p.388).

Kevin Stein says that by 1964, when Frank O'Hara's *Lunch Poems* appeared, US poetry was

> already embroiled in a wrenching poetic revolution. The rebellion had been initiated variously in the fifties by the Beats, by Charles Olson's theory and practice of projective verse, by the Black Mountain poets of the Objectivist tradition issuing from William Carlos Williams, and by Robert Bly and James Wright, who late in the decade abandoned the 'square poem' for an imagistic, intuitive mode modeled after foreign influences.
>
> (in Elledge, 1993, p.358)

Stein goes on to point out that O'Hara dated each of his poems, arguing that this makes it clear that he had rejected the 'New Critical manners which had dominated American poetry since the thirties' (in Elledge, 1993, p.358). What Stein is getting at is that the New Criticism's insistence on the words on the page was ahistorical; in contrast, by publishing dates of writing, sometimes even making dates part of the poem itself, as in 'The Day Lady Died', O'Hara insists on the importance of context. Stein concludes that in the mid- to late 1950s 'no one else was doing anything quite like him' (*ibid.*).

In spite of all this, Ashbery's qualifying phrase, 'indeed unlike poetry', brings the very nature of O'Hara's work into question: how else can it be described, and where exactly does its difference lie? To answer this question I want to consider O'Hara's 'The Day Lady Died'. The poem is an elegy, which simply means a lament: in this case for the celebrated jazz singer Billie Holiday, who was popularly, respectfully and affectionately known as 'Lady Day'. The elegiac convention has its origins in Classical literature, though at different times the term has been used to describe more general meditative, serious or reflective verse. Conventionally, many elegies begin with an invocation to the gods, like O'Hara's own 'For James Dean' (1955), which begins:

> Welcome me, if you will,
> as the ambassador of hatred
> who knows its cause
> and does not envy you your whim
> of ending him.
>
> For a young actor I am begging
> peace, gods. Alone
> in the empty streets of New York
> I am its dirty feet and head
> and he is dead.

(O'Hara, [1971] 1995, p.228)

Now read 'The Day Lady Died' (Appendix). Compare the opening lines with the opening stanza of 'For James Dean' quoted above.

While both poems have a strong sense of speaking voices, the tone of each is very different. 'For James Dean' has a formal quality: the tone is serious, appropriately enough given the conceit that it is 'the gods' who are being addressed, and it conveys a sense that the poet is acutely conscious of writing within a tradition. The poem is not written *for* James Dean, but pleads for peace on his behalf. It is much more difficult to decide who is being addressed in 'The Day Lady Died'. Might the speaker simply be talking to himself? Although the poems are very different, I was struck by the abruptness of 'and he is dead' and 'with her face on it'.

The tribute to Billie Holiday, 'The Day Lady Died', is of the moment and of the city, points of reference to which O'Hara constantly returns in his verse. In 'For James Dean', the 'empty streets of New York' are evoked and the speaker identifies himself directly as the city's 'dirty feet and head', but 'The Day Lady Died' is even more deeply rooted in New York.

Ashbery testifies to the vitality of the writing, paying tribute to its diversity and its range of reference. But does the innovation really just reside in 'ramblings' or are there other issues at stake? **Read 'The Day Lady Died' again. Try to relate the questions raised by Ashbery to the debate about mass culture that we have started to explore.**

The speaker consumes mass culture, buying a hamburger, a malted milk, cigarettes and – in a slightly different market, but nevertheless one dependent on the technology responsible for mass-produced goods – a volume of Paul Verlaine's poetry. This last is chosen only after much deliberation. The books all come from Europe, but such is the global market that the consumer can even see the work of poets in Ghana. City life is inscribed in O'Hara's work to such an extent that anti-pastoral becomes a theme: 'the country is no good for us', he writes in 'Walking' (1964), 'there's not enough / poured concrete' (1995, p.477); in 'Meditations in Time of an Emergency', he rejects nature in favour of the city: 'I can't even enjoy a blade of grass unless I know there's a subway handy, or a record store or some other sign that people don't totally *regret* life' (*ibid.*, p.197).

Now read 'Getting Up Ahead of Someone (Sun)' (Appendix) and compare it with 'The Day Lady Died'.

'Getting Up Ahead of Someone' provides us with a phrase to describe O'Hara's method of composition: waking and pouring himself a bourbon, he begins 'to write one of my "I do this I do that" / poems in a sketch pad'. The stuff of his daily life becomes the substance of the poem in the same way that choosing presents for friends, getting his shoes shined and eating a hamburger do in 'The Day Lady Died'. Much earlier in the twentieth century, James Joyce and Virginia Woolf insisted that it is not in heroic acts, but in daily activity that significance is found. O'Hara is fuelled by his own daily activity, and New York is as vital to his work as Dublin and London were to Joyce and Woolf.

'I do this I do that' describes the way in which the Billie Holiday elegy unfolds. Clause is piled on breathless clause, as each successive action is catalogued. The only punctuation – beyond line breaks – consists of four commas. One is in the second line; two serve to parenthesize 'but I don't', as the speaker weighs up and rejects alternative books to buy for Patsy. The fourth makes us pause between the cigarettes and the newspaper, preparing us for the front page. The effect is one of seamless activity. The apparently simple syntax builds to a climax: 'and' is repeated nineteen times, but eleven of those instances come in the last ten lines of the poem. There are no full

Figure 2.2   Frank O'Hara at 441 East 9th Street, New York City, on 26 September 1959; photograph by Fred W. McDarrah. (Copyright © by Fred W. McDarrah.)

stops, not even at the end: like Billie Holiday herself, readers are left permanently unable to draw breath, permanently diminished by her death. A line break and gap for a new paragraph arrest our reading as O'Hara is arrested by 'Her face' on the front of the newspaper. In an extravagant gesture, 'She' is never mentioned by name, though this is a tribute: by implication, she is too famous and the event too momentous to require it; what other death could be the subject? Only in the inversion of the poem's title is 'Lady Day' identified.

The immediacy of the date, time and place, the refusal to offer consolation or to distance the subject, and the sudden shock of grief all work to make this important poem stand in stark opposition to the elegiac tradition, while inevitably calling that tradition to mind. Unlike in John Milton's 'Lycidas' (1637) or Thomas Gray's 'Elegy Written in a Country Church Yard' (1751), nature provides no consolation; 'The Day Lady Died' is an urban anti-pastoral. Like Alfred Tennyson in 'In Memoriam' (1850), O'Hara finds 'she is not here' and so 'On the bald street breaks the blank day' (in Trilling and Bloom, 1973, p.444). There is not, however, the remotest suggestion that religion offers any resolution, as it does, eventually, in Tennyson's poem. It is the enduring moment of first hearing of a death, not the process of grief, that is O'Hara's subject here. 'A Step Away From Them' (Appendix) works in a similar way: the speaker walks through the streets of New York during his lunch hour, noticing workmen eating lunch, women's skirts 'flipping / above heels', and a moment's flirtatious connection between a black guy and a 'blonde chorus girl'. There are, he observes,

> several Puerto
> Ricans on the avenue today, which
> makes it beautiful and warm. First
> Bunny died, then John Latouche,
> then Jackson Pollock.

In the middle of the bustle, interest and warmth of the city, with no warning, death is introduced.

What are the effects of the insistence on the present moment in 'The Day Lady Died'?

The painter Grace Hartigan described O'Hara's 'In Memory of My Feelings' as a poem about 'how to be *open* but not violated, how *not to panic*' (quoted in Perloff, 1998, p.141; Hartigan's emphasis); the phrase is equally applicable to 'The Day Lady Died'. Attention to the present moment is one way of avoiding the feeling of physical assault that may result from unexpected news like this ('and I am sweating a lot by now'). Yet it also points to one of the poem's temporal anomalies: the relentless catalogue of doing this, doing that, written in the present tense, serves as distraction, a kind of denial. Significantly, however, all the 'doing' that takes place happens *before* the speaker has heard of the death, when actually there is no need to avoid anything. Absorbing the news brings activity to an end. For all the use of the present tense, the moment of writing is inscribed in the poem, retrospectively; there *is* prior knowledge of the event and the poem is actually a self-reflexive artifice that reviews the day's pursuits in the light of the shock of death.

Analyse the last four lines of the poem closely. What is their effect on the poem?

The last four lines intensify the emotional level of the poem. They take us back almost seamlessly to a memory of hearing Holiday in a night club – only the past tense 'whisper*ed*' confirms that this is in fact a memory and not an intention for the future ('I am ... thinking of / leaning on the john door'). The paratactic structure, so apparently simple and artless, complicates the last line and overlays past with present: was 'she' singing to 'Mal Waldron *and* everyone', including O'Hara; did those in the audience collectively hold their breath because the voice was, literally, breathtaking? Or again, does everyone *now* stop breathing because she has breathed her last, in (for this poem) an unusual moment of elegiac exaggeration. Both readings are simultaneously present, so the poem ends on an appropriate note of uncertainty. Although O'Hara's use of pronouns is usually subtle, typically creating complex and rapidly shifting perspectives, throughout this poem the focus is unequivocally on 'I'. Only the word 'everybody' widens participation in mourning right at the end. The overriding effect of the poem is an intensely personal response to the death of a famous figure.

Now think back to Ashbery's description of O'Hara's mind as 'open to the point of distraction'. In what ways might it be justified in the light of this poem?

Far from 'distraction', the catalogue of times and dates in the opening six lines might suggest an intent, concentrating, focused mind. But there is certainly a wide and eclectic range of reference in 'The Day Lady Died', so perhaps Ashbery is right. The question is difficult to answer without asking more: who are Verlaine, Bonnard, Hesiod, Richmond Lattimore, Brendan Behan, Mal Waldron and Genet, and do they have anything in common? Are Mike, Patsy and Linda Stillwagon from the bank equally important? What is the significance of *New World Writing* and the train times for Easthampton, beyond that of realistic detail? Why mention the time, but leave readers to work out the exact date in July, by reference to Bastille Day? The name-dropping and cultural references certainly derive from O'Hara's own preoccupations, but is there any further significance in the apparently random inclusion?

Ashbery felt there was not. He sees no significant patterning or connection between the figures mentioned in the poem. In his opinion, O'Hara's poetry 'does not speak out ... in favour of civil rights ... it does not attack the establishment ... [it is] a source of annoyance for partisans of every stripe' (quoted in Ward, 2001, p.136). Paul Carroll suggests that the reference to Bastille Day will lead readers to expect an elegy 'on the tormented life of one of the great artists of American jazz':

> Not only was Billie Holiday hounded and persecuted by police and FBI agents because of her addiction to drugs, but she was forbidden in her last, wretched years to work or live in New York City. In an elegy for her, then, the Bastille Day might develop into a symbol similar to what it originally represented to the Parisian mob that stormed it on July 14, 1787: namely, the hated symbol of despotism, the 'insolence of office', and the cruel perversions of justice by the establishment in general.
>
> (in Elledge, 1993, p.373)

But, Carroll goes on to argue, O'Hara fails to develop the allusion to the French national holiday 'in anyway whatsoever' (in Elledge, 1993, p.373). Geoff Ward, on the other hand, cites the 'innumerable pointedly favourable references in O'Hara's poetry to black friends and artists' – such as the black jazz pianist Mal Waldron – and argues that his poems are 'insistently libertarian precisely because of their basis in personal encounter, feelings, friendships and tastes' (2001, pp.136–7). Billie Holiday died of a drug overdose, Brendan Behan of alcoholism; mention of the gay, ex-convict French writer Jean Genet and the characters in *Le Balcon* ('The Balcony'; 1956) introduce 'the motif ... of the artist punished for his or her deviance' (Perloff, 1998, p.xix). The bank clerk's last name – Stillwagon – may, in this reading, imply both being 'on the wagon' and, perhaps, a whisky still. Bastille Day – which is *not* the day on which Holiday died – has resonance of tyranny overcome. The accumulated references to surface detail are not, therefore, as random as they may seem; or, if O'Hara's mind is as open as Ashbery suggests it is, it performs some subconscious selection on its own account. Whatever conclusion you may have reached, bear this discussion in mind when you come to read Allen Ginsberg's impassioned protests in 'Howl' and 'America'. Their tone is very different and a comparison might well convince you that O'Hara had little interest in creating a public voice.

Like Ashbery, Carroll argues that O'Hara is writing a new kind of poetry. He 'seems to assume the role of poet as a mirror or tape recorder or movie director in the sense of Andy Warhol allowing the camera to grind away for hours on end, filming without editing the top of the Empire State Building, or a man sleeping or eating a mushroom' (in Elledge, 1993, p.377). Carroll goes on to say that reading a poem by O'Hara is similar to seeing one of Claes Oldenburg's hamburgers in a museum for the first time, or Warhol's canvas of Campbell's soup cans (in *ibid.*, p.378). 'Unpoetic' details, like the shoeshine or buying cigarettes, are included for their own sake as a 'bare existential reality' (in *ibid.*), not as part of an organic structural pattern. It is this that makes O'Hara's work so exciting; what makes 'The Day Lady Died' a poem is, in Carroll's opinion, 'the nerve evident in the very act of writing it' (in *ibid*, p.378); the audacity itself is exciting.

Personism

In 1959, O'Hara was persuaded to write down his ideas about poetry for a journal. 'Personism: A Manifesto' was first published in the journal *Yugen 7* in 1961; it appeared elsewhere during the 1960s (in the journal *Audit*, for example), and is quoted in full in the Introduction to *An Anthology of New York Poets* (1970), edited by Ron Padgett and David Shapiro. More than a decade after it was written, the editors – poets themselves – said that 'it is a hard piece to top and ... in many ways it speaks for us all' (Padgett, 1970, p.xxxi).

Read 'Personism: A Manifesto' now (Reader, Item 33). How serious do you think the tone is, and what questions does O'Hara address?

The piece is deliberately provocative, iconoclastic and witty. O'Hara's language is casual: he draws his metaphors and comparisons from romantic relationships, sex and popular culture (the cinema and, in the first paragraph, college sports). However, his lack of solemnity does not signify lack of serious intent. He considers the reception of his poems by analogy with personal relationships: 'suppose you're in love and someone's mistreating ... you, you don't say "Hey, you can't hurt me this way, I care!"' In other words, he recognizes the ultimate lack of control writers are able to exert over how their work is read and interpreted. O'Hara goes on to ask whether poetry should 'improve' readers, a significant question at a time when the US government greatly concerned itself with public morality and censorship. But far from promoting an instrumental role for poetry, he concludes 'if they don't need poetry bully for them. I like the movies too. And after all, only Whitman and Crane and Williams, of the American poets, are better than the movies.' (I discuss Walt Whitman and William Carlos Williams later with reference to Ginsberg.)

In the first paragraph O'Hara advocates 'go[ing] on your nerve', rather than consciously working on rhythm, assonance and other stylistic devices. He develops this later: 'As for measure and other technical apparatus, that's just common sense: if you're going to buy a pair of pants you want them to be tight enough so everyone will want to go to bed with you. There's nothing metaphysical about it.' Poetic devices should be like tight pants: their function, to draw attention not to themselves, but to what lies within; they are there to generate desire. It is not so surprising, therefore, to find that a particular emotion ('I was in love') is incorporated into this statement about the function of poetry. As we have seen, 'Personal Poem' registers violence, racial hatred and disease, but without comment: the speaker's emotional well-being is the focus. As in so many of his poems, the particular moment – 'after lunch with LeRoi Jones on August 27, 1959' – is inscribed into the essay. Going back to work and writing a poem, not for LeRoi, but for a blond, O'Hara realized that he could simply telephone and speak to the person instead: 'and so Personism was born'. Instead of doing away with the need for a poem altogether, which might be one logical conclusion to this insight, he sees this as a way of making the poem (what is said) more important. He uses a startling metaphor to express this: 'Lucky Pierre' refers to the man in the middle of a three-way sexual encounter. Instead of being cancelled out, the poem, like the hypothetical Pierre, 'is correspondingly gratified'. O'Hara is being deliberately outrageous here, but 'Personism' ends on a slightly different, though still light-hearted, note to make a point he felt strongly about: 'The recent propagandists for technique on the one hand, and for content on the other, had better watch out.' The 'propagandists for technique' include poets subscribing to the New Criticism, which had 'dominated American poetry since the thirties' (Kevin Stein, in Elledge, 1993, p.358). As I said at the beginning of this chapter, O'Hara's work stands in opposition to them. As we have seen, it is 'anti-literary': 'The majority of pieces in *Lunch Poems* refuse both regular metric and rhyme patterns ... They make use of a varied language, welcoming both hieratic and demotic phrasing; and they abandon the then-popular mythic references in favour of a more personal allusion, often to close friends and familiar New York locations' (*ibid.*).

Everything that is absent in O'Hara's work, we would expect to find in poems by the 'propagandists for technique'. O'Hara's use of the word 'propagandists' has a distinctively pejorative ring. Whatever conclusion you reached after considering Ashbery, Carroll and Ward's opinions on whether or not O'Hara espouses causes, in the final sentence of 'Personism' O'Hara puts technique and content in opposition to each other, and rejects them both.

Gay New York in the 1950s: cinema, movie stars and mass culture

In 'Personism', O'Hara is both open and restrained about his homosexuality. The phrase 'Lucky Pierre' had a very specific – gay – meaning at the time, and although he explains that 'the poem is at last between two persons instead of two pages', O'Hara's gloss conveniently sidesteps the sexual aspect of his metaphor. It is there as a kind of code for those in the know, an acknowledgement that he has two audiences.

Actors and directors in the US film industry had evaded censorship in similar ways for decades, largely because, as Charles Kaiser says, 'in this era the American establishment was uncomfortable with *all* public manifestations of sexuality, not just homosexuality' (1998, p.67). But the film industry was one of several arenas where gay people did have an identity: by 1926, all the major studios employed dress designers, 'a majority of whom were men, a majority of whom were gay' (Barrios, 2003, p.28). Richard Barrios argues that Hollywood's writers and directors, 'who were constantly aiming their product toward the average lay mind, knew full well that the world of haute couture ... was, like the theatre, a safe haven for homosexual behaviour' (*ibid.*). By 1934, the Production Code was established to ensure strict censorship of all Hollywood movies:

> Every picture needed its seal of approval; without one, filmmakers risked a disaster at the box office because of a boycott ordered by the Catholic Legion of Decency. The code's purpose was clearly stated: 'No picture shall be produced which will lower the moral standards of those who see it. Hence the sympathy of the audience shall never be thrown to the side of crime, wrongdoing, evil or sin' and 'correct standards of life ... shall be presented'

because 'correct entertainment raises the whole standard of a nation. Wrong entertainment lowers the whole living conditions and moral ideals of a race.'

(Kaiser, 1998, p.66)

In spite of this, Barrios shows that the cinema had an efficient and 'surprisingly cultivated syntax' for representing gay and lesbian sexuality (2003, p.168). One of his countless examples comes from a scene in *Bringing Up Baby* (1938), where Cary Grant, inexplicably wearing Katherine Hepburn's negligee, says 'I just went *gay* all of a sudden' (the word 'gay' itself was not overtly used to describe homosexuality at the time). Barrios says this is 'coded enough to make it through the Breen gauntlet' (Joseph Breen was at that time responsible for making sure the Production Code was enforced). What confirms the status of 'gay' in this context is the line of dialogue that follows: 'I'm sitting in 42nd Street, waiting for a bus!' This, says Barrios, is 'the true subversive line, targeted directly to the insiders', for loitering was entirely legitimate on 42nd Street, a major transport terminus; men – and women – could cruise and pick up with impunity (2003, p.154).

Kaiser describes gay life in New York City in the 1950s as 'by turns oppressive and exhilarating, a world of persecution and vast possibilities ... Knowingly serving a drink to a gay person automatically made a bar disorderly under state law, and it was illegal for two men to be on a dance floor without a woman present' (1998, pp.83–4). Andrew Ross reminds us that in many ways the 1950s was a 'prepolitical' age: 'an age that predates the more explicit formation, in the sixties, of the kind of political culture which most of us have come to live and breathe'. The 1950s was a period of 'prelapsarian' innocence, 'before the break-up of consensus liberalism, before the conspiracy climate of all post-Kennedy ideology, before the Sixties "changed everything"' (1989, p.383). It is worth remembering too that the 1950s world of O'Hara's poems also predates the Stonewall riots in 1969, when police raided the Stonewall Inn, a gay bar in New York, and found violent resistance for the first time in many routine raids. Like Rosa Parks's refusal to give up her place on a bus for a white passenger in Alabama, which heralded the civil rights movement, the Stonewall riots became a defining moment, marking the beginning of gay pride. Frank O'Hara had died three years before.

In Kaiser's opinion,

> Gay life acted like a bracing undertow, exerting a powerful opposite pull beneath waves of conformity. Because being a rebel is almost always an essential part of one's homosexuality, it was both especially difficult and especially satisfying to be gay in an

age like this ... The sterility of mass culture made the life of an outsider particularly attractive to writers, artists, actors and painters.

(Kaiser, 1998, pp.88–9)

Now read 'Steps' (Appendix). Do you have a sense of a 'powerful ... pull beneath waves of conformity'? Is it possible to see where Kaiser's difficulties and satisfactions lie? And do you have a sense of 'The sterility of mass culture'?

The first three lines of the poem set a tone of joyous exuberance: New York itself is being addressed, and it is exciting and ebullient like a red-haired, tap-dancing movie star. It is also slightly out of kilter: even the church's authority is skewed, 'leaning a little to the left'. This is a love poem when love is going well: instead of war ('D-days'), we have victory ('V-days') and acceptance. The simplicity of 'all I want is a room up there / and you in it' gives way to a fantasy where out on the street crowds of people on their way to work are locked together, suggesting that everyone experiences a version of sexual fulfilment as gloriously as O'Hara has the night before. The importance of reality follows immediately though: at work, checking a photographic slide, he says 'that painting's not so blue'. Perhaps there is a 'pull' between gay life and conformity, but interestingly enough, in his working persona as museum curator O'Hara demands accurate representation.

Do you see any tensions in 'Steps'?

In this particular poem satisfactions outweigh any notion of difficulties. The world of the poem includes stars such as Lana Turner and Greta Garbo (neither in their public roles), while aspiring dancers and 'worker-outers' from the gym – along with 'everyone' who removes coats to show off torsos – seems body-conscious and self-aware. The impression is of a society in complete harmony, if not of a Hollywood musical. The gay couple who moved 'to the country for fun' should have stayed longer to enjoy the day O'Hara describes in the city, where, certainly in this poem, there is no discrimination.

In this way, conformity is pulled towards gay life rather than the reverse. O'Hara embraces mass culture, which seems anything but sterile. He celebrates the wealthy and famous, the young and fit, cheers with the winning football team, and does not exclude the old man who sits drinking beer on a crate on the sidewalk – or his bad-tempered wife. As we saw earlier, in 'Personal Poem', O'Hara records the violence of city life but he does not comment on it. He mentions 'the stabbings' but, in a moment of black humour, even they are given a positive spin by 'helping the population explosion'. The line that follows is particularly interesting, as it can be read in two ways. First, other parts of the world are overpopulated, so stabbings in New York do not help. But it could also suggest a measure of patriotism and thus conformity – New York is in 'the wrong country' for depopulation measures, not what one might expect from a man who risked arrest if he were rash enough to be open about his sexuality in the wrong company. All 'those liars' have left the United Nations too, but political issues are not sustained, and we move swiftly back to frivolity, the pronoun significantly plural now, with 'not that we need liquor (we just like it)'.

O'Hara's poems testify to his enthusiasm for the cinema. 'Ave Maria' (Appendix) begins with an imperative:

> Mothers of America
> > let your kids go to the movies!
> get them out of the house so they won't know what you're up to
> it's true that fresh air is good for the body
> > > but what about the soul
> that grows in darkness, embossed by silvery images
> and when you grow old as grow old you must
> > > they won't hate you
> they won't criticize you they won't know
> > > they'll be in some glamorous country
> they first saw on a Saturday afternoon or playing hookey

This is pure escapism; the movies provide an alternative 'glamorous' world, which offers distraction from the vicissitudes and humdrum of ordinary life. When O'Hara saw Judy Garland's show at the Palace Theatre, he was exhilarated: 'Well, I guess she's *better* than Picasso', he told John Button (quoted in Gooch, 1993, p.327). References to Lana Turner, James Dean, Ginger Rogers and Greta Garbo in his poems create a background of glamour, representing O'Hara as a fan, in touch with this particular aspect of popular culture. The title of his poem 'Rhapsody' is a reference to a film starring Elizabeth Taylor that came out in 1955 (Gooch, 1993, p.126), although other films mentioned specifically in the poems reproduced in the Appendix came out quite a bit earlier: 'Fantasy' refers extensively to *Northern Pursuit* (1943), starring Errol Flynn; 'Five Poems' refers to *The Blue Angel* (1930), starring Marlene Dietrich, while at the beginning of 'Steps', as we have seen, New York is compared to Ginger Rogers in the musical *Swingtime* (1935).

To put these references in context, read the extracts from Jim Elledge's essay 'Never Argue with the Movies: Love and the Cinema in the Poetry of Frank O'Hara' (Reader, Item 34). In its edited form, the essay focuses on two particular poems. What exactly is Elledge's argument?

Elledge begins by considering O'Hara's poetic strategies in relation to cinematic technique, then moves on to establish his joyful and extravagant commitment to the cinema above any form of high culture. Elledge's main argument is that the films O'Hara refers to are 'decidedly romantic', promoting love triumphant over adversity. After discussion of 'Ave Maria' and 'Fantasy', Elledge concludes that film in the poems is an authority that can teach, console and entertain. It offers 'an ideal or perfect situation which, in O'Hara, is always related to love'. **Now read 'Fantasy' and 'Poem' ('Lana Turner Has Collapsed!') (Appendix) and reread 'Steps'. Is Elledge's argument adequate to describe them?**

Although his discussion of 'Fantasy' is decidedly helpful, not least in supplying details of the film *Northern Pursuit* that allow us to appreciate O'Hara's imaginative self-projection into the action, it is worth remembering that Elledge began by insisting that film was chosen as a 'decidedly heterosexual medium by which to investigate love'. In spite of this, he resorts to describing O'Hara's 'pop/camp sensibility' in 'Fantasy' to account for his inadequacies: even in an imaginary role, O'Hara is diffident about measuring up to received ideas of masculinity. His skiing is inept and he fails to anticipate an unexpected spy, although he does triumph in the end: 'Well, that takes care of him.' But the camp persona cannot be abandoned altogether, not even in a fantasy: in character, Errol Flynn would be unlikely to finish an action scene with the throw-away remark 'boy were those huskies hungry'.

'Poem' is about a star, not a specific film. Andrew Ross argues that it relies on a camp, not a heterosexual, response for its humour. The last four lines ('I have been to lots of parties / and acted perfectly disgraceful / but I never actually collapsed / oh Lana Turner we love you get up'), which relate the star's experience to O'Hara's own, testify to 'survivalist exhortations' that

lie at the very heart of camp's insistence that the show must go on, that irony and parody can redeem even the most tragic *and* sordid events, which color everyday life ... In the prepolitical climate of O'Hara's day, this survivalism found expression in the highly ironized flamboyance of the camp ethic – 'laughing to keep from crying' – which structured a whole subculture around the act of imagining a *different* relation to the existing world of too strictly authorized and legitimized sexual positions. In this respect, camp has to be seen as an imaginative conquest of everyday conditions of oppression, where more articulate expressions of resistance or empowerment were impossible ... The suggestion that role-playing, and the destabilizing of fixed sexual

> positions, could actually add to the exercise of sexual power was a very attractive suggestion for the gay male, who knew that his sexuality, in everyday life, was likely to get him into trouble.
>
> (in Elledge, 1993, pp.387–8)

Although I am unconvinced that the poem speaks only to a camp audience, this imagining of a 'different relation to the existing world' is exactly what happens in 'Fantasy'. Ministering to Allen Ginsberg's hangover with home-made Alka Seltzers, O'Hara adopts a nurturing role, equally at odds with that of hero (however inept). What is striking, however, is that in this poem, these roles coexist without anxiety: O'Hara's identity is secure. In 'Steps', which we considered earlier, his identity is so secure that the existing world accommodates itself to his mood. Perhaps this is another way in which his poems resemble the movies he loves: they offer alternative versions of reality. As Ross says, this is why camp is protopolitical: 'it is a response to politically induced oppression, but at the same time it is a response that accepts its current inability to act in an explicit political manner to combat that oppression' (in Elledge, 1993, p.388). Whereas Ginsberg is open about his sexual orientation in his work, O'Hara, in poems published in his lifetime, relies on 'many covert forms and baroque systems of disclosure, not least in heavily coded speech repertoires and intonations of gay vernacular' (*ibid.*).

Great effort was expended on ensuring that mass entertainment promoted moral values, but as we have seen, movie directors and actors alike found ways of circumventing puritan strictures. Often, innocence on the part of Production Code Boards, and indeed the general public in cinema audiences, meant that double meanings and visual and verbal asides (as with *Bringing Up Baby* mentioned above) in popular films were not recognized. Parallels can be found in O'Hara's poetry, too. In 'Personal Poem', for example, the statement that 'even we just want to be rich / and walk on girders in our silver hats' can be read in several ways, as obviously the rich have no need to undertake hard labour of this kind. The construction workers represent glamour, physical confidence and masculinity, qualities that in stereotyped representations supposedly appeal to gay men (and indeed heterosexual women, there being a sense in which the lexicon has been 'borrowed'). But there is another 'straight' reading: white-collar workers do not have to be gay to romanticize physical outdoor work.

Now read 'Mass Culture in America: The Post-War Debate' (Reader, Item 35), in which John Storey summarizes a number of arguments current at the time O'Hara was writing, including Dwight Macdonald's that we considered earlier in the chapter. How might these debates relate to what you have learned of O'Hara's poetry?

Storey begins by quoting three positions in the debate about mass culture identified by Ross. There is no reason why any one of them should neatly fit attitudes in the poems we have read, but the first, the 'aesthetic–liberal' stance, decrying popular demand for second- and third-rate culture rather than high culture, certainly does not come close. I would not argue for the 'corporate–liberal' position either, although it is clear that O'Hara is at home in the new capitalist–consumerist society. 'Having a Coke with You' (Appendix), for example, celebrates love and the pleasures of consumption: drinking Coke in this company is 'even more fun than going to San Sebastian'. The fact that the Coke is being consumed after a visit to a museum or art gallery testifies to O'Hara's ease in both worlds of high and mass culture. The declaration 'I look / at you and I would rather look at you than all the portraits in the world' leads to qualification and complication that makes no concessions to readers' knowledge of art history: 'except possibly for the *Polish Rider* occasionally and anyway it's in the Frick' – another New York Gallery. References to Futurism, Marcel Duchamps's *Nude Descending a Staircase*, Leonardo da Vinci and Michelangelo follow. Each is invoked for the sense of movement their work conveys, an underlying association of ideas relating to Vincent Warren, the dancer with whom O'Hara is sharing a Coke, and who looks like a 'better happier St Sebastian' in an orange shirt. Of course, none of this is explained.

Of all the arguments Storey summarizes, Edward Shils perhaps comes closest to the ethos of O'Hara's poems. He rejects the ' "utterly erroneous idea that the twentieth century is a period of severe intellectual deterioration and that this alleged deterioration is a product of mass culture" '. The problem, as Storey explains, is not mass culture but the response of intellectuals to mass culture. Feeling threatened, they argue to protect their own positions.

Dwight Macdonald believed that mass culture is 'at best a vulgarized reflection of High Culture' (in Rosenberg and White, 1957, p.61), while according to Storey, Leslie Fiedler feels that those who oppose mass culture 'are also against industrialization, mass education and democracy'. The attack, in Fiedler's opinion, is a symptom of conformity and timidity: ' "the fear of the vulgar is the obverse of the fear of excellence, and both are aspects of the fear of difference: symptoms of a drive for conformity on the level of the timid, sentimental, mindless-bodiless genteel" '. In the words of Shils, those who welcomed changing cultural values in the 1950s stress vitality and energy as ' "the fruits of the liberation of powers and possibilities inherent in mass societies" '. I would suggest that the way in which O'Hara incorporates mass culture in his poems – as part of his daily experience – is very far from a sign of cultural impoverishment. It is not a mark of the 'de-individualization of life' but on the contrary suggests and opens up endless possibilities.

Poetry rarely features on bestseller lists in the way that romantic fiction, science fiction, thrillers, detective and adventure novels do. It is often considered to be a minority interest – 'difficult', reserved for an intellectual and educated elite. But in O'Hara's work we have recognized a personal voice that negotiates between high and popular culture, refusing to recognize boundaries, and yet remaining conversational and engaging. It is difficult to imagine it existing at all without consumerism. At the end of the chapter I will return to O'Hara to compare his attitude to consumerism with Ginsberg's.

Allen Ginsberg

> In the fall of 1955 a group of six unknown poets in San Francisco, in a moment of drunken enthusiasm, decided to defy the system of academic poetry, official reviews, New York publishing machinery, national sobriety and generally accepted standards to good taste, by giving a free reading of their poetry in a run down secondrate experimental art gallery in the Negro section of San Francisco ... They got drunk, the audience got drunk, all that was missing was the orgy ... The reading was such a violent and beautiful expression of their revolutionary individuality ... that the audience, expecting some Bohemian stupidity, was left stunned, and the poets were left with the realization that they were fated to make a permanent change in the literary firmament of the States.
>
> (Ginsberg, 1986, p.165)

This account was the way Allen Ginsberg and Gregory Corso remembered the evening at the Six Gallery when Ginsberg's long poem 'Howl' was first read to an unsuspecting public. The gallery was very small, but if everyone who later claimed to have been present really had been, the venue would have needed to be about the size of Shea Stadium. In decades to come, Ginsberg worked with popular icons, such as the Beatles, the Rolling Stones, Bob Dylan and the Clash. A poetry reading he gave in London filled the Albert Hall in 1965, attracting a great deal of media attention and establishing his reputation in Britain. Just before he died in 1997, MTV were planning a Ginsberg *Unplugged* programme; Paul McCartney, Patti Smith, Bob Dylan and Ornette Coleman were among those keen to take part; Johnny Depp was to introduce the programme. Although Ginsberg never inspired the same following of fans as the Beatles or the Stones, his influence was pervasive during the second half of the twentieth century.

A year after that first reading at the Six Gallery, in September 1956, Richard Eberhart published an article in the *New York Times Book Review* about the young writers who were rapidly becoming known as 'The Beat Generation'. It was not long before the 'New York publishing machinery', with its standards of 'academic poetry' and 'official reviews', became aware of a growing enthusiasm for this new poetry. Based on the west coast of the USA, mainly in the San Francisco area, the Beats were challenging

Figure 2.3 Allen Ginsberg in Mexico City, with Lucien Carr's dog. (© The Allen Ginsberg Trust.) The photograph was taken during a visit to Joan Burroughs while William Burroughs was in South America, 4 May 1950.

expectations and commanding new audiences, who expected to make their presence felt in what sounds, from Eberhart's description, more like a collective performance than a conventional reading:

> Hundreds from about sixteen to thirty may show up and engage in an enthusiastic, freewheeling celebration of poetry, an analogue of which was jazz thirty years ago. The audience participates, shouting and stamping, interrupting and applauding. Poetry here has become a tangible social force, moving and unifying its auditors, releasing the energies of the audience through spoken, even shouted verse, in a way at present unique to this region.
>
> (in Hyde, 1984, p.24)

The audience was young, lively and engaged; its members were likely to describe themselves, and those they admired, as 'hip'. This term, borrowed from the bebop language of 1940s jazz, was chosen specifically to distance the followers of Beat poetry further from the world of conventional poetry appreciation.

Norman Podhoretz was less enthusiastic in his essay in the *New Republic*: its title, 'A Howl of Protest in San Francisco', neatly reduced Eberhart's expansive 'West Coast Rhythms' to a more circumscribed single-city location. Podhoretz considers two or three of the group to be 'good writers', half a dozen more have 'mediocre talents', the rest he sums up as 'worthless'. What they all have in common, he says,

> is the conviction that any form of rebellion against American culture ... is admirable, and they seem to regard homosexuality, jazz, dope-addiction, and vagrancy as outstanding examples of such rebellion. Most of them like using bop-language, and though they are all highly sophisticated, they fancy themselves to be in touch with the primitive and the rugged. They talk endlessly about love; they are fond of Christian imagery.
>
> (in Hyde, 1984, p.34)

Rebellion is a key term here, but it is also tempting to see the beginnings of a time of peace, love and flower power in the endless talk about love – although this was not to arrive until the 1960s. Podhoretz is unimpressed, but even his account testifies to the liveliness and energy that the new poetry generated. He also makes an exception for Ginsberg's poem 'Howl', which he, like Eberhart, considers 'remarkable'. Both writers feel the need to explain this cultural phenomenon to their readers, which in itself says something significant about the novelty involved.

Who exactly were the Beats? The term was coined around the time Jack Kerouac published his first novel, *The Town and the City*, in 1950. Kerouac himself, Ginsberg, William Burroughs and Gregory Corso were all considered 'Beats' at various stages of their writing careers. Their shared experience, as Anne Charters says in her Introduction to Kerouac's *On the Road* (1957), was historical and political, 'based on the tumultuous changes of their times: the historic events that began with America dropping the atomic bomb on Japan to bring World War II to an end, and the political ramifications of the ensuing cold war and wave of anti-Communist hysteria that followed in the United States in the late 1940s and the 1950s' (1991, pp.xvi–xvii).

The word 'beat' has many associations. It was a slang term used by jazz musicians: being 'dead beat' meant being down and out, not having a cent to your name and being physically and emotionally exhausted. Ginsberg remembered the 'original street usage' as meaning being 'at the bottom of

Figure 2.4   Allen Ginsberg, Gregory Corso, Jack Kerouac, and Peter and Lafcadio Orlovsky in Mexico City, September 1956. (© Allen Ginsberg/CORBIS.) According to Allen Ginsberg's notes: 'Peter Orlovsky brought his younger brother Lafcadio to stay with us in SF ... Later that year 1956 we all took off with Gregory Corso to Mexico to visit Kerouac who wrote about these "Darlovsky Brothers" in *Desolation Angels*.'

the world, looking up or out, sleepless, wide-eyed, perceptive, rejected by society, on your own, streetwise' (quoted in Charters, 1992, p.xviii). As we shall see, this description sums up the characters in the first part of 'Howl'. 'Beat' quickly acquired additional meanings: the musical sense of beat – keeping time – was important because of the jazz connection. This too has formal implications for Ginsberg's long poem. It implied being 'in the groove', in step with like-minded others, 'the alienated, the dispossessed and even the nominally insane' (Gray, 1990, p.299). Beat poetry was also considered to be 'typewriter jazz', aimed at 'catching the abrupt, syncopated rhythms, the improvizational dash and *bravura* of jazz, bebop, and swing' (*ibid.*). In addition, it incorporated the religious term 'beatitude', implying innocence, blessedness and a spiritual state achieved through meditation, poetry, music or drugs. Ginsberg, quoting the nineteenth-century French poet Arthur Rimbaud, insisted that the poet 'becomes a seer through a long, immense, and reasoned derangement of all the senses. All shapes of love, suffering, madness. He searches himself, he exhausts all poisons in himself, to keep only the quintessences' (quoted in Charters, 1992, p.xi).

In Kerouac's opinion, the Beats were 'basically a religious generation' (quoted in Charters, 1992, p.xxiv); you will be able to judge this for yourselves as you read Ginsberg's poems. Perhaps above all, they were an extraordinary social phenomenon, 'part of a decade that seemed suddenly to have invented adolescence and rebellion' (Gray, 1990, p.299).

Now read the opening lines of 'Howl', printed below. You may choose to read the whole poem – if you have not done so already – but the opening should be sufficient for the moment to give you an initial idea of the content and style. Inevitably, the extract below stops rather arbitrarily, as the sentence which opens the poem does not reach its resolution until the end of part I, seventy-nine lines later (when Ginsberg numbered the lines for a much later edition, he referred to them as 'strophes', counting each unit as a single strophe or line; there are only five lines printed below). **What is this extract about, and how would you describe the tone, style and language of this writing?**

> I saw the best minds of my generation destroyed by
>   madness, starving hysterical naked,
> dragging themselves through the negro streets at dawn
>   looking for an angry fix,
> angelheaded hipsters burning for the ancient heavenly
>   connection to the starry dynamo in the machin-
>   ery of night,
> who poverty and tatters and hollow-eyed and high sat
>   up smoking in the supernatural darkness of
>   cold-water flats floating across the tops of cities
>   contemplating jazz,
> who bared their brains to heaven under the El and
>   saw Mohammedan angels staggering on tene-
>   ment roofs illuminated,
>
> (Ginsberg, 2002, p.9)

The opening suggests that if 'the best minds' of the speaker's generation are destroyed by madness, then there is something very wrong, either with his perception of what constitutes 'the best', or with a society that fails to agree with him. The opening of the poem, then, confirms Podhoretz's feelings about rebellion against US culture. The poem is also about altered states of consciousness: use of the past tense in the opening line tells us that mental destruction has already happened; there is also a desire for spiritual communion, apparent in the mystical 'ancient heavenly connection'. The language is strong, there are no half measures here: people are described as 'starving', 'hysterical', 'angry' and 'burning'; the scene is urban and seedy ('cold-water flats' describes apartments without hot water). The landscape is also unfamiliar: there are 'Mohammedan angels' on the roofs of the tenements. What, we might ask, is the 'starry dynamo in the machinery of night'? Is it simply a reference to the movement of the constellations in the night sky, or is it another way of describing a deity? There are two references to heaven in this short passage, and the word 'angel' identifies the hipsters – whose 'angry fix' may well be responsible for their visions – as well as the angels on the roofs. Who, then, is holy? The staggering angels, or the hipsters? And if this is a spiritual quest, to whom does it belong? All quests worthy of the name are a test of endurance, and if you find reading 'Howl' difficult, you may decide that readers, as well as those 'best minds' that are the subject of the text, are being tested as the poem progresses.

Although you may only have read the very beginning of the poem so far, can you identify any structuring devices in the lines you have read?

As the layout of the lines on the page shows, repetition is very important. Many begin with 'who' followed by a verb ('who bared', 'who passed', 'who cowered', 'who got busted'), conveying a sense of action and movement. As you become more familiar with the rest of the poem, you should try to decide whether this sense of movement results in progress: do the active verbs work in contradiction to the repetition? Line 4 does not conform grammatically: 'who poverty and tatters and hollow-eyed and high sat up smoking'. The line might make more conventional sense if it read 'who *in* poverty and tatters', and if we changed the word order to 'who sat up smoking in poverty and tatters'. This helps us to identify a couple of Ginsberg's characteristic techniques: ellipsis and unconventional word order. By eliding certain words and placing others in uncertain relations to each other, he conveys intensity and a sense of urgency through the verse movement – an appropriate technique for rendering his vision of the world out of kilter.

Like O'Hara, Ginsberg was dissatisfied with the possibilities that mid-twentieth-century US poetry offered for expression. His father, Louis Ginsberg, was an established poet whose work was published in the *New Yorker*, the *Atlantic Monthly*, the *New York Herald-Tribune* and the *Times Literary Supplement*. But the formal qualities of his verse seemed inadequate to communicate the world his son felt compelled to write about. Louis Ginsberg's poem 'Atomic' is a good example, especially as it takes up subject matter that also preoccupied his son:

> The splitting apart
>   Of man from man
> Dooms more than splitting
>   The atom can.
>
> In one blaze, will
>   All things be gone:
> The Empire State,
>   The Parthenon?

And must the sudden
  Atom's flash
Turn cities, statues,
  And poems to ash?

Quick! The foe
  In us is curled,
More fearsome than any
  Foe in the world!

(L. Ginsberg, 1970, p.25)

Louis Ginsberg's use of regular stanza form, rhythm and rhyme here is characteristic of his work, and very different from his son's. 'I have resisted this mode as an anachronism in my own time', Ginsberg wrote in his Introduction to a collection of his father's poems (A. Ginsberg, 1970, p.14), adding his appreciation of Louis's ability to 'transform the old "lyric" form' to 'the deepest actualization of his peaceful mortal voice' (*ibid.*, p.15).

You have already read an extract from David Lehman's book *The Last Avant-Garde* (Reader, Item 32) when working on O'Hara. **Reread it now to remind yourself of the conflict Lehman identifies between what he calls 'academic' and 'antiacademic' poetry.** His claim that 'the wild beasts' of US poetry did not draw on a literary tradition needs some qualification, especially as far as Ginsberg is concerned: though Ginsberg certainly rejected the poetic orthodoxy that his father subscribed to, he was well read and acknowledged debts to European as well as earlier US poets.

The first draft of part I of 'Howl' was written at one sitting; as Ginsberg later said, it was 'typed out madly in an afternoon' (quoted in Hyde, 1984, p.80). It is worth bearing in mind Lehman's phrase 'a sense of moral earnestness', which, in his opinion, characterized US poetry of the 1950s, for although Ginsberg's moral sense may differ from that of the poets Lehman sees as academically approved, you may come to feel that the whole impetus of 'Howl' was a moral one.

Now read to the end of the poem, bearing in mind the following quotation:

The 'form' of the poem is an experiment. Experiment with the uses of the catalogue, the ellipsis, the long line, the litany, repetition, etc.

(Ginsberg, 1986, p.152)

How do these techniques function in the poem?

A 'litany' is a collective prayer of supplication, led by a priest, with responses from the congregation that involve repetition. It is no accident that the word is a religious one: Ginsberg is trying to make his readers see the world with a sense of spiritual awe. 'Footnote to Howl' insists on reinvesting every aspect of the world with holiness, and it does so by relentless repetition. You may have felt that the piling up of clauses makes the poem little more than an uncontrolled rant. The lack of full stops and the relentlessly deferred ending of the sentence contribute to this and it is certainly one of many valid responses to the poem. But did you think that this relentlessness contributed to a sense of moral earnestness and sincerity?

Ginsberg sent the poem to his friend and mentor Jack Kerouac, who thought it powerful in spite of some reservations, which Ginsberg later explained: Kerouac 'didn't want it arbitrarily negated by my secondary emendations made in time's reconsidered backstep – he wanted my LINGUAL SPONTENAITY or nothing'. He 'wouldn't read hackled handicapped poetry manuscripts' (Ginsberg, 1986, p.149). (It is worth noticing the characteristic and idiosyncratic style of expression there; even his prose is unorthodox.) Ginsberg protested that what he had sent *was* spontaneous, not realizing that Kerouac's objections were to *any* amendments, second thoughts or crossings out made during the process of composition.

'First thought, best thought' was a commandment the Beats had taken from the Romantic poet William Blake; they believed that only by allowing the mind to roam free and unfettered could significant associations and connections be made and truths surface. 'The lines are the result of long thought and experiment as to what unit constitutes *one speech breath thought*', Ginsberg wrote (1986, p.153; his italics). Kerouac gives a helpful explanation of this, using a musical analogy linking it to jazz and bop. Ginsberg's strophes work 'in the sense of a, say, a tenor man drawing a breath and blowing a phrase on his saxophone, till he runs out of breath, and when he does, his sentence, his statement's been made' (quoted in Plimpton, 1999, p.121). 'We think and speak rhythmically all the time,' Ginsberg said. 'Given a mental release which is not mentally blocked, the breath of verbal intercourse will come with excellent rhythm, a rhythm which is perhaps unimprovable' (1986, p.153). Music is an important underlying analogy here.

Instead of making the thought fit a rhythm, his first concern is to say what he wants to say, varying the length of his lines accordingly. 'Mental release which is not mentally blocked' was an idea espoused by all of the Beat writers: in other words, they did not believe in rewriting or revising, for the process would act as a form of censorship imposed on the original ideas. Kerouac's method of avoiding self-censorship and revision was to type on a twelve-foot-long roll of paper made from sheets he had taped together (Charters, 1991, p.xix). The poem, Ginsberg believed, should be 'discovered in the mind' (Gray, 1990, p.302), which should not be allowed to censor itself. In spite of this, 'Howl' certainly went through many drafts and revisions before publication.

Ginsberg published an annotated draft facsimile of 'Howl' in 1986, showing that the changes he made were considerable and thus posing questions about the extent to which he practised what he preached (Figure 2.5). Lines were reordered and grouped thematically, linked 'by my own associations or external logic' (Ginsberg, 1986, p.11) – two quite different means of organization – allowing a progression to emerge, often based on a chronological series of events in his life, or with incidents from lives of his friends and acquaintances, which are seamlessly subsumed into his narrative. (Including names of people like this with no explanation is a characteristic he shares with O'Hara.) Such characters and events will, of course, still not be evident to readers unfamiliar with Ginsberg's life or with no access to annotations he made later, which offer exhaustive explanations. **Read through the rest of the poem again now, including 'Footnote to Howl'. This time, aim to get a sense of the overall form and structure.**

The poem is in three parts. Part I describes the symptoms of madness in society – specifically the wasted genius and talents of the speaker's own generation; part II offers a diagnosis; in part III the speaker identifies with Carl Solomon, a friend incarcerated in a psychiatric institution. Part I concludes with the ambiguous statement 'with the absolute heart of the poem of life butchered out of their own bodies good to eat a thousand years'. Remember that 'their' refers to the 'best minds of my generation' from the opening of the poem, the 'who' who initiate most of the lines. It is worth noticing the self-reflexive reference to 'the heart of the poem' too, something to which I will return later.

The second and third parts are much shorter than the first. Part II takes as its keynote Moloch, an Old Testament fire god of Canaa, to whom parents sacrificed their children – a practice the Lord forbids to the Israelites when he leads them from Egypt: 'And thou shalt not let any of thy seed pass through the fire to Moloch' (Leviticus 18:21; 20:1–5). Ginsberg may also be remembering Milton's *Paradise Lost* (1667):

> Moloch, horrid king besmeared with blood
> Of human sacrifice, and parents' tears,
> Though for the noise of drums and timbrels loud
> Their children's cries unheard, that passed through fire
> To his grim idol

> (1.392–6; Milton, 1966, pp.221–2)

Ginsberg explains his use of the image as 'the vision of the mechanical feelingless inhuman world we live in and accept', adding that the key line is 'Moloch whom I abandon' (1986, p.152). A compelling hallucinatory scene

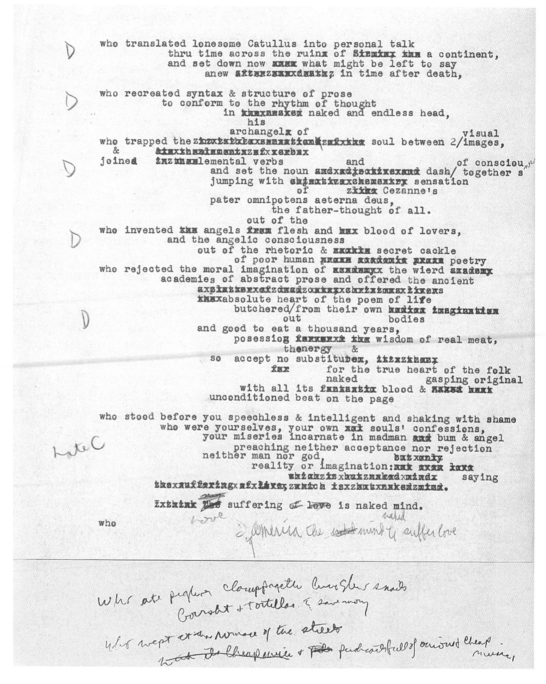

Figure 2.5 'Howl', Part 1: Draft 1 'Howl for Carl Solomon', in John Clellon Holmes's holograph, inscribed 'sent by Kerouac to me Aug.30, 1955 JCH', lines 76–115 (plus four lines added in manuscript). (Reproduced from Allen Ginsberg, *Howl*, ed. by B. Miles, Harmondsworth: Viking, 1986, p.24.) The extensive revisions on this page are characteristic of the amount of revision on the manuscript as a whole.

from Fritz Lang's futuristic film *Metropolis* (1927) uses similar imagery of workers consumed by the mouth of a monstrous underground machine (Figure 2.6).

References to Moloch and the Old Testament may make you think again about antecedents for the rhythms of Ginsberg's long line, and perhaps revise earlier ideas about tone; the long line may seem more familiar in this context: the declamatory voice can be seen as prophetic and the tone of the poem can be seen as a lamentation. But remember that the lines of 'Howl' have also been described as equivalent to the breath a jazz saxophonist or trumpeter may take to embody a musical idea, complete in itself though related to what goes before and to what follows. As far as 'hard' bop players like Miles Davis and Charlie Parker were concerned, the ability to improvise during live performance became the defining characteristic of the music. Given the amount of repetition in 'Howl', the jazz analogy works in terms of variations on a theme too.

Part III repeats 'I'm with you' to Carl Solomon, to whom the poem is dedicated – although 'Howl for Carl Solomon' can also be read as an imperative. Ginsberg and Solomon met when they were both patients in the Columbia Presbyterian Psychiatric Institute in 1947. Solomon had been admitted because he turned up there on his twenty-first birthday and requested a lobotomy. The incident becomes the basis for a line in part I of

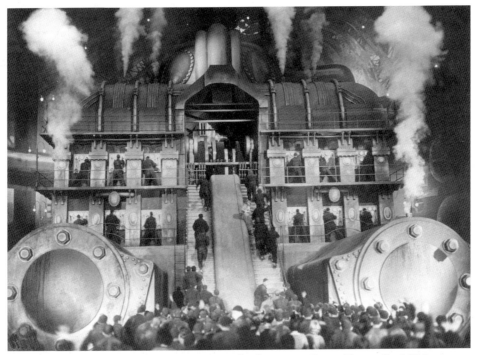

Figure 2.6   Cannibal dynamo in Metropolis Centrum, from *Metropolis*, 1926, directed by Fritz Lang. (Photo: UFA/The Kobal Collection.)

'Howl': it was Carl 'who threw potato salad at CCNY lecturers on Dadaism and subsequently presented themselves on the granite steps of the madhouse with shaven heads and harlequin speech of suicide, demanding instant lobotomy'. The movement from fact to poetic fiction is apparent in this line as the (literally) singular Carl becomes, in Ginsberg's poetic representation, plural. The fictionalizing point is further made by a letter from Solomon where he states categorically: 'I was never in Rockland [a psychiatric institution] ... Neither of us has ever been in Rockland. Ginsberg never even on a tour.' Graciously – or pedantically, possibly even humorously, it is hard to catch the exact tone – Ginsberg includes this in his annotations, adding 'Not at the time, though I visited a friend of Leary's there later 60s. – AG' (1986, p.143). The title of 'Footnote to Howl' declares a relationship to the earlier parts, even though it is sometimes treated as a separate poem. It was originally intended as part III of the poem, and was written before what is now part III (*ibid.*, pp.88, 97).

Now that you have some background to the poem, to what extent do you think this really is a new venture in poetry? Do you think the poem is a spontaneous utterance, or a carefully crafted piece of work?

The effect, I think, is one of spontaneity, but there is also a weight of tradition behind the poem that needs to be recognized; forms familiar from other contexts are retrieved and represented with a sense of urgent modernity. So, for example, the idea of *'one speech breath thought'* (Ginsberg, 1986, p.153) takes us directly back to the Romantics, although the idea of poetic inspiration predates them too. Inspiration is literally the drawing in of breath. A lone voice crying in the wilderness, prophesying and lamenting is intimately linked to the notion of spontaneous utterance, significantly emphasizing the spoken word rather than the written. Old Testament prophets, the poet as madman or shaman, speaking from a sense of heightened awareness, from a trance-like state induced by fasting, meditation, drugs or a combination of these, are all antecedents. William Blake was a direct influence: Ginsberg described the unforgettable mystical experience he had of hearing Blake's voice speaking aloud 'Ah! Sunflower' and 'The Sick Rose' from *Songs of Innocence and Experience*, with the book open before him (Miles, 2000, pp.98–9). He also collected an anthology of precursors in the 1986 facsimile edition of 'Howl'. His 'Model Texts' include Percy Bysshe Shelley's 'Ode to the West Wind' (1820), and an extract from Shelley's 'Adonais' (1821), as well as works by European poets Guillaume Apollinaire, Kurt Schwitters, Vladimir Mayakovsky, Antonin Artaud, Federico García Lorca and the Americans Hart Crane and William Carlos Williams. His anthology begins with an extract from the 'Jubilate Agno' of

Christopher Smart. **Read the lines from that extract printed below, briefly comparing subject matter and techniques with those of 'Howl':**

> the Lord endue us with
> temperance & humanity, till every cow have her mate!
>
> For I am not without authority in my jeopardy, which I
> derive inevitably from the glory of the name of the Lord.
>
> For I bless God whose name is Jealous – and there is a
> zeal to deliver us from everlasting burnings.
>
> For my existimation is good even amongst the slanderers
> and my memory shall arise for a sweet savour unto the
> Lord.
>
> For I bless the PRINCE of peace and pray that all the guns
> may be nail'd up, save such as for the rejoicing days.
>
> ...
>
> For I have glorified God in GREEK and LATIN, the conse-
> crated languages spoken by the Lord on earth.
>
> For I meditate the peace of Europe amongst family bick-
> erings and domestic jars.

(quoted in Ginsberg, 1986, p.176)

Most obviously, the poems share repetition at the beginning of lines. Through a sense of apparently logical progression Smart achieves an argument ('let this happen, because I have done this'), whereas Ginsberg endlessly defers resolution of his first long sentence. Both poets are concerned with war and peace, something I will return to with reference to 'Howl'. 'Jubilate Agno' is a Christian poem: subject matter, form and voice recall the Old Testament Psalms. Ginsberg's lines tend to be considerably longer than Smart's, but the tone is similar. Ginsberg shows his awareness of poetic convention when he notes Smart's 'variable measure', which differs from 'the powerful ten-syllable balances of Milton' (1986, p.175). This is not to say that either Smart's line or his own is not powerful – just that neither wrote in iambic pentameters. Ginsberg says that 'technical and syntactical ease' are necessary in order to make 'anything significant' of the long line. In other words, he was acutely aware that spontaneous ramblings did not constitute poetry: writers will always aim to find the most appropriate form – and that includes rhythm – for what they want to say.

Ginsberg does not name Walt Whitman in his notes to 'Howl', but he certainly admired Whitman and learned a great deal from the nineteenth-century poet. He draws attention to this by using a quotation from Whitman's 'Song of Myself' as epigraph to 'Howl'. Whitman too was unconventional; like Ginsberg he used long, unrhymed lines in his verse with no regular metre or stanza form; like Ginsberg (and O'Hara, who also admired Whitman) he was homosexual; and like Ginsberg he insisted that everything was holy:

> Through me forbidden voices,
> Voices of sexes and lusts, voices veil'd and I remove the veil,
> Voices indecent by me clarified and transfigur'd.
>
> ...
>
> I believe in the flesh and the appetites,
> Seeing, hearing, feeling, are miracles, and each part and tag of me is a miracle.
>
> Divine am I inside and out, and I make holy whatever I touch or am touch'd from,
> The scent of these arm-pits aroma finer than prayer,
> This head more than churches, bibles, and all the creeds.

> ('Song of Myself', lines 516–18 and 522–6; Whitman, 1996, p.87)

These lines show that there was a precedent for 'Footnote to Howl', where Ginsberg insists that: 'Everything is holy!' Whitman was accused of obscenity, something else he has in common with Ginsberg, as we shall see. An anonymous late Victorian reviewer did recommend his collection *Leaves of Grass*, which includes 'Song of Myself', albeit with qualifications – advising that 'once the reader can overcome his antipathy to the boisterous, unkempt manner, once his ear is willing continually to be baulked of music, there is the generous tingling message of democracy glowing before him' (*The Academy*, 28 August 1897). Whitman insists that through him 'many long dumb voices', including those of prisoners and slaves, are heard and he urges 'Unscrew the locks from the doors! / Unscrew the doors themselves from their jambs!' ('Song of Myself', lines 501–2; Whitman, 1996, p.86). It is no wonder that he appealed to Ginsberg, who used those lines as an epigraph, and was 'more than willing to assert that radicalism was radicalism, that to be outside the sexual order was to be outside the political order, which was to be outside the racial order' (Gobel, 1999, p.84).

Now read 'A Supermarket in California' (p.29). How does Ginsberg express his admiration for Whitman in this poem?

Perhaps the most surprising thing about the poem is that Ginsberg chooses a supermarket for his imagined meeting with Whitman. Having learned something of his beliefs, you might reasonably have expected the title to suggest an indictment of consumerism, whereas the poem itself overturns any such expectations, focusing instead on sensual aspects of display. The supermarket is a desirable place where, in a state of mental 'hungry fatigue', Ginsberg goes 'shopping for images'. There may be a store detective to prevent theft, but Whitman and the poet taste artichokes and possess 'every frozen delicacy' while 'never passing the cashier'. Whole families become part of this surreal vision – 'wives in the avocados, babies in the tomatoes' – and there is no notion of lists or weekly shopping. The description of Whitman as a 'childless, lonely old grubber, poking among the meats in the refrigerator' is hardly flattering. '[E]yeing the grocery boys' identifies his sexual orientation, although the questions Ginsberg imagines Whitman asking these grocery boys are hardly seductive: 'who killed the pork chops? What price bananas? Are you my angel?' Ginsberg 'wanders in and out of the brilliant stacks of cans' following his mentor – an analogy to reading Whitman's poems – in search of elusive images. The reference to Federico García Lorca 'down by the watermelons' helps Ginsberg place himself in relation to these major literary figures: García Lorca also wrote a poem in tribute to Whitman, 'Oda a Walt Whitman' (1933), which Ginsberg translated and adapted (Ginsberg, 1986, pp.185–6).

With all this background in mind, it is important to reconsider exactly what Eberhart meant when he described the poetry that contemporary audiences in San Francisco applauded as determinedly new and exciting, iconoclastic in its rejection of poetic techniques of the past. As we have seen, there is a whole weight of earlier poetry that Ginsberg acknowledges as significant for his own work. The freshness of his voice in the 1950s, then, is derived from the way in which disparate traditions come together with his own idiosyncratic style. This development relates to David Johnson's comments in the Introduction to Part 1: neither Matthew Arnold, nor F.R. Leavis, nor Dwight Macdonald (whose ideas about mass culture we considered in relation to Frank O'Hara) would quarrel with the merits of Milton, Blake or Shelley as part of the great literary tradition. But in Ginsberg's case, familiarity with these and other canonical writers failed to provide him with a 'buffer against the anarchy of the Populace that was menacing the world' (p.7): instead, they helped him to serve that anarchy. Let us return to 'Howl' to consider one more aspect of his 'newness' and how it challenged US values.

Ambiguity

Eberhart celebrates the newness of 'Howl' by rejoicing in the way that 'Ambiguity is despised, irony is considered weakness, the poem as a system of connotations is thrown out in favour of long-line

denotative statements. Explicit cognition is enjoined. Rhyme is outlawed' (in Hyde, 1984, p.25). **How true are these generalizations of 'Howl'?**

Rhyme is not used as a structuring device in the poem, and the long-line statements are a distinctive feature, as we have seen. Whether ambiguity is generally despised or not, there is plenty of it to be found in 'Howl'. The title is a case in point: is 'Howl for Carl Solomon' a dedication or an instruction? Long after publication Ginsberg and his editor Barry Miles established that it was intended to be the former, but whatever the intention, the ambiguity remains and the possibilities are the richer because of it. There is ambiguity everywhere, and you will have found your own examples. I was particularly struck by the startling juxtaposition of 'hydrogen jukebox':

> who sank all night in submarine light of Bickford's
> floated out and sat through the stale beer after-
> noon in desolate Fugazzi's, listening to the crack
> of doom on the hydrogen jukebox

(p.11)

Ginsberg later glossed this strophe, explaining that he had mopped floors at Bickford's, a cafeteria in Manhattan, when he was a college student. Fugazzi's was a Sixth Avenue Greenwich Village bar in the 1950s and some 'end-of-the-world of apocalyptic vibration' was noticed in the 'roaring' of its jukebox: thus 'hydrogen [bomb] jukebox' (1986, p.125). But does this literal explanation account for the effects of the juxtaposition? A jukebox is for entertainment; linking it to the notion of a hydrogen bomb makes it sinister. Seen against a background of mass culture, consumerism and the cold war, these two words could be said to encapsulate the whole argument of the poem: an indictment of modern US society.

Spontaneous utterance and self-reflexivity

Ginsberg explains his techniques within the poem itself, suggesting that spontaneity is an illusion, and that readers are invited – or expected – to share that contradiction. **How do the following lines comment on themselves, and how effective are they?** Towards the end of part I, the exclamation 'ah, Carl, while you are not safe I am not safe' is offered as the reason behind this action:

> and who therefore ran through the icy street obsessed
> with a sudden flash of the alchemy of the use
> of the ellipse the catalog the meter & the vibrat-
> ing plane,
> who dreamt and made incarnate gaps in Time & Space
> through images juxtaposed, and trapped the

> archangel of the soul between 2 visual images
> and joined the elemental verbs and set the noun
> and dash of consciousness together jumping
> with sensation of Pater Omipotens Aeterna
> Deus
>   to recreate the syntax and measure of poor human
> prose and stand before you speechless and intel-
> ligent and shaking with shame, rejected yet con-
> fessing out the soul to conform to the rhythm
> of thought in his naked and endless head,
>   the madman bum and angel beat in Time, unknown,
> yet putting down here what might be left to say
> in time come after death

(pp.19–20)

References to poetic devices ('ellipse' [ellipsis], 'catalog', 'meter'), parts of speech ('verbs', 'noun') and 'syntax' direct attention to the way in which the verse has been achieved – to its artificiality, if you like. The use of 'alchemy' in this context is important too, providing a metaphor for the very function of metaphor itself: for example, the speaker explains that the struggle to express 'the archangel of the soul', can be solved by '2 visual images': base metals become gold in a mysterious, mystical process. (In an annotation to line 9, 'who got busted in their pubic beards', Ginsberg says: 'The phrase comes by a simple mechanical method of intensifying a line by unusual juxtaposition of things or concepts.') The 'madman bum and angel … unknown yet putting down here' refers to Ginsberg himself, an unknown poet, and to the process of writing this poem, with the result that the moment of composition is inscribed within the finished text, collapsing the time of writing with the time of reading. You could argue that this adds to the immediacy of the writing, while being aware that it is playful manipulation: 'Time' with an upper case initial letter, 'time' and eternity are themes of the whole poem that converge here.

Minimal punctuation lends speed and urgency to the verse movement, mirroring the speaker running through an icy street and conveying a sense of danger. A variant danger is taken up two lines later. Here, it is an emotional risk that is being taken: the speaker is 'shaking with shame' at the nature of his confessional verse and what he reveals of himself and his sexuality, yet he is determined to communicate in spite of fear of misunderstanding and rejection. Word choice – 'dash of consciousness' and 'jumping with sensation' – also aids the sense of movement, while 'beat' is doubly potent, functioning as both verb and noun.

The self-reflexive techniques in these lines focus on the process of describing and transcribing thought processes. Ginsberg deliberately draws attention to a contradiction in the conscious use of technical devices to convey a 'rhythm of thought'. Formal rules of grammar are acknowledged, then treated with scant respect, but if you think about it, even the most inspired and unconventional outpourings must conform to some linguistic order – even a howl would have little meaning without a context or a tradition in which to understand it.

The intention of 'Howl' is not to shock; it is, instead, a sincere attempt to convey the writer's/speaker's consciousness. The attempt is not without humour and self-deflating asides: the phrase 'stanzas of gibberish' certainly raises a laugh from the audience on the 1959 recording of Ginsberg reading the poem. The word 'speechless' too is (surely?) a joke, given the preceding seventy-four long lines, while the desire to 'recreate the syntax and measure of poor human prose' is another wry comment.

Reception and obscenity trial

The image of the poet 'shaking with shame' at exposing his sexual proclivities before an audience and the sense of risk involved in his utterance were expressed by Ginsberg in a letter to Eberhart after publication: 'I have released and confessed and communicated clearly my true feelings tho it might involve at first a painful leap of exhibition and fear that I would be rejected' (1986, p.152). His poem was not originally intended for publication: it was written as an exercise in free expression, an attempt to free himself from the conventional forms and constraints of subject matter of his earlier verse. But the rapturous reception 'Howl' received when he read it at the Six Gallery in San Francisco on 7 October 1955 changed all that. According to Gregory Corso:

> The most brilliant shock of the evening was the declamation of the now-famous rhapsody, *Howl*, by Allen Ginsberg ... The poem initiates a new style in composition in the US, returning to the bardic-strophic tradition ...
>
> The reading was delivered by the poet, rather surprised at his own power, drunk on the platform, becoming increasingly sober as he read, driving forward with a strange ecstatic intensity, delivering a spiritual confession to an astounded audience – ending in tears which restored to American poetry the prophetic consciousness it had lost since the conclusion of Hart Crane's *The Bridge*, another celebrated mystical work.
>
> (in Ginsberg, 1986, p.165)

(The idea of 'a new style' 'returning' to an older tradition suggests the note of contradiction we have already noted in 'Howl'.) Lawrence Ferlinghetti, co-owner of the City Lights Bookstore and publisher of *Howl and Other Poems* was astute enough to ask William Carlos Williams, a well-respected established poet, to write an Introduction to the City Lights Pocket Poets series edition. **Read Williams's Introduction (pp.7–9) and decide how he thought the book might be received. What is the tone, and to what extent do you think it a carefully considered, calculated strategy on Williams's part?**

While there is some praise, there is also defensiveness in the tone. Williams reveals some biographical details: in the first paragraph he establishes Ginsberg's credentials as 'son of a well-known poet', going on to depict him as physically and mentally sensitive and vulnerable. (However, he was certainly not alive 'during those first years after the First World War': he was not born until 1926.) He admires the strength of character that survives these traits and notes an uncompromising toughness and a refusal to ignore unpleasantness. Williams tells us that the wonder is not Ginsberg's survival, but that he has found 'a fellow whom he can love, a love he celebrates without looking aside in these poems'. In other words, readers are going to be confronted by homosexuality – perhaps the word 'fellow', used twice in the piece, was carefully chosen to soften the blow to delicate sensibilities, avoiding 'man'. But readers should be reassured, too: according to Williams, there is no doubt that what Ginsberg produces is most definitely art. His experiences are validated by analogy with Christ's passion at Golgotha (a word repeated in the poem), as well as the persecution of the Jews in the Second World War. Is this taking things a step too far? Not if readers agree to see the beaten Ginsberg as a mid-twentieth-century symbol representing the end result of the whole weight of two thousand years of history. Williams persuades readers to agree with him: 'But this is our own country' – he is an American speaking to Americans – and he finishes by using the collective pronoun in the statement 'we believe'. Suffering and the perfection of the poet's art are the means by which Williams both celebrates and apologizes for his friend. The last sentence – 'Hold back the edges of your gowns, Ladies, we are going through hell' – takes on a different tone. It could be read as high camp, offering a challenge, but the tenor of the whole Introduction educates readers in the way that Williams, who is sympathetic to the poem, thinks it ought to be read.

Williams anticipated hostility and works hard to get readers on Ginsberg's side in the hope of deflecting it. The Beats were already subject to media attention, but not all readers were as liberal as Williams hoped they would be. Lawrence Ferlinghetti and Shigeyashi Murao – publishers, and owners of the City Lights Bookstore – were prosecuted for publishing obscene material, a fact that made a major contribution to Ginsberg's subsequent fame. An obscenity trial is a first-class way to attract attention to a writer's work, and 50,000 copies of *Howl and Other Poems* were sold in the first year of publication. This figure is modest indeed compared to three million copies of Mickey Spillane's anti-communist novel *One Lonely Night*, published in 1951, but in terms of poetry, *Howl* was a bestseller.

Ferlinghetti, credited with creating much of the interest in contemporary poetry at the time, took the precaution of submitting the manuscript of *Howl and Other Poems* to the American Civil Liberties Union before it was sent to Britain to be printed; the Union agreed to defend it if necessary. The first edition came back and was published at the City Lights Bookstore in the autumn of 1956. However, when the second edition arrived from the printers in March 1957 it was seized by the Collector of Customs on the grounds that 'The words and the sense of the writing is obscene.' '[Y]ou wouldn't want your children to come across it', he added (in Hyde, 1984, p.43). With those copies confiscated, Ferlinghetti sidestepped Customs altogether by having the next edition printed in the USA. He defended the poem in the San Francisco *Chronicle*, arguing 'It is not the poet but what he observes which is revealed as obscene. The great wastes of "Howl" are the sad wastes of a mechanized world, lost among atom bombs and insane nationalisms ... Ginsberg chooses to walk on the wild side of this world ... mostly in the tradition of philosophical anarchism' (in *ibid.*, p.44).

In explanation and defence of the poem, Ferlinghetti quotes (or slightly misquotes) from 'Howl' itself –

> What sphinx of cement and aluminium bashed open their skulls
> and ate up their brains and imagination?
> Moloch! Solitude! Filth! Ugliness! Ashcans and unobtainable
> dollars! Children screaming under the stairways! Boys
> sobbing in Armies! Old men weeping in parks!

– and comments wryly, 'a world, in short, you wouldn't want your children to come across' (in Hyde, 1984, p.44).

The police arrested Ferlinghetti and Murao with the aim of proving lewd intent in publishing *Howl and Other Poems*. Ferlinghetti was delighted. *Life* magazine ran a big article on the poems and the trial; Ginsberg, temporarily living in Paris, began to receive regular royalty cheques. Barry Miles, his biographer, says that Ginsberg 'emerged from the trial a famous literary figure, and upon his return to the States, the press seized upon him as the leader and spokesman of the scene' (2000, p.245).

The trial did not just draw the public's attention to the poem, inevitably it generated critical attention. According to the editor of *Poetry* magazine, Henry Rago, *Howl and Other Poems* 'is a dignified, sincere and admirable work of art' (in Hyde, 1984, p.45); Robert Duncan and Ruth Witt-Diamant of the San Francisco State College Poetry Center praised it for being 'rhapsodic, highly idealistic and inspired in cause and purpose', stating firmly that 'Only by misunderstanding might these tortured outcryings for sexual and spiritual understanding be taken as salacious' (in *ibid.*, p.46). The two expert witnesses for the prosecution did not come close to the clout of the nine expert witnesses for the defence. The likes of Mark Schorer and Leo

Lowenthal from the University of California, the poet Kenneth Rexroth and novelist Vincent McHugh spoke up in favour of the book's seriousness of purpose, its contribution to poetry and literature in general, and its sincerity and overall merit. As Ferlinghetti later observed, they presented as good a one-sided critical survey as could be hoped for (in Hyde, 1984, p.47).

Vindicating Ferlinghetti and Murao, the Counsel for the Defense summed up by identifying the main theme of 'Howl' as social criticism. Judge Horn agreed, apparently having done rather more homework than the witnesses for the prosecution:

> The first part of 'Howl' presents a picture of a nightmare world; the second part is an indictment of those elements in modern society destructive of the best qualities of human nature; such elements are predominantly identified as materialism, conformity, and mechanization leading to war. The third part presents a picture of an individual who is a specific representation of what the author conceives as a general condition ... 'Footnote to "Howl"' seems to be a declamation that everything in the world is holy, including parts of the body by name. It ends in a plea for holy living.
>
> (in Hyde, 1984, pp.52–3)

Even the judge could see that the poem had a beginning, a middle and an end; in that respect, it is both traditional and conventional.

Ginsberg had supported himself on his income from poetry for two years when he returned to the USA from Europe in July 1958 (Miles, 2000, p.245). In 1959, Fantasy Records released an LP of him reading from *Howl and Other Poems*. The record was available continuously until 1985, and was reissued as a CD in 1998. The cover of the original album declares that 'Howl' is not obscene or pornographic, and quotes from Judge Horn's summing-up: 'A work may be deemed obscene only if it intends to deprave or corrupt readers by exciting lascivious thoughts or inciting to immoral actions and there is no obscenity in a work which has "redeeming social importance".' While this declaration clears the work, it also functions to keep the trial in the public mind, doubtless contributing to the reputation and continuing sales of both book and record. The recording itself focuses attention back on the notion of utterance, reminding us that 'Howl' was read to enthusiastic audiences before a decision was made to publish it.

The USA in the 1940s and 1950s

If Ginsberg became a popular poet, he certainly began, and continued throughout his life, to be a proponent of a counter-culture. The end of the Second World War did not establish a new era of peace and harmony in the USA. The Japanese bombing of Pearl Harbor and the US bombs dropped on Hiroshima and Nagasaki left an indelible mark on the nation's consciousness, and the arms race intensified when the Soviet Union tested its first A-bomb in 1949. The Communist People's Republic of China was established in 1949; in 1950, US troops went to South Korea in response to invasion by communist North Korea. Fear of communism was widespread, fuelled by the Democratic administration under President Truman, who in 1946 instigated investigation of Americans for un-American activities: the message was that communists could be found anywhere and vigilance was the only answer. What became popularly known as 'McCarthyism' came later with the advent of Senator Joseph McCarthy in 1950. Writers, actors and artists were accorded particular attention. The House Un-American Activities Committee (HUAC) was most active in the early 1950s, but as early as 1947 the film industry was subject to scrutiny, and 'those in education were hard hit, both university professors and teachers' unions, and charges of subversion in school caused an atmosphere of extreme paranoia as different institutions raced to cleanse themselves of possibly suspect material in textbooks and assigned readings' (Jenkins, 1997, p.239).

In spite of this, the voice of scepticism was still heard. John Hersey, for example, published *Hiroshima* (1946), which aimed to present to fellow Americans an accurate picture of the death, destruction and continuing suffering caused by radiation inflicted by US atomic bombs, giving the lie to Truman's statement that 'The world will note that the first atomic bomb was dropped on Hiroshima, a military base. That was because we wished in this first attack to avoid, insofar as possible, the killing of civilians' (quoted in Zinn, 1999, p.424). The official report of the US Strategic Bombing Survey said the opposite, 'Hiroshima and Nagasaki were chosen as targets because of their concentration of activities and population' (quoted in *ibid.*). Ferlinghetti, like O'Hara, was in the navy during the war. He recalls visiting Nagasaki a few weeks after the bomb was dropped, showing that even eye witnesses were ignorant of the truth: 'we didn't even know what radiation was in those days. We just went in there like tourists ... We didn't have any protective gear. Nobody knew it was harmful. We didn't know that a whole culture had been destroyed in the blink of Satan's eye' (quoted in Plimpton, 1999, p.343). Less than a decade later, Kerouac's character Levinsky in the novel *The Town and the City* (1950) – who was based on Ginsberg – is obsessed with atomic contamination and disease, which has become his metaphor for the horror of modern life. It is worth remembering that the USA exploded its first hydrogen bomb in 1951, with the Soviet Union only two years behind in 1953.

Sceptics asked to what extent the US government was simply protecting investments by fuelling the cold war, rather than supporting 'high-minded' anti-communist ideals. The historian Howard Zinn's answer is that the atmosphere was one of such fear and repression that the government would have no trouble in finding mass support for a policy of rearmament:

> The system, so shaken in the thirties, had learned that war production could bring stability and high profits. Truman's anti-Communism was attractive. The Business publication *Steel* had said in November 1946 ... that Truman's policies gave 'the firm assurance that maintaining and building our preparations for war will be big business in the United States for at least a considerable period ahead'.
>
> (Zinn, 1999, p.437)

Now reread the first part of 'Howl' with this background in mind, looking for evidence of Ginsberg's attitudes. How are they expressed?

The earliest direct reference to war comes in line 6 – 'who passed through universities with radiant cool eyes hallucinating Arkansas and Blake-light tragedy among the scholars of war'. Lines of demarcation are carefully drawn: the best minds of Ginsberg's generation retain their 'radiant cool eyes', quite separate from those who study war. The next reference (which we considered earlier) is less direct: they 'sit listening to the crack of doom on the hydrogen jukebox' (line 15). However, the use of the word 'hydrogen' at the time was a potent reminder of the development of the fusion bomb, even more destructive than the fission atom bomb.

Fifteen lines later, our heroes have left university and begun travelling. After Kansas, Idaho, Oklahoma and Mexico they reappear on the west coast, comically parodying the authorities, their appearances a blueprint for beatniks in Europe as well as the USA, marching to Ban the Bomb in the years to come. They are 'investigating the FBI in beards and shorts with big pacifist eyes sexy in their dark skin passing out incomprehensible leaflets'. Self-inflicted cigarette burns protest against the 'narcotic tobacco haze of Capitalism', an image that works literally and metaphorically; they also distribute 'Supercommunist pamphlets' (line 32) – a counterblast to the millions of pamphlets distributed among the population of the USA in the early 1950s, such as 'One Hundred Things You Should Know About Communism' (Zinn, 1999, p.435). Subsequently, references in the poem to 'the wartime blue floodlight of the moon' (line 46) and to those

> who were burned alive in their innocent flannel suits
> > on Madison Avenue amid blasts of leaden verse
> > & the tanked-up clatter of the iron regiments
> > of fashion & the nitroglycerine shrieks of the
> > fairies of advertising & the mustard gas of sinis-
> > ter editors

(p.16)

indicate a new way to consider the imagery of the poem. There is a great deal of martial language, and by juxtaposition Ginsberg diagnoses the causes of war; fashion, advertising, publishing and war are all driven by capitalist interest. The part that 'sinister intelligent editors' play makes them just as responsible, for 'leaden verse'.

Now reread part II, which begins with the question 'What sphinx of cement and aluminium bashed open their skulls and ate up their brains and imagination?' How does the rest of the part answer it?

In this mass of detail, Moloch stands for all the evils of US society, and, indeed, might also represent the USA consuming its children. Lines 2–10 repeat the name 'Moloch' thirty-nine times, to relentless effect. There is no escape except through madness or suicide, which is described in the last four lines. Everything is wrong with the world: there is poverty and unequal distribution of wealth, evident in 'Ashcans and unobtainable dollars'. Moloch's mind is 'pure machinery', it has no human qualities of sympathy, pity or imagination.

Apart from the initial question, each phrase or sentence in this part ends with an exclamation mark. It is the first time in the poem that Ginsberg has used this form of punctuation, and he does not use it again until 'Footnote to Howl', where again use is extensive and precludes the need for full stops. In both part II and 'Footnote to Howl' the exclamation mark denotes certainty: in the former, that Moloch signifies everything that is wrong with society; in the latter, that everything is holy. Ginsberg's use of exclamation marks is biblical – it is no accident that part II and the footnote set up an opposition between evil and good. The declamatory style draws on prophetic voices of the Old Testament, while the very last words of the poem insist on the supernatural 'extra brilliant intelligent kindness of the soul!'

Now read 'America'. Compare and contrast it with 'Howl'.

As far as the form is concerned, repetition is an important structuring device once again, but lines are generally shorter, and usually endstopped. The result is a series of statements, as well as nine questions in the first part of the poem. In some ways, 'America' is more straightforward than 'Howl'. 'America when will you send your eggs to India' offers clear comment on one nation that has excess and its duty to help out another whose people suffer from starvation, but 'America when will we end the human war' only seems straightforward until it is examined closely. Why is the pronoun 'we' rather than 'you', and why is the war referred to as 'human'? Careful scrutiny reveals apparently simple statements to be cryptic. Some of the imagery is familiar from 'Howl': 'Your machinery is too much for me', for example, seems to follow a line of thought from the 'Moloch' section; 'I can't stand my own mind' continues the theme of madness.

There are many autobiographical elements to the poem, as there were in 'Howl'. Ginsberg's mother did take him and his brother to Communist Party meetings in the 1930s, and 'The Red Flag' and the union song 'On the Line' were among the first songs he learned (Miles, 2000, p.13). The speaker is a man who is obsessed with *Time* magazine but never buys it. He sees it for sale every time he slinks 'past the corner candystore', but reads it for free in the Berkeley Public Library. In a line that brings O'Hara to mind, he is described as poor, possessing 'two dollars and twentyseven cents' on 'January 17, 1956', but unlike O'Hara, he refuses to enter into the world of consumerism. It is *Time* magazine that tells him about responsibility and the commercial world: 'Business / men are serious. Movie producers are serious. / Everybody's serious but me'. Seriousness has been equated with capitalism, and Ginsberg will take no part in it.

Like 'Howl', 'America' is not without humour: 'It occurs to me that I am America. / I am talking to myself again' marks a turning point in the poem as well as raising a smile. The lines that begin the next sentence can be read as following directly on, so that 'me' is actually America: 'Asia is rising against me. / I haven't got a chinaman's chance'. National resources consist of a collection of the speaker's private belongings – two joints of marijuana and 'unpublishable' private writing – together with numerous mental institutions, prisons and the homeless poor. Then the voice becomes one of megalomania, having abolished brothels in France, 'Tangiers is next to go', but the alliance cannot continue: voice and country separate once more in the lines that follow. Ginsberg imagines his poetry – 'strophes' – as a commodity for sale, in part-exchange, and goes on to side with the unrepresented poor: the Scottsboro boys, for example, were nine black youths convicted of raping two white girls on negligible evidence by all-white juries in Alabama in 1931.

The last twelve strophes of the poem are satirical. War is something that Russia and China want, not America; oil is an issue – 'Him big bureaucracy running our fillingstations'. Language breaks down into stereotyped, deliberately racist speech patterns, ironically drawing attention to the diversity of the US population: 'Her wants to grab Chicago'; 'Ugh. Him make Indians learn read'; 'Him need big black niggers'. That particular strophe ends 'Her make us all work sixteen hours a day. Help', suggesting – at first – that the speaker subscribes to the fear. 'America this is quite serious' appears to reinforce the preceding xenophobia, it is only with the following line, 'America this is the impression I get from looking in the television set', that we realize the extent of the satire. Physical and mental disabilities prevent Ginsberg from signing up or doing munitions factory work – he would not subscribe to either in any case. He will, however, 'get right down to the job' of bringing America to her senses in an alternative way, appropriately enough putting his 'queer shoulder to the wheel'. Like 'Howl', 'America' is a poem of protest against paranoia, the cold war and big business.

Ginsberg's attacks against mainstream US values were recognized in, and indeed helped to shape, the popular culture of the 1960s. He met Bob Dylan in 1963 but was already aware of Dylan's songs, such as 'A Hard Rain's A-Gonna Fall' and 'Masters of War'. Photographs showing a beardless and top-hatted Ginsberg backstage at a concert in Princeton appear on the back of Dylan's *Bringing It All Back Home* (1965) album sleeve. Some years later, in an essay written to introduce a volume of his father's poems, Ginsberg described Dylan as one of a generation of 'minstrel poets' who '*sang* their poems aloud in contemplative rooms black alleyways or bardic halls thru microphones and a new consciousness that had broken thru the crust of old lyric forms like my father's evolved lyrics back to the same forms refreshed with new emotion and new subtleties of accent and vowel articulated in consequence of deep breath'd song' (A. Ginsberg, 1970, pp.13–14).

Dylan's 'Desolation Row' (1965), however, owes its relentless piling up of clauses and catalogue of characters on the margins of society more to Ginsberg's 'Howl' and 'In the Baggage Room at Greyhound' than it does to lyric poetry – so formal experiment worked both ways.

Conclusion

O'Hara and Ginsberg have both been credited with creating new voices for US poetry, and yet each is quite different from the other. O'Hara's voice is urbane, often flippant, informal, conversational and intimate; Ginsberg is declamatory, much less ironic than O'Hara, and passionate about his beliefs. It would be more accurate to say that the new US poetry of the mid-twentieth century was distinguished from what went before by a new plurality of voices – and clearly mass culture played a large part in shaping these. The mechanized world represented and deplored in Ginsberg's poems suggests everything that (as David Johnson says in the Introduction to Part 1 of this book) Matthew Arnold and F.R. Leavis feared from the popular. Dwight Macdonald would have agreed, and yet none of these arbiters of taste and defenders of high culture would value Ginsberg's work, even though, as we have seen, Ginsberg acknowledges a whole weight of poetic tradition by reference and allusion in *Howl and Other Poems*. O'Hara's consciousness of poetic tradition is also apparent, but he celebrates daily life, embraces consumerism, delights in the popular and shows a fine disregard for cultural divisions.

Works cited

Ashbery, J. (1971) 'Introduction', *The Collected Poems of Frank O'Hara*, ed. by D. Allen, Berkeley: University of California Press, pp.vii–xi.

Barrios, R. (2003) *Screened Out: Playing Gay in Hollywood from Edison to Stonewall*, New York: Routledge.

Berkson, B. and LeSeur, J. (eds) (1978) *Homage to Frank O'Hara*, Bolinas: Big Sky.

Burt, S. (2000) 'Hi Louise!', *London Review of Books*, 20 July, pp.27–9.

Charters, A. (1991) 'Introduction', J. Kerouac, *On the Road*, Penguin Twentieth-Century Classics, Harmondsworth: Penguin, pp.vii–xxxiii.

Charters, A. (ed.) (1992) *The Penguin Book of the Beats*, Harmondsworth: Penguin.

Eliot, T.S. (1974) *Collected Poems 1909–1962*, London: Faber & Faber.

Elledge, J. (ed.) (1993) *Frank O'Hara: To Be True to a City*, Ann Arbor: University of Michigan Press.

Ginsberg, A. (1970) 'Confrontation with Louis Ginsberg's Poems', in L. Ginsberg, *Morning in Spring and Other Poems*, New York: William Morrow.

Ginsberg, A. (1986) *Howl*, original draft facsimile, ed. by B. Miles, Harmondsworth: Viking, Penguin.

Ginsberg, A. ([1956] 2002) *Howl and Other Poems*, San Francisco: City Lights.

Ginsberg, L. (1970) *Morning in Spring and Other Poems*, New York: William Morrow.

Gobel, M. (1999) ' "Our Country's Black and White Past": Film and the Figure of History in Frank O'Hara', *American Literature*, 71.1, March, pp.57–92.

Gooch, B. (1993) *City Poet: The Life and Times of Frank O'Hara*, New York: HarperPerennial.

Gray, R. (1990) *American Poetry of the Twentieth Century*, Harlow: Longman.

Herring, T.S. (2002) 'Frank O'Hara's Open Closet', *Proceedings of the Modern Language Association*, 117.3, May, pp.414–27.

Hyde, L. (ed.) (1984) *On the Poetry of Allen Ginsberg*, Ann Arbor: University of Michigan Press.

Jenkins, P. (1997) *A History of the United States*, London: Macmillan.

Joyce, J. ([1916] 1977) *Portrait of the Artist as a Young Man*, London: Granada.

Kaiser, C. (1998) *The Gay Metropolis 1940–1996*, London: Weidenfeld & Nicolson.

Kerouac, J. ([1957] 1991) *On the Road*, ed. and intro. by A. Charters, Penguin Twentieth-Century Classics, Harmondsworth: Penguin.

Kerouac, J. ([1950] 2000) *The Town and the City*, intro. by D. Brinkley, Penguin Modern Classics, London: Penguin.

Lehman, D. (1999) *The Last Avant-Garde: The Making of the New York School of Poets*, New York: Anchor Books.

Miles, B. (2000) *Ginsberg: A Biography*, London: Virgin.

Milton, J. (1966) *Poetical Works*, ed. by D. Bush, London: Oxford University Press.

O'Hara, F. (1964) *Lunch Poems*, San Francisco: City Lights.

O'Hara, F. (1991) *Selected Poems*, ed. by D. Allen, Harmondsworth: Penguin.

O'Hara, F. ([1971] 1995) *The Collected Poems of Frank O'Hara*, ed. by D. Allen, Berkeley: University of California Press.

Padgett, R. (1970) 'Introduction', *An Anthology of New York Poets*, ed. by R. Padgett and D. Shapiro, New York: Random House.

Perloff, M. (1998) *Poet among Painters*, Chicago: University of Chicago Press.

Plimpton, G. (1999) *Beat Writers at Work*, London: Harvill.

Rosenberg, B. and White, D.M. (eds) (1957) *Mass Culture: The Popular Arts in America*, Glencoe, IL: The Free Press.

Ross, A. (1989) *No Respect: Intellectuals and Popular Culture*, London: Routledge.

Trilling, L. and Bloom, H. (eds) (1973) *Victorian Prose and Poetry*, New York: Oxford University Press.

Ward, G. (2001) *Statutes of Liberty: The New York School of Poets*, Basingstoke: Palgrave.

Whitman, W. (1996) *The Complete Poems*, ed. by F. Murphy, London: Penguin.

Zinn, H. (1999) *A People's History of the United States 1492–Present*, New York: HarperCollins.

Further reading

Charters, A. (ed.) (1992) *The Penguin Book of the Beats*, Harmondsworth: Penguin. A wide-ranging anthology of Beat writing.

Elledge, J. (ed.) (1993) *Frank O'Hara: To Be True to a City*, Ann Arbor: University of Michigan Press. The first part of this book consists of contemporary reviews of O'Hara's poetry, the second part collects general essays, while the third concentrates on essays on particular poems and themes.

Gooch, B. (1993) *City Poet: The Life and Times of Frank O'Hara*, New York: HarperPerennial. Gooch's biography, with illustrations, places O'Hara firmly in the context of New York in the 1950s and 1960s.

Gray, R. (1990) *American Poetry of the Twentieth Century*, Harlow: Longman. This comprehensive survey of twentieth-century US poetry includes sections on the New York School of poets and on the Beats.

Miles, B. (2000) *Ginsberg: A Biography*, London: Virgin. This biography includes critical appreciations of a number of Ginsberg's major poems.

Perloff, M. (1998) *Frank O'Hara: Poet among Painters*, Chicago: University of Chicago Press. Perloff's study involves close analysis of many of O'Hara's major poems and also explores his work at the New York Museum of Modern Art and his relationship with the painters Larry Rivers, Jasper Johns, Mike Goldberg, Willem de Kooning and Jackson Pollock.

Plimpton, G. (1999) *Beat Writers at Work*, London: Harvill. This book mainly consists of a series of interviews with Beat writers – William Burroughs, Jack Kerouac and Allen Ginsberg among them. It also includes 'A Semester with Allen Ginsberg', an account by Elissa Schappell of her experiences of Ginsberg's writing classes at New York University.

CHAPTER 3

Philip K. Dick, *Do Androids Dream of Electric Sheep?*

ANDREW M. BUTLER

Overview

After a brief introduction, I begin by discussing science fiction, the genre to which Philip K. Dick's novel *Do Androids Dream of Electric Sheep?* most obviously belongs, and examine three alternative definitions of it. I then introduce Dick and his historical context in more detail, before moving on to examine the critical approaches that have most frequently been applied to Dick's work: Marxism and postmodernism. In the next section, I examine the critical reception of this novel, before considering whether science fiction as a genre is gendered. By way of conclusion, I look at the status of *Do Androids Dream of Electric Sheep?* in an attempt to establish whether it is an example of 'high' or popular literature. There are other critical paradigms that I could have used in my readings of the novel, such as structuralism, psychoanalysis, feminism or ecocriticism – indeed, at various points in the chapter I will discuss issues surrounding gender and race – but I have been guided by the prevailing trends in academic analysis of Dick's writings. You should feel free to use any of these approaches – and to question them.

Introduction

There is a passage in a letter written by Dick in 1981 where he responds to a critical article he has been sent and confesses that he finds it unreadable. He writes: 'Criticism, to be valuable, must make sense and must relate in some way to that which it analyses.' Dick was objecting to an academic critic who had used the ideas of the German philosopher Immanuel Kant to examine one of his novels. Was Dick right to suggest that philosophy has nothing to do with popular fiction, or that a popular genre does not relate to abstract thought? Certainly, in his own non-fiction (see, especially, Dick, 1991, 1995), as well as in his novels, there are direct references to philosophers such as Plato, Parmenides, Heraclitus, David Hume and Martin Heidegger. Such a contradiction shows the danger of always taking an author at his or her own word, and in this chapter I will examine how philosophy may help to provide a reading of an example of popular fiction.

One consequence of examining Dick's novel in relation to philosophy is that it may prompt a reconsideration of whether science fiction should be classified as a popular genre. The case for arguing that science fiction is a popular genre rests on the substantial sales figures achieved by certain science-fiction writers – Arthur C. Clarke, Douglas Adams and Robert A. Heinlein are three such examples. The assertion is reinforced by reference to science fiction's generic cousin fantasy, which has also had many popular successes – witness the spectacular sales of writers such as J.R.R. Tolkien, J.K. Rowling, Terry Pratchett and Philip Pullman. The patronizing tone adopted by many cultural commentators should also be noted – the hysteria and despair generated by Tolkien's success in polls for the best book, and the hiving off of reviews of science fiction from literary novels in literary supplements. However, this evidence has not convinced all critics, and the case against treating science fiction as a popular genre has been made by Farah Mendlesohn, who argues in *The Cambridge Companion to Science Fiction* that 'whatever else it is, sf [science fiction] literature is not *popular*, even while "sci-fi" movies pack the cinemas' (2003, p.1). Mendlesohn points to the relatively small sales of the vast majority of science-fiction literature compared with other genres, as well as to its originality and intellectual ambition, and, like most writers on science fiction, rejects the popular term 'sci-fi' (originally coined in 1954 as a self-conscious echo of 'hi-fi') because it has so often been used in a derogatory tone. As you read the chapter, keep in mind the debate over whether science fiction is 'popular'; I will return to it in the concluding section.

The genre of science fiction

I would like to begin my examination of science fiction by taking a look at the opening of the novel. **Read the first chapter of *Do Androids Dream of Electric Sheep?* What things do you find strange? How is Dick portraying social relations in his imagined future?**

Right at the start we are introduced to the 'mood organ' next to Rick Deckard's bed, the device that has awakened him. Iran Deckard's awakening is less successful and this seems to be linked to something called a 'Penfield', which appears to be another name for the mood organ (this is confirmed later in the chapter). The Penfield has a number of settings – perhaps linked to electricity voltages – that can somehow change how the user feels. As the scene progresses, we learn about various different moods that can be dialled up. The mood organ can not only induce cheerfulness but also, as Iran has discovered, cause feelings of depression. It seems likely that Dick took the name Penfield from the scientist Wilbur Penfield, who in the 1930s and 1940s conducted experiments to map the human brain by using electricity to stimulate various parts of the brains of live patients. In particular, Penfield located the areas of the brain that deal with movement and the senses. The Penfield Mood Organ is an imaginative extension of this real scientific study.

The next mystery is why Rick and Iran have an electric sheep instead of a real pet – indeed, why they would wish to have a farm animal rather than a domesticated one. An electric sheep should remind us of the novel's title (which was settled on by the publisher after various suggestions by Dick: *The Electric Toad, Do Androids Dream?, The Electric Sheep* and *The Killers Are Among Us! Cried Rick Deckard to the Special Man*). The Deckards have an electric sheep and dream of – in the sense of yearn for – a real live one. The reasons for this ambition should become clearer as the novel progresses. The question posed by the title seems to be whether androids (artificial humans) desire to have electric sheep (artificial sheep). The choice of animal might also refer to the practice of counting sheep to facilitate sleep, although we do not normally think of machines sleeping – they are either on or off.

In Rick's conversation with his neighbour Bill Barbour it becomes clear that their relationship is based on a comparison of what they own, with Rick's artificial sheep indicating relative poverty. In this post-nuclear-war world, animals have become commodities to buy and sell, with a directory – *Sidney's* catalogue – listing their exchange value. Some animals are extinct, and cannot be bought. But there is more to the animals than what they are worth in monetary terms: they also clearly bring a kudos with them that relates to the as-yet-unexplained process of Mercerism. Anyone without an animal is looked down on by the rest of society – so much so that Rick is willing to risk having a fake animal. For Rick, work is a means of getting money to purchase and look after a real animal.

Dick's portrayal of Rick and Iran's relationship also has an economic dimension: it is made clear that Rick is the breadwinner and that Iran stays at home, and is dependent on Rick's money. It may be the future – or at least 3 January 1992 was in the future when the novel was first published – but the relationship between the sexes is not dissimilar to how it was before the 1970s. On an emotional level, the detail that they sleep in separate beds suggests distance between them, but it also recalls the chastity implied by separate beds in films and sitcoms of the 1950s and 1960s. This is a relationship under some kind of stress. In the next few pages there seems to be little for Iran to do, except for watching television and experimenting with the mood organ. Only the latter seems particularly fulfilling, and then only when she or Rick programs it to determine her mood in a particular way.

Dick's use of language contrasts Rick with Iran. Rick's 'multicolored pajamas', reflect his cheerful mood; the electricity is described, somewhat unusually, as 'merry' (Dick, [1968] 2001, 1; p.3; all subsequent references are to this edition). In contrast, Iran has 'gray, unmerry eyes', a 'dark, pert face', and is much more subdued. In their dispute she calls him a murderer and accuses him of killing 'andys' (1; p.4). Just what 'andys' are is not explained here. As we learn over the next two chapters, 'andy' is an abbreviation for 'android', a partly organic robot in the shape of a human. Rick makes a distinction between killing humans and killing androids, although Iran seems to have some sympathy for the latter (you may consider this a point in her favour). Later in the novel, Rick's apparent lack of compassion will become an important issue.

The novel begins with a domestic scene, the perhaps familiar experience of early morning grumpiness as a couple awake. The first chapter establishes that this is a post-nuclear future, and that Rick, like other surviving members of the human race on earth, wants a real animal to care for. From the start we are presented with the peculiar mix of the familiar and the strange that is typical of science fiction.

Now think about the genre of science fiction in more detail. What science fiction have you previously encountered? What do you understand by the term?

Science fiction as a mode has cut across virtually all forms of cultural production: television and radio programmes, films, books, plays, comics, magazines, computer games, adverts, fashion and so on. You may well have watched episodes of *Doctor Who* on television (1963–89) or seen one of the many versions of *Star Trek*. You may also have seen blockbuster films such as *Star Wars* (1977), *Independence Day* (1995) or the *Matrix* trilogy (*The Matrix*, 1999, *The Matrix Reloaded*, 2003, and *The Matrix Revolutions*, 2003), which offer action adventures, and provide the viewer with a series of spectacles and special effects to enjoy. The action can take place in some exotic location, separated from the here and now either by distance – a planet in a distant galaxy, say – or by time – anything from a few years to a century or a million years into the future. In science fiction set in the here-and-now, an element of the exotic is introduced by the discovery that the history of the fictional Earth is different from the history of the one we know, or by the arrival of something strange on Earth, such as alien invaders. Science fiction also examines imagined technologies, and their impact on fictional characters.

Alongside science fiction on film and television, there is a wide variety of science fiction in written material, published in books, magazines and now online on the world wide web. What constitutes the first written example of science fiction is a matter of some controversy – I will return to this topic later in the chapter – but Mary Shelley's *Frankenstein* (1818), with its exploration of the results of creating an artificial being, is a strong candidate. Its story of a creation turning on its creator has been mimicked in numerous science-fiction narratives. At the other end of the nineteenth century, H.G. Wells's 'Scientific Romances' examined time travel (*The Time Machine: An Invention*, 1895), vivisection (*The Island of Dr Moreau*, 1896), invisibility (*The Invisible Man: A Grotesque Romance*, 1897), alien invasion (*The War of the*

Worlds, 1898) and travel to the moon (*The First Men in the Moon*, 1901), as well as other ideas that were to become science-fiction staples. Still in the more serious camp, there are the various dark or ambiguous visions of future societies, such as Aldous Huxley's *Brave New World* (1932) and George Orwell's *Nineteen Eighty-Four* (1949).

Although certain recurrent themes and structures can be identified in these films and novels – the importance of technology, the utopian or dystopian future, the resourceful male hero who overcomes difficulties in an exotic or alien environment, the side-lining of female characters – such a partial listing is not in itself a definition of science fiction. Indeed, the definition of science fiction is much contested: Gary K. Wolfe lists nearly forty definitions in his *Critical Terms for Science Fiction and Fantasy* (1986, pp.108–11); Neyir Cenk Gökçe's web page (1996) offers over fifty; the second edition of John Clute and Peter Nicholls's *The Encyclopedia of Science Fiction* (1993, pp.311–14) spends nearly three thousand words trying to define the genre.

Look at one of the better-known definitions of science fiction, from Brian Aldiss's *Billion Year Spree* (1973), a history of science fiction. This is the first of three definitions that I will examine. How does it connect science fiction to literary history and what function does it describe the genre as serving?

> the search for a definition of man and his status in the universe which will stand in our advanced but confused state of knowledge (science), and is characteristically cast in the Gothic or post-Gothic mould.
>
> (Aldiss, 1973, p.8)

Aldiss sees science fiction as a development from an earlier genre, the Gothic, which flourished in the latter half of the eighteenth century and the first half of the nineteenth. The Gothic novel often featured exotic, wild landscapes and melodramatic plots, in which individuals were put in peril. There were two broad categories of Gothic novel: the supernatural, in which there are ghosts, zombies, vampires, spirits and so on – typified by Matthew Lewis's *The Monk* (1795) – and the rational, where all the mysterious events are revealed to be a fraud or a hallucination – typified by Ann Radcliffe's *The Mysteries of Udolpho* (1794). Science fiction falls into the latter category because of its use of science as an explanatory narrative. Aldiss suggests that the purpose of science fiction is to define the status of man in terms of rational science, as opposed to showing him as a spiritual being or one connected to a God. He also suggests that there is a philosophical dimension to science fiction in this investigation – it could question earlier moral values by showing alternatives to them.

Note the gender used here: despite the emergence of a new wave of feminism in the late 1960s, and even though *Billion Year Spree* begins with Mary Shelley, a female writer, Aldiss refers to 'man' rather than humanity. Admittedly science fiction was – and arguably still is – dominated by male writers, with women writers often hiding behind male pseudonyms (André Norton, James Tiptree), ambiguous names (Leigh Brackett) or initials (C.L. Moore). There were a few 'openly' female science-fiction writers in the 1950s and 1960s, such as Marion Zimmer Bradley, Ursula Le Guin, Joanna Russ and Anne McCaffery, but it was from the late 1960s that the most important feminist science fiction began to be published. However, when Aldiss (with David Wingrove) revised his history as *Trillion Year Spree* (1986), he altered 'mould' to 'mode' but left 'man' and 'he' unchanged (p.25).

Aldiss's history is contested in other ways, with the historical timeframe of science fiction disputed. Aldiss puts forward *Frankenstein* as the first science-fiction text, whereas other critics have suggested both earlier and later starting points for the genre. For example, the following works have all been categorized as early forms of science fiction: utopian writings such as Plato's *The Republic* (*c.*350 BCE) and Thomas More's *Utopia* (1516), fantastic voyages such as Homer's *Odyssey* (*c.*800 BCE) and Lucian of Samosata's *The True History* (second century CE, which includes a voyage to the moon and a space battle), and poems such as Geoffrey Chaucer's *House of Fame* (*c.*1380) and John Milton's *Paradise Lost* (1667). In contrast, other critics, notably Gary Westfahl (1998), have argued that science fiction *as a self-conscious genre* only begins in the 1920s, in the specialist pulp magazines.

A great deal of popular fiction had been published during the nineteenth century in magazine form and in cheap and sensational pamphlets, described as 'penny dreadfuls', which sought the maximum possible general audience. But as the century wore on, magazines began to occupy specific niches, especially in the North American market. There were those that featured westerns or detectives, and others with stories about war, spies, airships or aeroplanes – each area offering a family or genre of narratives, styles, themes and characterization. It is in such publications that the genre of science fiction emerged and was recognized. In April 1926, a Luxembourgian immigrant to the USA, Hugo Gernsback, launched the magazine *Amazing Stories*, which would be entirely devoted to what he called 'scientifiction'. In his editorial for the first issue he wrote that: 'By "scientifiction" I mean the Jules Verne, H.G. Wells and Edgar Allan Poe type of story – a charming romance inter-mingled with scientific fact and prophetic vision' (1926, p.3). Gernsback's *Amazing Stories* was one of his many attempts to promote inventions, such as radio sets, which he hoped to sell to his readers. Gernsback acknowledged earlier pioneers and enthusiasts of modern science and serialized works by Verne and Wells. At an early stage, 'scientifiction' was renamed 'science fiction' and became a genre that authors would consciously write and people would willingly seek out as readers.

Gernsback had begun the practice of encouraging feedback from his readers in order to gauge the success of stories. This was part of his more general ambition to popularize technology and encourage his readers to train as engineers, technicians and plumbers. He lost control of *Amazing Stories* on being forced into bankruptcy – although the magazine continued to be published under a different editor – and started publishing *Science Wonder Stories* (1929–30) and *Scientific Detective Monthly* (1930), as rivals exploited and broadened the market with *Astounding Science Fiction* (1930 to date, but called *Analog* since 1960), *Marvel Science Stories* (1938–41), *Unknown* (1939–43), *Planet Stories* (1939–55), *If* (1952–74) and many more. By the 1930s, the readers began writing to each other, setting up fan groups, publishing their own magazines (fanzines) and holding get-togethers (conventions). Some of the readers – Isaac Asimov and, a few years later, Philip K. Dick – became professional writers in their own right.

The second definition of science fiction I want to consider is Dick's own, from an article titled 'My Definition of Science Fiction' (1981). What relationship does he draw between the fictional world and the real world, and what impact does he believe reading science fiction has on the reader?

> [Science fiction is about] a society that does not in fact exist, but is predicated on our known society – that is, our known society acts as a jumping-off point for it ... *this* is the essence of science fiction, the conceptual dislocation within the society so that as a result a new society is generated in the author's mind, transferred to paper, and from paper it occurs as a convulsive shock in the reader's mind, *the shock of dysrecognition.*
>
> (in Dick, 1995, p.99)

Dick's definition emphasizes that science fiction is set in a world that is not real, although the fictional world is inspired by or extrapolated from the world in which the author lives. Dick's definition therefore rests on how the genre differs from realist fiction. Realist fiction is about a society that *does exist,* and the reader's pleasure occurs with the shock of *recognition*; science fiction is about non-existent society and the reader's pleasure occurs with *dysrecognition.* The distortion in science fiction between the real and fictional worlds makes us think afresh about the world that we and the author know, and offers some kind of commentary on it.

The science-fiction writer and critic Samuel R. Delany has argued that 'Science fiction is not "about the future". Science fiction *is in dialogue with the present*' (1984, p.176). The present-day context of *Do Androids Dream of*

Electric Sheep? – written in 1966, first published in 1968 and set in 1992 – was the 1960s, a decade dominated by the anti-Vietnam-War movement, the civil rights movements, the women's movement and, at the end of the decade, the gay rights movement. It seems that for Dick the disorientating thrill of reading a text that misrepresents or allegorizes such issues is a defining feature of science fiction.

The two definitions of science fiction so far have been offered by practitioners, and are perhaps descriptive of their own fiction. The third definition I want to examine, which is more academic in nature, was coined by the critic Darko Suvin. **Read the extract from Suvin's essay 'Cognition and Estrangement' (1979) (Reader, Item 36). Here, he defines science fiction as 'a literary genre whose necessary and sufficient conditions are the presence and interaction of estrangement and cognition, and whose main formal device is an imaginative framework alternative to the author's empirical environment'. How does he situate science fiction as a distinct genre within literature? How does his definition draw on ideas from the work of Bertolt Brecht?**

Suvin lists a range of earlier subgenres – utopias and anti-utopias, the 'fortunate island' and 'fabulous voyage' stories, and the 'planetary' and 'state' novels – that science fiction resembles, as opposed to ' "naturalistic" or empiricist fiction', which I take to mean 'realist' fiction. Suvin notes that from the eighteenth to the twentieth century much fiction has aspired to extreme realism, but before this there existed a whole range of imaginative fictions. He also notes that such imaginative fictions still live on in the genres of fairytale, myth and so on, but that these serve a different social function and take a different approach from science fiction. Suvin attempts to place science fiction within a historical continuum while identifying its uniqueness.

Suvin argues that the encounter with difference in fiction – the next valley, a distant island, the moon, utopias, foreigners, strangers – opens up a way of seeing how the prevailing social order might be different, and that readers of such fiction might as a consequence reassess their own social environments. In other words, the fictional representation of difference is a misrepresentation of the familiar. This transformative experience is labelled 'estrangement' by Suvin, drawing on Brecht's concept of *Verfremdung*, which in turn drew from the Russian literary theorist Viktor Shklovsky's concept *ostranenie* (defamiliarization). Estrangement in Shklovsky and Brecht is an attempt at representation that makes the familiar unfamiliar and still allows it to be recognized – particularly in Brecht's usage, it encourages critical thought.

The *Verfremdungseffekt* (discussed by Walder (2005) in relation to Brecht's *Life of Galileo*) is usually translated into English as 'alienation effect'. However, it is important to distinguish between *Entfremdung* ('alienation') and *Verfremdung* ('estrangement'). The former refers to the experience of the worker under capitalism who has sold his or her labour to a capitalist and has been made into an object or commodity. Because of this alienation, the worker is not fully aware of his or her exploited position within society. The latter term is derived from Brecht and is an aesthetic technique that might make the worker aware of his or her alienation – we might call it a 'shock of *dysrecognition*'. Suvin uses the term 'novum' – borrowing the word from the Marxist philosopher Ernst Bloch – to refer to the textual unit that describes something new and thus causes an estranging effect – such as the Penfield Mood Organ, discussed above. Suvin argues that 'SF is distinguished by the narrative dominance or hegemony of a fiction "novum" (novelty, innovation) validated by cognitive logic' (1979, p.63). The use of the novum – or in practice several nova – is central to science-fiction narratives. The difference between the world of the novum and the world that the reader knows leads the reader to realize that the environment being described is imaginary. Through this contrast, and by the foregrounding of the structures that underpin the imagined environment – its politics, laws, social systems, taboos, sexual politics, prejudices, working patterns, leisure practices and so on – the reader gains a new perspective in observing or recognizing equivalent structures and ideological operations in his or her own world.

The importance that Suvin places on 'cognition' and 'cognitive logic' lets us make a distinction between science fiction and other non-naturalistic genres, such as the folktale or fairytale. 'Cognition', for Suvin, involves knowledge, specifically scientific knowledge. Suvin quotes Brecht, who describes the astronomer Galileo watching the swing of a chandelier: ' "He was amazed by that pendulum motion as if he had not expected it and could not understand its occurring and this enabled him to come at rules by which it was governed".' The unfamiliarity of the chandelier behaving like a clock pendulum caused Galileo to look at the world with new eyes, to realize something he had not known before and to work out the mathematics of the pendulum.

Cognition, or scientific understanding, and its relations to philosophy, promotes a notion of being able to deduce abstract principles from the environment and use them to predict phenomena such as the direction and speed of the movement of a swinging chandelier. Suvin does not just define science as physics, biology and chemistry, but as a wider body of rigorous knowledge about history, psychology, sociology, anthropology and other human sciences. According to this view, the world can be understood, thought about and logically comprehended, rather than being simply accepted as mystical, magical or transcendent. Science-fiction texts therefore aspire to a consistent logic or rationality within their imagined worlds, unlike fairytales, where the illogical/irrational/magical is a necessary element of the text. Cognition becomes both a means of comprehending the estranging environment that is described and a part of the aesthetics of the genre. On the one hand, the author is presenting us with an estranging event or location; on the other, there is the sense that we can get to know and understand it, and relate it to our own world. For Marxists, of course, the possibility of imagining a different but possible world would be an aid to changing our own world into something better.

Suvin's theories about science fiction have been hugely influential on academic studies of the genre. It is fair to say that 'many of the most sophisticated studies of sf have been either explicitly Marxist in orientation or influenced by Marxist concepts adopted by feminism, race-criticism, queer theory and cultural studies' (Csicsery-Ronay, 2003, p.113). This is true of much of the academic work on Dick's writings. One of the reasons why this is the case is that Dick often appears sympathetic to the Marxist 'project' in his fiction, while denying he is a Marxist in real life – although, as ever, one cannot always take an author's statements about his or her work at face value.

Philip K. Dick and his historical context

By 1976, Dick could be described as a writer of 'self-consistent social allegories of a more-or-less Marxist bent' (Disch, [1976] 1983, p.23). But what was his attitude towards Marxism and how did he come to write *Do Androids Dream of Electric Sheep?* Dick was born in Chicago on 16 December 1928, the survivor of a pair of twins; Jane, his sister, died at one month old. His childhood was difficult: his parents divorced, and by 1936 he had moved to California, to Washington and back to California. He was brought up by his mother, with baby-sitters he later described as being members of the Communist Party (Rickman, 1988, p.120). In the early 1940s, he started reading science fiction, and began to write in the genre himself. At the end of the decade, in about 1949, he spent a semester at the University of California, Berkeley, before dropping out. Berkeley was a centre of radicalism in the USA, and in 1949 there was a crisis over lecturers at the university refusing to take loyalty oaths to the state.

As you saw in Chapter 2, the 1950s was a period of cold-war paranoia – about possible Chinese or Soviet infiltration of the USA, about Marxism, about the nuclear bomb. At the same time, there was the fear that patriotic counter-measures – especially the actions of the House Committee on Un-American Activities and of Senator Joseph McCarthy in exposing and persecuting individuals who were allegedly members of the Communist Party – were producing a dangerous, conformist society. In Hollywood some writers, directors and actors were blacklisted and were unable to work under their own names for many years. Science fiction was one of the few genres able to critique the various forms of McCarthyism – it is not clear whether this was because it was widely considered to be marginal and thus escaped surveillance, or because its use of displacement, distortion and allegory allowed any political subtext to be disowned by its creators. The film *Invasion of the Body Snatchers* (1956), released after the downfall of McCarthy in late 1954, is one such text. In a small town, people are being taken over by identical vegetable pods when they fall asleep – and only one man and his girlfriend resist the body snatchers. The studio insisted on softening the bleak ending of the film, but at the close at least one town has been lost and more may have followed. This film has been read as an allegory of the possibility of communist infiltration, as well as a satire on the paranoia of McCarthyism. Equally, it could be viewed as an attack on how conformist the USA had become – the pod people go about their daily lives without emotion and are seen by some critics as undistinguishable from dull suburbanite Americans.

Dick's fiction of the 1950s exhibited similar preoccupations to *Invasion of the Body Snatchers*. However, in Dick's fiction it would be the large US corporation or the US government that would be the threat to the individual, rather than Russians or communists. The cold war seemed remote, whereas the US state and large corporations appeared more immediately menacing. For example, at the start of *Eye in the Sky* (published 1957, but written 1955), Dick shows Jack Hamilton, a scientist, being suspended from his job because of the political beliefs of his wife, Marsha Hamilton – beliefs Dick shared: ' "She signed the Stockholm Peace Proposal. She joined the Civil Liberties Union ... She signed the Save the Rosenbergs Appeal ... she spoke at the Almeda League of Women Voters in favor of admitting Red China to the U.N. – a communist country ... she contributed money to the Society for the Advancement of Coloured People" ' (Dick, [1957] 1971, pp.10–11). The twist of this novel – in which characters move through a series of fake universes defined by totalitarian ideologies – is that it is the security officer who turns out to be the real Soviet agent.

The 1950s also saw an increased interest in psychology and psychoanalysis, and more people went into therapy. The 1948 report *Sexual Behaviour in the Human Male* was followed in 1953 by *Sexual Behaviour in the Human Female*; both were based on research run by Alfred Kinsey and shocked many Americans, not least because the reports revealed that the level of sexual activity, including homosexual activity, was higher than had previously been assumed. Dick could only really hint at even heterosexual sex in his science fiction – but throughout the 1950s and early 1960s he also wrote a series of quasi-realist novels set in California or in small west coast towns that focused on sexual jealousy, love-triangles, and sex between the teenaged and the middle-aged – a former pupil and his teacher – or across the racial divide. With one exception, none of these appeared in print in his lifetime – and even that exception, *Confessions of a Crap Artist*, was not published until 1975.

A counter-culture rose through the 1950s and into the 1960s, as mass campaigns were fought for an end to US involvement in Vietnam, for women's equality, for civil rights for African Americans and for acceptance of homosexuality, which at that time was widely regarded as a psychological disorder. There was a renewed growth in drug-taking, including marijuana, heroin, amphetamines and LSD, especially among the young (Dick sustained his long periods of all-night writing by taking amphetamines). While the USA was scandalized by the drug-inspired nightmares of William Burroughs's *The Naked Lunch* (1959), the heroin bar in Dick's *The World Jones Made* (1956) seemed to pass without mention.

Do Androids Dream of Electric Sheep? has its origins in a short story called 'The Little Black Box', which appeared in *Worlds of Tomorrow* (August 1964). In an unspecified future, the US government is fearful of a new religion based on people's ability to empathize with the suffering of one Wilbur Mercer via the little black boxes of the title. The government seizes all the devices, unaware that instructions on how people can make their own empathy boxes are being secretly distributed. In a 1978 note to the story, Dick writes: 'Here, a religion is regarded as a menace to all political systems; therefore it, too, is a kind of political system, even an ultimate one ... In this story it is never clear whether Mercer is an invader from some other world. But he must be; in a sense all religious leaders are' (in Dick, 1990, p.389). In *Do Androids Dream of Electric Sheep?* the empathy boxes take up much less of the narrative, and the setting is a post-nuclear-holocaust world rather than a totalitarian USA. The novel was completed by the end of June 1966 and published by Doubleday in March 1968. By April it had sold 1,733 copies, earning back much of Dick's advance of $1,500. This was good news for Dick as he usually had to write several novels a year to pay the bills – in some years in the 1960s he wrote as many as six.

It is now time to return to analysis of the novel itself. As I have already indicated, I will offer two sets of analyses: the first drawing on Marxist ideas of class, economics, commodities and cognitive estrangement; the second drawing on a range of ideas and questions that are associated with postmodernism. Before proceeding, I should emphasize that these approaches are offered as *possible* readings rather than as the only readings.

Marxist readings of *Do Androids Dream of Electric Sheep?*

Marxism is the name given to the group of ideas derived from the writings of the nineteenth-century German thinker and political activist Karl Marx. In *The Communist Manifesto* (1848), Marx and his long-time collaborator Frederick Engels argued that

> The history of all hitherto existing society is the history of class struggles.
>
> Freeman and slave, patrician and plebeian, lord and serf, guildmaster and journeyman, in a word, oppressor and oppressed, stood in constant opposition to each other, carried on an uninterrupted, now hidden, now open fight.
>
> (Marx and Engels, [1848] 1992, p.3)

In nineteenth-century Europe, Marx and Engels continued, the two major contending classes were the capitalists and the workers, with the former making profits (what they termed 'surplus value') by exploiting the labour of the workers. The next step in their argument was that in every instance, the economic system ('means of production' or 'material conditions') and its associated form of class struggle – for example, a slave economy's conflict between freeman and slave, a feudal economy's conflict between lord and serf, or a capitalist economy's conflict between capitalist and worker – would fundamentally influence the political, social and cultural ideas (including literature) of that society. In *The German Ideology* (1845–6), Marx illustrates this point as follows: 'we can say, for instance, that during the time when the aristocracy was dominant, the concepts honour, loyalty, etc. were dominant, during the dominance of the bourgeoisie the concepts freedom, equality, etc.' (Marx and Engels, [1845–6] 1970, p.65). However, Marx and Engels rejected crude economic determinism, and accordingly explained the relation between a society's economic system and its political/cultural system in general terms. In *The German Ideology*, for example, Marx and Engels argued that

> The production of ideas, of conceptions, of consciousness, is at first directly interwoven with the material activity and the material intercourse of men ... Conceiving, thinking, the mental intercourse of men, appear at this stage as the direct efflux of their material behaviour. The same applies to mental production as expressed in the language of politics, laws, morality, religion, metaphysics, etc. of a people.
>
> (Marx and Engels, 1970, p.47)

Marx was optimistic that capitalism was doomed. He and Engels declared in *The Communist Manifesto* that

> The weapons with which the bourgeoisie felled feudalism to the ground are now turned against the bourgeoisie itself.
>
> But not only has the bourgeoisie forged the weapons that bring death to itself; it has also called into existence the men who are to wield those weapons – the modern workers – the proletarians.
>
> (Marx and Engels, 1992, p.9)

With a dramatic flourish, they concluded that 'what the bourgeoisie therefore produces, above all, are its own grave-diggers. Its fall and the rise of the proletariat are equally inevitable' (Marx and Engels, 1992, p.16).

However, capitalism has proved remarkably resilient. A substantial part of the reason for its resilience is explained by Marx and Engels themselves in *The German Ideology* in their discussion of 'Ruling Class and Ruling Ideas' (1970, pp.64–8). They argue that 'The class which has the means of material production at its disposal, has control at the same time over the means of mental production, so that thereby, generally speaking, the ideas of those who lack the means of mental production [the workers] are subject to it' (*ibid.*, p.64). In other words, the ruling class also controls the means of mental or ideological production (churches, schools, newspapers and so on), and through these various institutions disseminates a version of reality that reinforces the system of material production (the economy). As a result, the economic system with its built-in inequalities (as Marx and Engels see it) appears as natural, as the only possible way of organizing society, and workers are thus prevented from understanding the nature and extent of their exploitation. Certain kinds of popular literature form part of the ruling class's 'means of mental production' in at least two ways: first, they repeat and reinforce the ruling class's understanding of society, and secondly, they provide a degree of pleasure for workers who read them, thus making their exploitation slightly more tolerable. There are moments of crisis in capitalist societies when the dissemination of ruling-class ideas is insufficient to secure the obedience of the workers, and in such moments of rebellion (even revolution), the ruling class has at its disposal forms of coercive power – the police, army, the prisons – to protect its interests. Indeed, at all times, but assuming different forms, the ruling class combines ideological and coercive means to protect its power.

A Marxist literary critic would concur broadly with Marx and Engels's diagnosis of western capitalism, but might take a more optimistic line with regard to the role of literature. In the first place, the Marxist critic might identify any number of popular works that do not reproduce the ruling class's version of social reality; indeed, they would point to many popular texts that expose hidden class struggles and the processes of alienation, and reveal how ideology functions in obscuring the realities of economic exploitation. Secondly, following Marx and Engels's insistence in *The German Ideology* that 'the production of ideas ... is directly interwoven with the material activity and material intercourse of men', the Marxists critic would emphasize how popular literary works (including those that support the status quo) are determined by/related to their socio-historical context.

It should already be clear that in *Do Androids Dream of Electric Sheep?* there is an economic imperative on individuals – at least on males – to work, with the ideological pressure of aspiring to own a genuine animal, or at least a convincing simulation. Women are placed firmly in the home; Marx argued that gender relations in the industrial age are often set up to support the processes of capitalism, with a particular focus on reproduction and the family. When the economics of the society change, so will the dynamics of the family: 'The bourgeois family will vanish ... with the vanishing of capital' (Marx and Engels, 1992, p.22). As capital clearly continues to exist, presumably the bourgeois family survives in Dick's future. Further, as the position of women is so dependent on capital's requirements – which include the reproduction of the system – Dick's placement of Iran in the domestic sphere, in a fictional world where many people are infertile, allows the reader to infer that a renewed importance may have been placed on childbirth and that women are forbidden from working outside the home in order to avoid too much exposure to radiation.

Now read to the end of Chapter 2. How does the second chapter build up our knowledge of the world that Dick has imagined?

We are told a lot at the start of this chapter. The setting has changed to a less salubrious district, and to what appears at first to be an empty building containing a television. The state of the building is used to contrast the reader's present, the imagined world's past and the imagined world's present. An idyllic community has been shattered by the emigration of its wealthy inhabitants, and by the ravages of the radioactive fallout from the war. It is not clear between whom the war was fought, nor what it was fought over, but the consequences have been devastating. From a Marxist standpoint it is irrelevant: war pits worker against worker, irrespective of nationality.

The effect of the fallout is to decimate animal life – hence the value of sheep and goats in the first chapter, as scarcity increases value – and to pose a medical threat to any human who has remained in the area. Society has split into several factions: those who can afford to emigrate to a safer location, those who can afford to protect themselves from the effect of the radiation and those affected by radiation and thus unable or forbidden to reproduce. This brings us to one of the characters introduced in this chapter – John or J.R. Isidore. John is squatting in the building, and has suffered from the effects of radioactive fallout. His genes are 'distorted' (2; p.17), and he has low intelligence; he is dismissed by society as a 'special', which would seem to be a euphemism, or a 'chickenhead', a more obviously abusive term.

The description of his status and the transcription of his thoughts are contrasted with the sales pitch of the television broadcast, which extols the virtues of the colony world to which he will not be able to emigrate because of his status. The colony is presented as a great adventure and an escape from the hell of Earth, as an unnamed announcer interviews Mrs Maggie Klugman about her new life on New Mars and asks her about her android servant. We have already been told that these servants are developments of the Synthetic Freedom Fighters built for World War Terminus.

The second half of the chapter moves to something more mystical and mysterious. Before John goes to work at the Van Ness Pet Hospital (actually a false-animal repair firm, possibly the same firm that Rick has used for his false pet, Groucho), he turns on something called an empathy box, holds its handles and first sees, then appears to become, an old man named Wilbur Mercer, who is climbing a hill on an alien planet. As we are shown John having this experience – which includes having rocks thrown at him – we are also told about Mercer's love of animals, his ability to reverse time and bring animals back to life, and his punishment with radioactive cobalt. The sequence introduces a note of menace and suffering into the novel, as well as reinforcing the significance of caring for animals, and letting us know that donkeys and toads are extinct. I will return to Mercer's role in the novel later in this chapter.

The close of Chapter 2 brings John back to his surroundings, and a sudden awareness that he is no longer alone in the building. The identity of his new neighbour is not yet revealed – the reader has to wait until Chapter 6 to find out, as the next chapters return to describing Rick Deckard's day – but John immediately decides to take his new neighbour a gift: 'You take them something, he decided. Like a cup of water or rather milk; yes, it's milk or flour or maybe an egg – or, specifically, their ersatz substitutes' (2; p.23). Given the scarcity of birds, hen's eggs are presumably not available, and meadows and wheat fields are likely to be too polluted to allow for wheat for flour or grass for cows to turn into milk. The staples of living need to be made artificially.

Now read Chapters 3–8. What do we learn about the androids here? What picture is given of the corporate world?

For a start, the androids are more intelligent than specials such as John (3; pp.26–7), and so can cope better in some situations, but they have 'no regard for animals … no ability to feel [empathic] joy for another life form's success or grief at its defeat' (3; p.28; there is a typographical error and 'emphatic' is printed in the text here). It is worth noting this distinction, and confirming whether we see androids failing to show emotions or empathy when they appear later in the novel. Any emotional response in an android is supposedly a programmed reflex and therefore not the result of genuine empathy for others. The humans have evolved a way of measuring empathy – the Voigt-Kampff test.

The androids are manufactured by a number of multinational corporations, of which the most significant – the Rosen Association – appears to be a family business, although this must be questioned as the only relation of Eldon Rosen's that we meet is Rachael, and she turns out to be an android. On the one hand, the corporation seems to be outside the control of governments, whether western or Soviet, who wish them to stop the manufacture of Nexus-6 units (androids); on the other, the fortunes of the

Rosen Association are tied to the government colonization programme – the corporation presumably has a contract to supply androids for the colonists. There is an air of corruption about the Rosen Association, which either 'invests its surplus capital on living animals' (4; p.36) that the general population believe to be extinct (note that the use of the term 'surplus capital' might be meant to recall the Marxist term 'surplus value', i.e. profit), or creates convincingly fake animals that could raise a fortune on the black market or undermine the open economy.

While Rick meets Rachael, in the parallel plot John meets Pris Stratton, although she initially announces herself to be Rachael Rosen. It later transpires that Pris is another android – perhaps she had intended to pass herself off as Rachael indefinitely. Given the emotionless nature of androids, we ought to begin to suspect her true identity from John's impressions of her: 'Now that her initial fear had diminished, something else had begun to emerge from her. Something more strange. And, he thought, deplorable. A coldness. Like, he thought, a breath from the vacuum between inhabited worlds, in fact from nowhere: it was not what she did or said but what she did *not* do and say' (6; p.58). John does not think that she is an android, but then his inability to tell the fake from the real is further demonstrated by the sequence in Chapter 7 when he attempts to recharge a real animal (7; pp.61–2).

At this point I wish to break off my chapter-by-chapter reading of the novel in terms of economics, class and social relations. As you continue to read the novel, you should note the behaviour of Rick and John as workers, and how they – especially Rick – are to some extent alienated by the work that they do. The androids, of course, are also workers, who have slipped their shackles and returned to Earth. In my mention of 'shackles', I am perhaps shifting analytic gears: I am suggesting that the androids might be seen/understood as slaves – although as I have already noted, race-conscious analysis to some extent borrows terminology from Marxism: '[racism is] frequently model[led] ... on bourgeois ideology, as racial hegemony ... is modelled on the capitalist mode of production' (Csicsery-Ronay, 2003, p.113). You will recall that Marx and Engels specify the conflict between freeman and slave as one form of class struggle.

Slave labour had been exploited in the Americas, but the practice was being outlawed in the mid-nineteenth century. This led to the American Civil War (1861–5), which began as the southern states threatened to secede from the Union if they could not continue to keep slaves. The northern states wished to maintain the Union, but it was only after 1863 that they fought for the emancipation of the slaves. They eventually prevailed, effectively occupying the south. The legal interference and economic deprivation that resulted left a deep-seated resentment by the south of the north and a continued segregation of whites and African Americans.

This racial segregation manifested itself in the form of separate areas for living, education, seeing plays and films, sitting on buses and drinking from water fountains. When the Supreme Court overturned local legislation, African Americans still took their lives in their hands if they ventured into previously whites-only territory. The biggest white fear was miscegenation, the interbreeding of the races, especially of an African American man and a white woman. By the mid-1950s, a civil rights movement was beginning to make progress, and in 1955 Martin Luther King led a bus boycott in Montgomery, Alabama after Rosa Parks had refused to give up her seat on a bus to a white person. King later helped to organize a march on Washington in 1963. He was assassinated in 1968. In parallel to King's advocation of non-violent seeking of equality, Malcolm X advocated black separatism using violence if necessary, first via the Nation of Islam movement and then with the Organization for Afro-American Unity. **Reread Chapter 2 of the novel and read the extract from Kevin McNamara's essay '*Blade Runner*'s Post-Individual Worldspace and Philip K. Dick's *Do Androids Dream of Electric Sheep?*' (Reader, Item 37). How useful do you find McNamara's article as a guide to understanding the link between US slavery and Dick's novel?**

McNamara suggests that Dick's novel began from an exploration of a racist regime's records (those of the Nazis), and moves on to express 'the American legacy of racism'. *Androids* openly makes the connection between the androids and slavery, in an overheard television broadcast in the chapter you have just reread:

> '– duplicates the halcyon days of pre-Civil War Southern states! Either as body servants or tireless field hands, the custom-tailored humanoid robot – designed specially for YOUR UNIQUE NEEDS, FOR YOU AND YOU ALONE – given to you on your arrival absolutely free, equipped fully, as specified by you before your departure from Earth; this loyal, trouble-free companion in the greatest, boldest adventure contrived by man in modern history will provide –'
>
> (2; p.16)

McNamara highlights the technological advance from the slavery of the southern states to the androids in Dick's novel. Although the southern plantation owners could specify certain requirements when purchasing a slave, and would require slaves to follow all their orders, they could not order 'custom-tailored' slaves in the way humans order androids to meet their personal needs in the novel. Further, in pre-Civil War USA, slaves were bought and sold, whereas androids in the novel are provided free to humans on the Martian colony. There are, however, striking similarities: both US slaves and Dick's androids have to obey their owners' every order; they both have to carry out all duties prescribed for them; and they both have limited lifespans (androids wear out after four years, and plantation slaves had notoriously short life expectancies).

McNamara goes on to discuss the 'bio-logic of the scientific racism' of the late nineteenth century, which argued that racial identity is based on blood and therefore that miscegenation led to an adulteration of the purity of the blood-line. McNamara focuses in particular on how fears of miscegenation (between European Americans and African Americans) in nineteenth-century America contrasts with miscegenation (between human and android) in Dick's novel. The fear of African American men raping white women was widespread in the nineteenth century, especially after the American Civil War, but in *Androids* 'the sterile male android's threat to human women is never established' (and you might recall that Iran sympathizes with male androids). As regards miscegenation between white men and African American women, there are many recorded instances of white male overlords raping and impregnating African American female slaves in nineteenth-century America. In *Androids*, the taboo outlawing male humans having sex with female androids is clearly frequently flouted (16; p.166). The analogy in the novel between owner–slave miscegenation and human–android sexual intercourse is ultimately limited by the fact that the androids have no blood to dilute, and their menace (including their sexual menace) is therefore more imagined than real. Equally, the model of race as being a matter of different types of blood should be rejected – the novel might even be questioning such 'bio-logic' in the apparent breakdown of the analogy, suggesting that slaves are not a threat either.

As the novel progresses and more androids are 'retired', this reading of the novel as an allegory for race relations within the USA becomes more problematic – if the androids are analogues for African American slaves, does the book endorse their slaying? McNamara argues that 'The novel ... humanizes Deckard at the same time that it reinstates traditional gender roles', but under this reading it might also appear to reinstate the rest of white, male, middle-class, patriarchal, heterosexual and capitalist ideological power relations.

Before dismissing Dick or his novel as racist, it might be worth examining his attitudes to race elsewhere in his life and work. He was certainly aware and supportive of the civil rights movement; indeed, in the 1960 presidential election between Kennedy and Nixon, Dick wrote in Martin Luther King's name on the ballot. Consensual sexual relations between people of different races are significant in at least two of Dick's non-science-fiction novels that remained unpublished during his lifetime: in *Mary and the Giant* (written 1954–5, published 1987) Mary Anne Reynolds becomes the lover of an African American lounge singer named Carlton Tweaney and in *Humpty Dumpty in Oakland* (written 1960, published 1986) Al Miller goes off with an

African American real estate agent at the end, apparently to start an affair. A similar integration can be seen in Dick's science fiction: at the end of *Eye in the Sky* the white protagonist Jack goes into business with an African American college graduate, Bill; *Dr Futurity* (written 1953–9, published 1960) features a non-white (specifically Native American) future and *The Crack in Space* (written 1963–4, published 1966) includes an African American presidential candidate. Jake Jakaitis, one of the few critics to analyse race in Dick's works, suggests that 'Dick's attempts to resolve his own ambiguous, personal relation to African Americans succeed mainly in elevating to a painful level of consciousness his own racial fears, his own sense of liberal guilt' (1995, pp.191–2). In most cases, the solution to institutionalized racism is on the level of an individual rapprochement between people of different races rather than a wider shift in society.

The white relationship with slaves or the human relationship with androids can be read in terms of racial difference and perceived inferiorities and superiorities. At the same time it has to be emphasized that these relationships can also be mapped onto a model of contending classes – in this case they are clearly masters and slaves. From the perspective of class analysis, any focus on specifically racial discrimination is a distraction from the exploitation of workers by capitalists. Rick and the androids have more in common as workers than not, and Rick is simply eliminating competing workers – and as slaves were not paid, they were cheaper to employ than non-slaves. Workers can achieve greater autonomy and freedom from alienation only through collective endeavour that overcomes difference. Carlo Pagetti argued that in this novel 'society must defend itself against the overwhelming power of an industry of mechanical devices that introduces to the market automata so perfect as to be confused with men and take their place' (1975, p.28). The question is whether 'society' means the working classes, who feel usurped, or whether it means the capitalists, who have potentially lost control of the processes of exploitation.

The possibility that the novel acts to endorse the dominant ideology could be examined in the light of the ideas of the Marxist theorist Theodor Adorno. You have already encountered Adorno in the Introduction to Part 1, but we need to consider his attitude to mass culture in relation to *Androids*. In the previous chapter, you also encountered Dwight Macdonald, who saw mass culture as democratic – homogenized, perhaps, but equally available to all; his ideas are also relevant here. Writing in the Marxist tradition, Adorno is concerned with why the 'inevitable' progression from capitalism to communism that Marx predicted has failed to unfold, and he looks closely at the culture industry for an explanation. **Read the following extract from his 'How to Look at Television' (1954). How has culture changed with mass production?**

Today the commercial production of cultural goods has become streamlined, and the impact upon the individual has concomitantly increased. This process has not been confined to quantity, but has resulted in new qualities. While recent popular culture has absorbed all the elements and particularly all the 'don'ts' of its predecessor, it differs decisively inasmuch as it has developed into a system. Thus, popular culture is no longer confined to certain forms such as novel or dance music, but has seized all media of artistic expression. The structure and meaning of these forms show an amazing parallelism, even when they appear to have little in common on the surface (such as jazz and the detective novel). Their output has increased to such an extent that it is almost impossible for anyone to dodge them; and even those formerly aloof from popular culture – the rural population on one hand and the highly educated on the other – are somehow affected. The more the system of 'merchandising' culture is expanded, the more it tends also to assimilate the 'serious' art of the past by adapting it to the system's own requirements.

... The repetitiveness, the selfsameness and the ubiquity of modern mass culture tend to make for automatized reactions and to weaken the forces of individual resistance.

(in Adorno, 1991, pp.137–8)

For a start, culture is no longer something made by just a few isolated individuals or lone geniuses. It has been 'streamlined', which is to say, made more efficient and concentrated – obviously the ability to print thousands or even millions of copies of a novel has made writing into an industry alongside the other manufacturing industries. Mass production of anything tends to produce uniformity: although you can pay someone to tailor a suit to your precise measurements, most suits are made in a limited number of sizes and a small selection of designs. Mass production, and mass distribution, has also made manufactured objects more ubiquitous. At one time, you were only able to hear the Halle Orchestra if you went to one of its concerts, but the invention of radio broadcasting and various sound recording technologies means that in theory almost anyone can listen to that orchestra.

There is a homogenization of popular cultural products, and in a sense this has the advantage of offering familiarity to the consumer, who is thereby comforted and consoled. Although popular music might include improvization, there are set musical and other patterns to which most commercial popular music conforms. The same rule applies not only to music, but also to literature, so that for Adorno, jazz and the detective novel alike are characterized by a 'repetitiveness' and 'selfsameness' that enforces 'automatized reaction' in mass audiences and ultimately destroys the workers' capacity to resist and defeat their capitalist oppressors. For

Adorno, the ideology underlying all forms of mass culture is one that supports the existing power structures in society. In detective fiction, for example, a murder is portrayed as the rare act of an individual criminal rather than the result of a wider alienation of society, and the murderer is no match for the competent individual detective. According to Adorno, the mass audience in the era of mass communications is bombarded with such texts and has no choice but to accept the ideological subtext and internalize it. Extending Adorno's argument to science fiction, the limited range of narratives and themes of the genre enforce conformity and obedience in mass audiences.

Adorno perhaps underestimates the intelligence and discernment of the audience, which he seems to assume will behave in a predictable way. In reality, relatively few records aimed at a mass market, for example, become hits, or even make back the initial investment in them, which is difficult to square with the idea of corporations force-feeding us cultural products that we unquestioningly swallow. Subsequent research on actual audiences (for example those watching the 1970s news magazine programme *Nationwide* (Morley, 1980) or the US soap opera *Dallas* (Ang, 1985)) has shown that the dominant ideology of an individual programme can be rejected or negotiated (partially questioned) by the individual audience members. Audiences are not necessarily passive but can become producers of meaning in their own right. This is particularly true of science-fiction audiences and science-fiction fans who discuss texts with their friends, whether in the course of everyday life, at an organized event, such as a convention, or in written form, from the fanzines that developed in the 1930s to the various computer-based discussion lists, chatrooms, web pages and LiveJournals that exist today. Far from passively accepting products aimed at them by a multinational corporation (whether a television network or a publisher), some audience members even attempt to have an impact on the way the product is made, for example in campaigns to save *Star Trek* or *Farscape*, or to demand a gay character in *Star Trek: The Next Generation*. There are signs of resistance in Dick's novel itself: Iran refers to 'that awful commercial ... the one I hate' (1; p.5), and she has also been able to find settings on the mood organ for despair rather than happiness.

Postmodernist readings of *Do Androids Dream of Electric Sheep?*

By the mid-1980s, there was a shift in academic thinking away from the unified masses towards individuality and notions of difference. Consciousness-raising for the previous two or three decades had stressed the importance of group endeavours within the black, gay and women's movements, with an awareness that class struggle did not necessarily coincide with the aims of these different constituencies. While power imbalances operate in broadly equivalent ways, there was a growing interest in the multiple identities of the individual, including class, sex, race, sexual orientation and so on, with difference being stressed over similarity. This was made more complicated by the notion that class, sex, race and sexual orientation were ideologically constructed categories rather than fixed biological certainties – and so at times it was barely possible to identify a distinct, autonomous individual, let alone locate a collectivity. Such blurring of boundaries, categories, certainties and hierarchies was characteristic of what was increasingly being labelled postmodernism. Just as varieties of Marxism were the dominant ways of reading Dick's works in the 1970s – especially in the special issue of *Science Fiction Studies* devoted to his works in 1975 – in the 1980s, forms of postmodernism were increasingly used to explicate his novels. The second special issue of *Science Fiction Studies* devoted to Dick – published in 1988 – was very much within a postmodernist paradigm. There is not the space here to outline postmodernism in all of its bewildering, conflicting and challenging incarnations, but a few central figures and ideas can be identified (Katie Gramich will return to some of these ideas in Chapter 4).

Postmodernism is characterized by a mood of uncertainty and doubt. For example, Jean-François Lyotard's *The Postmodern Condition* (1979) argues that we no longer trust metanarratives, those ideological structures which reassure us that what we do is legitimate. Metanarratives include Christianity, science, Marxism and feminism. Perhaps the most significant metanarrative was the idea that rationality would lead to democracy and thus to progress, which would set us free. But Lyotard points out that rationality led to industrialization, and that – in the eyes of some postmodernists – led to trench warfare, concentration camps and the nuclear bomb. In the aftermath of Nazism and Stalinism, metanarratives should (postmodernists argued) be viewed with caution.

Fredric Jameson, who wrote a foreword to the English translation of *The Postmodern Condition* and had contributed an article on Dick to the 1975 special issue of *Science Fiction Studies*, argued that the contemporary world had changed because the economy had changed: we were now in an age of post-industrial capitalism. Multinational corporations were now beyond the control of national governments – think back to the beginning of Chapter 3 of *Do Androids Dream of Electric Sheep?* and how neither the western nor Soviet governments could legislate against the Rosen Association. Jameson characterized the postmodern as follows:

> the following [are] constitutive features of the postmodern: a new depthlessness, which finds its prolongation ... in a whole new culture of the image or the simulacrum; a consequent weakening of historicity, both in our relationship to public History and in the

> new forms of our private temporality ... [and] the deep
> constitutive relationships of all this to a whole new technology,
> which is itself a figure for a whole new economic world system.
>
> (Jameson, 1991, p.6)

Jameson's final feature is worth taking up first because he writes as a Marxist critic of postmodernism, and as such (like Marx and Adorno) he is concerned to investigate how material conditions (the economic organization of society) determine consciousness and ideology. Accordingly, as regards the postmodern age, he argues that the 'new technology' and 'the whole new economic ... system' dominated by capitalist multinationals, new computer and communications technology and the global movement of capital and labour has determined the rapid shift to the ideology of postmodernism. Jameson is at pains to emphasize the complexity of the relationship between global capitalism (economics) and postmodernism (culture). In this passage, he identifies features of postmodern culture such as the emphasis on the 'image' and 'simulacrum' and the weakening sense of historical perspective, both collective and individual. In the balance of the essay, he lists further aspects of the postmodern: the loss for individuals of any sense of agency, the collapse of older forms of community based on work or location, and the proliferation in art, architecture and literature of nostalgia and pastiche.

Jameson does not, unfortunately, discuss *Do Androids Dream of Electric Sheep?* directly, but he does analyse *Time Out of Joint* (1959). In this novel a character retreats mentally from a war-torn 1990s present day into the apparent comfort of the 1950s, and so the Earth government constructs a fake 1950s town so that he can continue (unwittingly) to help them in their war against the Luna colonists. Seeing the 1950s as a golden age with a corrupt underside, Jameson argues that 'of the great writers of the period, only Dick himself comes to mind as the virtual poet laureate of this material [i.e. the 1950s]' (1991, p.280). The 1950s and 1960s, when Dick's sensibilities found their voice, was when the world changed for many postmodernists.

The third significant postmodern thinker is Jean Baudrillard, who, in the words of the cultural critic Dick Hebdige, 'introduced Philip K. Dick into the body of "serious" social and critical theory rather like a mad or malevolent scientist might assist the *Invasion of the Body Snatchers* by introducing a pod from outer space into a small, quiet mid western town' (1986/7, p.9). Among other things, Baudrillard discussed the way in which image has come to dominate over substance. In part, there is the sense that mechanized reproduction has cut us off from original, authentic objects – and this was being debated before the CD, the DVD and the internet facilitated precise copies of artistic products as data. Baudrillard discusses the pollution of the real by the 'simulacrum', the copy with no original.

Read the first passage, from Baudrillard's *Simulations*, and compare it to the second, from 'How to Build a Universe that Doesn't Fall Apart Two Days Later' written by Dick in about 1978. What do they have to say about what is real? What do you think are the advantages of a fake animal over a real one?

Disneyland is there to conceal the fact that it is the 'real' country, all of 'real' America, which *is* Disneyland ... Disneyland is presented as imaginary in order to make us believe that the rest is real, when in fact all of Los Angeles and the America surrounding it are no longer real, but of the order of the hyperreal and of simulation. It is no longer a question of a false representation of reality (ideology), but of concealing the fact that the real is no longer real, and thus of saving the reality principle.

(Baudrillard, 1983, p.25)

Suppose some night all of us sneaked into the park [at Disneyland] with real birds and substituted them for the artificial ones. Imagine the horror the Disneyland officials would feel when they discovered the cruel hoax. Real birds! And perhaps someday even real hippos and lions. Consternation. The park being cunningly transmuted from the unreal to the real ... They would have to close down.

(in Dick, 1995, p.264)

Disneyland is obviously a fake: it has been built, manufactured, to resemble in part an idealized US town, in part a fairytale castle and so on. With its costumed characters, amusement rides and robotic simulations, it is clearly a great source of pleasure to the many visitors it receives every day. But Baudrillard argues that this obviously bogus location distracts us from the way in which the rest of Los Angeles and the rest of the USA have become fakes because fake images of them have been so relentlessly transmitted to increasingly global audiences. As long as we hold onto the idea that Disneyland is fake, we are able to believe in the opposite concept of the real Los Angeles and USA outside Disneyland.

In the passage by Dick, the fakery of Disneyland becomes somehow preferable to reality (to park officials at least), perhaps because robotic birds, hippos and lions are more reliable and can perform on cue for visitors. Real animals need caring for and feeding, and some kind of management. The park, geared to the fake, would have to close down if replaced with the real. The confusion of real and fake, and the inability to be certain which is which, remained one of Dick's major themes throughout his career, whether he has characters pass into a hallucinated environment or discover that their environment is faked (in *Time Out of Joint*, for example) or whether it becomes impossible to label anything as real or fake. You have already seen the problems when a false-animal repair company tries to service a real dying animal, but a third of the way through the book, Rick Deckard begins to doubt his own reality as do we as readers. Is he human or android?

Read Chapters 9–12. What developments in the plot and characterization make us question who is human and who is an android double? Do we know for certain who is human by the end of the sequence?

Rick attends a rehearsal of Mozart's opera *The Magic Flute*, where the android Luba Luft is singing the part of Pamina. Her voice is great, comparable to that of Elizabeth Schwarzkopf, and he begins to doubt whether she is an android. He attempts to administer the Voigt-Kampff test, which distinguishes androids from humans, and tells her that her lack of care for androids is itself a sign of being an android: they have no empathy for other androids. When confronted in this way, she turns the tables on him: if he can kill androids then he can have no empathy for them and he could be an android himself. ' "This test you want to give me," ' she asks, ' "Have you taken it? ... Maybe there was once a human who looked like you, and somewhere along the line you killed him and took his place. And your superiors don't know" ' (9; p.87). At this point, when I first read the novel, I did begin to wonder whether she might be right. Rick may have his wife and his memories, but the androids Roy and Irmgard Baty also form a family unit. Any memories Rick has of the past may be false, and part of what he has been programmed to remember.

Luft becomes suspicious of his questions and accuses him of being a sexual deviant. She calls the San Francisco police, who have not heard of Rick Deckard, nor of his superior officer Inspector Harry Bryant. His retirement of Polokov begins to look like it has been a cold-blooded murder after all – and cold-bloodedness is one of the symptoms of being an android. We begin to oscillate between worrying what will happen to Rick if he has been arrested by androids – who are likely to be hostile to a bounty hunter – and wondering whether we have been wrong to think of Rick as human. It seems as if the entire law enforcement system has a double: 'It makes no sense, he said to himself. Who are these people? If this place has always existed, *why didn't we know about it?* And why don't they know about us? Two parallel police agencies ... ours and this one. But never coming in contact – as far as I know – until now' (19; p.97). The head of this police agency is Inspector Garland, who is also on Rick's list of androids to kill.

By the end of Chapter 10 it has been established that Polokov is an android, and Rick demands that Garland is tested. Inspector Garland is posing as someone in charge of anti-android activities – although his purpose in doing so is unclear. Garland is insistent that bounty hunter Phil Resch is an android, with false memory implants to help him at his job as bounty hunter. It is not until towards the end of Chapter 12 that the issue is resolved, after Rick Deckard has become increasingly worried about Resch's attitudes towards life and what Resch might do if he discovered himself to be an android. The Voigt-Kampff test reveals Resch to be human although ' "There is a defect in [his] empathic, role-taking ability" ' (pp.120–1). Resch is a strange figure: to humans he may seem more like an android than a human, but it is hard to be certain and it seems that among the androids he may have unwittingly been passing as an android.

The androids – Roy, Irmgard, Max, Luba, Pris, Rachael – could be seen as Baudrillardian simulacra, copies without originals, and these might distract us from appreciating the human characters such as Rick, Iran, Phil and John. Throughout the novel there is a complex set of mirrorings. **Now read to the end of the novel, looking out for duplicates, doubles, parallels and false identities. Then read the extract from Patricia Warrick's 'Mechanical Mirrors, the Double, and _Do Androids Dream of Electric Sheep?_' (Reader, Item 38). What doublings does she locate?**

Like many postmodern theorists, Warrick analyses the world as a 'wasteland' to which the only response is a 'schizoid' splitting of the individual. (It should be noted that postmodern thinkers use the term schizophrenia in terms of Jekyll and Hyde type divisions rather than in the true sense of the medical condition.) Rick, as alienated worker, splits (on a metaphoric level?) into a logical/rational side – that of the androids – and an emotional/anxious side – that of John. Throughout the course of the novel Rick's and John's days are paralleled. Rick is setting out to kill androids, whereas John welcomes them into his home. Each of them encounters three androids. Rick confronts 'Max Polokov ... an aggressive killer; Luba Luft ... an artist' and Rachael. John comes into contact with 'Roy Baty ... the aggressor; Irmgard the warm, responsive female' and Pris, who at first passes herself off as Rachael. Whereas John offers them shelter, the killer Rick finds that it is increasingly difficult to kill those he identifies as androids, and in Phil Resch he is presented with an extreme version of himself as cold killing machine: 'Rick recognizes that he may have become what he abhors in Phil Resch. Resch is a man unable to feel empathy.' This leads to some desperate acts – an attempt to fuse with Mercer and allowing himself to be seduced by Rachael (which Warrick describes as 'mak[ing] love', although the sexual politics of this sequence are uncomfortable). This makes it even more difficult for him to face the final three androids; meanwhile, the events in John's narrative offer parallels: his love is rebuffed by another destructive female android.

The two media figures, Wilbur Mercer and Buster Friendly, are also doubles of each other. Mercer is really Al Jarry, a drunken bit-part actor who is playing a role as a messiah to human beings, whereas Buster Friendly is really an android, who acts as a messiah to other androids because his exposure of the faked Mercer removes another means of distinguishing humans from androids. They are also opposites: as Warrick says, 'One acts; one talks. One creates faith; one destroys it.'

In the distinction between Rick and Phil, in the failure of empathy, we come to what for me is the crux of the novel, and indeed all of Dick's work. Baudrillard's theory of doubling applied to Dick's novel raises two related questions, namely, 'What is real?' and 'What is human?' The two questions are not entirely separate, as Dick acknowledged in 'How to Build a Universe that Doesn't Fall Apart Two Days Later': 'Over the twenty-seven years in which I have published novels and stories I have investigated these two interrelated topics over and over again' (in Dick, 1995, p.260). The answer, I believe, lies with empathy. In the description of androids I quoted earlier, they are seen as having 'no ability to feel [empathic] joy for another life form's success or grief at its defeat' (3; p.28). In Rick's interrogation of Luba he observes: ' "An android ... doesn't care what happens to another android" ' (9; p.86). John Isidore's kindness to his android guests is different from how they would treat him in the reverse situation. According to the leader of the androids, Roy Baty: ' "If he was an android ... he'd turn us in about ten tomorrow morning" ' (14; pp.140–1).

Read the following two quotations from Dick's non-fiction, the first from 'How to Build a Universe that Doesn't Fall Apart Two Days Later' (1978), and the second from 'The Android and the Human' (1972), and think about how they distinguish the human from the android.

> The authentic human being is one of us who instinctively knows what he should not do, and, in addition, he will balk at doing it ... even if this brings down dread consequences to him and to those whom he loves. This, to me, is the ultimately heroic trait of ordinary people; they say no to the tyrant and they calmly take the consequences of this resistance ... I see their authenticity in an odd way: not in their willingness to perform great heroic deeds but in their quiet refusals. In essence, they cannot be compelled to be what they are not.
>
> (in Dick, 1995, pp.278–9)

> Becoming what I call, for lack of a better term, an android, means as I said, to allow oneself to become a means, or to be pounded down, manipulated, made into a means without one's knowledge or consent – the results are the same ... Androidization requires obedience. And, most of all, *predictability*. It is precisely when a given person's response to any given situation can be predicted with scientific accuracy that the gates are open for the wholesale production of the android life form.
>
> (in Dick, 1995, p.191)

For Dick, empathy becomes the defining characteristic of the human, along with the desire to do good for others and a refusal to do bad. Humans cannot be made into machines, made predictable and measurable like a piece of factory equipment, nor can they be made into a tool for others – the authentic human being retains agency and the power to decide his or her own actions. Those that lack such humanity are to be considered androids. For Dick, humanity seems to be an ethical, rather than an ontological, category. In other words, humanity is determined by actions rather than a state of being. At any point an individual might ignore ethical duties and fall into an android state, using another human as a tool; equally, at any point an android might redeem itself by showing humaneness.

In many ways this is a crisis that has been facing humanity since the Industrial Revolution and the onset of what we might call the modern era. As Pagetti argues: 'the great capitalistic forces and the authoritarianism innate in state apparatus tend to extend their power in an ineluctable process that leaves less and less liberty to the individual' (1975, p.29). As we become tools of a rational industrial capitalism, we become simply a means of producing more capital. As Marx writes in *Capital*, volume 1:

> In the factory we have a lifeless mechanism which is independent of the workers, who are incorporated into it as its living appendages. 'The wearisome routine of endless drudgery in which the same mechanical process is ever repeated, is like the torture of Sisyphus; the burden of toil, like the rock, is ever falling back upon the wornout drudge.'
>
> (Marx, [1867] 1990, p.548)

The individual is compelled to repeat mundane tasks and fulfil the wishes of others, to become a machine. It is precisely this kind of alienation that Suvin wishes to break away from with the estrangement or alienation effect. This is to say that either Marxism has already analysed this crisis, or has failed to avert it. The different versions of postmodernism sometimes simply acknowledge the alienation, or offer us some pretty distractions from the situation, or in some cases suggest we embrace the alienation.

Empathy and being human

The central ethical issue of the novel is: 'Is it right to deny human agency or human rights to those who lack empathy?' Such a question has consequences for how we perceive our own world if we as readers are making judgements about the empathic abilities of the characters within the novel. To put the ethical question in more concrete terms: if alienated workers of the twentieth century have lost their capacity for empathy as a consequence of being subordinated to the industrial labour process, does it follow that they should be treated like androids and denied human rights? Furthermore, does the act of treating alienated workers as androids disclose a lack of empathy on the part of those passing judgement (like Rick)? Marxism aims to change the world so that exploitation of workers does not exist, but Rick functions as an individual judge and accuses the various androids of not being human, thus risking losing his own (human) status. But do readers who condemn Rick for his lack of empathy in turn reveal a lack of empathy of their own?

The Voigt-Kampff test is the means by which the bounty hunters of Rick's police department attempt to make the distinction: a series of questions is asked of the subject, and his or her emotional response is measured. It seems likely to be based on a test designed by the mathematician Alan Turing. Turing published theoretical papers on the mathematical basis of computers and artificial intelligence from 1936; in 1943, he helped Thomas Flowers build Colossus, the first electronic computer. Turing's work in cryptography and with calculating machines helped to crack the Nazi Enigma codes at Bletchley Park during the Second World War. Turing foresaw that there would come a point when scientists would have to decide whether a particular machine was actually thinking for itself as a kind of artificial intelligence rather than simply following through the implications of a (particularly complicated) computer program. The test requires an interrogator, who is isolated from the two test subjects – a computer programmed to mimic human behaviour and a human being. Communication between the interrogator and the two subjects is via the written word. The interrogator asks the machine and the other human a series of questions, and from the answers has to decide which of the two is the machine. If the interrogator gets it wrong, or is unable to decide between the two, then the machine is deemed to be intelligent and actually thinking. Sceptics would argue that even though the *appearance* of thinking has been given throughout the experiment, the electronic medium of the computer is entirely different from the way that human cells are behaving within the brain. There is a semantic distinction being made: what a machine does is not thinking, precisely because it is a machine, whereas what a human being does can be thinking because it is a human. Turing had anticipated such an objection and pragmatically asked: ' "May not machines carry out something which ought to be described as thinking but which is very different from what a man does?" ' (quoted in Hofstadter, 1980, p.597).

Rick and the other bounty hunters are only interrogating one subject at a time, and make it easier for themselves by measuring all kinds of biological responses to their questions, but they are clearly comparing the responses to what a human's would be. With statements such as ' "You have a little boy and he shows you his butterfly collection, including his killing jar" ', they are attempting to measure empathy, which would seem to be an indicator of genuine intelligence. As Douglas Hofstadter has argued, 'I simply can't believe emotions and thought can be divorced. To put it another way, I think emotions are an automatic by-product of the ability to think' (1986, p.502). Again the question is what to do if the human/android is not accurately identified by the test. Rick has had a conversation with his boss, Inspector Bryant, in which the latter spoke of a group of Russian scientists who wanted to test ' "a carefully selected group of schizoid and schizophrenic human patients. Those, specifically, which reveal what's called a *flattening of affect*" ' (4; p.33), in other words an inability to empathize – and an anticipation of one of Jameson's characteristics of postmodern, the waning of affect. Bryant and Rick both agree that such individuals would be in mental institutions rather than in a position to be wrongly identified as androids, but the possibility remains. However, on that very day Rick meets the bounty hunter Phil Resch, who might well fail the test if he continues along his present behavioural course, and so perhaps would no longer have the right to be considered a human. The next generation of androids may be able to fake empathy convincingly – Luba, Irmgard and Rachael all have their moments of care or concern – or even be able to experience real emotions.

The postmodern philosopher Emmanuel Levinas offers insights into empathy and what involves 'being human'. Levinas was a student of the Freiburg philosophy professor Martin Heidegger, and his ideas on empathy were developed in response to Heidegger's thought, as well as being influenced by his own work on Judaism. Heidegger is a significant reference point for our purposes: Dick also read him, several decades after Levinas, and (presumably unaware of Levinas's engagement with Heidegger) confessed in a letter to Uwe Anton that 'One thing I am trying to do is fuse early Hebrew monotheism with the philosophy of Heidegger – which no one has ever done before' (1980, p.1). What fascinated both Levinas and Dick about Heidegger's philosophy was his sustained interrogation in *Sein und Zeit* (*Being and Time*; 1927) of what 'being human' entails. Heidegger argues that the individual self is 'thrown' into 'Being', and can at any moment be 'thrown' out of 'Being' – in other words, can die at any time. As a result, the self is constantly anxious about this precarious state of 'Being', and so seeks to preserve him/herself by using the surrounding world, including other people, as distractions. For Heidegger, other people function as tools for the individual self struggling to avoid or stave off the fear of 'not-Being', to be treated in the same casual manner as, say, a hammer or a pencil. They are simply temporary extensions of the self.

Levinas contests Heidegger's bleak view of 'being human', and proposes a different conceptualization of the individual self's relation with other people. **Read the following passage by Levinas, and identify what responsibility he believes the individual 'self' or 'I' has for the 'Other'. Does Levinas prescribe limits to the 'self's' obligations towards the 'Other'?**

> The Other becomes my neighbour precisely through the way the face summons me, calls for me, begs for me, and in so doing recalls my responsibility, and calls me into question.
>
> Responsibility for the Other, for the naked face of the first individual to come along. A responsibility that goes beyond what I may or may not have done to the Other or whatever acts I may or may not have committed, as if I were devoted to the other man before being devoted to myself. Or more exactly, as if I had to answer for the Other's death even before being. A guiltless responsibility, whereby I am none the less open to an accusation of which no alibi, spatial or temporal, could clear me ... A responsibility for my neighbour, for the other man, for the stranger or sojourner, to which nothing ... binds me – nothing in the order of the thing, or the something, of number or causality.
>
> (in Hand, 1989, pp.83–4)

The awkward syntax of the passage might make for difficult reading, but it is nonetheless clear that in contrast to Heidegger, Levinas is arguing here that the 'self' or 'I' has substantial responsibilities towards 'the Other' and has to display altruism. The self's responsibility for the Other is initiated by any person who 'summons me, calls for me, begs for me'. No previous obligation or prior history of responsibility is required to establish a relation between the self and Other, a relation that Levinas describes elsewhere as the self's ethical commitment to the Other. The second paragraph suggests that there is no limit to the self's responsibility towards the Other: it is a responsibility 'that goes beyond what I may or may not have done to the Other', and 'no alibi, spatial or temporal' can clear the self of responsibility towards the Other.

Levinas's views on the relation between the self and the Other can be elaborated further. For Levinas, the self can only have meaning in connection with the Other, the 'not-I'; a failure of connection between self and Other traps the self in an enclosed cycle of only being interested in the self, a feedback loop (think of the shrieking sound made when a microphone records the sound from the loudspeaker it is connected to, or of a video camera filming its own monitor). In an essay, 'Power and the Relationship with the Other', he explains the identity of the Other as follows: 'The Other as Other is not only an alter ego; the Other is what I myself am not. The Other is this, not because of the other's character, or physiognomy, or psychology, but because of the Other's very alterity. The Other is, for example, the weak, the poor, "the widow and the orphan" [quoted from the Old Testament], whereas I am the rich and the powerful' (Levinas, [1947] 1987, p.83; also in Hand, 1989, p.48). The self, Levinas insists, must acknowledge the radical alterity (otherness) of the Other in an un-self-interested fashion in order to demonstrate the empathy that defines being human – the Other is separate from the self, not an extension of the self. To extend Levinas's example, the 'rich and the powerful' (the 'I' or self) are only 'being human' insofar as they empathize in an un-self-interested fashion with 'the weak, the poor, "the widow and the orphan"' (the Other).

Levinas's philosophical exploration of the relation between the self and the Other parallels in important respects Dick's concern in *Androids* with the place of empathy in defining what it means to be human. **Bearing in mind Levinas's ideas on the self and the Other, reread the passages in *Androids* that describe Mercerism: John Isidore's description of Wilbur Mercer in Chapter 2 (pp.19–23), and the later encounters with Mercer in Chapters 15, 18 and 19 (pp.152–3, 176–84 and 189–90). How does Dick understand the relation between being human and empathy?**

Mercer is an amalgam of Moses and Jesus. Mercer's discovery in a river recalls Moses' basket in the bulrushes, and Mercer is destined to be a leader of people journeying to a better world. Like Christ, Mercer performs miracles, is persecuted for his actions and is eventually killed. He descends into Hell, where there is a battle to free the souls of the dead – the Harrowing of Hell – before he (He) can re-ascend. Whereas in Christian belief, Jesus suffered for humankind's sins so that all people might be saved, here all people fuse with Mercer and suffer on his behalf – they substitute for him, and their suffering is an expression of compassion. Mercer differs from Christ further in that he makes it clear that he is no saviour, declaring 'How can I save you ... if I can't save myself? Don't you see: There is no salvation?' (15; pp.152–3). His fundamental function appears to be to provide a vivid pretext for humans to demonstrate their capacity for empathy; by demonstrating empathy, by caring for others, they save themselves. The practice of Mercerism requires the individual to fuse with the figure of Wilbur Mercer on his endless climb, and experience his difficult ascent: '[John Isidore's] own feet now scraped, sought purchase, among the familiar loose stones; he felt the same old painful, irregular roughness beneath his feet and once again smelled the acrid haze of the sky' (2; p.20). The believers like John Isidore are more than simply concerned with Mercer's plight; they empathize with him, sharing in his plight and suffering along with him. Dick himself underlined the centrality of the human capacity for empathy in his 1978 note to the story 'The Little Black Box': 'The concept of *caritas* (or agape) shows up in my writing as the key to the authentic human. The android, which is the unauthentic human, the mere reflex machine, is unable to experience empathy' (Dick, 1990, p.389). Accordingly, in the novel the androids' lack of empathy means that they are unable to engage in the practice of Mercerism, and are therefore determined to expose Mercer as a media fraud. Their success in exposing Mercer in the final chapters of the novel, however, thus removes one more means of distinguishing between androids and humans.

The central place of empathy in defining being human in the workings of Mercerism closely resembles Levinas's understanding of the relation between the self and the Other. However, in other respects Dick's novel throws up a number of awkward anomalies with regard to the relation between being human and empathy, particularly with respect to the character of Rick. In the novel Rick refuses a call for help in his encounter with the individual androids as neighbours, strangers or sojourners. As Luba reminds him, Rick has to suspend his empathy to kill the androids. Granted, it might be revenge for undermining the human ethical system, but such revenge hardly seems ethical. In the physical appearance of Mercer to Rick, in the apparent permanent fusing that he feels thereafter, a blessing seems to be given to the killing of the androids. If Rick has heard the call to show empathy, he has apparently rejected it, with the blessing of Mercer. **What are we as readers meant to conclude from this failure of empathy?**

A number of possibilities suggest themselves; here is what I came up with. First, Levinas's model of empathy may actually be wrong, and while we may be better or worse people because of what we do, it has no further significance. Second, Rick is simply one character within the novel. If we consider Rick as an anti-hero then we are not necessarily meant to agree with his choices – indeed he may not have made the correct choice to kill the androids. Empathy is an ideal we do not always live up to. If we interpret the novel as being about John Isidore, we see someone succeeding in becoming ethically human even if in legal terms he is not granted full humanity. Third, Rick may have been 'polluted' in his encounters with the androids, and has begun to share their lack of empathy for others. Fourth, even though in an ideal world we should have empathy for others and honour our neighbours, there are perhaps some occasions when a line has to be drawn and a violent act has to take place for the greater good. Fifth, Mercer has indeed been exposed as a fraud rather than a human with strange powers and so his appearance may be that of a charlatan and has no real meaning, let alone a blessing. Equally, although there is an experience to be gained from using the empathy box, it is not a fusing with Mercer and it has no spiritual or ethical significance. Perhaps, at the end of the novel, it is Iran who is the most ethical character. On her first appearance she is showing empathy for the androids, and at the end she is looking forward to caring for a toad. Her empathy exists irrespective of the status of the Other. I will leave it to you to decide on the meaning of the novel with regard to empathy; I do not think there is a simple answer to the matter. As I have already stated, Dick notes that empathy in the form of *caritas* is a concept that he explored throughout his writing career.

The reception of the novel

Is *Do Androids Dream of Electric Sheep?* a popular novel? It depends on what you mean by popular. I noted at the outset that it has never been a bestseller like novels by Robert A. Heinlein, Arthur C. Clarke, Douglas Adams, Isaac Asimov or Iain M. Banks, so it cannot be considered popular in terms of mass sales. The tangled publishing history of *Androids*, which has been published by several companies on either side of the Atlantic, means that precise sales figures are difficult to establish. It sold just under two thousand copies in the month of publication in the USA, enough to earn back much of the advance but not a bestselling figure.

Read the following five extracts from reviews and critical assessments of Dick's work. Do any of them match your opinion of the novel?

Judith Merril

Perhaps the best thing I can say is that there were still some ideas I'm not sure I know whether I liked, or agreed with, or fully understood – but I assume I will see them from some other angle the next time around [in his next novel].

And I can say with some certainty that the Happy Ending is *supposed* to make you weep.

(Merril, 1968, p.23)

Harry Harrison

The book is beautifully constructed, yet disappointing ... [H]is plot is weak and a little trivial, his characters are standard constructions, and his style makes the book difficult to read.

(Harrison, 1969, p.59)

Stanislaw Lem

we see the sad spectacle of an author who squanders his talent by using brilliant ideas and inspirations to keep up a game of cops and robbers. This is far worse than putting together a valueless whole from valueless parts.

(Lem, 1975, p.85)

Darko Suvin

[The novel is] an outright failure ... with its underlying confusion of androids as wronged lower class and as inhuman menace.

(Suvin, 1975, p.20)

Thomas M. Disch

[Dick's] single most compelling vision of man's unredeemably material nature.

(Disch, 1983, p.24)

Judith Merril was clearly bemused by the whole book, and tries to put it into the context of Dick's on-going concerns as a novelist – although this task is made more difficult as the novels were not published in the order he wrote them. Harry Harrison, like Merril an author and editor as well as a critic, admires the overall artistry, but seems bored by the whole thing. Stanislaw Lem, a Polish novelist best known for *Solaris* (1961), was contemptuous of all US science fiction that aimed itself at a market, although he usually exempted Dick from this hostility. Here, he seems more disappointed by a work that apparently uses a mundane vehicle for interesting ideas. Suvin is perhaps more worried that the novel does not sufficiently match his conception of what Dick should be writing about (which is to say, a Marxist critique of capitalism); could he be confusing the ideas of the novel's characters with Dick's own opinions? Thomas M. Disch, writing an introduction for a hardback reprint of another Dick novel in 1976, is the only author here to be entirely smitten by *Androids*. It should be noted that the novel was held in little regard during Dick's lifetime, and it might be argued that a reconsideration of the book was occasioned by the release of Ridley Scott's very loose adaptation *Blade Runner* (1982), a film which itself attracted indifferent reviews initially.

The studio asked Dick to suppress the original book and to write a version based on the film *Blade Runner* in return for $400,000. At the same time, his editor David Hartwell offered him a contract for two new novels, *Bishop Timothy Archer* (published as *The Transmigration of Timothy Archer*, 1982) and *The Owl in Daylight* (unfinished at the time of Dick's death in March 1982), and for a reprint of *Confessions of a Crap Artist* (written in the summer of 1959, published 1975). According to Dick, he would have made about $7,500 for *Bishop Timothy Archer* and claimed 'I don't have use for $400,000 anyway' (in Rickman, 1988, p.212). His agent, Russell Galen, has since pointed out that there was nothing to stop Dick from writing the novelization *and* the two novels (Sutin, 1989, pp.227–8). It also seems to presuppose a lot of books being sold – it is more likely that the $400,000 would have included a cut of the film's take at the box office as well as merchandizing. Whatever the embroidering of the tale, Dick seems to have wanted his novel to remain in circulation, rather than selling out to Hollywood and big money. In any case, Dick died in March 1982, before the release of the film.

As it was, tie-in editions of the novel were released with covers using poster artwork from the film – but the film itself quickly sank from the box-office charts. The release of *Blade Runner* in 1982 coincided with Steven

Spielberg's *ET: The Extra-Terrestrial* and audiences clearly wanted their science-fiction films to be sentimental that year. It was only after overseas sales and income from the growing home-video rental and sales markets that the film broke even. The film continued to have an afterlife as a cult, in particular as its fans probed at some of the details – for example, at the identity of the sixth android, which we are told about but never see. (There was growing speculation that Rick Deckard, as played by Harrison Ford, was also an android.)

The audience for Dick could also be described as cultish, with the author being more appreciated during his lifetime by small groups of fans in France and Britain than by mass audiences in the USA. The audience grew after Dick's death, with individuals zealously promoting his work. Mainstream publications and broadcasts took an occasional interest in him, with features in the *Independent*, the *Economist* and the *New Republic*, a BBC Arena documentary and an edition of BBC Radio 4's *Kaleidoscope*. In October 1991, an entire weekend was devoted to his life and works at a college in East London; in March 1992, the ICA in London held an evening to commemorate the tenth anniversary of his death, at which the star attraction was meant to be Fay Weldon – although she was unable to make it. Increasing numbers of conferences in both the USA and Italy have been devoted to Dick. The recent examples of critical attention attest as much to the novel's greater popularity as to its steady incorporation into more elite cultural spheres.

Is science fiction gendered?

Undoubtedly most of what Philip K. Dick wrote was science fiction, which from the outside might be perceived as very much a boys' club, with male writers producing stories for male readers. Science, with its insistence on logic and rigour, has been gendered as masculine by society, along with technology and engineering. It therefore might follow that a fiction based to some extent on scientific ideas and discourse would be more attractive in that society to a male audience than to a female one. The sense that science fiction shies away from fully rounded characterization, and especially from emotional relationships, also contributes to the picture of the genre as masculine – although much characterization in many popular genres does tend towards the archetype or stereotype, with the emphasis put on a character's function within the plot. Such views of the masculine nature of the genre perhaps reach their most extreme in the words of the US academic Fred Pfeil, who writes of the 'prepubescent technotwit satisfactions supplied by a whole ... branch of SF, from Jules Verne to Heinlein and Asimov, through great dollops of masculinist space-jockeying adventure and "amazing" technogadgetry for sexually terrified twelve- and thirteen-year-old boys of all ages' (1990, p.84).

Can Dick's portrayal of female characters be labelled sexist? Reread the extract from McNamara's essay (Reader, Item 37) and clarify his position on the issues.

The narrative is largely about men and their interaction: Rick's day and his eventual showdown with Roy Baty; John's day; the phenomenon of Wilbur Mercer, a male messiah. Iran is absent for much of the book, apart from the start and finish, and a phonecall or two home. Dick wrote in a letter to a female editor 'I tend to take it for granted in a novel that a man's wife is not going to help him; she's going to be giving him a bad time, working against him' (1983, p.10). This seems partially true of Iran, at least from Rick's point of view, and McNamara picks out some of Rick's feelings for her in his essay. All of the other female characters are androids: Luba is an opera diva and seems to be very capable; Irmgard is described sympathetically as warm and responsive. Rachael and Pris represent another of Dick's recurring female types, the seductive woman who is usually younger than the male protagonist, and who causes him difficulties, sometimes with his boss, sometimes with his wife, because of his desire for her. Pris is perhaps the colder of the two, but Rachael's act of revenge might lead you to assume that androids do have emotions after all. In all these cases, gendered roles are portrayed – but is Dick endorsing them? In Iran's case, Dick could be critiquing – as he did with Marsha Hamilton in *Eye in the Sky* and elsewhere – the limited options available to a woman who has to stay in the domestic sphere and make a home for her husband, with no apparent outlet for her intelligence or creativity. Her caring side is a triumph of the novel, despite the risk of it falling into a stereotype of female-as-nurturer.

In the science-fiction industry in general there are in fact more women involved than are generally given credit – alongside the important male editors who have shaped the field, such as Gernsback, John W. Campbell, Antony Boucher, Terry Carr and, more recently, Gardner Dozois, are figures such as Cele Goldsmith, Judith Merril, Susan Allison, Beth Meacham and Ellen Datlow. Following on from the female authors listed above in the discussion of Aldiss's definition of science fiction were Lois McMaster Bujold, Octavia Butler, Pat Cadigan, Suzy McKee Charnas, Storm Constantine, L. Timmel Duchamp, Karen Joy Fowler, Lisa Goldstein, Nicola Griffith, Nalo Hopkinson, Gwyneth Jones, Nancy Kress, Vonda McIntyre, Marge Piercy, Melissa Scott, Lucy Sussex, Sheri Tepper, Karen Traviss, Joan Vinge, Connie Willis, Jane Yolen and scores of others. Since *Star Trek* in the 1960s, more women have become viewers and consumers of science fiction and many of the leading convention organizers and fanzine editors are female. There is still not a parity in numbers, but women's roles in science fiction have often been invisible to male commentators.

Conclusion: popular or high culture?

To some extent, science fiction has been pre-eminently a fiction of the people: since its inception as a genre there has been an emphasis on interaction between writers and fans. Readers could write to authors and authors attended conventions and wrote for fanzines. Even today, conventions, electronic discussion lists and web pages bring together professional writers, fan writers and academics. The science-fiction community did not simply uncritically accept everything published as science fiction, but formulated critiques of it, in short reviews in hand-printed fanzines, at conferences and in quasi-academic journals. Such localized exchanges were necessary because the main outlets of publication – first pulp magazines, then paperback novels – were rarely reviewed, if ever, in the non-specialist press. At times, being on the margins was useful – the pro-communist or anti-McCarthyite opinions of writers such as Philip K. Dick, Theodore Sturgeon and Isaac Asimov were expressed without apparent reprisals.

It is precisely the vulgar origins of science fiction that made it appeal to a generation of academics who saw in postmodernism a chance to destroy a conservative canon and remove elite–popular distinctions. Some of these academics had been readers of science fiction for many years – some science fiction was taught in universities in the 1960s, and the process was speeded up in the USA in the aftermath of student unrest in the late 1960s. Other academics leapt on the bandwagon and some made grand statements based on the handful of texts they had read. The wish to sweep away the canon might be laudable, but in its place some postmodern academics installed a smaller corpus of texts: the novels of Thomas Pynchon, a handful of Dick's novels, William Gibson's *Neuromancer* (1984), *Blade Runner* and little else.

In the Introduction to Part 1 it was noted how 'the canonical' changes over time. Since the 1970s, a much wider range of writers have been studied, in part reflecting a wider mix of students; most universities in the English-speaking world with English Literature, Literature or English Studies departments now feature courses that study popular fiction, including science fiction. The science-fiction readers of previous generations are the syllabus-setters of today. The canon is being rejected, or being reformulated. There is also the sense that a US canon already exists – encompassing Herman Melville, Walt Whitman, Ralph Waldo Emerson, Ernest Hemingway and William Faulkner – that more clearly offers traditions to which popular writers such as Allen Ginsberg and Philip K. Dick could belong. When discussing the canon we also need to be clear whether works gain entry through critical praise (an elitist canon) or because a large number of people read them (a populist canon).

The academic attention paid to Dick since the early 1970s is part of the process that previously admitted popular writers such as Charles Dickens to the canon – although Dickens was read more widely than Dick ever was. The fact that *Do Androids Dream of Electric Sheep?* was taught as a book or in connection with the film has kept the book in print since the early 1980s. Meanwhile, a number of novels and short stories by Dick under option to become films – on the back of efforts such as *Blade Runner, Total Recall* (1988), *Impostor* (2002) and *Minority Report* (2002) – may bring Dick to a more popular audience, while also selling popcorn, nachos, soft drinks and the ideology of consumerism.

There is a danger in this kind of appropriation of the popular by the academy, which can make inflated claims for writers previously neglected by academic critics. The popular feminist science-fiction writer Ursula Le Guin described Dick as 'our own homegrown Borges' (1989, p.152) and Fredric Jameson has called him 'the Shakespeare of science fiction' (1982, p.17). Fay Weldon, in an introduction to *The Three Stigmata of Palmer Eldritch*, cast Dick as 'the William Blake of North California ... so exhilarated and entertained by his own inventions he can scarcely keep his feet on the ground, his words on the paper' (1996, p.1). Clearly, I agree that Dick is worthy of academic study, and that his novels and short stories can stand up to elitist theorizing. But I do not want to make Dick out to be a special case who transcends the genre of which he was part, and I often worry that the attention paid by critics to Dick is at the expense of other worthy cases such as Theodore Sturgeon, Clifford D. Simak, Alice Sheldon/James Tiptree and Gwyneth Jones, to pluck four names at random. I hope that this chapter has shown that just because a book is popular, or just because a book is a bestseller, it does not mean that it is not saying something profound, nor that we cannot analyse it from any number of theoretical perspectives.

In this we risk looking foolish, or looking pretentious. But it is a risk that needs to be taken – whether the author would be happy with us or not. I think, for example, that Dick would have rejected some of the academics who have made use of his writings to make sense of postmodernism. To return to the letter from Philip K. Dick on a Kantian reading of one of his novels that I quoted at the outset of this chapter:

> [E]verything bad about academic literary criticism is found in this article; it is dull, it is pointless, and its only purpose – if indeed it has a purpose – is to exhibit the education of its author, who, I feel, really should read fewer books and, instead, play frisbie in a park somewhere with some little kids (and I might take that advice myself, in view of my recent writings). Perhaps we are all spending too much time thinking and reading and writing when we should be out in the sun.
>
> (Dick, 1981)

Works cited

Adorno, T.W. (1991) *The Cultural Industries: Selected Essays on Mass Culture*, London: Routledge.

Aldiss, B. (1973) *Billion Year Spree: The History of Science Fiction*, New York: Doubleday.

Aldiss, B. with Wingrove, D. (1986) *Trillion Year Spree: The History of Science Fiction*, London: Gollancz.

Ang, I. (1985) *Watching 'Dallas': Soap Opera and the Melodramatic Imagination*, London: Methuen.

Baudrillard, J. (1983) *Simulations*, trans. by P. Patton, P. Foss and P. Beitchman, New York: Semiotext(e).

Burroughs, W. ([1959] 2001) *The Naked Lunch*, London: Flamingo.

Clute, J. and Nicholls, P. (eds) (1993) *The Encyclopedia of Science Fiction*, London: Orbit.

Csicsery-Ronay, I. (2003) 'Marxist Theory and Science Fiction', in E. James and F. Mendlesohn (eds), *The Cambridge Companion to Science Fiction*, Cambridge: Cambridge University Press, pp.113–24.

Delany, S.R. (1984) *Starboard Wine: More Notes on the Language of Science Fiction*, Elizabeth Town, NY: Dragon Press.

Dick, P.K. (1956) *The World Jones Made*, New York: Ace.

Dick, P.K. (1959) *Time Out of Joint*, Philadelphia: Lippincott.

Dick, P.K. (1960) *Dr Futurity*, New York: Ace.

Dick, P.K. (1966) *The Crack in Space*, New York: Ace.

Dick, P.K. ([1957] 1971) *Eye in the Sky*, London: Arrow.

Dick, P.K. (1975) *Confessions of a Crap Artist*, New York: Entwistle Books.

Dick, P.K. (1980) Letter to Uwe Anton, 25 February, photocopy of original.

Dick, P.K. (1981) Letter to Erwin H. Bush, 16 September, photocopy of original.

Dick, P.K. (1982) *The Transmigration of Timothy Archer*, New York: Timescape.

Dick, P.K. (1983) 'A Letter from Philip K. Dick February 1 1960', *PKDS Pamphlet*, 1.

Dick, P.K. (1986) *Humpty Dumpty in Oakland*, London: Gollancz.

Dick, P.K. (1987) *Mary and the Giant*, New York: Arbour House.

Dick, P.K. (1990), *The Little Black Box: Part 5 of the Collected Stories of Philip K. Dick*, London: Gollancz.

Dick, P.K. (1991) *In Pursuit of VALIS: Selections from the Exegesis*, ed. by L. Sutin, Novato, CA: Underwood-Miller.

Dick, P.K. (1995) *The Shifting Realities of Philip K. Dick: Selected Literary and Philosophical Writings*, ed. by L. Sutin, New York: Pantheon.

Dick, P.K. ([1968] 2001) *Do Androids Dream of Electric Sheep?*, SF Masterworks, London: Gollancz/Orion.

Disch, T.M. ([1976] 1983) 'Towards the Transcendent: An Introduction to *Solar Lottery* and Other Works', in J.D. Olander and M.H. Greenberg (eds), *Philip K. Dick*, New York: Taplinger, pp.13–26.

Gernsback, H. (1926) 'A New Sort of Magazine', *Amazing Stories*, 1, p.3.

Gökçe, N.C. (1996) 'Definitions of Science Fiction' [online]. Available from: http://www.panix.com/~gokce/sf_defn.html [accessed 10 August 2004].

Hand, S. (ed.) (1989) *The Levinas Reader*, Oxford: Blackwell.

Harrison, H. (1969) Review of *Do Androids Dream of Electric Sheep?*, *New Worlds*, 190, p.59.

Hebdige, D. (1986/7) 'A Report on the Western Front: Postmodernism and the "Politics" of Style', *Block*, Winter, pp.4–26.

Heidegger, M. ([1927] 1962) *Sein und Zeit (Being and Time)* trans. by J. Macquarrie and E. Robinson, Oxford: Blackwell.

Hofstadter, D.R. (1980) *Gödel, Escher, Bach: An Eternal Golden Braid*, Harmondsworth: Penguin.

Hofstadter, D.R. (1986) *Metamagical Themas: Questing for the Essence of Mind*, Harmondsworth: Penguin.

Jakaitis, J. (1995) 'Two Cases of Conscience: Loyalty and Race in *The Crack in Space* and *Counter-Clock World*', in S.J. Umland (ed.), *Philip K. Dick: Contemporary Critical Interpretations*, Westport, CT: Greenwood, pp.169–95.

Jameson, F. (1982) 'Futurist Visions that Tell Us about Right Now', *In These Times*, 6.23, 5–11 May, p.17.

Jameson, F. (1991) *Postmodernism or, The Cultural Logic of Late Capitalism*, London: Verso.

Le Guin, U.K. (1989) *The Language of the Night: Essays on Fantasy and Science Fiction*, London: The Women's Press.

Lem, S. (1975) 'Science-Fiction: A Hopeless Case With Exceptions', in B. Gillespie (ed.), *Philip K. Dick: Electric Shepherd*, Carlton: Norstrilia Press, pp.69–94.

Levinas, E. ([1947] 1987) *Time and the Other*, trans. by R.A. Cohen, Pittsburgh: Duquesne University Press.

Lyotard, J.-F. ([1979] 1984) *The Postmodern Condition: A Report on Knowledge*, trans. by G. Bennington and B. Massumi, Manchester: Manchester University Press.

Marx, K. ([1867] 1990) *Capital: A Critique of Political Economy*, vol.1, intro. by E. Mandel, trans. by B. Fowkes, Penguin Classics, Harmondsworth: Penguin.

Marx, K. and Engels, F. ([1845–6] 1970) *The German Ideology*, ed. by C.J. Arthur, trans. by W. Lough, C. Dutt and C.P. Magill, London: Lawrence & Wishart.

Marx, K. and Engels, F. ([1848] 1992) *The Communist Manifesto*, trans. by S. Moore, ed. by D. McLellan, Oxford World's Classics, Oxford: Oxford University Press.

Mendlesohn, F. (2003) 'Introduction', in E. James and F. Mendlesohn (eds), *The Cambridge Companion to Science Fiction*, Cambridge: Cambridge University Press, pp.1–12.

Merril, J. (1968) Review of *Do Androids Dream of Electric Sheep?*, *The Magazine of Fantasy and Science Fiction*, 35.2, pp.22–3.

Morley, D. (1980) *The 'Nationwide' Audience*, London: BFI.

Pagetti, C. (1975) 'Dick and Meta-SF', *Science Fiction Studies*, 2.1, pp.24–31.

Pfeil, F. (1990) *Another Tale to Tell: Politics and Narrative in Postmodern Culture*, London: Verso.

Rickman, G. (1988) *Philip K. Dick: In his Own Words*, Long Beach, CA: Fragments West/Valentine Press.

Sutin, L. (1989) *Divine Invasions: A Life of Philip K. Dick*, New York: Harmony Books.

Suvin, D. (1975) 'PK Dick's Opus Artifice as Refuge and World View', *Science Fiction Studies*, 2.1, pp.8–22.

Suvin, D. (1979) *Metamorphoses of Science Fiction: On the Poetics and History of a Literary Genre*, New Haven: Yale University Press.

Walder, D.J. (2005) 'Bertolt Brecht, *Life of Galileo*', in R.D. Brown and S. Gupta (eds), *Debating Twentieth-Century Literature: Aestheticism and Modernism 1900–1960*, London: Routledge in association with The Open University, pp.324–74.

Weldon, F. (1996) 'Introduction', in P.K. Dick, *The Three Stigmata of Palmer Eldritch*, London: Voyager, pp.1–2.

Westfahl, G. (1998) *The Mechanics of Wonder: The Creation of the Idea of Science Fiction*, Liverpool: Liverpool University Press.

Wolfe, G.K. (1986) *Critical Terms for Science Fiction and Fantasy: A Glossary and Guide to Scholarship*, New York: Greenwood Press.

Further reading

Broderick, D. (1995) *Reading by Starlight: Postmodern Science Fiction*, London: Routledge. A superb overview of theoretical thinking about written science fiction, including a variety of postmodern perspectives, by an Australian science-fiction novelist.

Butler, A.M. (2000) *Philip K. Dick*, Harpenden: Pocket Essentials. A short novel-by-novel guide to Dick's writings.

Butler, A.M. and Ford, B. (2003) *Postmodernism*, Harpenden: Pocket Essentials. Entry-level guide to postmodernism – Jameson, Baudrillard, Lyotard and many more.

Docherty, T. (1993) *Postmodernism: A Reader*, London: Harvester Wheatsheaf. A useful collection of extracts covering the entire range of postmodern theory, with all the major names featured.

Freedman, C. (2000) *Critical Theory and Science Fiction*, Hanover: Wesleyan University Press. A fascinating application of theory to science fiction, from one of the leading Marxists working in the field.

Mullen, R.D., Csicsery-Ronay, I., Evans, A.B. and Hollinger, V. (eds) (1992) *On Philip K. Dick: Forty Articles From Science-Fiction Studies*, Terre Haute: SF-TH. Reprints of the many useful articles on Dick from the North America-based journal from its inception to 1992; includes the two Philip K. Dick special issues.

Palmer, C. (2003) *Philip K. Dick: Exhilaration and Terror of the Postmodern*, Liverpool: Liverpool University Press. This volume pulls together Palmer's many interesting articles on Dick's fiction, with a postmodern perspective on the books. However, it only deals with *Do Androids Dream of Electic Sheep?* in passing.

CHAPTER 4

Manuel Puig, *Kiss of the Spider Woman*

KATIE GRAMICH

> Mothers of America. Let your kids go to the movies ...
> it's true that fresh air is good for the body
> > but what about the soul
> that grows in darkness, embossed by silvery images
>
> ('Ave Maria'; O'Hara, 1964, p.51)

Overview

This chapter is a detailed exploration of the novel *Kiss of the Spider Woman* (1976) by the Argentinian writer Manuel Puig. It constitutes a brief introduction to Puig's life and work, setting them in the context of the 'boom' in Latin American literature. It shows how a late twentieth-century novel enters into a productive intertextual relationship with what is arguably the century's most powerful and influential medium: film. The primary focus is on the ways in which Puig's novel breaks down traditional boundaries between popular and 'high' cultural forms. Having introduced the author in his specific cultural context, the chapter goes on to discuss the perils and complexities of working with a text in translation and to embrace theoretical perspectives drawn from the work of Mikhail Bakhtin and from psychoanalysis, looking at how Puig interweaves serious social and political themes with a demonstration of the seductive power of popular art. The chapter's secondary focus is on the ways in which the novel offers a radical interrogation of gender, sexuality and power relations within an experimental postmodernist structure.

Introduction

Born in 1932, Manuel Puig Delledonne was brought up in a small town called General Villegas in the remote Argentinian pampas in the 1930s and 1940s. As he put it, 'I grew up on the pampa in a bad dream, or rather a bad western' (quoted in Levine, 2001, p.2). From a very early age, Puig was an avid devotee of contemporary Hollywood movies (often B-movies) since his mother took him to the local cinema on a daily basis. (B-movies were made as supporting features for the main film, in the days when a trip to the cinema involved watching at least two films. B-movies usually had low budgets and were made relatively quickly.) He later trained in Italy to be a film director but instead of making films he turned to literature, publishing his first novel, *La traición de Rita Hayworth* (*Betrayed by Rita Hayworth*) in 1968. He published eight novels during his lifetime; *El beso de la mujer araña* – *Kiss of the Spider Woman* – is the fourth, first published in 1976. All his work is experimental in form, incorporating diverse elements of popular culture; it is also perennially concerned with gender roles and sexuality, and is profoundly influenced by cinema in its forms, language and themes.

Because Puig set out to represent contemporary Argentinian culture and society, which he regards as a *mestizaje* ('hybrid'), made up of the flotsam and jetsam of other cultures, he deliberately rejects the established, 'pure' forms of 'high art'. Instead, he habitually turns to popular cultural forms, notably Hollywood movies (such as in his first novel, *Betrayed by Rita Hayworth*, and in *Kiss of the Spider Woman*), Mills-and-Boon-type serial romance (in *Boquitas pintadas* (1969), translated as *Heartbreak Tango*), the detective novel (in *The Buenos Aires Affair*; 1973) and popular Latin American songs, such as the *bolero*, which pervade all his works. He once said of himself: 'Yo soy profundamente cursi' ('I am profoundly vulgar') (Sosnowski, 1977, p.36) and this proclamation can be taken as an apt description of his work: it draws on the everyday, the popular, the clichéd, and transforms those things into an unexpectedly profound exploration of a deracinated, hybrid, postcolonial society.

Puig consistently avoided highbrow literary modes, arguably because he felt that they would not be a true reflection of contemporary Argentina, a postcolonial society made up of fragments of different cultures. Gladys, his sculptress heroine in *The Buenos Aires Affair*, makes works of art from flotsam and jetsam she picks up on the beach and she explains her work in a fictional interview with the US magazine *Harper's Bazaar* like this:

> 'Ahora sé por qué no había pintado o esculpido en todo ese tiempo: porque los óleos, las témperas, las acuarelas, los lápices de pastel, la arcilla, los bastidores, todo ello era un material precioso, de lujo, que a mí no me estaba permitido tocar ... Por eso durante años no hice nada, hasta que descubrí las pobres criaturas hermanas que rechaza cada mañana la marejada.'
>
> (Puig, 1973, p.56)

> ('Now I know why I didn't paint or sculpt in all that time; because oils, tempera, water colours, pastel crayons, clay, frames, all that was precious, luxurious material, which I wasn't allowed to touch ... Because of that for years I did nothing, until I discovered the poor sister creatures which the tide rejects every morning.')
>
> (my translation)

Gladys's words are a reflection of her own lack of self-esteem, yet her basic artistic technique is not dissimilar to Puig's own. A number of critics have labelled this technique *bricolage* (an assemblage of haphazard or incongruous elements), a technique used by some modernist artists but more commonly and characteristically by postmodernists. As Roberto Echevarren states: 'It is legitimate to equate the use of film material by Molina to *bricolage* ... He fabricates his myths from bits and pieces of previous readings in an already given universe of culture' (1991, p.583).

You may already be familiar with debates surrounding modernism and attempts to define it; similar debates revolve around postmodernism. Some would argue that there is no real break between modernism and postmodernism but that the latter is just a continuation of some of the experiments initiated by the modernists. Others would argue that postmodernism is radically different from modernism. There is no room here to do justice to this debate. For the moment, I think we can see something of Puig's novel in the following definition of postmodernism: *The Penguin Dictionary of Literary Terms and Literary Theory* states that it is characterized by 'an eclectic approach, [by] aleatory writing [i.e. dependent on random choices and chance] and by parody and pastiche' (Cuddon, 1988, p.734).

In *Heartbreak Tango*, Puig used the model of the popular *folletin* ('serial romance') to write a novel that undermined many of the values and preconceptions usually found in this popular genre. Similarly, in *The Buenos Aires Affair*, Puig takes another genre of popular literature, the detective novel, and deliberately transforms its perspective. Yet Puig's intention is not to parody these forms; he has stated in an interview that: 'I've been told that *The Buenos Aires Affair* is a parody of detective novels and that *Boquitas pintadas* is a parody of serials. That's not right. At least that was not my intention. I like those two underrated genres and I tried to use them seriously, downright artistically' (in Christ, 1977, p.55). Later in the same interview, he again denies that he is a conscious parodist:

> Parody is a word I don't trust too much, because it carries some degree of scorn. I don't let myself go in the direction of scorn very often. The character [Molina in *Kiss of the Spider Woman*] is parodic in itself. If he's mimicking a woman of the '40s, a film character of the '40s, he's already parodic. It's not me who's doing the parody. Greer Garson wouldn't have liked me to do that.
>
> (in Christ, 1977, p.56)

The humorous reply is nevertheless telling. Puig denies parody because he rejects scorn; he absolutely refuses to be placed in a position of authority, to become a member of an elite. There is a clear class dimension to Puig's stance. The debased cultural forms that he enjoys and incorporates into his own works are the cultural forms associated with the working class from which he emerged. To a degree, this class allegiance explains Puig's lifelong opposition to his compatriot Jorge Luis Borges, whom he regarded as a patrician who was out of touch with the realities of everyday life. Thus, at the same time as Puig takes a subtle political stand against what he sees as the elitism of high modernism, he is moving towards the eclectic intertextuality of postmodernism.

Puig's novels were written against the background of the political instability and repression in Argentina in the 1960s and 1970s. In the 1940s and early 1950s, under Juan Perón and under the influence of his first wife Eva Perón, real efforts had been made to improve the lot of the urban poor: the charismatic Eva concentrated her efforts on helping the *descamisados* ('shirtless ones'). However, after her death in 1952, there was an abrupt change in Peronist policies, and successive military regimes took over throughout the later 1950s, the 1960s and the 1970s. By the late 1970s, Amnesty International had launched a major campaign in protest against the thousands of 'missing persons' of Argentina. There was harrowing evidence of torture, murder and interrogation in prison camps, while thousands of people 'disappeared' in the so-called *guerra sucia* ('dirty war') waged by the military despots against dissidents of any description. Puig wrote *Kiss of the Spider Woman* during this politically turbulent period while he was in exile in Brazil and, later, in the USA, since his work had been the subject of controversy and censorship in Argentina from the start and he had begun to receive death threats. However, before leaving Argentina he was able to interview a number of men who had been arrested and tortured as political prisoners; what happens to Valentin in the novel is therefore based very much on the horrific reality of Argentina in the mid-1970s.

If you have not already done so, please read the novel now.

Structure

Kiss of the Spider Woman is structured as a long dialogue and debate between two antagonistic individuals. As such, it is a particularly apt text to consider in this book, which is based on the premise that twentieth-century literature can be viewed as a series of on-going dialogues and debates. While the novel has been adapted both as a feature film and as a Broadway musical, suggesting its debt to popular cultural forms, its status as a dialogue also harks back to classical models of philosophical dialogue and debate, such as those in the works of Plato (for example, in the *Crito*, which is set in Socrates' prison cell). The technique of a storyteller narrating a story over many nights, leaving the listener in suspense each time, is also reminiscent of the *Thousand and One Nights* (the collection of folk-tales of Persian, Indian and Arab origin, in which the vizier's daughter, Scheherezade, cunningly spins out her tales during a thousand and one nights to delay her execution by the cruel King Shahriyar), with Molina playing the role of Scheherezade and Valentin as the potentially violent king. Other literary models invoked by *Kiss of the Spider Woman* include the device of the ill-matched masculine pair, such as Don Quixote and Sancho Panza or Tom Sawyer and Huckleberry Finn, also exploited in US movie culture in comedies such as *The Odd Couple* (with Jack Lemmon and Walter Matthau) and those featuring Laurel and Hardy and Bob Hope and Bing Crosby. However, *Kiss of the Spider Woman* goes further than these literary and filmic precursors in that it makes explicit the homoerotic undercurrents that fuel the relationship.

In addition to these disparate literary and filmic models that feed into its structure, the novel is itself a patchwork of diverse discourses, derived from Hollywood films, popular song, drama, scholarly works, dreams and domestic life. You might expect that an author would attempt to draw all these disparate threads and patches together with a unified and unifying narrative voice. This Puig notably refuses to do. In fact, the novel is characteristic of Puig's habitual structural technique in that it lacks a single, authoritative narrative voice. A number of voices speak in the novel – those of Molina, Valentin, the prison warden, the undercover policeman, the author of the footnotes (of which more later) and so on – but it is difficult to identify which of these is 'in charge' of the novel. Moreover, there are lengthy departures into interior monologue that counterpoint the spoken narrations. Puig's fictional method eludes traditional definitions of literary style: he presents a series of conflicting but often mutually illuminating discourses, though the resulting whole may be said to have a style in the sense of a pervasive mood or tone.

Literature and film

Beginning with his first novel, *Betrayed by Rita Hayworth*, Puig used Hollywood films to provide an underlying pattern to his fiction. For example, each of the chapters of *The Buenos Aires Affair* has an epigraph consisting of a snippet of dialogue from a Hollywood movie, a snippet that has parallels in the action of the novel. But Puig is not simply mocking the impossible ideal worlds of the movies. He understands people's need for them because he has shared this need:

> Up until I was twenty-five I had always rejected reality. I wanted to believe that the reality of life was MGM films ... I thought that somewhere – in Europe, in Hollywood – I would be able to live at that level of glamour, of explicit, clean passion. I was even ready to suffer. But to suffer with glamour ... Simultaneously, though, I

had the need to face reality, to come to terms with myself ...
What helped me in literature was that I could put both things
together – reality and beauty. If not in life, at least in literature.

(in Christ, 1977, p.53)

Kiss of the Spider Woman is punctuated by a series of stories derived from
films, told by Molina to entertain his cell-mate, Valentin. **Make a list of the
various films that feature in the text. How many are there? What, if
anything, do they have in common?**

I have identified seven films in all. In each case, I have included some
additional details about the plot, the cast and the director/producer.

1   The first film recounted by Molina (Chapters 1–2) is a version of *Cat
    People*, a 1944 Hollywood B-movie, directed by Jacques Tourneur and
    produced by Val Lewton. Despite its low budget, and the censorship to
    which it was subject, this became a cult classic, and was remade in the
    1980s by Paul Shrader, with Natassja Kinski in the lead role.

2   The second film (Chapters 3–4) is a Nazi propaganda film entitled *Her
    Real Glory* (*Destino* – 'Destiny' – in the original Spanish text). This is
    fictional, though Puig imbues it with a strong sense of realism by
    including a footnote on it which is, ostensibly, a press release from the
    Berlin film studio that made it. We should bear in mind that Puig actually
    studied cinematography in Europe and conducted detailed research on
    the contents of Nazi propaganda films of the Second World War period.
    He had a number of models in mind, including *Die grosse Liebe* ('The
    Great Love'), a 1942 film starring Zarah Leander, one of Puig's favourite
    female stars. Moreover, the description of the film's heroine, Leni, calls
    to mind Leni Riefenstahl, the great film-maker who made the Nazi
    propaganda epic *Triumph des Willens* ('Triumph of the Will') in 1934; she
    was at one time a film actress and often played the beautiful femme
    fatale.

3   The third film (Chapter 5) is one that Molina merely thinks about, rather
    than recounting out loud, since Valentin is busy reading. It is a love story
    between a plain servant-girl and a mutilated pilot, narrated by a blind
    pianist. Critics have identified this film as being based on *The Enchanted
    Cottage* (1946), directed by John Cromwell.

4   The fourth (Chapter 6) is a 'man's film' according to Molina, told to
    cheer up Valentin after his illness. It involves a South American racing
    driver in Europe, who has revolutionary hopes for his native country;
    there is a complex mother–son relationship, a tale of doomed love and
    parental betrayal. It is likely that Molina makes up this narrative to please
    Valentin, though he bases its elements on many of the films he has seen.

5   The fifth film (Chapters 9–10) returns us to the real Hollywood B-movie, namely *I Walked with a Zombie* (1943), another film directed by Jacques Tourneur and produced by Val Lewton.

6   The film in Chapters 12–14 is a doomed love story set in Mexico involving a beautiful singer, a reporter/poet and an oppressive tycoon. Again, one suspects that Molina/Puig is inventing this story, though it is based on a number of melodramatic Mexican movies from the 1930s and 1940s, such as *Mujer del puerto* ('Woman of the Port'; 1933) and *Aventurera* ('Adventuress'; 1949).

7   In the last chapter (Chapter 16), which consists largely of Valentin's hallucinatory dream under the influence of morphine, after he has been brutally tortured, there is a film-like fiction created by Valentin's disordered mind; it might be entitled *The Kiss of the Spider Woman*, though this does not appear to be based on any real movie.

If you did not count the narratives which occur in the protagonists' minds, your list will be shorter than mine. If it was longer, you have clearly spotted some which I missed!

Did you spot any similarities between the films?

Each of the films has a central, glamorous female protagonist, with whom Molina overtly identifies (see the end of Chapter 1, where Valentin asks 'Who do you identify with? Irena or the other one?', to which Molina replies 'With Irena, what do you think? She's the heroine, dummy. Always with the heroine'; Puig, [1976] 1991, Chapter 1; p.25; unless otherwise stated, all subsequent references are to this edition).

Although the heroines are different, they share certain similarities. Usually, for instance, the heroine is an artist of some kind; inevitably, she falls in love with the hero. The heroines' clothes and hairstyles are described in great detail by Molina, sometimes to Valentin's annoyance ('Don't waste so much time, tell me what happens'; 3; p.50). In Molina's descriptions, the heroines share some psychological characteristics: Irena in *Cat People* is described as 'all wrapped up in herself' (1; p.4); the singer of the sixth film is 'completely wrapped up in herself' (13; p.238); the poor zombie woman, the 'sleepwalker, somnambula' (14; p.258), can hardly help but be wrapped up in herself.

How do you think these descriptions relate to Molina?

Each of the heroines, like Molina, is isolated and eventually becomes either a victim or a martyr. Molina identifies with Irena because both share a sexual secret: they are outside the rules and regulations of a patriarchal society that imposes strict codes of sexual behaviour. Both are marginalized, outsider figures who do not belong in the world in which they find themselves. All are essentially gentle and artistic people and yet they harbour dreadful secrets that stem from their innermost sexual or psychological selves. On a more straightforward level, it is clear that Molina fantasizes about being these glamorous heroines ('since a woman's the best there is ... I want to be one'; 1; p.19).

Despite Molina's positive view of his heroines, three of the female protagonists are intimately connected with animals or monsters: Irena in *Cat People* (it is worth noting that the Spanish title of this film is *La mujer pantera*, 'The Panther Woman', foregrounding the female protagonist), the zombie woman and the spider woman. **How do you read this association of the female with monstrosity?**

It is capable of being read as an indication of male fears about the female body and female sexuality. This is not necessarily a reflection of Molina's own neuroses, but certainly there is something of this encoded into the original Hollywood films. The female figures are ambivalent: both desirable and fatal. If Molina is identified as one of his beloved heroines, we can also see that in a macho world of compulsory heterosexuality, his overt effeminacy would be regarded as monstrous. There is a shift of emphasis in this figure of the monstrous female. Irena is clearly predatory, a terrifying panther woman who will devour men if they dare to kiss her – that is, if she dares to unleash her sexuality. The zombie woman is the opposite: the embodiment of passivity and victimhood. In Molina's version of the story (though not in the real film) she is even subjected to repeated rape by the wicked witch-doctor. The spider woman, imagined by Valentin, is overtly identified with Molina, and appears to combine these two extremes: she traps men in her predatory web but at the same time she herself is trapped by the web that emerges from her own body (16; p.280).

Can you think of other ways in which Molina can be regarded as a spider woman?

Molina is also a spinner and weaver of webs in that he is the tale-teller, the mesmerizing Scheherezade figure who keeps listeners in thrall. He often leaves his listener in suspense until the next instalment. Often the thread/web imagery is explicit: 'I left you hanging' (2; p.46), an accurate rendition of 'Te dejé colgado'. Elsewhere, when Molina's memory fails him, he laments: 'That's the piece of thread that sometimes slips out of my fingers' (2; p.42). There is a further, psychological, dimension to the image of the spider woman and her webs, as indicated by Puig's comment in a late interview:

> Among the twentieth-century writers, I admire Kafka especially. What is he interested in? Cobwebs, the world of the unconscious, the system that somehow manipulates us, the bars we're not aware of but which are there and don't let us act freely ... And the more common the characters are ... the more they interest me. Because they're in the same cell with millions.
>
> (in Christ, 1991, p.574)

So, the webs woven by Molina can be taken to represent the world of the unconscious, the traps, the labyrinths, the hidden dusty corners. Moreover, we can see that Molina, despite his idiosyncrasies, is meant by Puig to be a kind of Everyman, not a hero – or even a heroine, as he would like to be. We know that Molina cannot regard himself as other than a woman, and in this role he is called 'Carmen' (3; p.65), after the doomed *mujer fatal* (femme fatale) heroine of Georges Bizet's opera (1875). We also know something about Molina that Valentin never knows: that he has been bribed with the promise of an early release by the authorities to try to win Valentin's confidence, so that he can gain secret information about the revolutionaries. We do not definitively receive this information until the interview with the warden at the beginning of Chapter 8, though we may have had a suspicion before this point. **Now reread Chapter 8. How do you react to the revelation that Molina is being bribed to betray Valentin?**

It may prompt you to reassess your view of Molina, who, up until this point, has been viewed in quite positive terms, as naive and emotional. Now we are tempted to view him differently, even negatively. **Does this negative view persist, though?**

I would say not. Molina is clearly a very reluctant collaborator. And it becomes increasingly apparent that Molina is trapped in his own web of seduction, so that he comes to admire and finally to love Valentin. There comes a point when he knows that he can never betray him, in spite of the rewards offered for doing so. From this point on, he is adamant that he does not want Valentin to tell him anything about his revolutionary activities or friends.

In the role of spider woman, Molina can also be compared to mythical antecedents, such as Arachne and Ariadne. Arachne is metamorphosed into a spider as a punishment for her hubris: she is so proud of her skill in weaving that she challenges even the gods to a competition which, of course, she loses. Ariadne, on the other hand, is a selfless heroine who helps her beloved, Theseus, to find his way out of the Cretan labyrinth with a ball of thread. In a sense Molina, the spider woman, vacillates between these two female roles: the reader is kept in suspense over whether he will prove to be a self-aggrandizing Arachne or a selfless Ariadne. Moreover, as Susan Bassnett has pointed out in an essay on Latin American women writers, whom she sees as Ariadne-like, weaving a mass of threads through the labyrinth: 'Once back among men and treated as a conquering hero, Theseus abandoned Ariadne and sailed off to find new adventures ... Now that myth is being rewritten' (1987, p.266). Puig's novel, too, offers a rewriting, and draws on this myth, reinscribing the roles of hero and heroine. What kind of Theseus will Valentin prove to be?

Let us pause now before analysing the novel in more detail and take a step back to think about Puig's use of popular culture in this novel in more general terms.

High and low

Puig's novels represent the kind of literary text that made the traditional distinction between high and low cultural forms increasingly untenable. Earlier in the twentieth century, the views of F.R. and Q.D. Leavis (outlined in the Introduction to Part 1) were dominant. As F.R. Leavis argued:

> In any period it is upon a very small minority that the discerning appreciation of art and literature depends: it is (apart from cases of the simple and familiar) only a few who are capable of unprompted, first-hand judgement. They are still a small minority, though a larger one, who are capable of endorsing such first-hand judgement by genuine personal response ... The minority capable not only of appreciating Dante, Shakespeare, Baudelaire, Hardy (to take major instances) but of recognising their latest successors constitute the consciousness of the race (or of a branch of it) at a given time ... Upon this minority depends our power of profiting by the finest human experience of the past; they keep alive the subtlest and most perishable parts of tradition. Upon them depend the implicit standards that order the finer living of an age, the sense that this is worth more than that, this rather than that is the direction in which to go. In their keeping ... is the language, the changing idiom upon which fine living depends, and without which distinction of spirit is thwarted and incoherent. By 'culture' I mean the use of such language.
>
> (Leavis, 1930, pp.3–4)

What kind of attitude towards literature is embodied in Leavis's statement? Who do you think 'the minority' is?

It is clear that Leavis is putting forward a very elevated view of literature as something special and complex, so it is not surprising that only a privileged few can appreciate it. The minority might include enlightened literary critics (such as himself!) and those few who have the intellect and the education to recognize 'great Literature'. Leavis's attitude was not particularly unusual at the time and is a view held by some today; it is part of an ideology which holds that literature constitutes a unique category of aesthetic objects, one made up of a strictly limited number of approved, canonical works. We can see that there is a strong sense of conservatism in Leavis's rhetoric and a sense that these 'high' literary forms have to be protected from the grubby hands of the masses who would, in any case, not be capable of understanding them. During the 1960s, this attitude would be challenged on two fronts: from within the academy, by a new generation of cultural critics, and from outside it, by creative writers. The Hispanic literary establishment has tended to share Leavisite views of the literary canon. This is why it took some time for Puig to be recognized as an important writer, since he overtly experimented with popular forms (not part of the canon), though younger critics and fellow experimental novelists, such as Guillermo Cabrera Infante, consistently championed his work. Today, the fact that part of a book such as this should be entitled 'Varieties of the popular' is a direct result of what can only be called a transformation in literary studies since the 1960s. Nevertheless, you might feel that there *is* still some worth in attempting to define a literary canon and to retain notions of literary judgement and taste. (These notions are by no means superseded, as the debates outlined in Part 2 of this book will show.)

However, to remain with the backlash against 'high' literary culture for the moment: we can take as an example of this Antony Easthope's 1991 book, *Literary into Cultural Studies*. Here, Easthope declared that 'the old paradigm has collapsed ... and ... a fresh paradigm has emerged' (1991, p.5). He claimed that the critical practices of the believers in high culture, typified for him by the 'New Criticism' advocated by influential figures such as I.A. Richards and Cleanth Brooks, had been utterly discredited and disproven. Easthope argued that the whole notion of the literary canon as in some way a 'transhistorical essence' is utterly false, since every text is subject to the forces of its time, place and circumstance, and is susceptible to being read in divergent ways by different readers at different times. **Pause for a minute and think about how this view compares with the view put forward by Leavis in the passage above.**

I hope you will agree, Easthope's position is at the opposite end of the spectrum from that of Leavis. There is no need for you to decide whether you think either of these positions is right or wrong; just bear the debate in mind as you explore Puig's novel further. While thinking of the novel in these general terms, we should not forget that we are reading it – like thousands of others across the world – in a translated form.

Translation

To begin, think about the version of *Kiss of the Spider Woman* that we are analysing. How might it differ from the original Spanish version, *El beso de la mujer araña*?

Although you should be aware that you are reading the novel in an English translation from the original Spanish, it is perhaps reassuring to know that Puig himself was multilingual and collaborated closely with his translators in producing the English, Italian, French and Portuguese versions of his novels. Indeed, he wrote one novel originally in English (*Eternal Curse on the Reader of these Pages*, 1980) and another (*Sangre de amor correspondido*, 1982) in Portuguese, when he was living in New York and Rio de Janeiro, respectively.

Translations have been crucial to Puig's fame and popularity as a writer, as they have to several of the Latin American writers of the twentieth century (of whom more later). To date, *Kiss of the Spider Woman* has been translated into twenty-seven languages. Puig's initial literary fame was a result of acclamation in the French press, which hailed *Betrayed by Rita Hayworth* (translated into French and published by Gallimard in 1969) as one of the best novels of the year. Puig outlined his approach to translation in an interview in 1979, where he said:

> A chapter in *Heartbreak Tango* is resolved in the Spanish original [*Boquitas pintadas*] through a reading of tarot cards performed by a gypsy. Nevertheless, in France and Great Britain, this special type of Spanish cards is not known. So I had to rewrite the segment. I had to transform everything, to adapt the images to a poker game. It was a deliberate act of rewriting. And there are many more examples like this one. More than anywhere else, I had to rewrite a lot in *Kiss of the Spider Woman*. And as you well know, translating theatre is a very difficult task. It's not only a matter of changing words; you have to adapt the meaning from one language into another. That's why in the United States people never say 'This is a translation of the work of such and such playwright or dramaturge,' but 'An English adaptation ... or an English version, of the works of such and such playwright.' A different thing happened with Italian, which is so similar to Spanish. French is less so, and English is very different, so I had much to change. The translator's task is to create, in his or her own language, the same tensions appearing in the original. That's hard!
>
> (*Review of Contemporary Fiction*, 1991, p.167)

The translation of *Kiss of the Spider Woman* by Thomas Colchie certainly uses a US idiom. You might regard this as appropriate, given that Puig and his characters have been profoundly influenced by the cinema culture of the USA. Certainly, the colloquial, conversational tone of much of the text is true to the original Argentinian Spanish, though the characters' language is rather coarser and more informal in the English version. British readers might find some of the US slang terms, or even the general vocabulary used, slightly puzzling: a 'duster' [*batón* in the original] (9; p.161), is a kind of dressing-gown or negligée; when a character 'gets pissed' [*se pone mal*] (6; p.116), he is actually getting angry, rather than drunk; a woman who is 'really stacked' [*pechugona*] (6; p.118) has a large bust. Generally, the translation is accurate, with only a few slips – for example, in Chapter 6 the racing driver does not 'climb into the shell' [*y se coloca el casco*] (6; p.115) but simply puts his helmet on. One example of a 'deliberate act of rewriting', as Puig calls it, is that the drink brought to the prisoners in the morning is *maté* (a distinctive South American tea) in the original, but coffee in the US translation – a good example of translation as cultural transposition. Nevertheless, there are some subtleties of language that remain untranslatable.

One of these is the word play on 'cannelloni' (15; p.265) – this provides a puzzle both for the undercover policeman who is making his report and for the translator. Molina is talking to his Aunt Chicha on the telephone and joking about his childish mispronunciation of his favourite dish, cannelloni, but which he pronounced as 'calne de leones', a slightly mispronounced 'carne de leones' ('lion meat'). Perhaps one of the attractions of this delicious food was that the child actually thought he might be eating the flesh of lions. Here, the translator has to use his ingenuity and translates 'calne de leones' as 'camel only' – this is good in that it mimics the sound of the word 'cannelloni' and conjures up an incongruous large animal, but somehow the cachet of eating camel meat is not quite equal to feasting on the king of the jungle. Another, more significant, difficulty is the Spanish word *loca*, a word habitually used by Molina to describe himself, which is translated into English as 'gay'. Literally, this word means 'madwoman', but in common parlance it also means a homosexual or 'queen'. The original Spanish word, with its connotation of madness, links the character with the figure of the female madwoman/dissident in a range of novels, from Charlotte Brontë's *Jane Eyre* (1847), through Charlotte Perkins Gilman's *The Yellow Wallpaper* (1899), to Jean Rhys's *Wide Sargasso Sea* (1966), and even including Daphne du Maurier's *Rebecca* (1938). Sadly, the English translation conveys none of this.

Translation in a wider sense is a thematic and structural issue in the novel, too. From the abrupt opening, where the speaker, Molina, is beginning to tell the story of a film he has seen years before, we see that the novel is engaged in 'translating' from one cultural medium into another. Puig's character is translating film language into oral storytelling, which is in turn translated into the form of the novel; arguably, the readers then 'translate' Molina's words back into visual images in their mind as they read the novel. It is an interesting demonstration of the endless cultural transactions that take place in modern, hybridized cultures such as our own. In the next section I consider in greater depth the film narratives that many readers find the most striking and dramatic features of Puig's text.

Parallel narratives

Think about how the film narratives relate to the main plot of the novel and the developing relationship between Molina and Valentin. Reread the version of *Cat People* told by Molina in Chapters 1 and 2 (pp.3–41). Make a note of the connections you perceive between the two layers of the narrative (that is, between the main plot of the novel and the plot of the film).

The story begins without any introduction or framing narrative. We are plunged directly into Molina's narrative, except that at this stage we do not know who is speaking, where, nor to whom – it is just a voice telling a story. (I was reminded here of Joseph Conrad's *Heart of Darkness* (1899), where Marlow's voice emerges eerily from the darkness to tell his story.) The focus from the start is on the female character, the heroine, and her difference from the crowd. Indeed, the syntax of the first sentence in the original Spanish emphasizes this further, reversing the usual word order so that the second word is 'she' – 'A ella se le ve que algo raro tiene, que no es una mujer como todas' ('She, you can see that there's something strange about her, that she's not a woman like all the others'). Immediately, the speaker's descriptive skills are evident: he is building up an atmospheric mental picture for his listener, not simply recounting a plot. The other voice is the interrupter, the questioner, and there is a distinctly mocking, commonsensical tone to some of the questions, counterpointing the rather flowery language of the story. (One example of this is the description of the woman as *ensimismada*, translated as 'all wrapped up in herself' (1; p.10), but which suggests to me 'in a reverie', literally 'inside herself'.) The questioner constantly breaks the flow of the narrative, making logical objections and requests but also wanting to know quickly what happens next. In this respect, he seems to stand for the reader. The storyteller is an artist – skilful at description but also at suspense and drama. Note the sudden 'And who's there behind her?' (1; p.4), which immediately elicits a response from the audience of one in the novel (and from us): 'Who is it?'

Within the space of two pages, the antagonistic attitudes of the two main characters are already established, although we do not yet even know their names. Moreover, it becomes clear by the first break in the narrative (1; p.9) that the narrator identifies completely with the cat woman heroine, whereas the questioner regards her merely as an erotic object ('a real piece'; 1; p.5) who is less attractive than her rival, the architect's assistant. We can also discern some parallels between the two stories that are unfolding simultaneously: for example, the caged birds in the film narrative and the description of Irena as a 'prisoner' (1; p.6) echo the situation of the two protagonists, in more ways than the literal. In retrospect, you might also suggest that there is a parallel between the fact that 'the war [is] ... still going strong at the time' (1; p.7) of the film's action and the fact that Valentin at least is engaged in a war against the repressive state. Irena, Molina and Valentin are all in a sense marginalized, displaced persons; as we shall see, they are afflicted by personal neuroses that might be regarded as analogous to the ancient curse of the cat people.

As Molina continues building up the fictional world of the film, there is a strange disjunction between the enormous visual detail of the film setting as described by Molina (see, for example, 1; p.10) and the sparse scraps of information we receive about the circumstances in which the two protagonists live. The first direct reference to 'this filthy cell' is delayed until two-thirds of the way through Chapter 1 (p.17).

What do you think is the effect of this deferral of information?

In one way, it exploits one of the classic techniques of narrative: the deferral of information-giving arouses the reader's curiosity and builds up suspense. On another level, the technique makes us work actively to build up a mental picture of a scene that remains undescribed. As a result, the 'realist' dimension of the novel (that which occurs in the Buenos Aires prison) is perversely bereft of the usual realistic descriptive techniques, whereas the 'fantastic' elements of the novel are lavishly endowed with realistic detail. This topsy-turveydom might be seen as a symptom of the novel's postmodernity; it is certainly 'an eclectic approach', one of the characteristics of postmodernism identified in the definition quoted earlier.

Now look in more detail at the elements of the *Cat People* story. What are the implications of the part of the narrative that explains the origins of the cat people (1; pp.12–13)?

The story suggests a grotesque sexual coupling between the woman who makes a pact with the devil and the black panther, but we notice that Molina skirts around this issue, saying 'I don't know what happened' (1; p.12). Just as the original film was subject to the rigid sexual censorship prevalent in the 1940s, so Molina censors himself; he is entranced more by the surface glamour than by the raw sexual undercurrents of the story. The story itself is like a myth or fairytale and, in common with many such tales, seems to convey certain male Freudian anxieties about predatory female sexuality. Valentin does begin to offer psychoanalytical readings of the film (1; p.15), but his analysis suggests that the film is about *female* fears of sexuality rather than male fears of the female.

As the *Cat People* story and the relationship between Molina and Valentin both develop, their stories are joined by yet another voice: that of the footnotes, to which we will turn our attention presently. For the moment, we can note that the myth about the origin of the cat women may also be linked to the developing story in the footnotes about the origins of homosexuality. Both the film narrative and the footnotes are attempting (using starkly different discourses – mythical and scientific) to explain the origin of a human conundrum that is mysteriously connected with sexuality.

In the above reading, two levels of narrative are identified and the interconnections between them are traced. Effortlessly, and using only the most 'vulgar' of materials, Puig is telling two stories simultaneously. The Russian theorist Mikhail Bakhtin has suggested that the modern novel as a genre is characterized by this kind of 'polyphony' or double-voiced discourse.

Art and ideology

In his influential work 'The Hero in Dostoevsky's Art', Bakhtin draws a distinction between the novels of Leo Tolstoy and those of Dostoevsky; the latter he suggests are dialogic (or polyphonic) in form, whereas Tolstoy's novels are monologic. As he puts it, 'Tolstoy's discourse and his monologically naïve point of view permeate everywhere, into all corners of the world and the soul, subjugating everything to its unity' (Bakhtin, 1984, p.56). What he means by this is that Tolstoy exerts a strong authorial control over his characters and although they may speak in a range of different idiolects (i.e. individual styles of speech), one is aware of the authoritative control of the author over them. Conversely, according to Bakhtin, Dostoevsky's novels are polyphonic in that their many characters and voices seem to range freely and autonomously, interweaving with one another on the page. It is as if Dostoevsky's characters are not predetermined and fixed by the external hand of the author but rather have their own independence and self-consciousness, which only they can reveal.

Would you say that Puig's novel is dialogic or monologic?

It might be possible to argue that the novel is monologic, for example if you were to take the voice of the erudite footnotes as the voice of the author, exerting control over and 'explaining' his creations. However, I think it would be easier to see the novel as dialogic, in that the author does not appear to impose a hierarchy on the polyphony of different voices and discourses that interweave in the text. In arguing against a monologic reading, you could cite the apparently innocent shopping list that we find near the beginning of Chapter 11 (p.200), which is as significant in displaying the operation of power relationships as many of the footnotes. **So, there are certainly different voices but what about the characters? Do you think they are 'fixed' or do they appear to have their own self-consciousness and autonomy?**

Bakhtin said that 'In a human being there is always something that only he himself can reveal, in a free act of self-consciousness and discourse, something that does not submit to an externalising secondhand definition' (1981, p.60). Dostoevsky's characters resemble human beings in this way; arguably, so do Puig's. The reader gains access to the thoughts and dreams of both Molina and Valentin in the course of the novel; they reveal to us things that only they can reveal. They also surprise us with their actions, which do not appear to be predetermined. You may disagree with this view, but for the moment let us continue with this Bakhtinian reading of Puig's novel.

Now read 'Dialogism in Manuel Puig's *Kiss of the Spider Woman*', by Michael Dunne (Reader, Item 39). How does Dunne explain the relationship between the footnotes and the main text? Are you convinced by this Bakhtinian analysis?

Dunne argues that the footnotes form part of the polyphony of the text, part of its dialogic structure. He goes on to elaborate on this, suggesting that a double-voiced discourse operates in the text, with at least two 'versions' of meaning implicit in every utterance. Thus, the footnotes not only comment on the main narrative and vice versa, as I have suggested above, but both the main text and the footnotes are each in a sense telling two simultaneous stories.

Can we take Dunne's analysis a stage further and suggest that the double-voiced nature of the novel is connected to its engagement with both 'high' and 'low' cultural forms?

You might argue that the traditional hierarchy of genres is deliberately subverted in Puig's text. Serious, academic discourse is relegated to the footnotes, while the discourse of trivial, ephemeral forms such as boleros is privileged by being sung centre-stage, as it were, in the main narrative. Similarly, the serious works of political science studied assiduously by Valentin are never actually represented in the text at all – they are erased in favour of Hollywood B-movies. To a degree we can see a broadly political motivation for such a literary strategy. The dismissal of popular forms as inferior and unworthy of attention may be regarded as an elitist ideology that succeeds in dismissing the mass of consumers of these forms as stupid, or at best misguided. This is the kind of attitude adopted by Valentin at the novel's outset: he is contemptuous of these movies and, to a degree, contemptuous of Molina for consuming them.

What do you think Dunne means when he says: 'We must constantly resist the temptation to interpret the polyphony of this novel monologically?'

I think Dunne is suggesting that we should not try to extract a single authorial voice or 'message' from the text. The novel works as an interplay of dissonant discourses; trying to harmonize them in a coherent, 'totalizing' reading of the book would be to go against the spirit of the novel. It would be to impose a 'grand narrative' on the whole, to reinsert the authority that Puig has so carefully excised from his work. However, you might also note that Dunne's stricture is itself authoritative: it attempts to prescribe and perhaps to limit the possible readings that might be made of the text.

In another influential work, 'Discourse in the Novel' (1981), Bakhtin discusses the nature of characters and their speech in the novel:

> The decisive and distinctive importance of the novel as a genre [is that] the human being in the novel is first, foremost and always a speaking human being; the novel requires speaking persons bringing with them their own unique ideological discourse, their own language ... The speaking person in the novel is always, to one degree or another, an *ideologue*. A particular language in the novel is always a particular way of viewing the world, one that strives for social significance.
>
> (Bakhtin, 1981, p.333)

Bakhtin then goes on to contrast the novel as a genre with the epic, concluding that 'In the epic there is one unitary and singular belief system. In the novel there are many such belief systems, with the hero generally acting within his *own* system' (1981, p.334).

How do you think Bakhtin's ideas about the novelistic character as *ideologue* might apply to *Kiss of the Spider Woman*?

Bear in mind that, according to Bakhtin, the dialogic novel does not privilege any of its ideologues. Rather, they produce their different discourses, which interweave polyphonically on the page. Thinking about *Kiss of the Spider Woman* in these terms, we can see that Valentin might well be identified as an ideologue, who has embraced Marxist ideology and who speaks according to that belief system for much of the novel. **Is Molina an ideologue, though? And what about the warden? To consider those questions adequately you might need to think about the ideology of the text as a whole. Does the novel advocate a particular ideological or political position?**

In order to consider this question adequately, we will have to move from the Bakhtinian emphasis on genre to a Freudian consideration of gender. It does seem that for much of the novel it is as if the worlds of politics and art (albeit popular, rather 'low' art) are being polarized, along with masculinity and femininity, in the figures of Valentin and Molina. In Freudian terms, Molina might be regarded as the advocate of the pleasure principle, while Valentin represents the reality principle (see Freud, [1920] 2001a), constantly pulling Molina back from wallowing in pleasure for its own sake and reminding him of his social responsibilities. Although Molina is in some ways a ludicrous figure, since he is the narrator for much of the time it is inevitable that readerly sympathy tends to be with him and therefore in partial opposition to the overtly political ideologue, Valentin. But we can see that the text gradually undoes its own polarities as it progresses. As Molina weaves his narrative web, something else is being unwoven. **What is that 'something else', do you think?**

One of Puig's main concerns in all his novels is the imprisoning quality of the masculine and feminine roles that are imposed on people in a patriarchal society. He has stated in a number of interviews that he was brought up in this constricting patriarchal ideology, which creates a false polarity between males and females, and constructs a powerful myth concerning gender and sexuality. His novels set about exposing these myths and attempting to deconstruct them. *Kiss of the Spider Woman* is the novel in which we can see most clearly the way in which Puig is attempting this deconstructive task. He does so in the microcosm of the prison cell, the 'island' (as Valentin calls it in his final dream; 16; p.278) where Molina and Valentin, initially the most unpromising of subjects, manage to break down those imposed roles and come together as human individuals. Puig dramatizes this as a gradual, reciprocal process: by Chapter 4, Valentin is saying 'art's not just something for women' (p.76); by Chapter 7, he seems to accede to Molina's statement that 'boleros contain tremendous truths' (p.139). Meanwhile, Molina's actions – both in the prison (his clever manipulation of the warden) and when he is released – show that he, too, has been influenced and partially enlightened by his contact with Valentin. The scene at the end of Chapter 11, when Molina puts his hand to his face to touch a mole that is actually on Valentin's face is an emblem of the way in which those binary oppositions have been completely broken down; as Molina says, mimicking the words of romantic films: 'like I wasn't me anymore. As if now, somehow ... I ... were you' (p.219).

The transformation of gender relations is seen as a prerequisite for fundamental social change. But we should not underestimate the extent to which *Kiss of the Spider Woman* is a direct political exposé. In the context of the mid-1970s it was necessary for someone to speak out about the hidden atrocities that were occurring every day in Argentina. The novel uses all its cinematic power to evoke the atmosphere of fear and repression that real people were experiencing at the time.

We can see that the text does propose an ideology, but it does not do so through one or other of its ideologues. In this sense, the novel cannot be entirely contained by the Bakhtinian view of dialogism, which is posited on the novel having no overarching ideology at all. Moreover, although the dismantling of patriarchal society is a profoundly revolutionary ideology, it is different from the direct political revolution that Valentin is working towards. Indeed, it is suggested that Valentin and his comrades are not particularly enlightened when it comes to sexual politics. They believe that the root causes of society's ills are economic and class-based, but the plot of the novel seems to tell a slightly different story: not that Marxism is wrong but that the pernicious system of political repression and torture in which both Valentin and Molina suffer is caused by patriarchal domination as well as by class oppression. An apparently innocent statement by Molina underlines this point: 'if men acted like women there wouldn't be any more torturers' (2; p.29), to which Valentin is forced to reply: 'You've got a point there, a flimsy one, but still, it's a point.'

Freud: masculinity and femininity

One of the central debates in the novel is about the definition of masculinity and femininity. Molina and Valentin argue over the issues both openly and in a more concealed way in their behaviour towards each other, while the voice of the footnotes also contributes to the discussion. Initially, Puig had intended to dramatize the entire debate through the characters' dialogue but found that he was unable to incorporate the more theoretical material convincingly into the narrative. However, he felt that it was very important to include the material in the footnotes because, as he puts it,

> well, the information's been violently denied, so I'll violently incorporate it into the narration ... Part of my interest in giving all the information on homosexuality came from thinking about the young reader in Spain, who has suffered the most violent denial of information of any reader in Western Europe in our time. They had censorship for almost forty years!
>
> (in Christ, 1991, p.577).

The novel was first published just after the end of the repressive Franco regime in Spain.

Freud figures largely in the footnotes and, more generally, in the construction of the text. We have noted the way in which the dialogue format mimics various literary models, but it also mimics closely the therapeutic method pioneered by Freud in his treatment of patients: the so-called 'talking cure'. Typically, the patient lies on a couch and tells stories – especially dreams – partly in response to the analyst's probing questions. Immediately we see how Molina takes the role of the patient and Valentin, the analyst. Indeed, Valentin explicitly identifies with the psychiatrist in the narrative of *Cat People* (1; p.25). As Molina conjures up the silvery, dream-like images, Valentin analyses them, perhaps with the suggestion that Molina is actually in need of a cure for his sexual malaise (fetishism, fixation, masochism?). **How does Molina respond to Valentin's analyses?**

At first he is impatient ('Wait, will you?; 1; p.15), then suspicious that Valentin is simply making fun of him; later, he accepts Valentin's suggestion – 'I'd like us to discuss the thing a little' (1; p.6). This is a key moment in the relationship because a true dialectic begins between the two voices, not simply a counterpoint between a speaker and a heckler. Valentin becomes actively engaged in the process, and this is vividly shown in the passage where they discuss the hero's mother (1; pp.16–17). Note that this is a character who does not actually appear in the film at all: Valentin is encouraging Molina to use his imagination. From this interchange we can extrapolate information about some of the two characters' outside relationships – for example, with their own mothers, one of the key relationships in psychosexual development, according to Freud.

In response to his 'analyst's' prompting, Molina gives a definition of the perfect mother: 'A lovely lady, who gave her husband every happiness and her children too, always managing everything perfectly' (1; p.16). She is the embodiment of self-abnegating femininity, another version of some of the film heroines. It is clear that Molina has completely accepted and internalized an ideal of femininity which is propagated by the dominant patriarchal ideology; it is an ideal that Valentin consistently tries to reveal as a sham: 'But don't you see how all that's nothing but a deception? If you were a woman you wouldn't want that' (2; p.44).

But do all the film narratives recounted by Molina project a similar ideal of femininity? Look at the film narrated in Chapters 3–4 and read the footnote relating to it, ostensibly taken from the press-book of the Tobis-Berlin Studios (pp.82–5). What might the ideal of femininity embodied in this discourse be?

Puig did extensive research on Nazi films in order to invent this footnote. He spent weeks in the New York Public Library listening to the recorded speeches of Joseph Goebbels and Adolf Hitler and at the same time viewed many propaganda films of the period held at the Museum of Modern Art. As mentioned above, much of the film is based on an actual movie from 1942 called *Die grosse Liebe* ('The Great Love'). Although this footnote is invented, it gives an accurate representation of Nazi gender ideology. The role of women, according to this, is to be mothers of the future generation of racially pure offspring; they must confine themselves to the domestic sphere and eschew all forms of 'decadence'. Quoting the Führer himself, the footnote declares: 'Her single mission is to be beautiful and bear the sons of the world. A woman who bequeaths five sons to the Volk has made a greater contribution than that of the finest woman jurist in the world.' The tone of this footnote is strange: at times it is so ludicrous that it is almost funny (Leni is apparently a rather alarming cross between a 'gymnast' and a 'healthy shepherdess', for example), whereas at other times it comes horrifyingly close to the actual anti-Semitic language of Goebbels (Jews are described as 'these locusts of Jehovah ... the master criminal ... the monster ... the Hebraic Moloch'). In terms of gender, though, the extreme right-wing ideology of Nazism is shown to be only an exaggeration of 'normal' patriarchal codes. Women have their place, later to be described by German feminists as 'Küche, Kinder, Kirche' ('Kitchen, Children, Church'), and they venture out of it at their peril.

Puig was an enthusiastic supporter of feminism. He said:

> The women's liberation movement is one of the most important things that ever happened. At first women thought that they had to be weak, frail, in order to BE, especially when searching for sexual pleasure. That was the big trap, the big lie ... When I wrote *Rita Hayworth*, I still believed in Clark Gable as a force of

Nature. I thought it was a cruel nature that had made this strong man and these weak Harlows, but that it was, in fact, Nature's law. Now I am convinced that Clark Gable is an historical-cultural product, not Nature's creature.

(in Christ, 1977, p.58)

Intellectually, the novel can be said to project Valentin's view exactly – that traditional gender roles are a sham; emotionally, the novel has much invested in the feminine world of the old Hollywood illusion. There is an ambivalence about the novel and I think we should not try to resolve this (or impose a monologic reading on the text, as Dunne would put it). The dialogue between Molina and Valentin about the Nazi propaganda film makes clear that Molina perceives its falseness and yet is utterly seduced by it. This is what has led Ronald Christ to describe Puig's vision as 'essentially bi-focal'; Christ says that Puig's characters 'suck the thumb of popular culture to avoid chewing the gristle of reality' (1973, p.63). Even *recognition* of self-deception does not necessarily ensure liberation from it, for Puig's characters or perhaps even for Puig's readers.

The other side of the coin is masculinity. Reread Chapter 3, from 'What's masculine in your terms …' to 'it's not as possible as you think …' (pp.61–3) and the footnote towards the end of Chapter 10 (pp.195–6). How do the conceptions of masculinity held by Molina and Valentin, respectively, compare with those of the theorists cited in the footnote?

As we have seen above, it is clear that Molina has completely internalized the notion of submissive femininity which he appears to have learned from the movies. He confesses to Valentin in a moment of intimacy that he cannot enjoy sex without an element of fear and pain inflicted on him by the dominant man who penetrates him (13; pp.243–4). Femininity, for Molina, is a construct imposed by the dominant ideology of compulsory heterosexuality. It leads him to a quasi-masochistic state, in which he is exceptionally vulnerable to exploitation. Moreover, he is politically inactive, and lacks both self-esteem and the ability to defend himself.

In *What a Man's Gotta Do*, Antony Easthope draws attention to the fact that

the forms and images of contemporary popular culture lay on a man the burden of having to be one sex all the way through. So his struggle to be masculine is the struggle to cope with his own femininity ... masculinity is an effect, and a contradictory one. In so far as men live the dominant version of masculinity ... they are themselves trapped in structures that fix and limit masculine identity. They do what they *have* to do.

(Easthope, 1986, pp.6–7)

Puig himself unconsciously echoes Easthope's theory when he says in an interview: 'In that cell there are only two men, but that's just on the surface. There are really two men, and two women. I agree with Theodore Roszack when he says that the woman most desperately in need of liberation is the woman every man has locked up in the dungeons of his own psyche' (in Christ, 1991, p.576).

It is notable that Molina does not recount any film narratives from westerns, which were an enormously popular genre in the Hollywood movie industry of the 1940s and 1950s. It is perhaps easy to see why. The western tends to be an aggressively masculine genre, focusing on the male hero, rather than on a heroine. Moreover, the cowboy has a specifically Argentinian manifestation in the *gaucho*, a figure who in a sense epitomizes everything about compulsory Latin masculinity that Puig spent his life battling against. You will remember that Puig once noted 'I grew up on the pampa in a bad dream, or rather a bad western' (quoted in Levine, 2001, p.2)

Freud spent much of his career analysing male and female sexuality, but his work is also profoundly concerned with the development of sexuality from infancy. The developmental aspect of Freud's theories is strongly represented in Puig's footnotes and in a different way also in the main narrative of the novel. Freud ([1905] 2001b) talks about the stages of human sexuality which individuals go through in infancy, labelling them the oral, the anal and the genital. **In what ways is sexual development reflected in the story of Molina and Valentin?**

There are interesting parallels to be made between these three stages and the plot of the novel. Molina initially gives pleasure to Valentin through oral narrative. Then Valentin is poisoned and regresses to an infantile stage where Molina has to clean him up (it is described in terms reminiscent of changing a baby's nappy). This spells the end – in a very literal, graphic way – of Valentin's anal retentiveness. Finally, the characters reach the genital stage when they have sexual intercourse. However, this subtext does not necessarily represent Valentin's 'conversion' to homosexuality. Puig himself frequently spoke out against exclusivity, the ghettoization which he saw as occurring in gay communities in the USA. It is no accident that Freud's description of infantile sexuality as 'polymorphously perverse' is discussed in the final footnote (11; p.205); there is a hint of utopianism in the suggestion that undifferentiated and, importantly, unoppressive sexuality is an ideal. Puig has said, perhaps somewhat mischievously:

> For me, the only natural sexuality is bisexuality; that is, total sexuality. It's all a matter of sexuality, not homosexuality, not heterosexuality. With a person of your own gender, with a person of the opposite gender, with an animal, with a plant, with

anything. Just as long as it's not offensive to the other party ... I
see exclusive homosexuality and exclusive heterosexuality as
cultural results, not as natural outcome.

(in Christ, 1991, p.578)

It is, on the face of it, curious that Valentin, who is an avowed Marxist,
should be so well informed about Freudian psychoanalysis, since many critics
tend to see Marxism and Freudianism as mutually antagonistic theoretical
positions. (This issue is explored further in the discussion of *Do Androids
Dream of Electric Sheep?* in Chapter 3.) Basically, Freudian theory is
frequently viewed by Marxists as ahistorical and far removed from the
economic bases of society, whereas Marxism is regarded by Freudians as a
system that ignores the fundamental unconscious drives of the individual.
However, we see that Valentin is a psychoanalytically inclined Marxist and,
though Marx himself is not directly quoted in the footnotes, the German
Marxist philosopher Herbert Marcuse is referred to extensively and not
fortuitously, since Marcuse's work demonstrates that Marxism and
Freudianism need not be mutually exclusive. His influential works *Eros
and Civilization* (1955) and *One-Dimensional Man* (1964) anatomize the
various unconscious repressions to which we are subject in civilized society,
and decry modern consumer society, which stimulates and satisfies false
desires, keeping individuals in a state of repression. Puig manages to
insinuate the presence of this commodity culture even into a prison cell.
How does he do this?

One of the techniques he employs is to introduce Molina's shopping lists
and show us the two prisoners feasting on the contents of those two brown
paper bags. The concern with food in the novel is understandable enough,
given the circumstances of the two prisoners and their sensual deprivation.
But an obsessive concern with food is also found in other novels by Puig,
such as *Betrayed by Rita Hayworth*. Food is often fetishized (think of the slice
of glazed pumpkin in *Kiss of the Spider Woman*), reflecting the preoccupations
and values of the society that consumes it. According to Marcuse, consumer
society, dominated by the mass media, creates a false situation whereby
individuals *appear* to choose things they really want, but these 'choices' have
actually been imposed on them by the system. In other words, your own
views and attitudes have been sold to you by the popular media: there is a
vast manipulation going on, under the guise of a free society. Molina is very
clearly the victim of this manipulation but he is largely unaware of it. His
loving descriptions of clothes and interior furnishings in his film narratives
show that he is in thrall to consumerism. It is fitting, therefore, that his
'profession' should be that of window-dresser. Puig continually demonstrates
the alienating and manipulative effects of popular culture but at the same
time reveals its seductiveness.

We have already looked at a Bakhtinian interpretation of the footnotes in *Kiss of the Spider Woman* and their role in the polyphonic structure of the novel. Let us think further about their function now in terms of the Freudian and Marcusian ideas they contain. The voice of the footnotes is very different from the voices of Molina and Valentin, who continue to converse, as it were, in the main body of the text, while a footnote goes on – and on. The voice is erudite and scholarly, taking it for granted that we as readers are interested in theories of psychology and sexuality. Many real theorists are cited, including Freud, Marcuse, Norman Brown *et al.* The footnotes are structured as a continuing debate among different theorists who interpret human behaviour and human society in differing ways; thus, the footnotes mirror the debates going on in the main narrative, involving Molina and Valentin. Moreover, the footnotes are clearly meant to relate to the main narrative in a more direct way. **How do you think this works?**

As the characters of Molina and Valentin are gradually revealed to us through their dialogue, we can see that both of them suffer from various kinds of repression and obsession, which are open to analysis in psychoanalytical terms. Most prevalent in the footnotes is the attempted explanation of homosexuality: why do individuals like Molina exist, why do they behave as they do? Puig, as a homosexual writer, is understandably concerned with both the origins of homosexuality and the meanings attached to it in society at large. It is clear that there is, at one level, a political statement about the unjust treatment and persecution of homosexuals. But at another level, Puig is suggesting that the homosexual individual, like Molina, has a subversive and even revolutionary social potential. You can see how the focus of the footnotes changes gradually as the novel proceeds: the first (3; pp.59–65) concentrates on theories about the physical origins of homosexuality, and is suddenly elicited from the main text by Valentin's confession of ignorance about 'people with your type of inclination' (3; p.59). Later, in Chapters 5, 6 and 7, the footnotes delve into Freudian interpretations of homosexuality and sexuality more generally (e.g. pp.97–101, 129–32, 137–43), moving on, in Chapters 8 and 9, to theories of repression and possible liberation (pp.151–4, 163–9). In the last of these, Kate Millett's ideas about sexual politics and Marcuse's ideas on sexual liberation are introduced. At the point in the main narrative where Valentin has succumbed to a violent outburst, and Molina resists his pleas for forgiveness, the footnote introduces this key reference to Marcuse: 'The social function of the homosexual is analogous to that of the critical philosopher, since his very presence is a constant reminder of the repressed elements of society' (10; p.195). At the same time, Marcuse condemns the ' "strong man" stereotype' since it affirms the validity of violence (10; p.196).

The final footnote addresses the role of the homosexual, who is the perennial outsider, the person who is marginalized and anathematized by a society in which ostensible heterosexuality is compulsory. And yet Puig demonstrates through the character of Molina that the revolutionary potential of the homosexual as dissident is continually undermined by the action of the mass media, which reinforces false notions about femininity and masculinity through the insidiously seductive operations of mass-cultural forms such as films and songs. The plot of *Kiss of the Spider Woman*, such as it is, enacts a liberation of the dissident potential of the homosexual but, paradoxically, the dissident action is motivated by an idyllically conceived personal relationship: love.

The footnotes may also be seen as an indirect reflection of Valentin's reading. We know that he is studying serious works of political science, but it may be that he is semi-secretly also reading psychoanalytical works. He certainly offers very astute psychoanalytical readings of several of the film narratives that Molina relates. Moreover, as we have seen, he identifies explicitly with the psychiatrist character in the story of *Cat People*, the first film that Molina recounts. Indeed, in many ways Valentin functions as an emblem of the reader, constantly asking questions, making objections, titillated by cliff-hanger endings, endlessly interpreting and judging. In this sense, one could argue that Valentin functions as one of the many self-reflexive devices in the novel, calling attention to the way in which narratives work and to the role of the reader in deciphering them.

Most of the footnotes refer to well-known scholars, but the last one cites the work of a Danish female psychologist named Anneli Taube. Actually, this person does not exist. **Why do you think Puig has invented her and what is the significance of the work she is supposed to have carried out?**

Anneli Taube could be seen as a spokeswoman for Puig himself, in that her research points out the necessity for homosexuals to awake from their political quiescence and to organize themselves for full participation in politics, where their dissident, marginal status has such revolutionary potential. However, Taube's voice is not privileged any more than the voices of the other – genuine – footnote authors. Jonathan Tittler (1992, p.51) has suggested that the invented footnote may be Puig's playful tribute to the work of his compatriot Jorge Luis Borges, whose fictions are full of footnotes alluding to imaginary but nonetheless extremely erudite scholars. Given that Puig generally did not share the critical regard for Borges, it might, however, be considered as more of a parody than a tribute. Nevertheless, both Puig and Borges can be seen to be playing with readers' expectations about footnotes – we expect them to be authentic. Our assumptions about how far we can rely on writers are being challenged. In this sense, the footnotes mirror Molina's dubiously authentic film narratives – how far can we rely on the veracity of either?

Stephanie Merrim's article 'Through the Film Darkly: Grade "B" Movies and Dreamwork in *Tres tristes tigres* and *El beso de la mujer araña*' explores the differences between the actual films and Molina's account of them, offering a detailed Freudian analysis of the zombie film narrative in *Kiss of the Spider Woman* (pp.158–213). Read this now (Reader, Item 40), bearing in mind your own experience of reading this section of the novel. Are you convinced by Merrim's analysis and argument?

Merrim accurately points out the degree of distortion that the real film texts undergo in Molina's narratives. They undergo the censorship of Freudian dreamwork but at the same time they are being manipulated by the invisible author, Puig. Everything in this polyphonic text is subject to several levels of mediation. It is also interesting to note the explicit parallel Merrim makes between Molina's zombie narrative and Hitchcock's *Rebecca*; you might like to reflect on how du Maurier's novel and Puig's complement each other in terms of their representation of gender.

It is certainly true that in Jacques Tourneur's film *I Walked with a Zombie* there is no hint that the first wife, who is a zombie, is raped by anyone and the wicked witch-doctor does not exist. Moreover, the film has a conventional moral message: the first wife, Rebecca-like, has had an affair with the hero's brother and they wish to run away together; at the end of the film, the would-be adulterers are punished and killed, being pursued into the sea by a zombie man, leaving the hero free to marry the heroine. Molina rejects this moral message and turns the narrative into something far more passionate and transgressive, perhaps to titillate his listener (and us?), perhaps to satisfy his own masochistic fantasies.

Merrim's conclusions about the novel are somewhat negative. She suggests that far from being 'happy' (the last word of the book), the ending simply reveals the continuing self-deception of the two protagonists and the endless repetition of systems of oppression and exploitation. This is certainly one possible reading of the novel, though one might argue that it is a reading that closes off possibilities more emphatically than Puig's 'open' technique invites.

Vulgarity and popular forms

As I mentioned earlier, Puig often professed to be 'profundamente cursi' ('profoundly vulgar' – *cursilería* is usually defined as 'bad taste'), not a self-description that many people would willingly embrace, but one that Puig proudly presents to his interviewers as a statement of defiance and challenge. In fact, what would be defined by many as 'bad taste' is often found in his works: in *Kiss of the Spider Woman*, for example, Molina's films are generally vulgar, as are the boleros he sings, while some readers will find tasteless the reference to Valentin's diarrhoea. (This is to omit those readers who will find the sexual acts between the two men offensive, since I do not think this is likely to be from finding the description of them in bad taste but rather from a moral objection to homosexual acts per se.) But we can also see that this use of vulgarity is a deliberate narrative strategy on Puig's part. **What do you think is the purpose of this insistent vulgarity in the text?**

This is perhaps best answered in Puig's own words:

> I am very interested in what has been called 'bad taste'. I believe that the fear of displaying a soi-disant bad taste stops us from venturing into special cultural zones, some of which are even beyond bad taste. I am very interested in those areas and I allow my intuition to lead my path towards them. For instance, in the gruesomeness of certain tangos I see the possibility of a different kind of poetry. I am also attracted to the excessive sentimentalism of a certain kind of cinema. I wonder, what's beyond that? What kind of audience uses these products? What kind of intellectual or intuitive need is satisfied with this type of 'culture'? Yes, I'm interested in exploring the different manifestations of bad taste. But of course, not with a cold approach. I am only interested in bad taste if I can enjoy a gruesome tango or watch a movie that makes me cry.

(in Corbatta, 1991, p.170)

In addition to popular films and popular song, the novel also alludes to and draws from the genre of romance. Clearly, most of the films narrated by Molina are to some extent romances and it is therefore natural that they should share some of the features of mass-market romances largely aimed at a female readership. In Chapter 1, Nicola Watson explored the use of the romance genre in du Maurier's *Rebecca*; **can you think of ways in which the interpolated narratives and, indeed, the main story involving Molina and Valentin conform to the conventions of the romance genre?**

Popular romances pay meticulous attention to the material details of women's dress and interior furnishings. This is very much a characteristic of Molina's narrative style, one that occasionally irritates his listener, Valentin: as a male 'reader', he wants Molina to 'get to the point' rather than to dwell lovingly on detailed descriptions. **What do you think the function of such descriptions are?**

You might say that these descriptions reveal the extent of Molina's alienation – in Marxist terms, the extent to which he is a dupe to consumer society. However, as a romance element of the text, these descriptions can be read in a more sociological and rather more positive way. Janice A. Radway has suggested the following:

> Despite its willingness to acknowledge stylistically that its tale is a fantasy, the popular romance also goes on to exhibit a marked attention to the material details of the world in which that fantasy is set. The effect is so overpowering that the technique may well persuade the reader that the tale need not be considered a fantasy at all. The romance's consequent equivocation about its status as myth or realism could conceivably be the mark of its authors' and readers' deep-seated unwillingness to admit that the perfect union concluding the story is unattainable in life.
>
> (Radway, 1987, p.193)

We have already noted some of the ambivalences of the text, which, on the one hand, appears to be proposing a radical programme of sexual revolution while, on the other, appears to be admitting the seductiveness of the existing, reactionary order. Radway's analysis of the way in which the romance operates as a genre allows us to add another layer of ambivalence to our reading of the text.

Intertextuality, hybridity, postmodernism

The French psychoanalytical theorist Julia Kristeva has argued that all texts are interdependent and that every individual work is actually a tissue of quotations and cross-references, allusions and rewriting. This 'intertextuality', as she and others have termed it, makes of the literary text a kind of palimpsest, in which one type of discourse is transformed into another (Moi, 1986). This view of literature is clearly very different from the Romantic view of literary creation as the inspired work of a solitary genius, who is distinguished by his (he is usually male) unprecedented originality. From the Romantic period until the modernist theories of T.S. Eliot, value judgements regarding literary quality commonly rested on the criterion of originality, whereas earlier models (such as those prevalent in the eighteenth century) relied instead on the criterion of successful imitation of previous models from the high points of literary culture, especially classical ones. Since the publication of Eliot's 'Tradition and the Individual Talent' (1919), the Romantic cult of originality has lost its power, but at the same time there has been no return to an eighteenth-century ideal of imitation. Instead, in the twentieth century there has increasingly occurred a mixing of 'high' and popular literary forms, a blurring of different discourses, leading to the creation of a self-consciously hybrid literary tradition characterized by ironic and parodic modes of discourse. Puig's novel presents a rich example of this shift to intertextuality. You may also think that this notion of intertextuality is quite similar to the ideas put forward by Bakhtin about the 'polyphonic' novel. Puig's novel is a text made up of a wide variety of different texts and discourses, which clash and intermingle with each other on the page. We have already analysed some of the various different texts incorporated in the novel. **Now try to make a comprehensive list of the different texts and discourses that you have identified in the novel. Identify each item in your list as 'high' or 'popular', according to what level of culture you think it comes from. What is your conclusion: is Puig mainly exploiting popular or 'high' cultural forms?**

My list of texts and discourses includes the following: bolero songs narrated and probably sung by Molina; a coded letter from Valentin's girlfriend; the film narratives based on 1940s Hollywood B-movies; the thoughts, dreams and nightmares of the two protagonists; footnotes; prison reports on the two prisoners; dialogues between Molina and the prison warden; Molina's shopping lists; the secret police report in diary form. This list is not exhaustive – you may well have identified others. The texts and discourses are discordant, clashing with each other, seemingly incongruous. The erudite speaker in the footnotes, which refer extensively to a range of psychoanalytical and cultural theorists, is a voice that speaks in direct contrast to the sentimental language of Molina's film narratives, the domestic detail of the shopping list or the sinister documentary of the undercover policeman's diary. In this novel that lacks an authoritative third-person narrator, it is the juxtaposition of these diverse texts and voices, the structuring of the novel in other words, that embodies the ideology of the novel as a whole. What I mean is that Puig does not pass judgement explicitly on his characters and their actions; instead, the judgement is apprehended by the reader through the strategic juxtaposition of texts.

Puig's method can be said to take away narrative neutrality; he writes in such a way that no single voice can dominate or stand above or outside the drama of the narrative, but at the same time he highlights that each voice is that of an ideologue. The palimpsest of different texts that make up *Kiss of the Spider Woman* suggests that Puig is deliberately rejecting the role of the authoritative narrator. He has expressed his suspicion of the authoritative narrative voice in a number of interviews. Some critics suggest that the rejection of this narrative voice connotes a broader rejection of authority on Puig's part, and an explicit refusal to speak according to the 'Law of the Father'. The latter is a term borrowed from the post-Freudian theorist Jacques Lacan, who suggested that the infant enters into the 'symbolic order' once it acquires language, and that it constructs its identity in relation to this symbolic order, which is inescapably patriarchal. The Law of the Father constitutes, in other terms, the patriarchal ideology and assumptions that mould and repress the individual (Lacan, 2004). Puig's technique can be seen as a challenge to the Law of the Father and a testing of the limits imposed on him as an author by all kinds of authorities – state, literary, familial and so on.

One of the ways in which Puig apparently rejects authorial authority is by inserting gaps in the text, which we as readers need to work to try to interpret and fill. We have seen how crucial information is deferred in the narrative, such as the information that Molina is in effect being blackmailed by the prison authorities to try to betray his cell-mate. But there are other omissions, too. Although the text is constructed rather like a play script, consisting almost entirely of direct speech (with the exception of the footnotes), there are passages of silence in the text, as there often are in staged plays. **Can you think of any examples?**

There are many, but for me the most obvious ones are those indicated by suspense points ('...') in Chapter 14, for example on pages 260–3. **What do these punctuation marks indicate?**

At this late stage in the narrative, the two prisoners have become lovers, so some of the silences surely denote actions, such as kissing and caressing. Bear in mind that this novel was first published in 1976, when explicit description of homosexual lovemaking would have been quite shocking to a general reading public. Indeed, perhaps you as a reader initially found these passages shocking. Puig may not wish to alienate a heterosexual reader with graphic descriptions of homosexual sex, nor does he wish to incur the wrath of the censors (since his work had already been afflicted by censorship from the very beginning – the publication of *La traición de Rita Hayworth* was delayed for three years because of such problems). At the same time, you could argue that the silences indicate the limitations of language. In moments of intimacy, such as are depicted here, words are inadequate or superfluous to express feelings. Thus, the text draws our attention to the way language breaks down; this forms part of the recurring pattern of self-reflexivity that we have seen in other aspects of the text, and is certainly a characteristic of postmodernist writing.

Another aspect of these gaps in the text is that they force us, as readers, to become active participants in the construction of the narrative. The author does not tell us what happens in these gaps: we have to fill them for ourselves. Again, this process is one that is often associated with postmodernist texts, which acknowledge that the traditional author has lost his patriarchal authority and that the reader has become what the Latin American writer Julio Cortázar has termed a *lector cómplice* ('a complicit reader') – one who actively participates in creation, rather than simply consuming what has been created for him or her. (See also Roland Barthes's seminal text 'The Death of the Author' (1968); in Barthes, 1977.)

Puig's novel is *scriptible* ('writerly'), to use the term coined by Barthes. This means that the reader is not simply a passive consumer of the novel but an active producer of its meaning. Barthes distinguishes between the 'writerly' and the 'readerly', the latter being the kind of classic realist text where, according to him, the reader simply accepts the given of the text, without having to work at creating the meaning for him/herself. Barthes sees the goal of literature as being to make the reader into an active producer of literature, rather than a passive consumer. Given that Puig's novel is so concerned with the pleasures and dangers of consumption, the fact that it is difficult for the reader to consume the novel itself passively might be taken as a demonstration of Barthes's theory about what literature should do. Actually, neither Molina nor Valentin is a passive consumer of cultural products; they are active interpreters, mimicking our own role as readers of the novel. Puig says: 'I try to give the reader all the possible data. I don't want my judgement to be oppressive. The reader should have space in which to make up his own mind' (in Christ, 1991, p.572). However, you might argue that even the insertion of gaps in the text is an authorial act, an intentional strategy on Puig's part. He *could* be seen as effacing himself as author and simultaneously and rather surreptitiously retaining authorial authority. As Bakhtin points out, the whole dialogic technique is itself an artifice:

> Thus the freedom of a character is an aspect of the author's design. A character's discourse is created by the author, but created in such a way that it can develop to the full its inner logic and independence as someone else's discourse, the word of the character himself. As a result it does not fall out of the author's design, but only out of a monologic authorial field of vision. And the destruction of this field of vision is precisely a part of Dostoevsky's [and Puig's?] design.
>
> (Bakhtin, 1984, p.58)

Now consider some of the other discourses in the novel. Reread Chapter 15 (pp.264–74). What kind of voice is speaking here and to what extent is it possible to identify a double-voiced discourse?

The last days of Molina are chronicled in the cold prose of surveillance, presented in the form of an undercover policeman's diary. For the first time, we are distanced from Molina, viewing him from afar, through the eyes of the 'enemy', as it were. The policeman's voice is unemotional; obeying his orders, he chronicles the minutiae of Molina's life, noting down trivial details in case they are in some way coded messages. Despite the cold detachment of the prose, there are moments of ironic humour, which occur because we can 'read' Molina's actions, whereas the policeman is frequently baffled by them. One example of this is the banter between Molina and his 'girlfriends', who call one another by a variety of female names, often derived from those of movie stars. The plodding policeman initially suspects that these false names are coded political messages, though we know that the code is simply a part of what we might call Molina's 'queer discourse'. The juxtaposition between this banter and the policeman's chronicle is deliberately incongruous. It highlights the limitations of documentary realism and in a sense champions the playfulness of Molina's language. In this way, we can see that the double-voiced discourse is also self-referential, drawing attention to the postmodernist techniques being used by Puig.

The policeman can be seen as another in a series of would-be readers and interpreters in the text. Just as Valentin has offered readings of Molina's film narratives, and the prison warden has tried to interpret Molina's words, so the hapless policeman tries to 'read' Molina's life. His reading is clearly inadequate; he perceives that there are gaps in the text but he does not have the imaginative wherewithal to try to fill them. One example of this is his observation that Molina repeatedly 'star[es] in a northwesterly direction, which is to say toward intersection of Calle Juramento and Bauness, or – to give more precise location – the existing site of the present penitentiary' (15; p.268). We as readers can interpret this nostalgic gaze as a sign of Molina's attachment to Valentin, who is still incarcerated in the penitentiary. Similarly, we can read Molina's new self-confidence in responding to a bullying godfather – ' "You never spoke to me in that tone before, is that what you learned in prison?" ' (15; p.267) – as his determination to act on one of Valentin's final pieces of advice to him: ' "promise me ... that you're going to make them respect you, that you're not going to allow anyone to treat you badly, or exploit you" ' (14; p.261). Thus, the inert prose of the policeman tells two stories, one of which is revealed only to us as experienced readers. It is almost as if the novel has been a reading primer up to these last two chapters and in these final stages we are 'set free' to read for ourselves. The death of the author (in this case, Molina) leads to the birth of the reader, as Barthes (1977) puts it. Molina's death is itself a story capable of many interpretations. On one level, it is a parody of the death of the heroine in the romantic movies to which Molina is addicted. And yet there is certainly a 'heroic' quality to Molina's end, particularly since his actions make clear that he is more or less prepared for martyrdom. Molina's end is worthy of the melodramatic climax of a Hollywood B-movie, but it is narrated in a deliberately flat, factual way that robs it of its glamour. But the other voice of the discourse, the one we as readers discern but to which the policeman is deaf, endows the scene with a terrible poignancy. It is the poignancy often found in popular forms, such as the bolero, which, as Molina says, 'contain tremendous truths', despite the painful gap between the clichéd language and the real emotions that language expresses. Puig has said of this: 'in many cases I work with alienated languages. But then, what language is not alienated? ... I believe I've always used those degraded languages in order to make them significant, to turn them into signs' (in Christ, 1977, p.55). Although Puig consistently denies being a parodist, there are hints of both parody and pastiche in this section, traits that are highly typical of the ironic mode of postmodernity.

Molina is an unlikely hero, a marginal figure whose complete identification with the impossibly beautiful heroines of the movies (and the opera), particularly the femme fatale stereotype, is faintly absurd. Puig was not the only Latin American author of this period to choose such a marginalized figure as a protagonist; the Chilean novelist José Donoso set his 1966 novel *El lugar sin límites* ('The Limitless Place') in a brothel, and the main character is the homosexual transvestite La Manuela. (Incidentally, Puig adapted Donoso's novel as a film script, which won the prize for the best script at the San Sebastián film festival in 1978.) Almost all of the main characters in the film narratives told by Molina are marginalized figures in some sense and they are also subject to outside forces over which they have no control. **Can you think of examples?**

Irena in *Cat People* is apparently the victim of an ancient curse, from which she can never break free; similarly, the zombie woman is utterly powerless and must obey her master; the pilot in *The Enchanted Cottage* is forced to go to war, while the servant-girl is marginalized both by her lack of economic power and by her lack of beauty, in a society that defines female worth according to those criteria. The operation of power is clearly a central concern in the novel, and Puig has chosen to explore it by stripping it down to its most basic form: two individuals marooned on a metaphorical, unidyllic desert island.

Power, domination, subjugation

At the time of the publication of *El beso de la mujer araña*, Puig was living in exile in New York. He wanted to attack the repressive regime that was in place in his native Argentina at the time, bringing it to the attention of the USA, in the hope that something could be done to stop the terrible dirty war that was destroying so many lives. Some Latin American historians would undoubtedly point to the contradiction inherent in Puig's devotion to US popular culture at a time when the USA either covertly or openly supported many of the oppressive regimes in power in Latin America. (For a polemical view of the involvement of the USA in Latin American politics, see Eduardo Galeano's *Open Veins of Latin America*, 1998.) At any rate, it is worth noting that the novel did not appear in an uncensored form in Argentina until the advent of a democratic government in 1983. Nevertheless, Puig generally sees political transformation as occurring on an individual level. Both Molina and Valentin undergo a political education during their time in Pavilion D, Cell number 7. Initially, as we have seen, Valentin seems to have all the answers. He is an avowed Marxist at the start of the text and an avowed Marxist at its end. **So what, if anything, has he learned during the course of the novel?**

He has learned, at first hand, how power relations work and how he himself has the propensity to be tyrannical, if he succumbs to it. He has dedicated his life to the cause of overthrowing tyranny and yet, in the initial stages of the novel, he behaves towards Molina like a petit-bourgeois tyrant. It is to his credit that he comes to realize this himself. At the same time, he also realizes that sexuality and personal relations are intimately connected with the political struggle and that it is not possible to repress forever, as he has attempted to do, his sexual, emotional and artistic impulses, all for the sake of 'the cause'. **To trace the change in Valentin's attitudes, have another look at the following passages: 'Do you like the picture? ... I'm sorry' (3; p.56); 'Then it's a German garden ... Sure?' (4; p.76); 'Tell me something ... Fine. Ciao' (4; p.104); 'Honestly, my friend ... Shut up!!!' (10; p.93); and 'That's the natural thing ... Because I don't, and that's that' (13; p.244).**

At first, Valentin sneers quite openly at Molina. He looks down on him intellectually and exhibits some distaste for his way of life, particularly his lack of political awareness. Gradually, though, he begins to acknowledge that some of the debased art forms to which Molina is devoted, such as Hollywood movies and boleros, might have some validity. He admits that 'art's not just something for women' (4; p.76), even confessing that he initially went to university to study architecture (like Puig himself). Towards the end we see him relishing the emotional lushness of the movies almost as much as Molina himself, and acknowledging that popular forms like sentimental songs may embody some truths. He realizes that he has treated Molina badly, taking advantage of him (taking his food, for instance), and he tries to bolster Molina's self-esteem and to disabuse him of the belief that femininity necessarily entails suffering and martyrdom. It is interesting to note that at the end of the novel Molina has become a political martyr, which was the role supposedly assigned to Valentin, while the latter is being tortured sexually (he has atrocious burns in his groin), the role for which Molina's sexual masochism appears to have prepared him. Through his plot Puig has changed the typical script of the Hollywood B-movie. His 'female' is not submissive and his male is not triumphantly dominant. Unfortunately, both are dead or dying by the end of the novel.

The context and after-life of *Kiss of the Spider Woman*

The 'boom' in Latin American fiction

Before the 1960s, Latin American literature was little known outside Central and South America and its former colonizers, Spain and Portugal. But a sudden change occurred in the 1960s, which saw a number of Latin American writers achieve fame through multiple translations and widespread critical recognition; their work was regarded as new and exciting, partly because it combined the readability of bestsellers with the kind of literary experimentation more usually associated with 'high' culture. Carlos Fuentes, himself one of the new writers of this generation, has attempted to explain this combination of the popular and the revolutionary, stating that: 'En paises sometidos a la oscilación pendular entre la dictatura y la anarquía, en los que la única constante ha sido la explotación, el novelista individual se vió compelido a ser, simultáneamente, legislador y reportero, revolucionista y pensador' (1969, p.23). ('In countries subject to the continual oscillation between dictatorship and anarchy, in which the only constant has been exploitation, the individual novelist was compelled to be, simultaneously, a law-maker and a reporter, a revolutionary and a thinker'; my translation.)

In 1967, the Nobel Prize was won by the Guatemalan novelist Miguel Ángel Asturias, followed fifteen years later by the Colombian Gabriel García Márquez. Other writers, such as Carlos Fuentes (Mexico), Juan Carlos Onetti (Uruguay), Guillermo Cabrera Infante (Cuba), Julio Cortázar (Argentina), Alejo Carpentier (Cuba), José Donoso (Chile), Mario Vargas Llosa (Peru) and, most importantly for us, Manuel Puig, came to prominence during the 1970s. It was not until the 1980s that Latin American women writers began to be recognized as part of this powerful new literary movement, authors such as Isabel Allende (Chile) and Clarice Lispector (Brazil). In some ways, Puig's work in the 1970s may be seen as a stepping-stone for these women writers, since he himself championed feminism and dedicated his oeuvre to a contestation of the typical Latin American machismo that made it difficult for women to be recognized as creative artists.

Certainly, there had been important individual authors before this period, notably Puig's older compatriot, Jorge Luis Borges, who began publishing in the 1940s, and who many critics believe should have been awarded the Nobel Prize. As early as 1945, the Chilean woman poet Gabriela Mistral had received the Nobel Prize, but both she and Borges to a degree are singular figures, not part of a recognizable literary movement.

Why did the 'boom' occur when it did? Many commentators have explained this with reference to *desarrollismo*, the industrial and commercial development of these countries, which had hitherto remained largely underdeveloped and rural. José Donoso talks in his 'personal history' (1977) about the expectations that were placed on him as a Latin American writer in the early days of his career – to be a realist, to write clearly and simply, and to eschew experimentation. It was his friendship with Fuentes that encouraged him to break away from these limiting expectations. He, like Puig, was from then on to reject such literary conventions as the authoritative narrator and the exclusively realistic mode of representation. The new techniques adopted by writers such as Puig, Donoso, Fuentes, García Márquez, Cabrera Infante and many others should not be regarded as simple aesthetic choices but as part of a social and political process. Literary technique can never be neutral. Many of these writers, including Puig, have been labelled 'magic realists', a description which attempts to encapsulate the blurring of the boundary between fantasy and reality that often characterizes their works. The Cuban writer Alejo Carpentier is often credited with coining the term, though the phrase he actually used in an essay of 1949 was 'lo real maravilloso' ('the marvellous real'; see Carpentier, 1976). Carpentier, influenced by French Surrealism, felt that a new mode of magic realism was the only way of conveying the peculiar reality of Latin America, a combination of myth, fantasy and a 'dirty' realism. Nevertheless, what has come to be known as 'magic realism' is not a mode exclusively confined to Latin American authors; writers such as Italo Calvino, Angela Carter, Günther Grass and Salman Rushdie have also been described in this way. Indeed, 'magic realism' may be regarded as one manifestation of a postmodern trend in literature that was an international phenomenon, not confined to a particular country or even a particular continent.

Another important reason for the boom was that these new, experimental works began to be widely translated. According to Donoso, before 1960 it was uncommon to hear people speak of 'the Latin American novel' as a single entity (Donoso, 1977); rather, the novels of each individual country, such as Argentina and Chile, were confined within that country's borders. But the new generation of writers was outward-looking, influenced by European and US artists such as Albert Camus, Günther Grass, Alberto Moravia, Alain Robbe-Grillet, Jack Kerouac, Henry Miller and others, as well as by the classics of modernism, such as the work of James Joyce, Franz Kafka and William Faulkner. A number of them, including Puig and Cabrera Infante, were profoundly influenced by film. (Puig cites the film directors Ernst Lubitsch, Joseph von Sternberg and Alfred Hitchcock as his major influences.) Donoso regards the modern Latin American novel as a *mestizaje*, a hybrid, drawing on a huge variety of outside sources. In this sense, it is a characteristically postcolonial literature, drawing not only on the imposed canonical tradition (in this case Hispanic) but also on indigenous and popular sources, and embracing a range of other cultural influences, from the USA and from Europe.

However, it is important to remember that Latin American countries on the whole gained their independence from European colonizers much earlier than those nations colonized by the British. Argentina, for example, gained its independence in 1810, a century and a half before Guyana (formerly British Guiana), in the same continental land mass, gained hers. The Spanish had conquered Argentina in the early sixteenth century but it remained somewhat neglected and underpopulated, since it did not have the promise of the gold that lay in Peru and Bolivia. There is still a native population in Argentina, living mainly in the remote areas of the north-west, but the large majority of Argentinians are the descendants of nineteenth-century European immigrants, not only from Spain but from Italy, Germany, Eastern Europe and Britain. It does not have a large black population, because it did not have a plantation economy during the years of the slave trade. It is interesting to note that one of the nightmares that afflicts Valentin in Puig's novel involves his shameful consciousness of racist disdain towards the native Indian girl who appears in his dream; this may be a reflection of the racism in Argentine society towards indigenous peoples, who still live a largely traditional way of life in remote corners of the country, in contrast to most Argentines, who like to think of themselves as sophisticated city-dwellers.

Early Latin American literature, according to Fuentes (1969), had as its true protagonist Nature itself, which was untameable and threatened constantly to engulf human beings. He takes as emblematic the final words of *La vorágine* ('The Whirlpool'; 1924) by José Eustasio Rivera: 'Se los tragó la selva!' ('The jungle swallowed them up'). The conflict was one encapsulated in the title of the much earlier, seminal work of the Argentinian writer Domingo Sarmiento: *Civilización y barbarie* ('Civilization and Barbarism'; 1848). In other words, this was a colonial literature, in which writers represented the primal encounter between the civilized European settler (or his descendant) and the intractable wildness of the land he wished to subdue.

Argentina has its own specific literary tradition, which Puig largely ignores or deliberately challenges. One of the most important figures in Argentine literature is the *gaucho* or cowboy, a highly romanticized representation of the independent, nomadic cattle-herders who roamed the pampas during the nineteenth century. The most famous example of this figure is Martín Fierro, eponymous hero of an enormously popular epic poem written by Jose Hernández in 1872. This is still regarded as the 'national' poem. Although Puig's writing may be seen as an attack on the macho ideology of such a text, it is also possible to see an unconscious debt to Hernandez's poem, which is structured as a song contest between guitar-playing gauchos. The dialectic so characteristic of *Kiss of the Spider Woman* mirrors the form of the national epic, although Puig would certainly have viewed this as reactionary.

In the 1920s, there was an attempt to reassert Argentinian nationalism in opposition to European and US models; this was reflected in works such as the classic gaucho novel *Don Segundo Sombra* (1925) by Ricardo Güiraldes. This nationalism was a reaction to mass European immigration in the late nineteenth century, as Argentina became a centre for European food production. The expansion in production actually led to the end of the traditional nomadic life of the gaucho. Puig's writing is largely in opposition to this nationalist vein of writing, which often refers to indigenous customs and beliefs. Instead, Puig is internationalist in outlook and seems to accept cheerfully the hybridity of contemporary Argentinian society – he does not search for 'pure' origins. His first novel, *Betrayed by Rita Hayworth*, does allude to gaucho myths of the pampas, only to subvert and substitute them with alternatives derived from Hollywood movies.

Roberto Echevarren has described the effect that Puig's novels had on the Hispanic reading public like this: 'When Manuel Puig's early novels were published in the late sixties, they shook the literary consciousness of the time. He was the first novelist writing in Spanish who consistently utilized popular culture and the products of the show-business industry, in order to articulate his fiction' (1991, p.583). Perhaps because of this Puig had continual difficulties in getting his books into print and often found his works on 'banned' lists, particularly in his homeland. Puig initially had some difficulty in publishing *El beso de la mujer araña*. In exile from an Argentina suffering under a brutal dictatorship and with his works banned in his homeland, he had no opportunity to publish there. Seix Barral, the prominent Spanish publishers, based in Barcelona, eventually agreed to publish, but initial reviews were lukewarm. Nevertheless, publication came at the right time, when Spain was just being engulfed in a wave of euphoric liberation after the Franco years. A younger generation of Spanish artists, such as the by-now renowned film director Pedro Almodóvar, were ready for and receptive to Puig's daring new novel. Gradually, translations into English, French, Italian, German and other languages began to appear; the Italian translation, *Bacio della donna ragno*, first published by Einaudi in 1978, was particularly successful.

Transformations

However, the true popularity of the work did not really materialize until Puig produced a play version, which was staged across many European and US cities. Then the novel was filmed in 1985, becoming a surprise box-office hit, and winning several Academy Awards, even though the conservative Reagan era was at its height. Some gay audiences have objected to the depiction of Molina as reactionary; Puig consistently defended his right to show 'gays as unexceptional human beings, in this case gentle and muddled, but at the same time courageous and loving' (Levine, 2001, p.262). Privately, he called his detractors 'Stalinist queens' (*ibid.*). After Puig's death, *Kiss of the Spider Woman* achieved even greater popularity in a musical version written for the stage.

The musical was in fact written shortly before Puig's premature death at the age of fifty-seven in 1990; it premiered in Toronto and then had a long and successful run on Broadway, winning the 1993 Tony Award for best musical. Puig himself approved of the adaptation and contributed to it, suggesting some modifications after the early performances. It might seem surprising that a novel which deals with homosexuality, anal intercourse and torture should be regarded as suitable material for a musical. However, it is also apt that it should have been 'translated' once more into one of the most popular of contemporary genres. Arguably, the novel's translation into other forms, notably the film and the musical, succeeded in stripping it of its radical edge, omitting such features as the footnotes and capitalizing instead on its potential for sentimentality. Moreover, the physical absence of women from the text is negated in both film and stage versions, where actual women embody and make 'present' the figures of fantasy, such as the spider woman. You might also argue that the authoritative narrator, whom Puig took such pains to try to efface, reappears and takes control in the film, where the camera controls and shapes everything the audience sees. Nevertheless, despite the possible losses, there is an undeniable poetic justice in the novel's translation into these popular forms. The original novel is suffused with spectacle and performance, as well as with boleros, so in a sense Puig's debt to popular forms is being repaid. Moreover, the translation to another genre (along with the translations into twenty-seven languages) has proved that Puig's intensely Argentinian text can be successfully transposed to have relevance to a contemporary US and European audience.

Some critics have explained the enormous popular success of *Kiss of the Spider Woman, The Musical* by suggesting that it is an allegory of AIDS in the USA (see Román and Sandoval, 1997). Indeed, some commentators hold that Puig himself died of complications as a result of AIDS, while others, including his biographer, maintain that he suffered a heart attack following a routine gall-bladder operation. The musical's success might be viewed in a positive light, as an indication of the way in which overt censorship and repression have decreased over the decades of the twentieth century, at least in some western countries. However, away from the glitter of the Broadway stage and the allure of Hollywood, in many countries of the world the patriarchal culture against which Puig rebelled and which he continually undermined in his works is still going strong.

Manuel Puig's novel demonstrates vividly the way in which traditional barriers between high and low cultures, between the popular and the elite, have been dismantled in the late twentieth century. It does more than that, though; it shows that the novel genre, which some had regarded as being exhausted and outmoded, is capable of continuous renewal through daring structural and stylistic experimentation and through imaginative engagement with contemporary issues.

Works cited

Bakhtin, M. (1981) *Dialogic Imagination: Four Essays*, ed. by M. Holquist, trans. by C. Emerson and M. Holquist, Austin: University of Texas Press.

Bakhtin, M. (1984) *Problems of Dostoevsky's Poetics*, Manchester: Manchester University Press.

Barthes, R. (1977) 'The Death of the Author', in *Image–Music–Text*, trans. by S. Heath, London: Fontana, pp.142–8.

Bassnett, S. (1987) 'Coming out of the Labyrinth: Woman Writers in Contemporary Latin America', in J. King (ed.), *Modern Latin American Fiction: A Survey*, London: Faber, pp.247–67.

Carpentier, A. (1976) 'De lo real maravilloso americano', in *Tientos y diferencias*, Buenos Aires: Calicanto Editorial, pp.83–99.

Christ, R. (1973) 'Fact and Fiction', *Review* (New York Center for Inter-American Relations), Fall, pp.61–70.

Christ, R. (1977) 'An Interview with Manuel Puig', *Partisan Review*, 44.1, pp.52–61.

Christ, R. (1991) 'A Last Interview with Manuel Puig', *World Literature Today*, 65.4, Autumn, pp.571–9.

Corbatta, J. (1991) 'Brief Encounter: An Interview with Manuel Puig', *Review of Contemporary Fiction*, 11.3, Special issue on Puig, Fall, pp.165–76.

Cuddon, J.A. (1988) *The Penguin Dictionary of Literary Terms and Literary Theory*, London: Penguin.

Donoso, J. (1977) *The Boom in Spanish American Literature: A Personal History*, New York: Columbia University Press.

Donoso, J. ([1966] 1995) *El lugar sin límites*, Barcelona: Seix Barral.

Easthope, A. (1986) *What a Man's Gotta Do: The Masculine Myth in Popular Culture*, London: Flamingo.

Easthope, A. (1991) *Literary into Cultural Studies*, London: Routledge.

Echevarren, R. (1991) 'Manuel Puig: Beyond Identity', *World Literature Today*, 65.4, Autumn, pp.581–5.

Freud, S. ([1920] 2001a) 'Beyond the Pleasure Principle', in *Beyond the Pleasure Principle, Group Psychology and Other Works*, trans. and ed. by J. Strachey, *The Standard Edition of the Complete Psychological Works of Sigmund Freud*, vol.18: *(1920–22)*, London: Hogarth Press, pp.7–64.

Freud, S. ([1905] 2001b) 'Three Essays on Sexuality', in *A Case of Hysteria, Three Essays on Sexuality and Other Works*, trans. and ed. by J. Strachey, *The Standard Edition of the Complete Psychological Works of Sigmund Freud*, vol.7: *(1901–05)*, London, Hogarth Press, pp.125–243.

Fuentes, C. (1969) *La nueva novela hispanoamericana*, Mexico: J. Mortiz.

Galeano, E. (1998) *Open Veins of Latin America: Five Centuries of the Pillage of a Continent*, New York: Monthly Review Press.

Lacan, J. (2004) *Écrits: A Selection*, trans. by B. Fink, New York: W.W. Norton.

Leavis, F.R. (1930) *Mass Civilisation and Minority Culture*, Cambridge: Minority Press.

Levine, S.J. (2001) *Manuel Puig and the Spider Woman: His Life and Fictions*, Madison: The University of Wisconsin Press.

Marcuse, H. (1964) *One-Dimensional Man: Studies in the Ideology of Advanced Industrial Society*, London: Routledge & Kegan Paul.

Marcuse, H. ([1955] 1969) *Eros and Civilization*, London: Sphere.

Moi, T. (ed.) (1986) *The Kristeva Reader*, New York: Columbia University Press.

O'Hara, F. (1964) *Lunch Poems*, San Francisco: City Lights.

Puig, M. (1968) *La traición de Rita Hayworth*, Buenos Aires: Jorge Alvarez. Trans. by S.J. Levine as *Betrayed by Rita Hayworth*, New York: Dutton, 1971.

Puig, M. (1969) *Boquitas pintadas: folletín* Buenos Aires: Sudamericana. Trans. by S.J Levine as *Heartbreak Tango*, New York: Dutton, 1973.

Puig, M. (1973) *The Buenos Aires Affair: novela policial*, Buenos Aires: Sudamericana. Trans. by S.J. Levine as *The Buenos Aires Affair*, New York: Dutton; London: Arena, 1976.

Puig, M. (1976) *El beso de la mujer araña*, Barcelona: Seix Barral. Trans. by T. Colchie as *Kiss of the Spider Woman*, New York: Knopf, 1979.

Puig, M. (1980) *Maldición eterna a quien lea estas páginas*, Barcelona: Seix Barral. Originally written in English by Manuel Puig as *Eternal Curse on the Reader of these Pages*, New York: Random House, 1982.

Puig, M. (1982) *Sangre de amor correspondido*, Barcelona: Seix Barral. Trans. by J.L. Grayson as *Blood of Requited Love*, New York: Random House, 1984.

Puig, M. ([1976] 1991) *Kiss of the Spider Woman*, trans. by T. Colchie, London: Vintage.

Radway, J.A. (1987) *Reading the Romance: Women, Patriarchy and Popular Literature*, London: Verso.

Review of Contemporary Fiction, 11.3, Fall 1991, Special issue on Puig.

Rivera, J.E. ([1924] 1998) *La vorágine*, Mexico City: Porrúa.

Román, D. and Sandoval, A. (1997) 'Latinidad, AIDS, and Allegory in *Kiss of the Spider Woman, The Musical*', in C.F. Delgado and J.E. Muñoz (eds), *Everynight Life: Culture and Dance in Latino/a America*, Durham, NC: Duke University Press, pp.255–87.

Sosnowski, S. (1977) 'Entrevista a Puig', *Hispanamérica*, 3, pp.69–80.

Tittler, J. (1992) *Manuel Puig*, New York: Twayne.

Further reading

If you have enjoyed this novel and wish to explore Latin American fiction further, you may like to begin with Puig's other novels and then some of the following (readily available English translations only are given, though all were initially published in Spanish).

Borges, J.L. (2000) *Labyrinths*, trans. by J.E. Irby and D.A. Yates, Penguin Modern Classics, Harmondsworth: Penguin.

Cabrera Infante, G. (1990) *Three Trapped Tigers*, trans. by D. Gardner and S.J. Levine with the author, London: Faber & Faber.

Carpentier, A. (1991) *The Lost Steps*, trans. by H. de Onís, London: Minerva.

Castellanos, R. (1992) *The Book of Lamentations*, trans. by E. Allen, Penguin Twentieth-Century Classics, Harmondsworth: Penguin.

Donoso, J. (1982) *The Obscene Bird of Night*, trans. by H. St. Martin and L. Mades, Boston: David R. Goldine.

Fuentes, C. (1968) *A Change of Skin*, trans. by S. Hileman, London: Cape.

García Marquez, G. (2000) *One Hundred Years of Solitude*, trans. by G. Rabassa, Essential Penguins, Harmondsworth: Penguin.

PART 2

Judging literature

Introduction to Part 2

DAVID JOHNSON

One of the pleasures of reading or watching literary works is the activity of passing judgement on them. Whether we prefer J.K. Rowling's Harry Potter books to Philip Pullman's trilogy *His Dark Materials*, or enjoy Shakespeare's *Twelfth Night* more than his *Richard III*, at some level we make judgements on the literary works we encounter. Sometimes, we do not own up to our judgements (as, for example, in cases of the 'guilty pleasures' of popular fiction discussed in Part 1), but most of the time we test our own judgements against those of other readers, audiences, reviewers or critics. Confronted with more persuasive judgements, we might change our initial assessments of certain literary works, and at times we might even strategically parrot the judgements of more authoritative readers (such as lecturers or tutors), while secretly sticking to our original likes or dislikes. But in all these cases, the activity of judging literature involves both a personal assessment by the individual literature-lover, and, in most cases, an on-going social exchange in some form of conversation or debate. Social institutions that enable the judging of literature include book clubs, the reviews and letters pages of newspapers and journals, the education system (where the judgements of education boards or teachers precede the setting of literary works) and the committees of literary prizes.

In Part 2, you will consider the literary, aesthetic, political and economic issues involved in judging literature. The discussion of these issues is anchored in case studies of two major institutions dedicated to publicly judging literature: the Nobel Prize for Literature and the Booker Prize for Fiction. The Nobel Prize is awarded to the writer 'who shall have produced in the field of literature the most outstanding work in an ideal direction' and the Booker Prize is awarded to the 'best work of fiction by a British or Commonwealth writer'. In this part you will consider the debates that these deceptively simple criteria for judging literature have generated and focus in particular on four literary texts that have been judged by the committees for these two literary prizes.

In Chapter 5, Suman Gupta introduces the Nobel Prize for Literature in more detail, and discusses 1969 Nobel Prize-winner Samuel Beckett's play *Waiting for Godot*. Discussion of the Nobel Prize continues in Chapter 6, where Richard Danson Brown analyses the poetry of the 1995 Nobel Prize-winner Seamus Heaney. The focus shifts in Chapter 7 to the Booker Prize, which Susheila Nasta introduces in more detail before moving on to discuss the 1994 Booker finalist, *Paradise* by Abdulrazak Gurnah. In the final chapter, Lynda Prescott continues the discussion of the Booker Prize, and focuses on the winner of the 1995 Booker Prize, Pat Barker's *The Ghost Road*.

The activity of judging literature is prominent in the case of literary prizes such as the Nobel and the Booker, where an accredited panel of judges declares one writer or literary work superior to all competitors, but the ubiquity of literary judgements in all contexts should be registered. In the first part of this book, for example, you encountered literary judgements in the form of the distinction between high/elite/minority literature on the one hand, and low/popular/mass literature on the other. Are literary works that are appreciated by an educated elite superior to those consumed by a mass audience? How we judge the literary works discussed in Part 2 is ultimately determined by how we weigh both these and many other criteria. Literary works judged superior by influential critics, or by mass audiences, have been added to the literary canon. Anton Chekhov's *The Cherry Orchard* (1904), T.S. Eliot's *Prufrock and Other Observations* (1917) and Daphne du Maurier's *Rebecca* (1938) now appear as natural features of British cultural landscape, whereas others – for example *Labyrinths with Path of Thunder* (1971) by the Nigerian poet Christopher Okigbo – have for a variety of reasons been judged less positively, and occupy a more peripheral status. As we focus on the last decades of the twentieth century, we are ourselves active participants in the process of judging literature, and by extension, canon-formation. Both the Nobel and Booker Prizes in their acts of judgement canonize certain authors and works of literature, and on a much more modest scale, the chapters of Part 2 endorse their positive judgements of Beckett, Heaney, Gurnah and Barker by adding their works to our list of set texts.

Before I discuss the activity of judging literature in the chapters to follow, it will help to establish working definitions of three familiar words that recur throughout Part 2.

- **Taste.** The primary meaning of 'taste' as a physical sense has been in use in English since the thirteenth century, but its specific association with matters of art and literature occurred only in the eighteenth century. In the philosophical writings of, among others, Lord Shaftesbury and Edmund Burke, 'taste' was defined as discrimination in the judging of art and literature, and in popular usage 'taste' was taken to be 'a generalized polite attribute associated ... with the notion of *Rules*, and elsewhere, with *Manners*' (Williams, 1983, p.314). It was therefore a prerequisite for producing 'tasteful' works of literature or art that the prescribed rules of art be observed. At the close of the eighteenth century, the Romantics rejected 'taste' as profoundly limited, and insisted instead that original works of literature or art *exceed* or *disrupt* the conventional standards of 'good taste'. In the twentieth century, the notion of 'taste' has been tied to the idea of consumption, so that literary appreciation is increasingly expressed in the vocabulary of consumers choosing products according to their tastes.

- **Aesthetic.** Despite its Greek form, the word 'aesthetic' came into English from the German, where it had been introduced by Alexander Baumgarten in his works *Reflections on Poetry* (1735) and *Aesthetica* (1750–8). Baumgarten distinguished two meanings of 'aesthetic': (1) the science of how knowledge is apprehended through the senses, and (2) the philosophical critique of judgement in art. Subsequent eighteenth-century German philosophers, notably Johann Christoph Gottsched and Johann Gottfried Herder, attempted to integrate these two meanings of 'aesthetic' in their competing theories of how beauty might be judged through the apprehension of the senses. This eighteenth-century German tradition culminated in the writings of Immanuel Kant, who in his influential *Critique of Judgment* (1790) focused on the second meaning of aesthetic as 'a critique of taste', and established a sophisticated model of adjudication. The twentieth-century meaning of 'aesthetic' insists on the central role of philosophy in judging literature.

- **Canon.** Originally referring to the books of holy scripture authorized as authentic by religious leaders, in the context of the study of literature 'the canon' refers to those literary works judged to be worthy of academic study. In the final quarter of the twentieth century, much critical energy was directed towards understanding how certain literary works became canonical (for example, those of Shakespeare), and how others were excluded from the canon (for example, those of Aphra Behn). As a result of this kind of research, the literary canon has itself been transformed, with the (formerly) non-canonical at times acquiring a greater cachet than the canonical. Debates about canon-formation – another form of judging literature – are of course not restricted to literary works of the past; differences of opinion over which current works will in time be canonized divide readers of all kinds, from members of the reading public, to students and teachers, to members of literary prize committees.

Writers and critics from Plato to the poststructuralists have expressed strong and divergent views on what judging literature involves. At the beginning of the twenty-first century there has been a flood of publications on aesthetics, particularly anthologies – Alan Singer and Allen Dunn's *Literary Aesthetics: A Reader* (2000), Clive Cazeaux's *The Continental Aesthetics Reader* (2000), Richard Kearney and David Rasmussen's *Continental Aesthetics: Romanticism to Postmodernism* (2001) and Berys Gaut and Dominic McIver Lopes's *The Routledge Companion to Aesthetics* (2001), to name but four – and they all attest to the scale and complexity of the debates over the judging of literature, and of art more generally. Selecting thinkers and arguments from such a plethora of learned opinion is inevitably somewhat arbitrary, and in what follows I try to do no more than highlight key concerns. The following subsections discuss four extracts, each of which puts forward different ideas about judging literature. The first extract is from Immanuel Kant's eighteenth-century treatise the *Critique of Judgment*, and the other three extracts are from the late twentieth century, from the period when our set literary texts were published and judged.

Read through the following subsections, and study each of the four extracts carefully. Note down the ideas and the problems raised in each passage about how literature should be judged.

Immanuel Kant

Kant's *Critique of Judgment* (1790) is the third work in his critical trilogy, and followed his examination of theoretical philosophy in *Critique of Pure Reason* (1781, rev. 1787), and of practical philosophy in *Critique of Practical Reason* (1788). The *Critique of Judgment* in fact comprises two critiques – the first examining the aesthetic judgement of taste, and the second looking at teleological judgement – but it has been acclaimed principally as the founding text of modern aesthetics, studied in isolation from other branches of philosophy. The *Critique of Judgment* remains 'arguably the text that has most consistently informed and sustained debates about artistic taste and aesthetic value over the last two hundred years' (Singer and Dunn, 2000, p.103). Kant's definition of 'genius' provides one important key to how he believes literature ought to be judged:

> Genius is the talent (natural endowment) that gives the rule to art ... What this shows is the following: (1) Genius is a *talent* for producing something for which no determinate rule can be given, not a predisposition consisting of a skill for something that can be learned by following some rule or other; hence the foremost property of genius must be *originality*. (2) Since nonsense too can be original, the products of genius must also be models, i.e. they must be *exemplary*; hence, though they do not themselves arise through imitation, still they must serve others for this, i.e. as a standard or rule by which to judge.

> (Kant, [1790] 1987, pp.174–5)

For Kant, the two fundamental qualities of a work of genius (including literary works) are therefore that: (1) it must be original and (2) it must be exemplary. Both these requirements require elaboration. First, Kant insists that a literary work of genius does not follow extant, pre-given rules; rather, a work of genius creates or invents its own rules of judgement, and these rules are discovered in the experience of apprehending the work. Secondly, a work of genius must serve as a model for other works by functioning as a standard or rule. Crucially, the model 'cannot be couched in a formula or serve as a precept ... [r]ather, the rule must be abstracted from what the artist has done, i.e. from the product' (Kant, 1987, p.177). Can Kant's rules for identifying works of genius serve as a guide to judging the literature of the late twentieth century? Attempting a crude paraphrase, a neo-Kantian might advise the Nobel or Booker judges as follows: derive your standards for judging literary works from the works themselves rather than by following extant rules of literary judgement; look to exemplary works of genius for guidance in judging the work before you; treat such works as models, and never reduce them to a list of determinate rules, formulae or precepts.

Kant's complex and controversial ideas in the *Critique of Judgment* are notoriously resistant to brief summary, and his work on aesthetics is perhaps best read as an extended reflection on the difficulties involved in judging literature. Nonetheless, simplified versions of his ideas on genius were taken up with great enthusiasm by the Romantic movement in Germany, and indeed in the rest of Europe. As these borrowed ideas have proved if anything more influential than Kant's own carefully qualified formulations, this Romantic understanding of literature should be noted. Key terms used by Kant – 'aesthetic', 'genius', 'imagination', 'art', 'universal', 'disinterested' – were appropriated by figures such as Johann Wolfgang von Goethe and Samuel Taylor Coleridge, and reworked into an understanding of judging literature that was built on a combination of the following assumptions: (1) aesthetics is entirely separate from other forms of knowledge (philosophy, history); (2) the poet/artist/genius has unique insight and expresses truths inaccessible to others; (3) the imagination is the faculty (highly developed in the poet/artist/genius) that enables and elevates literature; (4) literature should be judged on its own terms, and with no reference to extra-literary criteria; and (5) judging literature in this way produces judgements that are disinterested and universal. These assumptions have frequently been challenged – G.W.F. Hegel, for example, challenged the ahistorical universalism of the followers of Kant, asking: 'if we look at the works of art of those extra-European peoples ... which their fancy has originated as venerable and sublime, they may appear to us as the most gruesome idols, and their music might sound to our ears as the most horrible noise; while they, on their side, will regard our sculptures, paintings and musical productions as trivial or ugly' (Hegel, [1820–1] 1993, pp.49–50). Nonetheless, the Romantic position on judging literature has proved remarkably resilient, and it continues to provide the necessary philosophical base for the institutions and procedures of literary prizes.

Pierre Bourdieu

Bourdieu was a French sociologist who undertook a number of studies into how people's taste is socially determined and exercised. For example, in 1967–8, he and his researchers selected 1,217 respondents, categorized them in terms of their education and social origins, and interviewed them about their likes and dislikes in painting, music and literature. In one exercise, the respondents were played three pieces of music – *The Well-Tempered Clavier* by Johann Sebastian Bach, George Gershwin's *Rhapsody in Blue* and the *Blue Danube* waltz by Johann Strauss – and asked to rank them in order of personal preference. The results revealed a remarkably close correlation between education/class origins and musical tastes: 3 per cent of manual workers as opposed to 33 per cent of higher education teachers favoured *The Well-Tempered Clavier*, whereas 50 per cent of manual workers as opposed to 0 per cent of higher education teachers favoured the *Blue Danube*. In his book *Distinction: A Social Critique of the Judgement of Taste* (1979), on the basis of many such research studies, Bourdieu drew the following general conclusion:

> scientific observation shows that cultural needs are the product of upbringing and education: surveys establish that all cultural practices (museum visits, concert-going, reading, etc.), and preferences in literature, painting or music, are closely linked to educational level (measured by qualifications or length of schooling) and secondarily to social origin ... To the socially recognized hierarchy of the arts, and within each of them, of genres, schools or periods, corresponds a social hierarchy of the consumers. This predisposes markers of tastes to function as markers of 'class'.
>
> (Bourdieu, [1979] 1984, p.1)

In *Distinction*, Bourdieu develops a critical vocabulary to describe how questions of taste are ultimately tied to economic and social structures, with education particularly influential in determining taste. France's ruling classes not only have economic capital, which is produced and sustained by the labour of workers; they also have 'cultural capital' (Bourdieu, 1984, p.12), which enables them to universalize and naturalize their own aesthetic preferences at the expense of the working classes and their cultural preferences. Bourdieu shifts to a religious metaphor to describe how the ruling classes secure their taste in society: they 'consecrate the cultural élite' (*ibid.*, p.25), who make aesthetic judgements on their behalf. From this brief summary, it should be clear that Bourdieu is hostile towards Kantian ideas of disinterested or universal models of aesthetic judgement; as a consequence, his attitude towards the Nobel or Booker Prizes might be surmised with some confidence. Briefly, Bourdieu might characterize literary prizes as symbolic rituals performed by consecrated judges predisposed to enshrining literary works that endorse the aesthetic tastes of the ruling classes, and at the same time exclude literary works favoured by the working classes.

Christine Battersby

Battersby writes as a late twentieth-century feminist philosopher engaging with the tradition of aesthetics elaborated by Kant. Her work is self-consciously polemical, as it identifies the gender biases in the Romantic tradition of judging literature, in particular the masculine bias in the concept of 'genius'. In *Gender and Genius: Towards a Feminist Aesthetics* (1989), she states:

> Henry Miller, D.H. Lawrence, Rousseau and Schopenhauer remain 'geniuses' – or in more fashionably euphemistic terms, 'great innovative writers' – despite the narrowness of their sexual vision.
>
> (Battersby, 1989, p.180)

Reflecting later on the prospects for a feminist aesthetics, Battersby argues further:

> [Feminists] lack most of the basic historical scholarship that would reveal gender bias in the history of our aesthetic vocabulary. Terms like 'universal', 'rational', 'abstract', 'form', 'structure', 'matter', 'organic', 'natural', 'functional', 'imaginative', 'beautiful', 'sublime' are commonly used in art criticism; but all require a feminist analysis of the type that I have elsewhere supplied for 'genius' ... Feminist aesthetics must fracture the ideal of one universal, historically-timeless canon of 'great art' discoverable by any 'disinterested' observer ... and must also resist the rhetoric of one universally constant, unchanging 'feminine essence' governing art by women. But holding these resistances in tandem is not contradictory.
>
> (Battersby, 1991, p.42)

Battersby notes in the first instance that designated geniuses – or 'great innovative writers' such as Lawrence – remain in the pantheon of geniuses despite the 'narrowness of their sexual vision'. Their continued presence in the line-up of geniuses is because the positive categories of western aesthetic appreciation – not only 'genius', but also many other terms – have historically been inscribed in western culture as masculine. The judging of art and literature in these terms therefore has an inevitable masculine bias, and the challenge, according to Battersby, is to develop a feminist aesthetics that fractures this inherited vocabulary and tradition. Battersby adds a crucial proviso: any such feminist aesthetic must refuse the view that there exists a 'feminine essence' governing art by women. In other words, feminist philosophers should interrogate (1) the masculine bias in the western aesthetic tradition, and (2) the idea that there is a feminine essence characterizing art by women. It is worth noting that Battersby's hostility towards Romantic aesthetics is qualified: she recommends sustained engagement ('historical scholarship') with the received terms of aesthetic judgement; this suggests that she does not see aesthetic judgement as terminally contaminated by masculine bias, and as a consequence unsalvageable for feminist political culture. Rather, despite its history, the activity of judging literature (with its long-entrenched masculine bias) can be reconceptualized along different political lines. Applying Battersby's objections to the Nobel and Booker Prizes, Battersby's advice to Nobel and Booker judges seeking guidance on criteria for judging literature might be along the following lines: historically, masculine values have been inscribed in the neo-Kantian aesthetic vocabulary of 'genius', 'imagination' and so on, and in judging literature by these standards, implicit masculine criteria have long prevailed. However, with self-conscious scholarship and criticism, alternative criteria that recognize and correct this long-entrenched bias might be forged, and might ultimately produce a more inclusive aesthetic.

Chidi Amuta

Amuta writes as a late twentieth-century African literary theorist confronted, on the one hand, by the western tradition of aesthetics that has universalized its own criteria for judging literature and in the process denigrated African literature, and on the other hand, by an African aesthetic tradition premised on an essential, undifferentiated African identity and experience. In *The Theory of African Literature* (1989) he rejects both traditions in the following terms:

> Characteristically, the answer to this question [as to whose values should inform the evaluation of African literature] has been formulated in terms of a simplistic polarization between African and Western values with the obvious conclusion that African values should inform the evaluation of African literature ... [However, i]n most African societies, we can distinguish at least three levels of aesthetic perception and valuation. These are the aesthetics of the rural peasantry, of the urban poor and of the bourgeoisie (both urban and rural). In this formation ... the aesthetics of the bourgeois elite, who also furnish the ruling class, has acquired a hegemonistic status. The artistic appetite and standards of this class are conditioned and dictated from the familiar New York–Paris–London axis. The literary intelligentsia belongs to this class also, and accordingly derives its standards of aesthetic valuation from Western 'high' literary culture which it proceeds to use its *power* to enthrone into an African aesthetic ... Thus, to insist on a monolithic and undifferentiated African

aesthetic in literature is the height of bourgeois arrogance, for it neglects and negates the heterogeneity and complexity of the African cultural universe.

(Amuta, 1989, pp.120–1)

Amuta notes that it has become a truism to argue that western standards of literary judgement are relative, and that African literature should therefore be evaluated in terms of African values. He maintains, however, that such a generous-sounding formulation is limited, as it fails to register the complexity of African societies. Amuta identifies three distinct African aesthetics – those of the rural peasantry, of the urban poor, and of the rural and urban bourgeoisie – but contends that the aesthetic of the 'bourgeois elite' within 'the ruling class' dominates and effectively effaces all other competing African aesthetics. Further, this ruling-class 'African aesthetic' is fatally contaminated by being influenced by, indeed derived from, the western aesthetic of the literary intelligentsia along the 'New York–Paris–London axis'. In a similar spirit to Battersby, Amuta thus renounces the neo-Kantian possibility of a universal, objective, exclusively literary standard of judgement, and proposes an alternative aesthetic that insists on the heterogeneity of literary production, reception and evaluation. What advice might Amuta give on criteria for judging literature? It is clear that Amuta would reject any set of criteria derived from singular works of literary genius, whether western or African in origin. Instead, he would direct critical attention to the 'complexity of the African cultural universe', and seek criteria in the economic, political and cultural contexts that frame all literary production. In specifically African contexts, the massively unequal power relations between the West and Africa must be registered not only in economic and political terms, but also in terms of literary judgement. Both the Nobel and Booker Prizes are of course based in the West, and constitute their terms of literary judgement accordingly. Does Amuta's idea of multiple African aesthetics derail these western criteria? You will return to this question in discussions of the Booker, and the problems involved in judging postcolonial novels such as Gurnah's *Paradise*, both in the West and beyond.

The writers I have briefly discussed here are but four of many philosophers and critics who have grappled with the difficulties involved in judging literature; in Part 2 the chapter authors will try to relate the ideas of these writers to the Nobel and Booker Prizes and to the four set texts. Note that there is no simple progression in ideas from Kant to Amuta; all four extracts represent plausible approaches to judging literature that in their different ways are sophisticated, provocative and deserving of serious consideration.

As you turn to the first chapter, on the Nobel Prize and Beckett, bear in mind the following questions.

- Think back to the discussion of Kant and his Romantic successors, and give some thought to their argument that works of literary genius generate their own rules of judgement, and should never be valued in terms of extant, pre-given rules. As you read each of the four texts in Part 2, does this approach strike you as adequate? **Can literary works be judged on their own terms, according to exclusively literary criteria?** The Nobel and Booker Prize committees claim to proceed – at least at the level of official discourse – as if literary considerations are the only ones they bring to bear in selecting their winners. **Do you find their claims convincing?**

- In the closing decades of the twentieth century, philosophers and critics argued that the disinterested judgement of literature in the Romantic fashion is misconstrued because all such aesthetic judgements are inevitably skewed by class bias (Bourdieu), masculinist bias (Battersby) or Eurocentric bias (Amuta). **What weight and significance should we attach to such biases in the judging of literature?**

- In particular, do you find convincing the arguments of Battersby and Amuta about the unarticulated sexist and racist biases in the dominant western forms and practices of judging literature? If you *do* find their arguments convincing, what is the appropriate response? **Should alternative criteria be laid down for judging women's literature and African literature?** Should literary prizes rewarding appropriate literary works be established (like the Orange Prize for women's fiction, and the Caine Prize for African short stories)? Or do such separatist strategies consign women's writing or African writing to a literary ghetto?

- **Finally, what is the relationship between judging literature and the institutions of publishing, the education system and the wider political culture?** How do these various contextual considerations affect the adjudication of the Nobel and Booker Prizes?

These are difficult questions that are often suppressed when we think about literature. You are invited now, however, to give them your careful attention.

References

Amuta, C. (1989) *The Theory of African Literature*, London: Zed.

Battersby, C. (1989) *Gender and Genius: Towards a Feminist Aesthetics*, London: The Women's Press.

Battersby, C. (1991) 'Situating the Aesthetic: A Feminist Defence', in A. Benjamin and P. Osborne (eds), *Thinking Art: Beyond Traditional Aesthetics*, London: ICA, pp.31–43.

Bourdieu, P. ([1979] 1984) *Distinction: A Social Critique of the Judgement of Taste*, trans. by R. Nice, London: Routledge.

Cazeaux, C. (ed.) (2000) *The Continental Aesthetics Reader*, London: Routledge.

Gaut, B. and Lopes, D.M. (eds) (2001) *The Routledge Companion to Aesthetics*, London: Routledge.

Hegel, G.W.F. ([1820–1] 1993) *Introductory Lectures on Aesthetics*, trans. by B. Bosanquet, Harmondsworth: Penguin.

Kant, I. ([1790] 1987) *Critique of Judgment*, trans. by W.S. Pluhar, Indianapolis: Hackett.

Kearney, R. and Rasmussen, D. (eds) (2001) *Continental Aesthetics: Romanticism to Postmodernism*, Oxford: Blackwell.

Singer, A. and Dunn, A. (eds) (2000) *Literary Aesthetics: A Reader*, Oxford: Blackwell.

Williams, R. (1983) *Keywords: A Vocabulary of Culture and Society*, London: Fontana.

CHAPTER 5

Samuel Beckett, *Waiting for Godot*

SUMAN GUPTA

Overview

In the first section of this chapter, I examine the criteria on the basis of which the Nobel Prize in Literature is awarded, and attempt to understand Samuel Beckett's reputation in terms of these criteria. The relationships between some of the texts and performances of *Waiting for Godot* are considered in the second section, and this is followed by a section called 'Technical nuances', in which I offer a close analysis of both the text and its performance. In the two subsequent sections, I outline the interpretations and debates through which *Waiting for Godot* acquired its reputation as a particularly 'open' play that arises out of, but transcends, specific contexts. In the final section, I briefly assess the international impact of Beckett's work in terms of the more recent examples of *Waiting for Godot* in performance, and thus return to the issue of Beckett's reputation and the criteria governing the award of the Nobel Prize raised in the first section.

The Nobel Prize in Literature

In his will of 27 November 1895, Alfred Nobel stipulated that one part of a prize fund to be set up from capital realized from his estate should go every year to 'the person who shall have produced in the field of literature the most outstanding work in an ideal direction' (Nobel, 1895). He made it a condition that 'in awarding the prizes no consideration whatever shall be given to the nationality of the candidates, but that the most worthy shall receive the prize, whether he be a Scandinavian or not' (*ibid.*). In the history of the Nobel Prize in Literature a frequent concern has been the matter of how the term 'ideal' (*idealisk* in the original Swedish) has been interpreted in different periods. The problem of interpretation arose as early as the first award of the prize, to Sully Prudhomme, in 1901. In his 'Addresses to the Swedish Nation' (1910), the playwright August Strindberg objected to the prize having been awarded to Prudhomme, on the grounds that his writing was 'idealistic', rather than demonstrating 'an ideal direction' (a speculative discussion of what Strindberg might have meant by this distinction is available in Allén, 1997). Doubts about the meaning and nuances of 'an ideal direction' have persisted, and the terms of Nobel's will have consequently been adapted as necessary throughout the twentieth century, with different criteria used at different periods. In a survey of the Nobel Prize, Kjell Espmark (1999) discerns the following phases: from 1901 to 1912, prizes were given to writers who demonstrated 'a lofty and sound idealism'; from 1912 to 1920, a 'literary policy of [political] neutrality' was followed; in the 1920s, award-winners were marked as possessing a classical 'great style'; in the 1930s, 'universal interest' was considered key; from 1946 to 1977, writers were chosen who had made a 'pioneering' contribution; from 1978 to 1985, attention was given to 'unknown masters'; from 1986 onwards, the emphasis has been on recognizing the literary productions of the 'whole world'. Despite apparent ambiguities and inequities, Espmark (1986) maintains that, in its selection procedures for and deliberations about the award, the Swedish Academy, as executor of Nobel's will, has at all times striven to be true to its spirit.

The Nobel Prize is now widely regarded as giving a stamp of *universal* literary value that is untainted by commercial considerations or insular social or political affiliations. The prize is also understood as according this recognition not to a specific text (as do most other literary prizes around the world) but to a body of texts, and thereby emphatically to the *author* of the texts. Underlying the Nobel Prize is an uncomplicated understanding of the author as the source of a body of works and as the person responsible for its effects.

However, a closer look at the history of the Nobel Prize in Literature clouds the universalist evaluations that the award-makers, with whatever emphasis, have apparently sincerely followed. Of the fifty-nine Literature Nobel Laureates between 1901 and 1964 – I will explain in a moment why I stop at 1964 – all were awarded the prize for their writings in European languages. A prize was awarded to the Indian poet Rabindranath Tagore in 1913 and to the Chilean poet Gabriela Mistral in 1945. Apart from these, all the other recipients were from Europe or the USA (six up to 1964), and twelve were from Scandinavian countries. Between 1945 and 1964, only one prize was awarded across the great ideological divide of the cold war – to the Soviet writer Boris Pasternak in 1958. However, the award was politically controversial, and Pasternak was compelled by the Soviet authorities to reject it. The Russian emigré Ivan Bunin was awarded the prize in 1933, but on the understanding that he was a 'stateless domicile in France'. Indeed, the exceptions to the tacit European/US domination of the award until 1964 are in fact not very exceptional. As an Indian, Tagore was, naturally, a subject of the British Empire. He was and is revered in India for his substantial body of works in the Bengali language – a corpus that encompasses poetry, drama, fiction and criticism – and for his paintings. He had himself translated some of his poetry and prose into English. He was given the prize for making his 'poetic thought, expressed in his own English words, a part of the literature of the West'. In the presentation speech by Harald Hjärne, chairman of the Nobel Committee at the time, it was explained that Tagore's translations of his work had:

> made them accessible to all in England, America, and the entire Western world for whom noble literature is of interest and moment. Quite independently of any knowledge of his Bengali poetry, irrespective, too, of differences of religious faiths, literary schools, or party aims, Tagore has been hailed from various quarters as a new and admirable master of that poetic art which has been a never-failing concomitant of the expansion of British civilization ever since the days of Queen Elizabeth.
>
> (Hjärne, 1913)

It was also made clear that: 'The true inwardness of this work is most clearly and purely revealed in the efforts exerted in the Christian mission-field throughout the world' (Hjärne, 1913). Indeed, much of the presentation speech was about the Christian mission. The Chilean Nobel Laureate of 1945, Gabriela Mistral, had the advantage of writing in French, and had close contact with the USA and Europe (she had been Chilean consul to Naples, Madrid and Lisbon). Similarly, the only Greek Nobel Laureate before 1964, Giorgos Seferis (1963), also had a distinguished career as a diplomat, which culminated in his serving as Greek ambassador to the UK between 1957 and 1961.

In 1964, the French philosopher, novelist and playwright Jean-Paul Sartre voluntarily declined the Nobel Prize. On becoming aware that the Swedish Academy intended to award it to him, Sartre wrote on 14 October that he would have to decline it 'pour des raisons qui me sont personelles et pour d'autres qui sont plus objectives' ('for reasons that are both personal and more objective'; quoted in Brochier, 1995, p.40). The decision of the Swedish Academy was, however, irrevocable; the prize had been awarded for Sartre's work, 'which, rich in ideas and filled with the spirit of freedom and the quest for truth, has exerted a far-reaching influence on our age' (Swedish Academy, 1964) and, in the Academy's view, his refusal had no effect on the validity of the award. In a press statement published in *Le Figaro* on 23 October 1964, Sartre explained his reasons further. His main personal reason was his belief that a writer with political convictions should not seek institutional sanction, or allow himself to be identified with a particular institution. He pointed out that, in the same spirit, he had already refused the Légion d'honneur and membership of the Collège de France, and would also refuse the Lenin Prize from the Soviet Union were it offered him. The freedom that Sartre claimed for himself and other intellectuals is explained at greater length in a series of lectures he gave in Kyoto, Japan in 1965 – published in 1972 as *Plaidoyer pour les intellectuals* ('A Plea for Intellectuals';

Sartre, 1974). Among Sartre's objective reasons he cited the ideologically partisan nature of the Nobel Prize in Literature. His own convictions were socialist, and he regarded the award as guided by a capitalist western bloc ideology. He complained that the prize had never been awarded to those supporting decolonization, observing that, had he been awarded the prize at a time when he was championing the cause of Algerian guerrilla independence fighters, he might have viewed it differently. However, it was awarded to him only after the independence movement had run its course. He regretted that the prize had been awarded to the dissident Pasternak but not to Mikhail Sholokov, who enjoyed (despite occasional hitches) the official approval of the Soviet authorities. He noted that the communist South American (Chilean, to be precise) poet Pablo Neruda and the communist French writer Louis Aragon had not yet received the award. (The complete statement is available in Brochier, 1995, pp.41–5.)

Sartre's rejection and criticism of the Nobel Prize effectively undermined its reputation for recognizing universal value. Generally, historians of the prize (notably Espmark, 1986) choose to play down the embarrassing matter of Sartre's rejection. But it seems reasonably clear that the rejection did have an impact, for after 1964 the character of the prize distinctly changed. In 1965, Sholokov received the award; in 1966, it was shared by Nelly Sachs and, more importantly, the Israeli writer Samuel Agnon, who wrote in Hebrew (thus making him the first Nobel Laureate writing in a non-European language to receive the prize); in 1967, it went to the Guatemalan novelist Miguel Ángel Asturias (who had received the Lenin Prize in 1966), for being 'deep-rooted in the national traits and traditions of Indian peoples of Latin America' (Swedish Academy, 1967); and in 1968, it was given to the Japanese novelist Yasunari Kawabata for his work in Japanese. It is quite possible that this sudden opening up of the prize to the larger world, and to non-western ideologies, cultures and languages, had something to do with Sartre's refusal and criticisms of the award.

In 1969, the Nobel Prize came back to the West – it was awarded to Samuel Beckett. Beckett was a most uncontroversial choice. As an Irishman who lived in Paris and wrote in French and English, he was squarely located in Europe, but he and his work seemed simultaneously to transcend both that location and any narrow political consideration. It was this quality that in some sense, and at a tricky moment, both made Beckett the ideal Nobel Laureate and reaffirmed the reputation of the award as one that recognizes the universally valuable in a non-partisan manner. To give the prize to Beckett, and have it accepted, could be regarded as a healing of wounds dealt by political controversies, especially since 1964. As it happens, there is a touch of Sartre about Beckett's writing, and a similar air of uncompromising idealism and probity. However, it might be argued that, by accepting the prize, Beckett allowed himself to acquire exactly the kind of institutional sanction that Sartre had wished to avoid. In some sense, Beckett subsequently became associated with the prize, as the Laureate who best embodies the most charitable interpretation of the spirit in which it is given. Some critics have understandably regarded Beckett's career before and after the Nobel Prize as almost distinct phases. Thus, for instance, Carla Locatelli's interesting 1990 book on Beckett's later prose work is described in its title as discussing 'prose works after the Nobel Prize' (though actually it has little direct reference to the implications of Beckett's receiving that award).

Beckett had toyed with the idea of rejecting the Nobel Prize. According to one of his biographers, Anthony Cronin:

> He had frequently discussed the prize with his friends, saying that he would be inclined to refuse the supposed honour as Jean-Paul Sartre had done but that Sartre had to some extent queered the pitch: to do so now would seem to be imitating him. Besides, he told Lindon, Sartre's refusal had been 'inelegant' and at one point he instructed Lindon that if enquiries came from the Swedish Academy he was to intimate that Beckett would prefer not to be offered the prize ... Of course, Beckett was fully aware that the prize was a questionable honour, that it was largely given out on a rotatory basis and often for political reasons.
>
> (Cronin, 1996, pp.543–4)

Beckett was in Tunisia when the prize was announced, and, though he accepted it, he did not go to Stockholm to receive it – his friend and agent, Jerome Lindon, received it on his behalf. Beckett gifted most of the prize money to needy writers (the experimental novelists Djuna Barnes and B.S. Johnson were beneficiaries).

Nevertheless, the award and acceptance of the Nobel Prize undoubtedly consolidated Beckett's image as a writer whose work is both located in specific contexts and yet transcends those contexts. In the presentation speech, Karl Ragnar Gierow of the Swedish Academy identified Beckett as a 'paradoxical' Irishman; clarified that the award was addressed to 'one man, two languages and a third nation, itself divided'; and went on to describe Beckett's work as a 'miserere from all mankind' (Gierow, 1969). The award was given to Beckett 'for his writing, which – in new forms for the novel and drama – in the destitution of modern man acquires its elevation' (Swedish Academy, 1969). The writings that were singled out for particular attention in the speech included *Waiting for Godot* (the others, published in both English and French between 1947 and 1961, were the trilogy of novels, *Molloy, Malone Dies* and *The Unnamable*, the novel *Watt* and the play *Happy Days*). To what extent this evaluation of Beckett's work, which appeared to be consolidated by the Nobel Prize, stands up to close scrutiny will be considered in the remainder of this chapter, with particular reference to *Waiting for Godot*.

Text and performance

Now read *Waiting for Godot* (Beckett, [1955] 2004; all subsequent page references are to this edition). The edition I refer to in this chapter contains the text as used for the first English production of the play at the Arts Theatre, London in 1955, directed by Peter Hall. The play was originally written in French, entitled *En attendant Godot* (literally translated as 'While Waiting for Godot'), in 1949, and first performed in Paris at the Théâtre de Babylone, directed by Roger Blin. The translation into English was done by Beckett himself, and first published by Faber in 1956. The earliest performances were directed with constant input from Beckett, who was very particular about precisely how the play should be translated to the stage. Interestingly, in the 1955 English production directed by Hall, Beckett had permitted the use of extra props – a barrel and a tree stump – which did not exist in the first published French or English versions.

Waiting for Godot makes specific (and at the time pioneering) use of theatrical conventions. In addition to studying the textual content of the play, it is therefore also important to understand how the stage is used in performance. You will therefore find it useful to watch a performance of the play before going further. Seeing the play being performed, whether on stage or screen, reveals theatrical qualities that are not conveyed in the text – much of the humour of the play is physical and visual, for instance. I particularly recommend the film version directed by Michael Lindsay-Hogg (as part of the Beckett on Film project produced by Michael Colgan and Alan Moloney, and first screened in the UK on Channel 4 television on 18 October 2001). There are some interesting differences between the text of the play, in the edition to which I refer in this chapter, and this performance of it. For instance, in the film version the 'mound' in the set is changed into a 'stone', and the stone is specifically mentioned by Vladimir later, though not in the 2004 text. In fact, this film version follows a different performance text, but one that also bears the stamp of Beckett's intervention – indeed, more emphatically so than does the 1955 performance directed by Hall. The film's text is based on the German version of the play, which was performed at the Schiller Theatre, Berlin in 1975 and directed by Beckett himself. (Beckett's performance text with notes has since been published; Beckett, 1993.) The Beckett on Film project in general, and therefore the film, was intended by the producers (at the insistence of the Beckett estate) to convey as precisely as possible the author's own vision of his dramatic work. In an interview in the *New York Times* (11 June 2000), Colgan explained that the Beckett estate specified that 'no cuts, no gender-bending', no 'adaptations or "inspired by" stuff' would be permitted, and that directors 'with the sense of the importance of the text' would be chosen. However, a film camera allows a flexibility of perspective that a theatre audience is unlikely to have. In the film version, for instance, the action is sometimes viewed from above.

Even at this preliminary stage, it is possible to make a few inferences about Beckett's role as author of *Waiting for Godot*. **Does anything strike you as unusual about Beckett's authorship of the play?**

I was struck by the absence of a definitive author-sanctioned text or performance. The text of the play is remarkably fluid, largely because the act of authorship appears to be an on-going process over an extended period of time and through different media. This is demonstrated by the fact that the play was originally written in French, then translated into English by the author, and then altered in the German version, again by the author. Contributing to this fluidity is the fact that Beckett was closely involved with most of the well-known early performances of the play, and yet these are all significantly different from the version that he directed himself and that was later sanctioned by his estate. The confusion is exacerbated by Beckett permitting different texts and performances to be published/recorded at various times. In other words, Beckett took the liberty of exerting his authority as author constantly to modify the text, and to mediate and intervene in performances of the play. This constant modification renders the act of authorship an extended process, different stages of which are visible in different texts and performances. An obvious consequence is that, even in its making, *Waiting for Godot* embraces different contexts (places and times). The play's extended creation process also means that there is an extraordinarily vital relationship between text and performance.

Although you should be aware of the difficulties that may arise as a result of this lack of a definitive author-sanctioned text and performance of the play, you need not worry too much about them. For the purposes of this chapter, you are, somewhat arbitrarily, *given* a specific text to study. By and large, the essential points regarding *Waiting for Godot* can be made with reference to this text, and without detailed reference to differences between the various texts and performances of the play.

Technical nuances

The effect of a play depends to a large extent on how it makes use of certain theatrical conventions. These conventions depend on a shared understanding between the audience and all those concerned with the performance (playwright, director, set-designers, actors, etc.). One such convention, for instance, is that a theatrical performance takes place within a circumscribed space (typically, a stage), to which, given a few hints, the audience is expected to adjust itself. So, with a few simple props and words, the playgoers can be expected to understand that the action is set in a room, or a forest, or on a mountain, or, for that matter, in a playhouse – and perhaps in some country or city at some broadly identifiable period. Another convention is that a play has a fixed duration (typically, two or three hours) in real time, but that by means of some simple artificial devices this duration can be made to represent extended periods, or overlapping periods, or repeated periods, of time. Yet another convention is that the medium of theatre allows for a range of performance styles. These can be markedly artificial (characters may sing instead of speak, wear masks, have exaggerated gestures, be excessively melodramatic or subdued, and so on; abstract ideas such as Time or Everyman may be personified), but the audience must nevertheless temporarily accept them as being somehow meaningful and consistent. These conventions enable a play to be presented to an audience and enable an audience to identify relevant details (in terms of its context) from that presentation.

In brief, we might say that theatrical conventions allow audiences to negotiate between the artificial world of the theatre and the real everyday world. It follows, of course, that theatre works on the basis of having a flexible and engaged audience. The whole business of theatre is complicated further by the fact that, despite numerous efforts, from Aristotle onwards, to fix the conventions of theatre performance/spectatorship, these have been subject to change. Sometimes, theatrical conventions have evolved spontaneously; at other times, they have been deliberately questioned and challenged by playwrights. Interrogation of theatrical conventions in this way is found particularly in the work of twentieth-century playwrights such as Anton Chekhov and Bertolt Brecht. Stylistic techniques such as the apparently diffuse and unstructured naturalistic flow of Chekhov's *The Cherry Orchard* (1904) (which undermines clear ideological interpretations) and the alienation techniques and distancing effects that draw attention to theatrical artifice (and to a conscious ideological agenda) in Brecht's *Life of Galileo* (first written in 1939), both represent challenges to and questionings of theatrical conventions that compel audiences to rethink their approach to theatre. In these examples, and numerous others, the audience is required to make almost instantaneous and radical readjustments in its expectations and therefore in its methods of making sense of a play in terms of (and with reference to) the real world. Naturally, different members of an audience may make sense of a play in vastly different ways, but the point is that this kind of readjustment is necessary for *any* sense to be made at all. Clearly, some resent this demand and some refuse to make the effort – but the success of plays such as those of Chekhov and Brecht demonstrates that on the whole such readjustments and renegotiations of theatrical conventions are possible.

A final observation is worth making in this generalizing, theoretical vein, before I look closely at *Waiting for Godot*. Each questioning of theatrical conventions in a play, and each renegotiation on the part of an audience, throws into relief the medium of the theatre and its assumptions. The process involves not only a straightforward engagement with a specific play (with its particular aesthetic qualities, ideological bent and focus on issues), but also a clarification of what engaging with theatre in general entails. Plays that question theatrical conventions and compel renegotiation and readjustment from the audience are inevitably, therefore, *about* theatre itself to some extent: in them, theatre becomes an issue to be engaged with. Twentieth-century playwrights who have compelled audiences to rethink in this way have done so by creating theatre that is deliberately self-reflective. Brecht's plays are significant examples of such self-reflective work (see, for example, Walder, 2005). Luigi Pirandello's play *Six Characters in Search of an Author* (1921) is another. In this play, Pirandello stages a debate between six conceived but not yet wholly realized characters and their author about the exigencies of characterization in theatre. Beckett's plays, especially *Waiting for Godot*, are undoubtedly – indeed emphatically – of that order.

With these general observations in mind, list some of the features of *Waiting for Godot* that appear to question theatrical conventions – in each case make a note of the conventions in question. I suggest that you break down your answer into the following categories: 'overall structure', 'setting', 'protagonists', 'dialogue' and 'action'.

Some of the features that seem to me to be noteworthy are as follows.

Overall structure

Vivian Mercier aptly described *Waiting for Godot* as a play 'in which nothing happens, *twice*' (1977, p.xii). Structurally, the play's two acts are similar: two tramps who are waiting for someone called Godot by a country road beside a tree spend most of their time talking to each other, meet an odd pair called Lucky and Pozzo towards the middle of the act, and are informed by a boy at the end that Godot will not be able to come. The broadly repetitive quality of the two acts undermines the habitual expectation of any audience that there will be some sort of development or progression (of plot, in characterization, in elaboration of themes, etc.) between the acts. However, this bald statement does not convey the excruciating deliberation with which habitual audience expectations are played with. In detail, of course, there are some promising features that are inserted to tempt the audience to look for development. The tree that was bare in the first act has a few leaves in the second, and an audience (envisage here any first-time group of spectators) is tempted to rub its hands and cleverly infer that some time has passed – time enough for the tree to grow a few leaves and perhaps even shed some. The audience, in other words, falls back on its grasp of theatrical conventions for interpreting props. The reader of the play text is told at the beginning of Act 2 that it is the 'Next day' (p.47). To make sense of the change in the tree, the reader will have to infer that it is a different tree – which is a readerly convention that is equivalent to the theatrical convention of interpreting props. With similar hopefulness an audience might grasp at other straws promising development – has not Pozzo gone blind in the interim and Lucky dumb? Something terrible must have happened to them, something that will help develop these characters further. But these conventional expectations are lightly, fleetingly suggested – only, it appears, to make sure that they are gleefully not met. Unlike the audience, who are initially certain that some time has passed, Vladimir, Estragon and Pozzo seem to struggle with uncertainty about the passage of time (pp.50, 55 and 77). Vladimir and Estragon discuss the tree and are unable to decide whether it is in fact the same tree (p.50). Readers who, from the directions at the beginning of the act, might have supposed it was a different tree, are likely to find themselves immediately contradicted by the specificity of the definite article in '*the* tree'. There is no explanation of why Pozzo is now blind and Lucky dumb:

> POZZO I woke up one fine day as blind as Fortune. (*He pauses*) Sometimes I wonder if I'm not still asleep.
>
> VLADIMIR And when was that?
>
> POZZO I don't know.
>
> VLADIMIR But no later than yesterday —
>
> POZZO (*violently*) Don't question me! The blind have no notion of time. The things of time are hidden from them too.
>
> (p.75)

Estragon and Vladimir also consider the possibility that the boots in Act 2 are those left behind by Estragon in Act 1 (pp.56–7), and Vladimir wonders whether the boy in Act 2 is the same boy as in Act 1 (pp.79–80); in each case there is more than a grain of uncertainty. Each promise of development between the acts dissolves in disappointed expectation. It gradually becomes evident that to some extent what Vladimir and Estragon are doing on stage mirrors what the audience is likely to be doing – *waiting* for something to develop (ultimately, for the appearance of Godot), grasping at straws that seem to mark development only to have them tantalizingly withdrawn.

It is, of course, not strictly true that 'nothing happens'. Plenty of things happen in a literal sense. But here's the rub – a 'happening', for an audience engaging with theatre (and perhaps a person engaging with the world generally), is likely to be marked as happening only in relation to other happenings, within some frame of development or progression (such as a chronological frame, a chain of events, highlights of memory). If that frame is withdrawn, each individual happening simply seems to become unremarkable, almost indistinguishable, almost unmemorable: 'nothing happens' describes a series of unremarkable, almost indistinguishable, almost unmemorable theatrical happenings. In overall structure, *Waiting for Godot* presents two sets of equally unremarkable, almost indistinguishable, almost unmemorable happenings in two very similar acts.

Setting

I have already discussed the main prop, the tree, to show how it is used to undermine conventions for interpreting theatre props. But that is only one of the ways in which it acquires a rather late significance at the beginning of Act 2. In fact, the tree is undeniably significant from the very beginning: it is the *only* noteworthy prop. Only the tree is there to attract Vladimir and Estragon's typically confusing attention:

> ESTRAGON What is it?
>
> VLADIMIR I don't know. A willow.
>
> ESTRAGON Where are the leaves?
>
> VLADIMIR It must be dead.
>
> ESTRAGON No more weeping.
>
> VLADIMIR Or perhaps it's not the season.
>
> ESTRAGON Looks to me more like a bush.
>
> VLADIMIR A shrub.
>
> ESTRAGON A bush.

(p.5)

In anticipation of Act 2, the leaflessness of the tree has been noted. But more than that, the presence of the tree in the desolate landscape draws attention to the bareness of the landscape/stage. The effect of desolation created by the single leafless tree needs to be visualized to be understood, and every production of *Waiting for Godot* has played on this in different ways. In the film version recommended above, the tree appears in the midst of stony rubble.

In the absence of other props, the audience has to try to make the best of the one prop that is there (though any inference made from it is doomed to failure), just as Vladimir and Estragon try to make the best of the few things at their disposal. The emptiness of the set accords an unusual significance to the few things that are there – both for Vladimir and Estragon, and for the audience. The two main characters spend as much time as possible

Figure 5.1 K. Herm, S. Wigger, H. Bollmann, C. Raddatz and Samuel
Beckett during a rehearsal of *Waiting for Godot* at the Schiller Theatre,
Berlin (1975). (Photo: A. Heuer.)

Figure 5.2 Scene from *Waiting for Godot* at the Royal Court Theatre,
London (1965). (Photo: Zoë Dominic, London.)

Figure 5.3 Barry McGovern as Estragon and Tom Hickey as Vladimir in *Waiting for Godot* at the Gate Theatre, Dublin (1988). (Photo: Tom Lawlor.)

Figure 5.4 Samuel Beckett in Alberto Giacometti's studio with the tree designed by the artist for the Paris revival of *Waiting for Godot* (1961). (Photo credited to Georges Pierre.)

Figure 5.5 Pierre Latour, Lucien Raimbourg and Jean Martin in *Waiting for Godot* at the Théâtre de Babylone, Paris (1953), produced by Roger Blin. (© Agence Bernand.)

Figure 5.6 Philippe Faure and Daniel Znyk in *Waiting for Godot* at the Théâtre de Gennevilliers, France (2002), produced by Bernard Sobel. (© Pascal GELY Agence Bernand.)

discussing their boots and hats and, of course, the tree, and the appearances of Pozzo and Lucky or of the boy/boys are veritable windfalls of entertainment ('Vladimir: At last! ... Reinforcements at last!', p.67). Equally, though, by acquiring this kind of significance, the single prop, the few objects for discussion, also reveal their inability to add up to a recognizable scene; they stand out, without becoming a part of something as complete and cohesive as a scene. These are not objects that are *used* to compose a scene; if that were the case, the characters and the audience would probably pay them little attention (just as an audience is unlikely to notice a chair placed on stage with other furniture in a scene depicting a drawing-room). These are objects that are focused on by the characters, and indeed by the audience, because they are there as themselves without becoming part of a scene. Inevitably, an air of desperation attends the attempts by Vladimir and Estragon to get much entertainment out of the tree, the hats, the boots – and therefore an audience's attempt to interpret them in a meaningful way – which simply conveys more starkly than ever that these objects add up to nothing more than themselves.

Protagonists

All the play's protagonists are constrained in different ways. The main characters are inhibited by their ailments. Estragon has something wrong with his feet and suffers from insomnia; Vladimir's bladder is not too good and hurts when he laughs; Pozzo becomes weak and goes blind; Lucky, weak too, suffers from a speech impediment that makes him veer between excessive loquacity and complete silence (he is dumb in Act 2). All, even the boy, suffer from a loss of short-term memory that renders them unable to distinguish between days or exercise the ability to link happenings. The only memories that surface occasionally are either vague (more a sense of familiarity, or déjà vu, than a distinct memory) or remote, fragmented images, ideas and stories from the past (Estragon's recollections of maps of the Holy Land, p.3; Vladimir's recollection of the story of the two thieves, pp.3–4; Estragon's story of the Englishman in the brothel, p.7; Vladimir's song, pp.47–8; Vladimir's recollection of the Macon country, p.51) or compulsively immediate (Estragon's recollection of being beaten and spending the night in the ditch, pp.1, 49; the realization that they are both obliged for some reason to wait for Godot). All the characters are bound to each other (or defined by each other) in different ways. Vladimir and Estragon seem not to be able to leave each other and panic when momentarily parted; a rope connects Lucky and Pozzo in an eternal interdependence; even the boy probably has an identical brother. The bonds that hold them to each other seem to work on a principle of attraction of opposites: Vladimir's optimism and assertiveness are expressed against

Estragon's pessimism and defeatism; Pozzo's masterful vehemence against Lucky's (generally) dumb submissiveness. And the invisible Godot seems unable to appear.

The depiction of constraints or impediments working in/on characters (from the Aristotelian notion of a tragic flaw in an individual character to the societal/ideological barriers that define aspirations in the plays of Chekhov and Brecht) is a familiar theatrical device that most audiences would recognize, though probably with different emphases. Generally, these constraints allow characters to fulfil their parts meaningfully within specific situations – a series of happenings – to highlight the issues, themes, ideas that usually form the substance of plays. An audience may be expected to apply the convention of recognizing constraints in/on theatrical characters with a view to apprehending some larger message or realization. In *Waiting for Godot*, the constraints working in/on characters are simply there – they lead on to no larger realization than that these characters *are* constrained. Their constrainment is a condition rather than an explanation for what happens. The most obvious example in the play is the condition of being constrained by a need to wait for Godot without knowing who or what Godot is and why waiting is necessary. The realization on the part of an audience in relation to this is really no more than the understanding that the characters in the play themselves have about it:

> ESTRAGON (*chewing, swallowing*) I'm asking you if we're tied.
>
> VLADIMIR Tied?
>
> ESTRAGON Ti-ed.
>
> VLADIMIR How do you mean, tied?
>
> ESTRAGON Down.
>
> VLADIMIR But to whom. By whom?
>
> ESTRAGON To your man.
>
> VLADIMIR To Godot? Tied to Godot? What an idea! No question of it. (*He pauses*) For the moment.
>
> ESTRAGON His name is Godot?

(p.12)

Dialogue

Mostly the dialogue consists of quick, sharp exchanges between the protagonists, but even in such exchanges there is a range of rhythms – an aural quality akin to music or poetry.

There are dissonant exchanges:

> ESTRAGON Who?
>
> VLADIMIR What?

ESTRAGON   What's all this about? Abused who?

VLADIMIR   The Saviour.

ESTRAGON   Why?

VLADIMIR   Because he wouldn't save them.

ESTRAGON   From hell?

VLADIMIR   Imbecile! From death.

ESTRAGON   I thought you said hell.

VLADIMIR   From death, from death.

ESTRAGON   Well, what of it?

VLADIMIR   Then the two of them must have been damned.

ESTRAGON   And why not?

VLADIMIR   But one of the four says that one of the two was saved.

ESTRAGON   Well? They don't agree, and that's all there is to it.

(p.4)

The laboured perambulations and misdirections through which Estragon's conclusion is reached is itself, of course, a demonstration of that conclusion: a perfectly natural communication of disagreements and confusions.

There are assonant exchanges:

ESTRAGON   Oh I say.

VLADIMIR   A running sore!

ESTRAGON   It's the rope.

VLADIMIR   It's the rubbing.

ESTRAGON   It's inevitable.

VLADIMIR   It's the knot.

ESTRAGON   It's the chafing.

(pp.17–18)

There are splendidly harmonic exchanges:

ESTRAGON   In the meantime let us try and converse calmly, since we are incapable of keeping silent.

VLADIMIR   You're right, we're inexhaustible.

ESTRAGON   It's so we won't think.

VLADIMIR We have that excuse.

ESTRAGON It's so we won't hear.

VLADIMIR We have our reasons.

ESTRAGON All the dead voices.

VLADIMIR They make a noise like wings.

ESTRAGON Like leaves.

VLADIMIR Like sand.

ESTRAGON Like leaves.

Silence

VLADIMIR They all speak together.

ESTRAGON Each one to itself.

Silence

VLADIMIR Rather they whisper.

ESTRAGON They rustle.

VLADIMIR They murmur.

ESTRAGON They rustle.

(pp.52–3)

The harmony (reminiscent of T.S. Eliot's poem 'The Hollow Men'; 1925) is evidently a demonstration of 'calm' conversation.

And there are purely repetitive exchanges:

ESTRAGON Then adieu.

POZZO Adieu.

VLADIMIR Adieu.

POZZO Adieu.

Silence. No-one moves

VLADIMIR Adieu.

POZZO Adieu.

ESTRAGON Adieu.

Silence

POZZO And thank you.

VLADIMIR Thank *you*.

POZZO Not at all.

ESTRAGON Yes yes.

POZZO No no.

VLADIMIR Yes yes.

ESTRAGON No no.

(pp.38–9)

Usually there is a constant and rapid shift between these and other kinds of rhythm.

I have reproduced these passages here to allow you to focus on their aural qualities, to *listen* to them, without reference to where in the play they appear and why. I will not comment on them specifically, but hope that their aural quality is self-evident. **What impression do passages such as these make on you? What purpose (if anything in the play can be said to have a purpose) does their aural quality serve?**

To me, such passages (and they make up the larger part of the play) convey a sense of the deliberately and ostensibly *performed* air of the play. This sense of the play's progressing via a series of deliberately performed dialogues, or set pieces, is not confined only to the aurally rhythmic passages, but extends to some of the thematically playful passages, such as the convoluted logic games that the characters sometimes indulge in (the whole exchange about the two thieves, pp.3–4; the section about Vladimir and Estragon hanging themselves from the tree, pp.8–9; the discussion about why Lucky holds Pozzo's bags, p.23; the debate as to whether the boots in Act 2 are Estragon's, p.57), or the snappy interrogation–response passages (mainly between Vladimir and the boy/boys, pp.41–4 and pp.79–81). The dialogue does not progress purposefully with relation to situations, developing the characters and the plot around them. Nor does it stick consistently to a characteristically artificial style to which the audience can get accustomed (as, say, in drama in verse or a witty comedy of manners). The dialogue largely goes through a series of set pieces, which are presented in a way that particularly draws attention to their artificial quality. Unsurprisingly, the dialogue in *Waiting for Godot* has often reminded critics of sketches and short dramatic routines in early twentieth-century British music hall or American vaudeville, or 1930s German cabaret.

The audience is made aware of the set quality of much of the dialogue because the characters constantly draw attention to it. Phrases like the following are thrown in between dialogues with increasing frequency: 'Come on, Gogo, return the ball, can't you, once in a way?' (p.4); 'That passed the time' (p.40); 'let us try and converse calmly' (p.52); 'That's the idea, let's contradict each other' (p.53); 'That's the idea, let's ask each other questions' (p.54); 'That wasn't such a bad little canter' (p.54), and so on. In fact, as the play progresses, the set quality of the dialogue grows more and more emphatic because Vladimir and Estragon grow gradually more weary of having to wait, of having to perform, of having to keep the show going; gradually the audience grasps what was the case from the beginning – that the dialogues are designed to dissolve the distinction between actor and character.

The deliberately performed quality is nowhere more evident than in some of the monologues. Pozzo's brief disquisition on the firmament (pp.28–30) begins with a set of commands that turn his companions into a compliant audience: 'A little attention, if you please', 'Look', 'that's enough'; he then goes on to demonstrate a series of contrary modulations between lyrical, prosaic and dramatic until '*His inspiration leaves him*'; he ends by demanding an assessment of his performance: 'How did you find me? ... Good? Fair? Middling? Poor? Positively bad?' Lucky's extraordinary speech (pp.34–6) – of which I will have more to say later – is begun ('Think, pig!', p.33) and finished by demand, while he is positioned precisely (p.34) in relation to his audience. Vladimir's sudden ascendance into a generalization of their condition ('all mankind is us') in Act 2 (pp.68–9) has all the rhetorical flourish of a rousing speech that no-one is convinced by.

Action

Charting the movements of the actors across the stage in a performance of *Waiting for Godot* is a useful exercise. Figure 5.7 is my attempt to do this, using the first five pages of the 1955 performance text (which corresponds to the first five pages of the 2004 text, but includes fuller stage directions). I have tracked only movements left and right. Figure 5.7 clearly shows that even in the relatively tranquil first five pages there is substantial movement – indeed, the whole stage is traversed several times from right to left and back by both characters. The picture can be further complicated by similarly charting the movements backwards and forwards. Add to that, in different sections, the characters looking up and down, constantly sitting and rising, struggling with shoes and playing with hats, gesticulating, rushing off stage, falling down and sometimes staying down, meeting and parting. It is obvious – even if in the flow of the dialogue this might have been obscured – that there is constant and sometimes hectic action on the stage.

Juxtapose all that action on what is essentially an almost bare stage, and you will have some sense of the impression that a performance of the play makes in the theatre. In the absence of significant props (except for the tree) or scenery, these movements acquire a somewhat unusual character. The effect is exacerbated by the absence of any conventional theatrical 'happenings' or plot development. In conventional theatre, the scenery and props, in combination with the exigencies of plot, largely define movement on stage. In *Waiting for Godot*, however, the total effect of the action is to

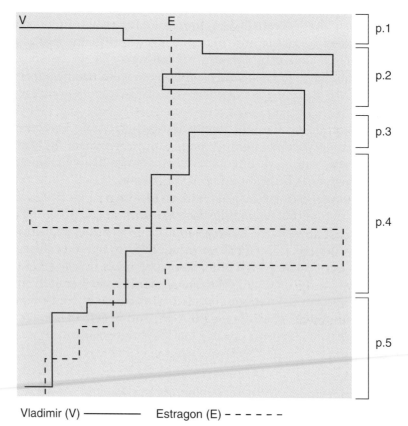

Vladimir (V) —————— Estragon (E) – – – – – –

Figure 5.7   An attempt to track the movements of characters across the stage in the first five pages of the text used for the first English production of *Waiting for Godot* in 1955, directed by Peter Hall (Beckett, [1955] 1957).

establish more emphatically a sense of the circumscribed performance space; a more essential relation appears to be established between the stage and those on it. The 'acted-ness', to coin a word, of particular movements is emphasized with relation to the stage – all the more so because the ailments from which various characters suffer often render these movements visibly painful. Equally, the 'staginess' of the stage with relation to those moving on it is brought out.

To summarize: under the five categories I suggested for your responses to the question, you may have noted down theatrical features of *Waiting for Godot* that coincide with some of those I have discussed. You may also have recalled a general point I made earlier: that in plays where theatrical conventions are questioned and an audience is compelled to readjust or renegotiate its expectations, the nature of theatre itself becomes an issue – that is, such plays are to some extent theatre about theatre. **To what extent**

do you think *Waiting for Godot* is theatre about theatre? In what ways do the theatrical features described above contribute to this view of the play?

I feel reasonably convinced that *Waiting for Godot* is theatre about theatre to a substantial extent. Its questioning of the theatrical conventions familiar to audiences is so persistent and pervasive, and the kinds of renegotiation of expectations that it demands are so unavoidable, that it inevitably opens theatre as a medium to renewed consideration and discussion. But beyond simply challenging conventions, a consistent *turning inwards* is manifest at every level. The play's overall structure undermines the idea of structure itself by rendering redundant the notion of progressive happenings or development; the setting is so minimalistic and so averse to purposeful interpretation that an audience's attention is likely to be drawn to the objects on the stage as merely objects and no more; the protagonists are presented with several layers of constraints operating on/in them in ways that fix them uncomfortably – and inexplicably for the audience – as merely being there; the dialogues are, by and large, suggestive of deliberately pre-prepared set pieces, which are mechanically gone through, and which effectively dissolve the distinction between character and actor; the continuous and hectic action has the effect of laying bare the 'staginess' of the stage and the 'acted-ness' of the movements. At each level, therefore, *Waiting for Godot* seems designedly to obscure the boundary between *being* theatre and *doing* theatre.

You may, though, and perfectly legitimately, think that my focus on the technical nuances of theatre and the conventions of watching plays, at the expense so far of any attempt to discern contextual placements and possible universal relevance, has actually thrown me into a somewhat circular argument. I have determinedly engaged with the play in terms exclusively of its use of the medium of theatre, and so it is hardly surprising that I see the play as being *about* the medium of theatre. This is an argument against which I have no sound defence. Nevertheless, I do feel that the discussion above makes a strong case for regarding *Waiting for Godot* as theatre about theatre. In addition, it provides a serviceable description of the play that can be used to elucidate possible contextually specific or universally applicable interpretations.

I will be focusing on contextual interpretations in the following section. Before I leave this section on technical aspects, however, I would like briefly to discuss one final point: the fact that Beckett first wrote *Waiting for Godot* in French and then translated it into English. Actually, to be precise, the English version should not be thought of as a translation; in none of the published English texts is it described as such, and Beckett probably regarded it as a stand-alone work, since it carried the stamp of his own authorial signature in every respect. This takes us back to the issue of the fluidity of the text and the extended period of authorship involved. It is more accurate to think of Beckett approaching the English text of the play through the French. The question, of course, is why Beckett chose this approach (given that English was his first language, though he was fluent in French), and what impact it might have had on the play.

This question has received some stimulating critical attention (e.g. Batty, 2000; Cockerham, 1975; Cohn, 1967; Kenner, 1970). Clues as to why he chose to approach the play via French are available in some of Beckett's interviews and letters. The following indicative sentiments were expressed in a letter Beckett wrote on 9 July 1937 to a German friend, Axel Kaun, who wished to have letters addressed to him in English but to whom Beckett insistently wrote in German:

> It is indeed becoming more and more difficult, even senseless, for me to write an official English. And more and more my own language appears to me like a veil that must be torn apart in order to get at the things (or the Nothingness) behind it. Grammar and Style. To me they seem to have become as irrelevant as a Victorian bathing suit or the imperturbability of a true gentleman. A mask. Let us hope the time will come, thank God that in certain circles it has already come, when language is most efficiently used where it is being most efficiently misused. As we cannot eliminate language all at once, we should at least leave nothing undone that might contribute to its falling into disrepute. To bore one hole after another in it, until what lurks behind it – be it something or nothing – begins to seep through; I cannot imagine a higher goal for a writer today.
>
> (Beckett, 1983, pp.171–2)

On a similar, and less verbose, note a conversation recalled by Mel Gussow is also suggestive:

> Why did he write *Godot* in French rather than in English?
> 'Because English was too easy. I wanted the discipline.'
>
> (Gussow, 1996, p.32)

It seems likely that Beckett wrote the play first in French *because* it was the language in which he was less comfortable. Arguably, the use of French imposed a certain caution about using words, a certain deliberation about the connotations of phrases, and deterred habitual, flowing, idiomatic usage that can often unthinkingly – or deliberately – suggest more than is strictly necessary. It seems to me that some such consideration led Beckett to start by writing the play in French; possibly, the effect he sought was one in which language would be used with frugality and deliberation. It would be language that was not wholly transparent, not a window onto the world, but a screen. Windows are generally unnoticed, but screens draw attention to themselves.

This is similar in spirit to Beckett's use of the theatre medium to draw attention to the medium itself. Possibly, he felt it would be easier to write a version in French that produced the effect he wanted, and then transfer the effect into an English version. It seems he did that too cautiously: Mercier observes that at times the French version is more colloquial and idiomatic in effect than the deliberately slightly formal English version (1977, p.46).

Social/political contexts

Postwar France

Waiting for Godot was written between 9 October 1948 and 29 January 1949, shortly after the end of the Second World War. The war was a period of such massive disruption throughout most of Europe and her colonial satellites that it seems very unlikely that it would not have been on Beckett's mind at the time. Beckett had spent the entire period of the war in France, going through the same vicissitudes of danger, displacement and uncertainty as most of the civilian population of France. Remarkably, for someone who professed no strong political convictions, Beckett was involved from a relatively early stage with the resistance against the German occupation and the Nazi-collaborating Vichy regime (from roughly 1941, when the resistance consisted of scattered groups following their independent agendas without significant coordination). In later life Beckett tended to play down these activities, but it was a courageous path to follow, and his bravery was honoured with the Croix de Guerre with gold star. His involvement showed that Beckett, however determinedly apolitical, could not but be hostile to fascism. This was only to be expected given his loyalty to friends (Beckett was deeply saddened by the treatment of his Jewish friends, especially the death of Paul Léon in a concentration camp), his artistic inclination (which always possessed an uncompromising radicalism that was inimical to the muscular conservatism of much fascist art) and his philosophic disposition (tending to extend to all humanity, and especially the downtrodden). Beckett's decision to dedicate his services to war-torn France rather than neutral Ireland was a deliberate choice: early in the war, he had unsuccessfully sought recruitment in the French Army and later the ambulance service. This probably indicates a powerful desire to be in the thick of things, in the happening world, rather than – as one might expect from a reclusive character – in retreat.

Living in postwar France may have been for Beckett a disquietingly quiet experience. The movements and uncertainties and activity of war were replaced by a period of uneasy transition from total disruption to a gradual return to normality. This period was an especially extended one in France. The fact that France had been largely either occupied or under the Vichy regime meant that the ravaged urban landscape of postwar London, or of cities in Germany and Poland, was not to be seen there. Yet the entire infrastructure had been unsettled, communications had broken down, civic services were provided only in a sporadic and makeshift fashion, and a massive economic crisis was looming. General de Gaulle's decision not to impose serious austerity measures meant that the unsettled condition was extended somewhat longer than it might otherwise have been. Immediately after the war, France also unusually found itself to be no longer counted among the great and the powerful – Britain, the Soviet Union and the USA started off postwar settlements with little regard for the recently occupied France (a situation that soon changed for strategic reasons).

But behind these immediate realities the larger horrors of the war and the rankling ideological uncertainties following it were beginning to sink in. The true scale and industrial methods of the Holocaust began to be slowly assessed and absorbed after 1945. In France, with its recent experience of being either occupied by the German army or, in the unoccupied territories, ruled by the collaborating Vichy regime, these revelations were received with a mixture of guilt and shame, which triggered manoeuvres to distance the French from the atrocities and to glorify the resistance. Commenting on the attitude in France towards Jews during the war, Michael Marrus has the following to say:

> Working in France, Robert Paxton and I discovered in prefectoral reports on public opinion widespread indifference to the Jews' fate until the latter half of 1942. Broadly speaking, while the anti-Semitic campaign of the collaborationist Vichy regime left most Frenchmen unmoved, their protests against it were few and far between. Anti-Jewish feeling was widespread, and the public seemed to follow the lead of right-wing politicians at Vichy who built an anti-Semitic program into the 'National Revolution' they prescribed for France. A common (and quite mistaken) assumption was that persecution affected mainly foreign Jews and that, to some degree at least, this was justified, given the 'preponderant influence' Jews were supposed to have had in French society.
>
> (Marrus, 1987, p.102)

Of the 76,000 foreign Jews (and those divested of their citizenship) handed over by the French police to the Nazis, only 2,500 survived (Rousso, 1991, p.100). In fact, serious historical research on and analysis of the Holocaust appear mainly after the Eichmann trial in Jerusalem and the publication in 1961 of Raul Hilberg's *The Destruction of the European Jews*.

More confusingly, though, there seemed to emerge in France after the Second World War a sort of 'moral crisis' – as Uhlmann (1999), in his study of Beckett's French context, calls it. Though the destructive nature of fascism became clearer, and attempts to distance the French from it were under way, it was evident that the state machinery continued to employ codes and systems in government similar to those operating during the war:

> There had been an apparent complete reversal of system of government from Fascist to non-Fascist, yet under both of these systems it was the French national interest that was presented as the transcendental Good against which a more fluid Evil might be defined. The leaders of the Vichy government which collaborated with the Nazis, Pétain and Laval, and de Gaulle, who resisted them from London and later became president of France (and was president when Papon instigated the massacre of Algerians [in 1961]), all appealed to the notion of *La France*, to the unchallengeable good of the French nation state to justify the actions of their governments.
>
> (Uhlmann, 1999, p.103)

The new French government seemed to cling to France's colonies ever more tenaciously and aggressively, and would soon unleash its own series of atrocities. On the other hand, the socialist alignments, which had emerged from the war in a positive light (especially after Hitler's invasion of the Soviet Union), and towards which many intellectuals in France were sympathetic, could also be viewed with a degree of scepticism. After all, at the beginning of the war these alignments had denounced it as a bourgeois matter in which they would not intervene, at least while the Molotov–Ribbentrop pact (the Nazi–Soviet non-aggression pact signed in 1939) stood.

Beckett must have been aware of these circumstances, arising as they did in his adoptive homeland, and at a period of his life when he was as involved in social and political concerns as he had ever been or was ever likely to be again. At any rate, this postwar period was the one in which he was most prolific: between 1947 and 1949 he wrote a trilogy of novels (*Molloy, Malone Dies, The Unnamable*), and the plays *Eleuthéria* and *Waiting for Godot*. **What bearing might the postwar social/political events briefly sketched out above have on *Waiting for Godot*?**

The overwhelming impression conveyed by the play is one of uncertainty: about whether the day is the day Vladimir and Estragon think it is or the place is the place they believe it to be; whether the shoes are Estragon's shoes or the tree is the one they vaguely remember; whether Godot is likely to turn up; whether the boy they meet is the boy they had met before; whether Lucky is dependent on Pozzo or Pozzo on Lucky; whether the second thief of the gospels was saved or not; whether they need to wait or not; whether they really need to do anything or not; whether there is a God or not; whether there is any purpose in their existence or not. So profound is this uncertainty, from which the characters *in the play* suffer, and which the *play itself* appears to be designed to convey, that little remains to be ascertained by the audience except that what is before them is a play. There is an air of resignation about this excessively subversive self-consciousness, and yet there is simultaneously a desire for clarification that keeps the main characters waiting and the audience watching until the ending – which is not really an ending at all. This debilitating uncertainty could, of course, be regarded as a somewhat jaundiced view of the human condition itself – but equally it could be understood as the expression of the postwar context within which Beckett was writing. The uncertainty had a particular resonance for those who had lived through the dislocations and upheavals of war. More importantly, the 'moral crisis' that was evident in France, and the protracted period of transition to relative stability in the late 1940s, meant that a sense of war-engendered uncertainty persisted long after the war had ended.

Moreover, despite the lack of dramatic happenings in *Waiting for Godot*, there is a feeling that things become increasingly fraught and tense as the play progresses. The sense of unproductiveness in Act 2 builds on that in Act 1; the growing despair of Vladimir and Estragon gains in intensity through repetition. The gradual disintegration of Lucky and Pozzo is all too manifest. Quite possibly, this sense of intensification through lack of progression, of disintegration without evident causes, was Beckett's comment on the perpetuation of moral and ideological ambiguities from fascist to non-fascist France. The starkness of the landscape may have chimed with the ravaged landscapes of postwar Europe; the experience of being stuck, which Vladimir and Estragon, Lucky and Pozzo, and the audience, share in the course of the play, coincides with a postwar France where things no longer seem to work. Towards the end of the play, Pozzo spits out:

> One day, is that not enough for you, one day like any other day, one day he went dumb, one day I went blind, one day we'll go deaf, one day we were born, one day we shall die, the same day, the same second, is that not enough for you? (*Calmer*) They give birth astride of a grave, the light gleams an instant, then it's night once more.
>
> (p.78)

The bitterness with which he says this is perhaps the bitterness with which people confronted a world that had produced something as unspeakably brutal as the Holocaust.

The Irish background

The immediate postwar French context is not the only one that is relevant to Beckett's work. Inevitably, his Irish heritage and upbringing has also been examined with a view to understanding his writing, and provides another context. Beckett was the son of Protestant Irish parents; his school and university education was in Ulster and Dublin. In the 1930s, he wrote occasional pieces on Irish literature, and had a particular interest in Irish poetry (see Beckett, 1983). He settled in Paris in 1937 at the age of twenty-one but maintained contact with his family and visited Ireland intermittently thereafter. Of his literary friends in Paris, the one who influenced him most profoundly was the Irish writer James Joyce. In 1929, Beckett wrote an essay entitled 'Dante ... Bruno, Vico ... Joyce' (Beckett, 1972) about Joyce's work, which is important for an understanding of Beckett's own literary development and attitudes. Undoubtedly, Beckett's Irish background and connections contribute to his writings – however muted the connection might appear at first sight. In some cases (especially in the novels), his Irish sensibility is gently implied by, for instance, giving the central protagonists Irish names (Murphy, Moran, Molloy, Malone). However, no such hint of an Irish context is obvious in *Waiting for Godot*. In the placing of the two tramps at the centre of the play, some critics have seen an indication of Gaelic tradition: Declan Kiberd, for instance, traces Beckett's figure of the tramp to representations of the uprooted bard, from the works of the *spailpín* ['wandering labourer'] poets of the seventeenth and eighteenth centuries to those of W.B. Yeats and J.M. Synge (Kiberd, 1995, p.538). This seems plausible, but if that was Beckett's intention he clearly chose to disguise it, by giving the characters Russian and French names. In the film version recommended above, the two tramps do in fact speak with Irish accents. It has also been argued that the figure of Pozzo is reminiscent of the English landlord (*ibid.*, p.542; Mercier, 1977, p.53), especially to all who are sensitive to Irish colonial history (and indeed other colonial histories). But the person whom he oppresses, Lucky, is not self-evidently Irish. Lucky's background is vague at best: his name suggests a symbolic significance; his extended speech suggests an acquaintance – or mimicked awareness of – European academic conventions and jargonizing (and therefore a more genteel education than his appearance might suggest). Some critics have detected an Irish source in the religious themes that seem to linger in the background. In a vigorous exchange of letters in the *Times Literary Supplement* in 1956, the poet and critic William Empson accused Beckett of revealing in the play a religious sentimentality to which, Empson believed, the Irish are especially susceptible (*TLS*, 30 March 1956, p.195). A reader, John J. O'Meara, acidly retorted in a letter the following week: 'It is obtuse to interpret the play in terms of the experience of any national' (*TLS*, 6 April 1956, p.207).

Any attempt to understand Beckett in terms of his Irish background, and as belonging to an Irish literary tradition, is necessarily part of a larger debate about what it means to be Irish. This is a complicated matter because political imperatives (particularly of decolonization and nationalist unification) have frequently dictated the critical construction of an Irish literary tradition. This critical construction has essentially been made with the ambition of discerning consistent features that characterize writings by Irish writers over an extended period of time – incorporating both those whose Irish affiliations are central to their writing (a reasonably easy task) and those (such as George Bernard Shaw, Oscar Wilde and Samuel Beckett) whose Irish connections are not immediately visible in their works (a task that is usually problematic). The aim of bringing such writers under the banner of 'Irish literature' is also complicated by the fact that most of them have written in English and have been allocated positions of distinction in a well-established *English* literary canon. They have, in other words, been appropriated or assimilated by the colonizer's literary tradition. One example of such an attempt to construct an Irish literary tradition (which is relevant to Beckett and which tries to incorporate him within it) is Vivian Mercier's *The Irish Comic Tradition* (1962). Mercier maintains that *all* Irish writers, irrespective of how aware or unconscious they are of their Irishness, show a peculiar kind of wit, a penchant for word play and grotesque humour, that reveals a 'characteristic Irish mind' (1962, p.12). Beckett, Mercier argues, is one of those writers who are largely ignorant of the Gaelic tradition and remote from Irish preoccupations, and yet are unconsciously possessed of such a 'characteristic Irish mind' and therefore belong to the Irish literary tradition: 'We have the peculiar case here of an Anglo-Irishman who, like Swift, seems to fit comfortably into the Gaelic tradition yet has almost no conscious awareness of what that tradition is' (*ibid.*, pp.75–6). The logical riposte to that almost biogenetic characterization of Irishness and an Irish literary tradition is found in a critique of the book by another Irish writer, Conor Cruise O'Brien:

> The idea that there is 'an Irish mind,' continuing with its own peculiar quirks, not shared even by other Europeans, from medieval times to the days of Samuel Beckett, seems to me implausible ... There is probably no continuous and distinctive 'Irish mind,' but there has been since the 16th century at least an Irish predicament: a predicament which has produced common characteristics in a number of those who have been involved in it.
>
> (O'Brien, 1965, p.104)

Given the above observations about past attempts to place *Waiting for Godot*, and Beckett generally, in terms of Beckett's Irish background and connections, to what extent is it possible to analyse the play in those terms?

I think two points are reasonably clear. One is that, in terms of the situations, characters and ideas that the play presents, where it was written and the immediate audiences to which it was addressed, it is difficult to discern a self-evident Irish context. The other is that, given Beckett's essentially Irish background and connections (i.e. Beckett *was* Irish by birth and upbringing, though he made little conscious effort to present himself as such), it is nevertheless plausible to locate the play within such a context in terms of past and on-going debates about Irish history, culture and politics. These two points suggest that to contextualize the play in this direction we (readers, critics, audiences) need to possess or cultivate an informed perspective on Irish history, culture and politics, and the debates relevant to these. I do not feel that I can do this here, in a chapter engaging with the play from a range of perspectives. But if you happen to be informed in this respect, or are particularly curious about this aspect of the play, you may wish to follow up these ideas (see the 'Further reading' section at the end of the chapter).

Contexts of ideas

The bareness of the stage, the economy with which props are used, the arbitrary constraints that work on the characters, the artifice of the dialogues, and so on – all those factors that give *Waiting for Godot* the quality of being theatre about theatre – have not particularly encouraged attempts at social/ political contextualization. It has been generally assumed that the play operates on a level of communication that is larger than any particular social and political context, or is relevant to a range of vastly different social/ political contexts. In other words, the play communicates most effectively in a realm of abstraction and generality – of acontextual and universal human interests. How this assumption has influenced performances of the play in different countries and languages is something that I discuss below. Ironically, though, it has not ensured any consensus about the abstract and general ideas with which the play deals; on the contrary, it has simply become clear that here, too, contextualization operates – a kind of contextualization in domains of ideas rather than in social and political domains. However, this still offers the possibility of seeing the play in terms of specific social and political contexts; after all, even the most universal-sounding and generalized philosophical ideas have their specific political and social conditions and imperatives.

We need not dwell too closely on this paradox, for it is one that continues to occupy much critical thinking and is yet to be (perhaps cannot be) resolved. The point is that interpretations of and debates about *Waiting for Godot* have more often been aired in terms of ideas than social and political contexts. The first reviewer of the Paris performance, Sylvian Zegel in *Libération* (7 January 1953), decided that the tramps 'represent all humanity, [and] utter remarks as we might utter' (in Graver and Federman, 1979, p.89); the noted French playwright Jean Anouilh, in the same year, opined that the play was 'a masterpiece that will cause despair for men in general and playwrights in particular' (in *ibid.*, p.92). In a similar vein, early reviewers of the London performance in 1955 – such as Harold Hobson and Kenneth

Tynan – took it for granted that the play says something about humanity in general or the human condition (in *ibid.*, pp.93–7). For the English spectator and reader of *Waiting for Godot*, these suggestions were given flesh in the pages of the *Times Literary Supplement*, following a review by G.S. Fraser of the first published English text of the play. In this review, Fraser interpreted *Waiting for Godot* as 'a modern morality play, on permanent Christian themes', which, by confronting liberal doubts about religion and human purpose, manages to convey a 'message of religious consolation' rather than nihilistic despair (*TLS*, 10 February 1956, p.85; also in Graver and Federman, 1979, pp.99). In subsequent weeks, a large number of responses to this interpretation followed: Katherine M. Wilson argued that the play was not a Christian allegory but 'preached obvious and straightforward existentialism' (*TLS*, 2 March 1956, p.133; I will discuss 'existentialism' later in this chapter); J.S. Walsh asserted that 'the play is neither a Christian allegory nor an existentialist parable, but ... states a simple eternal truth – that in a world of materialism, brutality, ignorance and despair the only hope of survival lies in the spiritual awareness of the few' (*TLS*, 9 March 1956, p.149); Philip H. Bagby maintained that the play's 'strength clearly lies in its uncertainties, in the fact that it gives us no final answer, no decisive reason to prefer either hope or despair' (*TLS*, 23 March 1956, p.181). This debate appears to mark out the main directions that critical engagement with the play has taken since. All parties seem to concur that the play should be approached as addressing matters of large theoretical import – the condition of humanity itself, the purpose of life, the nature of certainty and uncertainty and faith. However, several different emphases are apparent in how the play is understood: as being informed by a religious sensibility; as promoting an existentialist view; and as departing from and yet alluding to both in an original fashion.

In the following discussion, I examine the play in terms of religious and existentialist perspectives. I then look at some other contexts of ideas, which are related to and yet distinct from both these perspectives.

The religious perspective

Please reread the play, and note the passages that seem to you to allude directly to religious motifs and themes. Bearing in mind these passages, do you think the play presents a coherent religious or anti-religious perspective?

The exchange about the two thieves who were crucified with Jesus – 'The Saviour' – (pp.3–4) is the first obvious scriptural reference in the play. It alludes to an apparent difference in the accounts given by Luke (23:43), who speaks of one of the thieves being saved, and Matthew (27:44), who reports that both abused Jesus on the cross (and therefore presumably both were damned). The brief exchange works in several different ways in the play.

Vladimir points out the apparent contradiction in the gospels, and seems to question the certainty of gospel truth. Vladimir's somewhat pedantic preoccupation with the difference in the gospel accounts set against Estragon's obvious lack of interest in it suggests that the extent to which this is perceived as important is relative. What Vladimir complains about is not so much the veracity of one account over another but that people have privileged Luke's account for no particular reason. This leads to Estragon's sweeping denunciation of people as 'bloody ignorant apes' – in other words, this exchange concludes on a note not of religious uncertainty but of scepticism about human understanding. The point of the dialogue constantly seems to miss the mark, to evade clarity, because of the slippages in the exchanges between Vladimir and Estragon.

Another passage that alludes to religion is Lucky's speech (pp.34–6), which appears to start off by suggesting a conception of God. This passage has exercised every critic who has engaged with the play, and numerous fairly plausible interpretations of it have been proposed. And yet, the speech is so clearly designed to defeat clear construction and sequential development that one cannot help feeling that to try to interpret it is to distort its effect. I do not think Lucky's speech is open to any single conclusive, or even persuasive, interpretation of an argument or a structure – it could well be taken simply as nonsense. Nevertheless, for the sake of giving some semblance of order to this unwieldy passage let me have a stab at interpreting it (if only to emphasize how inadequate such interpretations are). Leaving aside the themes it tries, but does not quite manage, to elaborate, the speech has some unusual organizing principles. First, it is entirely unpunctuated, thus leaving the pauses and full stops unclear or open to choice, and giving the whole a certain unstoppable momentum (in performances, Lucky generally goes faster and faster as he proceeds). Second, every possibly meaningful assertion in it is referenced, in pseudo-academic fashion, to certain usually unfinished or lost works by invented persons, such as 'Essy-in-Possy of Testew and Cunard' (*esse-in-posse* is a legal term meaning 'being in potential', and Testew and Cunard are thinly veiled obscenities – clearly tongue-in-cheek). Third, it contains recognizable names with recognizable associations (place names such as Peckham, Fulham, Clapham, Connemara; personal names such as Miranda, reminiscent of the character in *The Tempest*, and the eighteenth-century philosopher Bishop Berkeley), and yet these associations do not seem to throw much light on Lucky's meaning. Fourth, the beginning of the speech mixes up fragments of meaningfully constructed speech that are large enough to be amenable to understanding (*almost* whole sentences can be discerned early in the speech); later in the speech the sensible fragments become smaller, the sense of fragmentariness increases and sub-clauses from elsewhere, which have little immediate connection to the surrounding words, seem to collide in an *almost* haphazard fashion.

With these organizational principles in mind, the speech seems to be divisible into three broad thematic sections. The first part (ending roughly with the words 'Fartov and Belcher') introduces the idea of an indifferent and yet benevolent and ultimately inscrutable God; the second part (ending roughly with the second mention of 'Steinweg and Peterman') expands on the meaninglessness of human activity (emphasized as physical activity); and the third part (to the end of the speech) envisions the collapse of the world and communication itself into chaos.

If this reading of Lucky's speech is taken as plausible, the speech can be seen to work in several different ways: it presents the despair of a vision of purposelessness; it reveals the limits of communication in relation to attempts to understand something as large and abstract as human and divine purpose; it is no more than a pseudo-academic, deliberately irreverential and ultimately incoherent and desperate *performance* done to order (and as such conveys no more than Lucky's condition of servitude).

On the theme of religious motifs, the following exchange toward the end of Act 1, when Estragon announces that he will leave, stands out as peculiarly relevant:

> VLADIMIR But you can't go barefoot!
>
> ESTRAGON Christ did.
>
> VLADIMIR Christ! What's Christ got to do with it? You're not going to compare yourself to Christ!
>
> ESTRAGON All my life I've compared myself to him.
>
> VLADIMIR But where he lived it was warm, it was dry!
>
> ESTRAGON Yes. And they crucified quick.

(p.45)

Estragon's comparison of himself to Christ points towards some of the play's symbolic resonances with Christian mythology: just as Christ represents a sympathetic understanding of the human condition, the two tramps can be seen as embodying and eliciting sympathy for the human condition; Christ's humanness includes a self-conscious assumption of suffering as an inevitable aspect of being human, and Estragon and Vladimir too suffer self-consciously; whereas in the Christian universe Christ's martyrdom holds out to humankind the possibility of hope, in the play, ironically (in a world where divinity does not manifest itself with any certainty), martyrdom does not occur and there is no promise. However, even as these symbolic resonances *may* be recognized, the purely pragmatic air of the dialogue undermines their full effect. Vladimir's concern is not with the symbolic possibilities of Estragon's announcement, but with the exaggeration in it and with its immediate failure. Vladimir takes the comparison Estragon makes in a narrowly materialistic (and in those terms irrefutable) fashion: Christ was able to walk barefoot because he lived in a warm country, Estragon really should worry about the effects of a night-time chill. Nevertheless, to some extent these symbolic resonances – with the Christian references muted – recur briefly in Act 2, in:

> VLADIMIR   (*sententiously*) To every man his little cross. (*He sighs*) Till
> he dies. (*With an afterthought*) And is forgotten.

(p.52)

They recur in a more extended fashion when Vladimir responds to Pozzo's cries for help with the following:

> Let us do something, while we have the chance! It is not every
> day that we are needed. Not indeed that we personally are
> needed. Others would meet the case equally well, if not better. To
> all mankind they were addressed, those cries for help still ringing
> in our ears! But at this place, at this moment of time, all mankind
> is us, whether we like it or not. Let us make the most of it, before
> it is too late! Let us represent worthily for once the foul brood to
> which a cruel fate consigned us!

(pp.68–9)

There are other elements in the play that are suggestive to those aware of Christian mythology. The lone tree, for example, may remind readers of the tree of knowledge in paradise, or the burning bush that Moses found, or the cross; there is a mention of maps of the Holy Land (p.3); Vladimir and Estragon wonder whether Pozzo may be Abel or Cain (p.72). Some critics have argued that Godot, who is always expected and does not appear, may stand for God (the sound of the name itself points in that direction, it has been proposed, but tenuously – it does not work in French, for instance); that Godot's representatives – the boys – are shepherds is also suggestive in that sense.

However, it seems to me that none of the above references to Christian mythology is more than suggestive; none of them amounts to a decisive indication of religious conviction or lack of it. Christian religious perspectives provide a frame of reference at certain points in the play, but not much more than that. To allude to that frame of reference does not endorse it or otherwise; it is no more than one way of expressing something of the human condition as portrayed in the play and given the contexts in which the play is performed and received. Undeniably, such allusions are made with so much performative self-consciousness and deliberation that it is impossible to regard them as statements of any sort. In my discussion above, I repeatedly come back to the various, simultaneous and contradictory ways in which such allusions may operate. It seems to me that to expand these few explicit references into an interpretive structure that sees the whole play as a Christian (or anti-Christian) or religious (or anti-religious) allegory (as Fraser and others have done) requires an extrinsic conviction in the efficacy of religious perspectives. Perhaps it needs some conviction in religion itself, or at any rate some sense of a religious world-view, to begin with. As with so many other interpretative approaches to *Waiting for Godot*, there is quite possibly enough in the play to make such an approach productive, but not enough to make it sufficiently comprehensive and satisfactory.

The existentialist perspective

In the *TLS* debate outlined above, one of the contributors cited existentialism as the key to the play. Indeed, earlier in this chapter I remarked in passing that there is some affinity between Beckett's work and that of Sartre – an exponent of a particular existentialist position. A number of rather complex late nineteenth- and twentieth-century philosophical works (mainly by Søren Kierkegaard, Friedrich Nietzsche, Edmund Husserl, Karl Jaspers, Martin Heidegger, Martin Buber, Jean-Paul Sartre, Maurice Merleau-Ponty and Albert Camus) are usually understood as contributing to the existentialist 'school'. These works employ different sets of philosophical terminology and a variety of inferential processes, and often have different emphases (e.g. some of them hit upon existentialist formulations by reflecting on religious principles, others do so with secular and political imperatives).

Although existentialism may appear complex, the main idea that characterizes an existentialist approach is in fact not difficult to grasp. It can be put as follows: any philosophical approach depends on first identifying that which can be regarded as an absolute certainty, or an inevitable starting point of thinking, and then determining what can be inferred from it to enable the thinker to understand the world (or any aspect of it) and the place of people in it. Thus, Plato, for instance, decided that the form of things (or their essences) – that is, the abstract ideas underlying different perceived things – can be regarded as an absolute certainty and that these ideas are therefore the place to start thinking about the world. So, for example, according to Plato, behind every material tree that can be perceived there is an essential form of a tree, which is real, and in terms of which philosophy can proceed. This can also apply to conceptual notions: Plato believed, for instance, that behind different manifestations of just actions there is an essential form of justice. From certain religious philosophical perspectives (such as those of St Augustine or Thomas Aquinas), the absolute certainty that has to be assumed is that of a supernal intelligent godhead from which everything originates. For the philosopher René Descartes, the absolute certainty from which philosophy can begin to approach the world is the fact of thinking itself – because one thinks, one knows that there is something that exists which can be thought about (hence the famous 'I think therefore I am', or *cogito ergo sum*, formulation).

Different versions of thinking as a beginning point, or of essence as a beginning point, or of an originator, account for most traditional philosophical approaches and systems. In these, as you may have noticed, the fact that the world exists and that we exist is taken as a secondary matter, something that follows from the primary positioning of essences or ideas or creation. In the existentialist approach, this is reversed: it is maintained that the fact that the world exists and that we exist in it is the absolute certainty, and everything else – how we think about the world, how it is organized for us, what we can do within it – follows. Or, as Sartre argued in *L'Être et néant* (1943; translated as *Being and Nothingness*, 1956), existence, or being, precedes essence, perception and cogitation.

That is the key idea, but before returning to Beckett and the play it is worth sketching out briefly a few of the powerful inferences that can follow from this. One is that there is nothing external to the existence of the world, and more importantly to the existence of humans, to justify the fact of that existence. So, humans exist for no greater purpose than to exist: how we choose to conduct our lives is not determined by any external reason, it is entirely up to us. If we believe there is an external purpose – say, a moral purpose determined by a creator – that belief is arbitrary and cannot be or does not need to be justified (this is roughly Kierkegaard's line: he was concerned with the mechanics of faith).

The existentialist realization that we have this choice enjoins on us a unique freedom, which opens up an infinity of choices. These choices may turn out to be constructive or creative, good or bad, and so on, but the actual making of any choice is ultimately arbitrary (even if, later, we attribute reasons for making it, or just delude ourselves that the possibilities are somehow limited). Those who grasp this sense of freedom and live accordingly (existentialist humans) are likely to feel a certain dread or anxiety about being put in this position of unlimited freedom without extrinsic direction (Kierkegaard described this as 'angst') and to be captured by a sense of the absurdity of the institutions and beliefs we live by (described most convincingly in Camus's *Le Mythe de Sisyphe* (1942; translated as *The Myth of Sisyphus*, 1955)). Apart from worrying about the nature of faith and the workings of human psychology, some existentialists – notably Sartre – also saw such existentialist freedom as being politically effective: the freedom that existence itself permits is a natural human right, and all institutions/ persons that restrict that freedom beyond certain reasonable limits (say, the limit that restrains one person's freedom so that others can exercise theirs) are unjust and unacceptably coercive.

Interestingly, it appears that Beckett had subscribed to some of these ideas at an early stage in his career. In his long essay on Proust (written in 1931), which is actually as much a vehicle for presenting some of his own philosophical convictions as a critique of the French author, one gets a sense of this. Consider the following:

> Habit is a compromise effected between the individual and his environment, or between the individual and his own organic eccentricities, the guarantee of a dull inviolability, the lightning conductor of his existence. Habit is the ballast that chains the dog to his vomit. Breathing is habit. Life is habit. Or rather life is a succession of habits, since the individual is a succession of individuals; the world being a projection of the individual's consciousness ... the pact must be continually renewed, the letter of safe-conduct brought up to date ... The periods of transition that separate consecutive adaptations ... represent perilous zones in the life of the individual, dangerous, precarious, painful, mysterious and fertile, when for a moment the boredom of living is replaced by the suffering of being ... The suffering of being: that is, the free play of every faculty.
>
> (Beckett, 1965, pp.18–20)

The 'suffering of being' that Beckett understands as occurring in the transitions between different phases of habitual existence has clear analogues with the condition of existential awareness briefly described above. The 'suffering of being' is evidently a matter of awareness (it is the 'free play of every faculty'); it reveals the full experience of *being* – or existence – itself. It releases an unnerving sense of freedom, which is alluring ('mysterious and fertile') and yet gives rise to a sense of dread or angst ('dangerous, precarious, painful'). The state of 'suffering of being' is obviously contingent on being or existing consciously – it is, in some sense, an inevitable truth that we can scarcely avoid. But because it is painful and alluring and dangerous it is more comfortable and secure to try to disregard it, and the easiest way to do so is to bind ourselves in a habitual (ritualistic and arbitrary) existence. Beckett sees the condition of being human (a view he feels he shares with Proust) as a constant struggle between a blinkered, habitual existence and the inevitable 'suffering of being' that threatens to reveal itself. The existentialist aspect of this is, I think, self-evident.

Given the above sketchy outline of existentialist formulations, how might some of these apply to the play?

The following are some of the ways in which, I would suggest, such existentialist formulations may apply to *Waiting for Godot*.

First, the central thread that holds the play together – waiting for an unknown person for unknown reasons – could be regarded as a metaphor for the existential human condition itself: the purposes and expectations that people give themselves are as arbitrary and purposeless and inconclusive as waiting for Godot. As Ruby Cohn put it: 'Beckett's play tells us plainly who Godot is – the promise that is always awaited and not fulfilled, the expectation that brings two men to the board night after night. The play tells us this dramatically and not discursively' (1973, p.132).

Second, the almost bare stage, with props that curiously draw attention to themselves as props, has the effect of emphasizing the *presence* of the protagonists/actors on it (a point made by Alain Robbe-Grillet, 1965). The constant and visibly painful movements of the protagonists/actors have the same effect. This emphasized *presence* could be regarded as the only affirmable and uncontroversial fact about the play – and, from an existentialist point of view, about people and things in the world (the beginning point of this philosophical approach). All the other things with which the protagonists/actors occupy themselves (ultimately waiting) are uncertain, equivocal, make-believe, performed.

Third, the repetitive two-act structure of the play conveys the feeling of habitual existence. There is enough day-to-day (act-to-act) ritualistic activity to ensure a comfortable and secure and also dull and uninspiring sameness. And yet, there are also inevitable day-to-day (act-to-act) changes – such as the appearance of leaves on the tree, the changes in Pozzo and Lucky, etc. – which constantly threaten the insertion of an unnerving 'suffering of being'. The dualistic nature of the characterization also contributes to an understanding of the struggle between habitual existence and the 'suffering of being'. Vladimir and Estragon, Lucky and Pozzo cling tenaciously to their mutual dependence and their roles relative to each other because they choose to – not because they have to. There is no evidence (despite the appearance of coercion in Pozzo's behaviour to Lucky) that Lucky is being *forced* into slavery. If characters cling to each other it is because the absence of the other is more terrifying (this terror is manifest at several points); it brings the 'suffering of being' starkly to the fore. And yet there is also the allure of facing that 'suffering of being' – Vladimir and Estragon therefore often contemplate leaving each other. In a perverse way, Lucky is lucky because the relation that binds him to Pozzo relieves him so completely of any choice, any sense of the 'suffering of being' (though, paradoxically, his only speech shows that he, too, thinks of it).

Fourth when the characters reflect on their condition in the broadest terms, when they see themselves as representative of the human condition itself or of humanity at large, they express clearly the despair of realizing the purposelessness of existence, and the dread of absolute existential freedom. It is in this spirit that Vladimir describes humanity as 'the foul brood to which a cruel fate consigned us' (p.69) and Pozzo announces that 'They give birth astride of a grave, the light gleams an instant, then it's night once more' (p.78).

To read/watch the play as a dramatization of existentialist formulations and ideas is an obviously attractive way of making sense of it. The limitations of this approach are to some extent the limitations of existentialist philosophy itself. Theodor Adorno in *Jargon der Eigentlichkeit* (1964; translated as *The Jargon of Authenticity*, 1973) argued plausibly that existentialist philosophy assumes a language (the 'jargon of authenticity' of the title) that seems to issue in an oracular fashion from existential being in the abstract – that effectively lacks a sense of its own social and political context, its own communicative performance. To get drawn into this mode of understanding the play means to get drawn away from those social and political contexts that I discussed earlier. It also draws us away as critics from the exigencies of communication and literature/art into a field of abstract philosophical ideas and grand generalizations. Beckett himself and those who have critically engaged with *Waiting for Godot* have, however, generally been aware of the exigencies of communication and literature/art, and a closer consideration of this gives a somewhat different slant to the play.

Theatre of the Absurd

What do you think is the relationship between the play's existentialist themes and its self-reflexive theatrical methods?

You may, justifiably, feel that I have covered most of the ground that answers this question in my discussion of the play as theatre about theatre. However, it is worth returning to this issue, now that the thematic aspects of the play have been elucidated further. One of the peculiarities of the play that has become better defined in the course of this chapter is the extent to which it *performs* its preoccupations rather than *talks about* them. It so happens that existentialist philosophers like Sartre and Camus wrote influential literary texts, including plays, to communicate their ideas. It is instructive to have a look at some of these if you have not come across them before. In the plays of Sartre and Camus, dramatic situations are presented using conventional theatrical techniques, which allow characters to ponder and talk to each other about their (often existentialist) realizations. So, for instance, in Camus's play *Caligula* (1944; an English translation is available in Camus, 1965), the eponymous Roman emperor goes through a series of extreme and shocking actions with a destructive sense of his existentialist free choice and the absurdity of moral expectations and institutional sanction. In the course of doing this, his existentialist self-awareness is *talked about*, but the dramatic action, and its effect on the audience, is predicated on the conventional form of the play. The play works by shocking, rousing pity and terror in an Aristotelian fashion, by using a form that still depends on certain (distinctly non-existentialist) moral ideas and norms being tacitly accepted. By contrast, those features discussed above that render *Waiting for Godot* a possibly existentialist play are to do with the dramatic form itself and not with what is talked about within the play. The characters do not talk about anything very substantial and certain at all – almost nothing, as we have seen above, is said that is unequivocal or straightforward. Nevertheless, existentialist impressions are conveyed through the manner in which the play adapts theatre to its purposes: through its formal construction (the bare stage, the artifice of the props, the presence of the characters, the deliberateness of the dialogues, the repetitive two-act structure, etc.). The existentialist themes (if these are what we see in it) are conveyed by the features that make it self-reflexive of theatre itself, by its being theatre about theatre.

In *Waiting for Godot*, then, a quite unusual method of communicating ideas, or of self-contextualizing in a field of extant ideas, is in evidence: one in which communication occurs almost against the grain of itself, by reflecting on its own limitations, and to some extent despite itself. The techniques employed are, to a small degree, analogous to the defamiliarization effects that Brecht employed – there is an air of deliberate strangeness about the performance of the play that makes us reflect on theatre and communication, and on the ideas underlying them. But it is defamiliarization taken to a level of purity beyond that of Brecht; in Brecht's plays the theatre still talks, symbolizes its ideas, announces its ideology, whereas in Beckett's plays it does not do any of these things with any degree of success, and the play works because of this. *Waiting for Godot* makes a virtue of the inability to be certain or to communicate successfully. This particular mode of communicating or failing to communicate is something that Beckett cultivated with the greatest circumspection and deliberation, and something that he admired greatly in the works of other artists in different media. The idea of self-defeating communication is elaborated in 'Three Dialogues', an essay about three painters that is presented in dialogic form. **An extract from this essay is reproduced in the Reader (Item 41). Please read it now.**

In an influential book, written in 1961, Martin Esslin labelled this particular use of uncertainty and ambiguity in theatre, which appeared to him to be closely linked to the philosophy of Sartre and Camus, as the 'Theatre of the Absurd'. The word 'absurd' here brings together the existentialist sense of the absurdity of human institutions, beliefs and purposes with the sense of absurdity that results from techniques that interrogate and undermine theatrical conventions. It has proved an apt and abiding label that has stuck to Beckett's plays, and those of others who appear to employ similar techniques to similar ends, often under Beckett's influence, such as Eugène Ionesco, Arthur Adamov, Jean Genet and Harold Pinter. Esslin described the 'Theatre of the Absurd' as follows:

> The Theatre of the Absurd has renounced arguing *about* the absurdity of the human condition; it merely *presents* it in being – that is, in terms of concrete stage images. This is the difference between the approach of the philosopher and that of the poet; the difference, to take an example from another sphere, between the *idea* of God in the works of Thomas Aquinas or Spinoza and the *intuition* of God in those of St John of the Cross or Meister Eckhart – the difference between theory and experience.
>
> (Esslin, [1961] 1980, p.25)

It is worth remembering, though, that Beckett was notoriously reluctant to have his work categorized or placed in any group of any sort.

Structuralism/post-structuralism and modernism/postmodernism

Clearly, the existentialist perspective (attractive as it is) provides only one of many possible approaches to the play. The peculiarities of the play's communicative means (in terms of language and performance) are not confined to existentialist interpretation alone. In fact, from various critical perspectives the communicative peculiarities of Beckett's play, as much as the world-view it presents thereby, have been a matter of interest in themselves, outside the context of existentialist philosophy. As you have been reminded often in preceding chapters, literary critical thinking has its own contexts and emphases, and has appropriated or situated specific literary texts accordingly. To a significant extent, twentieth-century literary criticism was concerned with the role of language and communication. Instead of looking on language and other communicative media as transparent – or as mere vehicles for conveying an external reality and politically or socially or morally effective ideas – it has been argued with a somewhat different emphasis that communicative media mould transmission and reception, that ideological inclinations and organizational structures are embedded within them in inevitable ways. This view has ranged from the conviction that the structures of language themselves impose clarifying frameworks on all areas of knowledge (structuralist criticism), to the feeling that language introduces unresolvable ambiguities and slippages in the quest for knowledge, which render the frameworks it provides unreliable and even partisan (post-structuralist criticism). Inevitably, for those who engage with these issues the communicational peculiarities of *Waiting for Godot*, strikingly original as it was when it appeared, are of particular interest. In addition, that these communicative practices are so self-consciously employed in the play makes it an ideal subject for study.

In the dialogues from the play that have been examined above, two points in particular have been noted. First, many of them operate like set pieces, which are performed along certain predictable lines with the pairs of characters issuing instructions to each other ('Come on, Gogo, return the ball, can't you, once in a way?', p.4; 'Take your time', p.10; 'Worse than the pantomime.' / 'The circus.' / 'The music hall.' / 'The circus', pp.26–7; 'How did you find me? ... Good? Fair? Middling? Poor? Positively bad?', p.30; 'Think, pig!', p.33; 'That passed the time', p.40; 'That's the idea, let's contradict each other', p.53, etc.). Second, they often work in several ways simultaneously. For example, the dialogue about the two thieves crucified with Jesus questions gospel truth, expresses doubts about the understanding of gospel readers and highlights the relativity of the importance attached to concepts; all these can be inferred simultaneously from the dialogue. The slipperiness of language is a constitutive element of the play: characters are often slow to understand each other, sometimes because their speech is enormously pat and quick; they talk at cross-purposes and so misunderstand each other; they talk for the sake of talking; they sometimes refuse to talk to each other and lapse into uncomfortable silences. Most remarkably, though, the impression that the play conveys – its communication, if you will – is not *in* the dialogue at all. It is brought about in several ways. First, it is the result of the conjunction of different theatrical elements, including dialogue, in the performance. Second, it occurs because the theatrical elements, in being thus brought together, make us reflect on the nature of theatre itself – that is, the performance is self-reflexively theatre about theatre. Third, the communication emerges in an insidious way from *between* what is straightforwardly presented and said and done. The slipperiness of language is, I feel and others have felt, extended to the slipperiness of theatre as a medium of communication – but, paradoxically, communication does *happen*. If we go back to the brief description above of structuralist and post-structuralist criticism, it is tempting to think of *Waiting for Godot* as a demonstration of the slipperiness and unreliability of language and communicative media posited by the post-structuralist viewpoint – while ironically allowing successful communication. It does with theatre what many post-structuralist theorists (notably Jacques Derrida) have tried to do with language itself: express the slipperiness and unreliability of language by and while using it.

The manner in which the play uses language and communication practices naturally relates to its positioning as a modernist and/or postmodernist text. A certain amount of critical attention has been devoted to the placement of Beckett's work with respect to modernism and postmodernism. These terms are used with wide application and are not in themselves particularly clear. The following is a brief summary of their usage, with an emphasis appropriate for the purpose of the discussion at this point.

Twentieth-century literary modernism (a contested term with varying connotations in different contexts) in general could be thought of as a *searching* approach to understanding the contemporary world in literature.

The perception of different kinds of crisis (changes in traditional institutions, loss of conviction about older value and belief systems, unequal development in technology and society, etc.) leads to a need to develop new ways of thinking, institute new social/cultural/political institutions and create new modes of expression. It is expected that from this effort some reasonably defined new direction will emerge in which the contemporary world can be steered. So, modernist literature concerns itself with trying to grasp the contemporary world through new ways of thinking. This could entail recycling mythic systems, envisaging a new Christian order, developing fascist ideologies or working with socialist theories of different sorts, trying to recruit developments in physics or psychoanalysis to the social arena, and so on. The next step is to develop stylistics and aesthetics – communicative practices – that are appropriate to the contemporary world thus apprehended. In literature this involves the kind of experimentation with language and form that characterizes the work of, among others, T.S. Eliot, Virginia Woolf, Bertolt Brecht and Christopher Okigbo.

Literary postmodernism could be regarded as a coming to terms with the limitations of the modernist effort; it involves the realization that the modernist expectation that it might be possible to find broad, holistic ways of coming to grips with the contemporary world, and to discover reasonably defined directions for the future, is unrealistic. In contrast, the postmodern perspective accepts that there could be a multitude of simultaneously relevant and reasonable ways of grasping the contemporary and looking to the future, and that communicative practices and expressions therein have to be sensitive to a plurality of means (some of which may well be contradictory). In literature this may involve the use of multiple styles in writing, presenting ideological contradictions and positions as being unsynthesizable, showing how different points of view in different contexts cannot be resolved into a universal whole.

These brief outlines of modernism and postmodernism should not be regarded as definitions, but more as provisional descriptions which any close examination of texts containing these terms is likely to complicate. No clear chronological order attaches to these descriptions; although it is broadly understood that postmodernism follows modernism, in terms of the modernist effort there may well be writers writing now who are more modernist than postmodernist in temper (or indeed who do not fit into either category).

Now read the extract from Hans Bertens's _The Idea of the Postmodern_ (Reader, Item 42). Do you feel that Beckett's play can most appropriately be described as 'modernist' or 'postmodernist'?

There is no clear consensus about how _Waiting for Godot_ should be placed with respect to modernism and postmodernism as described above. In some respects the play does seem to possess a modernist character. This has mainly to do with the sense of despair that many critics have noted in it; certainly the protagonists (Vladimir, Estragon, Pozzo, Lucky) at different points in the play powerfully express *their* sense of hopelessness and angst. Pozzo's equation of birth and death, Vladimir's cutting remarks about the human species, the disappointment with which the tramps receive the news that Godot will be unable to appear, the manner in which they contemplate suicide, the frenzy with which all the characters cling to each other and talk, their fear of the emptiness of not having anything to do – all these are elements in the pessimistic impression the play may make. Whether these expressions of despair from the protagonists amount to the play itself being a pessimistic affair is a debatable issue. This pessimism, or sense of dissatisfaction with the world and the human condition, gives rise to the need to look for something more (to wait for Godot, as it were) – and could be thought of as expressing a modernist sensibility. It is comparable in that sense to Eliot's rather dark view of the contemporary world in the poems of *Prufrock and Other Observations* (1917), and his reaching out towards some more ideal condition (a Christian utopia as it turned out).

However, in *Waiting for Godot* it is also reasonably clear that Godot will not ultimately turn up. More importantly, the uncertainty about Godot is perfectly matched with the uncertainty that seems to be a condition of the play itself. All the characters are uncertain about pretty much everything, and though this makes them unhappy at times, in general they live with it without greater expectations – in general they accept uncertainties as being inevitable. This is not confined to the characters *in* the play; the entire form of theatre is exposed to a questioning of conventions and a self-consciousness that draw the audience in. Though in no conventional sense could this play be regarded as having a beginning, a middle and an end (or any kind of dramatic theme and resolution), it has the effect of a complete artefact. You may recall that one of the participants in the 1956 *TLS* debate outlined earlier maintained that the play's 'strength clearly lies in its uncertainties, in the fact that it gives us no final answer, no decisive reason to prefer either hope or despair'. In this sense, *Waiting for Godot* appears to reach a postmodernist realization of the need to accept uncertainty and ambiguity as the condition of human existence and the world, and gives it a suitably open-ended postmodernist expression.

Closer analysis of the text may help you to make up your mind about whether it could be more firmly placed in one context or another – this is an enterprise that I will leave to you.

Iconic status and international relevance

The social and political contexts and the ideas that have been discussed above have been the substance of the main critical interpretations of and debates about *Waiting for Godot* (though, inevitably, there are others that I have not touched on here). **Looking back on these, are there any general observations about the manner in which the play has been interpreted and debated that you can discern?**

The following are some of my own responses to this question.

First, the uncertainties that are highlighted in the play seem to spill over into critical engagements with the play. While some of the interpretations that have been put forward are attractive in themselves, it is difficult to feel convinced that any one interpretation is more obviously correct than any other. Or, to put it another way, the play seems to be designed not to direct its implied readers/spectators towards a specific social or political context or a specific set of ideas, but to be suggestive of several contexts. In itself – in its allusions, structure, style, etc. – the play does not invoke any specific context that the critic may therefore feel justified in giving particular attention.

Second, to some extent this means that critics have received the play as being more acontextual, or more open to appropriation in different contexts, than is usual. The tendency of much critical thinking has been to understand the play in terms of broad philosophical and theoretical generalizations – as saying something about the human condition and the contemporary world, or addressing the nature of belief and faith, or reflecting something about communication and the lack thereof, and so on.

Third, to a significant degree, the 'openness' of the play has meant that critics who have wished to place it squarely in a particular context have had to depend on their own scholarly interests to provide this contextual emphasis. Thus, those who have seen the play as making some sort of religious statement have done so because they have been able to bring extrinsic theological material and experience usefully to bear on it, and similarly for those who have chosen to see it as reflecting a postwar French context, or an Irish sensibility, or a postmodernist perspective, and so on. Undoubtedly, any critical appraisal of a literary text/performance does this to some degree, but it seems to me that this kind of *fitting* of *Waiting for Godot* into different contexts, this kind of self-conscious appropriation, has been more pronounced – and more inescapable – than usual. I doubt whether any critic has felt fully convinced that he or she has found a key to the text/ performance.

It was precisely this openness, this acontextual appearance and assimilability in different contexts, this sense of relevance to immediate and universal contexts in this and other works by Beckett that was perceivably given the seal of approval by the Nobel Prize in Literature. As I observed in the opening section of this chapter, it also arguably gave direction to the universalist aspirations (i.e. hoping to recognize and reward literary production that is of universal value, that has an 'ideal direction' without limitation as to context) of the Nobel Prize award-makers. It brought a momentary closure to the controversies that had dogged the Nobel Prize in preceding years.

In recent years, there has been some discussion of the manner in which controversies about the Nobel Prize, such as those in the 1960s, have themselves become part of the prestige of the prize – and have been appropriated by the media, by publishers and other interested parties to raise the profile of the award and give it added significance. **Now read the extract from James F. English's essay 'Winning the Culture Game: Prizes, Awards, and the Rules of Art' (Reader, Item 43).** As English argues, the fact that literary prizes such as the Nobel Prize, the Booker Prize and the Orange Prize have received adverse criticism has ironically been used to raise the profile of these prizes and give them added cultural value. They derive their prestige from the controversies that have surrounded them. Likewise, writers who have created controversy after being given awards – as Sartre did by refusing the Nobel Prize, or as John Berger did when he denounced the Booker Prize and what it stood for in his acceptance speech in 1971 – have also found that controversy has served them well by bringing them to public attention and giving them a certain added cultural value. Much was made of Beckett's own dithering about accepting the Nobel Prize, of his absence at the award ceremony, of the fact that he gave away most of the prize money. However, it is not in the controversial nature of the award or its reception (this once, I would argue, the Nobel Prize and the recipient came together to heal controversies) but in its uncontroversialness that the impact of the Nobel Prize on Beckett's career – or more to our purpose, the career of *Waiting for Godot* – has to be assessed.

This is how the matter seems to me to stand: on receiving the Nobel Prize, Beckett, and *Waiting for Godot*, as his best-known work, were understood firmly and widely as being valuable in precisely the ways in which critical debates and interpretive engagements had already indicated. The play was seen as a particularly open text/performance, one that is of acontextual universal interest or appropriable in a range of different (or even in all) contexts. At the same time, the Nobel Prize itself was seen as being confirmed in what it had always claimed, recognizing work in an 'ideal direction' without limitation as to context. This dual affirmation pulled Beckett, and particularly *Waiting for Godot*, out of the limited sphere of admiring literati and cognoscenti, and into an international domain. Beckett became a kind of international icon, with *Waiting for Godot* as his calling card – a process that caused Beckett himself some unease, as we will see, and one that he could not control. Everyone everywhere now had a claim to Beckett's works, and nowhere has this claim been more inventively and consistently exercised than in performances of *Waiting for Godot*.

The result, to put it briefly, is that *Waiting for Godot* has been made the repository of contextually determined values in a manner that Beckett could not have anticipated. Because he believed very strongly (and after his death his estate has followed that lead faithfully) that an author should have absolute control over his work, this has not always been to his (or his estate's) liking. That Beckett had a powerful sense of authorial control has been illustrated in passing already: I have noted how Beckett constantly changed and allowed different versions of the text of *Waiting for Godot* to be brought into the public forum, and how he intervened in different performances and directed the play himself. What I have not yet noted with sufficient emphasis – and do now – is that he was fiercely protective of this control: while he himself felt entitled to change the text, introduce new props and add stage directions to different performances of the play, he was absolutely adamant about not allowing anyone else (directors or producers or performers) to take similar liberties.

In the performances of *Waiting for Godot* after the award of the Nobel Prize, therefore, can be seen the consequences of the iconization of Beckett and the internationalization of the play, and the disgruntlement of Beckett (and his estate) about that process. There were both some remarkable context-specific appropriations of the play in performance and some memorably obstructive behaviour regarding a few of these by Beckett (and his estate). A brief outline of some of these makes this final point and brings this section – and this chapter – to a close.

The defining moment of Beckett's reclaiming of authorial control over *Waiting for Godot* occurred in the production at the Schiller Theatre, Berlin, which he directed himself in 1975. I have mentioned this already because it is the performance that is most closely followed in the film version recommended above. As I have observed before, Beckett took several liberties with the original text in this (see Beckett, 1993, for further details), inserting occasional phrases and stage directions that were not there before – liberties that he certainly would not have permitted any other director to take. The end result, according to those who watched it, was quite unlike any previous production. Most admired it, but some had mild reservations; the writer, director and critic Susan Sontag, who had watched the Schiller Theatre performance, had this to say (also interesting because it draws a parallel between Chekhov and Beckett in their desire to control performances of their texts): 'I was actually quite shocked by his production. To my surprise ... it was very funny, it was fast, as if someone had taken literally Chekhov's declaration that the *Three Sisters* was a comedy. I found it in short much too amusing' (quoted in Bradby, 2001, p.135).

The first Dutch production in 1988 at Haarlemse Toneelschuur departed from the usual all-male performances of the play by introducing an all-woman cast. The text and directions were not changed in any respect, and the female actors in fact played their roles as male. However, Beckett sued through the Société des Auteurs et Compositeurs Dramatique, arguing that he had not been informed of this casting decision when his permission was sought (later defending himself weakly by saying that 'women don't have prostates'; Worth, 1999, p.153). In this event the judge dismissed the case on the grounds that 'since the play was about the human condition in general, it transcended the sexual identity of men and women' (Bradby, 2001, p.157). *Waiting for Godot* has been used to introduce gender issues elsewhere. In 1994 in Japan, Yukio Ninagawa directed twin productions of the play on alternate nights at Theatre Ginza Saison in Tokyo, one with an all-male cast and another with an all-female cast. The Beckett estate refused permission for an all-female *Waiting for Godot* to be performed by the Grimy up North company at the Edinburgh Festival of 1998. On a different note, the play has also been used in specific contexts to reflect on-going racial and ethnic conflicts. Memorably, Donald Howarth produced the play with a multiracial cast in Cape Town in 1980, at the height of apartheid in South Africa. In this production, Pozzo was dressed as a Boer farmer. In a similar vein, the play was directed by Ilan Ronan in Haifa, Israel in 1984 with two Arab actors. Here Vladimir and Estragon spoke Arabic to each other and Hebrew to Pozzo, who used Arabic to give orders to Lucky. In 1998, Joy Zinoman directed *Waiting for Godot* for the Studio Theatre, Washington, with black actors playing Vladimir and Estragon, and white actors playing Pozzo and Lucky, and using some elements of the black vaudeville tradition (black acts originally featured as interludes). The Beckett estate tried to block this production through their US agents and Zinoman went public about the 'bullying and intimidating' tactics of the representatives of the estate (*Washington Post*, 10 November 1998). The play was successfully produced and presented nevertheless. Other noteworthy productions include the first Yugoslav performance of the play in Sarajevo, directed by Susan Sontag in 1993, at the height of Serb bombardment of the city. In November 2001, Richard Schechner was refused permission by the Beckett estate to produce the play in its entirety for the Confrontations Theatre Festival in Lublin, Poland, because of the experimental nature of Schechner's directing.

We can thus see that *Waiting for Godot* has come to stand for far more than even the author had expected (or his representatives now understand). It has become a global cultural phenomenon, a powerful statement of discontent and hope in a variety of different contexts – potentially anywhere.

Works cited

Adorno, T. (1973) *The Jargon of Authenticity*, trans. by K. Tarnowski and F. Will, London: Routledge & Kegan Paul.

Allén, S. (1997) 'Topping Shakespeare? Aspects of the Nobel Prize for Literature', *Nobelprize.org*, Stockholm: The Nobel Foundation [online]. Available from: http://nobelprize.org/literature/articles/sture/index.html [accessed 17 September 2004].

Batty, M. (2000) 'Acts With Words – Samuel Beckett, Translation, Mise en Scène and Authorship', in C.-A. Upton (ed.), *Moving Target: Theatre, Translation and Cultural Relocation*, Manchester: St Jerome Press.

Beckett, S. ([1955] 1957) *Waiting for Godot*, London: Samuel French.

Beckett, S. (1965) 'Proust', in *Proust and Three Dialogues*, London: John Calder.

Beckett, S. (1972) 'Dante ... Bruno, Vico ... Joyce', in *Our Exagmination Round his Factification for Incamination of Work in Progress*, London: Faber & Faber, pp.1–22.

Beckett, S. (1983) *Disjecta: Miscellaneous Writings and a Dramatic Fragment*, ed. by R. Cohn, London: Calder.

Beckett, S. (1993) *Theatrical Notebooks of Samuel Beckett: Waiting for Godot*, ed. by D. McMillan and J. Knowlson, New York: Grove.

Beckett, S. ([1955] 2004) *Waiting for Godot*, London: Samuel French.

Bradby, D. (2001) *Beckett: Waiting for Godot*, Cambridge: Cambridge University Press.

Brochier, J.-J. (1995) *Pour Sartre: le jour où Sartre refusa le Nobel*, Paris: J.C. Lattès.

Camus, A. (1965) *Caligula*, trans. by S. Gilbert, in *The Collected Plays of Albert Camus*, London: Hamish Hamilton, pp.2–66.

Camus, A. (1955) *The Myth of Sisyphus*, trans. by J. O'Brien, Harmondsworth: Penguin.

Cockerham, H. (1975) 'Samuel Beckett, Bilingual Playwright', in K. Worth, *Samuel Beckett the Shape Changer*, London: Routledge & Kegan Paul, pp.139–59.

Cohn, R. (1967) 'Samuel Beckett Self-Translator', *PMLA*, 76, pp.613–22.

Cohn, R. (1973) *Back to Beckett*, Princeton, NJ: Princeton University Press.

Cronin, A. (1996) *Samuel Beckett: The Last Modernist*, London: Flamingo.

Espmark, K. (1986) *The Nobel Prize in Literature: A Study of the Criteria Behind the Choices*, Boston: G.K. Hall.

Espmark, K. (1999) 'The Nobel Prize in Literature', *Nobelprize.org*, Stockholm: The Nobel Foundation [online]. Available from: http:// nobelprize.org/literature/articles/espmark/index.html [accessed 17 September 2004].

Esslin, M. ([1961] 1980) *The Theatre of the Absurd*, Harmondsworth: Penguin.

Gierow, K.R. (1969) 'The Nobel Prize in Literature 1969: Presentation Speech', *Nobelprize.org*, Stockholm: The Nobel Foundation [online]. Available from: http://nobelprize.org/literature/laureates/1969/press. html [accessed 17 September 2004].

Graver, L. and Federman, R. (1979) *Samuel Beckett: The Critical Heritage*, London: Routledge & Kegan Paul. (Reviews of *Waiting for Godot*, pp.88–115.)

Gussow, M. (1996) *Conversations With (and About) Beckett*, London: Nick Hern.

Hilberg, R. (1961) *The Destruction of the European Jews*, London: W.H. Allen.

Hjärne, H. (1913) 'The Nobel Prize in Literature 1913: Presentation Speech', *Nobelprize.org*, Stockholm: The Nobel Foundation [online]. Available from: http://nobelprize.org/literature/laureates/1913/press. html [accessed 17 September 2004].

Kenner, H. (1970) 'Beckett Translating Beckett Translating Beckett: *comment c'est*', *Delos*, 5, pp.194–211.

Kiberd, D. (1995) *Inventing Ireland: The Literature of a Modern Nation*, London: Vintage.

Locatelli, C. (1990) *Unwording the World: Samuel Beckett's Prose Works After the Nobel Prize*, Philadelphia: University of Pennsylvania Press.

Marrus, M. (1987) *The Holocaust in History*, Harmondsworth: Penguin.

Mercier, V. (1962) *The Irish Comic Tradition*, Oxford: Clarendon Press.

Mercier, V. (1977) *Beckett/Beckett*, London: Souvenir Press

Nobel, A. (1895) 'Alfred Nobel's Will', *Nobelprize.org*, Stockholm: The Nobel Foundation [online]. Available from: http://nobelprize.org/nobel/ alfred-nobel/biographical/will/will-full.html [accessed 17 September 2004].

O'Brien, C.C. (1965) *Writers and Politics*, London: Chatto & Windus.

Robbe-Grillet, A. (1965) 'Samuel Beckett or "Presence" in the Theatre', in M. Esslin (ed.), *Samuel Beckett*, Englewood Cliffs, NJ: Prentice Hall, pp.108–16.

Rousso, H. (1991) *The Vichy Syndrome: History and Memory in France Since 1944*, Cambridge, MA: Harvard University Press.

Sartre, J.-P. (1956) *Being and Nothingness*, trans. by H.E. Barnes, New York: Washington Square Books.

Sartre, J.-P. (1974) 'A Plea for Intellectuals', in *Between Existentialism and Marxism*, trans. by J. Matthews, London: NLB, pp.228–85.

Swedish Academy (1964) 'The Nobel Prize in Literature 1964', *Nobelprize.org*, Stockholm: The Nobel Foundation [online]. Available from: http://nobelprize.org/literature/laureates/1964/index.html [accessed 17 September 2004].

Swedish Academy (1967) 'The Nobel Prize in Literature 1967', *Nobelprize.org*, Stockholm: The Nobel Foundation [online]. Available from: http://nobelprize.org/literature/laureates/1967/index.html [accessed 17 September 2004].

Swedish Academy (1969) 'The Nobel Prize in Literature 1969', *Nobelprize.org*, Stockholm: The Nobel Foundation [online]. Available from: http://nobelprize.org/literature/laureates/1969/index.html/ [accessed 17 September 2004].

Uhlmann, A. (1999) *Beckett and Poststructuralism*, Cambridge: Cambridge University Press.

Walder, D.J. (2005) 'Bertolt Brecht, *Life of Galileo*', in R.D. Brown and S. Gupta (eds), *Aestheticism and Modernism: Debating Twentieth-Century Literature 1900–1960*, London: Routledge in association with The Open University, pp.324–74.

Worth, K. (1999) *Samuel Beckett's Theatre*, Oxford: Clarendon Press.

Useful websites

The Nobel Foundation: Nobel Prize in Literature (http://nobelprize.org/
   literature/). The website contains a translation of Alfred Nobel's will,
   lists all the Nobel Laureates and gives brief biographies and the Nobel
   presentation speeches. It also has an archive of articles about the
   Nobel Prize.

The Samuel Beckett On-Line Resources and Links Page (http://samuel-
   beckett.net/). This provides an enormous variety of links to Beckett-
   related websites.

Further reading

Essif, L. (2001) *Empty Figure on an Empty Stage: The Theatre of Samuel
   Beckett and his Generation*, Bloomington: Indiana University Press. This
   study begins with a discussion of the philosophical, socio-cultural and
   theatrical implications of emptiness. Beckett's drama and performance
   are examined in this context, along with those of other dramatists of
   his generation.

Gordon, L. (2002) *Reading Godot*, New Haven: Yale University Press.
   Gordon approaches the play scene by scene, exploring the text
   linguistically, philosophically, critically and biographically. It is argued
   that the play portrays more than the rational mind's search for self and
   worldly definition.

Junker, M. (1995) *Beckett: The Irish Dimension*, Dublin: Wolfhound. Five
   plays, including *Waiting for Godot*, are examined in terms of Beckett's
   Irish heritage. There is a particularly useful discussion of the influence
   of Irish language usage on Beckett.

McDonald, R. (2001) *Tragedy and Irish Writing: Synge, O'Casey, Beckett*,
   Basingstoke: Palgrave. It is suggested here that in Irish theatre tragedy
   appears in terms of a communal sense of loss. Beckett's plays are
   discussed in that context.

CHAPTER 6

The poetry of Seamus Heaney

RICHARD DANSON BROWN

Overview

This chapter presents Seamus Heaney's poetry alongside extracts from his criticism and reviews of his work. My central concern is to consider Heaney as a Nobel Laureate, and to explore the tensions between critical readings of his poetry, his own defence of poetry and the poems themselves. In the first section, I consider Heaney's work and career in the light of the Nobel citation and his own judgements about the value of poetry. In the second section, I address Heaney as an Irish poet writing in English at a time of political upheaval and violence in his native Northern Ireland, and examine his complex relationship to the English poetic tradition. I develop this in the third section, by investigating the debate about the ethics of the so-called 'bog poems' in his 1975 collection, *North*, and the extent to which Heaney can be seen as a 'laureate of violence'. In the final section, I consider an example of Heaney's creative use of translation in the context of *North* and his profile as a prize-winner. In brief, this chapter juxtaposes the discourse of prize-winning with the rich ambiguity of the work itself and its critical reception. The main poems discussed are: 'The Stone Verdict', 'Sloe Gin', 'Requiem for the Croppies', 'Anahorish', 'Broagh', 'A New Song', 'Bog Oak', 'The Grauballe Man', 'Punishment', reproduced in *New Selected Poems 1966–1987* (Heaney, 1990; unless otherwise stated, all Heaney's poetry is quoted from this edition), and 'The Digging Skeleton' (see Appendix).

'Crediting poetry': Heaney and the Nobel Prize

Judgement figures strongly in the poetry of Seamus Heaney. Typically, he focuses not on literary judgements but on moral evaluation. 'The Stone Verdict' imagines the fate of a taciturn man, who Michael Parker (1993, p.211) links with Heaney's father, Patrick, who died in 1986:

> It will be no justice if the sentence is blabbed out.
> He will expect more than words in the ultimate court
> He relied on through a lifetime's speechlessness.
>
> Let it be like the judgment of Hermes,
> God of the stone heap, where the stones were verdicts
> Cast solidly at his feet ...
>   maybe a gate-pillar

Or a tumbled wallstead where hogweed earths the silence
Somebody will break at last to say, 'Here
His spirit lingers,' and will have said too much.

(p.222)

In this stern poem, the form of the 'verdict' is more important than 'the sentence' which the man receives: he 'expect[s] more than words in the ultimate court'. Heaney conjures up a pagan ritual 'like the judgment of Hermes' through which the sentence will be conveyed. The 'gate-pillar' and 'tumbled wallstead' translate divine judgement into the solid, physical terms of a pastoral landscape that the man seems to have inhabited, 'With his stick in his hand and the broad hat / Still on his head'. It would seem that for Heaney, judgement is at once a serious and a formal business: proper evaluations should be made in an appropriate way. When he was awarded the Nobel Prize for Literature in 1995, the terms of that judgement focused on the moral and formal dimensions of his work: he was praised 'for works of lyrical beauty and ethical depth which exalt everyday miracles and the living past' (Swedish Academy, 1995). As you have seen in the case of Samuel Beckett (Chapter 5), the criteria used for the Nobel Prize have tended to privilege such abstract and idealized qualities. This chapter will read Heaney's poetry in the light of these qualities, and in terms of critical debates about him, to help you form your own verdict on his work.

Heaney was born in Mossbawn, County Derry, in 1939 to Catholic parents who owned a small farm (Parker, 1993, pp.1–4); in his own words, he was 'Sprung from an Irish nationalist background' (Heaney, 1999, p.xxiii). He is the author of ten major collections of poetry, from *Death of a Naturalist* (1966) to *Electric Light* (2001), and four volumes of critical essays; he has translated poetry and plays from languages including Irish, Latin, Ancient Greek, Italian, French, Dutch, Polish and Anglo-Saxon. *New Selected Poems 1966–1987* gathers poems from his first seven collections alongside prose poems from the pamphlet *Stations* (1975) and excerpts from his translation of the Irish poem *Sweeney Astray* (1983). One of the most eulogized of contemporary writers, Heaney has been described by the American poet Robert Lowell as 'The greatest Irish poet since [W.B.] Yeats', and by the critic John Carey as 'The greatest living poet writing in English' (quoted in Andrews, 1992, p.1). His work has produced large numbers of critical essays and monographs; he is already a major canonical figure inasmuch as his work is widely taught in schools and universities. Unlike most poets, Heaney's work sells in thousands of copies. For a poet, prize-winning is directly linked to visibility and marketability in that it creates an interest in a literary form that is usually ignored by the media. Heaney's Nobel success has arguably raised interest in and awareness of poetry.

Yet praise has not been universal. As Elmer Andrews's curiously hesitant sentence indicates, alongside critical hyperbole, there remains an undertow of suspicion: 'There are not many critics anywhere in the world who would deny that Heaney is a very good poet' (1992, p.1). Andrews's cautious formulation implies that there *are* critics who have denied, or at least queried, Heaney's quality. In Andrews's own collection of essays, James Simmons draws attention to what he sees as Heaney's aesthetic limitations: 'He is a very skilful poet, dedicated to the work, with terrible blocks in his mind and imagination that frustrate that beautiful dedication' (1992, p.65), while David Lloyd, writing from a Marxist perspective, condemns him as 'a minor Irish poet' whose work embodies the 'contradiction between ethical and aesthetic elements of bourgeois ideology' (1992, pp.113, 88).

Why does Heaney simultaneously provoke such adulation and such resistance? Your own reading should ultimately guide you in answering this question, but before turning to the poetry, it is worth knowing something about his extraordinarily successful career. While he was a student at Queen's University, Belfast, in the early 1960s, Heaney was encouraged by Philip Hobsbaum, a lecturer in the English department. Hobsbaum put him in touch with influential figures in literary London. Soon after, in 1965, Heaney's first collection was accepted by Faber & Faber, the most important publishers of poetry in the English-speaking world (Parker, 1993, pp.49, 58). Faber's list included Ezra Pound, W.H. Auden and Louis MacNeice; T.S. Eliot had been a director of and an editor at the firm. At a stroke, the twenty-six-year-old Heaney was taken into the heart of London's literary establishment. In Hobsbaum's words, 'Seamus Heaney has won all of the competitions, and deserves to; no poet has had more startling success in his youth' (1985, p.37): *Death of a Naturalist* received enthusiastic notices from critics such as Christopher Ricks (Curtis, 1985, p.8); the next two volumes, *Door into the Dark* (1969) and *Wintering Out* (1972), were also highly praised. As we shall see, reaction to *North* (1975) was less uniform; nonetheless, Heaney's central importance to the contemporary scene was established from his first publications, and has remained largely unchallenged since then.

As Andrews observes, the object of this praise was slightly at odds with the prevailing Zeitgeist:

> Old ways and dying arts were what Heaney offered the Swinging Sixties ... [He] was absorbed by the family farm, playing around its barns and wells and fields with an imagination schooled in the traditional Eng. Lit. canon of Wordsworth, Keats, Hopkins, Frost and Eliot. At a time when the streets of London and the excitements beyond of Europe and America were more on the mind than tilling the native sod, Heaney emphasised 'roots in the soil'.
>
> (Andrews, 1992, p.2)

You can get a sense of what Andrews means by reading such poems as 'Blackberry-Picking' (dedicated to Hobsbaum), 'Follower' and 'Thatcher': these are, to quote the latter, 'Bespoke' (p.10), crafted texts which sympathetically evoke traditional skills and lifestyles. There is little sense here of the urban 'excitements' that stimulated Allen Ginsberg and Frank O'Hara a decade earlier. One of the main reasons for Heaney's early fame is precisely that his work is self-consciously traditional, rooted not only in the canon of 'Eng. Lit.', but also in traditions of farming and family life. Yet Heaney was writing these poems at a moment of political turmoil in Northern Ireland. Though his work in the 1970s does, as we shall see, engage with the Troubles, his first impulse as a writer was not explicitly political. This is perhaps one of the reasons for the eulogies and brickbats Heaney has received. On the one hand, if you think that poets should not take partisan positions and should write about things they know about in a recognizable formal idiom, his traditionality seems to establish him as a 'proper' poet. On the other, if you think that it is the business of poets to be, in Percy Bysshe Shelley's formulation, 'the unacknowledged legislators of the World' (Reiman and Powers, 1977, p.508), such traditionality can be seen as a cop-out, a deliberate avoidance of a political perspective. Of course, you do not have to endorse either of these approaches: each depends on contrasting assumptions about what poetry 'ought' to be or to do, and each grotesquely oversimplifies Heaney's poetry. Nonetheless, his rise to fame was meteoric – or as meteoric as poetic fame could be in the later twentieth century – and it may be reasonable to suggest that this success is connected with the fact that his poetry is amenable to traditional expectations about poetic form and language. More than any poet of his generation, Heaney has been seen to have what 'Thatcher' admiringly calls the craftsman's 'Midas touch' (p.10).

This takes us back to the terms of the Nobel citation, which identify Heaney as a 'lyric' poet. Deriving from the Greek word *lyra* and the practice of singing songs to the accompaniment of the lyre, 'lyric' is a loose term used to describe any short poem that 'usually expresses the feelings and thoughts of a single speaker ... in a personal and subjective fashion' (Cuddon, 1982, p.372). Heaney's own analogy for poetry – 'like a harp asleep in some dark chamber, waiting to be touched' – echoes this idea of lyric poetry as an introspective activity, which remains closely rooted to its musical origins (2001, p.20). According to the Nobel Committee, Heaney's lyricism is yoked with 'ethical depth' to produce poems 'which exalt everyday miracles and the living past' (Swedish Academy, 1995). This implies that Heaney's poetry has a definite moral agenda, is in touch with tradition and is responsive to the spiritual possibilities inherent in ordinary things. But how well does it describe his poetry? Obviously, this is a thumbnail sketch of all of Heaney's oeuvre rather than of any single poem. Nevertheless, we should be able to see some of these qualities at work in a text such as 'Sloe Gin' from the *Station*

Island (1984) collection. **Now read 'Sloe Gin' (p.147). To what extent do you think the poem exemplifies the qualities singled out by the Nobel panel?**

The first thing you probably noticed about 'Sloe Gin' is its brevity. It is composed of four short stanzas, the lines of which are themselves truncated and unexpansive: the whole of line 11 is: 'and flamed'. The poem is written in what Edna Longley has called 'the skinny quatrain' (1985, p.88): a deliberately emaciated syntactic and metrical unit of four lines, which is one of Heaney's preferred measures. He has made a more portentous connection between these quatrains and 'drills or augers', suggesting that the thin form of the stanza is like a kind of poetic precision tool, which enables him to excavate deep seams of meaning (quoted in *ibid.*, p.88). In this case, we might suggest that Heaney's management of the quatrain is lyrically beautiful in its orchestration of different sounds and images. Note the way in which sibilance in the second stanza powerfully conveys the drinker's sensory delight in the drink:

> When I unscrewed it
> I smelled the disturbed
> tart stillness of a bush
> rising through the pantry.

These lines skilfully stage an encounter between the indoors world of the pantry and the outdoors world of the bush as the speaker opens the bottle. So the poem responds well to our definition of lyric poetry: it is short and expresses the thoughts of a speaker prompted by his drinking a glass of sloe gin.

The other terms used by the Nobel Committee are slightly harder to reconcile with 'Sloe Gin'. Certainly, it lacks the 'ethical depth' of a poem like Ginsberg's 'Howl', which, as you saw in Chapter 2, embodies a critique of mainstream American culture. But it is not without an ethical dimension: you might have paused over the final lines, in which the adjectives 'bitter' and 'dependable' seem to modify both the sloes and the 'you' the speaker 'drink[s] to'. These unusually paired adjectives provide both a description of the taste of the gin and a way of understanding the poem as a whole. As the woman feeds 'gin to sloes' in the first stanza (sloe gin is made by adding gin to sloes and sugar and allowing the mixture to macerate over a period of time), so the speaker in the rest of the poem relishes the finished drink. '[B]itter / and dependable' mixes the sensory impact of the gin on the palate with a sense of the ethical qualities of its maker; as such, the poem as a whole seems to be a form of graceful tribute-paying – an elegant 'thank you' in verse.

We might want to claim that the poem is an example of the exaltation of an 'everyday miracle' inasmuch as it celebrates a handmade drink and the woman who made it. Yet I am not sure that 'the living past' is visible in 'Sloe Gin', unless you argue that it broadly commemorates the traditional practice of gin-making. The problem with such a reading is that Heaney is more interested in the metaphoric evocation of the taste of the drink, which 'flamed / like Betelgeuse' (Betelgeuse is an enormous star in the constellation of Orion), than he is in the history of sloe-gin-making. Such a history may be inferred from the poem, but it is carefully buried below its surface.

To get a sense of how Heaney's work evokes 'the living past', we must look at other poems. 'Requiem for the Croppies' (p.12), taken from *Door into the Dark*, deals with a historical incident: the Irish Rebellion of 1798 against British rule, which culminated in the Battle of Vinegar Hill of 21 June in County Wexford. 'Croppies' was a term for the rebels who 'cut their hair short in sympathy with the French Revolution'; you may be familiar with the folk song 'The Croppy Boy', which laments the execution of one of these rebels (Hodgart, 1982, pp.258, 203–4). In his essay 'Feeling into Words', Heaney contextualizes the poem in terms of Northern Irish politics in the late 1960s and the fiftieth anniversary of the Easter 1916 uprising. He quotes from Yeats's poem 'The Rose Tree' (written in 1917), in which the condemned Republican leaders Patrick Pearse and James Connolly anticipate the regeneration of Ireland through the shedding of their 'own red blood' (Yeats, 1983, p.183):

> 'Requiem for the Croppies' ... was written in 1966 when most poets in Ireland were straining to celebrate the anniversary of the 1916 Rising. That rising was the harvest of seeds sown in 1798, when revolutionary republican ideals and national feeling coalesced in the doctrines of Irish republicanism and in the rebellion of 1798 itself – unsuccessful and savagely put down. The poem was born of and ended with an image of resurrection based on the fact that some time after the rebels were buried in common graves, these graves began to sprout with young barley, growing up from barley corn which the 'croppies' had carried in their pockets to eat while on the march. The oblique implication was that the seeds of violent resistance sown in the Year of Liberty had flowered in what Yeats called 'the right rose tree' of 1916. I did not realize at the time that the original heraldic murderous encounter between Protestant yeoman and Catholic rebel was to be initiated again in the summer of 1969.
>
> (in Heaney, 1980, p.56)

Now read 'Requiem for the Croppies' (p.12). What did you find most striking – its evocation of historical events or its use of language?

Since you have read the poem immediately after reading Heaney's account of the circumstances in which it was written, you were probably first struck by its evocation of the past. Using the first-person plural, Heaney gives voice to the dead Croppies, explaining their guerrilla tactics ('We'd ... stampede cattle into infantry') and their eventual undoing in the Battle of Vinegar Hill. As 'Feeling into Words' indicates, the poem is held together by the detail that the Croppies kept barley in 'The pockets of [their] greatcoats', which later grows up 'out of the grave'. As Heaney suggests, the poem's final lines are a symbolic recuperation of the Croppies' rebellion: though 'Terraced thousands died', the last line implies that they live on after their deaths. Metaphorically, the poem uses the 1798 rebellion as a form of what Heaney calls 'oblique implication': as the Croppies are transmuted into a fresh 'crop' of barley (the pun is carefully embedded in the poem's metaphoric structure), so it implies, their political ideals persist and can potentially be realized in the future. 'Requiem for the Croppies' cautiously reads the rebellion of 1798 as an augur of better times to come for Irish nationalists. Yet, as he admits in a later essay, 'Cessation 1994', soon after 1966, the poem 'could have been taken' – against its author's intentions – 'as a direct expression of support for the IRA's campaign of violence' (Heaney, 2002, p.46).

'Requiem for the Croppies' seems to be much more of a historically conscious poem than 'Sloe Gin'. Yet it would be a mistake to overlook its use of language: it is hard to describe it without engaging with its punning use of metaphor. Although we have read the poem primarily through context, its lyrical imagining of historical events is equally striking. Note the economy with which Heaney conveys the fact that the Croppies have barley in their pockets because they are conducting a guerrilla campaign: 'No kitchens on the run, no striking camp – / We moved quick and sudden in our own country'. Equally, though 'Feeling into Words' states that the rebellion was 'savagely put down', 'Requiem for the Croppies' aestheticizes the slaughter by its use of lavish imagery: 'The hillside blushed, soaked in our broken wave'. This line simultaneously personifies Vinegar Hill and endows the battle with a lush pictorialism. As we shall see, Heaney's aestheticization of violence is particularly contentious in the poems from *North*. For now, we should note that it is virtually impossible to separate Heaney's sense of the continuities between the past and the present from his commitment to the inherited forms of lyric poetry. As you may have noticed, 'Requiem for the Croppies' is a sonnet, one of the most traditional forms of English lyric; it could be seen as a formally conservative poem written in support of a rebellion against British imperial power.

My reading of 'Sloe Gin' and 'Requiem for the Croppies' suggests that the Nobel citation responds to some key elements in Heaney's poetry. A sense of Heaney the prize-winner can be developed by reading his Nobel lecture, 'Crediting Poetry'. The importance of this text is signalled by its inclusion as an 'Afterword' to *Opened Ground: Poems 1966–1996*; as Heaney explains: 'This seemed to make sense, since the ground covered in the lecture is ground originally opened by the poems which here precede it' (1998, p.vi).

Now read the extract from 'Crediting Poetry' (Reader, Item 44). What does Heaney tell us about his attitude towards poetry?

There is little ambiguity about Heaney's attitude towards poetry: it is one of profound reverence. If 'Sloe Gin' is a thank you to the maker of a drink, 'Crediting Poetry' is a more extended act of gratitude to the whole of the art of poetry: 'I credit it because credit is due to it, in our time and in all time, for its truth to life, in every sense of that phrase.' Heaney – to use one of his own favourite terms – grounds this credit in the story of listening to the radio as a child during the Second World War. Hearing transmissions from far-off places like Warsaw and Stockholm becomes the first step in Heaney's journeys 'into wideness of the world' and 'into the wideness of language'.

It is difficult to read a passage like this without picking up other frequencies; as Peter McDonald has observed, the lecture 'functions in ways that suggest [a] prose-poem' (2002b, p.83). Heaney's elaborate, oracular repetitions have a biblical resonance and grandeur; you might compare his repetition of 'time' and 'journeys' with the variations on 'days' and 'years' in Ecclesiastes 12:1:

> Remember now thy Creator in the days of thy youth, while the evil days come not, nor the years draw nigh, when thou shalt say, I have no pleasure in them.

The point I would underline is that if Heaney sounds like the Bible, this is not accidental: he wants to amplify and indeed inflate our credit in poetry, and he does this by using the most resonant prose idioms in the English language: those of the King James Bible.

Inevitably, connecting Heaney's Nobel lecture with the Bible raises other issues about his poetics. Though Heaney is usually careful not to take precise religious or political positions, his defence of poetry has become progressively more spiritual in inflection, arguably as he himself has become more of an established literary figure. His lectures as Oxford Professor of Poetry discuss what he calls 'the redress of poetry', which he explains as a 'salubrious effect' in which poetry can foster 'cultural and political realignment' as well as 'animat[ing] our physical and intelligent being' (1995, pp.191, 15). These formulations mirror 'Crediting Poetry', where poetry is credited partly 'for making possible a fluid and restorative relationship between the mind's centre and its circumference'. Like 'salubrious' (meaning conducive to good health), this clause unequivocally points to poetry as an instrument of psychic regeneration: reading poetry is literally 'good for you'. These are large claims to make of any art form, and one of your tasks will be to consider how far Heaney realizes them in his own work. Yet there has been resistance to this theory. McDonald's review of *Finders Keepers* (a collection of selected prose) balances admiration for Heaney's close readings of individual poems with a trenchant critique of his therapeutic poetic:

> At his best, Heaney reads himself and others with an utterly persuasive clarity, and expresses his own gratitude to both art and life with an old-fashioned delicacy and grace: the best of this criticism is, in the best sense, indeed good for us. Yet there is a sense in which Heaney only gives us the good news about literature, and this is the prose of a man whom the audience always applauds, and for whom the uncertainties, contradictions, difficulties, and ambiguities of language and memory are always going to be reassuringly resolved in the end.

> (McDonald, 2002a, p.79)

McDonald convincingly presents Heaney as the Nobel laureate whose discussion of poetry is always applauded and who edits out refractory critical issues; as Heaney himself has recently admitted, 'I find myself saying things that are actually a bit orotund' (Carvalho Homem, 2001, p.29). You may have found 'Crediting Poetry' 'a bit orotund', though the issue is not so much whether we endorse Heaney or McDonald, but that Heaney's characteristic presentation of poetry both before and after receiving the Nobel Prize in 1995 tends towards the universalist discourse of the Nobel Committee itself. You may have been struck by the similarity between Heaney's idea of poetry and Immanuel Kant's theory of judging literature as outlined in the Introduction to Part 2 of this book. The Nobel citation praises Heaney in the kind of critical idiom which he had evolved for the praising of poetry. Depending on your viewpoint, this is a virtuous or a vicious circle of mutual enforcement.

So the Nobel Prize emphatically confirmed the upward trajectory of Heaney's career. Robert Lowell's name-dropping accolade ('The greatest Irish poet since Yeats') anticipated Heaney's later success, since Yeats had won the Nobel Prize in 1923. The prize fixes Heaney as Yeats's successor and establishes his reputation. Heaney has long been conscious of Yeats's shadow: *Preoccupations* includes two essays on him, while in 'Crediting Poetry', he knowingly occupies the same space as his great predecessor. As well as summarizing Yeats's own Nobel address, he cites his 'Meditations in Time of Civil War' as a supreme example of poetry's capacity to satisfy 'the contradictory needs which consciousness experiences at times of extreme crisis' (Heaney, 1998, p.464). Heaney quotes 'The Stare's Nest by My Window' from Yeats's poem-sequence, which includes the famous lines:

We had fed the heart on fantasies,
The heart's grown brutal from the fare;
More substance in our enmities
Than in our love

(Yeats, 1983, p.204)

In Heaney's view, Yeats's poem simultaneously asserts that 'the massacre will happen again on the roadside' and testifies to 'the actuality of sympathy and protectiveness between living creatures' (1998, p.464). And yet Yeats was a very different writer: a representative of the Irish Ascendancy (the Protestant ruling elite of pre-independence Ireland), he was aristocratic in sympathy and autocratic in politics. As a Catholic Northerner, Heaney inevitably constructs a very different account of Ireland and Irishness. It is to this account we now turn.

'Difficult to manage': Heaney and Ireland

The Troubles have deep historical roots, ultimately deriving from the colonization of Ireland by England from the twelfth century onwards. The conflicts of the 1960s stem from the partition of Northern Ireland (also known as 'The Six Counties') from the Irish Free State after the civil war of 1922. This left Northern Ireland as a province within the United Kingdom, ruled via a devolved government dominated by the Protestant majority. During the late 1960s, Terence O'Neill's government collapsed after a deterioration in relations between Protestants and Catholics that resulted in rioting in major cities. The conflict arose from long-standing grievances between Catholics and Protestants about political representation and housing allocations (Arthur and Jeffery, 1988, pp.5–7). British troops were sent to Northern Ireland in August 1969, initially to 'contain the violence until a political solution could be found' (Goodby, 2000, p.141); however, they came to be seen by Catholics as an army of occupation, which perpetuated institutionalized discrimination against their community. In 1970, the IRA officially resumed its campaign of violence against British rule in Northern Ireland. As Jonathan Bardon summarizes:

> By 1969 Northern Ireland was in a state of near-revolutionary crisis ... Ancient hatreds welled to the surface in bitter violence ... as the Westminster government imposed direct rule on the region, Northern Ireland became the most continuously disturbed part of Europe since the ending of the Second World War.

(Bardon, 1992, p.623)

Heaney was strongly affected by the re-emergence of hostilities. His work is haunted both by 'Ancient hatreds' and by the sense that the conflict demands greater commitment from him as a poet. A section of 'The Flight Path' stages an exchange between an IRA man and the reluctant poet:

> 'When, for fuck's sake, are you going to write
> Something for us?' 'If I do write something,
> Whatever it is, I'll be writing for myself.'

(Heaney, 1996b, p.25)

The fictional context of this argument is important: it takes place 'One bright May morning, nineteen-seventy-nine' (1996b, p.24) – that is, several years after Heaney's poetry had first engaged with the Troubles. The point at issue between the poet and the terrorist is one of commitment: it is one thing to write poems of 'oblique implication' – such as 'Requiem for the Croppies' – which might be taken as a generalized support for the ideals of Irish republicanism; it is quite another to write 'Something for us' if that 'us' is the IRA. The fictional Heaney is categorical that he will 'be writing for [him]self'; though he recognizes and articulates the claims of such commitment, 'The Flight Path' rehearses these claims in order to refute them.

Although he refuses to write 'for' any political or paramilitary party, his poetry continuously reflects on the ethics and roots of sectarian conflict. As John Goodby puts it, 'No poet more completely embodied the encounter between poetry and the Troubles than Heaney' (2000, p.151). 'Feeling into Words' is again useful as a guide to Heaney's thinking:

> From [1969] the problems of poetry moved from being simply a matter of achieving the satisfactory verbal icon to being a search for images and symbols adequate to our predicament. I do not mean liberal lamentation that citizens should feel compelled to murder one another or deploy their different military arms over the matter of nomenclatures such as British or Irish. I do not mean public celebrations or execrations of resistance or atrocity ... I mean that I felt it imperative to discover a field of force in which, without abandoning fidelity to the processes and experiences of poetry ... it would be possible to encompass the perspectives of a humane reason and at the same time to grant the religious intensity of the violence its deplorable authenticity and complexity.

(in Heaney, 1980, pp.56–7)

Heaney articulates his reaction to the Troubles primarily as a poet. As in 'The Flight Path', his political reactions are deeply involved with his sense of his poetic vocation – his 'fidelity to the processes and experiences of poetry' remains constant. The Troubles meant that 'the problems of poetry moved

... to being a search for images and symbols adequate to our predicament'. Note how the rest of the paragraph painstakingly clarifies what this means: the 'search for images and symbols' correlates to 'a field of [poetic] force' which would encompass 'reason' and a sense that sectarian violence has both 'authenticity and complexity'. Heaney's reaction to the Troubles is very much that of a poet who wants to find a way to convey the paradoxical horror and logic of what was happening in Northern Ireland in the 1970s.

As we shall see, the poems that embody this paradox are some of the most debated in Heaney's oeuvre. But first we turn to poems from *Wintering Out* that reflect his position as an Irish poet writing in English. As he commented in his essay 'Belfast' (1972), 'I speak and write in English, but do not altogether share the preoccupations and perspectives of an Englishman. I teach English literature, I publish in London, but the English tradition is not ultimately home' (in Heaney, 1980, p.34). **Now read 'Anahorish', 'Broagh' and 'A New Song' (pp.21, 25, 27).** These are complex poems, which repay rereading and reading aloud, especially since they are so concerned with issues of pronunciation and intonation: do not be put off if the place names look and sound strange to you. A couple of notes may help with 'A New Song'. The final stanza includes several Irish words: 'bawn' means a fortified dwelling, particularly of the kind 'English planters built in Ireland to keep the dispossessed natives at bay' (Heaney, 1999, p.xxx); 'rath' means 'hill fort' and 'bullaun' is a 'hollowed stone mortar, found on archaeological sites' (Corcoran, 1998, pp.42–3). **After you have read the poems a few times, make some notes about their use of place names: what function do you think they have?**

Your first thought was probably how unavoidable place names are in these poems. '*Anahorish*' and '*Broagh*' stand out in italics; 'A New Song' takes the reader from Derrygarve via the Moyola to Castledawson and Upperlands. All of these places are close to Heaney's family home (Parker, 1993, p.7). The poems are 'about' these names, as when 'Anahorish' translates the word from the Irish in its first line – 'My "place of clear water" '– and then lyrically evokes the sound of the name, 'soft gradient / of consonant, vowel-meadow' (Murphy, 2000, p.23). 'A New Song' develops this technique further as place names are eroticized to become a 'Vanished music' that conveys both the sensual sound of the names and the sexual encounter between the speaker and the 'girl from Derrygarve': 'our river tongues must rise ... To flood, with vowelling embrace, / Demesnes staked out in consonants'. Landscape, language and the sounds of words literally 'embrace' one another; as Heaney has observed, these poems are 'erotic mouth-music by and out of the Anglo-Saxon tongue' (quoted in O'Donoghue, 1994, p.61). Morrison and O'Donoghue have connected these texts with traditional Irish forms, the *dinnseanches*, or 'poetry of locality'

(Morrison, 1982, p.41; O'Donoghue, 1994, p.59). So you might have felt that place names function as properties that Heaney turns into poems: that they are lyrical ornaments through which he fashions his poems.

But 'Broagh' directly indicates that place names are not only being used rhetorically. The name both evokes the place ('the shower / gathering in your heelmark / was the black *O* / ... / in *Broagh*') and differentiates native speakers from 'strangers'. The poem asserts that the '*gh*' in Broagh phonetically distinguishes those who can easily pronounce the name from those who find it 'difficult to manage': the place identifies those who successfully speak its name.

'Broagh' implies that these poems have a broader agenda, which Goodby has usefully described as a 'linguistic politics' (2000, p.154). Heaney's explanation of 'Broagh' reads it as a text that mediates issues of language and identity:

> its purpose was to bring ... Irish, Elizabethan English and Ulster Scots ... into some kind of creative intercourse and alignment and to intimate thereby the possibility of some new intercourse and alignment among the cultural and political heritages which these three languages represent in Northern Ireland ... The poem ... was just one tiny move in that big campaign of our times which aims to take cultural authority back to the local ground, to reverse the colonising process by making the underprivileged speech the normative standard. Whitehall ministers would have called the place *Broa*, but they would have been wrong ... But everyone native to Northern Ireland, Protestant or Catholic, Planter or Gael, whatever their separate myths of linguistic exile from Irish or Ulster Scots – every one of them could say *Broagh*, every one was fitted to dwell in at least phonetic amity with the other.
>
> ('Burns's Art Speech'; in Heaney, 2002, pp.351–2)

This puts us in a better position to understand these poems. By drawing poetic attention to Ulster place names and their roots in a number of different, but for Heaney complementary, languages and traditions, these poems both assert the authority of 'the local ground' against the colonizing authority of 'Whitehall' and metaphorically gesture towards the possibility of a deeper 'amity' between sectarian groups. Heaney's 'linguistic politics' embraces both a commitment to the local and an aspiration towards a broader 'vowelling embrace', which might encompass all Northern Irish speakers, no matter what their origins.

Another *Wintering Out* poem, 'Bog Oak' (p.19), articulates some of the ambiguities about Heaney's relationship with linguistic and literary tradition that his prose account of 'Broagh' rather muffles. Like the texts you have just studied, this poem is highly allusive, though its allusions are literary rather than geographical or linguistic. The 'Edmund Spenser' of the sixth stanza is the writer of the epic of English Protestantism, *The Faerie Queene* (1590–6), as well as the pastoral poem *The Shepheardes Calendar* (1579). He was also a leading representative of the Elizabethan colonization of Ireland: he had substantial lands in Munster including Kilcolman Castle, from which he was ejected by rebels during the Tyrone uprising of 1598 (Judson, 1945, pp.196–201). 'Bog Oak' does not quote from Spenser's poetry but from his political dialogue, *A View of the Present State of Ireland*. This text was so critical of the Elizabethan government's handling of Ireland that it was first published long after Spenser's death in 1633; it advocates a hardline approach to the native Irish and to colonial administration. In the view of Irenius, the speaker whose experiences most clearly mirror Spenser's own, Irish resistance to English rule should be forcibly suppressed. Heaney quotes from its most infamous passage, the eye-witness description of the Munster famine, which describes the starving Irish as 'anatomies of death' (see Appendix). It is hard to catch from 'Bog Oak', but Spenser's account is profoundly unsympathetic to the starving Irish. According to Irenius, the reduction of the Irish to cannibalism and starvation was entirely their own fault: 'sure in all that warre there perished not many by the sword, but all by the extremitie of famine, which they themselves had wrought'. **Now read 'Bog Oak' (p.19). Remembering Heaney's comments from 'Belfast' (p.273 above), how would you characterize this poem's attitude towards what he called 'the English tradition'?**

There are two different ways of approaching this question. If you read the poem as a whole in the light of the colonial context that Heaney sketches in the final stanzas, 'Bog Oak' is critical of the English tradition. It begins with a piece of timber preserved in a bog, which in turn evokes 'the moustached / dead': Heaney moves from the physical remains of a peasant past to the peasants themselves. Note how inaccessible they are: though the speaker 'might tarry' with them, 'or eavesdrop on / their hopeless wisdom', the pathos of these images lies in the fact that the physical evidence of Gaelic Ireland has all but disappeared. However, the speaker is able 'just' to 'make out / Edmund Spenser'. Thus Heaney juxtaposes Spenser's description of the Munster famine with Spenser himself as a disconnected poet 'dreaming sunlight' in the midst of extreme human misery. In this reading, 'Bog Oak' simultaneously suggests Spenser's callousness in the face of Irish suffering and asserts the 'genius' of the very people he disdained.

But you might not be convinced by this approach: despite the severity of Spenser's attitude towards the Irish, 'Bog Oak' is positively good-mannered in its treatment of him. And though it is self-evidently in sympathy with the 'geniuses who creep' from the pages of the *View*, the poem can be seen as a version of English pastoral: Heaney could be said to attack 'the English tradition' from the inside of that tradition. Like 'A New Song' or 'Anahorish', the poem articulates its cultural politics within the vocabulary of traditional poetry in English. This is evident not only in Heaney's sensuous handling of 'the skinny quatrain', but also in the way in which Spenser's own words are deftly incorporated within Heaney's poem. Though the *View* is recontextualized in 'Bog Oak', the poem draws a measure of its poetic energy from this source. Heaney's attitude towards Spenser is perhaps more equivocal than critical.

This is borne out by a passage in Heaney's Introduction to his translation of the Anglo-Saxon epic *Beowulf*, in which he contrasts an incident from that poem with Spenser's own life:

> every time I read the lovely interlude that tells of the minstrel singing in Heorot just before the first attacks of [the monster] Grendel, I cannot help thinking of Edmund Spenser in Kilcolman Castle, reading the early cantos of *The Faerie Queene* to Sir Walter Raleigh, just before the Irish would burn the castle and drive Spenser out of Munster back to the Elizabethan court.
>
> (Heaney, 1999, p.xxx)

This Spenser is a figure of pathos: a man in the wrong place at the wrong time, but nevertheless a genuine poet with whom Heaney sympathizes. (In fact, Heaney romanticizes Spenser's life by compressing events separated by about ten years.) Similarly, we could argue that 'Bog Oak' neatly enacts Heaney's dilemma as an Irish poet writing in English. Though the poem is critical of Spenser's abstraction from the sufferings of the Irish, it does not explicitly reject his poetry nor the traditions that he represents.

This reading suggests something of Heaney's adroit cultural politics in *Wintering Out*: while these poems are part of a broader movement to 'reverse the colonising process', they are also traditional texts which achieve their novelty through the accommodation of Irish place names and poetic techniques to the English language. As we have seen, Heaney is a Faber poet, publishing 'in London', marketed to a broad range of English-speaking readers. Arguably, it was precisely the universality of Heaney's appeal, and his ability to draw on different, apparently antagonistic, traditions, that made his work amenable to the universalistic ambitions of the Nobel Committee.

'Beauty and atrocity': the bog poems

If these texts mediate Heaney's ambivalent position as an Irish poet writing in English, it is with the bog poems that Heaney discovered what 'Feeling into Words' calls, again quoting from Yeats's 'Meditations in Time of Civil War', 'befitting emblems of adversity' (in 1980, p.57; Yeats, 1983, p.202):

Some of these emblems I found in a book that was published in English translation ... in 1969 ... entitled *The Bog People*. It was chiefly concerned with preserved bodies of men and women found in the bogs of Jutland, naked, strangled or with their throats cut, disposed under the peat since early Iron Age times. The author, P.V. Glob, argues convincingly that a number of these, and in particular the Tollund Man ... were ritual sacrifices to the Mother Goddess, the goddess of the ground who needed new bridegrooms each winter to bed with her in her sacred place, in the bog, to ensure the renewal and fertility of the territory in the spring. Taken in relation to the tradition of Irish political martyrdom for that cause whose icon is Kathleen Ni Houlihan, this is more than an archaic barbarous rite: it is an archetypal pattern. And the unforgettable photographs of these victims blended in my mind with photographs of atrocities, past and present, in the long rites of Irish political and religious struggles.

(in Heaney, 1980, pp.57–8)

Glob's work on Iron Age bog bodies provided Heaney with an emblematic vocabulary through which he could evoke 'Irish political and religious struggles'. The Iron Age goddess Nerthus becomes a metaphor for 'Mother Ireland' (present in this extract as 'Kathleen Ni Houlihan', a personification of Ireland about whom Yeats had written a patriotic play), who demands sacrificial appeasement (in Heaney, 1980, p.57). In Heaney's poem 'The Tollund Man', the Man is not only an offering to a rapacious Earth Mother – 'She tightened her torc on him / And opened her fen' – but also an emblem of more recent victims of 'archetypal' violence. The 'Stockinged corpses / Laid out in the farmyards' allude to Catholics murdered by Protestants during the civil war (pp.31–2; Parker, 1993, p.107). (Note that this edition misprints 'Grabaulle': it should read 'Grauballe'.)

Since Glob was crucial to Heaney, it is important to study some of the photographs he included in his book. Figure 6.1 shows the Tollund Man as he was initially excavated in 1950; Figure 6.2 is the photograph mentioned in Heaney's poem 'The Grauballe Man' (p.70); Figure 6.3 shows the decapitated female head described in 'Strange Fruit' (p.73); Figure 6.4 shows the head of the Windeby Girl, who is the subject of 'Punishment' (pp. 71–2). **How do you react to these photographs? Now read 'The Grauballe Man'. How does Heaney's poem differ from your first reaction to the photos?**

Taken simply as photographs, these are arresting and shocking images. As 'Feeling into Words' explains, the subjects are victims of Iron Age ritual: Glob estimates that the Grauballe Man died about 1,650 years before his excavation in 1952 ([1969] 1988, p.62). Yet despite their antiquity, these bodies are disquietingly fresh: you might have noticed the Windeby Girl's

Figure 6.1 The Tollund Man completely uncovered. (Photo: Lennart Larsen, The National Museum of Denmark.)

Figure 6.2 First picture of the Grauballe Man. (Photo: Moesgård Museum, Denmark.)

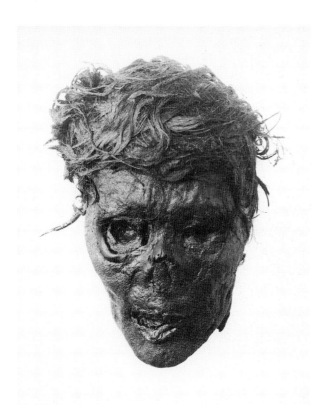

Figure 6.3   Head of decapitated girl from Roum. (Photo: Lennart Larsen, The National Museum of Denmark.)

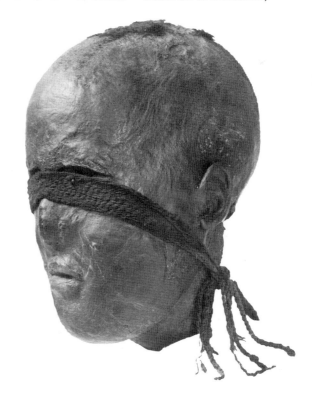

Figure 6.4   The Windeby Girl and the band with which she was blindfolded. (© Archäologisches Landesmuseum in der Stiftung Schleswig-Holsteinische Landesmuseen Schloss Gottorf, Schleswig, Germany, 2004.)

ear, or the Tollund Man's feet, which look almost like living tissue. Indeed, Glob records the controversy between archaeologists and local people, who claimed that the Grauballe Man was really the body of a peat-cutter who disappeared in the 1880s (*ibid.*, pp.59–62). But the true shock value of these images lies in the violent deaths they record. The Tollund Man, despite his foetal posture, is caught by the noose which probably strangled him (*ibid.*, p.32), the Windeby Girl is apparently blindfolded in preparation for execution (*ibid.*, p.114), while the Grauballe Man appears to have had his head beaten to a pulp (*ibid.*, p.39).

Heaney's poem registers the difference between a first reaction to this photograph and later thoughts:

> I first saw his twisted face
>
> in a photograph,
> a head and shoulder
> out of the peat,
> bruised like a forceps baby,
>
> but now he lies
> perfected in my memory ...

(p.70)

In this formulation, first sight gives way to a process of perfection through which the body of the Grauballe Man becomes metaphorically 'hung in the scales / with beauty and atrocity'. The body that Heaney's poem meticulously describes is simultaneously a beautiful thing and an emblem of 'atrocity'. The Man's death symbolizes religious and political violence in Northern Ireland, where victims of sectarian violence were also 'slashed and dumped'. Though you can probably see how Heaney has come to construe the Grauballe Man in this way, I suspect that the poem is very different from your first reaction to the photographs. Apart from 'bruised like a forceps baby' and 'the vent / of his slashed throat' – which evoke the Man's violent death – Heaney's poem is arguably more concerned with the construction of evocative similes than it is with the shock of the image that prompted it: note the way it begins with an elaborate comparison: 'As if he had been poured / in tar'.

Unsurprisingly, such texts have generated energetic critical debate. For Longley, 'Beauty on the whole has outweighed atrocity by the time we reach "the actual weight / of each hooded victim, / slashed and dumped"' (1985, p.76). Corcoran offers the opposing view:

> The precision and meticulousness of Heaney's metaphors, which may be thought to appropriate the human victim to the poem's own form and order ... are themselves criticized in the final stanza

where the victim – the man himself, then, and each murdered corpse, now – sickeningly thuds out of artistic 'repose' into the realistic brutality of 'slashed and dumped'.

(Corcoran, 1998, pp.71–2)

In effect, Longley and Corcoran agree that 'The Grauballe Man' records the process of how it became a poem: Heaney self-consciously draws our attention to the processes of art in the writing of a poem about violence. The debate centres on the moral legitimacy of such a strategy.

So you can begin to form your own judgement, now read through the extracts from *North* in *New Selected Poems 1966–1987* (pp.49–91). The poems you should particularly concentrate on are: 'Bog Queen', 'Punishment', 'Strange Fruit' and 'Exposure'. After you have done this, read the two reviews of *North* in the Reader (Items 45 and 46) and think about the following questions.

1 **What differentiates the two reviewers' readings of 'Punishment'?**

2 **Which reviewer do you find most convincing and why?**

In Conor Cruise O'Brien's view, 'Punishment', like *North* as a whole, articulates 'the tragedy of a people in a place: the Catholics of Northern Ireland'. The moment at which the poem concedes that its speaker 'understand[s]' the punishment both of the 'Little adulteress' and of her contemporary 'betraying sisters' is seen by O'Brien as a magnificently accurate piece of political realism: 'I have read many pessimistic analyses of "Northern Ireland", but none that has the bleak conclusiveness of these poems.' In contrast, Ciaran Carson disputes the whole basis of the analogy used in 'Punishment'. For him, the same passage is an example of sloppy thinking and bad writing: 'Being killed for adultery ... is one thing; being tarred and feathered is another ... It is as if there never were and never will be any political consequences of such acts; they have been removed to the realm of sex, death and inevitability.' Carson's general comments about the volume amplify this unease: 'Heaney seems to have ... become the laureate of violence – a mythmaker, an anthropologist of ritual killing, an apologist for "the situation["], in the last resort, a mystifier'. For Carson, 'Punishment' is not an example of realism so much as an index of how Heaney has deteriorated as a poet, and how he has used his gifts to aestheticize violence. Where O'Brien praises Heaney for unpitying forensic accuracy, Carson lambasts him for exaggeration and for 'mystifying' the Troubles.

Your response to the second question will depend on your response to the *North* poems as a group, and your evaluation of the different arguments deployed by each critic. You might have felt that Carson's accusations against 'Punishment' are well grounded – you might have pointed to other poems, such as 'The Grauballe Man' or 'Bog Queen', where there is evidence of Heaney acting as a 'laureate of violence'. To quote from 'Punishment' itself, you might have felt that Heaney writes too much as an 'artful voyeur' (p.72) of the bog bodies, and that he culpably refuses to pass any form of judgement on the IRA. Equally, you may have been unpersuaded by Carson's strictures, and prefer to view the poems as precisely the kinds of 'emblems of adversity' that Heaney hoped they would be.

Despite their different readings, Carson and O'Brien agree that 'Punishment' does not question the IRA's right to punish people accused of betraying them; for O'Brien, the poem depends on 'a double assumption – that she did ... inform on the IRA and that informing on the IRA is a crime'. Yet, as O'Brien's review makes clear, he sees poems like 'Punishment' more as a general expression of the predicament of 'the Catholics of Northern Ireland' than as the views of Seamus Heaney as an individual. So one of the key questions raised by these poems is whether the speaker is Heaney himself or is a fictionalized projection, which allows him to voice attitudes and opinions that are not necessarily his own.

The evidence from the rest of Heaney's work is ambiguous. There are texts in *New Selected Poems* that are frankly autobiographical: 'Clearances' elegizes Heaney's mother Margaret: '*In memoriam M.K.H., 1911–1984*' (p.224); as we have seen, Parker views 'The Stone Verdict' as an elegy for Heaney's father. Even in *North*, there are several poems in which the first-person speaker is undeniably Heaney. 'Exposure' presents the poet in his Wicklow home, 'weighing and weighing / My responsible *tristia*' (p.90). As 'Crediting Poetry' explains, this is an allusion to the Russian poet Osip Mandelstam. Mandelstam was the writer of a collection of poems called *Tristia* (1923) (itself an allusion to poems written in exile by the Latin poet Ovid) who was murdered in the Stalinist purges in the 1930s. As Heaney glosses, 'Exposure' articulates his ambivalent feelings during the early 1970s in his self-imposed exile in the Republic of Ireland: 'Feeling puny in my predicament as I read about the tragic logic of Osip Mandelstam's fate ... feeling challenged yet steadfast in my non-combatant status' (1998, p.452). But this does not mean that we must read poems such as 'Punishment' in the same way. Although 'The Grauballe Man' records Heaney's first sight of the photograph in Glob, the poem itself is not cast as autobiography in the way that 'Exposure' is. Where 'Exposure' focuses on Heaney's predicament as a reluctant would-be spokesman ('For what? For the ear? For the people?'; p.90), 'The Grauballe Man' centres on the body of the victim. The identity of the speaker is largely tangential to the critical debate about the poem's ethical legitimacy.

But 'Punishment' poses rather different problems because it foregrounds the responses of the speaker to the 'Little adulteress' (even that phrase is pregnant with a kind of suppressed sensuality):

My poor scapegoat,

I almost love you
but would have cast, I know,
the stones of silence.
I am the artful voyeur

of your brain's exposed
and darkened combs

(p.72)

Again, the photograph on which this passage is based is illuminating. Figure
6.5 shows the Windeby Girl's exposed brain. Glob's commentary seems to
have informed Heaney's poem:

> When the brain was removed the convolutions and folds of the
> surface could be clearly seen, but even after a most thorough
> examination it remained uncertain whether there was any
> difference between this brain of about two thousand years ago and
> the brain of contemporary man.

(Glob, 1988, p.113)

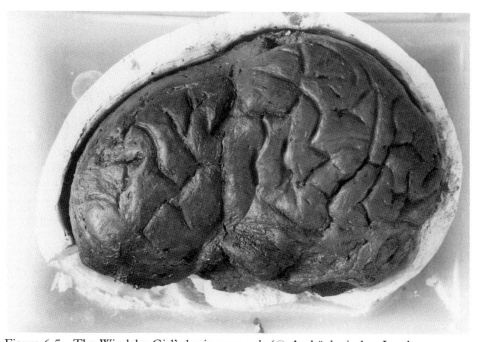

Figure 6.5   The Windeby Girl's brain exposed. (© Archäologisches Landesmuseum
in der Stiftung Schleswig-Holsteinische Landesmuseen Schloss Gottorf, Schleswig,
Germany, 2004.)

It seems to me that 'Punishment' tries to convey the shock and sense of guilty knowledge that are implicit in Glob's text and illustration. When we open Glob's book, or even this one, and look at these photographs, we become ourselves voyeurs of the Windeby Girl's 'exposed / and darkened combs'. Through its evocation of this act of voyeurism, 'Punishment' connects tribal complicity in ritual violence with sectarian complicity in political violence.

Like Glob's view of the girl's brain, Heaney sees no difference between the ancient and the contemporary. This is, I would say, the real force of 'artful'. This word admits the writer's agency – that he is using the Windeby Girl as a metaphoric device – and refuses to grant the figure of the poet any superior moral knowledge to the people who executed the Girl, or who tar and feather her contemporary 'betraying sisters'. The speaking voice of 'Punishment' is therefore that of a fictionalized poet through whom Heaney concedes his misgivings about his aesthetic procedures and admits his guilty understanding of 'the exact / and tribal, intimate revenge' (p.72). This sharply diverges from the 'orotund' defence of poetry that Heaney has subsequently developed in texts such as 'Crediting Poetry'. In the 1970s, Heaney was less confident about the reforming authority of poetry.

As we have seen, Heaney viewed such poems as Yeatsian 'emblems of adversity'. When Yeats won the Nobel Prize, he was praised 'for his always inspired poetry, which in a highly artistic form gives expression to the spirit of a whole nation' (Swedish Academy, 1923). Yeats's victory was as much a symbolic endorsement of Irish independence as it was a recognition of his work; he observed, 'I consider that this honour has come to me less as an individual than as a representative of Irish literature, it is part of Europe's welcome to the Free State' (Foster, 2003, p.245). Similarly, Heaney's victory in 1995 partly embodied optimism about Northern Ireland's future after the paramilitary ceasefires of 1994: in his Nobel lecture, he spoke of his hope that the partition between different communities would 'become a bit more like the net on a tennis court, a demarcation allowing for agile give-and-take' (in Heaney, 1998, p.461). Prize-winning is itself an emblematic activity, where literary figures can symbolize broader political aspirations. However, just as it is questionable whether Yeats's poetry did give expression to 'a whole nation', so we can query whether poems such as 'Punishment' are as 'ethical' or indeed as 'miraculous' as the Nobel citation suggests. Arguably, the strength of the bog poems is precisely their resistance to what 'Feeling into Words' calls 'liberal lamentation that citizens should feel compelled to murder one another' (in 1980, pp.56–7). Indeed, you might consider that 'Punishment' encapsulates the tension between Heaney's work and the terms of his canonization: though it evokes 'the living past' – paradoxically through the body of a dead girl – its 'lyrical beauty' does not sit easily with conventional understandings of 'ethical depth'. Rather, the poem insists on the long history of acts of violence and the moral plausibility of such acts to their perpetrators.

'Mementoes of anatomy': Heaney and translation

We turn now to a different sort of poem from *North*: 'The Digging Skeleton', a version of the nineteenth-century French poet Charles Baudelaire's 'Le Squelette laboureur' (see Appendix). Translation has been important to Heaney throughout his career: versions of passages from Dante and Virgil frame the *Field Work* (1979) and *Seeing Things* (1991) volumes.

'The Digging Skeleton' is the only translation in *North*, and it is in some ways a puzzling choice. Baudelaire is a much less respectable figure of poetic authority than Dante or Virgil. His major work, *Les Fleurs du mal* (*The Flowers of Evil*) (1857), was banned and subsequently expurgated on the grounds that it was prejudicial to public morality (Ruff, 1968, p.28). Both in his life and his work, Baudelaire exemplifies the notion of the poet as a dissolute, immoral, outcast who sets himself against bourgeois morality; were it not for his sedulous observance of the classical rules of French versification, he could almost be seen as a precursor of the Beats (Figure 6.6).

Figure 6.6   Charles Baudelaire, self-portrait, *c.*1860, pen, brown ink and red crayon, 31.5 × 2.4 cm. (Photo: RMN – Michèle Bellot.)

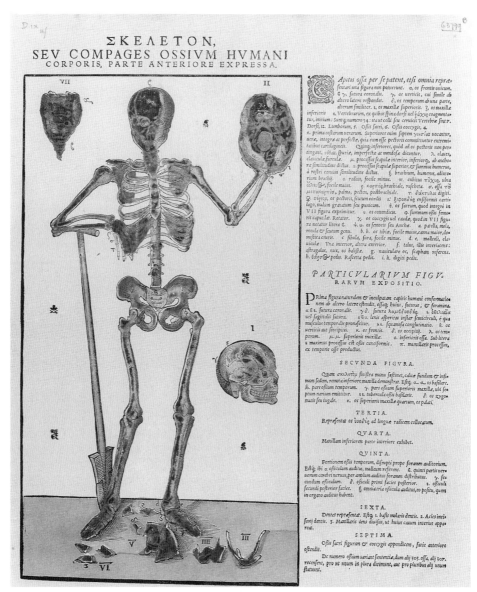

Figure 6.7 Skeleton, fugitive sheet published in Wittenberg by S. Groneberg, 1573. (Photo: Wellcome Library, London.)

'Le Squelette laboureur' is taken from the 'Tableaux Parisiens' ('Parisian Pictures') section of *Les Fleurs du mal*; it begins by describing the antiquarian bookstalls that are still found on the banks of the Seine. Like Heaney's bog poems, it is driven by the imagery of dead bodies. Baudelaire evokes 'les planches d'anatomie' ('anatomical engravings') from Renaissance anatomy textbooks, such as Andreas Vesalius' *On the Fabric of the Human Body* (1543), which show flayed corpses or skeletons performing tasks such as digging to

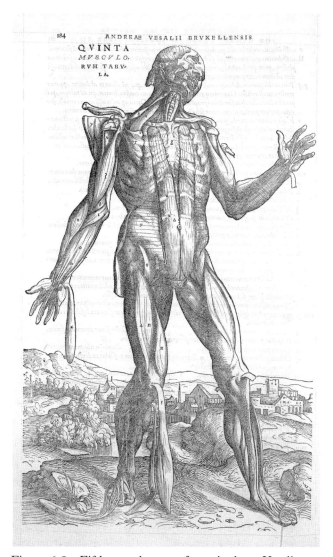

Figure 6.8   Fifth muscle man, from Andreas Vesalius, *De humani corporis fabrica libri septem [On the Fabric of the Human Body in Seven Volumes]*, Basle, J. Oporinus, 1555, p.224. (Photo: Wellcome Library, London.)

illustrate the body's musculature (Figures 6.7 and 6.8). Reproduced in the Appendix are three different versions of the poem: Heaney's translation, Baudelaire's original and a literal prose translation. **Now read these texts – if necessary, use the prose translation to help you with the French. How has Heaney altered Baudelaire's poem? What are the effects of these changes?**

Heaney has altered Baudelaire's poem in numerous ways. Consider the following phrases that he has added: 'red slobland around the bones' (which has no equivalent); 'Sad gang of apparitions' (which brilliantly paraphrases 'Manants résignés et funèbres': 'passive and sombre churls'); 'like plaited sedge' (which amplifies 'vos muscles dépouillés': 'your perished muscles'); 'by the sweat of our stripped brows / We earn our deaths' (which paraphrases and reinterprets Baudelaire's final stanza). More drastically, Heaney recasts the last two stanzas so that they are voiced by the skeletons rather than the poet. Though this is an ingenious solution to the difficulties of the French – the idea that the dead 'earn [their] deaths' through hard labour adds a macabre twist to the original – I think that it rather dilutes the horror of Baudelaire's text. In Heaney's version, the after-life of eternal drudgery is a certainty, whereas for Baudelaire it remains a matter of fearful conjecture: 'sempiternellement, / Hélas! il nous faudra, *peut-être* ... Écorcher la terre revêche' ('eternally alas! we must *perhaps* flay the rough earth'; my emphases). However, it is worth noting that Heaney largely preserves the technical effects of Baudelaire's poem. He mimics the original's eight- and nine-syllable lines, using four- and three-beat lines; and – through a proliferation of the half-rhymes in which he specializes – reproduces Baudelaire's ABBA rhyme scheme.

Heaney's changes have two main effects. In the first place, he delivers a striking version of Baudelaire which has sufficient verbal energy to stand as a poem in its own right. We could say that Heaney has responded to Baudelaire's Gothic imagery with an idiosyncratic fidelity. 'Mysterious candid studies / Of red slobland around the bones', though paraphrase rather than strict translation, registers the fascinating horror of the anatomical images, and gives the effect of representing Baudelaire in Heaney's own vocabulary. This is the second effect of Heaney's translation: he assimilates 'Le Squelette laboureur' to the topography and concerns of the *North* poems as a sequence. As Carol Clark and Robert Sykes suggest, Heaney's version fits into *North* as 'a dark meditation on the eternal nature of suffering' that 'echo[es] the terrain of the bog poems' (1997, p.135). This is what I would suggest is particularly revealing about reading 'The Digging Skeleton' alongside poems like 'Punishment', 'The Grauballe Man' and 'Bog Queen'. By translating 'Le Squelette laboureur', Heaney provides a compelling poetic pedigree for his own poems. The pessimism about the nature of violence and religious ritual that infuses Heaney's poems finds a root in Baudelaire's spiritual malaise. Compare the speech that closes 'The Digging Skeleton' with 'Bog Queen', a poem that is couched as a dramatic monologue by a bog body. In each case, death does not lead to the extinction of identity or salvation, but to a curious passivity, as the dead become subject to other forces. In 'Bog Queen', the speaker apprehends the process of her preservation – 'My body was braille / for the creeping influences ... the seeps of winter / digested me' (p.66) – whereas in 'The Digging Skeleton' the dead sombrely outline their regimen. Heaney's version encapsulates the gloomy fatalism that O'Brien sees as *North*'s leitmotiv: 'The void deceives. / We do not fall like autumn leaves / To sleep in peace'.

How do you think that translation connects with Heaney's profile as a winner of the Nobel Prize?

I would say that translation is important to Heaney's work precisely because it connects his original work with 'the living past'. Heaney is not a formally radical poet; he remains rooted in the traditions of European poetry. Translation – whether from Baudelaire's French or the Anglo-Saxon of *Beowulf* – is one of the chief means by which he asserts the integrity of the poetic tradition to which he belongs. It is also, as 'The Digging Skeleton' demonstrates, a way of assimilating older poetic practices to his own concerns. You might argue that Heaney's commitment to poetic translation is another of the ways in which he has positioned himself as a worthy Nobel winner. By revoicing the traditions that underlie contemporary poetry, Heaney emerges as a generous conduit for the dissemination of European poetries and helps to extend his readers' poetic literacy. In this way, he works within the same traditions as T.S. Eliot, who he has identified as a significant influence on his own conception of the 'poetic vocation' (in Heaney, 2002, p.38). If you would like to pursue the ways in which he has deployed translation, look at the extracts from *Sweeney Astray* (this is a translation of a medieval Irish poem about King Sweeney, who goes mad and is turned into a bird) and compare them with the 'Sweeney Redivivus' sequence from *Station Island* (pp.132–45, 194–209).

The poem with which I began, 'The Stone Verdict', conveys an 'old disdain of sweet talk and excuses' (p.222) alongside a suspicious, watchful reticence about the business of judgement. As with any living writer, our judgements of Heaney's work must be provisional: none of the verdicts dealt with in this chapter is, as it were, set in stone. Heaney's reaction to his critics is illuminating here. 'The Scribes' (from 'Sweeney Redivivus') admits 'I never warmed to them. / If they were excellent they were petulant ... [I] felt them / perfect themselves against me page by page'. In this fable, criticism is a 'jealous art' through which a class of professionals nurture 'myopic angers' against a writer they must nevertheless acknowledge: 'if I never belonged among them, / they could never deny me my place' (p.203). Of course, as a professional critic, Heaney realizes that this is an exaggeration, which is why the poem is voiced by King Sweeney. Yet the conceit of a conflict between an inspired poet and his 'petulant' critics is at once intriguing and profoundly traditional – Yeats's 'The Scholars' is similarly dismissive of academic critics: 'Bald heads forgetful of their sins' (Yeats, 1983, pp.140–1). Yet poetry demands criticism if it is to be properly understood rather than just genuflected towards. It seems to me that a poem like 'The Scribes' encapsulates the ambivalence even a major poet like Heaney feels about judgement: as in 'The Stone Verdict', any form of judgement is seen as a sentence and an attempt to fix the writer definitively.

Are we any closer to clarifying why Heaney's work has provoked both adulation and resistance? His poetry is an unusual amalgam of disparate impulses. On the one hand, he is a profoundly traditional poet, whose 'fidelity to the processes and experiences of poetry' remains constant. Nonetheless he has used poetry written in English as a means of asserting Northern Irish cultural identity in poems such as 'Broagh'. In the next chapter, Susheila Nasta develops this concern by exploring an African novel written in English that just failed to win the Booker Prize. Poems such as 'Punishment' and 'The Digging Skeleton' undermine any comfortable expectations we might have of 'traditional' poetry. At its best, Heaney's work remains genuinely unsettling and self-consciously aware of its own procedures. Though the Nobel Prize sealed Heaney's canonization, and though his own criticism has increasingly espoused a therapeutic model of poetry, his strongest work remains resistant to easy evaluation.

Works cited

Andrews, E. (1992) 'Introduction', in E. Andrews (ed.), *Seamus Heaney: A Collection of Critical Essays*, Basingstoke: Macmillan, pp.1–11.

Arthur, P. and Jeffery, K. (1988) *Northern Ireland since 1968*, Oxford: Blackwell.

Bardon, J. (1992) *A History of Ulster*, Belfast: The Blackstaff Press.

Carvalho Homem, R. (2001) 'On Elegies, Eclogues, Translations, Transfusions: an Interview with Seamus Heaney', *The European English Messenger*, 10.2, pp.24–30.

Clark, C. and Sykes, R. (eds) (1997) *Baudelaire in English*, London: Penguin.

Corcoran, N. (1998) *The Poetry of Seamus Heaney: A Critical Study*, London: Faber & Faber.

Cuddon, J.A. (1982) *A Dictionary of Literary Terms: Revised Edition*, Harmondsworth: Penguin.

Curtis, T. (1985) 'Introduction', in T. Curtis (ed.), *The Art of Seamus Heaney*, Bridgend: Poetry Wales Press, Dufour Editions.

Foster, R.F. (2003) *W.B. Yeats: A Life*, vol.II: *The Arch-Poet: 1915–1939*, Oxford: Oxford University Press.

Glob, P.V. ([1969] 1988) *The Bog People: Iron-Age Man Preserved*, London: Faber & Faber.

Goodby, J. (2000) *Irish Poetry since 1950: From Stillness into History*, Manchester: Manchester University Press.

Heaney, S. (1980) *Preoccupations: Selected Prose 1968–1978*, London: Faber & Faber.

Heaney, S. (1990) *New Selected Poems 1966–1987*, London: Faber & Faber.

Heaney, S. (1995) *The Redress of Poetry: Oxford Lectures*, London: Faber & Faber.

Heaney, S. ([1975] 1996a) *North*, London: Faber & Faber.

Heaney, S. (1996b) *The Spirit Level*, London: Faber & Faber.

Heaney, S. (1998) *Opened Ground: Poems 1966–1996*, London: Faber & Faber.

Heaney, S. (trans.) (1999) *Beowulf*, London: Faber & Faber.

Heaney, S. (2001) 'Time and Again: Poetry and the Millennium', *The European English Messenger*, 10.2, pp.19–23.

Heaney, S. (2002) *Finders Keepers: Selected Prose 1971–2001*, London: Faber & Faber.

Hobsbaum, P. (1985) 'Craft and Technique in *Wintering Out*', in T. Curtis (ed.), *The Art of Seamus Heaney*, Bridgend: Poetry Wales Press, Dufour Editions.

Hodgart, M. (ed.) (1982) *The Faber Book of Ballads*, London: Faber & Faber.

Judson, A.C. (1945) *The Life of Edmund Spenser*, Baltimore: Johns Hopkins University Press.

Longley, E. (1985) '*North*: "Inner Emigré" or "Artful Voyeur"?', in T. Curtis (ed.), *The Art of Seamus Heaney*, Bridgend: Poetry Wales Press, Dufour Editions.

Lloyd, D. (1992) '"Pap for the dispossessed": Seamus Heaney and the Poetics of Identity', in E. Andrews (ed.), *Seamus Heaney: A Collection of Critical Essays*, Basingstoke: Macmillan.

McDonald, P. (2002a) 'Appreciating Assets: Seamus Heaney, *Finders Keepers: Selected Prose 1971–2001*', *Poetry Review*, 92.2, pp.76–9.

McDonald, P. (2002b) *Serious Poetry: Form and Authority from Yeats to Hill*, Oxford: Clarendon Press.

Morrison, B. (1982) *Seamus Heaney*, London: Methuen.

Murphy, A. (2000) *Seamus Heaney*, Tavistock: Northcote House.

O'Donoghue, B. (1994) *Seamus Heaney and the Language of Poetry*, Hemel Hempstead: Harvester Wheatsheaf.

Parker, M. (1993) *Seamus Heaney: The Making of the Poet*, Basingstoke: Macmillan.

Reiman, D.H. and Powers, S.B. (eds) (1977) *Shelley's Poetry and Prose: Authoritative Texts and Criticism*, New York: Norton.

Ruff, M.A. (ed.) (1968) *Baudelaire: Œuvres Complètes*, Paris: Éditions du Seuil.

Simmons, J. (1992) 'The Trouble with Seamus', in E. Andrews (ed.), *Seamus Heaney: A Collection of Critical Essays*, Basingstoke: Macmillan.

Swedish Academy (1923) 'The Nobel Prize in Literature 1923', *Nobelprize.org*, Stockholm: The Nobel Foundation [online]. Available from: http://nobelprize.org/literature/laureates/1923/index.html [accessed 17 September 2004].

Swedish Academy (1995) 'The Nobel Prize in Literature 1995', *Nobelprize.org*, Stockholm: The Nobel Foundation [online]. Available from: http://nobelprize.org/literature/laureates/1995/index.html [accessed 17 September 2004].

Yeats, W.B. (1983) *W.B. Yeats: The Poems. A New Edition*, ed. by R.J. Finneran, London: Macmillan.

Further reading

Coughlan, P. (1991) ' "Bog Queens": The Representation of Women in the Poetry of John Montague and Seamus Heaney', in T. O'Brien Johnson and D. Cairns (eds), *Gender in Irish Writing*, Milton Keynes: Open University Press. An essay that critically interrogates the bog poems from a feminist perspective.

Heaney, S. (trans.) (2004) *The Burial at Thebes: Sophocles' 'Antigone'*, London: Faber & Faber. Heaney's most recent translation, a version of the Ancient Greek tragedy about the conflict between human and divine law.

Johnson, D. (2003) 'Violence in Seamus Heaney's Poetry', in M. Campbell (ed.), *The Cambridge Companion to Contemporary Irish Poetry*, Cambridge: Cambridge University Press, pp.113–32. A useful recent essay that considers Heaney's poetry in terms of this central issue.

O'Brien, E. (2003) *Seamus Heaney: Searches for Answers*, London: Pluto. A critical study that focuses on all of Heaney's writing (including his prose and translations) and seeks to uncover major themes in his work.

Ramazani, J. (1994) *The Poetry of Mourning: The Modern Elegy from Hardy to Heaney*, Chicago: University of Chicago Press. A study of the elegy in modern poetry, the final chapter of which explores Heaney's work in this field.

Vendler, H. (1999) *Seamus Heaney*, London: Fontana. A study of Heaney's work by an influential scholar working in the traditions of close reading and textual analysis.

CHAPTER 7

Abdulrazak Gurnah, *Paradise*

SUSHEILA NASTA

Overview

Abdulrazak Gurnah's novel *Paradise* was one of six books on the shortlist for the 1994 Booker Prize. By the 1990s, this list had come to be seen by many readers in the West as the most reliable guide to the best in contemporary fiction. Set in East Africa, and written by an East African migrant long resident in Britain, *Paradise* raises a number of questions regarding the formation of literary taste, aesthetics and judgement. How, for example, should we read a novel like *Paradise* – an issue that seemed to perplex a number of its reviewers when it first appeared? Should we use the same aesthetic criteria to judge it as are used to judge novels by non-African writers? Does the novel in fact conform to certain pre-existing ideas of what makes a 'typical' Booker contender? Or does its rich mix – both literary and cultural – implicitly compel us to adjust our expectations and engage with a different set of aesthetic criteria for judgement – criteria that do not derive only from a western mindset?

This chapter opens with a discussion of the Booker Prize (originally the Booker McConnell Prize and now the Man Booker Prize). By incorporating on its shortlists a number of postcolonial texts, the prize is perceived to have played a role in changing the face of 'British fiction' in the aftermath of empire. I focus on this perceived role and highlight a number of debates concerning the cultural politics of the prize. I then examine the particular historical and cultural contexts of *Paradise* and consider Gurnah's literary location as a migrant writer from Zanzibar (now part of Tanzania) who has lived in Britain since 1968. *Paradise* is open to a number of possible readings, which stem from a variety of different cultural, literary and linguistic influences – East African, Arab, Islamic and European. The novel's deliberate intermeshing of fictional narratives with those drawn from history and myth provides the reader with ways of witnessing the process of history under construction as well as supplying the key to unravelling a complex series of linked frameworks of meaning. I examine Gurnah's narrative methods – his art as a storyteller – and consider the ways in which memory and the stories we create about ourselves have both a significant role to play in the invention of personal and national histories and the potential to give imaginative voice to the silences of the past.

Before going any further, read *Paradise* right through. As you read, make notes on your initial responses to the novel. You may find it helpful to base your notes on some of the questions raised in the first paragraph above.

The Booker Prize

The Booker Prize was launched in 1968 to provide a benchmark for the 'best of contemporary British fiction' by awarding a prize for what was deemed to be, in the joint opinion of the judges selected by the management committee, the most outstanding novel by a 'British or Commonwealth writer' in any given year. As such, it could be seen to mark the beginning of an important phase in Britain's post-imperial history, a phase in which questions of national identity have frequently been under scrutiny in an increasingly plural and global literary world. Writers from a number of previously colonized territories are eligible to be considered for the prize, whether or not they reside in Britain, as long as the work submitted was written in English and published in Britain. The Booker's remit suggests, therefore, that it is as much concerned with expanding the frontiers of the 'novel in Britain' as with 'British fiction'. In the remainder of this section I will examine the role of the prize in more detail.

The prize was set up initially by Tom Maschler, then an ambitious young literary editor at Jonathan Cape, following a successful approach for sponsorship to Booker Brothers, an agricultural and food company, now Booker plc. Maschler's stated goal was 'to found a prize' that was designed not solely to benefit the 'winner' but also to stimulate interest in 'serious British fiction as a whole'. This highly laudable objective – to open up the canon of 'serious British fiction' by heightening public awareness and hence the readership of contemporary literature – was, however, inextricably linked from the outset to a series of blatantly commercial objectives. These objectives are evident from Maschler's recollections of his original agenda: to catch 'the imagination of the press' and that of the general public by encouraging a 'competitive (and a promotional climate) which would be generated by announcing a shortlist each year' (Booker, 1998, p.15). In its first few years, the prize was slow to build up momentum – so much so that in the early 1970s the management committee actually contemplated its demise. Today, however, the Booker is not only an integral part of national culture, a temperature gauge for the literary taste of the nation, but also a major part of the British literary establishment, an 'institution ... rather like Derby Day' (*ibid.*, 1998, p.50). By 1993, the year in which Salman Rushdie's 1981 novel *Midnight's Children* was nominated as the 'Booker of Bookers', 'the Booker [had become] London's way of formally commemorating and coronating literary tradition ... the closest thing in writing to the movies' Academy Award' (Iyer, 1993, p.46). Each year on Booker night (the night on which the winner of the award is announced), literary London is gripped by a 'huge annual orgasm' (Kate Saunders; quoted in Booker, 1998, p.51). Surprisingly, perhaps, despite the media hype and razzamatazz increasingly associated with the Booker, it has remained one of the most prestigious accolades a contemporary writer of fiction can achieve. This badge of literary approval seems to apply as much to those shortlisted as to the lucky winner. As we will see, questions of judgement have not always been based solely on objective literary criteria, nor are they necessarily always determined by any convincing consensus between the judges concerning questions of quality.

One of the most successful shifts that took place in the prize's history and subsequent status was the management committee's strategic decision in the early 1980s to create a widely publicized shortlist but postpone the announcement of the winner until Booker night, thereby heightening the sense of suspense and contest attached to the prize. For publishers, this was an extremely effective marketing ploy. The build-up over a period of several months ensures that interest is maintained in all the contenders between the publication of the shortlist and the announcement of the winner, and provides the maximum opportunity for gossip in newspapers, coverage by literary critics and gambling at the betting shops. Of course, authors – both established figures and so-called 'outsiders', whose reputations are built on the widespread coverage created by prize publicity – receive an enormous boost in sales by being on the Booker shortlist. Just think of a typical display in any high-street bookshop, where many books, whether they are current contenders or subsequent novels by Booker winners, carry a prominent mention of the prize, to signal consumer approval. This boosting of sales, and hence the visibility of the prize, was further heightened when Penguin decided to publish the entire shortlist in paperback, thus ensuring a place for many on the lists of bestsellers in national newspapers as well as widespread distribution in bookshops across the country. The hype surrounding the prize turned it for some vocal dissenters into a debased 'scrum' rather than an objectively measured award. This hype has been further inflated in recent years by the coverage of the prize-giving on television as a national media event. It was initially televised by Channel 4 and then, most famously perhaps, by BBC2's *The Late Show*. The programme, which increasingly took the form of a 'chat show', attracted wide audiences keen to savour the literary wisdom of well-known celebrity reviewers, whose pearls of wisdom stressed further the prize's viability as 'the Mark One cultural prize event in British public life', the 'Grand National of culture' (Melvyn Bragg; quoted in Booker, 1998, pp.36–8). By the mid-1990s, 'Booker on the Box' had become an event in itself. It was remarkable both for its success in bringing literature to the forefront of the nation's consciousness, and for making what are often quite difficult novels appear accessible in a manner that seemed to democratize questions of literary judgement. This desire for democratization was reflected most recently, perhaps, in the strategic renaming of the Booker in 2002 on the official Man Booker website as the 'People's Prize'.

The suggestion that the impact and influence of the Booker may be tied to the cultural politics of a fairly cynical and market-driven prize industry is an argument you have already encountered in your reading of James F. English's essay 'Winning the Culture Game: Prizes, Awards, and the Rules of Art' in Chapter 5 (Reader, Item 43). You may also have noted that much of the commentary surrounding the prize blurs the boundaries between literary judgement, aesthetic criteria and questions of marketability – an issue raised by Suman Gupta in his discussion in the same chapter of the awarding of the Nobel Prize to Samuel Beckett. However, whereas the Nobel Prize provides 'a stamp of universal value' for a lifetime's work in any genre, the Booker is a prize for fiction alone and for only one novel in any particular year. As such, therefore, the Booker was not initially seen to be particularly remarkable. A relative newcomer, it could be distinguished neither by history nor by tradition, and the cash element was not particularly significant. Yet, from the early 1970s onwards, its status as a potent symbol of what Pierre Bourdieu describes as 'cultural capital' (Bourdieu, [1979] 1984, p.12) has continued to rise – a profile generated as much by the Booker's role as a school for literary and media scandal as by the works of fiction chosen for selection.

As witnessed by the annual disputes that accompany the prize, there has been a long-standing debate between its role as an authorized institutional mechanism for judging the artistic or aesthetic value of serious fiction and its more instrumental function as a thinly disguised marketing machine. Suggesting that such rows were deliberately staged, Mark Lawson summed up the aim of the prize as not in fact to 'promote the cause of serious fiction' but 'to provoke rows and scandals, which may, in due course, promote the cause of serious fiction' (Lawson, 1994, p.12). Interestingly, this has been a position adopted by a number of others critical of the politics of late twentieth-century prize culture, including many of the annually selected Booker judges themselves. In most years, there are at least five kinds of Booker row: the 'Judging Bust-up' (when one or more of the annual quintet of literary magistrates resign); the 'Inclusion Dispute' (when those selected for the given shortlist are noisily criticized by the literary media); the 'Exclusion Furore' (when those not included rail against their exclusion); the 'Category Spat' (when books that seem to fail to meet the prize's criteria are critiqued: as was the case with Paul Scott's *Staying On* in 1979 and Pat Barker's *The Ghost Road* in 1995, both of which were condemned for not being 'stand alone' novels); and finally, the 'Closed Shop Attack' (where judges are accused of bias owing to personal connection or the forming of narrow literary cabals). In other words, as Lawson succinctly put it, 'Never mind the plot, enjoy the argument' (Lawson, 1994, p.12).

Figure 7.1   Chris Garratt, cartoon published in the *Guardian*, 1993. (Courtesy Chris Garratt.) In 1977, the chair of judges, Philip Larkin, threatened to jump out of the window if Paul Scott's *Staying On* did not win the Booker Prize.

So does the prevalence of such now predictable disputes mean that the prize is taken less seriously? According to English, it seems that the opposite may in fact be the case. Paradoxically, perhaps, an undue emphasis on the more mundane and popular aspects of cultural life – aspects that have traditionally been kept separate from the criteria for judging great art – may in fact serve to 'reinforce belief' in the 'higher' artistic value of a particular book (English, 2002, p.5). In other words, the more coverage, however banal, a book receives, the more its significance and value seems to increase. What we may imagine, therefore, to be an impartial judgement based on criteria of literary value agreed on by a number of gurus in the academic and literary/critical industry, may in fact be determined by a large number of extra-literary and commercial factors.

As with all literary prizes, this process is driven by a number of different institutions and agents – including booksellers, publishers, judges, reviewers and readers – as well as by the conditions imposed by the prize regulations. These regulations stipulate, for example, that for a novel to be eligible for consideration, it must have been published in Britain (Man Booker Foundation, 2004). Further, a current condition of entry is that publishers submitting books must be in a financial position to enhance the marketing of those shortlisted to the order of at least £4,000. So, although in its rubric the prize encourages entries from the entire 'Commonwealth', it simultaneously restricts eligibility to those works published in Britain. This not only excludes a large number of writers and publishing houses worldwide but also fails to take into account the different conditions affecting their modes of production. Moreover, in its expectation of substantial marketing support, it restricts entry to well-established and affluent publishing houses.

Many critics have argued vehemently against such a materialist reading of the role of the Booker Prize in the assessment of literary merit. Alastair Niven, for example, has praised the Booker unequivocally for its impartial recognition of 'quality', its central role in redefining the 'state of the novel today' and its enhancing of the reputation of writers such as Salman Rushdie (little known before his novel *Midnight's Children* won the prize in 1981) or Ben Okri (similarly little known and published by specialist publishers such as Longman Drumbeat before his move to Jonathan Cape with *The Famished Road* in 1991), who would otherwise perhaps not have become honoured subsequently as 'writers of stature' (Niven, 1997, p.18). Yet even Niven's worthy defence of the Booker's commitment to advancing the cause of high-quality contemporary fiction in Britain and its key role in redefining the nation's view of itself after empire has been muddied by comments such as that of John Bayley, chair of the judges in 1994 and Warton Professor of English at Oxford. Discussing the state of the novel in that year, Bayley accused writers of conforming to fashionable agendas of political correctness. 'New fiction ... is at best ambitious and at worst pretentious', he was to proclaim on BBC's Radio 4, because many writers seem to adhere to a 'formula as though they [have] an idea in advance of what the reviewer was going to write' (quoted in Donovan, 1994, p.6).

I will return to some of these issues when I consider the particular controversies provoked by the prize in 1994, the year in which *Paradise* was shortlisted. For the moment, however, let us look back at one of the Booker's first major public scandals. In 1972, in a notoriously rude acceptance speech, John Berger (who had been awarded the prize for his novel *G*), famously denounced both the prize itself and the complicity of its patron, Booker McConnell, with Britain's dubious colonial history. The impact of this speech still resonated in 1992, when the *Guardian* newspaper reprinted it in the run-up to that year's Booker.

Read Berger's speech, reproduced below. What is his argument? Do you think his position represents a valid critique of the prize and its stated objectives?

> Since you have awarded me this prize, you may like to know, briefly, what it means to me. The competitiveness of prizes I find distasteful. And in the case of this prize, the publication of the short list, the deliberately publicized suspense, the whole

emphasis on winners and losers is false and out of place in the context of literature. However, prizes act as a stimulus – not to writers themselves but to publishers, readers and booksellers.

'G' took five years to write. Since then I have been planning the next five years of my life.

I have begun a project about the migrant workers of Europe. For this project it will be necessary to travel and stay in many places. This project will cost about £10,000. The award would make it possible to begin. Yet one does not have to be a novelist seeking very subtle connections to trace the £5,000 of this prize back to the economic activities from which they came. Booker McConnell has had extensive trading interests in the Caribbean for over 130 years. The modern poverty of the Caribbean is the direct result of this and similar exploitation. One of the consequences of this Caribbean poverty is that hundreds and thousands of West Indians have been forced to come to Britain as migrant workers. Thus my book about migrant workers would be financed by profits made directly out of them or their relatives and ancestors. This is why I intend to share the prize with those West Indians in and out from the Caribbean who are fighting to put an end to their exploitation. The London-based Black Panther movement has arisen out of the bones of what Booker and other companies have created in the Caribbean; I want to share this prize with the Black Panther movement because they resist both as black people and workers the further exploitation of the oppressed. The sharing of the prize signifies that our aims are the same. By the recognition a great deal is clarified. And clarity is more important than money.

(Berger, 1992, p.3)

What is interesting about this speech (apart from the scandal it provoked at the time) is the fact that Berger was publicly attacking the patrons and sponsors of the prize for their long and essentially dubious involvement in Britain's colonial history in Guyana – a history of commercial exploitation built on the back of a harsh slave and indentured labour system. Berger's decision to donate half of his prize money to the Black Panther movement (a major black activist group in the 1970s) and the rest towards his own work on the plight of migrant workers in Europe was a clear statement of his own political position in relation to what he regarded as the mercantile imperial system from which the gains of the prize money had originally evolved. It also pointed to a number of ironic inconsistencies at the heart of the prize itself –

a prize whose stated aim was to open its doors to so-called 'fictions' from 'Commonwealth' writers (as the Booker guidelines still term them) – what we might perhaps now more appropriately call 'postcolonial' literatures.

As you are no doubt aware, Britain is no longer a separate entity within the so-called Commonwealth but one of the many countries that jointly make up its constitution – an untidy conglomeration of many different nations united soon after independence to buoy up Britain's decreasing global power. The Commonwealth has always been linked to Britain, primarily because of her imperial past and because many of the countries were superficially unified by English as a language, imposed by their respective experiences of a colonial education system. Interestingly, strong ideological connections still remain between the idea of the Commonwealth perpetuated in such discourses and the British monarchy – a hierarchical relationship still mimicked in some ways by the language of the Booker Prize.

In one sense, Berger was right to draw attention to the past history of the prize's patron, Booker McConnell. For although today Booker plc is a large, successful and multinational agribusiness (employing over 20,000 people all over the world with an income in excess of 5 billion dollars), its origins can be traced to the early nineteenth century, when it functioned as a distribution system on the Demerera (now Guyana) sugar estates. The company flourished in Guyana until independence, in 1966, when it moved its headquarters back to Britain. Berger thus sees it as primarily deriving from an imperialist enterprise the capital of which was originally gleaned from the exploitation of the Caribbean as a market for cheap labour. In his opinion, the situation was still on-going in 1972 as a consequence of the continued exploitation of a large West Indian migrant labour force invited to Britain as a source of cheap labour in the aftermath of the Second World War. Interestingly, the Caribbean poet David Dabydeen (originally from Guyana but now resident in Britain) also notes the ironies of Booker's chequered past in his 1994 poem 'Song of the Creole Gang Women', in which 'Booker' is portrayed not only as an exploitative manager of the plantations but also as a predatory patriarchal figure guilty of harassing their powerless female labourers:

> Wuk, nuttin bu wuk
> Maan noon an night nuttin bu wuk
> Booker own me patacake
> Booker own me pickni [child]
> Pain, nuttin bu pain
> Waan million tous'ne acre cane

(Dabydeen, 1994, p.43)

You might see Berger's attack on the lucrative colonial history of Booker McConnell as being irrelevant to its current role as an apparently benevolent patron of the contemporary novel in Britain. However, he raises some important points that have significant implications today as far as the judging of the prize and the fictions it authorizes are concerned. These concern the cultural politics involved in the prize's perceived role in expanding the traditional canon of English literature and the manner in which it heightens the profile of postcolonial writers through its apparently generous incorporation of 'Commonwealth fiction' into its rubric.

Scrambling for 'otherness': the Booker and the postcolonial

If we look at a list of the prize-winners since 1970, there is little doubt that writers who have colonial and/or postcolonial links with Britain (whether Irish, Scottish, Indian, African, Caribbean, Canadian or Australian) figure prominently in the shortlists and among the nominees. Indeed, Booker's privileging of such works – which increased significantly in the period after 1972 following the impact of Berger's ferocious speech – has frequently been given as a reason for commending the international reach of the prize and its role in reinventing Britain by drawing attention to the plural nature of its multicultural history and the diversity of its imperial past. Among the winners have been writers such as V.S. Naipaul (a resident of Trinidad and Britain), Nadine Gordimer (South Africa), Salman Rushdie (India and Britain), Thomas Keneally (Australia), J.M. Coetzee (South Africa), Keri Hulme (New Zealand), Ben Okri (Nigeria and Britain), Michael Ondaatje (Sri Lanka, Canada and Britain), James Kelman (Scotland), Peter Carey (Australia) and Margaret Atwood (Canada). Shortlisted writers include Chinua Achebe (Nigeria), Anita Desai (India and Germany), Romesh Gunesekera (Sri Lanka and Britain) and Abdulrazak Gurnah (Tanzania and Britain). And, if this was not enough, a number of works in the early history of the prize, such as J.G. Farrell's *The Siege of Krishnapur* (1973) or Paul Scott's *Staying On* (1979), clearly demonstrate an explicit engagement with themes of empire – whether or not such preoccupations are seen simply as a further manifestation of Britain's narcissistic concern with questions of imperial loss in an era of waning global power or as the 'artistic counterpart', as Rushdie once put it, 'to the rise of conservative ideologies in modern Britain' (quoted in Huggan, 2001, p.112).

Go to the Man Booker website (http://www.bookerprize.co.uk/ aboutprize/previous.html) and examine the lists of prize-winning and shortlisted novels. Note down the titles of any novels that seem to deal with issues of empire or the rewriting of British identities and the names of publishing houses that have submitted winning or shortlisted entries (and that have thereby benefited financially from the prize). You may also find it interesting to look at the largely

metropolitan and establishment composition of the judging panels responsible (in Bourdieu's terms) for consecrating particular texts (Bourdieu, 1984, p.25). When you have done this, think once again about the political implications of Berger's 1972 speech.

What should be immediately clear to you from the titles alone (whether or not you are familiar with the works of any of these writers) is that certainly since 1981 – the year in which Rushdie's *Midnight's Children* won – at least half of the texts to win the prize have been engaged in a process of examining and revisioning the state of Britain post-empire. Often set outside Britain and penned by writers from Commonwealth or postcolonial backgrounds, such novels draw on the varied histories of a number of geographical regions and feature a mixture of cross-cultural literary influences which posit alternatives to commonly received narratives of British colonial history. The majority are works that not only have been published in Britain but also are, in the main, the submissions of large and mainstream publishing houses, such as Jonathan Cape, André Deutsch and Picador. In fact, this aspect of the Booker's history has been so significant that several books and reviews have been entirely devoted to examining the prize's role in ushering in the advent of a postcolonial canon in British fiction. In addition, given Berger's attack on the prize's relationship to the economic benefits of a past colonial history, it is important to note that the majority of texts submitted as well as the organs for valuing them derive from the cultural capital of the once imperial metropolis. By 1994, when *Paradise* was shortlisted, reviewers frequently offered readers a template for a winning Booker opus. One such piece by D.J. Taylor (1994, p.23) included a list (admittedly tongue-in-cheek) of common features, which I have summarized below.

1   Novels should focus on a subject that is not England.

2   They should be 'exotic' or 'strange'.

3   The content should be historical and revisionist, rewriting popular versions of slavery or stories of empire.

4   They should lay on 'imperial guilt', because Booker books are about making people feel 'bad'.

5   They should be written in a lush and poetic style.

6   If penned by a writer who has emerged from nowhere, they will have a better chance of winning, because Booker winners are often 'outsiders' or 'obscure'.

Now turn back to the notes you made when you first read *Paradise*. Did any features of the novel strike you as corresponding to one or more of these 'template' features?

A more serious approach to the relationship between Booker fictions and apparent trends in their subject matter is taken in Richard Todd's *Consuming Fictions* (1996), which argues that the prize has been a key factor in creating 'an increasingly global picture of fiction in Britain', reflecting 'a new public awareness of Britain as a pluralist society' (Todd, 1996, p.83). Todd argues therefore that contemporary Britain is as much a postcolonial world as those regions on the supposed peripheries that it previously colonized. Similarly, Luke Strongman's *The Booker Prize and the Legacy of Empire* concentrates primarily on the postcolonial aspect of the prize: '[it] is a crucial award in English letters because it is perceived as one which, from a former imperial centre, confers literary recognition on novels that reflect and portray the state of culture after empire' (Strongman, 2002, p.ix). Clearly, the 'state of culture [in Britain] after empire' can be viewed from a number of different perspectives. One is that the cultural range of the Booker enables postcolonial writers to assert their independence and establish distinctly 'new' and 'hybridized' works with identities that are distinct from the formerly dominant culture. Another is that such works (often by migrant writers whose cultural identities frequently straddle several worlds) could be seen to represent a late twentieth-century response to Britain as former imperial centre, a nation now 'enriched by the disparate ethnicities of its former Empire' which is seeking to refashion its 'own identity in post-imperial terms' (Strongman, 2002, p.ix). Such recent evaluations of the prize are keen to stress that it is not useful for Booker judges, or indeed for metropolitan readers, to continue to assess the value of such ground-breaking fictions by reverting to outdated critical paradigms that continue to privilege the authority of the metropolitan centre and thereby undermine the symbolic value apparently placed on the cultural products of the postcolonial margins – a practice that continues to locate the postcolonial writer as one writing back from the margins to the centre. In addition, drawing on the arguments of Edward Said in his major study *Culture and Imperialism* (1993, pp.84–90), Strongman stresses that the cultural forms spawned by the European modernist enterprise not only have always been inextricably intertwined with that of its colonial past but also were to a large extent defined by it (Strongman, 2002, p.xx).

The twentieth century witnessed many debates relating to the assessment of literary value. One example is the ways in which the cultural influences on the modernist poetics of the Nigerian poet Christopher Okigbo were attributed by critics earlier in the century. Okigbo's poetry encompassed various oppositions – Nigerian/European, colonial/postcolonial – and strategically played these out against each other (Richards, 2005). It is interesting therefore to discover that similar difficulties in assessing the value of cultural difference continue to rear their heads much later in the century in the politics of a prize such as the Booker. Reading between the lines of many commentaries on the prize – discussions that often purport to celebrate its very diversity – can reveal some interesting slippages and contradictions. These point to a failure to move beyond a fairly reductive, Eurocentric frame of reference for judging literature – a system that, in crude terms, continues to rely on a false binary division between the authority of a European 'self' and its colonial 'other' – and also reflect a blinkered unwillingness among the literary establishment in Britain to change the terms by which such literatures should be validated.

Now read two extracts in the Reader. The first is from Pico Iyer's 'The Empire Writes Back' (Item 47). The second is a response to Iyer by Graham Huggan entitled 'The Postcolonial Exotic' (Item 48). How does Iyer place the works of postcolonial writers in relation to the European canon? What terms does he use to judge such works? Can you see any problems with this approach? How convincing do you find Huggan's view of the 'postcolonial' as willing participant in creating a critical climate in the West for what he calls 'the postcolonial exotic'?

Iyer views the work of postcolonial writers as the empire writing back to the centre. Several difficulties emerge from this apparently celebratory stance, which also begs a number of important questions. First, in using this formula, Iyer inevitably recreates an essentially inequitable relationship between the metropolis (which seems to authorize the writing) and the particular locations and cultural contexts of the individual writers themselves. In the colonial period the imperial metropolis was the centre of power – through its creation of imperial mandates, systems of colonial administration and education. Now, even after independence, the metropolitan Euro-American space remains privileged. Iyer also inadvertently sets up the western 'canon' as the legislator of 'truth', 'meaning', 'knowledge' and 'value' and European modernity as the empowered face to which all such writers are either reacting or resisting. Little mention is made of other literary traditions or systems of value and influence from which these texts derive, or the fact that these works can exist without so-called 'frontiers' only when viewed from the insular perspective of a privileged western publishing context. So although Iyer stresses both the transformative and transcultural potential of much postcolonial writing, he not only fails to value the extent to which the cultural preoccupations of such works may exist beyond the borders of Europe but also turns their very 'difference' into a comfortable 'instrument' for easy metropolitan consumption.

Read in the manner that Iyer suggests, such fictions are homogenized, regardless of their very different individual preoccupations, histories or geographical/cultural locations. In addition, the writers themselves can be seen as cashing in on a situation where the consumer potential of 'postcoloniality' becomes, as Huggan puts it in his essay, less a 'marker of anti-imperial resistance' than 'a sales tag' for the 'exotic' and the 'international commodity culture of late (twentieth-century) capitalism'.

Such 'sales tags' are signalled by the seductive and 'exotic' labels Iyer attributes to this 'new' writing –'bright colors', 'strange cadences', 'foreign eyes', 'Janus-faced', and so on – and through the ways in which he glibly compares and writes over the linguistic and cultural differences of individual texts.

What, you might ask, has this to do with the Booker Prize for fiction and its role in enhancing the reputations of a number of now major writers from previously colonized Commonwealth and migrant British backgrounds? One way of answering this question is suggested by Huggan, although his approach is more sceptical.

As Huggan notes, late twentieth-century academic discourse frequently employs a critical rhetoric (typical of Iyer's piece) that privileges the 'exotic' or fashionable theories of 'otherness' common in contemporary postmodern parlance. This process is further compounded by the ways in which postcolonial fictions are received in the West, whether by the literary-critical establishment or by the global market. The Booker's celebration of the diversity of postcolonial fictions neatly matches such packaging and also diminishes the politics of resistance such novels often demonstrate. Instead, therefore, of truly acknowledging and celebrating cultural diversity and difference, the Booker creates a climate for a form of banal intellectual tourism, where difference is not only contained but becomes the 'stuff of ... spectacle' as the wider 'world becomes a theme-park'. Most worryingly, perhaps, this way of reading the 'other' relieves the general public and professional critics alike from the 'burdensome task of actually learning about' or confronting the diverse realities of 'other' cultures. At the same time, publishers benefit by having a ready-made and extremely profitable marketing machine, as is evidenced by the 'exotic' descriptions placed strategically on cover blurbs to allure readers.

In addition, although the notion of 'Commonwealth' writing was popular in the early 1960s and 1970s (the period in which Booker was first launched), it has increasingly been seen to be, as Huggan notes, a 'diplomatic dodo', a 'figment of the imperial imagination' (Rushdie) or a 'cultural hangover from the Empire' (Ahmad). The notion of the Commonwealth (whatever its arguable benefits as a loose political union) continues to advance a rhetoric that inevitably recreates an unequal filial relationship between Britain (the parent) and the colonies (its children), smacking of what many have come to regard as some of the worst forms of a liberal humanist 'colonial condescension'. Thus, the continued use of 'Commonwealth' as a category in the Booker's criteria for eligibility can be seen to be a way of still enabling the post-imperial centre to cast judgement on those who are supposedly writing back to it from 'outside'. This relationship fails either to reposition such writers as central players in the British canon or to value fully the extent to which their fictions resist and go beyond the need to simply counter familiar European cultural models.

The Booker Prize thus situates itself in an ambivalent position in relation to the fictions of those postcolonial writers it chooses (because of the consumability of their subject matter) to include. In addition, the writers themselves, whose own positions often do not coincide with the ways in which their books are marketed, face the difficult political dilemma of becoming assimilated into the global politics of a postmodern world. As Huggan explains, this is a world in which equivalence increasingly becomes the norm and the realities of cultural difference are significantly diminished.

There is no doubt that the Booker is ostensibly keen to applaud the art of writers from 'Commonwealth' backgrounds. However, such 'cultural capital' is often 'unevenly distributed' and circulates within a narrow 'series of interlocking hierarchical structures'. Whether or not you agree with the position Huggan outlines in his essay, it is important to recognize that such 'interlocking ... structures' do become important modes of cultural legitimation by which some writers are seen to be 'in' and others 'out'; the prize consecrates certain kinds of texts as special and therefore, in a sense, despite its best intentions and the supposed breadth of its reach, it canonizes them. It is worth noting here, too, that this kind of critique of the 'postcolonial' aspects of prize culture could usefully be extended to questions of gender and the ways in which, in the race to define contemporary British fiction, the prize paradoxically locates some shortlisted Irish, Scottish or Welsh writers as 'outsiders'.

The idea of the 'postcolonial exotic' put forward by Huggan is certainly a seductive one. Moreover, it is particularly evident, as we shall see later, when one examines the myopic critical rhetoric that informed the media reception of Booker novels such as *Paradise* in 1994. Huggan's view, though, has its limitations. While he accepts that many writers do not necessarily comply with his vision of a marketable 'postcoloniality' – that many texts in fact deliberately resist the construction of a palatable exoticism – it is a moot point how far it is possible to disentangle the literary agendas of individual writers from the materialist premise of Huggan's overarching message. Like that of Iyer and the Booker itself, Huggan's position has a diminishing effect because it homogenizes the artistic aims of different works.

Of course, Booker contenders are not unaware of the politics of these issues. Nor do they necessarily choose to enter their novels for the prize. Although all works submitted must by necessity be fictions written in English, that language is frequently transformed and the form of the novel itself hybridized. In addition, these postcolonial reinventions of 'other' linguistic–cultural–literary influences frequently reflect specifically situated regional cadences. They are often, therefore, highly individualized and complex fictional discourses, which straddle several worlds and interrogate several different systems of aesthetic and literary convention.

So far we have focused on questions of judgement as determined by the literary politics of the Booker Prize and the impact of western market forces in the publishing world. **By way of a contrast, now read Gurnah's essay 'Imagining the Postcolonial Writer' (Reader, Item 49). How does Gurnah, as a migrant African writer and critic, view the 'postcolonial'? You should also begin to consider whether his views are relevant in any sense to his fictional project in *Paradise*.**

Like Huggan, Gurnah points out some of the pitfalls of an overly simplified use of the term 'postcolonial' as a convenient category for defining books from 'elsewhere'. He also critiques its dangerous use as an umbrella term or a synonym in western post-structuralist academic discourse for 'otherness'. More importantly, he questions its efficacy as a tool to evaluate the complexity of literary traditions that derive not only from the particularities of very different cultural and historical contexts but also, in many cases, from different language systems. Discussing the specific issue of 'African' writing, a tradition from which his own work (as both critic and novelist) partially stems, he makes plain a number of important points. He is keen to stress that the western postcolonial model of interpretation, which focuses on the 'incommensurable difference between the European and the native', can only reduce the complex fragmentations and the heterogeneous language systems of colonized culture into 'a kind of necessary detail to the larger issue'. Such readings, he argues, perpetuate colonial mappings – geographical and political (of nations) or literary (of canons) – by creating a false vision of linguistic and cultural homogeneity. They thus continue to recycle a colonialist reading of the world as 'the West and the Rest'. In a continent as large and as culturally and linguistically diverse as Africa, as Gurnah illustrates, this is clearly a nonsense. Moreover, it is not simply a question of Eurocentrism. It would seem that even some distinguished African novelists of an earlier generation, such as the Nobel Prize-winner Wole Soyinka (Nigeria) or Ngugi wa Thiong'o (Kenya), were bound indirectly to 'historical accounts ... constructed by an imperial discourse' and, consequently, still tended to foreground the encounter with Europe. In 'An Idea of the Past', Gurnah has elaborated on the ways in which such questions affected him as a writer who followed on several decades later:

> When I first read Chinua Achebe's *Things Fall Apart* (1958) as a schoolboy, it was a million miles away from my experience, but I understood that I was to read it as if it was part of my experience ... Similarly, when I read Ngugi at about the same time, I was required, and did not resist, to see the rural environment of those early novels as familiar and 'natural', when it was not. I remember

we were encouraged to enter for a regional short story competition, and several of us wrote stories about village life and stealing chickens when our reality was as urban as could be imagined. Decolonization had heightened our sense of solidarity with 'Africa', and we understood that the appropriate way of reading such texts was as Africans who had that sense of progressive solidarity. Of course the texts invited such a reading because of the way they figured the past that was their subject.

(Gurnah, 2002, p.15)

I will return to this essay in the next section. What is interesting to note at this stage, however, is that Gurnah is not only problematizing the notion of what constitutes the supposedly typical 'African' novel or the typically 'African' subject, but also revealing some of the difficulties he encountered in writing *Paradise*. Moreover, as he suggests here, although 'classic' nationalist or independence novels of the African canon such as Achebe's *Things Fall Apart* (1958) or Ngugi's *Weep Not, Child* (1964) were crucial interventions in the decolonization process, they nevertheless continued to focus on the 'eternal contest' with the European settler as the normative and 'defining moment' of the archetypal 'African' experience.

Gurnah's novel is set at a similar time to *Things Fall Apart*, in the period prior to the outset of the First World War, but it deals with a very different history (the Islamic/Arab/Swahili history of coastal East Africa rather than that of the rural Ibo tribe in Northern Nigeria), and, as he intimates here, stems from a very differently determined colonial past. As some other scholars of African literature have also noted, the 'consolidation of traditionalist models of identity around notions of an authentic precolonial sensibility' (Wright, 1997, p.10) was an early response by writers to the decades post-independence – an attempt, in other words, to rescue a sense of 'African' value from the confusions resulting from a violent colonial and imperial history.

By the 1980s and 1990s, however, when writers of the post-national period such as Gurnah began to publish, it was no longer tenable simply to lay the blame for 'all the continent's woes' at the doors of western imperialism either by writing narratives of decolonization or by creating seamless or romanticized visions of an unsullied mythological African past (Wright, 1997, pp.10–11). In other words, there was a need to move beyond a culture of blame and address the fact that the psychic damage wrought by history extends to both colonizer and colonized. Fictions such as *Paradise* may therefore be less concerned with 'writing back' to 'Europe' (to return to Iyer again and the stance of many western Booker critics) than with setting up a dialogue with the already existing canon of 'African' fiction and the parallel difficulties of being judged within the confines of a narrowly defined African aesthetic, a question disputed by Chidi Amuta in *The Theory of African Literature* (1989) (discussed in the Introduction to Part 2).

The histories Gurnah presents us with in *Paradise* do not focus specifically on the colonial encounter between Africa and Europe. His concern is with the ways in which different accounts of the past – including those of the Omani Arabs, the indigenous Swahili, the migrant Asians, the black tribes of the interior, the Christians and the Muslims – compete with one another in a region dominated for centuries by a global trading history and a shifting hybrid multiracial population. Importantly, too, Gurnah's focus in *Paradise* on how the dehumanizing practice of domestic slavery was perpetuated in coastal East Africa (long after slavery was formally eradicated) contextualizes some of the scaremongering stereotypes of cruel Arab slavers in authorized European versions of the history of the area. At the same time, the region's own culpabilities in the perpetuation of such social practices are highlighted. We are led, therefore, to *compare* but not necessarily to *judge* the nature of the injustices imposed on the indigenous population by both Arab and European imperialisms as well as to consider the entrapped status of an indigenous figure such as Yusuf, the novel's main character, who is witness to the vying forces of this unforgiving world.

Bearing these questions in mind, let us now return to *Paradise* and consider how far the novel conforms to our expectations either of a typical Booker opus or a typical African novel. In what ways does Gurnah's fictional representation of history invite us to read against the grain? In other words, in what ways does it complicate our preconceptions of African literature? These are complex questions and you will not necessarily find easy answers to them in the text. However, be aware of them as you approach the material that follows.

Reading *Paradise*

Paradise does seem to contain many ingredients of the typical Booker opus, as discussed in the last section. It is set in East Africa in the period preceding the First World War. Its very title suggests the exploration of a universal literary theme and an 'exotic' setting; indeed, the eastern coast of Africa is now a popular western tourist destination, a contemporary 'paradisaical' location, if you like, for the western imagination. The style of the writing is lyrical, fabular and mythical; moreover, it takes a familiar scriptural tale – the story of Yusuf (in the Koran) or Joseph (in the Bible) – as the structure for its main plot. It seems also to present a reworking of history from the perspective of an 'insider', a supposedly representative 'postcolonial' voice. The novel also connects to the western canon through its implicit relationship to and interrogation of previous representations of 'Africa' in works such as Joseph Conrad's modernist novel, *Heart of Darkness* (1899).

Finally, through its emphasis on the fabular *Bildungsroman* narrative of the enslaved Yusuf and his journeys into the mountainous interior – a landscape as alien to the young Swahili boy from the coast as it would have been to the Victorian adventurers who explored the 'dark continent' – it presents readers with a sense of the unknown, the mysterious, as they voyage into a sensuous but threatening landscape. Yet these are only the superficial signifiers (signs) of the narrative. Gurnah consistently complicates his material by forcing his audience to engage from the outset with the complex realities of a fragmented multilingual world, the receptacle of several parallel histories poised on the brink of change.

Now reread the opening section of the novel, entitled 'The Walled Garden' (Gurnah, [1994] 2004a, pp.1–43; all subsequent page references are to this edition). In what ways are the central preoccupations of the book intimated? Make notes on the style and the ways in which Gurnah constructs the bleak parameters of Yusuf's innocent childhood world. Is any explicit or linear sense of historical time presented? If not, why not? You could fruitfully begin this task by doing a close reading of the first few pages of the novel, as I do below.

You will notice immediately that Yusuf is introduced 'first' as the subject of the main story, an ordinary young Swahili boy living out his life in the bleak context of an insignificant small town in a state of economic decline. He is not initially referred to by name: we see him simply as 'the boy'. His world, like that of his parents, is an impoverished and transient one. We are given several hints in this first paragraph, however, that Yusuf is to become a paradigmatic and symbolic figure who is situated both within and outside history. The prose style creates the sense of a fabular or mythical tale: 'he left his home suddenly during his twelfth year'; 'He remembered it was the season of drought ... Unexpected flowers bloomed and died ... The sun made distant trees tremble in the air', etc. Time is defined here through the eyes of a child rather than through the explicit imposition of any firm geographical or historical context determined by outside events. We witness the intimate details of the domestic routines that structure Yusuf's days, the passing of the seasons, the barren state of the landscape common for the time of year and the past histories of his parents' migrant lives.

In the next paragraph, Gurnah makes us aware of the existence of another world that is beginning to encroach on Kawa, a fictional name for Yusuf's home, which had once been a boom town, 'when the Germans had used it as a depot for the railway line they were building to the ... interior', but which has long been left abandoned and is going 'to Hell' (p.5). Here, Yusuf's sighting of his 'first' Europeans is not given much significance other than the fact that they have clearly been on the fringes of his world until this point as figures of legendary curiosity. For, as we are told, Yusuf has heard rumours that the Germans had superhuman powers: not only did they hang people 'if they did not work hard enough' but one had also 'put his hand in the heart of a blazing fire without being burnt, as if he were a phantom' (p.7). His over-reaction on the station platform, when the white man bares his teeth at him in what he perceives to be 'an involuntary snarl' (p.2), is therefore not surprising. Despite the unreal nature of the scene, as Yusuf runs for safety from the fangs of an imagined spectre, Gurnah nevertheless establishes the Germans as potentially dangerous predators. Such images recur later in the novel and merge with those of the prowling dogs that haunt Yusuf's nightmares while he is working under the tutelage of Khalil at Aziz's shop on the coast. We are also made aware of the flag flying on the station's mast.

Gurnah does not cast authorial judgement on the various perspectives he interweaves in these opening pages, which are filtered primarily through the eyes of Yusuf. 'Uncle Aziz', the Arab merchant, dressed in white and smelling of perfume and danger, appears therefore as a family friend, an intimate and trusted figure, despite his reputation for 'sharp-clawed' trading. Like Yusuf, who waits eagerly to receive his regular ten anna handout on each of Aziz's visits or fantasizes about the mysterious adventures of his trading caravans into the interior, we are encouraged to regard him with awe. And even though we are conscious that Aziz, like the Germans, is a potentially exploitative figure, we are made to accept the inequalities of the deal that is struck between this apparently benevolent figure and Yusuf's parents, who effectively sell off their son to him to settle an ancient debt. The ethics of the situation of Yusuf's bondage are further complicated by his parents' desire to maintain a sense of family pride by adhering to the strict social and religious codes of the society and their koranic teaching. As a representative of the Arabs, who have long held political and economic power in the region, Aziz has also long exploited such apparently 'filial' relationships with the indigenous Muslim Kiswahili population. Yusuf's parents, therefore, have no choice but to honour their debt to him.

Within a few pages, then, we are presented with a number of different stories and potentially conflicting versions of reality that will later have an impact on Yusuf and will determine the nature of his powerlessness as a domestic slave within the rigid social and racial hierarchies that surround him. Initially, we view events through Yusuf's uncritical eyes as he innocently accompanies his 'Uncle' on a train journey down to the coast. Later, Khalil, a fellow bondsman, attempts to set the record straight by making clear to the reader that the world of *Paradise* is not determined by filial affection but by a harsh mercantile agenda: 'You're here because your Ba owes the seyyid money. I'm here because my Ba owes him money'; 'He ain't your uncle ... You'd better learn that quickly ... He likes you to kiss his hand and call him seyyid. And in case you don't know what that means, it means master' (pp.24–5). The hierarchies of the Arab world Yusuf enters and the contrasting state of servility in which most of the native inhabitants live is consistently emphasized in the repeated descriptions of people bowing down to the merchant: 'He was impassive in the face of grovelling salutes and prayers, and when he had listened long enough not to seem discourteous, he continued on his way, slipping a handful of coins to the most abject of his courtiers' (p.22). And although we are told that the official days of slavery are over, Aziz's various trading caravans into the interior lands of the 'wild people' are supported by terrifying thugs such as Mohammed Abdalla, a 'demon' and 'hard-hearted twister of souls' (p.34), whom the apparently upright seyyid respects, despite his vices.

It is clear that the Arabs and the Germans are both culpable as representatives of two different but essentially exploitative imperial systems; they are not, however, the only awesome subjects of fear and myth in Yusuf's world. For, as his father frequently warns him, such threats also come from within: 'We are surrounded by savages ... Washenzi, who have no faith in God and who worship spirits and demons which live in trees and rocks. They like nothing better than to kidnap little children and make use of them as they wish' (p.6). Yusuf's own mother (his father's second wife) is condemned for being the descendant of one of the 'wild people' from the hills, and is told she should not give herself airs 'just because she had grown up on the coast among civilized people' (p.13); his father, too, was once called a 'savage' by the 'civilized' family of his first wife. Gurnah thus introduces a theme that is to be repeated in several different ways and through several voices throughout the book as Yusuf encounters on his travels a whole series of competing accounts of what constitutes the 'civilized' and/or the 'savage'. Such accounts include a variety of definitions of 'otherness', polarized constructions of identity and/or difference often articulated in ignorance or fear.

We are constantly made aware that the landscape of Gurnah's novel is far from the paradise that its title suggests. The word 'paradise' derives from a word meaning 'walled garden' in Farsi, the language of ancient Persia. However, despite the tranquil lure of Aziz's Islamic garden, separated only by a wall from Khalil's compound, we increasingly suspect that for Yusuf there is unlikely to be a paradise on this earth. On the surface, the novel appears to be a straightforward *Bildungsroman*, or novel of development – the story of an innocent young boy coming of age within the incomprehensible corruptions of an adult world. At its centre, however, lies a far more complex analysis of how the history of this particular region of coastal East Africa has suffered the psychological and material effects of a long history of disempowerment – a history that will continue to have an impact on human lives. It embraces a world reconstructed from a distance out of memories of the past, both real and imaginary; it draws on mythic fairy tales and legends as well as on the actual versions of history that Gurnah imbibed as a child growing up in Zanzibar prior to independence in 1963 and the bloody revolution that followed soon after in 1964, a revolution caused by the sultan being reinstated by the British as sovereign and the wealth of the country being handed back to the old Arab ruling families. Built on a cyclical series of journeys, the text moves from a meticulously rendered exploration of the hybrid social, political and religious culture of East Africa to the frontiers of the fabular, where the interwoven art of storytelling and the possibilities of the imagination expose the ambiguous 'truths' underlying the inventions of history and the harsh costs of human freedom.

The fictional landscape Gurnah creates in *Paradise* is a world in which everything, whether goods or human beings, is commodified. The Arabs are presented as callous materialists, fond, like Aziz, of 'sharp deals' (p.89) and exploiting a ready black market in illegal goods, an existence they would willingly die for. The Indian mukkhi, caught up in this corrupt system as middlemen and moneylenders, are driven by a similarly ruthless agenda and will 'sell you' their own mothers 'if there's profit in it' (p.133). Similarly, the Germans, though not directly involved in trading goods, are described by porters returning from the interior in terms of their callousness, immorality and brutality, as 'snakes in disguise' (p.73), here to '[take] it all' (p.185), who pretend to be their 'saviours' but have only imposed another oppressive system of colonial authority on the region:

> They take the best land without paying a bead, force the people to work for them by one trick or another, eat anything and everything however tough or putrid. Their appetite has no limit or decency, like a plague of locusts. Taxes for this, taxes for that, otherwise prison ... or even hanging. The first thing they build is a lock-up, then a church, then a market-shed so they can keep the trade under their eyes and then tax it.
>
> (p.72)

Gurnah's portrait of the black tribes of the interior is similarly unromantic, for they, like all the others, are happy to betray the interests of their own people. As Aziz tells Yusuf, remembering the recent history of slavery before it was abolished by a government decree, 'buying slaves from these parts was like picking fruit off a tree ... There were enough people eager to sell their cousins and neighbours for trinkets' (p.131). Moreover, Gurnah further satirizes the widespread corruption endemic to his 'paradise' by suggesting through the eyes of Aziz's brutal henchman, Mohammed Abdalla, that such trade is in fact a 'civilizing' activity. Mohammed Abdalla's righteous justification to Yusuf for his continued existence as a trader makes explicit the mercantile credo that lies at the heart of the book:

This is what we're on this earth to do ... To trade. We go to the driest deserts and the darkest forests, and care nothing whether we trade with a king or a savage, or whether we live or die. It's all the same to us. You'll see some of the places we pass, where people have not yet been brought to life by trade, and they live like paralysed insects. There are no people more clever than traders, no calling more noble.

(p.119)

This episode points to one of the central themes of the book: dramatizing the conflicts of the world of the pantheistic interior reveals that it is far from the earthly paradise it is reputed to be. It also focuses the reader's attention on the ways in which several parallel versions of history coexist, each creating its own 'truths', its own victims and oppressors and its own versions of 'otherness'. Mohammed Abdalla, as the sodomizing mercenary of the more dignified Arab merchant, Aziz, is accounting here for the profits of an age-old system of trade – in ivory, rhino horn, rubber and cloth – carried out for generations between the Arabs and the inland tribal kingdoms of the interior. We are aware, however, that the traces of a more sinister system of barter – the trade in human beings – took place within living memory and haunts the edges of the narrative. Moreover, as the formidable Mohammed Abdalla voices his faith in the moral virtues of his livelihood, his vision is counterpointed by the sense of both a superiority to and a growing fear of the new invaders, the 'ghostly' Europeans, 'famed breakers of nations', who 'look like skinless reptiles and have golden hair' (p.120). Mohammed Abdalla's almost heroic oral account is deflated first by his dismissal in one breath of the 'savages' and 'kings' of the interior and later by his superstitious demonizing and 'othering' of the Europeans who, as the older and wiser Aziz comments sardonically, are 'here for the same reason you and I are' (p.121). Both groups of outsiders – be they Islamic Arab or Christian European – are there with the same essentially materialist agenda, an agenda partially disguised in both cases by the 'morality' of their respective religious codes.

As Gurnah himself has commented, the novel is not simply concerned with countering the standard – and incomplete – narrative of European colonialism, a history that typically sees 'European intervention' in the 1890s 'as a benign deliverance' of the 'Africans from the Arab slavers'. Instead, it aims to examine how such a history came to be constructed, by exposing parallel ways of seeing the past that existed simultaneously with it (Gurnah, 2000, p.83). Gurnah also wanted to contest the comfortable notion of that 'benign' European intervention by 'showing the [full] complexity of what went on before – without *forgiving* it' (Gurnah, quoted in Jaggi, 1994, p.18; my emphasis). As he tells us in 'An Idea of the Past':

When I started to write, and I think probably long before then, but writing made a resolution imperative, I understood that the idea of the past which had become the legitimate African narrative of our times, would require the silencing of other narratives that were necessary to my understanding of history and reality ... I understood also that history, far from being a rational discourse, is successively rewritten and fought over to support a particular argument, and that, in order to write, you had to find a way through this competing babble.

(Gurnah, 2002, p.16)

Now read 'An Idea of the Past' (Reader, Item 50). How far does Gurnah's vision of history as outlined here correspond to some of the key features of the novel you have already observed?

Gurnah suggests that there is no one authentic version of history because all histories (whatever their particular agendas) are constructed by discourse. In other words, they rely for their authority and potency on a system of culturally encoded signs as well as a series of intertextual referents and stories that are open to interpretation and reconstruction depending on your perspective on the material represented. Further, he argues that the various narratives of history by which we live are often linked to questions of power. If one of such narratives becomes accepted as the authentic or legitimate version (as was the case, during his own schooling, with the authorized story of European colonial history), other, equally important, accounts of the past are often silenced. These attempts to impose different hierarchies of power apply not only, he argues, to the world-view imposed by the standard narrative of 'European' colonialism but also to other indigenous or 'African' narratives of decolonization that have subsequently been employed to counter them. While the writing of fiction is a process that, like history, operates within a pre-existing discursive field, the possibilities of the imagination can enable the creative writer to negotiate such discourses and discover the means to give voice to different versions of the past. The creative writer is thus able to raise questions about some of the positions naturalized in authorized historical accounts, which frequently only reaffirm their own political agendas by attempting to contain or write over the fragmented nature of such divergent realities and thus only seem to present one version of the 'truth'. In making clear that all reconstructions of the past – whatever the perspective of the speaker – are inevitably determined by our readings of the present, Gurnah points us both to his own location as a novelist writing back in time to an imagined past and to the inevitable provisionality of all forms of fictional reconstruction. The imaginative vision he presents us with in *Paradise* is thus his mediation from a distance of those past events and nothing more.

Gurnah's view of history and tradition is not an unusual one for a writer in his position. Salman Rushdie (also a migrant) has made similar comments on the interrelationship between fiction and history in some of his non-fictional essays collected in *Imaginary Homelands* (1991). The key factor to consider here is what role fiction (as imagined history) can play in negotiating the supposed 'truths' of authorized historical accounts – narratives that are supposed to be objective and based on verifiable events. Of course, all histories (whether documented or fictional) are open to the ideological persuasions of their authors. However, it is important to remember that fictional reconstructions are not necessarily reliant for their 'truths' on the corroboration of historical evidence. These are issues you should continue to ponder as you attempt to assess the means by which Gurnah evokes his fictional world in *Paradise*.

Gurnah's own perspective is partially determined by his position as a migrant writer (originally from Zanzibar, but currently resident in Britain). *Paradise* is a fictional reconstruction of a particular period in the history of colonial Tanganyika (now Tanzania) – a period that predates by at least forty years Gurnah's own experience of growing up under the colonial system as a Muslim boy in Zanzibar. However, Gurnah is writing from a geographical distance as well as a temporal one – from the perspective of being a 'stranger' in another land. Gurnah talks about his arrival in Britain from Zanzibar in 1968 in *Strangers in a Strange Land,* a programme broadcast on BBC Radio 4 in 2001. He explains:

> To write in the bosom of my culture and my history was not a
> possibility, and perhaps it is not a possibility for any writer in any
> profound sense. I know I came to writing in England, in
> estrangement and I realize now that it is this condition of being
> from one place and living in another that has been my subject
> over the years, not as a unique experience which I have
> undergone, but as one of the stories of our times.
>
> (Gurnah, 2004b)

Gurnah aligns himself here with other late twentieth-century writers in Britain who have similar migrant stories to tell – for example, Salman Rushdie, Timothy Mo, Kazuo Ishiguro, Caryl Phillips. He also makes it clear, as did John Berger earlier, that such narratives – which conjoin several worlds and stretch the English language across cultural and national boundaries – have become one of the major 'stories of our times'. And rather than taking up a rigid position, which consistently flags up oppositions and differences between, say, indigenous 'African' traditions and/or external western influences, cultural nationalism or black essentialism, Gurnah situates his fictional material from the outset as an integral part of that larger world.

Gurnah is not only an accomplished writer of fiction – the author of seven novels – but also a well-known critic, teacher and editor in the field of African and postcolonial literature. His knowledge, therefore, of previous literary and historical representations of 'Africa', as well as the ways in which such narratives have participated in creating stereotypical versions of the 'dark continent', frequently recycled in colonial histories, is therefore worth bearing in mind when considering his artistic project in *Paradise* and the complex weaving of the textual layers that inform it. A desire to make plain the difficulties involved in presenting any one unified or 'authentic' version of the past in the stories that we remember and tell to each other and succeeding generations has been a thematic preoccupation in all his published fiction to date: from his first novel, *Memory of Departure* (1987), set in the 1960s period of East African independence and disillusionment, to more recent works, partially set in Britain, such as *Admiring Silence* (1996) and *By the Sea* (2001).

Background and contexts

In *Paradise*, Gurnah draws on a wide range of literary and historical sources, and presents a variety of cross-cultural referents and perspectives on the history of East Africa between 1890 and 1914. The density of these discursive layers forms the backcloth to the novel's fictional landscape. Gurnah's artistry as a storyteller enables him to orchestrate these different ways of seeing into a powerful evocation of East Africa at a specific historical period. He shows us the history of the area through the eyes of his fictional characters – the oblique vision of the young Yusuf, for example – and through their imagined voices reveals the shifting political alliances and linguistic differences of a region that has long been susceptible to outside influences, and the limitations they impose on individual human freedoms.

At the centre of the novel, two ancient stories that derive originally from the religious texts of Islam (the Koran) and Judaeo-Christianity (the Bible) are examined in a modern context: the story of Yusuf/Joseph and the story of the Garden of Paradise. Both stories have long roots in literary traditions that date back over several centuries. Although Islamic versions of the walled Garden of Paradise are more sensual and carnal than those of the West, which focus more on purity, there are several correspondences between them – most notably in relation to the idea of desire, a world of bliss and perfection not easily attainable on this earth.

Like his biblical and koranic namesake, Gurnah's Yusuf is a beautiful boy, loved by all. A dreamer and a visionary, he is caught not like the scriptural figure, between the ancient rivalries of the Egyptians and the Hebrews, but between the equally competitive cultural and political agendas of the Arabs and the Europeans. For Gurnah's Yusuf, though, there is no relief from his bondage. From the novel's opening, even before he is bartered into domestic slavery with 'Uncle Aziz', he lives, as his nickname 'kifa urongo' suggests, a form of living death. In the next subsection, on narrative strategies, I will discuss in more detail how Gurnah uses the religious story of Yusuf/Joseph and ideas about the Garden of Paradise. In the remainder of this subsection, I will concentrate on another important context: earlier representations of 'Africa' in literary narratives.

You may already have realized that the novel is responding to earlier literary representations of 'Africa', both through its interrogation of Conrad's seminal text of 'European' modernism, *Heart of Darkness*, and through its implicit questioning of the nationalist premises of *Things Fall Apart*, Achebe's first novel, which explores the Nigerian encounter with European colonialism. In addition, the threatening landscape of the mountainous interior – a landscape frequently mythologized in imperialist accounts of the 'dark continent' by Victorian explorers such as David Livingstone, Henry Morton Stanley or Richard Burton – is viewed from a different angle in Gurnah's *Paradise*, and peopled with a range of characters, all of whom have individual viewpoints. This difference in perspective can also be seen as an implicit critique of V.S. Naipaul's narrow stereotyping of the native 'African' sensibility in his postcolonial novel, set in the Congo, *A Bend in the River* (1979).

As I have noted, *Paradise* does not set out to rewrite such earlier narratives – to create a counter-discourse with a view to deconstructing imperialist or other pre-existing stereotypes – but instead seeks to unravel the ambivalences engendered by such histories, which are situated at the threshold of a complex network of affiliations. In fact, the definition of the word 'ambivalence' provided in the *Oxford English Dictionary* is an instructive one when considering the function and significance of the intertextual references in Gurnah's novel. As the *OED* (2000 edn) tells us, 'ambivalence' can mean to look in two directions at once, thus enabling the 'coexistence of ... opposing feelings in a single context'. As many Booker critics were keen to show, correspondences between Conrad's *Heart of Darkness* and *Paradise* may be fairly easy to identify. Gurnah's concern, however, is less with the imperialist pretext of Conrad's novel as a symptom of some of the racist misconceptions about the continent that were circulating at that time – for example the idea of Africa as a symbol of otherness or a foil to Europe – than with creating a portrait of a colonial society from the viewpoint of those who actually lived through this period of its history. For *Paradise* is set at the moment when political and economic power passed from one intruder race (Arabs) to another (Europeans) without much consideration for the lives of its already mixed indigenous population. As Gurnah explains:

[*Paradise* is] not an attempt to rewrite *Heart of Darkness*, but – if
you like – [Conrad's] ironical view of the whole enterprise of
imperialism is useful to resonate against. This activity that
Conrad saw as destructive to the European mind also destroyed
the African mind and landscape.

(quoted in Brace, 1994, p.22)

In addition, like Conrad, who was keen to employ a double-edged and highly
ironical narrative mode that would offer ambiguous and shifting perspectives
on the dubious moral pieties of the imperial mission, Gurnah 'unashamedly'
makes use of a 'melange of racial stereotypes' in order to show 'unequivocally
that it does not matter on which side one stands: the colonial experience
corrupted and brutalised everyone' (Schwerdt, 1997, p.95).

**Figures 7.2 and 7.3 show two maps of East Africa, both of which
relate closely to the period in which the novel is set. Please examine
the two maps and think about the differences between them.**

Dating from 1873, the map in Figure 7.2 graphically portrays the
hinterland of Zanzibar prior to the so-called 'Scramble for Africa' that
followed the Berlin conference of 1884 and shows the network of ancient
Arab and indigenous trading routes that traversed the area before its spoils

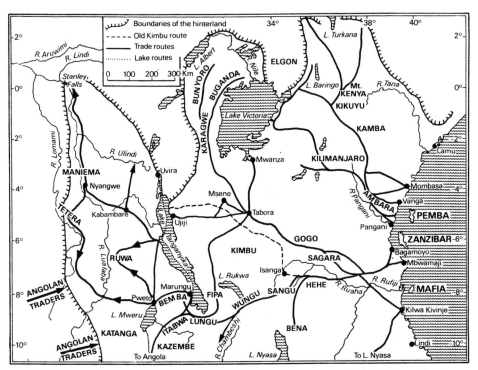

Figure 7.2   Map of the hinterland of Zanzibar, *c.*1873. (From Abdul Sherrif, *Slaves,
Spices and Ivory in Zanzibar: Integration of an East African Commercial Empire into the
World Economy, 1770–1873*, 1987, London: J. Currey, p.191.)

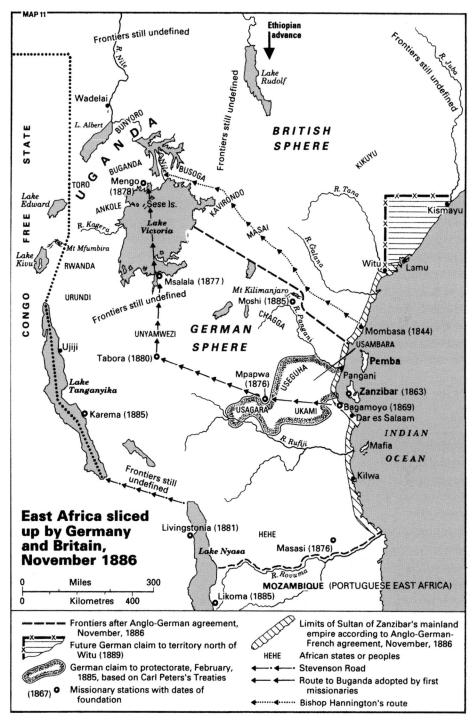

MAP 11

Frontiers still undefined

Ethiopian advance

R. Nile

Frontiers still undefined

R. Juba

Lake Rudolf

BRITISH SPHERE

Wadelai

L. Albert

STATE

Lake Edward

FREE

Lake Kivu

CONGO

BUNYORO

U G A N D A

TORO

BUGANDA

Mengo (1878)

ANKOLE

Sese Is.

Lake Victoria

R. Kagera

RWANDA

Mt Mfumbira

URUNDI

Ujiji

Lake Tanganyika

Karema (1885)

BUSOGA

KAVIRONDO

KIKUYU

R. Tana

MASAI

R. Galana

Kismayu

Witu

Lamu

Msalala (1877)

Frontiers still undefined

UNYAMWEZI

Tabora (1880)

Mt Kilimanjaro

Moshi (1885)

CHAGGA

GERMAN SPHERE

Mpapwa (1876)

USAGARA

R. Pangani

USEGUHA

UKAMI

R. Rufiji

Mombasa (1844)

USAMBARA

Pemba

Pangani

Zanzibar (1863)

Bagamoyo (1869)

Dar es Salaam

INDIAN

Mafia

OCEAN

Kilwa

East Africa sliced up by Germany and Britain, November 1886

Livingstonia (1881)

HEHE

Masasi (1876)

Lake Nyasa

Frontiers still undefined

| 0 | Miles | 300 |
| 0 | Kilometres | 400 |

R. Rovuma

MOZAMBIQUE (PORTUGUESE EAST AFRICA)

Likoma (1885)

- – – – Frontiers after Anglo-German agreement, November, 1886
- —x—x— Future German claim to territory north of Witu (1889)
- German claim to protectorate, February, 1885, based on Carl Peters's Treaties
- (1867) ○ Missionary stations with dates of foundation

- Limits of Sultan of Zanzibar's mainland empire according to Anglo-German-French agreement, November, 1886
- HEHE African states or peoples
- ◄–·◄– Stevenson Road
- ◄—◄— Route to Buganda adopted by first missionaries
- ◄······◄ Bishop Hannington's route

Figure 7.3 Map of East Africa sliced up by Germany and Britain, November 1886. (From Thomas Pakenham, *The Scramble for Africa 1876–1912*, London: George Weidenfeld & Nicolson, 1991, p.295. Courtesy of Weidenfeld & Nicolson, a division of the Orion Publishing Group.)

were arbitrarily divided up between the German and British imperial powers. The East African coast had been an integral part of a sophisticated system of world trade for at least two thousand years:

> [It] was a zone of interaction between two cultural streams, one coming from the African interior and one from the Indian Ocean, from which emerged a synthesis, the Swahili civilization, that at every step betrays its dual parentage.

> (Sheriff, 1987, p.8)

This 'dual parentage' was the result of a series of histories that were implicitly interconnected but at the same time straddled several worlds. The composition of the mixed populations of the east coast had evolved as a result of the impact and assimilation of a number of different cultural and religious systems – Persian, Portuguese, Omani Arab, Indian, Somali, German and British. This long history of cross-cultural permeation is epitomized by the etymological roots of the word 'Swahili' itself: deriving originally from the Arabic word for 'coast', it is now commonly used to refer to the Bantu language Kiswahili, an amalgam of a number of mixed linguistic and cultural roots. The term 'Swahili' also refers to the 'Waswahili', or coastal people, who – like Yusuf in Gurnah's *Paradise* – are native inhabitants of the area and frequently of Muslim origin.

The map in Figure 7.3, dating from 1886, comes from Thomas Pakenham's 1991 history, *The Scramble for Africa*. It presents a European perspective of the area just after the signing of the Berlin Treaty and draws attention primarily to the ensuing division of the region by the European colonial powers – Germany and Britain. You can see that the routes inland are attributed to and named after Christian missionaries and that frontiers marking the administrative borders of colonial rule have begun to be put in place. As the Pakenham map makes clear, these divisions were not agreed according to any particular rationale or with any intimate knowledge of the area; they were therefore as little understood by the colonizing powers as by those they controlled (Pakenham, 1991, p.xix). In many cases, however, they now mark the falsely imposed national boundary lines of a number of contemporary East African states, such as Uganda, Kenya and Tanzania. Most significantly, the arbitrary creation of these nation states by Germany and Britain in the late nineteenth century imposed a false sense of cultural homogeneity on a region that had previously existed as a heterogeneous mix of different racial, tribal and linguistic groups. The growing penetration of such lines of colonial administration and power are evident in the opening chapters of *Paradise* in the references to the German railway, which runs through Kawa and provides a link between the east coast and the western interior.

In what ways might the contrasting perspectives offered in the two maps aid your understanding of *Paradise*? Although these two maps clearly present contrasting topographies of the region, they are related in the sense that they both exhibit the mappings of an essentially mercantile history – whether that of the Muslim Arabs or the Christian European colonists. They also illustrate in clear graphic terms how different visions of history can be represented. *Paradise* frequently addresses the ways in which these two external forms of domination are superimposed on the area (either through the imposed lines of European occupation or the more seamless tracks of the ancient trading routes). It also attempts to map the predicament of other members of the population, such as the Asians – often affluent middlemen and moneylenders – and the Kiswahili characters, like Yusuf, who is caught between the impenetrable barriers of a world determined less by cultural differences than by territorial dominance and trade.

In the 1873 map, there is little evidence of any European presence, nor are there clear boundary lines demarking the different tribal, religious and linguistic regions it describes. The main focus is on the criss-crossing of trading routes linking the different areas, which were for several hundreds of years crucial arteries of communication. In fact, the kind of borderless landscape depicted in it is similar to the country through which Yusuf journeys on his many expeditions as rehani (servant/slave) to 'Uncle Aziz' in *Paradise*.

This area beyond the coastal strip around Zanzibar had long been open to the migrant passages of a number of different indigenous groups, well before the supposed 'discovery' by European explorers of an Edenic paradisaical world at the 'heart' of Africa. In fact, in many cases, the explorers depended on these ancient routes for their much publicized voyages of discovery. Western explorers were often guided by native Swahilis, hired porters from the interior or influential Arab slavers, such as the infamous mixed-race Tippu Tip (Figure 7.4). Stanley's expeditions, in the success of which Tippu Tip played a key, but little acknowledged, role, were reported in hugely popular Victorian publications such as *Through the Dark Continent* (1878) and *In Darkest Africa* (1890). In fact, Tippu Tip wrote his own fascinating accounts of these journeys in Swahili (see Farrant, 1975), accounts which cast a different perspective on Stanley's well-known publications as well as on the Arab slave trade itself.

Victorian missionaries and explorers frequently referred to the hinterland of Zanzibar and the area of the great lakes as a tropical El Dorado, or Garden of Eden. However, the passion to discover a world previously unmapped and unknown to European civilization and to lay claim to the fountains of a paradise buried in the 'heart of darkness' had a much longer history (Pakenham, 1991, pp.282–4). Interestingly, the legend of a temperate land of plenty, situated by the waters of two great lakes and a high snow-capped

Figure 7.4 E.C. Dias, Tippu Tip, *c*.1890, silver gelatine print, 20 × 15.2 cm. (Private collection. Courtesy Michael Graham-Stewart. Photo: The Bridgeman Art Library, London.) Like Gurnah's fictional character Aziz, Tippu Tip was a slave trader who commanded a great deal of respect and honour throughout East Africa.

mountain range, had its roots as early as 460 BCE in the speculations of the Greek historian Herodotus as well as in accounts by ancient Egyptians keen to discover the sources of the great river that nourished their plains and on which, in times of drought, the lives of their tribes depended. As Alan Moorehead puts it:

> No unexplored region in our times, neither the heights of the Himalayas, the Antarctic wastes, nor even the hidden side of the moon, has excited quite the same fascination as the mystery of the sources of the Nile. For over 2000 years at least, the problem was debated and remained unsolved.
>
> (Moorehead, 1960, p.13)

Significantly, such accounts of journeys into the lands of the 'mountains of the Moon' (Ptolemy; 2 CE) were frequently imbued with a religious and metaphysical significance. Gurnah's fictional territory is similarly fabular and luminous as Yusuf listens to the tales of elders about what might exist beyond the limits of their known worlds – worlds not enclosed by national boundaries but by tales of walls built by Gog and Magog (p.41), of frozen lakes (p.62) or of an earthly paradise surrounded by waterfalls but entered only through a gate of fire (pp.178–81). In addition, the landscape through which Yusuf travels (whether on the plains or in the mountains), often evokes the exile of his namesake in the Bible and the Koran, as we see during the course of the three journeys he makes in the novel.

Narrative strategies

I have looked at how Gurnah makes use of earlier literary representations of Africa. Now I will explore in more detail how he uses the koranic/biblical story of Yusuf/Joseph and the story of the Garden of Eden. As I mentioned earlier, the origins of the idea of Paradise, later the Garden of Eden – Jennet el Adn in Arabic – stems from a Persian (Farsi) word meaning 'walled garden'. This idea has been incorporated into both koranic and biblical accounts.

As already mentioned, like Yusuf/Joseph in the religious sources, Gurnah's Yusuf is gentle, beautiful and loved by all. Aziz (like the figure of Potiphar in the Koran and the Bible) becomes Yusuf's seyyid (master) and is not unkind to him; in fact, like many others, Aziz is increasingly impressed by the boy's wisdom, his prophetic sensibility and his intelligence. Like the religious figure, too, Yusuf rouses the passion of Aziz's wife Zulekha, who tears his shirt from behind. (In the religious stories she is referred to only as the wife of Yusuf/Joseph's master, but Gurnah is clearly elaborating on stories about Zulekha and Yusuf to be found in Islamic mystic poetry.) In contrast to the religious stories, however, Gurnah's Yusuf is not thrown into prison after Zulekha deliberately ensnares him, nor is he later redeemed and reunited with his family. In fact, for Gurnah's figure there is no possibility of redemption. Although a native of the coastal lands, he has no sense of belonging; his real family is lost to him forever and on the different journeys he undertakes with Aziz he frequently sees himself as an outcast, lost in the middle of nowhere, at the mercy of a 'displaced heart' that would be with him wherever he went, 'to diminish and disperse any plot he could hatch for small fulfilment' (p.236). Others are impressed by his visions and dreams, but to Yusuf they are the stuff of nightmares, filled with terrifying images of wild dogs and other predators – often human – that haunt the landscape. The scriptural story is therefore not to be repeated in real life. Moreover, although Yusuf is not unhappy under Aziz's patronage, he comes to recognize (particularly towards the end of the novel) that the mental habits he has developed as a result of his servitude will always inhibit his freedom. For him, as for Amina and Khalil, there is no escape, no fairytale happy ending. As more than one critic has observed, Yusuf's position does not change in the novel; he may reach a position of enlightenment and self-apprehension, but he cannot be redeemed. By the end of the novel, we come to recognize the fact that, despite the many journeys he has made, he has not really moved anywhere. His life has simply come full circle; he is still to all intents and purposes a 'slave', dispossessed and disempowered, an 'inner émigré' or stranger in his own land (Heaney, 1975, p.73; also quoted in Maslen, 1996).

Before we proceed further you should now now consider what function the Yusuf story has in the novel. In what ways are the koranic/biblical tales important? If you are unfamiliar with them, you might like to read the story of Yusuf in the Koran (Surah 12) or the Old Testament story of Joseph in the Bible (Genesis 37–47) before you proceed further. Both stories are readily available on the internet.

Think particularly about how the novel presents ideas relating to the Garden of Paradise. Note down any versions of this mythical realm that are suggested. Do they share any characteristics? Begin by rereading the passage in which Hamid and Kalasinga discuss different visions of Paradise, from 'Isn't it pleasant ...' (p.79) to '... ghouls and snakes as huge as islands' (p.84).

On his travels Yusuf hears many accounts of various earthly paradises. However, despite his status as a visionary and a prophet – a status that increases as the novel progresses – he remains trapped outside the rigid borders of the dominant Arab world, unable to enter any of the promised lands that he is offered in these tales. In fact, his life seems more like a kind of purgatory or living death. This is made clear in the final scenes of the book, when for once he follows his own heart and pursues his newly awakened sexual desire for Amina by entering the forbidden walled garden. Although at the opening of the book this garden is perceived to be a tranquil haven – full of fragrance and the sounds of water and music – Yusuf discovers that the reality hidden behind the walls of this apparently paradisaical world, a world in which Amina is entrapped, is more like a 'Hell on earth' (p.229).

During the course of the novel, a number of versions of paradise are proposed, each of which is subsequently deflated and deconstructed. Soon after Yusuf first arrives at Uncle Aziz's home town, we see him being debarred, by a single hand gesture from the merchant, from entering his earthly garden – a seemingly enticing place, lovingly tended by Mzee Hamdani. We later learn that this gardener is also bound to his role (albeit willingly), by servitude and an ancient pact of bondage to his mistress, Zulekha. Later, Yusuf tries to construct his own Garden of Paradise while living with Hamid in the 'mountain town'. Despite his attempts to clear a fertile space in the sterile bush, his efforts fail, as does his first experience of love and adolescent sexual awakening with Hamid's young daughter. At this time, he learns to read, studies the Koran and listens avidly to Muslim ideas of the seven heavens articulated by Hamid (pp.79–85). These conflict with those of the Indian Sikh, Kalasinga, who comments: 'We [too] have gardens like that in India, with seven, eight levels and so on ... Built by Mogul barbarians. They used to have orgies on the terraces and keep animals in the garden so they could go hunting when they felt like it' (p.80). However, as is apparent from Kalasinga's tales, such gardens are parodies of the original Persian version created by the Mughals. They are, therefore, not unlike Aziz's walled garden. Its beguiling streams and fruit trees are reminders of the rivers in early Islamic descriptions of Paradise, but Aziz's garden is in fact a prison for his two wives, Zulekha and Amina. Moreover, this man-made 'paradise' belongs to a man whose earthly riches derive in the main from his often illegal trading expeditions and the continued imposition of what is, to all effects, the perpetuation of a system of domestic slavery.

Similar divisions between harsh human realities and unattainable desires also occur in the world of the interior, where the searches of the merchants for the equivalent of the riches of a paradisiacal El Dorado remain unfulfilled. In fact, Gurnah frequently portrays the landscape of the interior as an inhospitable place: despite its seductive beauty, it is a world that has gone wild and reeks not only of disorder but of resistance and death. And, like many other Edenic gardens, it contains its own serpent:

> The appearance of the green landscape cheered them at first. The bushes shook and shuddered with birds ... Ancient trees towered over them ... But the glossy shrubs hid barbed creepers and were tangled with poisonous vines, and the most inviting shades were full of snakes. Insects bit them day and night. Clothes and flesh were torn by thorns and strange ailments befell the men.
>
> (p.126)

In the final scenes of the novel, when Yusuf returns to the coast, we realize that it is not beauty but decay that is the defining characteristic of such 'paradises' – whether they have been made by humans or by God.

Look at the section in which Yusuf enters the walled garden towards the end of the novel (pp.216–46). Why is this episode significant? At this point Gurnah draws more explicitly on the biblical and koranic stories, as Yusuf is not only tempted into the garden but also into the secluded female quarters of the house itself. It is here that he encounters Zulekha. In Gurnah's novel, Zulekha is disfigured, her face marked by a purple and throbbing wound. She longs for a release from her physical miseries, and entreats Yusuf to pray for her. Despite Khalil's repeated warnings about transgression, Yusuf visits Zulekha repeatedly, obeying her demands as a way of getting closer to Amina. Amina, of course, turns out to be another forbidden fruit, not only because she is the second 'wife' of Aziz (his seyyid and master) but also because she turns out to be the adopted sister of Khalil, his surrogate brother. She becomes the living embodiment of a further story of dispossession, entrapment and violence that Khalil has kept from him. In keeping with the religious stories, having failed to entrap Yusuf, Zulekha tears his shirt from behind and he flees from the house. Despite the fact that Yusuf is forgiven by the merchant on his return and is not thrown into prison, as in the religious story, the last thing Yusuf hears as the novel closes is the symbolic 'bolting' of the garden's door (p.247).

It is clear throughout that Gurnah's use of the religious story of Yusuf/ Joseph is a secular one. We are made to understand that there is no paradise available to Yusuf on earth. Whatever the magnitude of Yusuf's earthly virtues or his beauty, he cannot be rewarded, and his desires cannot be gratified; instead, he will remain entrapped by his historically determined position. Gurnah thus persistently deflates any possibility of redemption suggested by the authority of the Islamic and the Judaeo-Christian stories. At the same time, he draws our attention to the irony that, despite the apparent divisions between the Islamic and Christian world-views (as dramatized in the power conflicts between the Arabs and the Europeans), some of their primary fables for spiritual fulfilment derive from a shared ancient scribal source. In this sense, Gurnah's modern fictional character Yusuf has a living relationship to the stories of both traditions – Islamic and Christian – and functions as a symbolic amalgam in the novel for all the different stories that are told to him. He thus becomes a reservoir for many voices, a figure whose imagined vision might have the potential for reconciling the oppositions between such apparently contradictory worlds.

These final scenes serve to emphasize the extent to which Yusuf's position has been one of disempowerment throughout his life. In addition, his growth to 'manhood' or the independence that might come with age is frequently undermined by his feminization by others in the novel, whether as a consequence of his status as an enslaved bondsman, or because of his alluring physical beauty. Certainly, in the episode with Amina and Zulekha, he clearly rebels against his lifelong servitude to Aziz (seeing no point in any longer 'remaining in the merchant's service'; p.244). However, even his final act of self-determination – to follow behind the column of German soldiers who are passing through the town, scooping up cheap African labour to fight a war against the incoming British – suggests less the possibility of a real bid for freedom than the tragic continuation of a condition of servility, which will result only in a different form of subservience. As Gurnah intimates:

> The seyyid could travel deep into strange lands in a cloud of perfume, armed only with bags of trinkets and a sure knowledge of his superiority. The white man in the forest feared nothing as he sat under his flag, ringed by armed soldiers. But Yusuf had neither a flag nor righteous knowledge with which to claim superior honour.
>
> (p.237)

The bleak implications of this final scene draw our attention once again to the ironic reverberations of the novel's title and its function in deconstructing any comfortable notions of a precolonial paradise that existed prior to the European encounter. Moreover, Yusuf appears fated to remain bonded to a way of life that will continue to perpetuate another inequitable economic and political system, a world where questions of race, gender and power remain inextricably entangled. Most significantly, Yusuf's position, as he willingly gets taken up as a colonial mercenary just before the outbreak of the First World War, suggests the continuance of a more disturbing form of psychological passivity and stasis, a condition that Yusuf is ill-equipped to resist. There is one area, however, in which Yusuf does not feel displaced and that is in the world of the imagination, the magical landscape of words, of dreams and storytelling. And it is in this world – a world created by an imaginative vision that has the potential to transform the harshness of the novel's historical realities and create associative links between the competing cultural worlds that the bleak landscape of the novel straddles – that Gurnah offers us a possible recipe for Yusuf's redemption.

The art of storytelling

It is the way in which the stories are told that creates the novel's magic. They not only create and define the lives of those who listen to them, but also create the sense of a number of parallel histories in the making. In his frequent role as witness, listener and mediator, Yusuf is often the repository for these various tales. As he grows to adulthood and ventures further away from the coastal world he knows, the stories he hears are both a psychological solace and a source of spiritual nourishment. He listens to people who share similar views of the world, and who share the same cultural heritage, exchanging their myths and legends; he is also often an onlooker when those who disagree tell each other their own versions of tales – an activity that can result in conflict. Some stories (as in the ones that Khalil relays to Yusuf about the hellish 'wolfmen' early in the novel; p.29) blur the boundaries between history and reality, myth or actuality. In addition, elements that exist beyond the speaker's own world often reappear in different guises – as fables, fairy stories or oral narratives of individual lives. Both the speakers and the listeners seem to be aware that occasionally these different worlds collide. However, all the characters recognize that, no matter how unrealistic the world of storytelling and fable might be, it can often reveal important truths.

Reread the tale of the magic jinn who can conjure up gold and the tale of the jinn and the princess, from 'Do you remember the story ...' (p.188) to '... without hesitation' (p.189). What function do stories such as these have in the novel? You might also find it useful to read the text from 'Despite everything ...' (p.238) to '... to go inside so often' (p.240).

The harsh realities of the lives of characters such as Yusuf, Khalil and Amina are frequently framed by the stories of legend, koranic tradition and fable that both touch on actual events and embellish their individual histories. This is the case when Khalil finally reveals the 'truth' to Yusuf about his and Amina's childhoods and the story of how Aziz (also compared to a jinn; p.239) and Zulekha come to be married. Similarly, when we first meet Khalil's various renderings of the tale of the magic jinn, they appear as a form of straightforward oral entertainment, a means of escape from the gruesome world in which he and Yusuf exist. Yet if we examine these versions within the surrounding context of their original telling, they begin to have more significance. The tale is narrated at a point in the novel when we hear about Aziz's failing ventures as a trader, a moment when Khalil and others talk about the cunning magic he will need to redeem his failing enterprises. And later, when Gurnah presents us with yet another version of the jinn story, about the cruel jinn who is in love with a princess, we come to see that this story too has reverberations in real life. The princess in this story is imprisoned by the jinn (like Amina in Aziz's garden); she cannot remain faithful to him because she loves a woodcutter. When the powerful jinn discovers this, he turns the woodcutter into an ape and banishes him from the land. Although when he discovers his transgression with his wives Aziz does not turn Yusuf into an ape or banish him from the land, Gurnah clearly wants us to reflect on how such stories can shift swiftly from one world to another. This is made clear towards the end of the novel, when Yusuf wonders whether Aziz will 'turn him into an ape' just as 'the jinn had treated the woodcutter' (p.239). This deliberate shifting of the boundaries between myth, legend and the actual predicament of people's lives not only heightens our sense of how such stories can at times modify our perceptions of history but also serves as a narrative strategy for deconstructing the reductive notions of otherness on which such histories are often built.

As Elisabeth Maslen has observed, Gurnah's use of storytelling in *Paradise* frequently 'constructs personality' and 'culture' in terms of its 'otherness'; moreover, throughout the novel, Gurnah pursues this as an imaginative vehicle for interrogating the crucial role that such definitions hold in the creation of our notions of self (Maslen, 1996, p.53). Thus, binary terms such as 'civilized' or 'savage' are often voiced by a number of different speakers. Differences in race or colour are not emphasized; instead, Gurnah highlights, often to humorous effect, the ways in which different perceptions of reality and ways of existence come to be valorized in particular contexts. Furthermore, as different characters repeat such terms in varied cultural contexts, the words themselves become deconstructed and emptied of their larger meanings. They make sense, therefore, only within particular scenes (depending on who is 'othering' whom) and can never be seen as descriptive agents of overall authority or value. Hence, as Maslen (1996, p.55) points

out, the violent thrashing that Aziz's mnyapara is given by the 'savage' Chatu
is not dissimilar to the similarly horrific beating the mnyapara had carried
out on his 'savage' guide just a few days before (pp.145–62).

We have already seen this strategy at work in the debate on Paradise
between Kalasinga and Hamid (pp.73–90), a discussion in which Hamid
humorously defines himself as an upright Muslim in contrast to his
'blasphemer' friend, the 'hairy-arsed' and ignorant Sikh. Interestingly, at
moments when those who think themselves 'civilized' attempt to define their
own identities against those whom they regard (for whatever reason) to be
'savages', the comparison is not always incontrovertibly negative. For
example, on several occasions Mohammed Abdalla warns his men of the
dangers of encountering 'savages' in the interior (pp.59–60) who are, he tells
them, not 'made of the same cowardly metal as you' (p.59). Similarly, when
he describes the fearsome red Masai warriors as 'savages', he makes plain not
only that they are 'worth ten' (p.59) of any of his men but also that they eat
lion penises. Whether these warriors are to be held in awe as superhuman or
despised for their bestial traits is an ambiguity that is left for readers to
resolve.

While frequently drawing our attention to the ways in which such
categorizations of the 'other' often have reductive and negative effects,
Gurnah at the same time makes it plain that such stereotypes sometimes
form the only basis from which his often flawed characters can create and
affirm their own senses of identity and belief. In other words, the need to
construct personality in terms of 'otherness' may be a means of asserting
difference in particular contexts but is also highly questionable as a
convincing description of individual ways of life. This is apparent in his
interrogation of all the various ethnic identifications he gives voice to in the
novel but is particularly evident in the ways in which the Germans –
frequently stereotyped in reverse in the novel with the general signifier 'the
Europeans' – are both 'exoticized' and simultaneously deflated to being little
better than 'animals'. And we have here of course a neat ironic reversal of
certain long-held imperialist European stereotypes of 'Africa' or 'Africans'
that stressed the primitive, bestial and 'uncivilized' qualities of the landscape
and native populations in order to justify and valorize a one-sided and
misplaced sense of moral superiority.

**First read the following passages containing references to the
'legendary European': from 'In the dusty shadowlands …' (p.62) to
'… unless they were called' (p.63) and from 'Everywhere they went
…' (p.71) to '… snakes in disguise?' (p.73). Now read the passage in
which Chatu is summoned before 'the European': from 'The
merchant and Chatu …' (p.169) to ' "… he will take the whole
land," he said' (p.172). What is the cumulative effect of such stories?**

As such stories are recycled by different voices in different contexts, they begin to take on the more sinister function of actually affecting people's beliefs and the ways in which some characters perceive and recount history. The scene in which the powerful sultan Chatu (who, you will remember, had no difficulty in demolishing the formidable Aziz and his caravan) is reduced to a subordinate state by the arrival of the Germans, shows just how powerful such stories can be. Notably Chatu, like Mohammed Abdalla earlier, has heard it rumoured that 'the Europeans' can both 'eat metal' (pp.170, 171) and make others consume 'shit' (pp.169, 171). Despite his never having seen 'anything as strange looking as the shining red man with hair growing out of his ears' (p.170), the tales he has heard of the Europeans' superhuman powers make him submit passively to their authority. Although the merchant's men build up this story into a triumphant song of revenge about Chatu the python who is swallowed by a European jinn, the message is clear. For while, on this occasion, the merchant's honour is saved by the barking red man whose timely arrival makes Chatu return all his goods, we suspect that a similar fate lies in store for Aziz and his henchman, Mohammed Abdalla.

Significantly, Gurnah seems to be telling us that the negative impact of such stories belongs as much to those who are in power as to those they oppress. Moreover, as the Sikh Kalasinga warns, there is an irony involved for both sides in the ways that such stereotypes become perpetuated. This applies as much to the 'Europeans' as anyone else among the different ethnic communities in the novel. As Kalasinga says to Hussein, making plain the symbiotic relationship between 'self' and 'other':

> Learn who they are, then. What do you know about them apart from these stories about snakes and men eating metal. Do you know their language, their stories? So then how can you learn to cope with them ... They are our enemies. That's also what makes us the same. In their eyes we're animals, and we can't make them stop thinking this stupid thing for a long time.

(p.87)

Kalasinga's sense of identification through his ability to see both sides of the coin, as these different versions of 'otherness' collide, is a significant one. And while we know that the Europeans have already created their own versions of the 'civilized' and their own versions of the 'truth', we also know, as Hussein reminds Kalasinga, that such stories can only ever be partial representations: 'When they come to write about us, what will they say? That we made slaves' (p.87).

There is obviously a clear echo here of Gurnah's own stated aim in writing the novel, which was to complicate and to challenge the benign narrative of Europe's deliverance of the area from the corruptions of the Arab slave trade. Yet, in many senses, Hussein's view of a future under the colonial power of the Europeans is even more bleak. For this time, Hussein predicts not only that 'We'll lose everything', including the land and 'the way we live', but also that the next generation will become like the Europeans' puppets, speaking their language and reciting 'their laws and their story of the world as if it were the holy word' (p.87).

Judging *Paradise*

Now that you have considered the novel in some depth, it is time to return to some of the questions raised earlier concerning the Booker Prize, postcolonialism and questions of judgement. Gurnah's *Paradise* was shortlisted for the Booker in 1994 – a year in which the nominated novels were referred to notoriously as the 'Mogadon shortlist'. (Mogadon is a brand of sleeping pill.) It was also the year in which many earlier scandals associated with the prize came to light. Most significantly, perhaps, in that year the Booker also came under vehement attack as a prize seemingly open only to colonial 'dark horses' or unknown female 'outsiders'. According to the media at least, it was clearly no longer seen as a reliable register of the nation's inner feelings or as a prize for British fiction that was available to 'native' or 'home-grown' writers.

The most obvious pair of supposedly 'colonial' novels – in that they were set outside Britain – on the 1994 shortlist were Romesh Gunesekera's so-called 'lush' Sri Lankan 'nouvella' *Reef* and Gurnah's *Paradise* (the terms in quotation marks are those of Sarah Dunant – see below). Interestingly, two Scottish novels joined them in the 'outsider' category: George McKay Brown's *Beside the Ocean of Time* (a novel that featured a crofter's son and was set on the remote island of Norday) and James Kelman's *How Late It Was, How Late*. Written in an incomprehensible Glaswegian street dialect and containing at least 4,000 instances of the 'f' word, *How Late It Was, How Late* was condemned by Julia Neuberger, one of the judging panel, as a travesty of the prize and a 'disgrace' to the state of the novel in Britain and the English language. In fact, to Neuberger's much publicized disdain, it was Kelman's Glaswegian novel that won the 1994 prize. In his provocative acceptance speech, Kelman drew attention to the 'colonial' prejudices of metropolitan critics, vehemently declaring his right to use a non-standard form of Glaswegian street language. Neuberger's opinion, however, was echoed by many conservative reviewers in the southern counties, who launched a scathing attack on him. Most significantly, perhaps, the judges were seen once again not to have been in agreement – on the winning novel, on the aesthetic criteria for judging it or on the means by which they reached what was clearly an uneasy compromise.

The general sense of a growing scepticism in the objectivity and authenticity of the judging process was not helped by the level of misreading evident among some of the prize's most distinguished commentators. One such example occurred on the much publicized televised version of Booker night on BBC2's *The Late Show* (11 October 1994). During this programme, a brief introductory outline of each shortlisted novel was presented, followed by a discussion of the novel between the presenter Sarah Dunant (a novelist) and her guests Tom Paulin (a poet and critic), Germaine Greer (a professor of literature) and Antonia Byatt (a critic and novelist). Surprisingly, *Paradise* was described in the introductory outline as follows:

> *Paradise*, by Abdulrazak Gurnah, is set in Zanzibar in the 1940s and tells the story of twelve-year-old Yusuf, who is sold into slavery to pay his father's debts. The book is filled with folk legends, myths and religious fables, and explores the themes of colonialism and enslavement.

The novel is, of course, set not in the 1940s but in the period prior to 1914 – before the presence of the Germans and the English had really impinged on the East African coast or its hinterland. This major misrepresentation of the background to a Booker shortlisted novel, broadcast at prime viewing time, was subsequently repeated by Dunant, prior to the discussion with her celebrity guests – none of whom, it seems, corrected it.

Look back at my discussion on the rhetoric of the 'postcolonial exotic' and its effect on the reception of texts such as *Paradise* (p.305–8). In the light of this, read the following extract from a transcript of the programme, and consider the views presented in it. How do these critics assess the novel and in what ways, if any, do their critical perspectives differ from each other?

> SARAH DUNANT Let's move on to the second book of this pair, which is Abdulrazak Gurnah's *Paradise*, set in East Africa, again in the past in the *forties* [my emphasis], again a story of a young boy growing up. Germaine.

> GERMAINE GREER Well, [like Gunesekera's *Reef*,] I think it partakes of this same thing of making exotic something which probably ought to be experienced in a more straightforward way. It's still the black man in the bush. In this case it's the Black Muslim trader, going up country in a kind of version of the *Heart of Darkness*, except in this case it's not, it's the heart of something else. But the story doesn't have the courage to pin itself down anywhere. It occasionally makes gestures to German East Africa, to Tanganyika, or whatever it was called in those days, and occasionally invokes what the invasion felt like. But I think we are still stuck with this intermediate character, the beautiful boy, the Joseph who is

going to redeem everybody just on account of his beauty. And that ties into the way both of these writers have used rhetoric in a beguiling kind of way. But in the end, I feel as if I am clutching at shadows. I am being mocked by this book.

SARAH DUNANT And it's also true that both writers use the young boys to perceive a present happening which can only be seen obliquely because the narrators are young boys. They never face that fully.

ANTONIA BYATT I don't see why they shouldn't write novels about young boys ... People throughout history have written novels about young boys. And it seems to me that Abdulrazak Gurnah's book is completely different from Romesh Gunesekera's because it isn't really about youth. It's an extremely sophisticated novel about all the things that go on in your mind, which include layers of fairy tale, layers of religion, layers of bumping up against other religions. We, as westerners, think that African novels ought to be about the arrival of the Germans just as Germaine has said. It isn't. It's about the consciousness of being a Muslim in a society where you bump up against other spirit religions. You want your life to stay as it was and you want it not to. It's a very complicated book.

SARAH DUNANT Tom, are you agreeing with Antonia or Germaine here?

TOM PAULIN Well ... I don't know whether we are agreeing or disagreeing. I think I am with Germaine really. I mean, I think the problem is that you are led into it thinking that there's going to be a big colonial focus. Now, there isn't really, and the problem with this novel – which is very well written – ... is how does this novelist go beyond Chinua Achebe's great seminal founding novel *Things Fall Apart* and actually show a traditional society disintegrating under the impact of colonialism? Now, he doesn't because he doesn't, as Germaine says, really face the fact of the German colonists. They are on the fringes.

ANTONIA BYATT But all novels nowadays by persons of African origins or from Africa, are about the colonials. About the arrival of the people from the West. This is actually a novel about the enslavement of a black man by a black man ...

TOM PAULIN But it's in a western literary form so by definition it has got to be about it [colonialism].

ANTONIA BYATT   But can he not make a beautiful hybrid? He's mixed in Conrad. He's mixed in 'The Arabian Nights'. He's mixed in the Koran. He's mixed in the Bible, and you are telling me he ought to be doing something else!

(transcript from *The Late Show*, 11 October 1994)

In mistakenly locating the action of the novel in the 1940s, rather than before 1914, it would seem that both the BBC and the presenter had already categorized the book as a story concerned with a phase in East African history that immediately preceded independence and decolonization: in other words, *Paradise* is perceived as a form of nationalist resistance novel responding to the period of transition before the end of European colonialism. Whether such failures of perception (repeated twice on the programme) can simply be attributed to hasty reading or whether they are indicative of a more serious error of judgement, based on a reluctance (as is evident from Greer's comments) to fully engage with the particularities of the historical setting of the text is a moot point. We have already seen that Gurnah tends not to signal a timeframe in the novel that easily adheres to recognizable dates or points of origin in the European colonial calendar. What is important, therefore, in this misrepresentation and dismissal of the significance of the novel's historical setting is that the reading processes of two major western critics seem to have already been predetermined by their expectations.

It is worth considering to what extent such critics are looking for signs (often Eurocentric), which they can easily recognize and which are common to other postcolonial Booker fictions they might have read. Greer, for instance, refers to Gurnah's use of an 'exotic' and 'beguiling rhetoric' rather than attempting to engage directly with the complex representations of 'difference' that compose Gurnah's fictional world. Is Greer, like Paulin, unable to engage fully with such a book because it refuses to be pinned down to 'a colonial theme', to act out the predictable postcolonial 'story' of European colonialism, which it promises but does not deliver? Or is it because western readers (as Byatt suggests) 'think that African novels ought to be about the arrival of the Germans'? As Byatt makes clear, *Paradise* does not intend to tell us *one* story, nor should it be bound only to western tradition, as yet another version, for example, of *Heart of Darkness*. As we have seen, Gurnah's novel offers the reader a complex and 'hybrid' mediation of a whole host of important literary themes, which stem from a number of cultural traditions. Only *one* of Gurnah's many concerns, as Byatt suggests, is the impact of European colonialism. More significant is Gurnah's exploration in *Paradise* of the full range of the contradictory legacies of empire, a theme admirably illustrated by his main focus in the novel on the enslaving of the young black boy Yusuf (a native Swahili) by another black man, the Arab trader.

Paulin is unable to move beyond his opening position and insists on placing *Paradise* alongside Achebe's *Things Fall Apart*, a novel set in rural Nigeria and concerned in part, as discussed earlier, with the break-up of a traditional tribal society under the impact of colonialism. In insisting that Gurnah *should* have directly addressed the subject of the European colonial encounter in *Paradise*, Paulin homogenizes the potential scope and range of subsequent 'African' fictions. He also refuses to engage with the historical complexity of Gurnah's fictional world – a world which, as we have already seen, derives from a very different geographical and cultural context from that of Achebe, a different local history and a very different moment in contemporary African writing.

Not all reviewers of *Paradise* were so careless. Many praised Gurnah's fictional evocation of a young boy's growth from innocence to experience – his postcolonial interrogation of the *Bildungsroman* genre – and his portrait of Yusuf's powerless entrapment in a harsh and rigidly stratified mercantile society that would always deny him true liberty or freedom. The majority of reviews, however, failed to mention the novel's exploration of an area in East Africa that is the receptacle of several different and competing histories, or its deliberate interweaving of cultural traditions and language systems that predated the European encounter by at least two centuries. Instead, most critics dwelt on the novel's representations of the voices of a 'lost continent', its authentic recreation of an aural archive of Africa, highlighting its oedipal relationship to Conrad's *Heart of Darkness*. Few explored the strategies underlying Gurnah's fusion of the koranic and biblical elements of the Yusuf/ Joseph story (stressing, in the main, the biblical), or his exploration of the ancient Persian/Islamic literary tradition of the Garden of Paradise. Nor did such critics signal Gurnah's refusal to engage with a topography that would precisely locate, map and date Yusuf's various journeys – a mapping and naming of the area, in other words, that would be immediately identifiable to European eyes. Hence, as with Gunesekera's *Reef*, which was heralded by James Wood in the *Guardian*, as 'a kind of Asian *Tempest*, drenched in the unreal, tropical colours of a dream' (Wood, 1994, p.30), Gurnah's *Paradise* fitted most easily into the predictable western convention of reading 'Africa' as a continent full to the brim of mystery and darkness, superstition and magic, which, in the 'best' tradition of 'Conrad', reveals 'the ravishment of man's complex vulnerability' (Sherwood, 1994, p.22).

I will leave you to form your own opinion about how you regard such readings of *Paradise*. Before I draw this chapter to a close, however, I will return briefly to the notion of the postcolonial. As you will no doubt have gathered, since the late twentieth century terms such as 'postcolonial' have been subject to a number of interpretations; this is not the place to attempt to privilege any one view or provide a summary of its discontents (see Gurnah,

2000, for a historical overview of these debates). However, for the purposes of this discussion, it is worth noting a few points that will be useful as we move towards a conclusion.

First, modernism has not only been a European phenomenon. The history of modernism (both in Europe and elsewhere) has always been the result of a series of cross-cultural interchanges, borrowings and translations. This traffic has resulted in what we might call a complex archaeology of different cultural knowledges in which the theoretical discourse of migration, as advanced by a number of postcolonial theorists often based in the West, is perhaps of less significance than the migratory character of narrative itself. While such admixtures and borrowings may be linked to the history of European colonialism, they are by no means solely contingent on it. Second, the translation of these different cultural knowledges – by this I mean the ways in which they have been 'valued', whether in the West or elsewhere – has not always been an equitable one (Moore-Gilbert, 1997, pp.12–14). Third, as far as the cultural politics of metropolitan literary prizes such as the Booker are concerned, it is worth distinguishing between what Huggan calls two competing systems of postcolonial value: 'the postcolonial' as a symbolic system, which attempts to create equivalent space for what were previously marginalized literatures, and 'postcoloniality' as a commercial system, which coexists with the former but appropriates such literatures as western consumer products (Huggan, 2001, pp.6–8). Finally, it is important not to forget that the writers themselves, as well as the aesthetic aims and contexts of their work, have often been too narrowly circumscribed by such theoretical and critical frameworks – a situation in which, as Gurnah has noted, 'postcolonial theory' is often 'a triumph of the imagination over a more problematic reality, and the postcolonial writer, shed of her or his complicated difference, comes into being' (Gurnah, 2000, p.85).

In an essay on African writing, Gurnah provides an illuminating insight into his own view of a work of fiction:

> One of the ways fiction convinces is by suggesting that behind the surface lies an imaginatively more complex world which its construction in the narrative approaches but does not quite convey. Thus the narrative is able to hint at and realize what it is not possible to reveal fully, and to liberate the reader into seeing affiliated networks of knowledge and meaning.
>
> (Gurnah, 1993, pp.156–7)

The idea of liberating the reader as well as the text from the assumptions engendered by its location and reception – be it as 'postcolonial exotic', representative 'African' novel or a 'Booker-stamped' work of 'serious British fiction' – is an important one to keep returning to as you form your own judgement of Gurnah's aesthetic aims and his success in achieving them in *Paradise*.

Conclusion

In an essay entitled 'The Muse of History', Derek Walcott, the Nobel Prize-winning Caribbean poet, comments that 'revolutionary literature is a filial impulse, and that maturity is the assimilation of the features of every ancestor' (Walcott, [1974] 1998, p.36). He warns that in the 'New World servitude to the muse of history has produced a literature of recrimination and despair, a literature of revenge, written by the descendants of slaves or a literature of remorse written by the descendants of masters'. In this essay, Walcott puts forward the view that the 'truly tough aesthetic' for all writers of the New World should not be one of 'recrimination and despair' but rather to create a vision that is 'alive, alert and simultaneous', a vision that 'neither explains nor forgives history' (*ibid.*, pp.37–8, 64). Gurnah's attempt in *Paradise* to move beyond a rhetoric of blame and to interrogate the ways in which histories come to be written can be closely aligned to what Walcott urges writers to do in 'The Muse of History' (Gurnah, 2002, pp.6–17). We should keep in mind, however, the fact that both Gurnah and Walcott (as creative writers) are not attempting directly to challenge or to corroborate historical evidence as such; instead, they are problematizing the relationship between ideological bias and the difficulties in the colonial and postcolonial contexts of accepting any one version of verifiable historical 'truth'.

Although some readers have taken *Paradise* to represent an easily palatable version of 'Africa' or a rendering of the 'postcolonial exotic', it does not in fact in any way 'exoticize' its subject matter; nor, indeed, are we presented with a romantic or sentimentalized view of an unsullied precolonial past. Instead, Gurnah provides us with a detailed reconstruction of the coastal world of East Africa in the period before European colonialism. In so doing, he creates a fluid representation of both its latent corruptions and its lost potentiality. This is not a fictional landscape that can easily be reduced to polarized conceptions of difference or 'otherness', whether these are defined in terms of the binaries between self and other, black and white or victim and oppressor. All the participants in Gurnah's world are affected by a situation in which the politics of power are determined less by questions of difference than by economics, and all values, whatever their cultural origins, are commodified. This is an agenda that perhaps has significant ironic reverberations in the present, particularly in the context of the Booker Prize and the ways in which the subject matter of *Paradise* was consumed by some Booker Prize critics. In reading this text closely we witness the different stories of the region in all their complexity and see how stereotypes of otherness – black or white, native or savage, civilized and uncivilized – circulate as much among the indigenous communities as among those who invent such reductive 'myths' from outside. Significantly, too, Gurnah demonstrates that such contrasting perceptions of reality are not only generated by obvious differences in ethnic identification or cultural allegiance but also created by misapprehensions that result from the very different languages spoken by his many characters – languages that range from Arabic to Kiswahili, from the 'unnamed' dialects of the interior to German and English.

The world of *Paradise* is clearly a hybrid world, where a number of divergent literary and cultural traditions collide and where national boundaries have little place. And although on one level the novel presents an alternative history of East Africa, its purpose is not solely a political one. The excitement and energy of the narrative springs directly out of the ways in which this world is brought to life – through the artistry of Gurnah's storytelling, his recreation through memory of the immediacy of its fictional landscape and the testimony of his often flawed characters, which bears witness to a vanished way of life. In 'reconciling' these competing voices and in enabling 'different ways of seeing [to] slide against each other' (Gurnah, 2004b; radio transcript only), the novel demonstrates the potentiality of the creative work to build on 'the features', as Walcott puts it, 'of every ancestor', and enables the reader to make sense of and engage with the linked networks of meaning it unravels.

Paradise clearly 'fits' in some senses with the fashionable agendas of contemporary theories. As with many postmodernist texts, it can clearly be seen to question the 'authority' of the grand narratives of history and, in keeping with many postcolonial fictions, it problematizes the homogenizing binary between European 'self' and colonial 'other'. However, it is worth remembering that such theories are useful only in so far as they enable us to ask informed questions about our reading. How, for example, does Gurnah manage to both challenge and activate our postcolonial sympathies and by what terms should his representations of 'difference' be judged? Different theories clearly ask different questions and fictional texts often refuse their comfortable orthodoxies. Yet, as Gurnah's imagined world in *Paradise* makes plain, the language of fiction can sometimes travel where theory cannot go. The best literary works are challenging precisely because they are able to take us to the limits of what we can or must say in forms that cross and have always crossed the difficult boundary lines between critical judgement and theoretical definition.

Works cited

Amuta, C. (1989) *The Theory of African Literature*, London: Zed.

Berger, J. ([1972] 1992) 'Past Notes: Berger Shares Booker Prize', *Guardian*, 24 November.

Booker (1998) *Booker 30: A Celebration of 30 Years of Fiction*, St Ives: Booker plc.

Bourdieu, P. ([1979] 1984) *Distinction: A Social Critique of the Judgement of Taste*, trans. by R. Nice, London: Routledge.

Brace, M. (1994) 'Question Marks over the Empire's Decision', *Independent*, 10 September, p.24.

Conrad, J. (1899) *Heart of Darkness*, in *Youth – A Narrative and Two Other Stories*, London: Dent.

Dabydeen, D. (1994) *Turner: New and Selected Poems*, London: Jonathan Cape.

Donovan, K. (1994) 'A Booker of Surprises', *Irish Times*, 6 September, p.8.

English, J. (2002) 'Winning the Culture Game: Prizes, Awards, and the Rules of Art', *New Literary History*, 33.1, pp.113–35.

Farrant, L. (1975) *Tipu Tipp and the East African Slave Trade*, London: Hamish Hamilton.

Gurnah, A. (1987) *Memory of Departure*, London: Jonathan Cape.

Gurnah, A. (1993) *Essays on African Writing: A Revaluation*, Oxford: Heinemann.

Gurnah, A. (1996) *Admiring Silence*, London: Hamish Hamilton.

Gurnah, A. (2000) 'Imagining the Postcolonial Writer', in S. Nasta (ed.), *Reading the 'New' Literatures in a Postcolonial Era*, Cambridge: D.S. Brewer, pp.73–86.

Gurnah, A. (2001) *By the Sea*, London: Bloomsbury.

Gurnah, A. (2002) 'An Idea of the Past', *Moving Worlds: Reflections*, 2.2, pp.6–17.

Gurnah, A. ([1994] 2004a) *Paradise*, London: Bloomsbury.

Gurnah, A. (2004b) 'Writing and Place' (transcript of *Strangers in a Strange Land*, broadcast on BBC Radio 4, 2001), *Wasafiri*, 42, pp.58–61.

Heaney, S. (1975) *North*, London: Faber.

Huggan, G. (2001) *The Post-Colonial Exotic: Marketing the Margins*, London: Routledge.

Iyer, P. (1993) 'The Empire Writes Back', *Time Magazine*, 8 February, pp.46–52.

Jaggi, M. (1994) 'Glimpses of a Paradise Lost', *Guardian*, 24 September, p.31.

Lawson, M. (1994) 'Never Mind the Plot, Enjoy the Argument', *Independent*, 6 September, p.12.

Man Booker Foundation (2004) *The Man Booker Prize 2004*, London: Man Booker Foundation [online]. Available from: http://www.bookerprize.co.uk [accessed 15 November 2004].

Maslen, E. (1996) 'Stories, Constructions and Deconstructions: Abdulrazak Gurnah's *Paradise*', *Wasafiri*, 24, pp.53–6.

Moore-Gilbert, B. (1997) *Postcolonial Theory: Contexts, Practices and Politics*, London: Verso.

Moorehead, A. (1960) *The White Nile*, London: Penguin.

Naipaul, V.S. (1979) *A Bend in the River*, London: Penguin.

Niven, A. (1997) 'In Defence of the Booker Prize', *Guardian*, 18 September, p.18.

Pakenham, T. (1991) *The Scramble for Africa 1876–1912*, London: Weidenfeld & Nicolson.

Richards, D. (2005) 'The Poetry of Christopher Okigbo', in R.D. Brown and S. Gupta (eds), *Aestheticism and Modernism: Debating Twentieth-Century Literature 1900–1960*, London: Routledge in association with The Open University, pp.375–401.

Rushdie, S. (1991) *Imaginary Homelands*, London: Granta.

Said, E. (1993) *Culture and Imperialism*, London: Chatto & Windus.

Schwerdt, D. (1997) 'Looking in on *Paradise*: Race, Gender and Power in Abdulrazak Gurnah's *Paradise*', *Contemporary African Fiction*, Bayreuth Studies, 42, pp.91–101.

Sheriff, A. (1987) *Slaves, Spices and Ivory in Zanzibar: Integration of an East African Commercial Empire into the World Economy, 1770–1873*, London: J. Currey.

Sherwood, P. (1994) 'A Retailer of Tales', *Times Literary Supplement*, 11 March, p.22.

Strongman, L. (2002) *The Booker Prize and the Legacy of Empire*, Amsterdam: Rodopi.

Taylor, D.J. (1994) 'And the Winner Will Be...', *Independent*, 10 October, p.23.

Todd, R. (1996) *Consuming Fictions*, London: Bloomsbury.

Walcott, D. ([1974] 1998) 'The Muse of History', in *What the Twilight Says*, London: Faber, pp.36–64.

Wood, J. (1994) 'Cooks Tour of Former Paradise Island', *Guardian*, 30 July, p.14.

Wright, D. (1997) 'Introduction: Writers and Period', *Contemporary African Fiction*, Bayreuth Studies, 42, pp.5–15.

Further reading

Appiah, A. (1991) 'Is the Post in Postmodernism the Post in Postcolonial', *Critical Enquiry*, 17, pp.337–57. A useful discussion of the relationship between postmodern and postcolonial theory.

Ashcroft, B., Griffiths, G. and Tiffin, H. (eds) (1995) *The Postcolonial Studies Reader*, London: Routledge. Provides much reference material on key postcolonial debates.

Barber, K. (1995) 'African Language Literature and Postcolonial Criticism', *Research in African Literatures*, 26.4, pp.3–30. Examines the significance of indigenous languages in the context of postcolonial critical debates.

Brantlinger, P. (1986) 'Victorians and Africans: The Genealogy of the Myth of the Dark Continent', in H.L Gates (ed.), *Race, Writing and Difference*, London: Routledge, pp.185–223. A survey of the myth of the dark continent and how this discourse evolved.

Jeal, T. (1996) *David Livingstone and the Victorian Encounter with Africa*, London: National Portrait Gallery. Graphic illustrations of Victorian expeditions and much useful history.

Nasta, S. (2004) *Writing Across Worlds: Contemporary Writers Talk*, London: Routledge. A number of interviews with postcolonial writers, of whom many have won major literary prizes. Includes a discussion with Gurnah, pp.352–64.

Stanley, H. (1878) *Through the Dark Continent*, 2 vols, New York: Harper & Brothers. An interesting depiction by Stanley of the various expeditions he made. Contrasts with Gurnah's presentations in *Paradise*.

Tiffin, H. (1988) 'Post-colonialism, Post-modernism and the Rehabilitation of Post-colonial History', *Journal of Commonwealth Literature*, 23, pp.169–80. A useful essay setting out the difficulties of reading the postcolonial through the Eurocentric lens of postmodernism.

CHAPTER 8

Pat Barker, *The Ghost Road*

LYNDA PRESCOTT

Overview

The chapter begins by looking at the reading process itself, using brief comments from writers and theorists. You are then asked to record your own responses to Pat Barker's novel (these notes will be the jumping-off point for later questions in the chapter, so it is important that you complete this activity). A short summary of the two earlier novels in the *Regeneration* trilogy then leads into an account of the 1995 Booker Prize competition. In this section I will be building on the material introduced in Chapter 7, referring to two reviews in the Reader. A further review and extracts from an essay by A.S. Byatt underpin a discussion of historical fiction in the late twentieth century in the next section. Then I explore the interplay of fact and fiction in *The Ghost Road*, and the emphasis here on the structure of the novel continues into the section 'Divided Selves'. By the end of the chapter you will have reviewed and developed your own initial judgements about *The Ghost Road* before looking very briefly at the question 'What does fiction do?'

First impressions

You may already have read *The Ghost Road*, but if not, you should read it in its entirety before moving on to the next section of this chapter ('The *Regeneration* trilogy'). *The Ghost Road* is a little shorter than Abdulrazak Gurnah's novel *Paradise* (1994), which you studied in the preceding chapter, and you may find that you are able to read it at a slightly faster pace. If this is the case, it would be worth reflecting on the differences between the two reading experiences, as a way of beginning to pin down the nature of your response to Barker's novel. You will be asked shortly to register your initial ideas about *The Ghost Road*, and by the time you reach the end of this chapter you will, I hope, have developed some of these preliminary thoughts and arrived at your own judgement of the novel. But first it might be worth making explicit some of the assumptions we commonly hold about reading and rereading.

Reading novels for study purposes is a rather specialized kind of activity, involving more *re*reading than we would ordinarily engage in. Even allowing for the infinite variations in the way that individuals approach their reading, and for the amount of rereading that may be involved even in what we call our first reading of a novel, there is still, I think, an assumption that when we are reading a new novel 'purely for pleasure', a single reading is often enough. At the most literal level, the term 'novel' signifies something new, something original; our expectations of the novel as a genre may well include the idea that our interest and curiosity should be maintained for the duration of reading, and satisfied by the time we reach the end of the book, so that we can then move on to the next new fiction. It is easy to see how such expectations, especially as regards the contemporary novel, suit publishers and booksellers, and arguably the Booker Prize is part of this 'fiction industry'. But how does this consumerist approach to novel-reading sit with the questions about judging literature that we are concerned with in Part 2 of this book?

One widely accepted criterion of what makes a 'good' novel is that it will repay rereading. Often the value of rereading is seen in terms of the aesthetic pleasure it will give the reader. This line of argument relates to a critical debate about the meaning and purpose of literature in the early part of the twentieth century. Aestheticism was a late nineteenth-century movement whose adherents saw art as an end in itself ('art for art's sake'); it should serve, they thought, no moral, social or political purpose. This view can be contrasted with the instrumental view of literature – the idea that literary texts should serve a purpose beyond the purely literary sphere. The instrumental argument is that literature should teach or persuade readers with respect to particular moral, social or political values or attitudes. **Below are two short extracts: the first is from Oscar Wilde's dialogue 'The Decay of Lying', the second is from Virginia Woolf's essay 'How Should One Read a Book?' Read the extracts and consider the following questions.**

- **Is there any difference between the approaches to novel-reading that Wilde and Woolf propose?**

- **What relation does each of them assume between the activities of reading novels and judging novels?**

> There is no doubt that whatever amusement we may find in reading a purely modern novel, we have rarely any artistic pleasure in rereading it. And this is perhaps the best rough test of what is literature and what is not. If one cannot enjoy reading a book over and over again, there is no use reading it at all.
>
> (Wilde, [1891] 1966, p.977)

> The first process, to receive impressions with the utmost understanding, is only half the process of reading; it must be completed, if we are to get the whole pleasure from a book, by another. We must pass judgment upon these multitudinous impressions; we must make of these fleeting shapes one that is

hard and lasting. But not directly. Wait for the dust of reading to settle; for the conflict and the questioning to die down ... Then suddenly, without our willing it, for it is thus that Nature undertakes these transitions, the book will return, but differently. It will float to the top of the mind as a whole. And the book as a whole is different from the book received currently in separate phrases. Details now fit themselves into their places. We see the shape from start to finish; it is a barn, a pig-sty, or a cathedral. Now then we can compare book with book as we compare building with building.

(Woolf, [1932] 1986, pp.266–7)

Wilde's approach distinguishes between 'amusement' and 'artistic pleasure'. Novels that give the reader 'artistic pleasure' are worth rereading, whereas novels that are merely amusing are not. Wilde seems to assume that this rewarding aesthetic dimension of the work is immediately apparent, so presumably the judgement about which novels deserve the label 'literature' can be made on first reading. Incidentally, you will notice that, in spite of having written one novel himself, Wilde is clearly not at all impressed by the 'purely modern novel' of the late nineteenth century, and finds it fit only for 'amusement'. His comments remind us how much the status of the novel as a genre changed during the course of the twentieth century. From the perspective of the 1890s, the Booker Prize quest, a hundred years later, for the 'best novel' of the year would perhaps have seemed an unlikely focus for critical interest (though maybe its commercial interest would have been recognized).

Woolf takes a rather different approach, concentrating on separate stages of the reading process rather than distinguishing between different sorts of readerly pleasure. Initially the reader is 'receiv[ing] impressions', though this is not as passive as it sounds – earlier in the essay we are told that to read a novel 'you must be capable ... of great boldness of imagination'(Woolf, 1986, p.261). But this is not enough on its own: the second stage (which seems to happen in a rather mysterious way, according to Woolf, 'without our willing it', but it evidently involves a degree of reflection) is essential to complete the process. Woolf differs from Wilde, I think, in implying that the aesthetic worth of a book (is it a pig-sty or a cathedral?) can only be discerned *after* the initial reading experience is over. Interestingly, the metaphor of buildings is quite commonly used in discussions of novelistic structure. Matei Calinescu, in one of the few theoretical studies of rereading, points out that while critics usually describe first readings in terms of linear, temporal unfolding, the effects of rereading are often expressed in terms of spatial form. Calinescu quotes Rudolf Arnheim, a psychologist of visual perception in art, as saying:

> In order to comprehend an event as a whole, one must view it in simultaneity, and that means spatially and visually ... The curious paradox [is] that a piece of music, a drama, a novel or dance must be perceived as some kind of visual image if it is to be perceived as a structural whole.
>
> (quoted in Calinescu, 1993, p.26)

You will notice the similarities here with Woolf's language, when she talks about *seeing* the shape, and perceiving the book *as a whole*. In this model of (re)reading, the reader must thoughtfully process his or her initial impressions of a novel and *then* go a stage further in order to comprehend the work in its formal entirety. This has been a very influential argument in favour of rereading ever since modernist writers began placing so much conscious emphasis on the form of novels.

You may also have noticed how closely the perception of structure is related to the issue of judgement in Woolf's approach to reading: as we shall see, verdicts on Booker novels have been known to hinge on the question of structure. Finally, she emphasizes the comparative nature of judgements, as book is measured against book. The implication, followed through in the next section of Woolf's essay, is that the more we have read, the more finely we shall be able to discern the strengths and weaknesses of a particular book. Is breadth of reading, then, a prerequisite for making judgements? There is a danger here of making the reader's task so onerous that we might well be tempted, in Woolf's words, to 'remit this part of reading and to allow the critics ... to decide the question of the book's absolute value for us' (1986, p.268). (Arguably, one of the uses of literary prizes is to save readers some work by using the judges' decisions as a way of narrowing down the vast field of contemporary literature.) But in fact we never hand over the responsibility for judgement entirely because, says Woolf, 'there is always a demon in us who whispers, "I hate, I love", and we cannot silence him' (*ibid.*). This demon may lead us into *wrong* judgements, but then, as she says, critics sometimes make wrong judgements, too. While it is quite cheering to be reminded that critics are not always right, and to be assured that the individual element in our response to a book is important, we may well ask how we avoid being led into wrong judgements. Woolf's answer is: through the cultivation of taste.

Woolf's reliance on the concept of taste, a concept discussed in the Introduction to Part 2, and the rather mystical language she uses to describe the reading process (for example, 'without our willing it, for it is thus that Nature undertakes these transitions, the book will return') seem to belong to the eighteenth rather than the twentieth century. However, towards the end of her essay she argues quite strongly for the importance of readers in creating a literary climate that will influence authors. In this respect her approach anticipates some later twentieth-century ideas about the reception of literary texts. From the 1960s onwards, the role of the reader attracted more and more attention in literary studies. The French writer and critic Roland Barthes expressed this shift in dramatic terms: 'the birth of the reader must be at the cost of the death of the Author' (Barthes, [1968] 1977, p.148). The move away from authors and their intentions also entailed a move away from the idea of texts having stable, determinate meanings. The German theorist Hans Robert Jauss gave a clear statement of this new view of texts in his influential essay 'Literary History as a Challenge to Literary Theory':

> A literary work is not an object that stands by itself and that offers the same view to each reader in each period. It is not a monument that monologically reveals its timeless essence. It is much more like an orchestration that strikes ever new resonances among its readers and that frees the text from the material of the words and brings it to a contemporary existence.
>
> (Jauss, [1967] 1982, p.21)

Jauss's interest in literary history means that he focuses mainly on pre-twentieth-century literature and on readers in the plural – 'the public'. His colleague at the University of Constance, Wolfgang Iser, also made a significant contribution to reader-centred theory and criticism in the 1970s, but his focus is on the individual reader and his/her experience of the literary text.

Iser's studies of the 'implied reader' in prose fiction from the late seventeenth to the twentieth century suggest that, for the reader of the twentieth-century novel, reading involves a complex process of discovery concerning 'the functioning of our own faculties of perception' and 'the hitherto unconscious expectations that underlie all [our] perceptions' (Iser, 1974, p.xiv). Like Jauss, Iser sees the literary text as something indeterminate, 'a network of response-inviting structures' (*ibid.*, p.163), and he gives the reader considerable scope to create meanings within the potentialities offered by the text. But at the same time he argues that the text acts on the reader, not just in the ordinary sense of, say, influencing what the reader thinks or feels, but entangling (a favoured term of Iser's) the reader in the meanings that are being created. A reader produced by the text is, of course, not a real person but a theoretical construct, an 'implied reader', who lives a shadowy kind of life somewhere between the structure of the text and the mind of the critic. This peculiarity illustrates a common problem besetting reader-centred approaches to literature: the actual reading experience of individual readers is hidden from observation, so very often the critic falls back on his/her own perceptions as a reader and generalizes from them instead. This present chapter is no exception. Although a number of the questions and suggested activities here are centred on your encounters with Barker's novel as a first- or perhaps second-time reader, I have of course had no access to your responses when following up those questions. This is, self-evidently, a general feature of guided study texts, on whatever subject. You will by now have well-developed strategies for dealing with such texts, but, because our focus here is the reading process itself, I am asking you to exercise an even more conscious awareness of the interaction between your own reflections on the reading of particular passages from Barker's novel and the printed discussion. You may find it easier to tap into this extra level of self-consciousness if you can adopt an 'experimental' approach to your work on this chapter. In this way I hope that you can make productive links between questions about both the reading process and judging literature – the theme of this part of the book.

Both Jauss and Iser are concerned with the issue of how literary worth is established, and I will return to aspects of their work at the end of this chapter. Other exponents of reader-centred approaches, mainly from the USA, have helped to develop a new critical vocabulary to account for the way readers acquire and apply their understanding of literary conventions. There is not space here to discuss the practices usually grouped under the heading 'reader-response criticism' (as opposed to the 'reception theory' of the Constance School) but critics such as Jonathan Culler and Stanley Fish draw attention to certain facets of first readings that you might find helpful to bear in mind as you reflect on your own first reading of *The Ghost Road* (see, e.g., Culler, 1975; Fish, 1967). One is that first readings are, at least in part, creative. When we are not aware of what is coming next, we are continually formulating and revising predictions about the direction the narrative will take and about the total form that will emerge. Another important feature of first readings is that the predictions we entertain, however fleetingly, will be shaped not only by our own imaginations but also by assumptions about the kind of novel we are reading. Behind our first reading of any novel lie certain 'models of coherence' (Culler, 1975, p.159), which may be derived either from reality or from literature. We come to *The Ghost Road* with, no doubt, ideas about the First World War, some of which may well be traced back to literary sources, as well as some general ideas, conscious or otherwise, about what a historical novel is like and what we want novels to do for us. We may find that the text pulls against these ideas, for good or ill. First readings thus involve a complex interplay between our expectations, our prior reading experiences and our current experience of reading the text.

So, having established the importance of first readings, I would like you now to make some notes about your initial response to *The Ghost Road*. Since our eventual purpose is to analyse the process of judgement-forming I will refrain from offering specific prompts about what to look out for. However, if you find it difficult to know where to start, you might ask yourself what thoughts, feelings and possibly questions you were left with after you had closed the book. If this does not work (and it may not if you read the novel some time ago), try reminding yourself of those fundamentals of narrative – events and characters – and attempt a fifty-word summary of the novel; when you have done that, reflect on the choices you have made, what to include or exclude, to emphasize or play down, and you will perhaps recover a stronger sense of how the novel worked on you. You might also like to ask yourself whether the reputation of this novel as a Booker Prize-winner coloured your response: did the judgements that others had already made set up expectations that affected your reading, and in what way? **Record your responses to your first reading of *The Ghost Road* now** – we will return to these initial responses later, so it is worth taking some time over this activity. Once you have done this, we will come at the novel from a different direction, stepping back from your current or recent reading to the 1990s context of the novel's publication.

The *Regeneration* trilogy

The Ghost Road is, of course, the final novel in a trilogy. *Regeneration* was published in 1991 and *The Eye in the Door* in 1993, so when the third novel won the Booker Prize in 1995 some critics viewed this as an accolade for the trilogy as a whole rather than for *The Ghost Road* in its own right. (There was an earlier precedent, with the award of the prize to Paul Scott, for seeing the award as being based on cumulative achievement; see Chapter 7 of this book.) *Regeneration* and *The Eye in the Door* narrowly missed appearing on the Booker shortlist in their respective years, although both novels were highly acclaimed elsewhere, with *Regeneration* being nominated as one of the four best novels of the year by the *New York Times Book Review* and *The Eye in the Door* winning the *Guardian* Fiction Prize. So when *The Ghost Road* appeared on the Booker shortlist in 1995 there was perhaps a sense that the moment had come to recognize the quality of the complete novelistic enterprise.

As far as your own study of *The Ghost Road* is concerned, you may well be wondering whether you need to have read the two earlier novels in order to make sense of and enjoy the third part of the trilogy. My own view is that, although the reading experience is rather different if you approach this text with an established sense of the major characters and their previous interactions with each other, the novel can certainly be studied productively on its own. Even in the first few chapters, where there are frequent references back to earlier parts of the trilogy, the forward momentum of the narrative is strong, so that the 'new' reader is not unduly disadvantaged. You may, of course, have read *Regeneration* and/or *The Eye in the Door* before coming to *The Ghost Road*, and, if so, you may decide to skip the next two paragraphs. But if you are unfamiliar with the earlier novels, here is a brief summary.

Regeneration opens by quoting an actual historical document: the poet Siegfried Sassoon's manifesto for peace, which was read to the House of Commons in July 1917. A serving officer who had already been awarded the Military Cross, Sassoon defied military authority by stating that 'this war, upon which I entered as a war of defence and liberation, has now become a war of aggression and conquest' (Barker, 1991, p.3). The official response, aimed at discrediting his protest, was to send him to Craiglockhart War Hospital to be treated by Dr W.H.R. Rivers, the neurologist and social anthropologist who worked during the war as an army psychiatrist specializing in the treatment of war neuroses.

At this period there was little, if any, distinction between experimental neurology and psychiatry; Rivers's approach to treatment, as described by Barker, is influenced both by Sigmund Freud and by his own prewar practical experiments in nerve regeneration conducted with his colleague

Figure 8.1   William Brown, W.H.R. Rivers and Grafton Elliot Smith at Maghull Military Hospital, Liverpool, 1915.

Henry Head – one of several real-life characters peopling the novel. The best-known of these, though, are the poets: Robert Graves makes an appearance as Sassoon's friend and Wilfred Owen is another patient at Craiglockhart. The novel is set almost entirely in and around the hospital, near Edinburgh, but the realities of trench warfare are vividly present through the memories and dreams of Rivers's patients. Barker draws on some of Rivers's own writings for the case histories of these men, but the factual material is seamlessly blended with the purely fictional, notably in the character of Billy Prior. Second-Lieutenant Prior, a 'little, spitting, sharp-boned alley cat' (Barker, 1991, p.49), arrives at the hospital unable to speak or to remember the events that had precipitated his breakdown. To both Sassoon and Prior, Rivers becomes a kind of father-figure, though their relationships are marked by conflicts as well as protectiveness. At the end of the novel, with Prior discharged for home service and Sassoon returning to France, Rivers, whose business as a psychiatrist is to change people, reflects on the changes that have been brought about in himself through his encounters with these patients.

At the end of *Regeneration* Rivers takes up a new post at the Royal Flying Corps Hospital in London, attracted partly by the possibility of restoring some of his prewar academic contacts. Much of *The Eye in the Door* is set in London – Prior, who now takes on a more central role, is working at the Ministry of Munitions, and later in the novel Sassoon, wounded in France, is sent to a hospital in Lancaster Gate. As the lengthy 'Author's Note' at the end of the novel makes clear, there is again much blending of fact and fiction. The notorious 'Pemberton Billing Affair', which surfaces briefly in the final section of *Regeneration*, had been fuelling public hysteria in the early months of 1918. Its keynote was to link homosexuality with treachery, as the MP Pemberton Billing claimed knowledge of a German 'black book' containing the names of 47,000 eminent people in Britain whose private lives compromised their loyalty to their country. Oscar Wilde's friend and literary executor, Robert Ross, is another of the real-life characters featuring in this episode and a performance of Wilde's play *Salome*, authorized by Ross, becomes the focus of much publicity and prejudice as 'England's poor showing in the war [is blamed] on the plays of Oscar Wilde' (Barker, 1993, p.160). Barker also uses historical material more indirectly, as an alleged 'poison plot' against the prime minister, David Lloyd George, is transformed into the story of the working-class pacifist Beattie Roper and her son Mac, whom Prior has known since childhood. Visiting Beattie in prison, Prior sees that around the peephole in her cell door has been painted an eye, complete with iris, eyelashes and lid – a disturbing reminder of his horrific trench experience of holding a dead soldier's eyeball in the palm of his hand. The

Figure 8.2 Battle of Pilckem Ridge, Passchendaele; stretcher bearers carrying a wounded man to safety near Boesinghe, 1 August 1917; photograph by Lieutenant J. W. Brooke. (With permission of The Trustees of the Imperial War Museum, London, Q5935.)

effects of his combat memories eventually lead to a fracturing of his consciousness, as 'Billy Prior' alternates with his 'warrior double', who he says 'was born two years ago. In a shell-hole in France' (*ibid*., p.240).

But Prior's pathological condition is only the most extreme form of duality affecting many of the characters in the novel. Sassoon realizes 'I survive out there [in France] by being two people' (Barker, 1993, p.229) – the anti-war poet and the efficient soldier. Many homosexuals, like Prior's friend Manning, lead consciously double lives. Prior's own bisexuality represents another kind of fracturing. And Rivers, struggling unsuccessfully to reconcile his academic English self with his recollections of life as an anthropologist in Melanesia, begins to wonder whether integration is actually possible.

In a radio interview with Paul Vaughan in September 1995, Barker was asked at what point she had decided that *Regeneration* was going to be a trilogy. She replied that at the end of the first novel she could not get the characters out of her mind. 'And I was also aware, of course, that ... the whole business of the therapy at Craiglockhart Hospital has to be challenged in France ultimately' (Vaughan, 1995). So in *The Ghost Road* this test is set up as Billy Prior returns, eventually, to the front.

The 1995 Booker Prize

In this section I will be building on the account in Chapter 7 of the Booker Prize as a cultural and commercial institution, and looking at some early judgements on the quality of Barker's novel. *The Ghost Road* was published on 11 September 1995 by Viking, at £15 – at that date the average price for a new hardback novel. You are probably reading the novel in the form of a Penguin paperback, and, as you may be aware, the corporate link between the hardback imprint Viking and the paperback imprint Penguin (both of them owned by the media group Pearsons) is quite characteristic of late twentieth-century book publishing. During the 1980s and 1990s, the shape of the UK publishing industry changed dramatically as many of the older publishing houses were absorbed into larger international media groups such as News Corporation, Bertelsmann or Reed Elsevier. One particular consequence of this transformation that was making itself felt in 1995 was the collapse of the Net Book Agreement (NBA) in Britain. The NBA was a form of price-fixing by the Publishers' Association and Booksellers' Association that had been in place throughout the twentieth century. Its supporters maintained that for booksellers to retail all books at agreed prices was in the best interests of authors, publishers and booksellers themselves, particularly smaller ones. In the climate of international mergers and takeovers, the NBA was also seen as a way of protecting the UK publishing industry. However, by 1995 the NBA was beginning to succumb to small-scale erosion and in the autumn of that year it suffered several major blows, including a legal defeat for the Publishers' Association in the Restrictive Practices Court. The implications for 'serious literary fiction' were two-fold: most immediately, in an unrestricted market the promotional opportunities attached to literary prizes such as the Booker became ever more important; in the longer term there were anxieties that this unrestricted market might produce a general lowering of literary standards.

This was not the only way in which the world of literary fiction in English was, in 1995, dominated even more than usual by questions of finance. Martin Amis (who had been shortlisted for the Booker Prize in 1991 with *Time's Arrow*) secured an extremely large and controversial advance – reputed to be around £500,000 – for his new novel, *The Information*. Without the enhanced sales guaranteed by a Booker Prize win, it seemed unlikely that his new publisher, HarperCollins (newly acquired by News Corporation), would ever recoup their money. So speculation about the Booker Prize and its financial rewards for winning authors was very much in the air during 1995.

An unusually large number of novels, 141, was entered for the Booker that year. This group of novels was reduced during the summer to a 'long-list' of 13, but when the shortlist was announced on 28 September there were only 5 novels on it instead of the usual 6. This prompted speculation that the judges had pointedly rejected *The Information*. However, Waterstone's bookshops took immediate advantage of the collapse of the NBA by offering Amis's novel at just £5 to anyone buying one of the five shortlisted novels, thus making it a kind of loss leader in the 'Booker promotion'.

Two former winners of the Booker Prize appeared on the 1995 shortlist: Salman Rushdie, with *The Moor's Last Sigh*, and Barry Unsworth, with *Sacred Hunger*. Rushdie's name was of course well known – not just for his achievement in winning the prize in 1981 (and subsequently the 'Booker of Bookers' in 1993) with *Midnight's Children*, but also for the worldwide controversy that had erupted with the publication of *The Satanic Verses* in 1988. Like his earlier novel *Shame* (1983), *The Satanic Verses* made it to the Booker shortlist, but that was barely the start of its fame. Described by one critic as 'the most discussed but least read book of recent years' (Connor, 1996, p.113), *The Satanic Verses* was denounced by some Muslims, notably Ayatollah Khomeini of Iran, for the way it represented the beginnings of Islam. In February 1989, Khomeini charged Rushdie with blasphemy and proclaimed a fatwa, or death-sentence, against him. Rushdie was forced into hiding, under police protection, but continued to write, publishing a children's tale and a collection of short stories in addition to defending himself in print. *The Moor's Last Sigh* was Rushdie's first full-length work since *The Satanic Verses*, and he made his first pre-announced public appearance in over six years at its launch. The inclusion of this novel on the 1995 Booker shortlist was itself sufficient to guarantee public interest in the competition.

The second former Booker winner was Barry Unsworth, a major historical novelist, whose vast novel about the eighteenth-century slave trade, *Sacred Hunger*, had shared the prize in 1992 with Michael Ondaatje's *The English Patient*. Like Barker, Unsworth is from a northern working-class background, but his writing career began much earlier than hers, in the 1960s. *Morality Play*, his twelfth novel, is set in the north of England, at a very distant period: the late fourteenth century.

Completing the shortlist were two novels of contemporary life: *In Every Face I Meet* by Justin Cartwright, born in South Africa, and *The Riders* by the Australian novelist Tim Winton. These two, along with Barker, were considered 'outsiders' by bookmakers. Betting on the Booker Prize is usually described by journalists as 'frenetic', although a *Financial Times* writer, making the usual comparison between the Booker Prize and the Grand National, noted that *The Moor's Last Sigh* was such a clear favourite that 'this year, all bets are off' (McAfee, 1995). Rushdie, whose novel had already sold over 100,000 copies before the announcement of the prize (at the same stage *The Ghost Road* had sold only 10,000 copies), was in fact the first-ever odds-on favourite at 4–5, followed by Unsworth at 7–2.

The 1995 panel of judges was chaired by a slightly unusual figure, George Walden, a Conservative MP and newspaper columnist. Walden, a former diplomat, had spent much of his life overseas and took a rather pessimistic view of British (or rather English) culture in the mid-1990s. In an interview in the *Bookseller* magazine he said:

> Our politics have become tired. The debate about left and right is dead on its feet. As a country we have become provincial in the worst sense ... Our art hankers after the past ... Very few people write with any conviction about the present ... Reading 140 novels is valuable because it tells you so much about what is right and wrong with our culture. And there is so much that is wrong with our culture, with our politics.
>
> (quoted in Cowley, 1995, p.20)

The remaining panel members were all literary figures: two well-respected writers, Adam Mars-Jones and Ruth Rendell, and two experienced literary reviewers, Peter Kemp and Kate Kellaway.

Kemp and Kellaway both reviewed *The Ghost Road* (in the *Sunday Times* and the *Observer* respectively) as part of the early autumn flurry of reviews that appeared in the British daily and weekly press as well as in specialized journals like the *Times Literary Supplement* and the *London Review of Books*. I would like to begin looking at the reception of Barker's novel by comparing two of these short initial reviews published *before* the announcement of the Booker shortlist on 28 September. In the interests of establishing a range of responses, I have selected not Kemp's or Kellaway's reviews, but two that offer more grounds for contrast. **Read the reviews by Candice Rodd and Harriet Patterson (Reader, Items 51.1 and 51.2), asking yourself the following questions.**

- **What do these reviewers select as significant features of the novel?**

- **How is the structure of the novel described in each case?**

- **What kind of impact does each reviewer think that *The Ghost Road* will have on its readers?**

- **How good is the novel judged to be?**

(You may feel tempted to compare the responses of these professional reviewers with the 'first impressions' you noted down yourself at the start of this chapter. But, if possible, try to focus on the comparison between the two articles, holding on to a sense of your initial response as something provisional and open to development, and therefore still at a different stage from these published reviews.)

Reviewers trying to convey the flavour of a 70,000-word novel in just a few hundred words are, of course, going to be very selective, and differences in length (Rodd's article is about half as long again as Patterson's) will compound these variations. So despite there being much common ground, I was struck by differences between these two accounts of *The Ghost Road* in the kind of detail that is selected as well as in the judgements that are offered. (Your own first impressions may well have been different again.) So, what is *The Ghost Road* about? Patterson offers a very direct and immediate answer: it is, she says, about 'the psychological effects of war'. We might also infer from her sixth paragraph that questions about civilization versus primitivism are seen to be thematically important, too. Rodd offers a convenient list of Barker's themes at the end of her third paragraph: 'the nature of courage, kindness, cruelty and hypocrisy, what happens to minds at the lonely extremities of experience, what it means to be a man'. There is some overlap here with Patterson ('the psychological effects of war' and 'minds at the lonely extremities of experience') but you may have noticed that the last theme in the list, 'what it means to be a man' is picked up again at the end of Rodd's eighth paragraph with the reference to the young Rivers's question, 'What's wrong with boys?' (In fact, this is a slight misquotation: Rivers remembers the Reverend Charles Dodgson saying emphatically, '*Boys are a mistake*' (Barker, 1995, 2; p.26; all subsequent page references are to this edition). A little later, Rivers, with much stammering, asks his mother, 'Are we a mistake? Why are we?' and their conversation then turns on boys' need to fight; 2; p.32.) As other reviewers and commentators on Barker's work in general have remarked, Barker's exploration of the effects of war on both men and women, sexually and socially, is a noteworthy feature of *The Ghost Road* – and indeed of the trilogy as a whole. But more than that, to a degree that is still seen as unusual in a woman writer, she is interested in masculinity and writes about male experience in the same powerful way that, in some of her earlier novels, she explored female experience. Rodd indicates the importance of this theme in *The Ghost Road*.

When turning to the question of how these reviewers describe the novel's structure, you may have noticed more pointed differences between the two. I picked out Rodd's approving recognition, in her third paragraph, of the way Prior's current experiences in France alternate with Rivers's recollections of his prewar anthropological work in Melanesia: 'Either of these extended meditations would alone be powerful stuff. In tandem, they echo and illuminate each other in ways that both wrench your heart and make the hairs on the back of your neck stand up.' Rodd sees Rivers and Prior as equally important – '*The Ghost Road* belongs to William Rivers and Billy Prior' – and suggests that their separate, alternating narratives add up to more than the sum of the parts. Patterson also comments on the way that Rivers's Melanesian memories point up certain aspects of Prior's war-torn world, but on the whole she finds the anthropological 'flashbacks' a distraction from the novel's main business: 'The fact that Rivers really did this does not automatically make these sequences congruous with the rest of the book ... It all calls for a lot of emotional advance-and-retreat.' Although at the start of the review Patterson describes the trilogy as being 'based on the experiences of the neurologist William Rivers', it is his experiences as a wartime doctor to which she principally refers. Rivers, in this account, seems to be viewed mainly as a stable factual source for the novel's interesting depiction of war trauma and its treatment. I will return to the subject of the novel's structure, and to the role of Rivers, later in this chapter, but for the moment it is sufficient to note that for one reviewer the alternating narratives (in Parts Two and Three of the novel) are an important strength, and for the other they are something of a weakness.

In this discussion of the novel's structure I have also touched on the issue of the novel's impact on its readers. Rodd describes hearts being wrenched and hairs standing up on the back of readers' necks, suggesting that pity and horror are among the emotions the novel will evoke. As well as being moved, the reader can also expect to be amused at times (there is a reference to 'sly humour') and to enjoy Barker's 'tough, unself-important prose'. Patterson, too, refers to the emotional impact of parts of the novel, but also suggests that as readers we will respond to the historical dimension in the novel: early theories of psychotherapy are 'potentially fascinating', we are given a bogus-free sense of period and our understanding of what the First World War did to people will be enhanced. Patterson, it seems to me, sees the novel as a possible window on the past from the point of view of the present. In Rodd's review there is, clearly, a strong sense of the novel's historical dimension, but there seems to be less emphasis on the distinction between past and present. I am conscious of making a rather tentative distinction here, based on slight evidence, but Barker's approach to the past is one of the most interesting aspects of the novel, and this is another topic that I will be returning to in much more detail later.

Before we leave these two reviews, though, what kinds of judgements did you think they made about *The Ghost Road*? Rodd's language surely leaves us in very little doubt: she describes it as 'a book of ... dark brilliance' in the opening paragraph and 'a marvellous novel' in the closing paragraph. In between, the approval ranges across the characters ('complex and engaging'), the structure ('inspired and seamless welding of the real and imagined') and Barker's style ('unwavering commitment to vividly concrete ... narrative detail' and that 'tough, unself-important prose which nevertheless flexes effortlessly to encompass the narrative's many moods and voices'). In Patterson's review I think the praise is more muted. In the final paragraph there are some generalized comments, but they are expressed mainly in negatives: the novel offers a 'surprisingly unsentimental' view of war, the

Figure 8.3 A soldier saying goodbye at Victoria Station, London, on his way to the front in December 1914. (Photo: Topical Press Agency/Getty Images.)

sensationalist possibilities of violence are 'not over-exploited', and so on. Having chosen these two reviews from the many available mainly to provide a contrast in terms of judgement, I should add that most of the initial reviews inclined more to Rodd's estimate of the novel than Patterson's (it is repeatedly described by reviewers as 'remarkable', 'fine', 'brilliant'). However, I hope this comparison demonstrates that, in a year when 'big names' such as Rushdie and Amis were in contention for the Booker Prize, *The Ghost Road*'s initial reception did not mark it out unequivocally as a potential winner.

When the judges' verdict was announced on 7 November, there was, then, some surprise, though not nearly as much as when James Kelman won the prize the year before. John Walsh, writing in the *Independent* the following day, described *The Ghost Road* as a 'worthy winner', though the announcement apparently 'shocked many fans and devotees of Salman Rushdie'. Perhaps the second most interesting part of the proceedings was the chairman of judges' speech at the prize-giving dinner, in which Walden warmed to his theme of the decline of British culture. He described Barker's 'first-rate prose' as an exception to the prevailing mediocrity and warned again that 'the abolition of the Net Book Agreement will be a boon for ordinariness. It will drive highbrow books off the shelves and keep them where they belong: preferably behind the author's high brow' (Walden, 1995, p.15) This was not all. A further consequence of this declining culture, in Walden's view, was that it was driving good young writers into artistic introversion, so that more and more novels were about novelists and the writing of novels:

> Alternatively, they can escape into the past. I say this because so few of the Booker entries tackled modern England. Are our writers, by their silence, making a point? Is there something wrong with England? Why do they shy away from us? Do we give off a bad smell, like old vegetation? The flight from the present is becoming a general phenomenon. If the past is another country, then we are facing a sort of mass emigration. Nostalgia is becoming our heavy industry ... At some point you have to decide when an entire era is over, or whether you are going to re-live it endlessly. What do we want? Movement or stagnation? A vibrant country or a patch of overgrown vegetation? ... dead or alive?
>
> (Walden, 1995, p.15)

Walden was not alone in making this complaint, although he made it in unusually strong terms. You will recall D.J. Taylor's comments (quoted in Chapter 7) about Booker priorities and historical novels. Other critics, too, in the 1990s were puzzled by the scarcity of novels about contemporary England, though this was not a problem that seemed to afflict the Scottish, Irish or American novel to anything like the same degree. Genre fiction such as thrillers or romances continued to draw productively on contemporary social reality, whether urban or rural, but the 'literary novel' (Booker material) offered fewer representations of present-day England. *The Ghost Road* is, arguably, part of this 'flight from the present', though Walden did not explicitly make this point. Instead, he credited Barker with the extraordinary achievement of saying 'something new about the First World War'. So at this point we will look in more detail at late twentieth-century novelists' 'mass emigration' to the past and test out Walden's claim that Barker was doing something new in this sphere. This will also give you an opportunity to start developing the initial responses to *The Ghost Road* that you registered earlier, particularly in relation to your expectations regarding the genre of historical fiction.

Historical fiction in the late twentieth century

One earlier Booker Prize-winner, J.G. Farrell (*The Siege of Krishnapur*, 1973), declared that there was 'nothing worth writing about' in contemporary Britain (Farrell, 1970, p.217). Farrell had already turned to the recent past for his subject matter, with *Troubles* (1970), set in Ireland during the period of the Irish War of Independence, 1919–21, before moving even further back, to mid-nineteenth-century India, for *The Siege of Krishnapur*. Farrell's great theme was the decline of empire – the British Empire in this case – and the third novel in what he called his 'triptych' (though critics more often call it his 'Empire trilogy') dealt with the Fall of Singapore during the Second World War. In common with many writers of historical fiction in the late twentieth century, and indeed with many social historians, Farrell adopts a decentred view of history. The major events, the famous historical personages, are largely off-stage; instead Farrell focuses on the lives of fictional characters at the margins of these significant events, dramatizing the ideological conflicts that are shaping their particular 'moments'. Hindsight is, of course, an essential component of the historical novelist's vision, but there is more than one way of putting hindsight to use. In her book on history and politics in postwar British fiction, Margaret Scanlan identifies some characteristic ways in which writers like Farrell 'encode the before and after'. One of these is

> what might be called the historical variant of dramatic irony. The novelist frequently exploits the reader's awareness of the future that awaits characters who are secure in their certainty that 'Nuremburg is a city of tolerance' or that England will never surrender her claim to Singapore, India, Egypt, or Ireland. Part of the humor of *The Siege of Krishnapur* comes from the narrator's deadpan chronicling of the more bizarre theories of Victorian medicine. The multiple time shifts, characteristic of modernist fiction, in a historical novel similarly tend to keep both past and present visible, thus preventing the comfortable escape into the past that is characteristic of romantic fiction ... Shuttled between their own time and that of the characters, readers become implicated in the past.
>
> (Scanlan, 1990, p.11)

How does this compare with Barker's approach? A good place to look would be the start of the novel, since openings are always so important in orientating the reader. **Reread the first chapter of *The Ghost Road*, asking yourself whether you feel 'shuttled between [your] own time and that of the characters'.**

It is fairly common for historical novels to begin with some kind of period 'placing' – a date may be given, or a landmark event mentioned so that we, the readers, know where in the past we are. In Virginia Woolf's novel *Orlando*, for example, we are told after just a few pages that 'the sixteenth century had still some years of its course to run' (Woolf, [1928] 1998, p.16). Another brief example: Rose Tremain's *Restoration*, which was shortlisted for the Booker Prize in 1989, has a first-person narrator who tells us at the start of the novel that he is 'thirty-seven years old as this year, 1664, moves

Figure 8.4 Munitions workers seated at a bench at Woolwich Arsenal using primitive remote handling equipment to work with explosives, May 1918; photograph by G.P. Lewis. (With permission of The Trustees of the Imperial War Museum, London. Q27889.)

towards its end' (Tremain, [1989] 1990, p.13). There is nothing quite so explicit in *The Ghost Road*. To be sure, the references to the war, German snipers, yellow-skinned munitions workers, and so on, make the period setting clear, although we have to look for clues as to *which* summer of the First World War we are in (Prior was invalided home in 'April last year' (1; p.10) after three years in France (1; p.12) so this must be 1918). But before we reach any hint of the war, Barker gives us a seaside scene – bare-kneed men in deck-chairs, a small boy crying as his mother towels his legs dry – that could really belong to any part of the early twentieth century. It is worth noting how quickly the narrative pulls us in to this scene. A third-person narrator describes for us the Bradford businessmen in their deck-chairs, Prior leaning on the sea-wall, the family below him on the beach, but within a few lines, with the phrase 'my God, he'd be regretting it tomorrow' (1; p.3), the reader is positioned with Prior, the observer, hearing his thoughts (as well as the phrase 'my God', the word 'tomorrow' must belong to a character in the scene, since the third-person narrator would more probably say 'the next day'). This is reinforced a few lines later with 'Wet sand was the problem. It always was, Prior remembered. However carefully you tiptoed back from that final paddle, your legs got coated all over again, and the towel always hurt.' Use of the second-person pronoun, 'you', not only generalizes the experience but makes the reader complicit in the recollection.

Throughout the whole of this first chapter, I suggest, because the narrative is focalized through Prior and constantly slides into his thoughts and memories, the reader is mainly occupied in establishing a mental 'fix' on Prior and his world. A reader who has not met Prior and Owen via the two earlier novels might get a surprise on realizing that 'Owen' is Wilfred Owen, friend of Siegfried Sassoon (1; pp.14–15); possibly this entails some readjustment as the fictional world of Prior has to be meshed with the real-life existence of Owen. However, there was only one point in this chapter when I became very conscious that I was looking through a historical prism back at 1918: that moment comes near the end of the chapter as Owen emerges from his Medical Board:

> Owen started to speak and then, realizing the Board's secretary had followed him, raised a thumb instead. From which Prior concluded that Owen's chances of ending the year deaf, blind, dumb, paralysed, doubly incontinent, insane, brain damaged or – if he were lucky – just plain dead had enormously increased.

(1; pp.15–16)

Here Barker is, in Scanlan's words, 'exploit[ing] the reader's awareness of the future that awaits characters' in a variant of dramatic irony. The twist here is that in the literary history of the twentieth century, the death of Owen at the age of twenty-five, in November 1918, just a week before the end of the First World War, is an emblem of the tragic waste of that war, so to contemplate the prospect of his death as 'lucky' is at first startling. There is considerable force in the idea that a soldier's death might be preferable to the awful possibilities of mutilation listed by Prior, and although this idea is not unfamiliar it does involve some readjustment, probably, to our habitual assumptions about premature death. But more than that, because the soldier in question is Wilfred Owen, we have to switch between our twenty-first-century perception of Owen as, primarily, a poet, to a fellow-soldier's view of him in 1918 (Owen published a mere handful of poems during his lifetime: his poetic reputation grew only after 1919). So, looking back on the first chapter as a whole in relation to the question of whether readers are 'shuttled between their own time and that of the characters', I would say that 'shuttled' is too strong a term. Barker *does* offer us a fresh view of the past and that will sometimes involve a re-examination of our current perceptions, but for the most part the narrative draws us compellingly into the time of the characters. As we read on beyond the first chapter and adapt ourselves to the alternating points of reference – Prior's and Rivers's – another kind of dynamic is established, which, I suggest, pulls against the more familiar chronological perspective, such as that which features strongly in the review by Patterson you read earlier.

I will examine the braided effect of Prior's and Rivers's interwoven experiences and memories in more detail shortly. But, even within each narrative strand, the play of memory is complex enough to generate a sense of each character's present moment that demands the reader's full attention. As an example, we will look at the third chapter of the novel, in which we rejoin Prior in the evening of his Medical Board day. **Reread Chapter 3, noting the points at which memories, in one way or another, are foregrounded.**

You may have noticed that some of Prior's memories refer back to earlier points in the trilogy. The first recollection, prompted by writing a letter to Rivers earlier that evening, is of Craiglockhart:

> he drifted along, remembering the light flashing on Rivers's glasses, and the everlasting *pok-pok* from the tennis courts that somehow wove itself into the pattern of their speech and silence, as Rivers extracted his memories of France from him, one by one, like a dentist pulling teeth.
>
> (3; p.33)

Already a kind of layering effect is achieved: within Prior's almost casual, nostalgic memory of Craiglockhart, with its unthreatening sounds from the tennis courts, is embedded the painful but therapeutically crucial act of recovering his war-memory. A later stage in his relationship with Rivers is recalled further on in the chapter, on pages 43–4. In this memory Prior is suffering not the trauma of trench warfare but the pathological condition of alternating states of consciousness that surfaced during his period working as an intelligence agent for the Ministry of Munitions (in *The Eye in the Door*). The most terrible part of this is not remembering what he, or rather his alter ego, may have done and contemplating the possibility that he may have killed someone.

In this chapter Prior's actual memories of fighting in France are merely touched on, but the fear they carry with them is inescapable. At the fairground, people in the haunted house are screaming at cardboard terrors, but Prior is unable even to complete his thoughts about real skeletons and skulls: 'If they'd seen ... *Oh, leave it, leave it*' (3; p.34). He escapes from these sounds by going with a prostitute to her room, only to be assailed by deeper fears, triggered by a different sense:

> He was pulling his half-unbuttoned tunic over his head when he noticed a smell of gas. Faint but unmistakable. Tented in dark khaki, he fought back the rush of panic, sweat streaming down his

sides, not the gradual sweat of exercise but a sudden drench, rank, slippery, hot, then immediately cold ... He told himself there was no reason to be afraid, but he was afraid.

(3; p.38)

The encounter with Nellie, the prostitute, reminds Prior of Lizzie MacDowell and her 'patriotic gesture' on the first day of the war (3; pp.35–6). Another very different kind of sexual memory also surfaces as he recognizes and identifies with the expression on Nellie's face, 'waiting for it to be over' (3; p.41). This is a memory from childhood, a memory that from a late twentieth- or twenty-first-century perspective we would call 'child abuse', even though Prior's experience so quickly modulates into relish ('he'd been a forward child ... not so much resorting to prostitution as inventing it').

These examples alone (and you may have picked out others) would be sufficient to demonstrate that the act of remembering is essential to Prior's narrative. But just to clinch the point, at the end of the chapter, death and memory become transposed onto the living present as Prior remembers a line from Sassoon's poem 'Survivors':

'Cowed subjection to the ghosts of friends who died.' That was it exactly, couldn't be better put. Ghosts everywhere. Even the living were only ghosts in the making. You learned to ration your commitment to them. This moment in this tent already had the quality of *remembered* experience.

(3; p.46)

The boundaries between past and present are thus dissolved, and even the future is undifferentiated (the living are 'only ghosts in the making'). The reader who tries to maintain a conventional focus on 'the past' soon runs into difficulties because the past is not single. Instead, the reviewer Lorna Sage describes Barker's novelistic method as producing 'a powerfully ironic sense of imprisonment in the moment'.

Sage's review, 'Both Sides', appeared in the fortnightly *London Review of Books* in early October 1995. Sage was a widely respected academic with a reputation as an acute critic, and her review of *The Ghost Road*, longer and more substantial than the newspaper reviews you read earlier, was bound to be influential. It is still, to my mind, one of the best pieces of criticism on *The Ghost Road*, and I will refer to it several times in the remainder of this chapter. **Now read Sage's review (Reader, Item 52) and reflect on the following questions.**

- **To what extent does my analysis of Chapter 3 of *The Ghost Road* fit with her term 'palimpsest history'?**

- **Does this review offer any support for Walden's claim that Barker is saying 'something new about the First World War'?**

In the first paragraph of the review Sage talks about 'palimpsest history' in terms of the rapid switches from 'document to dream to memory to dialogue', and perhaps we would need to look more closely at the interplay between the Prior and Rivers narratives to grasp the full force of what she packs into the term. But essentially she is referring to the procedure (quite common before the invention of printing) of reusing paper or expensive parchment by erasing one text to make room for another. This process sometimes resulted in a 'superimposed' effect when the original text was not thoroughly effaced and remained still faintly visible beneath the new one. I would say that the layering of memories we have observed in Chapter 3 conveys the basic sense of 'palimpsest' in that one story is superimposed on another. But there is another feature of palimpsests that is relevant to the points Sage is making. In the monastic libraries of medieval Europe, where this recycling of parchment was fairly common, very often a 'pagan' text would be erased and overwritten with a Christian one. So palimpsests sometimes contain not just different texts but *opposing* texts. This understanding of the term is clearly relevant to the description of Prior's 'palimpsest personality', but it is also worth bearing in mind with reference to the kind of history Barker is offering her readers.

In the first place, as Sage points out, in *The Ghost Road* we have an effect of 'spread, not sequence'. This 'spread' enables Barker to move beyond the conventional boundaries of the First World War and incorporate, through Rivers's narrative, an anthropological perspective whose timescales and geographical reach are entirely different from those of the European conflict. Rivers's memories of the Melanesian people among whom he has recently worked are as vivid as his encounters with war-damaged soldiers in Britain. However, there is a profound tension between the familiar story of war on the Western Front as a tragic waste of life and the less familiar story from the other side of the Pacific of 'a people perishing from the absence of war' (14; p.207) at the same historical moment. A second point, more fully developed in Sage's review, is that Barker uses the overlapping of historical and fictional characters in the novel 'to rub in a bitter message about the invisibility of most people's lives and deaths'. There are thus really three categories of characters in the novel. When we talk about 'historical' figures we generally mean those who are named and whose existence we know about from other documents – Rivers, Owen, Colonel Marshall-of-the-Ten-Wounds, and so on. But Barker's 'Author's Note' at the end of the novel reminds us that 'Njiru, Kundaite, Namboko Taru, Namboko Emele, Nareti, Lembu and the captive child are also historical.' As Sage puts it, 'Rivers's Solomon Islanders were perfectly real, but nothing more is known of them than what he chose to record (and never got around to publishing).' The existence of this second category of characters – real but to most of us unknown – bridges the divide between the 'historical' figures and the fictional characters such as Prior, Sarah, Ada Lumb and the multitude of her neighbours at the séance in

Chapter 5 of the novel. The characters in the latter group are realistic, but the novelist has to invent them because their historical counterparts have lived and died without their identities having been marked. To be sure, the names of many of the soldiers who died in the First World War are recorded on the war memorials that sprang up in unprecedented numbers after the conflict, but the novel subtly reminds us of the unnamed widows and mothers who were also subject to the same forces of history. There is some continuity here, I think, between Barker's earlier novels, set in working-class communities with a major – though not exclusive – focus on women characters, and the concerns of her *Regeneration* trilogy.

So is Barker saying something new about the First World War? There are certainly no stale clichés in *The Ghost Road* about lost innocence or nostalgia for an Englishness that has vanished, and there is little trace of the 'shattered illusions' storyline that has marked many literary versions of the First World War from Erich Maria Remarque's *All Quiet on the Western Front* (1929) onwards. But much more important, to my mind, is what Sage describes as Barker's 'assault on the class distinction between real and unreal': this is, as she says, 'striking and disconcerting', and while it undoubtedly gives us a new

Figure 8.5 Two men on Kulumbangra, a large volcanic island near Gizo, Solomon Islands, 9 May 1910, silver gelatine print. (Photo: Royal Anthropological Institute, London.)

perspective on the First World War, as Walden suggests, its originality is not limited to this particular historical subject. Developing the point about Barker's handling of the real and the unreal, at the end of the review Sage says that 'There is a kind of horror or obscenity lurking in the way she breeds facts with fictions' and that this powerful new growth blots out 'the authorial power of the overview'. If it is true that Barker's method dissolves 'the one of the writer into the many of the written-about' then arguably she has achieved something new in fiction-writing.

Before I conclude this section on historical fiction in the late twentieth century, you may want to revisit the notes you made on your 'first impressions' of *The Ghost Road*. Now that you have read three reviews of the novel, with differing degrees of emphasis on its historical nature, and have looked more closely at Barker's technique in two chapters from Part One, do you want to modify in any way your initial response to the historical dimension of the novel? **Review your 'first impressions' notes now, picking out anything that touches on the novel's historical setting and/or Barker's approach to her historical material. Ask yourself whether your judgements about this aspect of the novel have shifted or developed at all in the light of the selective rereading you have now done, and, if so, revise your notes in whatever way you feel is appropriate.**

For the final reading in this section we will be placing *The Ghost Road* in the context of the preoccupation of late twentieth-century novelists not just with historical subjects in general but, more specifically, with the two world wars. This is not a new strain in Barker's writing. The novel she wrote immediately before the *Regeneration* trilogy, *The Man Who Wasn't There* (1989), is set during the Second World War, and before that, in *Liza's England* (originally titled *The Century's Daughter*; 1986), the impact of both world wars on the central character, Liza Jarrett, is carefully charted. A number of other novelists, such as Graham Swift, Julian Barnes and Sebastian Faulks, have also explored this territory, prompting much critical speculation about a heightened (millennial) need to recall that past which lies within living memory. The novelist and critic A.S. Byatt has written insightfully about narratives of war in her essay 'Fathers', based on a lecture originally given in the USA in 1999, in which she pays particular attention to Barker's *Regeneration* trilogy. **Read the extracts from Byatt's essay (Reader, Item 53) and make brief notes in response to the following questions.**

- **What explanations does Byatt offer for the flowering of historical fiction in the later decades of the twentieth century?**

- **What does she suggest is distinctive about Barker's 'recreation' of the First World War?**

In the fourth paragraph of the extract Byatt lists a number of reasons why so many novelists have 'taken to' history. The first comes out of developments in the discipline of history itself, developments that have unsettled confidence in 'master narratives' and foregrounded the artifice involved in the writing of history. In this climate of uncertainty ('we cannot know the past, we are told'), the narratives of fiction-writers and biographers may compete for validity with the narratives of historians, so they all have an equal claim on the subject matter of the past. Arising from this shift is 'the sense of a new possibility of narrative energy' – something that Byatt first refers to near the beginning of the essay. Counting these as two separate explanations, a third would be that 'novelists are trying to find historical paradigms for contemporary situations'. Understanding the past in order to understand the present is a need that is especially relevant, Byatt suggests, to the war novels under discussion, including Barker's. It is worth dwelling on this explanation because it complicates the picture offered by Walden in his 1995 Booker speech, according to which contemporary novelists *either* 'tackle modern England' *or* 'escape into the past'. Going outside Byatt's essay for a moment, there does seem to be some evidence that Barker sees parallels between the period of the First World War and the 1990s: in the radio interview mentioned earlier, she said:

> I think that at that time [of the First World War] men were questioning the ideas of manliness they had grown up with in a very open and honest and untrendy kind of way, and that fascinates me – I think it has parallels with ... certain developments that are going on today.
>
> (Vaughan, 1995)

It is entirely possible that we, as readers, may find further ways in which Barker's historical novel illuminates aspects of late twentieth-century society, but the novelist's own comments confirm that this 'find[ing] historical paradigms' is a conscious and deliberate element in choosing historical subject matter.

We have still not exhausted Byatt's list of explanations for the late twentieth-century flowering of historical fiction. At the end of her fourth paragraph there is a rather different kind of explanation, based on language and the relationship between past and present literatures. Then in the fifth paragraph we move to an explanation that will already be familiar to you from your study of *Paradise* – 'the political desire to write the histories of the marginalised, the forgotten, the unrecorded'. (Byatt mentions in particular the 'flourishing and brilliant culture of the post-colonial novel' but resists the critical commonplace that modern British writing owes its vitality solely to the energies of 'writers from elsewhere'.) As we have seen, the political desire to write about the people who have been neglected in conventional histories is certainly at work in *The Ghost Road*. You may remember that Sage emphasized this element in Barker's work at the end of her review with the comment: 'She is one of fiction's most dedicated levellers – not the one but the many, and the many in one.'

Near the end of the extract Byatt offers one further explanation for the turn to historical fiction that takes us into new territory altogether. She suggests that 'postmodern writers are returning to historical fiction because the idea of writing about the Self is felt to be worked out, or precarious, or because these writers are attracted by the idea that perhaps we have no such thing as an organic, discoverable, single Self'. The half-known quality of historical characters matches our contemporary sense that the Self is not as central as it would seem to be in the representations of the great modernist writers of the early twentieth century. This is the most far-reaching of Byatt's ideas about the attraction of historical subject matter, and you will notice that she arrives at this suggestion via Barker's trilogy, the work of Rivers and, behind him, Freud. This might count (moving on to our second question about this extract) as one of the distinguishing elements Byatt finds in Barker's 'recreation' of the First World War, as she dramatizes the way that the conflict fuelled changes in medical history and psychiatry. Not all critics, however, have been so approving about Barker's treatment of her scientific sources. Ben Shephard, in his history of twentieth-century military psychiatry, *A War of Nerves*, makes the following comment in relation to the *Regeneration* trilogy:

> Barker drew skilfully on some of the literature [from the period of the First World War], but she also projected backwards a great deal of modern baggage derived from the women's movement and the 1980s 'counselling culture'. She brought the subject back into the public mind, but in a lop-sided way.
>
> (Shephard, 2000, p.xx)

The anonymous German professor Byatt cites in her essay also, presumably, thinks that Barker brings to her material 'modern baggage derived from the women's movement' when he sums up the trilogy as being 'simply about the ideology of the feminization of society brought about by the war'. But Byatt disagrees with such a reductive judgement. She rejects the idea that Barker's novels are driven by any narrowly conceived ideology and talks instead about a much larger exploration of 'the enormous shifts and rifts in the structure of society, sexuality and psyche brought about by the war'. You may recall that Rodd, in her review of *The Ghost Road*, singled out masculinity and the question of 'what it means to be a man' as major issues in the novel. But in case it seems that this debate is dividing along gender lines, I should just like to add that by no means all male critics are with the German professor on this one. For example, Dennis Brown says in relation to Barker's treatment of the Pemberton Billing affair that

> The hysteria about homosexuality helps focus a Great War issue that Barker, unusually for a woman novelist, engages head-on: a crisis in ideas about masculinity. The topic of 'masculinities' has become of considerable recent interest. However, to my knowledge, male war experience has not featured largely in Gender Studies – despite its having been an actual or potential reality for Western men in most of the last century.
>
> (Brown, 2005, pp.192–3)

Brown, like Byatt, applauds Barker for moving outside 'the constraints of prescribed feminist subject-matter' and exploring the nature of courage and combativeness. But perhaps what Byatt finds *most* distinctive about Barker's trilogy is the 'formally inventive ... decision' to use the real-life Rivers as her central focus alongside other actual and fictional characters. It is nothing new for a historical novel to be peopled by a mixture of real-life and invented characters – this is a well-established convention of the genre. But Byatt suggests that Barker uses this technique in an original way, and that its success hinges on the figure of Rivers. I will investigate this claim in the next two sections, first by exploring the relationship between fact and fiction in the novel, then by analysing Rivers's pivotal role in more detail.

Factual fictions

Barker's 'Author's Note' at the end of *Regeneration* begins: 'Fact and fiction are so interwoven in this book that it may help the reader to know what is historical and what is not.' There are similar notes on historical sources at the end of *The Eye in the Door* and *The Ghost Road*. Although it is not so very unusual for a novelist, especially a historical novelist, to include such notes or even a bibliography as part of the book's apparatus, Barker's blending of fact and fiction in *The Ghost Road* has merited particular attention from critics. It has a bearing on the structure as well as the texture of the novel, so it is undoubtedly a feature that we need to take into consideration in our literary judgement of the text.

Barker uses the terms 'fact' and 'fiction' in the ordinary, everyday way, as antonyms. However, in the context of written narratives the easy distinction between 'fact' and 'fiction' is more problematic, and especially so in the case of novels. The possible overlap between the two terms is not just a consequence of postmodern doubts about the status of knowledge and self-consciousness about the construction of narrative forms. As far as the novel is concerned, the overlap goes back a long way. Terry Eagleton points out that

> In the English late sixteenth and early seventeenth centuries, the word 'novel' seems to have been used about both true and fictional events, and even news reports were hardly considered factual. Novels and news reports were neither clearly factual nor clearly fictional. Our own sharp distinctions between these categories simply did not apply.
>
> (Eagleton, 1983, pp.1–2)

When the realist novel as we know it took shape in the eighteenth century, it imitated closely the conventions and language of non-fiction such as biography, autobiography, diaries, letters, journalism and travel-writing, not to mention more formal kinds of history-writing. However, it is easy to overlook this mixed parentage in the conventional language of the novel because the kind of fictional realism forged in the eighteenth century and consolidated in the nineteenth has established itself so firmly as a distinct mode of writing. Indeed, it has remained the dominant novelistic mode, although tempered by various kinds of experimentation throughout the twentieth century. Before I quickly review some of these developments, it is worth making the point that the novel's debt to non-fictional forms of writing sometimes persists in a quite explicit way. A familiar convention is that of using letters, diary entries or other kinds of 'documents' *within* a third-person narrative. Where these insertions are letters or journals being read or written by characters in the novel, they have the effect of bringing the reader into a closer, more immediate relationship with the character concerned. Sometimes a novelist will insert part of a document that is actually or ostensibly from another published source – Sassoon's 1917 declaration against the war at the opening of *Regeneration* is a case in point. Another brief example occurs at the start of Part Three of *The Ghost Road*. **Reread the first section of Chapter 14 (pp.203–4): what is the effect on the reader of the newspaper headlines at the start of the chapter?**

You may have noticed that the words 'newspaper' and 'headlines' only appear at the end of the section; initially the novelist relies on the reader's understanding of typographical conventions (the headlines appear in two sizes of centred, upper-case print) and familiarity with the linguistic patterns of headlines to make sense of these dozen words. You may have wondered whether these headlines are real or invented; that unspoken question is of a different order from the question of whether the real-life Rivers had a boiled egg for breakfast on this particular morning in October 1918 because it impinges on the public record of the final stages of the war. Appearing as they do without quotation marks, the headlines propel the reader out into the world beyond the novel. You may have been struck by the word 'Huns', a slang term that was widely used during the war but is now considered to have pejorative overtones (contrast Prior's references to 'Germans') and the easy cliché 'Both Sides Pay the Price' (again, contrast the previous page or so of

Prior's diary). The phrase 'Sheer Fighting' is also arresting, conveying something like exhilaration, perhaps, but also suggesting the difficulty of describing the intensity of these engagements. The novelist Henry James made a remarkably prescient comment in March 1915:

> The war has used up words; they have weakened, they have deteriorated like motor car tires ... we are now confronted with a depreciation of all our terms, or, otherwise speaking, with a loss of expression through increase of limpness, that may well make us wonder what ghosts will be left to walk.
>
> (quoted in Bellringer, 1988, p.24)

One of the effects, I think, of Chapter 14's newspaper headlines is to remind us that language does change, and that the historical novel involves a negotiation between the languages of past and present. Drawing again on Sage's 'palimpsest' metaphor, this brief insertion at the beginning of Part Three rubs a hole in the surface of Barker's late twentieth-century prose and thus paradoxically makes that surface more visible. The overall effect is that the reader does not take the realist-fiction conventions so much for granted – the layering of fictional and non-fictional textures makes us more aware that each kind of language use has its own, different relationship to the realities it strives to express.

Variations within a realist novel such as the inclusion of diary entries, letters or other derivatives of non-fictional forms are readily understood by readers as belonging to long-established conventions. However, the experimentation that characterized some twentieth-century approaches to the novel depended on actually undermining conventions. Early twentieth-century modernists such as James Joyce, Franz Kafka, Virginia Woolf or William Faulkner attempted to express the complexity of human experience in the modern world by exposing, in a variety of ways, what lay beneath the narrative surface of their fictions, and by doing so they overtly acknowledged the 'fictitiousness' of novels. Despite some critical predictions that this kind of experimentation would prove to be either the death of the novel or, at best, a kind of cul-de-sac in its history, the novel as a genre in fact managed to absorb an enormous amount of self-questioning. In later twentieth-century fiction the term 'metafiction' was widely used to refer to the now familiar awareness of tension in the relationship between the world of fiction and the world outside it. Patricia Waugh offers the following definition of the term:

> Metafictional novels tend to be constructed on the principle of a fundamental and sustained opposition: the construction of a fictional illusion (as in traditional realism) and the laying bare of that illusion. In other words, the lowest common denominator of metafiction is simultaneously to create a fiction and to make a statement about the creation of that fiction.
>
> (Waugh, 1984, p.6)

Some novelists have gone so far as to discard the notion of fiction altogether in relation to the novel. The British novelist B.S. Johnson moved unequivocally in this direction with his novel *Trawl* (1966). This work was based even more firmly on his own experiences than his earlier novels had been, and his publishers wanted to classify it as autobiography. Johnson insisted that the book 'is a novel ... what it is not is fiction. The novel is a form in the same sense that the sonnet is a form; within that form, one may write truth or fiction. I choose to write truth in the form of a novel' (quoted in Bradbury, 1977, p.154).

Similar moves were being made in the USA where, in the 1960s, the term 'non-fiction novel' was applied to true stories written in the form of novels. Truman Capote claimed to have coined the term to describe his bestselling book *In Cold Blood* (1965), the story of a Kansas family murdered by two drifters in 1959. The decision to fashion a work in this form was based, he said, on a long-held theory that 'journalism, reportage, could be forced to yield a serious new art form ... On the whole, journalism is the most under-estimated, the least explored, of literary mediums' (quoted in Hollowell, 1977, p.64).

The 'true-crime story' has, of course, a long tradition, but Capote's promotion of this 'serious new art form', using the techniques of a variety of 'popular' writing – journalism – certainly served to arouse debate in 1960s America about the possibility of new directions for the novel. The debate was stimulated further by the publication in 1968 of Norman Mailer's *Armies of the Night*. The subject matter of Mailer's book is the 1967 march on the Pentagon and demonstration against the war in Vietnam, and its metafictional credentials are declared in its two-fold structure, revealed in the subtitle: 'History as a Novel, the Novel as History'. Mailer was directly involved in the events described, so his role was in many ways like that of the 'new journalist' of the 1960s. 'New Journalism', as practised by writers such as Tom Wolfe and Jimmy Breslin (in the *New York Herald Tribune*'s Sunday supplement), Joan Didion (in the *Saturday Evening Post*) and Gay Talese (in *Esquire*), used many of the techniques usually reserved for fiction. These included scene-by-scene construction and full dialogue, and a more openly subjective attitude towards the people and events described, in contrast to the supposed objectivity of standard news reporting. So in some respects this takes us back to the early seventeenth-century state of affairs described by Eagleton, in which there is no sharp distinction between 'novels' and news reports. New Journalism's influence on the literary world was considerable and this influence quickly spread beyond its American roots. For example, Adam Mars-Jones, one of the 1995 Booker judges, produced a distinguished piece of British New Journalism in his account of the trial of the 'Black Panther', Donald Neilson, entitled 'Bathpool Park' (in Mars-Jones, 1981).

The principles of the non-fiction novel and New Journalism could be applied to historical as well as contemporary subject matter. This was what happened when the Australian novelist Thomas Keneally stumbled upon the remarkable true story of Oskar Schindler, the German industrialist who, during the Second World War, managed to save hundreds of Polish Jews from Auschwitz by employing them in his enamelware and munitions factory. In his 'Author's Note' prefacing the novel, Keneally explains his choice of literary form:

> To use the texture and devices of a novel to tell a true story is a course which has frequently been followed in modern writing. It is the one I have chosen to follow here; both because the craft of the novelist is the only craft to which I can lay claim, and because the novel's techniques seem suited for a character of such ambiguity and magnitude as Oskar. I have attempted to avoid all fiction, though, since fiction would debase the record.
>
> (Keneally, 1982, pp.9–10)

In fact, this faithfully researched book was published as non-fiction in America, but Keneally's British publishers decided to catalogue the work as a novel. So when *Schindler's Ark* was awarded the 1982 Booker McConnell Prize for Fiction there was, understandably, some controversy. John Carey, the chairman of the Booker judging panel that year, endorsed the decision in terms that recall Johnson's separation of 'novel' and 'fiction':

> It seemed to me that the artistic and literary element lies in the structure of the book – in the way in which the author has put together the testimony and evidence he collected and the sequence in which he chooses to release the facts. There is no falsity in the book, but he has made a novel by structuring, placing and ordering.
>
> (quoted in Colvin, 1982, p.8)

Carey's emphasis on 'structuring, placing and ordering' as criteria for judging this novel actually closes the gap between novelistic and historiographic narratives and relegates the fact/fiction dichotomy to the periphery of this particular discussion.

How, then, does this brief elaboration of the term 'factual fictions' help us to further our understanding of *The Ghost Road*? First, it allows us to come at the question of the novel's structure from a slightly different direction, seeing the interplay between factual and fictional elements as a key *formal* consideration. Secondly, I hope it will provide a way of enlarging on one of the reasons that Byatt proposed for the enthusiasm of late twentieth-century novelists for historical subject matter – 'the sense of a new possibility of narrative energy'. This vitality derives, I suggest, from a more inclusive attitude not only towards non-fictional material but also towards the techniques of non-fictional writing. With these points in mind, we will return to *The Ghost Road*, and examine the shift in Part Two from third-person to first-person narration. **Reread Chapter 7 of the novel and consider the following questions.**

- **How is the change to journal form 'justified' in narrative terms?**

- **How does the chronology of this chapter mesh with that of Chapter 6?**

- **What is the effect of the comment on first-person narrators at the end of the chapter?**

In terms of naturalism, Prior's journal hardly needs much justifying. Paul Fussell, in *The Great War and Modern Memory*, points out that while the American Civil War was the first conflict in which large numbers of common soldiers were literate, 'by 1914, it was possible for soldiers to be not merely literate but literary' (1975, p.157). Like letters, the war-journal is an authentic literary form appropriate to this context, and it is entirely probable that the well-educated Prior should write one; it is even entirely probable that he should record the literary activity of his fellow-soldiers (7; p.115). Although this is a fictional journal, it is studded with facts and phrases from actual letters – those of Wilfred Owen, listed in the 'Author's Note' at the end of the novel. Since the two forms, war-letters and war-journals, are so closely related, factual material from the first can be smoothly transposed to a fictional version of the second. In the same move the novelist achieves that emphasis on '*the living moment*' (7; p.107) that the first-person diary-form affords.

You may have noticed that Barker goes to some lengths to establish the material form of Prior's diary, written on 'thick creamy pages', which will later be shared with his companions when the front-line paper-shortage – something Owen mentions in his letters – threatens to interrupt the steady flow of soldiers' writing (17; p.253). Prior says that he bought the blank-paged book in London 'quite a long time ago' and he begins writing his journal in it almost in a spirit of defiance: 'the thick creamy pages have been saying, Piss off, what could *you* possibly write on *us* that would be worth reading?' (7; p.107). Here Barker's 'levelling' drive is at work again, as she reminds us how economics and class impinge on the creation of what may become source material from which history will later be written. Prior does not set out to explain why he begins his journal (he will, later, in the midst of fighting (13; p.192) express the need to record extreme experiences), but we infer that departure from England is the stimulus and conventional starting point. The third-person narrator has already described, in the second half of Chapter 6, a significant part of this departure episode, namely the meeting between Prior and Rivers (their only actual encounter in this novel) the evening that Prior leaves London. However, Chapter 7 begins the day before that, with his arrival in London, meeting with Manning, and so on. You may have found this disruption to the linear sequence of the narrative a little jarring, although the break from Part One to Part Two perhaps prepares us for a shift in chronology as well as method of narration. But I think this can also be viewed as part of the novel's overall treatment of time. As we have seen, the emphasis on memory is an important feature of the narrative, looping back with the flow of recollection. In the journal sections we are made aware that even a first-person day-to-day account of action depends on memory, too: the idea of narrative sequence is again exposed as something of a literary illusion.

Another narrative expectation that Barker takes care to undercut is the illusion we always have that a first-person narrator must exist outside the timeframe of the story. As Prior puts it at the end of Chapter 7, 'First-person narrators can't die, so as long as we keep telling the story of our own lives we're safe' (p.115). There is psychological plausibility in Prior's explanation that for him, and for other soldiers writing their letters, diaries and even poems, the use of 'I' may be a way of claiming immunity from death. Being Prior, he immediately refutes this idea with 'Ha bloody fucking Ha', but his comments also serve to foreground the literary convention and to warn the reader not to place too much reliance on it. So although there is a touch of metafictive self-consciousness in the way that Barker lays bare the 'device' of the war-diary, because she does this *through* the character of Prior the overarching realism of her approach is not threatened.

From Chapter 7 onwards, then, the fictional story of Prior is presented mainly (though not entirely) in the pseudo-factual form of a diary, while the chapters focused on Rivers, using historical material from his anthropological notebooks, continue in conventional novelistic form. The alternation between the two 'stories' becomes more pronounced not only because of the switches from first-person to third-person narration but also because the 'Rivers' chapters, apart from the first page or so of Chapter 8, now consist entirely of prewar Melanesian material. In Chapters 10 and 12 Barker even dispenses with the association-prompts which have so far led us back from Rivers's life in London, 1918, to his recollections of Eddystone. So the final sentence of Chapter 8, ' "I'm afraid what we need is a proper death" ' (p.137), is picked up in the first sentence of Chapter 10: 'They didn't have to wait long for their proper death' (p.155). No apparent accommodation is made for the fact that in between we have had sixteen pages concerned with a week or so of Prior's time in France. Although Prior often thinks of Rivers (9; pp.145, 148), there is no overt connection between the two narrative lines at this stage, so the reader is nudged into awareness of parallels, echoes or contrasts that will hold the reading experience together. **Reread Chapters 8 and 9, noting any points of similarity or contrast between the two narrative sequences.**

At the most basic structural level, you may have commented on the fact that both chapters deal with journeys and arrivals. The final stage of Rivers's journey to Eddystone on a tramp steamer is made in the mixed company of his fellow-field worker, Hocart, a missionary, Father Michael, and the larger-than-life trader, Brennan. Prior travels by train from the French coast to join his battalion, also in rather mixed company (9; p.138), including Hallet, who is Prior's younger, untried companion in much the same way that Hocart is Rivers's. There are parallels, too, in that both journeys lead to unexpected kinds of arrival. Rivers is used to conducting his anthropological fieldwork on 'missionized islands where canoes paddled out to meet the incoming steamer' and smiling natives would carry their bags up to the mission station (8; p.124). Eddystone is different: no-one appears on the beach and Rivers and Hocart pitch their tent, rather uncertainly, in a clearing not too far from the village they can see from the bay. As the tropical darkness falls, so does a mysterious, expectant atmosphere, in which Rivers's senses are all alert: 'He was aware of the thick darkness of the bush around him, but more as a pressure on his mind than through his senses' (8; p.126). Prior's arrival in Amiens also has a mysterious quality. He is led in the darkness through unlit streets of ruined houses: 'The night, the silent guide, the effort of not slipping on broken pavements, sharpened his senses. An overhanging branch of laburnum flung a scattering of cold raindrops into his eyes and he was startled by the intensity of his joy' (9; p.140). His billet is a ruinous villa, complete with heavily scented roses hanging round a broken pergola, overgrown terraces and lace curtains behind shattered glass.

The magical atmosphere of the ruined house persists for Prior and his companions as, over the course of several leisurely days, apparently forgotten by the army, they create 'a fragile civilization, a fellowship on the brink of disaster' (9; p.143). Just as the Eddystone material is based on historical documents, Barker draws on another kind of factual source, Owen's letters to his mother, for this episode in Chapter 9:

> **Monday, 9 September 1918**
>
> ... It was frightfully nice of Haig to allow the French to be shelled out of [Amiens], & so leave us any amount of room & household goods. I have a good room in a large house, with a young officer, – quite bearable, – bound also for the 2nd. [Battalion] Man [chester Regiment]. There are no window panes, but the valuable hand-lace-curtains remain. I sleep on a table, for which a kind Kiltie has just found me a mattress. It's huge fun looting for furniture, & I sleep on my table in a serenity far different from, let us say, at Hastings ...

Tues. 10 September 1918

... I kick joyfully about the debris, and only feel a twinge of sadness when a little child's copy-book or frock or crumpled little hat is laid bare.

Near the Cathedral I picked up a delightful wee lace-surplice, my only souvenir so far.

Potts, that is my comrade – in billets –, chose a Toby jug, – in very bad taste.

Potts is a science student at Manchester; only 20; book learned in certain 'Subjects', but not without ideas. Indeed we talked 3 good hours last night.

... I had a strong poetical experience in a wrecked garden this afternoon, not an ordinary garden, but full of conservatories of tropical plants, aviaries, fish-ponds, palms & so on. I can't make a poem out of it, because of Shelley's 'Sensitive Plant' which you might turn up if you want the effect I enjoyed. I say enjoyed ...

(Owen, 1967, pp.574–6)

What follows Owen's ellipsis after 'enjoyed' is a prosaic shopping-list of requirements for his next parcel from home. The mood is abruptly broken, and we infer that his qualification of the term 'enjoyed' refers to the dark, melancholy mood that prevails at the end of 'The Sensitive Plant' (1820), when the Edenic garden Shelley has described in lush detail over the space of forty-odd quatrains turns to a wintry wilderness:

And the leaves, brown, yellow, and gray, and red,
And white with the whiteness of what is dead,
Like troops of ghosts on the dry wind passed;
Their whistling noise made the birds aghast.

(in Shelley, 1966, p.239)

The myth of the garden in Shelley's poem offers an elaboration on the theme of mutability, but, more than that, it is (in the words of Harold Bloom) 'a parable of imaginative failure ... another of the many Romantic versions of the Miltonic Eden's transformation into a wasteland' (in Shelley, 1966, p.xxxii). Presumably Owen feels that he cannot make a poem of his 'poetical experience' in the wrecked garden because Shelley has already expressed this particular experience in poetic form. However, on pages 145–7 of *The Ghost Road*, Barker transposes some of the details from Owen's letter of 10 September and something of the mood of Shelley's poem into a vividly realized journey through a garden-wilderness, culminating in the description of Hallet immersing himself in the 'overgrown goldfish pool'. This is a remarkable passage, linking the landscape of war with the landscape of ruined gardens ('splintered fences', 'bramble-filled craters') and drawing attention to the way these landscapes impact on the soldiers, and vice versa:

> Hundreds of men, billeted as they were in these ruined houses, had broken down every wall, every fence, forced a passage through all the hedges, so that they could slip unimpeded from one patch of ground to the next. The war, fought and refought over strips of muddy earth, paradoxically gave them the freedom of animals to pass from territory to territory unobserved.
>
> (9; p.146)

More powerful still is the description of Hallet, who does not know that he is observed by his comrades, undressing in the garden. The ambivalence of the language here makes his healthy young body sound almost corpse-like: 'Dappled light played across his body, lending it the illusion of fragility, the greenish tinge of ill-health' and without his uniform his body appears 'starkly white. Sharp collar-bones, bluish shadows underneath.' In one arresting phrase – 'he stepped out of his drawers and out of time' – Barker yokes together, through the grammar of her sentence, the prosaic and poetic elements of this scene. So, without ever jeopardizing her down-to-earth novelistic realism, she also manages to incorporate into this passage the 'strong poetical experience' Owen felt, with hints of the mythic qualities of Shelley's poem.

I have dwelt at some length on this particular part of Chapter 9 and its historical/literary underpinnings because I think it exemplifies the way that fictional writing based on factual sources can transform and enrich the original material. Rather than seeing 'fact' and 'fiction' as opposite poles, it seems more appropriate in this case to see them as being folded into each other, like geological strata. Beneath the 1995 fictional surface of Barker's novel we have the real-life 1918 letter from Owen to his mother, and, beneath that, Shelley's poem of 1820 lamenting the failure of imagination. It takes some deliberate digging to uncover these hidden layers, and you may feel that analysis of this kind, even if interesting as a literary exercise, does not make any real difference to the way we read Barker's novel. There is, I think, some validity in this point of view: allusion in postmodern writing does not usually carry the structural weight that it does in modernist works, so it is, in that sense, non-essential. However, I would argue that the passage we have looked at acquires a double richness from its intertextual links. There is the specificity derived from Owen's letters (down to details such as the 'souvenirs' of Owen and Potts: the 'child's lace-trimmed surplice' and toby jug) and the much wider but looser suggestiveness of Eden transformed into a wasteland that is derived from Shelley's poem.

But there is another way in which this passage acquires additional resonance, and – returning to our comparison of Chapters 8 and 9 – you may well have noted that Hallet's immersion in the goldfish pond has parallels with the passage in Chapter 8 when Hocart and Rivers bathe in the shallows of the Bay of Narovo. As Rivers wades out to join Hocart, 'he was joined by a shoal of little darting black fish who piloted him out into deeper waters – always a moment of absolute magic. Behind him, the bluish shadows of rocks crept over the white sand' (8; p.132). The colours here, blue and white, will be repeated in the description of Hallet's body, but although there are other parallels (the water in each case brings ease from the heat of the day, and the bathers relax into laughter), there are notable differences in atmosphere between the two scenes. In contrast to the overgrown and slightly incongruous wasteland setting of the garden in Amiens, the Bay of Narovo is open, clear and entirely natural. The phrase 'always a moment of absolute magic', referring to the motions of the little black fish, belongs to Rivers, and reveals that for him this is not an isolated incident but a recurring joy. Eddystone is, for Rivers, an 'idyllic' place; despite the 'points of darkness' generated by his anthropological enquiries into death and dying (12; p.188), he is clearly much more relaxed and happy in Melanesia than he is at home.

Later in the novel Prior recalls one of Rivers's characteristic silences during consultations: 'Sometimes I used to think he was back with his fucking head-hunters – he really does love them, his whole face lights up when he talks about them –' (15; p.215). For all the discomforts and perils of life on Eddystone, and despite the sorry decline of the population, paradisal touches remain. The 'bathing' passage in Chapter 8 embodies these, drifting to a simple ending: 'At last, driven back to shore by the cooling water, they snatched up their clothes and ran, laughing, back to the tent' (8; p.133). The parallel passage in Chapter 9 also ends with the sun going down and the pond growing cooler, but when Owen voices the possibility that they might continue to be forgotten (and thus go on living their charmed lives) the mood changes:

> Everybody touched wood, crossed fingers, groped for lucky charms: all the small, protective devices of men who have no control over their own fate. No use, Prior thought. Somewhere, outside the range of human hearing, and yet heard by all of them, a clock had begun to tick.

> (9; p.147)

You may have noticed other points of similarity and/or contrast between the two chapters, but I think these examples are sufficient to demonstrate the importance of 'structuring, placing and ordering', in John Carey's words, as Barker brings the parallel narratives of Rivers and Prior into a telling

Figure 8.6   W.H.R. Rivers (far left) and the Cambridge Anthropological Expedition, 1898. (Cambridge University Museum of Archaeology and Anthropology.) In *The Ghost Road*, Rivers looks at 'a photograph of himself and the other members of the Torres Straits expedition. Barefoot, bare-armed, bearded, sun-tanned, wearing a collection of spectacularly villainous hats, they looked for all the world like a low-budget production of *The Pirates of Penzance*' (6; p.88).

relationship with each other. If you have time, you may like to extend this kind of analysis to other consecutive chapters in Parts Two and Three of the novel.

You will remember that the initial reviews by Rodd and Patterson discussed near the start of this chapter made differing judgements about the novel's alternations between Prior's diaries and Rivers's Melanesian recollections. The comparisons we have just drawn between Chapters 8 and 9 tend to support Rodd's view of the two narratives echoing and illuminating each other. But you may have felt there was some justification in Patterson's view:

> Barker spends a lot of time flashing back to Rivers's pre-war experience as an anthropologist living among headhunters. The fact that Rivers really did this does not automatically make these sequences congruous with the rest of the book, apart from the obvious parallel between Rivers and the local healer-witch-doctor.

Patterson seems to be suggesting that Barker dwells on Rivers's anthropological work largely because, like his work as an army psychiatrist, it is part of the historical record. The historical novelist is, of course, free to select which facts should be incorporated within the fiction, but it seems that Barker does want to present us with a rounded, rather than a partial, characterization of Rivers. In the radio interview I referred to earlier, she mentions her surprise on discovering that the Rivers she knew about through the Sassoon connection was also the neurologist whose experiments were still taught to university students: 'For a long time I didn't realize they were the same man – it never occurred to me – and when I did realize it, of course, I was very interested' (Vaughan, 1995). She was even more surprised and 'not terribly pleased' when she discovered his family relationship with Lewis Carroll: 'I'd already got him having all these poets around him, it already seemed improbable, and then when Lewis Carroll popped up as well I thought, "Oh, no, no, I don't want this." But in *The Ghost Road* I think Lewis Carroll gets a lot more integrated' (*ibid.*). You may want to consider for yourself how the incorporation of Carroll and allusions to 'Alice in Hysterialand' (2; p.24) further the themes of the novel. However, the general point about 'improbable' connections is an important one for the writer of factual fictions. There is always a fall-back position for the non-fiction writer: 'truth is stranger than fiction'. But realism in the novel demands a degree of plausibility that may be at odds with the facts, and Rivers's multifaceted life is as much a challenge to the novelist as a gift. Perhaps the most obvious way for a novelist to meet this challenge would have been to place Rivers squarely at the centre of the novel, so that everything about his life, whether derived from factual sources or imagined using the kinds of techniques perfected in New Journalism, would have automatic validity. This is essentially what Keneally did with the stranger-than-fiction story of Oskar Schindler. But *The Ghost Road* is a very different kind of enterprise: juxtaposing the historical figure of Rivers with the fictional figure of Prior immediately complicates our readerly involvement with the characters. As Prior presses on towards an unknown future (you may already know that Owen will be killed at the Sambre–Oise Canal, but Prior's fate is in the hands of the novelist) we follow the unfolding of events, and the unfolding of his character, in a way that is familiar to us from the experience of reading many other novels. But our reading of the Melanesian episodes cannot be driven by plot and character in the same way – not simply because the person and life of Rivers are already constrained by the historical facts, but also because these episodes stand outside the 1918 timeframe of the novel's action. Or at least they do until the end of the novel, when Njiru makes his dramatic appearance on the ward of the Empire Hospital, Westminster. Up to this point Barker does seem to have renounced 'the authorial power of the overview', in Sage's words, by giving equal weighting to the alternating narratives and allowing the reader to hear the echoes between them. In the final section of the novel (which, like the final description of the 2nd Manchesters at the Sambre–Oise Canal, has moved into the present tense) Barker reasserts her authorial power – not the power of overview as such, but the power to unite past, present and future in a way that only fiction can do.

Before we leave the subject of factual fictions, I would like to examine one last passage from the novel alongside its factual source. **Read the last entry in Prior's journal (17; pp.255–8) alongside Owen's last letter to his mother (below), and ask yourself what Barker has achieved by attributing some of Owen's observations and sentiments to the fictional Prior.**

> **Thurs. 31 October [1918] 6.15 p.m.**
>
> Dearest Mother,
>
> I will call the place from which I'm now writing 'The Smoky Cellar of the Forester's House' ... the ground is marshy, & I have a slight cold!
>
> So thick is the smoke in this cellar that I can hardly see by a candle 12 ins. away, and so thick are the inmates that I can hardly write for pokes, nudges & jolts. On my left the Coy. Commander snores on a bench: other officers repose on wire beds behind me. At my right hand, Kellett, a delightful servant of A Coy. in *The Old Days* radiates joy and contentment from pink cheeks and baby eyes. He laughs with a signaller, to whose left ear is glued the Receiver; but whose eyes rolling with gaiety show that he is listening with his right ear to a merry corporal, who appears at this distance away (some three feet) nothing [but] a gleam of white teeth and a wheeze of jokes.
>
> Splashing my hand, an old soldier with a walrus moustache peels and drops potatoes into the pot. By him, Keyes, my cook, chops wood; another feeds the smoke with the damp wood.
>
> It is a great life. I am more oblivious than alas! yourself, dear Mother, of the ghastly glimmering of the guns outside, & the hollow crashing of the shells.
>
> There is no danger down here, or if any, it will be well over before you read these lines.
>
> I hope you are as warm as I am; as serene in your room as I am here; and that you think of me never in bed as resignedly as I think of you always in bed. Of this I am certain you could not be visited by a band of friends half so fine as surround me here.
>
> Ever Wilfred x
>
> (Owen, 1967, pp.590–1)

Owen himself does not appear in the final entry from Prior's journal, although he will be alongside Prior in the final attack (18; pp.261, 273). Barker is thus free to make her fictional character the author of this description of the crowded, smoky, candle-lit cellar full of men, variously telling jokes, sleeping, peeling potatoes or chopping damp wood for the fire. More than that, she also gives Prior Owen's head-cold and his remarkable sense of serenity in comradeship. Prior's account shows rather more consciousness of danger than Owen's does – he acknowledges the elated behaviour of men at the point of death, summed up in the word 'fey', and adds 'We all know what the chances are' (17; p.258). But we can hardly fail to notice that his final words express, albeit in a different idiom, exactly the same sentiments as Owen's. Prior looks around the faces in the dug-out and all he can think is: 'What an utter bloody fool I would have been not to come back' (*ibid.*). Owen assures his mother: 'Of this I am certain you could not be visited by a band of friends half so fine as surround me here.' In both statements negative constructions are turned to the same emphatic affirmation.

The last sentence from Owen's letter is justly famous – it was, says Owen's biographer Jon Stallworthy, 'perhaps the last he ever wrote' (Stallworthy, 1974, p.288). It rounds off the writing life of this undoubtedly courageous man, and echoes down the twentieth century as an assertion of the worth of ordinary companionship in the face of the terrible waste of the First World War. Lifting such distinctive sentiments from the famous literary hero and giving them to a fictional working-class character is perhaps Barker's boldest move in terms of *The Ghost Road*'s blending of fact and fiction. You may recall that towards the end of her review, 'Both Sides', Sage spoke about Rivers's efforts to persuade the mute to speak turning, paradoxically, into a way of silencing their protests:

> This seems to connect, for Barker, with the need to invent the disintegrated character of Prior: to have a figure who speaks in fiction, but didn't in fact, the kind of character born of the war, and largely lost and denied at its end.

The novel as a whole asserts the importance of the historically unnamed, and, in this last entry from Prior's journal, the people that Prior stands for are made the equals of those whose names and reputations happen to have survived. History may have denied the Priors of this world, but through fiction they can appropriate real voices.

Divided selves

So far we have kept the subject of ghosts at arm's length, but it may well have been a topic that you wanted to include when you registered your initial response to the novel. The novel's title and epigraph from Edward Thomas (another of the British poets killed in the First World War) suggest the ghostly return of the dead, unburdened soldiers, but there are many other ways in which the theme of ghosts pervades the novel. In approaching this theme I would like to refer briefly to Freud's 1919 essay 'The Uncanny'. I alluded earlier to the fact that Rivers's work as a psychiatrist had some affinities with Freud's. In his postwar writings Rivers, like Freud, developed a theory of the unconscious and explored the mechanisms of repression (see Slobodin, 1997, pp.54, 168), so approaching the theme of ghosts in Barker's novel via Freud can be fruitful.

Freud suggests in his essay that an 'uncanny' experience can occur 'when primitive beliefs which have been surmounted seem once more to be confirmed' (Freud, 1990, p.372). As an anthropologist Rivers had had extensive opportunities to study so-called 'primitive' societies – in this he had a clear advantage over Freud – and since we shall later be looking at a brief extract from Rivers's writing on 'The Primitive Conception of Death', it may be worth commenting here on early twentieth-century usage of the term 'primitive'. For social evolutionists, 'primitive' societies represented one end of the spectrum of human development; at the other end were the more sophisticated societies to which the social theorists themselves belonged. A different, more romantic view of primitivism was promoted by some anthropologists, such as Lucien Lévy-Bruhl, and the psychiatrist Carl Jung: in this view, primitive peoples were believed to have access to a magical, archaic consciousness which gave them a fundamentally different way of relating to the world. The real-life Rivers did not share this view of the 'primitive mind', but nor did he judge what he called 'low cultures' by the utilitarian standards of 'civilized' societies. The abundance of quotation marks in the last sentence is an ample reminder of the caution with which we now use terms that were much less problematic for Rivers and Freud. Barker's language in the novel neatly ducks under this kind of linguistic barbed wire by homing straight in on the particularities of Rivers's Melanesian experiences, but since in my general discussion here I can hardly avoid abstract phrases such as 'primitive superstition' they should be read in as neutral a way as possible.

For Freud, modern civilization and primitivism are quite distinct, but he recognizes that traces of the emotions triggered by animistic beliefs can seep into even a rational mind like his own. In his essay 'The Uncanny', in the context of distinguishing between 'primitive' beliefs about the return of the dead and 'modern' resistance to superstition, he offers an instance from his own experience involving a surprise encounter with his own mirror-image on a moving train – an image that he momentarily fails to recognize. The incident produces in Freud not, as might be expected, fear, but rather a feeling of dislike towards his own temporarily unfamiliar reflection. It is a striking anecdote, and it offers interesting parallels with the experiences of many of Barker's characters. The critic John Brannigan uses Freud's story as a point of entry for his discussion of the *Regeneration* trilogy in an essay subtitled 'History and the Hauntological Imagination', noting that the trilogy's characters frequently encounter doubles, ghosts and hallucinatory figures. In these encounters, as in Freud's personal anecdote, distinctions between the real and the imagined, the living and the dead, become problematic:

> Freud's lack of fear, confronted with the ghostly reflection of himself, certifies his modernity, his rational distrust of 'animistic beliefs'. There is some room for doubt in Freud's mind, however. Is it not possible, he asks, that his dislike of his double 'was a vestigial trace of the archaic reaction which feels the "double" to be something uncanny?'
>
> Freud's concern is that the archaic might seep into the modern, that the boundaries between primitive superstition and modern rationality are more permeable than he imagines ... The primitive belief in the 'uncanny' or ghostly appearance of the double, for Freud ... is the anachronistic trace of a different mode of knowing, a different way of seeing the world, which he experiences, if only briefly.
>
> (Brannigan, 2003, p.14)

In *The Ghost Road*, Rivers's encounters with doubles or ghosts are mostly at second hand, through his patients, and through his Melanesian experiences. But Prior, like many of the soldiers in the trilogy, has more direct experience of the uncanny. If you have read *The Eye in the Door* you will recall that the fracturing of personalities was a major theme in that novel. Traces of this linger on into *The Ghost Road* when Prior alludes to the unnerving experience of living with his demonic double:

> Prior peered into the small looking-glass behind the wash-basin, checking the knot in his tie. If they didn't send him back he was going to be awfully lonely, marooned among civilians with their glib talk. His reflection jeered, *Lonely, You? Oh, c'mon, duckie. You can always split in two.* At least the Board didn't know about *that*.
>
> (1; p.13)

As with his other patients, Rivers finds a rational explanation for this uncanny doubling. It is, in Brannigan's words, 'an all too transparent manifestation of the dissociation of self required under the disciplinary structures of modern society ... Prior is generating his own monster precisely to conduct the tasks he finds himself unable to do' (2003, p.16). His split personality is 'cured', as was his earlier mutism following a traumatic incident under fire in France, and Prior returns to the front as living proof of the efficacy of Rivers's methods. It is, however, almost inevitable that Prior will not be living for long. In his final letter to Rivers he succinctly recapitulates a major theme of the trilogy: 'My nerves are in perfect working order. By which I mean that in my present situation the only sane thing to do is to run away, and I will not do it. Test passed?' (17; p.254). In effect, another kind of dissociation of self is required for soldiers like Prior, who believe that there is no longer any rational justification for the war (9; p.144), to continue fighting.

This terrible contradiction is one that Rivers, the rationalist, has had to wrestle with throughout the trilogy. Sassoon's public protest against the war involves Rivers facing this contradiction in its most heightened form, and towards the end of *The Eye in the Door*, when he visits Sassoon in hospital, he confronts his own dual feelings:

> in the years before the war he had experienced a splitting of personality as profound as any suffered by Siegfried. It had been not merely a matter of living two different lives, divided between the dons of Cambridge and the missionaries and headhunters of Melanesia, but of being a different person in the two places. It was his Melanesian self he preferred, but his attempts to integrate that self into his way of life in England had produced nothing but frustration and misery. Perhaps, contrary to what was usually supposed, duality was the stable state; the attempt at integration, dangerous.
>
> (Barker, 1993, p.235)

In *The Ghost Road* Rivers does not merely recall occasional fragments of his Melanesian life, as he does in the earlier novels; the extended meditations beginning in Chapter 4 balance the 1918 narrative with a weight and vividness that constitutes, for the fictionalized Rivers, a reliving of these parts of his life. The experience of reading *The Ghost Road*, as we have seen, involves oscillating between two different narratives and two very different worlds. If the alternation were simply between Rivers's two selves, then from our readerly vantage point we could still maintain a single focus on Rivers's personality. But Barker complicates matters by switching our attention from Prior to Rivers and back again, from the 'living moment' to the recollected life, from fiction to anthropology, giving equal weight to each. The effect of this alternation is to give us a kind of reading experience that embodies in itself a kind of dividedness. In a very minor, muted way, the dynamics of reading give us access to the oppositions that afflict the novel's characters.

Your own experience of reading *The Ghost Road* may or may not chime with the comments I have just made about the novel's structure. But the importance of the Melanesian chapters lies in their thematic as well as their structural function. Njiru, Namboko Taru, Kundaite, Namboko Emele and all the other people of Eddystone provide Rivers – and the reader – with what Brannigan calls a 'different mode of knowing, a different way of seeing the world' (2003, p.14). Let us examine some of these differences by looking at a passage from Chapter 14 – the episode that Rivers reluctantly describes as a 'séance'. **Reread the passage, from 'Kundaite could interpret …' (p.208) to '… into the mouths of the dead' (p.212) and consider the following questions.**

- **What purpose does the meeting serve for the islanders?**

- **Why do you think Rivers finds himself 'moved in a way he'd never expected'?**

The ostensible purpose of the meeting is, as Kundaite explains at the beginning of the passage, to speak with the ghosts who will be coming to fetch the recently dead Ngea to his new home. This meeting, unlike the séance Prior and Sarah Lumb attend in Chapter 5 (pp.76–9), is thus part of a complex of rituals, in this case rituals surrounding the death of a great chief. It is a communal affair: apart from Njiru's notable absence, pretty well everyone seems to be present, from Ngea's widow to the baby Kwini and older children. Here again there is a marked contrast with the damaged community of Ada Lumb's 'spuggies', where there are 'Too many widows. Too many mothers looking for contact with lost sons' (5; p.77). But the meeting also serves another important purpose for the living islanders, in that 'the questions the ghosts had asked had all been questions the living people wanted answered' (14; p.211). Fortunately for Hocart and Rivers, these ghosts, according to Kundaite, are curious about the white men rather than suspicious. The absent Njiru perhaps takes a different view. Although there is much mutual respect and liking between Njiru and Rivers, Njiru understands the threat that the white men bring with them, and this makes him dangerous – the axe on Rivers's pillow is a reminder of Njiru's 'ordinary' power as well as his extraordinary powers as one who can control spirits.

The only defence the anthropologists have against hostility from the islanders is their own harmlessness, going around the islands unarmed and barefoot (16; pp.232–3). But although this defence is fragile, it also allows them access to experiences that would otherwise be closed off. Rivers's receptiveness to the atmosphere of the séance is perhaps partly due to the fact that he and Hocart have been allowed to penetrate one of the more mysterious aspects of the islanders' spiritual lives. On this occasion they hear *talk blong tomate*: the language of ghosts, something that, earlier, had not been permitted (10; p.164). Rivers is as sceptical about Kundaite as Prior is about the 'small, self-satisfied man with brown teeth' who acts as medium at the earlier séance (5; p.77). Rivers wonders 'whether the attempt to induce a trance state was genuine or merely histrionic' (14; p.209), but there is something inexplicable about the ghosts' whistles, which neither he nor

Hocart can locate. When Kundaite announces that Ngea himself is in the room, silence falls and Rivers feels the hairs on his arms rise. A few sentences later Barker's prose intensifies: 'By now the room was full of whistles, slithering up and down the walls and all across the floor. At times the sounds seemed almost to be a ripple running across the skin' (14; p.211). The synaesthetic effect of sounds becoming kinetic, almost tangible, conveys a sense of powerful mystery without recourse to the vocabulary of emotions. Rivers, despite his intellectual detachment, might well be moved. Of course, Hocart and Rivers do not fully share the islanders' experience – neither the swish of the paddles from the ghosts' canoes (14; p.210) nor the blowing of the conch (14; p.211) is audible to them – but the way that Barker describes the non-supernatural sounds, and silences, of the séance allows us to see that extraordinary sensations are loose here. Scientific observation has not been discarded, but something unexpected has happened. The issue is nothing to do with belief or lack of belief in the ghosts, but everything to do with openness to 'a different mode of knowing'. In his reflections on this memory ten years later Rivers is able to connect the experience of hearing *talk blong tomate* with Sassoon's experience of ghosts and arrive at a new insight about the questions that perturb the living: they become 'more insistent, more powerful, for being projected into the mouths of the dead' (14; p.212).

In his London lodgings, earlier in the novel, Rivers catches a glimpse of his landlady's 'shrine' to her dead son and is reminded of the skull houses he had visited with Njiru:

> Difficult to know what to make of these flashes of cross-cultural recognition. From a strictly professional point of view, they were almost meaningless, but then one didn't have such experiences as a disembodied anthropological intelligence, but as a man, and as a man one had to make some kind of sense of them.
>
> (8; p.117)

An important feature of the Melanesian episodes in the novel is that we see Rivers not merely making observations but having experiences, some frightening, some comical, some – as at the séance – yielding new personal understandings. To some extent the novel does show us Rivers the man making sense of these 'flashes of cross-cultural recognition', and the novel's recurring motifs (ghosts and skulls leap to mind) also make the cross-cultural possibilities more visible to the reader. But I think Barker's emphasis on the division Rivers feels between his English personality and his Melanesian one, most directly expressed in the passage from *The Eye in the Door* I quoted earlier, also speaks of a late twentieth-century dilemma about the relationship between culture and the concept of self. The postcolonial critic Homi Bhabha, talking in 1990 about cultural difference and identity, said:

> However rational you are ... it is actually very difficult, even impossible and counterproductive, to try and fit together different forms of culture and to pretend that they can easily coexist ... the possibility of producing a culture which both articulates difference and lives with it could only be established on the basis of a non-sovereign notion of self.
>
> (Bhabha, 1990, pp.209–12)

Bhabha is writing about late twentieth-century multiculturalism, but the fact of Rivers being an anthropologist, and thus keenly aware of the diversity of cultures, gives Barker a neat opportunity to project backwards, as it were, from this 1990s viewpoint.

In the final part of the novel there is perhaps less urgency about Rivers's sense of having a divided personality. Under the pressure of illness, then overwork, his notion of self becomes submerged and indeed his sense of cultural difference weakens as his Melanesian memories bleed into his relentless hospital duties. It feels as though Rivers is moving towards some melting down of personality just as inevitably as Owen, and probably Prior, are moving towards death in battle. As this dual movement gathers pace, one question that I think becomes more insistent for the reader is whether and how Rivers's prewar explorations of the islanders' beliefs about death and ghosts will connect with the narrative about the final stages of the First World War.

In 1912 Rivers published an article on 'The Primitive Conception of Death' in which he drew extensively on his Eddystone data. The main purpose of this article is to refute Lévy-Bruhl's view that the mentality of primitive peoples is 'prelogical' because it is not disturbed by contradictions. The argument as a whole is interesting, but what is most germane to our discussion is Rivers's elaboration of the concept of death itself. Here he articulates the significance of this subject:

> Death is so striking and unique an event that if one had to choose something which must have been regarded in essentially the same light by mankind in all times and in all places, I think one would be inclined to choose it in preference to any other, and yet I hope to show that the primitive conception of death among such people as the Melanesians is different, one may say radically different, from our own.
>
> (Rivers, 1912; quoted in Slobodin, 1997, p.210)

The Ghost Road coaches the reader in some of the topics that Rivers addresses in the course of his article. Probably the most important is the existential state of *mate*-ness (where *mate* is 'a state of which death is the appropriate outcome'; see 8; pp.134–5), which can apply to the sick and the very aged as well as the dead. By the time we reach the last terrible stages of Hallet's dying

(18; pp.264–5) we can appreciate the force of *mate*-ness as a concept. Rivers's article draws a clear contrast between the view of death in civilized society as a 'unique and catastrophic event' and the Melanesian view that death is 'merely a condition of passing from one existence to another, forming but one of a number of transitions' (Rivers, quoted in Slobodin, 1997, p.218). In the character of Hallet we have, then, a kind of cultural cross-over. From the moment when Prior rescues him from the flooded crater (13; p.196) he embodies death-in-life, and Prior, having thought about killing him at the time, is still wondering a week later whether bringing him back was 'the right thing' (15; p.215). But Hallet still has an important function to fulfil in the novel: in the hospital ward, out of his condition of *mate*-ness, he utters a judgement on the war that is all the more powerful for being, initially, as mysterious as the whistling of the ghosts on Eddystone: '*Shotvarfet*' (18; p.274).

In the final Melanesian episode in the novel (18; pp.267–9) Rivers remembers his last evening on the island, when Njiru revealed the nature of the spirit Ave and the words of exorcism that gave him power over Ave. Njiru's description of Ave is recalled in the darkness of a hospital ward filled with the terrible casualties of war and understaffed because of the Spanish influenza epidemic that would claim twice as many lives as the war had done:

> Ave lives in Ysabel. He is both one spirit and many spirits. His mouth is long and filled with the blood of the men he devours. Kita and Mateana are nothing beside him because they destroy only the individual, but Ave kills 'all people 'long house'. The broken rainbow belongs to him, and presages both epidemic disease and war. Ave is the destroyer of peoples.
>
> (18; p.268)

Ave belongs to the world of primitive superstition, but in the closing months of 1918, when modern rationality could be seen to have failed quite spectacularly, the boundaries between the two worlds are as permeable as they were, briefly, for Freud confronted by his reflection in the train mirror. So, apart from the particularities about the spirit's habitat, blood-filled mouth, and so on, it is quite easy to transpose this description of Ave to the context of the 1914–18 war. But one important difference between the two forces of destruction is that Ave can be subdued. The words of exorcism that Njiru teaches Rivers are part of his extraordinary, hard-won, carefully guarded store of knowledge, and when he appears to Rivers on the hospital ward at the very end of the novel these are the words that he speaks. The words themselves are enigmatic:

*There is an end of men, an end of chiefs, an end of chieftains' wives,
an end of chiefs' children – then go down and depart. Do not yearn for
us, the fingerless, the crippled, the broken. Go down and depart, oh,
oh, oh.*

(18; p.276)

It is tempting to look for a 'message' in Njiru's words. But the effects of the
novel's ending are as complex as anything that has gone before. This timely
'haunting' does at last draw the two narrative strands firmly together and thus
affords a kind of satisfaction to the reader. But there is little comfort in the
words themselves – no healing for 'the fingerless, the crippled, the broken',
just as there was no saving Prior, Owen or Hallet. Rivers himself seems to be
approaching a state of *mate*-ness, and the coming of daylight, so often a
symbol of hope, has already been divested of such associations in the
description of the sun rising over the dead bodies of the 2nd Manchesters
(18; pp.275–6). Brannigan suggests that this final scene indicates

> a traumatic shift in historical consciousness, from one in which
> time unfolded progressively towards healing, to one in which time
> is structured around loss, absence and otherness. History, after
> the Great War, Barker's trilogy suggests, is continually haunted by
> the memory of loss, and is constantly striving to regenerate the
> past.
>
> (Brannigan, 2003, p.24)

Figure 8.7 The Sambre–Oise Canal, November, 1918. (From
Archibald Armar Montgomery-Massingberd, *The Story of the Fourth
Army in the Battles of the Hundred Days, August 8 to November 11,
1918*, London: Hodder & Stoughton, 1920, pl. 92, opp. p.241.)

You may have responded differently to the novel's ending. But now that we have revisited a number of passages from Parts Two and Three, you may like to return to your initial judgements about *The Ghost Road*. **Reread your 'first impressions' notes, including any alterations you made as a result of the activity on p.368, and answer the following questions. (The last question is the most important.)**

- **Have your views about the structure of the novel changed?**

- **Do you want to revise or extend any points you made about the Melanesian episodes?**

- **Have your initial opinions about the literary quality of the novel changed or been confirmed?**

- **Can you identify the factors on which your assessment of the novel's quality rests?**

What does fiction do?

Lying behind the final question in the list you have just worked through is another question: what do we want from novels? Writers, of course, have their views on what fiction should do. Here are just two examples, from the earlier and later parts of the twentieth century:

> It is the way our sympathy flows and recoils that really determines our lives. And here lies the vast importance of the novel, properly handled. It can inform and lead into new places the flow of our sympathetic consciousness, and it can lead our sympathy away in recoil from things gone dead.
>
> (Lawrence, [1928] 1990, p.105)

> It seems to me that the active imaging of a world accurately is one of the most truthful tools that human beings have as a way of understanding what's going on around them. That's what fiction does.
>
> (Rushdie, 1983, p.4)

Despite the contrary directions implied in these two quotations – Lawrence looking inward to the 'flow of our sympathetic consciousness', Rushdie looking outwards to what is going on around us – one does not rule out the other. In fact, you may feel that the best novels operate both on our 'sympathetic consciousness' and on our 'understanding [of] what's going on around [us]'.

As we have seen, Barker is interested in collective experience as well as the individual's, and she is able to use her historical material to explore issues of class, gender, war and culture that still preoccupy us now. If you agree with the statement I have just made, then it is possible that 'breadth' and/or 'relevance' might well have been qualities that you singled out in making your judgement about the novel. You might have felt, with George Walden, that *The Ghost Road* succeeded in saying something new about the First World War, or you might have judged the novel by other kinds of effects it had on you, aesthetic or emotional. You might have listed factors that have not even been touched on in this chapter, or, if you have not rated the novel as highly as I have done, your list might be expressed more in terms of negative qualities. So where does this leave us? Are there any reliable general criteria we can fall back on when judging literature?

At the start of this chapter we looked briefly at the work of Jauss and Iser and 'reception theory'. I hope that those initial points about the process of reading will have helped you reflect more self-consciously on your own experience of reading *The Ghost Road*. Both Jauss and Iser also have something to say about how we judge the quality of what we read, and in the same sort of spirit – helping you hone your own ideas about literary judgements rather than offering a definitive (and impossible) last word – I would like to conclude by returning briefly to these reception theorists.

Jauss equates literary quality with a text's ability to change the literary landscape. Taking a historical view, he argues that literature that has been deemed to have lasting value has always, it turns out, gone beyond the expectations and norms current at the time of its production. Jauss's concept of a prevailing 'horizon of expectations', and measurable divergence from it, made quite an impact on literary theory in the late 1960s, but the idea was not as objective or unproblematic as it sounded at first. You may well have identified similarities between such an approach and the modernist ideal of unsettling conventions – Jauss himself later acknowledged this unspoken bias. Such a leaning towards originality, the capacity for 'making it new', has, however, been a persistent aesthetic touchstone throughout the twentieth century. Another feature of Jauss's approach that I noted earlier in this chapter and that it is worth reminding yourself of here is that he is concerned with readers in the plural, and the public reception of works of literature. The historical thrust of Jauss's work means that he is interested in the process of canon formation, but he sees this process as dynamic, involving continual interplay between past and present. If you find this idea of literary judgements evolving through dynamic social processes a persuasive one, you might like to look back at the Introduction to Part 2 and perhaps reflect on the final question about the relationship between judging literature and the institutions of publishing, the education system and the wider political culture. What part, if any, do you think that literary prizes play in the process of canon formation?

For a rather different slant on the issue of judgement we can turn back to Iser. You will recall that Iser focuses on the individual reader, even if that reader is more hypothetical than actual, and thus on personal acts of judgement. He conceives of texts as structures full of gaps which the reader actively fills in, so anticipation, and subsequent adjustment, are crucial to the production of meaning. The value that Iser attaches to freshness and discovery as key elements in the individual reading process perhaps parallels Jauss's emphasis on originality as a mark of literary value. But in the preamble to his essay 'The Reading Process: A Phenomenological Approach', Iser hints that the desire to 'make it new' can go too far, and leave the reader behind. On the other hand, texts that are too predictable (and he consigns 'popular' literature to this category) do not give the reader enough creative satisfaction:

> A literary text must therefore be conceived in such a way that it will engage the reader's imagination in the task of working things out for himself, for reading is only a pleasure when it is active and creative. In this process of creativity, the text may either not go far enough, or may go too far, so we may say that boredom and overstrain form the boundaries beyond which the reader will leave the field of play.

> (Iser, 1974, p.275)

I leave you to decide how far your judgement of *The Ghost Road* might have been influenced by the extent to which your reading experience engaged your imagination in the task of working things out for yourself. Although our emphasis in the second half of this book has been on *public* judgements about literature by means of prizes, I hope that bringing the individual reader firmly into the critical frame will have enabled you to find a more prominent place for your own reading experience in the discussion about judging literature. From this vantage point, you may want to revisit the questions at the end of the Introduction to Part 2 and link them to the debate about the meaning and purpose of literature that was briefly rehearsed at the start of the present chapter. The question at the heart of this debate – 'what is literature for?' – is one that inevitably grows larger the more we examine it, and the process of refining our self-awareness as readers helps us approach that question from the inside as much as from the outside.

Works cited

Barker, P. (1991) *Regeneration*, London: Penguin.

Barker, P. (1993) *The Eye in the Door*, London: Penguin.

Barker, P. (1995) *The Ghost Road*, London: Penguin.

Barthes, R. ([1968] 1977) *Image – Music – Text*, trans. by S. Heath, London: Fontana.

Bellringer, A.W. (1988) *Henry James*, Basingstoke: Macmillan.

Bhabha, H. (1990) 'The Third Space' (interview), in J. Rutherford (ed.), *Identity, Community, Culture, Difference*, London: Lawrence & Wishart, pp.207–21.

Bradbury, M. (ed.) (1977) *The Novel Today*, Glasgow: Fontana.

Brannigan, J. (2003) 'Pat Barker's *Regeneration* Trilogy: History and the Hauntological Imagination', in R.J. Lane, R. Mengham and P. Trew (eds), *Contemporary British Fiction*, Oxford: Polity Press, pp.13–26.

Brown, D. (2005) 'Pat Barker's Trilogy: Total War, Masculinities, Anthropology and the Talking Cure', in S. Monteith, M. Jolly, N. Youraf and R. Paul (eds), *Critical Perspectives on Pat Barker*, Columbia: University of South Carolina Press, pp.187–202.

Calinescu, M. (1993) *Rereading*, New Haven: Yale University Press.

Colvin, C. (1982) 'Can Fact Make Winning Fiction?', *Sunday Times*, 3 October, p.8.

Connor, S. (1996) *The English Novel in History, 1955–1995*, London: Routledge.

Cowley, J. (1995) 'Cultural Pessimism and the Booker Prize', *Bookseller*, 22 September, pp.20–1.

Culler, J. (1975) *Structuralist Poetics*, London: Routledge & Kegan Paul.

Eagleton, T. (1983) *Literary Theory*, Oxford: Basil Blackwell.

Farrell, J.G. (1970) 'No Matter', *Spectator*, 29 August, p.217.

Fish, S. (1967) *Surprised by Sin: The Reader in 'Paradise Lost'*, London: Macmillan; New York: St Martin's Press.

Freud, S. (1990) 'The Uncanny', in Freud, S., *Arts and Literature*, ed. by A. Dickson, Penguin Freud Library, vol.14, London: Penguin.

Fussell. P. (1975) *The Great War and Modern Memory*, Oxford: Oxford University Press.

Hollowell, J. (1977) *Fact and Fiction*, Chapel Hill: University of North Carolina Press.

Iser, W. (1974) *The Implied Reader*, Baltimore: Johns Hopkins University Press.

Jauss, H.R. ([1967] 1982) *Toward an Aesthetic of Reception*, trans. by T. Bahti, Brighton: Harvester Press.

Keneally, T. (1982) *Schindler's Ark*, London: Hodder & Stoughton.

Lawrence, D.H. ([1928] 1990) *Lady Chatterley's Lover*, London: Penguin.

McAfee, A. (1995) 'Under Starter's Orders for the Literary Race', *Financial Times*, 29 September, p.17.

Mars-Jones, A. (1981) *Lantern Lecture*, London: Faber & Faber.

Owen, W. (1967) *Collected Letters*, ed. by H. Owen and J. Bell, London: Oxford University Press.

Rushdie, S. (1983) Interview, *Book Four News*, 9 October, pp.2–4.

Scanlan, M. (1990) *Traces of Another Time: History and Politics in Postwar British Fiction*, Princeton, NJ: Princeton University Press.

Shelley, P.B. (1966) *Selected Poetry*, ed. by H. Bloom, New York: New American Library.

Shephard, B. (2000) *A War of Nerves*, London: Jonathan Cape.

Slobodin, R. (1997) *W.H.R. Rivers: Pioneer Anthropologist, Psychiatrist of 'The Ghost Road'*, Stroud: Sutton Publishing.

Stallworthy, J. (1974) *Wilfred Owen*, London: Oxford University Press/ Chatto & Windus.

Tremain, R. ([1989] 1990) *Restoration*, London: Hodder & Stoughton.

Vaughan, P. (1995) Interview with Pat Barker, *Kaleidoscope*, BBC Radio 4, 12 September.

Walden, G. (1995) 'Why Pat Barker Won the Booker', *The Times*, 8 November, p.15.

Waugh, P. (1984) *Metafiction*, London: Methuen.

Wilde, O. ([1891] 1966) 'The Decay of Lying', in *Complete Works of Oscar Wilde*, London: Collins, pp.970–92.

Woolf, V. ([1932] 1986) 'How Should One Read a Book?', in *The Common Reader*, 2nd series, ed. by A. McNeillie, London: Hogarth, pp.258–70.

Woolf, V. ([1928] 1998) *Orlando*, ed. and intro. by R. Bowlby, Oxford World's Classics, Oxford: Oxford University Press.

Further reading

Monteith, S. (2002) *Pat Barker*, Tavistock: Northcote House. A useful introduction to Barker's novels, from *Union Street* to *Border Crossing*; Chapter 5 is devoted to the *Regeneration* trilogy.

Monteith, S., Jolly, M., Youraf, N. and Paul, R. (eds) (2005) *Critical Perspectives on Pat Barker*, Columbia: University of South Carolina Press. A collection of critical articles on Barker's work, some of them dealing with the *Regeneration* trilogy. The volume also includes an interview with Barker on writing the trilogy and an annotated list of criticism.

READER REFERENCES

Chapter 1   Daphne du Maurier, *Rebecca*

du Maurier, D., 'The House of Secrets', in *The Rebecca Notebook and Other Memories*, London: Victor Gollancz, 1981, pp.130–5 (Reader, Item 30).

Freud, S., 'Female Sexuality', in *On Sexuality: Three Essays on the Theory of Sexuality and Other Works*, ed. by A. Richards, trans. by J. Strachey, Penguin Freud Library, vol.7, Harmondsworth: Penguin, 1991, pp.371–8, 380–3 (Reader, Item 31).

Chapter 2   The poetry of Frank O'Hara and Allen Ginsberg

Lehman, D., *The Last Avant-Garde: The Making of the New York School of Poets*, New York: Anchor Books, 1999, pp.332–5, 337 (Reader, Item 32).

O'Hara, F., 'Personism: A Manifesto', in *The Collected Poems of Frank O'Hara*, ed. by D. Allen, Berkeley: University of California Press, 1995, pp.498–9 (Reader, Item 33).

Elledge, J., 'Never Argue with the Movies: Love and the Cinema in the Poetry of Frank O'Hara', in *Frank O'Hara: To Be True to a City*, Ann Arbor: University of Michigan Press, 1990, pp.350–2, 355–7 (Reader, Item 34).

Storey, J., 'Mass Culture in America: The Post-War Debate', in *Cultural Theory and Popular Culture: An Introduction*, London: Prentice Hall, 2000, pp.28–33 (Reader, Item 35).

Chapter 3   Philip K. Dick, *Do Androids Dream of Electric Sheep?*

Suvin, D., 'Cognition and Estrangement', in *Metamorphoses of Science Fiction*, New Haven: Yale University Press, 1979, pp.3–5, 5–7, 7–8, 9–10, 14–15 (Reader, Item 36).

McNamara, K.R., '*Blade Runner*'s Post-Individual Worldspace and Philip K. Dick's *Do Androids Dream of Electric Sheep?*', *Contemporary Literature*, 38.3, 1997, pp.432–3, 436–7 (Reader, Item 37).

Warrick, P.S., 'Mechanical Mirrors, the Double, and *Do Androids Dream of Electric Sheep?*', in *Mind in Motion: The Fiction of Philip K. Dick*, Carbondale: Southern Illinois University Press, 1987, pp.122–4, 124–9 (Reader, Item 38).

Chapter 4   Manuel Puig, *Kiss of the Spider Woman*

Dunne, M., 'Dialogism in Manuel Puig's *Kiss of the Spider Woman*', *South Atlantic Review*, 60.2, May 1995, pp.121–36 (Reader, Item 39).

Merrim, S., 'Through the Film Darkly: Grade "B" Movies and Dreamwork in *Tres Tristes Tigres* and *El beso de la mujer araña*', *Modern Language Studies*, 15.4, Fall 1985, pp.302–12 (Reader, Item 40).

Chapter 5   Samuel Beckett, *Waiting for Godot*

Beckett, S., 'Three Dialogues', in *Disjecta: Miscellaneous Writings and a Dramatic Fragment*, ed. by R. Cohn, London: Calder, 1983, pp.138–9 (Reader, Item 41).

Bertens, H., 'Introduction', in *The Idea of the Postmodern: A History*, London: Routledge, 1995, pp.3–11 (Reader, Item 42).

English, J.F., 'Winning the Culture Game: Prizes, Awards, and the Rules of Art', *New Literary History*, 33.1, 2002, pp.113–35 (Reader, Item 43).

Chapter 6   The poetry of Seamus Heaney

Heaney, S., 'Crediting Poetry', in *Opened Ground: Poems 1966–1996*, London: Faber & Faber, 1998, pp.447–50 (Reader, Item 44).

O'Brien, C.C., 'A Slow North-East Wind', review of Seamus Heaney's *North* in *The Listener*, 25 September, 1975, pp.404–5 (Reader, Item 45).

Carson, C., 'Escaped from the Massacre? *North* by Seamus Heaney', *The Honest Ulsterman*, 50, 1975, pp.183–6 (Reader, Item 46).

Chapter 7   Abdulrazak Gurnah, *Paradise*

Iyer, P., 'The Empire Writes Back', *Time*, 8 February, 1993, pp.46–52 (Reader, Item 47).

Huggan, G., 'The Postcolonial Exotic', *Transition*, 64, 1994, pp.22–9 (Reader, Item 48).

Gurnah, A., 'Imagining the Postcolonial Writer', in S. Nasta (ed.), *Reading the 'New' Literatures in a Postcolonial Era*, Leicester: The English Association, Essays and Studies, 2000, pp.73–86 (Reader, Item 49).

Gurnah, A., 'An Idea of the Past', *Moving Worlds*, 2.2, 2002, pp.6, 13–17 (Reader, Item 50).

Chapter 8 Pat Barker, *The Ghost Road*

Rodd, C., 'Spirits in Waiting / Booker Nomination; *The Ghost Road* by Pat Barker', *Independent on Sunday*, 10 September, 1995 (Reader, Item 51.1).

Patterson, H., 'Trench Trauma and Jungle Ghosts: The Final Part of Pat Barker's War Trilogy Explores a Society with the Lid Off', *The Independent*, 23 September, 1995 (Reader, Item 51.2).

Sage, L., 'Both Sides: *The Ghost Road* by Pat Barker', *London Review of Books*, 5 October, 1995, p.9 (Reader, Item 52).

Byatt, A.S., 'Fathers', in *On Histories and Stories: Selected Essays*, London: Vintage, 2001, pp.9–13, 26–32 (Reader, Item 53).

APPENDIX

Charlotte Brontë
Jane Eyre, Chapter 10

> This extract from *Jane Eyre* (1847) is included here for comparison with *Rebecca*. A comparison not only reveals that the two texts are affiliated to the genres of romance and Gothic romance, but suggests that *Rebecca* consciously reworks *Jane Eyre* in its story of marriage between a 'plebeian' bride (Jane Eyre) and a quasi-aristocrat (Mr Rochester) founded upon the imperfectly repressed crime of the husband. The extract is taken from Chapter 10, which deals with the night before the wedding. Jane's state of anxiety about the change of identity that marriage will bring is elaborated. In the next chapter, after the aborted wedding, Rochester's secret comes to light. His wife is alive, insane and incarcerated on the third floor of Thornfield Hall. This demonic figure clearly stands behind du Maurier's creation of Rebecca and her surrogate, Mrs Danvers.

The month of courtship had wasted: its very last hours were being numbered. There was no putting off the day that advanced—the bridal day; and all preparations for its arrival were complete. *I*, at least, had nothing more to do: there were my trunks, packed, locked, corded, ranged in a row along the wall of my little chamber; to-morrow, at this time, they would be far on their road to London: and so should I (D.V.),—or rather, not I, but one Jane Rochester, a person whom as yet I knew not. The cards of address alone remained to nail on: they lay, four little squares, on the drawer. Mr. Rochester had himself written the direction, 'Mrs. Rochester, —Hotel, London,' on each: I could not persuade myself to affix them, or to have them affixed. Mrs. Rochester! She did not exist: she would not be born till to-morrow, some time after eight o'clock A.M.; and I would wait to be assured she had come into the world alive, before I assigned to her all that property. It was enough that in yonder closet, opposite my dressing-table, garments said to be hers had already displaced my black stuff Lowood frock and straw bonnet: for not to me appertained that suit of wedding raiment; the pearl-coloured robe, the vapoury veil, pendent from the usurped portmanteau. I shut the closet, to conceal the strange, wraith-like apparel it contained; which, at this evening hour—nine o'clock—gave out certainly a most ghostly shimmer through the shadow of my apartment. 'I will leave you by yourself, white dream,' I said. 'I am feverish: I hear the wind blowing; I will go out of doors and feel it.'

It was not only the hurry of preparation that made me feverish; not only the anticipation of the great change—the new life which was to commence to-morrow: both these circumstances had their share, doubtless, in producing that restless, excited mood which hurried me forth at this late hour into the darkening grounds; but a third cause influenced my mind more than they.

I had at heart a strange and anxious thought. Something had happened which I could not comprehend; no one knew of or had seen the event but myself: it had taken place the preceding night. Mr. Rochester that night was absent from home; nor was he yet returned: business had called him to a small estate of two or three farms he possessed thirty miles off—business it was requisite he should settle in person, previously to his meditated departure from England. I waited now his return; eager to disburthen my mind, and to seek of him the solution of the enigma that perplexed me. Stay till he comes, reader; and, when I disclose my secret to him, you shall share the confidence.

I sought the orchard: driven to its shelter by the wind, which all day had blown strong and full from the south; without, however, bringing a speck of rain. Instead of subsiding as night drew on, it seemed to augment its rush and deepen its roar: the trees blew stedfastly one way, never writhing round, and scarcely tossing back their boughs once in an hour; so continuous was the strain bending their branchy heads northward—the clouds drifted from pole to pole, fast following, mass on mass: no glimpse of blue sky had been visible that July day.

It was not without a certain wild pleasure I ran before the wind, delivering my trouble of mind to the measureless air-torrent thundering through space. Descending the laurel-walk, I faced the wreck of the chestnut tree; it stood up, black and riven: the trunk, split down the centre, gaped ghastly. The cloven halves were not broken from each other, for the firm base and strong roots kept them unsundered below; though community of vitality was destroyed—the sap could flow no more: their great boughs on each side were dead, and next winter's tempests would be sure to fell one or both to earth: as yet, however, they might be said to form one tree—a ruin; but an entire ruin.

'You did right to hold fast to each other,' I said: as if the monster-splinters were living things, and could hear me. 'I think, scathed as you look, and charred and scorched, there must be a little sense of life in you yet; rising out of that adhesion at the faithful, honest roots: you will never have green leaves more—never more see birds making nests and singing idyls in your boughs; the time of pleasure and love is over with you; but you are not desolate: each of you has a comrade to sympathize with him in his decay.' As I looked up at them, the moon appeared momentarily in that part of the sky which filled their fissure; her disk was blood-red and half overcast: she seemed to throw on me one bewildered, dreary glance, and buried herself again instantly in the deep drift of cloud. The wind fell, for a second, round Thornfield; but far away, over wood and water, poured a wild melancholy wail: it was sad to listen to, and I ran off again.

...

> The restless and apprehensive Jane eventually walks to meet Rochester returning from London, and they sit down to supper together.

'Take a seat, and bear me company, Jane: please God, it is the last meal but one you will eat at Thornfield Hall for a long time.'

I sat down near him; but told him I could not eat.

'Is it because you have the prospect of a journey before you, Jane? Is it the thoughts of going to London that take away your appetite?'

'I cannot see my prospects clearly to-night, sir; and I hardly know what thoughts I have in my head. Everything in life seems unreal.'

'Except me: I am substantial enough:—touch me.'

'You, sir, are the most phantom-like of all: you are a mere dream.'

He held out his hand, laughing: 'Is that a dream?' said he, placing it close to my eyes. He had a rounded, muscular, and vigorous hand, as well as a long, strong arm.

'Yes; though I touch it, it is a dream,' said I, as I put it down from before my face. 'Sir, have you finished supper?'

'Yes, Jane.'

I rang the bell, and ordered away the tray. When we were again alone, I stirred the fire, and then took a low seat at my master's knee.

'It is near midnight,' I said.

'Yes: but remember, Jane, you promised to wake with me the night before my wedding.'

'I did; and I will keep my promise, for an hour or two at least: I have no wish to go to bed.'

'Are all your arrangements complete?'

'All, sir.'

'And on my part, likewise,' he returned. 'I have settled everything; and we shall leave Thornfield to-morrow, within half an hour after our return from church.'

'Very well, sir.'

'With what an extraordinary smile you uttered that word, —"very well," Jane! What a bright spot of colour you have on each cheek! and how strangely your eyes glitter! Are you well?'

'I believe I am.'

'Believe! What is the matter? —Tell me what you feel.'

'I could not, sir: no words could tell you what I feel. I wish this present hour would never end: who knows with what fate the next may come charged?'

'This is hypochondria, Jane. You have been over excited, or over fatigued.'

'Do you, sir, feel calm and happy?'

'Calm? —no: but happy, —to the heart's core.'

I looked up at him to read the signs of bliss in his face: it was ardent and flushed.

'Give me your confidence, Jane,' he said: 'relieve your mind of any weight that oppresses it, by imparting it to me. What do you fear? —that I shall not prove a good husband?'

'It is the idea farthest from my thoughts.'

'Are you apprehensive of the new sphere you are about to enter? —of the new life into which you are passing?'

'No.'

'You puzzle me, Jane: your look and tone of sorrowful audacity perplex and pain me. I want an explanation.'

'Then, sir, —listen. You were from home last night?'

'I was: I know that; and you hinted a while ago at something which had happened in my absence: —nothing, probably, of consequence; but, in short, it has disturbed you. Let me hear it. Mrs. Fairfax has said something, perhaps? or you have overheard the servants talk? —your sensitive self-respect has been wounded?'

'No, sir.' It struck twelve—I waited till the time-piece had concluded its silver chime, and the clock its hoarse, vibrating stroke, and then I proceeded.

'All day, yesterday, I was very busy, and very happy in my ceaseless bustle; for I am not, as you seem to think, troubled by any haunting fears about the new sphere, et cetera: I think it a glorious thing to have the hope of living with you, because I love you. —No, sir, don't caress me now—let me talk undisturbed. Yesterday I trusted well in Providence, and believed that events were working together for your good and mine: it was a fine day, if you recollect—the calmness of the air and sky forbade apprehensions respecting your safety or comfort on your journey. I walked a little while on the pavement after tea, thinking of you; and I beheld you in imagination so near me, I scarcely missed your actual presence. I thought of the life that lay before me—*your* life, sir—an existence more expansive and stirring than my own: as much more so as the depths of the sea to which the brook runs, are than the shallows of its own strait channel. I wondered why moralists call this a world a dreary wilderness: for me it blossomed like a rose. Just at sunset, the air turned cold and the sky cloudy: I went in. Sophie called me up stairs to look at my wedding-dress, which they had just brought; and under it in the box I found your present,—the veil which, in your princely extravagance, you sent for from London: resolved, I suppose, since I would not have jewels, to cheat me into accepting something as costly. I smiled as I unfolded it, and devised how I would teaze you about your aristocratic tastes, and your efforts to masque your plebeian bride in the attributes of a peeress. I thought how I would carry down to you the square of unembroidered blonde I had myself prepared as a covering for my low-born head, and ask if that was not good enough for a woman who could bring her husband neither fortune, beauty, nor connections. I saw plainly how you would look; and heard your impetuous republican answers, and your haughty disavowal of any necessity on your part to augment your wealth, or elevate your standing, by marrying either a purse or a coronet.'

'How well you read me, you witch!' interposed Mr. Rochester: 'but what did you find in the veil besides its embroidery? Did you find poison, or a dagger, that you look so mournful now?'

'No, no, sir; besides the delicacy and richness of the fabric, I found nothing save Fairfax Rochester's pride; and that did not scare me, because I am used to the sight of the demon. But, sir, as it grew dark, the wind rose: it blew yesterday evening, not as it blows now—wild and high—but "with a sullen, moaning sound" far more eerie. I wished you were at home. I came into this room, and the sight of the empty chair and fireless hearth chilled me. For some time after I went to bed, I could not sleep—a sense of anxious excitement distressed me. The gale, still rising, seemed to my ear to muffle a mournful undersound; whether in the house or abroad I could not at first tell, but it recurred, doubtful yet doleful at every lull: at last I made out it must be some dog howling at a distance. I was glad when it ceased. On sleeping, I continued in dreams the idea of a dark and gusty night. I continued also the wish to be with you, and experienced a strange, regretful consciousness of some barrier dividing us. During all my first sleep, I was following the windings of an unknown road; total obscurity environed me; rain pelted me; I was burdened with the charge of a little child: a very small creature, too young and feeble to walk, and which shivered in my cold arms, and wailed piteously in my ear. I thought, sir, that you were on the road a long way before me; and I strained every nerve to overtake you and made effort on effort to utter your name and entreat you to stop—but my movements were fettered; and my voice still died away inarticulate; while you, I felt, withdrew farther and farther every moment.'

'And these dreams weigh on your spirits now, Jane, when I am close to you? Little nervous subject! Forget visionary woe, and think only of real happiness! You say you love me, Janet: yes—I will not forget that; and you cannot deny it. *Those* words did not die inarticulate on your lips. I heard them clear and soft: a thought too solemn perhaps, but sweet as music—"I think it is a glorious thing to have the hope of living with you, Edward, because I love you." —Do you love me, Jane? repeat it.'

'I do, sir—I do, with my whole heart.'

'Well,' he said, after some minutes' silence, 'it is strange: but that sentence has penetrated my breast painfully. Why? I think because you said it with such an earnest, religious energy; and because your upward gaze at me now is the very sublime of faith, truth, and devotion: it is too much as if some spirit were near me. Look wicked, Jane; as you know well how to look; coin one of your wild, shy, provoking smiles; tell me you hate me—teaze me, vex me; do anything but move me: I would rather be incensed than saddened.'

'I will teaze you and vex you to your heart's content, when I have finished my tale: but hear me to the end.'

'I thought, Jane, you had told me all. I thought I had found the source of your melancholy in a dream!'

I shook my head. 'What! is there more? But I will not believe it to be anything important. I warn you of incredulity beforehand. Go on.'

The disquietude of his air, the somewhat apprehensive impatience of his manner, surprised me: but I proceeded.

'I dreamt another dream, sir: that Thornfield Hall was a dreary ruin, the retreat of bats and owls. I thought that of all the stately front nothing remained but a shell-like wall, very high and very fragile looking. I wandered, on a moonlight night, through the grass-grown enclosure within: here I stumbled over a marble hearth, and there over a fallen fragment of cornice. Wrapped up in a shawl, I still carried the unknown little child: I might not lay it down anywhere, however tired were my arms—however much its weight impeded my progress, I must retain it. I heard the gallop of a horse at a distance on the road: I was sure it was you; and you were departing for many years, and for a distant country. I climbed the thin wall with frantic perilous haste, eager to catch one glimpse of you from the top: the stones rolled from under my feet, the ivy branches I grasped gave way, the child clung round my neck in terror, and almost strangled me: at last I gained the summit. I saw you like a speck on a white track, lessening every moment. The blast blew so strong I could not stand. I sat down on the narrow ledge; I hushed the scared infant in my lap: you turned an angle of the road; I bent forward to take a last look; the wall crumbled; I was shaken; the child rolled from my knee; I lost my balance, fell, and woke.'

'Now, Jane, that is all.'

'All the preface, sir; the tale is yet to come. On waking, a gleam dazzled my eyes: I thought—oh, it is daylight! But I was mistaken: it was only candlelight. Sophie, I supposed, had come in. There was a light on the dressing-table, and the door of the closet, where, before going to bed, I had hung my wedding dress and veil, stood open: I heard a rustling there. I asked, "Sophie, what are you doing?" No one answered: but a form emerged from the closet: it took the light, held it aloft and surveyed the garments pendant from the portmanteau. "Sophie! Sophie!" I again cried: and still it was silent. I had risen up in bed, I bent forward: first, surprise, then bewilderment, came over me; and then my blood crept cold through my veins. Mr. Rochester, this was not Sophie, it was not Leah, it was not Mrs. Fairfax: it was not—no, I was sure of it, and am still—it was not even that strange woman, Grace Poole.'

'It must have been one of them,' interrupted my master.

'No, sir, I solemnly assure you to the contrary. The shape standing before me had never crossed my eyes within the precincts of Thornfield Hall before: the height, the contour were new to me.'

'Describe it, Jane.'

'It seemed, sir, a woman, tall and large, with thick and dark hair hanging long down her back. I know not what dress she had on: it was white and straight; but whether gown, sheet, or shroud, I cannot tell.'

'Did you see her face?'

'Not at first. But presently she took my veil from its place; she held it up, gazed at it long, and then she threw it over her own head, and turned to the mirror. At that moment I saw the reflection of the visage and features quite distinctly in the dark oblong glass.'

'And how were they?'

'Fearful and ghastly to me—oh, sir, I never saw a face like it! It was a discoloured face—it was a savage face. I wish I could forget the roll of the red eyes and the fearful blackened inflation of the lineaments!'

'Ghosts are usually pale, Jane.'

'This, sir, was purple: the lips were swelled and dark; the brow furrowed; the black eye-brows wildly raised over the bloodshot eyes. Shall I tell you of what it reminded me?'

'You may.'

'Of the foul German spectre—the Vampyre.'

'Ah! —What did it do?'

'Sir, it removed my veil from its gaunt head, rent it in two parts, and flinging both on the floor, trampled on them.'

'Afterwards?'

'It drew aside the window-curtain and looked out: perhaps it saw dawn approaching, for, taking the candle, it retreated to the door. Just at my bedside, the figure stopped: the fiery eye glared upon me—she thrust up her candle close to my face, and extinguished it under my eyes. I was aware her lurid visage flamed over mine, and I lost consciousness: for the second time in my life—only the second time—I became insensible from terror.'

'Who was with you when you revived?'

'No one, sir; but the broad day. I rose, bathed my head and face in water, drank a long draught; felt that though enfeebled I was not ill, and determined that to none but you would I impart this vision. Now, sir, tell me who and what that woman was?'

'The creature of an over-stimulated brain; that is certain. I must be careful of you, my treasure; nerves like yours were not made for rough handling.'

'Sir, depend on it, my nerves were not in fault; the thing was real: the transaction actually took place.'

'And your previous dreams: were they real too? Is Thornfield Hall a ruin? Am I severed from you by insuperable obstacles? Am I leaving you without a tear—without a kiss—without a word?'

'Not yet.'

'Am I about to do it? —Why the day is already commenced which is to bind us indissolubly; and when we are once united, there shall be no recurrence of these mental terrors: I guarantee that.'

'Mental terrors, sir! I wish I could believe them to be only such: I wish it more now than ever; since even you cannot explain to me the mystery of that awful visitant.'

'And since I cannot do it, Jane, it must have been unreal.'

'But, sir, when I said so to myself on rising this morning, and when I looked round the room to gather courage and comfort from the cheerful aspect of each familiar object in full daylight—there, on the carpet—I saw what gave the distinct lie to my hypothesis, —the veil, torn from top to bottom in two halves!'

I felt Mr. Rochester start and shudder; he hastily flung his arms round me: 'Thank God!' he exclaimed, 'that if anything malignant did come near you last night, it was only the veil that was harmed. —Oh, to think what might have happened!'

He drew his breath short, and strained me so close to him I could scarcely pant.

Frank O'Hara

from *Lunch Poems*

Music

If I rest for a moment near The Equestrian
pausing for a liver sausage sandwich in the Mayflower Shoppe,
that angel seems to be leading the horse into Bergdorf's
and I am naked as a table cloth, my nerves humming.
Close to the fear of war and the stars which have disappeared.
I have in my hand only 25¢, it's so meaningless to eat!
and gusts of water spray over the basins of leaves
like the hammers of a glass pianoforte. If I seem to you
to have lavender lips under the leaves of the world,
    I must tighten my belt.
It's like a locomotive on the march, the season
    of distress and clarity

and my door is open to the evenings of midwinter's
lightly falling snow over the newspapers.
Clasp me in your handkerchief like a tear, trumpet
of early afternoon! in the foggy autumn.
As they're putting up the Christmas trees on Park Avenue
I shall see my daydreams walking by with dogs in blankets,
put to some use before all those coloured lights come on!
    But no more fountains and no more rain,
      and the stores stay open terribly late.

1953

A Step Away From Them

It's my lunch hour, so I go
for a walk among the hum-colored
cabs. First, down the sidewalk
where laborers feed their dirty
glistening torsos sandwiches
and Coco-Cola, with yellow helmets
on. They protect them from falling
bricks, I guess. Then onto the
avenue where skirts are flipping
above heels and blow up over
grates. The sun is hot, but the
cabs stir up the air. I look
at bargains in wristwatches. There
are cats playing in sawdust.
                        On
to Times Square, where the sign
blows smoke over my head, and higher
the waterfall pours lightly. A
Negro stands in a doorway with a
toothpick, languorously agitating.
A blonde chorus girl clicks: he
smiles and rubs his chin. Everything
suddenly honks: it is 12:40 of
a Thursday.
              Neon in daylight is a
great pleasure, as Edwin Denby would
write, as are light bulbs in daylight.
I stop for a cheeseburger at JULIET'S
CORNER. Giulietta Masina, wife of
Federico Fellini, *è bell' attrice.*

And chocolate malted. A lady in
foxes on such a day puts her poodle
in a cab.

       There are several Puerto
Ricans on the avenue today, which
makes it beautiful and warm. First
Bunny died, then John Latouche,
then Jackson Pollock. But is the
earth as full as life was full, of them?
And one has eaten and one walks,
past the magazines with nudes
and the posters for BULLFIGHT and
the Manhattan Storage Warehouse,
which they'll soon tear down. I
used to think they had the Armory
Show there.

       A glass of papaya juice
and back to work. My heart is in my
pocket, it is Poems by Pierre Reverdy.

1956

The Day Lady Died

It is 12:20 in New York a Friday
three days after Bastille day, yes
it is 1959 and I go get a shoeshine
because I will get off the 4:19 in Easthampton
at 7:15 and then go straight to dinner
and I don't know the people who will feed me

I walk up the muggy street beginning to sun
and have a hamburger and a malted and buy
an ugly NEW WORLD WRITING to see what the poets
in Ghana are doing these days
                I go on to the bank
and Miss Stillwagon (first name Linda I once heard)
doesn't even look up my balance for once in her life
and in the GOLDEN GRIFFIN I get a little Verlaine
for Patsy with drawings by Bonnard although I do
think of Hesiod, trans. Richmond Lattimore or
Brendan Behan's new play or *Le Balcon* or *Les Nègres*
of Genet, but I don't, I stick with Verlaine
after practically going to sleep with quandariness
and for Mike I just stroll into the PARK LANE
Liquor Store and ask for a bottle of Strega and

then I go back where I came from to 6th Avenue
and the tobacconist in the Ziegfeld Theatre and
casually ask for a carton of Gauloises and a carton
of Picayunes, and a NEW YORK POST with her face on it

and I am sweating a lot by now and thinking of
leaning on the john door in the 5 SPOT
while she whispered a song along the keyboard
to Mal Waldron and everyone and I stopped breathing

1959

Poem

Khrushchev is coming on the right day!
                                        the cool graced light
is pushed off the enormous glass piers by hard wind
and everything is tossing, hurrying on up
                              this country
has everything but *politesse*, a Puerto Rican cab driver
says and five different girls I see
                        look like Piedie Gimbel
with her blonde hair tossing too,
                          as she looked when I pushed
her little daughter on the swing on the lawn it was also windy

last night we went to a movie and came out,
                              Ionesco is greater
than Beckett, Vincent said, that's what I think, blueberry blintzes
and Khrushchev was probably being carped at
                                in Washington, no *politesse*
Vincent tells me about his mother's trip to Sweden
                                    Hans tells us
about his father's life in Sweden, it sounds like Grace Hartigan's
painting *Sweden*
                  so I go home to bed and names drift through my head
Purgatorio Merchado, Gerhard Schwartz and Gaspar Gonzales,
all unknown figures of the early morning as I go to work

where does the evil of the year go
                              when September takes New York
and turns it into ozone stalagmites
                        deposits of light
                      so I get back up
make coffee, and read François Villon, his life, so dark
    New York seems blinding and my tie is blowing up the street

I wish it would blow off

                though it is cold and somewhat warms my neck
as the train bears Khrushchev on to Pennsylvania Station
    and the light seems to be eternal
    and joy seems to be inexorable
    I am foolish enough always to find it in wind

1959

Personal Poem

Now when I walk around at lunchtime
I have only two charms in my pocket
an old Roman coin Mike Kanemitsu gave me
and a bolt-head that broke off a packing case
when I was in Madrid the others never
brought me too much luck though they did
help keep me in New York against coercion
but now I'm happy for a time and interested

I walk through the luminous humidity
passing the House of Seagram with its wet
and its loungers and the construction to
the left that closed the sidewalk if
I ever get to be a construction worker
I'd like to have a silver hat please
and get to Moriarty's where I wait for
LeRoi and hear who wants to be a mover and
shaker the last five years my batting average
is .016 that's that, and LeRoi comes in
and tells me Miles Davis was clubbed 12
times last night outside BIRDLAND by a cop
a lady asks us for a nickel for a terrible
disease but we don't give her one we
don't like terrible diseases, then

we go eat some fish and some ale it's
cool but crowded we don't like Lionel Trilling
we decide, we like Don Allen we don't like
Henry James so much we like Herman Melville
we don't want to be in the poets' walk in
San Francisco even we just want to be rich
and walk on girders in our silver hats
I wonder if one person out of the 8,000,000 is

thinking of me as I shake hands with LeRoi
and buy a strap for my wristwatch and go
back to work happy at the thought possibly so

1959

Rhapsody

515 Madison Avenue
door to heaven? portal
stopped realities and eternal licentiousness
or at least the jungle of impossible eagerness
your marble is bronze and your lianas elevator cables
swinging from the myth of ascending
I would join
or declining the challenge of racial attractions
they zing on (into the lynch, dear friends)
while everywhere love is breathing draftily
like a doorway linking 53rd with 54th
the east-bound with the west-bound traffic by 8,000,000s
o midtown tunnels and the tunnels, too, of Holland

where is the summit where all aims are clear
the pin-point light upon a fear of lust
as agony's needlework grows up around the unicorn
and fences him for milk- and yoghurt-work
when I see Gianni I know he's thinking of John Ericson
playing the Rachmaninoff 2nd or Elizabeth Taylor
taking sleeping-pills and Jane thinks of Manderley
and Irkutsk while I cough lightly in the smog of desire
and my eyes water achingly imitating the true blue

a sight of Manahatta in the towering needle
multi-faceted insight of the fly in the stringless labyrinth
Canada plans a higher place than the Empire State Building
I am getting into a cab at 9th street and 1st Avenue
and the Negro driver tells me about a $120 apartment
"where you can't walk across the floor after 10 at night
not even to pee, cause it keeps them awake downstairs"
no, I don't like that "well, I didn't take it"
perfect in the hot humid morning on my way to work
a little supper-club conversation for the mill of the gods

you were there always and you know all about these things
as indifferent as an encyclopedia with your calm brown eyes
it isn't enough to smile when you run the gauntlet
you've got to spit like Niagara Falls on everybody or

Victoria Falls or at least the beautiful urban fountains of Madrid
as the Niger joins the Gulf of Guinea near the Menemsha Bar
that is what you learn in the early morning passing Madison Avenue
where you've never spent any time and stores eat up light

I have always wanted to be near it
though the day is long (and I don't mean Madison Avenue)
lying in a hammock on St. Mark's Place sorting my poems
in the rancid nourishment of this mountainous island
they are coming and we holy ones must go
is Tibet historically a part of China? as I historically
belong to the enormous bliss of American death

1959

Five Poems
Well now, hold on
maybe I won't go to sleep at all
and it'll be a beautiful white night
or else I'll collapse
completely from nerves and be calm
as a rug or a bottle of pills
or suddenly I'll be off Montauk
swimming and loving it and not caring where

•

an invitation to lunch
HOW DO YOU LIKE THAT?
when I only have 16 cents and 2
packages of yoghurt
there's a lesson in that, isn't there
like in Chinese poetry when a leaf falls?
hold off on the yoghurt till the very
last, when everything may improve

•

at the Rond-Point they were eating
an oyster, but here
we were dropping by sculptures
and seeing some paintings
and the smasheroo-grates of Cadoret
and music by Varèse, too

well Adolph Gottlieb I guess you
are the hero of this day
along with venison and Bill

I'll sleep on the yoghurt and dream of the Persian Gulf

●

which I did it was wonderful
to be in bed again and the knock
on my door for once signified "hi there"
and on the deafening walk
through the ghettos where bombs have gone off lately
left by subway violators
I knew why I love taxis, yes
subways are only fun when you're feeling sexy
and who feels sexy after *The Blue Angel*
well maybe a little bit

●

I seem to be defying fate, or am I avoiding it?

1960

Ave Maria

Mothers of America
              let your kids go to the movies!
get them out of the house so they won't know what you're up to
it's true that fresh air is good for the body
                    but what about the soul
that grows in darkness, embossed by silvery images
and when you grow old as grow old you must
                  they won't hate you
they won't criticize you they won't know
                they'll be in some glamorous country
they first saw on a Saturday afternoon or playing hookey

they may even be grateful to you
            for their first sexual experience
which only cost you a quarter
            and didn't upset the peaceful home
they will know where candy bars come from
            and gratuitous bags of popcorn
as gratuitous as leaving the movie before it's over
with a pleasant stranger whose apartment is in the
            Heaven on Earth Bldg

near the Williamsburg Bridge
                      oh mothers you will have made the little tykes
so happy because if nobody does pick them up in the movies
they won't know the difference
                 and if somebody does it'll be sheer gravy
and they'll have been truly entertained either way
instead of hanging around the yard
                or up in their room
                     hating you

prematurely since you won't have done anything
    horribly
        mean yet
except keeping them from the darker joys
              it's unforgivable the latter
so don't blame me if you won't take this advice
             and the family breaks up
and your children grow old and blind in front of a
            TV set seeing
movies you wouldn't let them see when they were young

1960

Steps

How funny you are today New York
like Ginger Rogers in *Swingtime*
and St. Bridget's steeple leaning a little to the left

here I have just jumped out of a bed full of V-days
(I got tired of D-days) and blue you there still
accepts me foolish and free
all I want is a room up there
and you in it
and even the traffic halt so thick is a way
for people to rub up against each other
and when their surgical appliances lock
they stay together
for the rest of the day (what a day)
I go by to check a slide and I say
that painting's not so blue

where's Lana Turner
she's out eating
and Garbo's backstage at the Met
everyone's taking their coat off
so they can show a rib-cage to the rib-watchers

and the park's full of dancers and their tights and shoes
in little bags
who are often mistaken for worker-outers at the West Side Y
why not
the Pittsburgh Pirates shout because they won
and in a sense we're all winning
we're alive

the apartment was vacated by a gay couple
who moved to the country for fun
they move a day too soon
even the stabbings are helping the population explosion
though in the wrong country
and all those liars have left the UN
the Seagram Building's no longer rivalled in interest
not that we need liquor (we just like it)

and the little box is out on the sidewalk
next to the delicatessen
so the old man can sit on it and drink beer
and get knocked off it by his wife later in the day
while the sun is still shining

oh god it's wonderful
to get out of bed
and drink too much coffee
and smoke too many cigarettes
and love you so much

1961

Poem

Lana Turner has collapsed!
I was trotting along and suddenly
it started raining and snowing
and you said it was hailing
but hailing hits you on the head
hard so it was really snowing and
raining and I was in such a hurry
to meet you but the traffic
was acting exactly like the sky
and suddenly I see a headline
LANA TURNER HAS COLLAPSED!
there is no snow in Hollywood
there is no rain in California
I have been to lots of parties

and acted perfectly disgraceful
but I never actually collapsed
oh Lana Turner we love you get up

1962

Fantasy

(dedicated to the health of Allen Ginsberg)
How do you like the music of Adolph

Deutsch? I like
it, I like it better than Max Steiner's. Take his
score for *Northern Pursuit*, the Helmut Dantyne theme
was ...

and then the window fell on my hand. Errol
Flynn was skiing by. Down

down down went the grim
grey submarine under the "cold" ice.

Helmut was
safely ashore, on the ice.

What dreams, what incredible
fantasies of snow farts will this all lead to?

I
don't know, I have stopped thinking like a sled dog.

The main thing is to tell a story.

It is almost
very important. Imagine

throwing away the avalanche
so early in the movie. I am the only spy left
in Canada,

but just because I'm alone in the snow
doesn't necessarily mean I'm a Nazi.

Let's see,
two aspirins a vitamin C tablet and some baking soda
should do the trick, that's practically an

Alka
Seltzer. Allen come out of the bathroom

and take it.
I think someone put butter on my skis instead
of wax.

Ouch. The leanto is falling over in the
firs, and there is another fatter spy here. They
didn't tell me they sent

him. Well, that takes care

of him, boy were those huskies hungry.

Allen,

are you feeling any better? Yes, I'm crazy about
Helmut Dantyne

but I'm glad that Canada will remain

free. Just free, that's all, never argue with the movies.

1964

from *Collected Poems*

Getting Up Ahead of Someone (Sun)

I cough a lot (sinus?) so I
get up and have some tea with cognac
it is dawn
　　　　the light flows evenly along the lawn
in chilly Southampton and I smoke
and hours and hours go by I read
van Vechten's *Spider Boy* then a short
story by Patsy Southgate and a poem
by myself it is cold and I shiver a little
in white shorts the day begun
so oddly not tired not nervous I
am for once truly awake letting it all
start slowly as I watch instead of
grabbing on late as usual
　　　　　　　　where did it go
　　　　　　　　it's not really awake yet
　　　　　　　　I will wait

and the house wakes up and goes
to get the dog in Sag Harbor I make
myself a bourbon and commence
to write one of my "I do this I do that"
poems in a sketch pad
　　　　　　　it is tomorrow
though only six hours have gone by
each day's light has more significance these days

Radio

Why do you play such dreary music
on Saturday afternoon, when tired
mortally tired I long for a little
reminder of immortal energy?
All

week long while I trudge fatiguingly
from desk to desk in the museum
you spill your miracles of Grieg
and Honegger on shut-ins.

Am I not

shut in too, and after a week
of work don't I deserve Prokofieff?

Well, I have my beautiful de Kooning
to aspire to. I think it has an orange
bed in it, more than the ear can hold.

To the Film Industry in Crisis

Not you, lean quarterlies and swarthy periodicals
with your studious incursions toward the pomposity of ants,
nor you, experimental theatre in which Emotive Fruition
is wedding Poetic Insight perpetually, nor you,
promenading Grand Opera, obvious as an ear (though you
are close to my heart), but you, Motion Picture Industry,
it's you I love!

In times of crisis, we must all decide again and again whom we love.
And give credit where it's due: not to my starched nurse, who taught me
how to be bad and not bad rather than good (and has lately availed
herself of this information), not to the Catholic Church
which is at best an oversolemn introduction to cosmic entertainment,
not to the American Legion, which hates everybody, but to you,
glorious Silver Screen, tragic Technicolor, amorous Cinemascope,
stretching Vistavision and startling Stereophonic Sound, with all
your heavenly dimensions and reverberations and iconoclasms! To
Richard Barthelmess as the "tol'able" boy barefoot and in pants,
Jeanette MacDonald of the flaming hair and lips and long, long neck,
Sue Carroll as she sits for eternity on the damaged fender of a car
and smiles, Ginger Rogers with her pageboy bob like a sausage
on her shuffling shoulders, peach-melba-voiced Fred Astaire of the feet,
Eric von Stroheim, the seducer of mountain-climbers' gasping spouses,
the Tarzans, each and every one of you (I cannot bring myself to prefer
Johnny Weissmuller to Lex Barker, I cannot!), Mae West in a furry sled,
her bordello radiance and bland remarks, Rudolph Valentino of the moon,
its crushing passions, and moonlike, too, the gentle Norma Shearer,
Miriam Hopkins dropping her champagne glass off Joel McCrea's yacht
and crying into the dappled sea, Clark Gable rescuing Gene Tierney
from Russia and Allan Jones rescuing Kitty Carlisle from Harpo Marx,
Cornel Wilde coughing blood on the piano keys while Merle Oberon berate
Marilyn Monroe in her little spike heels reeling through Niagara Falls,

Joseph Cotten puzzling and Orson Welles puzzled and Dolores del Rio
eating orchids for lunch and breaking mirrors, Gloria Swanson reclining,
and Jean Harlow reclining and wiggling, and Alice Faye reclining
and wiggling and singing, Myrna Loy being calm and wise, William Powell
in his stunning urbanity, Elizabeth Taylor blossoming, yes to you

and to all you others, the great, the near-great, the featured, the extras
who pass quickly and return in dreams saying your one or two lines,
my love!
Long may you illumine space with your marvellous appearances, delays
and enunciations, and may the money of the world glitteringly cover you
as you rest after a long day under the kleig lights with your face
in packs for our edification, the way the clouds come often at night
but the heavens operate on the star system. It is a divine precedent
you perpetuate! Roll on, reels of celluloid, as the great earth rolls on!

Having a Coke with You

is even more fun than going to San Sebastian, Irún, Hendaye, Biarritz, Bayonne
or being sick to my stomach on the Travesera de Gracia in Barcelona
partly because in your orange shirt you look like a better happier St. Sebastian
partly because of my love for you, partly because of your love for yoghurt
partly because of the fluorescent orange tulips around the birches
partly because of the secrecy our smiles take on before people and statuary
it is hard to believe when I'm with you that there can be anything as still
as solemn as unpleasantly definitive as statuary when right in front of it
in the warm New York 4 o'clock light we are drifting back and forth
between each other like a tree breathing through its spectacles

and the portrait show seems to have no faces in it at all, just paint
you suddenly wonder why in the world anyone ever did them
                                                        I look
at you and I would rather look at you than all the portraits in the world
except possibly for the *Polish Rider* occasionally and anyway it's in the Frick
which thank heavens you haven't gone to yet so we can go together the first time
and the fact that you move so beautifully more or less takes care of Futurism
just as at home I never think of the *Nude Descending a Staircase* or
at a rehearsal a single drawing of Leonardo or Michelangelo that used to wow me
and what good does all the research of the Impressionists do them
when they never got the right person to stand near the tree when the sun sank
or for that matter Marino Marini when he didn't pick the rider as carefully
as the horse
                it seems they were all cheated of some marvellous experience
which is not going to go wasted on me which is why I'm telling you about it

Edmund Spenser
from *A View of the Present State of Ireland*

Iren[ius] The end will (I assure me) bee very short and much sooner then can be in so great a trouble, as it seemeth hoped for, although there should none of them fall by the sword, nor bee slaine by the souldiour, yet thus being kept from manurance, and their cattle from running abroad, by this hard restraint they would quickly consume themselves, and devoure one another. The proofe whereof, I saw sufficiently exampled in these late warres of Mounster; for not withstanding that the same was a most rich and plentifull countrey, full of corne and cattle, that you would have thought they should have beene able to stand long, yet ere one yeare and a halfe they were brought to such wretchednesse, as that any stony heart would. have rued the same. Out of every corner of the woods and glynnes they came creeping forth upon their hands, for their legges could not beare them; they looked like anatomies of death, they spake like ghosts crying out of their graves; they did eate the dead carrions, happy where they could finde them, yea, and one another soone after, insomuch as the very carcasses they spared not to scrape out of their graves; and, if they found a plot of water-cresses or shamrocks, there they flocked as to a feast for the time, yet not able long to continue therewithall; that in short space there were none almost left, and a most populous and plentifull countrey suddainely left voyde of man and beast; yet sure in all that warre, there perished not many by the sword, but all by the extremitie of famine, which they themselves had wrought.

Seamus Heaney

The Digging Skeleton

After Baudelaire

I

You find anatomical plates
Buried along these dusty quays
Among books yellowed like mummies
Slumbering in forgotten crates,

Drawings touched with an odd beauty
As if the illustrator had
Responded gravely to the sad
Mementoes of anatomy –

Mysterious candid studies
Of red slobland around the bones.
Like this one: flayed men and skeletons
Digging the earth like navvies.

II

Sad gang of apparitions,
Your skinned muscles like plaited sedge
And your spines hooped towards the sunk edge
Of the spade, my patient ones,

Tell me, as you labour hard
To break this unrelenting soil,
What barns are there for you to fill?
What farmer dragged you from the boneyard?

Or are you emblems of the truth,
Death's lifers, hauled from the narrow cell
And stripped of night-shirt shrouds, to tell:
'This is the reward of faith

In rest eternal. Even death
Lies. The void deceives.
We do not fall like autumn leaves
To sleep in peace. Some traitor breath

Revives our clay, sends us abroad
And by the sweat of our stripped brows
We earn our deaths; our one repose
When the bleeding instep finds its spade.'

Charles Baudelaire

Le Squelette laboureur

I

Dans les planches d'anatomie
Qui traînent sur ces quais poudreux
Où maint livre cadavéreux
Dort comme une antique momie,

Dessins auxquels la gravité
Et le savoir d'un vieil artiste,
Bien que le sujet en soit triste,
Ont communiqué la Beauté,

On voit, ce qui rend plus complètes
Ces mystérieuses horreurs,
Bêchant comme des laboureurs,
Des Écorchés et des Squelettes.

II

De ce terrain que vous fouillez,
Manants résignés et funèbres,
De tout l'effort de vos vertèbres,
Ou de vos muscles dépouillés,

Dites, quelle moisson étrange,
Forçats arrachés au charnier,
Tirez-vous, et de quel fermier
Avez-vous à remplir la grange?

Voulez-vous (d'un destin trop dur
Épouvantable et clair emblème!)
Montrer que dans la fosse même
Le sommeil promis n'est pas sûr;

Qu'envers nous le Néant est traître;
Que tout, même la Mort, nous ment,
Et que sempiternellement,
Hélas! il nous faudra peut-être

Dans quelque pays inconnu
Écorcher la terre revêche
Et pousser une lourde bêche
Sous notre pied sanglant et nu?

The Skeleton Digger

I

In anatomical engravings which languish on those dusty quaysides where many a cadaverous tome sleeps like an ancient mummy,

there are drawings to which the gravity and the cunning of an old artist, even though the subject matter is dismal, have given a kind of beauty,

we see, which makes these mysterious horrors more complete, digging like labourers, flayed men and skeletons.

II

From this ground which you dig, passive and sombre churls, with all the effort of your backbones or of your perished muscles,

say, what strange harvest, convicts dragged from the charnel house, do you hack out of the earth, and which farmer's barn must you fill?

Are you trying to tell us (vile and unambiguous symbol of a fate too harsh!) that even in the grave the sleep which we were promised is doubtful;

that towards us Nothingness is treacherous; that everything, even death, lies to us and that eternally alas! we must perhaps

flay the rough earth in some unknown country and push a heavy spade beneath our bleeding and naked feet?

(translated by Richard Danson Brown, with Jean Brown)

ACKNOWLEDGEMENTS

Grateful acknowledgement is made to the following sources for permission to reproduce material within this book:

O'Hara, F. (1964) 'Personal Poem', 'For James Dean', 'A Step Away From Them' and 'Ave Maria', *Lunch Poems*, City Lights Books.

Ginsberg, A. (2002) 'Howl for Carl Solomon', 'A Supermarket in California' and 'America', *Howl and Other Poems*, City Lights Books. HarperCollins Publishers, Inc. © 1956, 1959 by Allen Ginsberg. All Rights Reserved.

Ginsberg, L. (1970) 'Atomic', *Morning in Spring and Other Poems*. Copyright © 1970 by Louis Ginsberg. Reprinted by permission of HarperCollins Publishers, Inc.

Heaney, S. (1990) 'The Stone Verdict', 'Sloe Gin', 'The Grauballe Man', 'Punishment' and 'The Scribes', *New Selected Poems 1966–1987*, Faber & Faber Limited. © Seamus Heaney.

Yeats, W.B. in Finneran, R.J. (1983) 'The Stare's Nest by My Window', *W.B. Yeats: The Poems*, *A New Edition*, Macmillan London. © Copyright Michael Yeats 1983.

Heaney, S. (1996) 'The Digging Skeleton', *North*, Faber & Faber Limited. © 1996 Seamus Heaney.

Dabydeen, D. (1994) 'Song of the Creole Gang Women', *Turner: New & Selected Poems*, Cape Poetry. Curtis Brown Group Limited.

BBC *The Late Show*, 11 October 1994. Copyright © 1994 BBC.

O'Hara, F. (1964) 'Music', 'A Step Away From Them', 'The Day Lady Died', 'Poem' ('Khrushchev is coming on the right day!'), 'Personal Poem', 'Rhapsody', 'Five Poems', 'Ave Maria', 'Steps' and 'Fantasy', *Lunch Poems*, City Lights Books.

O'Hara, F., 'Poem' ('Lana Turner has collapsed!'), in Allen, D. (ed.) (1995) *The Collected Poems of Frank O'Hara*, University of California Press. City Lights Books.

'Getting Up Ahead of Someone (Sun)', 'Radio', 'To the Film Industry in Crisis' and 'Having a Coke with You' from *Collected Poems* by Frank O'Hara, copyright © 1971 by Maureen Granville-Smith, Administratix of the Estate of Frank O'Hara. Used by permission of Alfred A. Knopf, a division of Random House, Inc.

Every effort has been made to contact copyright owners. If any have been inadvertently overlooked, the publishers will be pleased to make the necessary arrangements at the first opportunity.

INDEX

Abstract Expressionists 63

Achebe, Chinua 302
    Things Fall Apart 308, 309, 319, 335, 337

Adamov, Arthur 249

Adams, Douglas 109, 142

Adorno, Theodor 10, 11
    'How to Look at Television' 127–9
    The Jargon of Authenticity 248

aesthetics
    African tradition 206–7, 309–10
    feminist 205–6
    meanings of 'aesthetic' 201
    and modernism 252
    and novel-reading 345, 346
    recent publications on 201

Africa
    in *Paradise* 319–25, 337
        and the hinterland of Zanzibar
            320–2, 323–5
        maps of East Africa 320–2
    Victorian explorers of 319

African aesthetics 206–7, 208

African fiction 308–10, 319–20
    see also Paradise (Gurnah)

Agnon, Samuel 213

AIDS, and *Kiss of the Spider Woman, The Musical* 193

Aldiss, Brian
    Billion Year Spree 112–13
    Trillion Year Spree 113

alienation
    in *Do Androids Dream of Electric Sheep?*
        136–7
    and science fiction 115–16

Allen, Donald 60

Allende, Isabel 188

Almodóvar, Pedro 192

Amazing Stories 113–14

Amis, Martin 359
    The Information 354, 355
    Time's Arrow 354

Amuta, Chidi 206–7, 208
    The Theory of African Literature 310

Analog 114

Anderson, Judith 41

Andrews, Elmer 264–5

Anouilh, Jean 239

Anthology of New York Poets (Padgett and Shapiro) 70

Anton, Uwe 138

Apollinaire, Guillaume 90

Aquinas, Thomas 244

Aragon, Louis 213

Argentina 189–91
    gaucho novels 190
    'missing persons', torture and murder in
        156, 171
    nationalism 190–1
    and Puig's novels 156
    racism in 189–90

Aristotle 217

Arnheim, Rudolf 346–7

Arnold, Matthew 93, 104
    Culture and Anarchy 6–7, 8

Artaud, Antonin 90

artificial intelligence 137

Ashbery, John, on O'Hara's poetry 62, 63, 64, 65, 69, 70, 72

Asimov, Isaac 114, 142, 144, 146

Astounding Science Fiction 114

Asturias, Miguel Ángel 188, 213

atomic bombs
    dropped on Japan 81, 100
    and Kerouac's *The Town and the City*
        100–1

in poetry
  Ginsberg's 'Howl' 101–2
  Louis Ginsberg's 'Atomic' 84–5

Atwood, Margaret 302

Auden, W.H. 264

audiences
  and Dick's fiction 144
  and popular literature 6, 8
  Rebecca and the Radio 4 Book Club
    48–51
  television and mass culture 129

Audit 70

Auerbach, Nina 40

Augustine, St 244

Austen, Jane
  Pride and Prejudice 6, 45
  and *Rebecca* 21, 41

avant-garde literature, and popular literature
    6, 8–9

Aventurera 159

Bagby, Philip H. 240

Bakhtin, Mikhail
  'Discourse in the Novel' 169–70
  'The Hero in Dostoevsky's Art' 168
  and intertextuality 181
  and *Kiss of the Spider Woman* 153,
    168–71, 177, 184

Banks, Ian M. 142

Bardon, Jonathan 271

Barker, Pat 200
  The Eye in the Door 350, 352–3, 364,
    387, 388, 390
  Liza's England 368
  The Man Who Wasn't There 368
  Regeneration 350, 351–2
  Regeneration trilogy 344, 350–3, 367,
    368
  see also The Ghost Road (Barker)

Barnes, Djuna 214

Barnes, Julian 368

Barrios, Richard 72–3

Barthes, Roland 348
  'The Death of the Author' 183
  on *Kiss of the Spider Woman* 183–4

Bassnett, Susan 161

Bastille Day, and O'Hara's 'The Day Lady
    Died' 69–70

Battersby, Christine 207, 208
  *Gender and Genius: Towards a Feminist
    Aesthetics* 205–6

Baudelaire, Charles 7
  'Le Squelette laboureur' 425–6
  translations 285–9, 424–7
  Les Fleurs du mal 285, 286

Baudrillard, Jean 23, 131–2, 135
  Simulations 132

Baumgarten, Alexander
  Aesthetica 201
  Reflections on Poetry 201

Bayley, John 299

'Beat Generation'
  and Baudelaire 285
  and Ginsberg's poetry 57, 58, 79–83,
    86, 97

the Beatles 79

Beauman, Sally 48
  Rebecca's Tale 13, 44, 45, 46–8, 53

Beckett, Samuel 200
  and the Booker Prize 297
  'Dante ... Bruno, Vico ... Joyce' 237
  Eleuthéria 235
  Happy Days 214
  Irish background 236–9
  and the Nobel Prize for Literature
    213–15, 254–6, 263
  in postwar France 233–6
  'Three Dialogues' 249
  trilogy (*Molloy, Malone Dies* and *The
    Unnameable*) 214, 235
  Watt 214
  see also Waiting for Godot (Beckett)

Behan, Brendan 69, 70

Behn, Aphra 201

Bellringer, A.W. 373

Benjamin, Walter 10, 11

Berger, John 317
 and the Booker Prize 255, 299–302

Berkson, Bill 60

Bertens, Hans, *The Idea of the Postmodern* 252

Bhabha, Homi 390–1

The Bible
 and Heaney's poetry 269
 and the story of Joseph in *Paradise* 318, 326

Bizet, Georges 161

Black Mountain poets 64

Black Panther movement 300

Blade Runner 143–4, 146, 147

Blake, William 86, 93
 Songs of Innocence and Experience 90

Blin, Roger 215

Bloch, Ernst 116

Bloom, Harold 379

Bluebeard's chamber story, and *Rebecca* 34, 36, 46

Bly, Robert 64

Booker Prize 199, 200, 204, 208, 295–310
 1991 shortlist 354–5
 1995 shortlist 355–60
 and African aesthetics 207
 and Beckett 297
 betting on the 355
 and colonialism 299–302
 and Commonwealth fiction 302, 306–7
 and the consumerist approach to novel-reading 345, 346
 and controversy 255
 disputes 297–8
 and feminist aesthetics 206
 and *The Ghost Road* 297, 350, 354–60
 history 295–7

John Berger's acceptance speech 299–302
 and *The Late Show* 296, 334–7
 and non-fiction novels 375
 and *Paradise* 294, 295–310, 333–8, 339
 and postcolonial literature 301, 302–10, 333, 336
 prize regulations 298–9
 publishers of shortlisted works 303
 and Scottish novels 333

Borges, Jorge Luis 156, 178, 188

Bourdieu, Pierre 203–4, 297
 Distinction 204

Brackett, Leigh 113

Bradley, Marion Zimmer 113

Bragg, Melvyn 296

Brannigan, John 387, 389, 393

Brecht, Bertolt 8, 225, 249, 252
 concept of *Verfremdung* 115–16
 Life of Galileo 115, 116, 217

Breen, Joseph 73

Breslin, Jimmy 374

Brief Encounter 31

Bringing Up Baby 73, 77

Bromley, Roger, on class in *Rebecca* 31–2

Brontë, Charlotte
 Jane Eyre
  Chapter 10 403–10
  and *Kiss of the Spider Woman* 165
  plot-summary of 34
  and *Rebecca* 9, 13, 34–40, 43, 44, 45, 48, 403
  and *Wide Sargasso Sea* 37–8

the Brontës, as literary classics 6

Brookes, Cleanth 64, 163

Brown, Dennis 371

Brown, George McKay, *Beside the Ocean of Time* 333

Brown, Norman 177

Brown, William 351

Buber, Martin 244

Bunin, Ivan 211

Burke, Edmund 200

Burroughs, William 81
   The Naked Lunch 119

Burt, Stephen 61

Burton, Richard 319

Button, John 75

Byatt, Antonia 334–5, 336, 371
   'Fathers' 368–70, 371, 375

Byron, George Gordon, Lord 7

Cabrera Infante, Guillermo 163, 188–9

Cage, John, 'Music of Changes' concert 63

Caine Prize 208

Calinescu, Matei 346–7

Calvino, Italo 189

The Cambridge Companion to Science Fiction 109

Camus, Albert 189, 244, 248–9
   Caligula 248
   The Myth of Sisyphus 245

canonical writers
   and culture 7
   defining the term 'canon' 201
   and Ginsberg's poetry 93
   and the Irish literary tradition 237–8
   judging literature and canon formation 395
   Leavis on 162–3
   and *Paradise* 310
   and postcolonialism 303, 305, 307
   and science fiction 146

capitalism
   and Ginsberg's poetry 57, 58, 102
   Marxist theories of 120–1, 122, 136
   and postmodernism 130–1

Capote, Truman, *In Cold Blood* 374

Carey, John 9, 263, 381

Carey, Peter 302

Carpentier, Alejo 188, 189

Carroll, Lewis 383

Carroll, Paul, on O'Hara's poetry 69–70, 72

Carson, Ciaran 281, 282

Carter, Angela 189
   The Bloody Chamber 34

Cartwright, Justin, *In Every Face I Meet* 355

Cat People 158, 159, 160, 166, 167, 172, 178, 186

Cawelti, John 33

Cazeaux, Clive, *The Continental Aesthetics Reader* 201

censorship
   and *Kiss of the Spider Woman* 183, 193
   and the US film industry 72–3

Charters, Anne 81, 82

Chaucer, Geoffrey, *House of Fame* 113

Chekhov, Anton 225
   The Cherry Orchard 200, 217
   Three Sisters 257

children's literature 5

Christ, R. 155, 158, 160, 174, 176

cinema *see* film

civil rights movement 73
   and Dick's fiction 115, 119, 125, 126

Clark, Carol 288

Clarke, Arthur C. 109, 142

the Clash 79

class
   and aesthetic judgements 204, 207
   in Arnold's *Culture and Anarchy* 6–7
   in *Do Androids Dream of Electric Sheep?* 127
   and Marxism 120
   and postmodernism 130
   in Puig's fiction 155–6
   in *Rebecca* 30–3
      and *Jane Eyre* 35
      and literary tourism 51, 52

middle-class female readership 38–9, 50

and the nameless narrator 20

Clute, John and Nicholls, Peter, *The Encyclopaedia of Science Fiction* 112

Coetzee, J.M. 302

cognition, and science fiction 116–17

Cohn, Ruby 247

Colchie, Thomas 164

cold war
and the 'Beat Generation' 81
and Dick's fiction 117, 118
and Ginsberg's poetry 57, 59, 94, 100–1, 104
and O'Hara's poetry 59

Coleman, Ornette 79

Coleridge, Samuel Taylor 203

Colgan, Michael 215

colonialism
and the Booker Prize 299–302, 335–6, 337
in East Africa, and *Paradise* 320–3, 335–6, 337

Colvin, C. 375

Commonwealth fiction 302, 306–7

communism
anti-communism in the USA 81, 100, 101
and science fiction 117–18
and Ginsberg's poetry 59, 103

computers, and *Do Androids Dream of Electric Sheep?* 137

Connolly, James 267

Conrad, Joseph
Heart of Darkness 166
and *Paradise* 310, 319–20, 334, 336, 337

consumerism
and Ginsberg's poetry 58, 93, 94, 103
and *Kiss of the Spider Woman* 176, 184
in O'Hara's poetry 78, 79, 103

consumption, and taste 200

Corbatta, J. 180

Corcoran, N. 280

Corso, Gregory 79, 81, 82, 96

Cortázar, Julio 183, 188

counter-culture
and Dick's fiction 119
and Ginsberg's poetry 57, 58, 100

Cowley, J. 356

Crane, Hart 90, 96

Cromwell, John 158

Cronin, Anthony 214

Crosby, Bing 157

Culler, Jonathan 349

cultural capital 204
and the Booker Prize 297, 307

cultural difference, and identity 390–1

cultural studies 5
and science fiction 116

culture, and popular literature 6–8

Dabydeen, David, 'Song of the Creole Gang Women' 301

Dante Alighieri 7, 8
and Heaney's poetry 285
Inferno 62

Davis, Miles 61, 89

Dean, James, in O'Hara's poetry 65–6, 75

Delany, Samuel R. 114

Depp, Johnny 79

Derrida, Jacques 251

Desai, Anita 302

Descartes, René 244–5

detective fiction
Adorno on 128, 129
and Puig's novels 154–5

Dick, Philip K. 5–6, 108–47
'The Android and the Human' 135

attitudes to race 126–7
audiences and critical attention 144
Bishop Timothy Archer (The Transmigration of Timothy Archer) 143
Confessions of a Crap Artist 118, 143
The Crack in Space 127
death 143
Dr Futurity 127
Eye in the Sky 118, 127, 145
and female characters 145
films of books 143–4, 147
historical context 117–19
'How to Build a Universe that Doesn't Fall Apart Two Days Later' 132–3, 135
Humpty Dumpty in Oakland 126–7
on literary criticism 108, 147
'The Little Black Box' 119, 140
Mary and the Giant 126
'My Definition of Science Fiction' 114
The Owl in Daylight 143
and philosophy 108–9
and popular or high culture 146–7
Time Out of Joint 131, 132
The World Jones Made 119
see also *Do Androids Dream of Electric Sheep?* (Dick)

Dickens, Charles 6, 147

Didion, Joan 374

Dietrich, Marlene 75

Disch, Thomas M. 143

Disneyland, fakery of 132

Do Androids Dream of Electric Sheep? (Dick) 3, 6, 9, 119–47, 176
androids and the corporate world in 123–4
Baudrillardian simulacra in 134
and *Blade Runner* 143–4
Chapter 1 109–11
Chapter 2 122–3, 125
empathy and being human in 136–41
empathy boxes in 119, 123
gender in 121–2, 126, 145
humans and android doubles in 133–4

Marxist readings of 119–29, 137
Penfield Mood Organ in 109–10, 116
postmodernist readings of 129–36
present-day context of 114–15
publication of 119
race in 124–7
reviews and critical assessments of 142–3
and the Voigt-Kampff test 133, 134, 137

Doctor Who 111

Donoso, José 188–9
The Limitless Place 186

Dostoevsky, Fyodor 168

drug-taking, and Dick's fiction 119

du Maurier, Daphne 5–6
and the Brontës 37
and Cornwall 14, 15, 51–4
dramatization of *Rebecca* for the London stage 41
'The House of Secrets' 15–19, 53
life-experiences of in *Rebecca* 49, 52–3
The Loving Spirit 15
The Rebecca Notebook and Other Memories 19, 26, 47
Vanishing Cornwall 53
see also *Rebecca* (du Maurier)

du Maurier, George, *Trilby* 15

du Maurier, Gerald 15

Duchamp, Marcel, *Nude Descending a Staircase* 78

Dunant, Sarah 333, 334, 335

Duncan, Robert 98

Dunn, Allen see Singer, Alan and Dunn, Allen

Dunne, Michael, 'Dialogism in Manuel Puig's *Kiss of the Spider Woman*' 169

Dylan, Bob 6, 79, 104

Eagleton, Terry 371–2, 374

Easthope, Anthony
Literary into Cultural Studies 163
What a Man's Gotta Do 174–5

Eberhart, Richard 79, 80, 81, 93–4, 96

Echevarren, Roberto 155, 192

elegiac tradition, in O'Hara's poetry 65, 67

Eliot, T.S. 8, 60, 252
    'Burnt Norton' 62
    and Faber & Faber 264
    and Heaney 289
    'The Hollow Men' 227
    Prufrock and Other Observations 200, 253
    'Tradition and the Individual Talent' 38,
        181

Elledge, Jim, 'Never Argue with the Movies'
    75–7

Emerson, Ralph Waldo 146

empathy, in *Do Androids Dream of Electric
    Sheep?* 119, 123, 136–41

Empson, William 64, 237

The Enchanted Cottage 158, 186

Engels, Friedrich *see* Marx, Karl, and
    Engels, Friedrich

English, James F., 'Winning the Culture
    Game' 255, 297

English literature, definition of 4

Espmark, Kjell 211

Esslin, Martin 249

estrangement, and science fiction 115–16

ET: The Extra-Terrestrial 144

Eustasio Rivera, José, *The Whirlpool* 190

existentialism
    and 'suffering of being' 246
    and the *Theatre of the Absurd* 248–50
    in *Waiting for Godot* 240, 244–8

Faber & Faber, and Heaney's poetry 264

factual fictions 371–85
    in *The Ghost Road* 371, 372–3, 375–85
    and metafictional novels 373
    and New Journalism 374–5, 383
    and 'non-fiction novels' 374–5

fairytales
    and *Rebecca* 18, 22
    and science fiction 116–17

fantasy, and science fiction 109

Farrell, J.G. 260–1
    The Siege of Krishnapur 302, 360, 361
    Troubles 360

Farscape 129

Faulkner, William 146, 189, 373

Faulks, Sebastian 368

female identity
    in *Jane Eyre* 35–6
    in *Rebecca* 22
        and romance 40–1

female sexuality
    in *Kiss of the Spider Woman* 159–60, 167
    in *Rebecca* 22–3, 24–6, 49
        and class 30–1
        Freudian theories of 26–30
        Hitchcock film 42–3, 44

femininity
    in *Kiss of the Spider Woman* 172, 173–4
    see also gender; women

feminism
    and aesthetics 205–6
    and domesticity in *Rebecca* 33
    and Gothic romance 33–4
    and *Kiss of the Spider Woman* 173–4, 188
    and middle-class female readers 38–9
    and science fiction 113, 116, 117

Ferlinghetti, Lawrence 96, 97, 98, 99, 100

fiction, purpose of 394–6

Fiedler, Leslie 78

Fierro, Martín 190

film
    cinema and gay New York in the 1950s
        72–9
    film industry and anti-communist
        hysteria 100
    Hitchcock's *Rebecca* 41–4, 47, 179
    and *Kiss of the Spider Woman* 153–4,
        155, 157, 157–62, 186

and femininity 173–4
Nazi propaganda films 158, 173,
174
and parallel narratives 166–8
and psychoanalytic theory 178–9
and Latin American fiction 189
and O'Hara's poetry 60
and science fiction 111, 118, 143–4

First World War
and domesticity 32
and *The Ghost Road* 362–3, 367–8,
368–71, 393, 395
reviews of 357–9, 366
Passchendaele 353
and the *Regeneration* trilogy 350–3

Fish, Stanley 349

Flowers, Thomas 137

Flynn, Erroll 75, 76

folk art, and 'high' culture 7–8

Fontaine, Joan 41

Ford, Harrison 144

Forster, E.M. 7

Fraser, G.S. 240

Freud, Sigmund
and Barker's *Regeneration* trilogy 351,
370, 386–7, 392
theories of sexuality
and *Kiss of the Spider Woman* 172,
175–6
and *Rebecca* 26–30
'The Uncanny' 386–7

Fuentes, Carlos 188–9, 190

Galeano, Eduardo, *Open Veins of Latin
America* 186

Galen, Russell 143

Garbo, Greta, in O'Hara's poetry 74, 75

García Lorca, Federico 90, 93

Garcia Márquez, Gabriel 188–9

Garland, Judy 75

Gaut, Berys and Lopes, Dominic McIver,
The Routledge Companion to Aesthetics
201

gender
and aesthetics 205–6, 208
in *Do Androids Dream of Electric Sheep?*
121–2, 126, 145
and genres of popular literature 6
and *The Ghost Road* 370–1
in *Kiss of the Spider Woman* 170–1,
172–5, 179
and Marxism 122
and science fiction 112, 113, 144–5
and *Waiting for Godot* 257
see also femininity; masculinity; women

Genet, Jean 69, 70, 249

genius, Kant's definition of 202–3

Gernsback, Hugo 113–14

The Ghost Road (Barker) 199, 344–96
'Author's Note' 366, 376
and the Booker Prize 297, 350, 354–60
Chapter 1 361–3
Chapter 3 and the layering of memories
364–5, 366
Chapters 8 and 9 378–81
fact–fiction relationship in 371, 372–3,
375–85
final section 384, 392–4
and gender 370–1
ghosts and doubles in 385–94
and historical fiction 360–71
judgements of 394–6
Melanesian material 366–7, 377–8,
381–3, 386, 387–93
responses to first reading of 349–50,
368, 394
reviews of 356–9, 365–8, 371, 383–4
shift to first-person narration 376–7

Gibbon, Lewis Grassic 15

Gibson, William, *Neuromancer* 146

Gierow, Karl Ragnar 214

Gilman, Charlotte Perkins, *The Yellow
Wallpaper* 165

Ginsberg, Allen 3, 5–6, 10, 79–104, 146
  'America' 57, 70, 103–4
  and autobiography 58
  and the 'Beat Generation' 57, 58,
    79–83, 86, 97
  and Bob Dylan 79, 104
  and canonical writers 93
  and Heaney 265, 266
  'Howl' 57, 70, 79, 81, 82, 85–92, 93–6,
    101–3, 104, 266
    ambiguity in 93–4
    and 'America' 102–3
    and Carl Solomon 87, 89–90
    drafts and revisions of 86–7
    Ferlinghetti on 98
    'Footnote to Howl' 85–6, 87, 90,
      92, 99, 102
    opening lines 83–4
    part I 87, 89–90
    part II 87–9, 102
    part III 89–90
    reading at Six Gallery, San
      Francisco 79, 96
    and the Romantic tradition 90
    self-reflexivity in 95–6
    and Smart's 'Jubilate Agno' 90–1
    spontaneity in 86, 90, 94–5
    structuring devices in 84
    techniques used in 85–6
    war in 101–2
    and Whitman's 'Song of Myself' 92
  Howl and Other Poems 96–9, 104
    LP/CD of Ginsberg reading from
      99
    obscenity trial 57, 97, 98–9
    sales figures 97
    Williams's introduction to 97
  'In the Baggage Room at Greyhound'
    57, 58–9, 104
  on the meaning of 'beat' 81–2
  'Oda a Walt Whitman' 93
  and O'Hara 57–8, 60, 70, 77, 84, 103
  'A Supermarket in California' 92–3
Ginsberg, Louis, 'Atomic' 84–5
Glob, P.V., The Bog People 277–80, 283
Goebbels, Joseph 173

Goethe, Johann Wolfgang von 203
Gökce, Neyir Cenk 112
Gone with the Wind 41, 45
Goodby, J. 272, 274
Gordimer, Nadine 302
Gothic novels, and science fiction 112
Gothic romance
  defining 33
  in Rebecca 33–4, 40–1, 44
Gottsched, Johann Christoph 201
Grant, Cary 73
Grass, Günther 189
Graves, Robert 352
Gray, Thomas, 'Elegy Written in a Country
  Church Yard' 67
The Great Love (Nazi propaganda film) 158,
  173
Greer, Germaine 334–5, 336
Güiraldes, Ricardo, Don Segundo Sombra
  190
Gunesekera, Romesh 302
  Reef 333, 334, 335, 337
Gurnah, Abdulrazak 200, 302
  Admiring Silence 318
  aesthetic aims 338
  By the Sea 318
  'An Idea of the Past' 308–9, 315–17
  'Imagining the Postcolonial Writer' 308
  Memory of Departure 318
  as a migrant writer 317–18
  in Strangers in a Strange Land 317
  see also Paradise (Gurnah)
Gussow, Mel 232
Guyana, and the Booker Prize 300, 301

Hall, Peter 215
Hand, Seán 139
Hardy, Thomas 7
Harrison, Harry 142, 143

Hartigan, Grace 68

Hartwell, David 143

Hawkins, Harriett 39

Head, Henry 352

Heaney, Seamus 199, 200, 262–90
    'Anahorish' 262, 273–4, 275
    background 263
    'Belfast' 273
    'Blackberry-Picking' 265
    'Bog Oak' 262, 274–6
    bog poems 276–85
    'Bog Queen' 281, 288–9
    'Broagh' 262, 273–4, 290
    career success 264
    'Cessation 1994' 268
    'Clearances' 282
    'Crediting Poetry' (Nobel lecture) 269,
        270, 282, 284
    critics on 263–4
    Death of a Naturalist 263, 264
    Door into the Dark 264, 267
    Electric Light 263
    'Exposure' 281, 282
    'Feeling into Words' 267, 272, 276, 284
    'Field Work' 285
    Finders Keepers 270
    'The Flight Path' 272
    'Follower' 265
    'The Grauballe Man' 262, 277–81, 282,
        288
    and Ireland 267–8, 271–6
        Northern Ireland and the Troubles
            262, 265, 271–3, 280, 281–2,
            284, 290
    as a 'lyric' poet 265–6
    New Selected Poems 262, 263, 281, 282
    'A New Song' 262, 273, 275
    and the Nobel Prize for Literature
        265–71, 276, 289, 290
    North 262, 264, 268, 281–2, 285, 288,
        289
    Opened Ground: Poems 1966–1996 269
    Preoccupations 270
    'Punishment' 262, 277, 281–5, 288,
        290

'Requiem for the Croppies' 262, 267–8,
    272
'Seeing Things' 285
'Sloe Gin' 262, 265–7, 268, 269
Station Island 266, 289
    'The Scribes' (from 'Sweeney
        Redivivus') 289–90
Stations 263
'The Stone Verdict' 262–3, 282, 289,
    290
'Strange Fruit' 277, 281
'Thatcher' 265
translations 285, 289
    Beowulf 276, 289
    'The Digging Skeleton' 262, 285–9,
        290, 424–5
    Sweeney Astray 263, 289
    Wintering Out 264, 273–6

Hebdige, Dick 131

Hegel, G.W.F. 203

Heidegger, Martin 108, 139, 244
    Being and Time 138

Heinlein, Robert A. 109, 142, 144

Hemingway, Ernest 146

Her Real Glory 158

Heraclitus 108

Herder, Johann Gottfried 201

Hernández, José 190

Herodotus 324

Herring, Terrell Scott 61

Hersey, John, *Hiroshima* 100

'high' culture
    and folk art 7–8
    and Ginsberg's poetry 104, 146
    and literary judgements 200
    and O'Hara's poetry 57
    and the 'popular' 54–5
    and Puig's novels 162–3
    and *Rebecca* 37–41
    and science fiction 146–7

Hilberg, Raul, *The Destruction of the
    European Jews* 234

Hill, Susan
 Mrs de Winter 13, 44–6, 47
 The Woman in Black 44

historical change, and psychoanalytic theory
 in *Rebecca* 29–30

historical contexts
 and Barker 360–5
 and Beckett 233–9
 and Dick 117–19
 and du Maurier 30–3
 and Ginsberg 79–83, 97–101
 and Gurnah 316–25
 and Heaney 267–8, 271–6
 and O'Hara 59, 65, 67, 69–70
 and Puig 156, 171, 187–92

historical fiction
 in Byatt's 'Fathers' 368–70, 371
 and *The Ghost Road* 360–71
 period 'placing' in 361–2

Hitchcock, Alfred 189
 film of *Rebecca* 41–4, 47, 179

Hitler, Adolf 173

Hjärne, Harald 212

Hobsbaum, Philip 264, 265

Hobson, Harold 239

Hofstadter, Douglas 137–8

Holiday, Billie, and O'Hara's 'The Day Lady
 Died' 65–70

the Holocaust, and *Waiting for Godot* 234,
 236

Homer, *Odyssey* 113

homosexuality
 in Dick's fiction 118, 119
 in *The Eye in the Door* 352, 353
 in *The Ghost Road* 371
 and Ginsberg's poetry 95, 96, 97
 in *Kiss of the Spider Woman* 167, 175–6,
  177–8, 179–80, 183, 192, 193
 O'Hara and gay New York in the 1950s
  72–9
 in *Regeneration* 352

Hope, Bob 157

Horkheimer, Max 10

Horn, Judge 99

Howarth, Donald 257

Huggan, Graham, 'The Postcolonial Exotic'
 305–6, 307, 338

Hulme, Keri 302

Hume, David 108

Husserl, Edmund 244

Huxley, Aldous, *Brave New World* 112

Hyde, Lewis 80, 81, 99

I Walked with a Zombie 159, 179

identity, and cultural difference 390–1

Imposter 147

Independence Day 111

intertextuality, and *Kiss of the Spider Woman*
 181–3

Invasion of the Body Snatchers 118, 131

Ionesco, Eugène 249

IRA (Irish Republican Army) 268, 271, 272

Ireland
 and Beckett 236–9
 and Heaney's poetry 271–6
  bog poems 277, 280, 281–2
  civil war 277
  Easter (1916) uprising 267
  and Edmund Spenser 275, 276
  Irish rebellion (1798) 267–8
  'linguistic politics' in 274
  the Munster famine 275
  Northern Ireland and the Troubles
   262, 265, 271–3, 280, 281–2,
   284, 290
  place names in 273–4
  and 'the English tradition' 275–6
  and the Tyrone uprising (1598) 275

Iser, Wolfgang
 'The Reading Process: A
  Phenomenological Approach' 396
 studies of the 'implied reader' 348, 349,
  395

Ishiguro, Kazuo 317

Isidore, John 140

Islam, and *The Satanic Verses* 355

Iyer, Pico, 'The Empire Writes Back' 305–6, 309

James, Henry 61, 373

Jameson, Frederic 130–1, 138, 147

Japan, US dropping of atomic bombs on 81, 100

Jaspers, Karl 244

Jauss, Hans Robert, 'Literary History as a Challenge to Literary Theory' 348, 349, 395, 396

Jews, in wartime France 233, 234

Johns, Jasper 60

Johnson, B.S. 214, 374, 375
    Trawl 374

Jones, Gwyneth 147

Jones, LeRoi (Amiri Baraka) 61

Joyce, James 7, 66, 189, 373
    and Beckett 237
    Portrait of the Artist as a Young Man 60

Judaism, and Heidegger 138

judging literature 199–208, 395–6
    and novel-reading 345–50
    see also aesthetics; Booker Prize; Nobel Prize for Literature

Jung, Carl 386

Kafka, Franz 189, 373

Kaiser, Charles 72, 73–4

Kant, Immanuel 108, 147, 205, 208
    Critique of Judgment 201, 202–3
    Critique of Practical Reason 202
    Critique of Pure Reason 202
    and Heaney's poetry 270

Katz, Alex 60

Kaun, Axel 232

Kawabata, Yasunari 213

Kearney, Richard and Rasmussen, David, *Continental Aesthetics* 201

Kellaway, Kate 356

Kelman, James 302, 359
    How Late It Was, How Late 333

Kemp, Peter 356

Keneally, Thomas 302
    Schindler's Ark 375, 383

Kerouac, Jack 82, 83, 189
    and Ginsberg's 'Howl' 86
    On the Road 81
    The Town and the City 81, 100–1

Khomeini, Ayatollah 355

Kiberd, Declan 237

Kierkegaard, Søren 244, 245

King, Martin Luther 125, 126

King, Stephen 50

Kinsey reports on sexual behaviour 118

Kinski, Natassja 158

Kiss of the Spider Woman (Puig) 3, 6, 9, 153–93
    art and ideology in 168–71
    and *bricolage* 155
    dialogic structure 156–7, 168, 169, 170, 184
    and film 153–4, 155, 157, 157–62, 186
    and femininity 173–4
    and parallel narratives 166–8
    and psychoanalytic theory 178–9
    footnotes 167, 169, 172, 176, 177–8, 182
    gender in 170–1, 172–5, 179
    and high and low cultural forms 162–3, 169, 182, 193
    homosexuality in 167, 175–6, 177–8, 179–80, 183, 192, 193
    and intertextuality 181–3
    and Latin American fiction 187–91
    and Molina as spider woman 160–1
    musical version 192–3
    and postmodernism 155, 167, 185–6
    power relations in 186–7
    publication 192

romance genre in 180–1
in translation 163–5, 192
vulgarity in 179–80

Kline, Franz 63

Kooning, Willem de 60, 63

Koran, and the story of Yusef in *Paradise* 318, 326

Kristeva, Julia 181

Lacan, Jacques 182

Lang, Fritz, *Metropolis* 89

Larkin, Philip 298

Latin American fiction, 'boom' in 187–91, 193

Laurel and Hardy 157

Lawrence, D.H. 7, 205, 394

Lawson, Mark 297

Le Guin, Ursula 113, 147

Leander, Zarah 158

Leavis, F.R. 8, 10, 11, 93, 104
on the literary canon 162–3
Mass Civilisation and Minority Culture 7

Leavis, Q.D. 8, 10, 11, 162
Fiction and the Reading Public 7

Lehman, David, *The Last Avant-Garde* 64, 85

Leigh, Vivien 41

Lem, Stanislaw 142, 143
Solaris 143

Lemmon, Jack 157

Léon, Paul 223

LeSeur, Joe, *Homage to Frank O'Hara* 60

Levinas, Emmanuel
on the individual self and the Other 138–40, 141
'Power and the Relationship with the Other' 139–40

Lévy-Bruhl, Lucien 386, 391

Lewis, Matthew, *The Monk* 112

Lewton, Val 158, 159

libraries, and popular fiction 7

Life magazine 63

Light, Alison, on *Rebecca* 44

Lindon, Jerome 214

Lindsay-Hogg, Michael 215

Lispector, Clarice 188

literary prizes
and canon formation 395
and novel-reading 347
see also Booker Prize; Nobel Prize for Literature

literature, definitions of 4–5

Livingstone, David 319

Lloyd, David 264

Lloyd George, David 352

Locatelli, Carla 214

London Review of Books 61, 356, 365

Longley, Edna 266, 280, 281

Lopes, Dominic McIver *see* Gaut, Berys and Lopes, Dominic McIver

Lowell, Robert 263, 270

Lowenthal, Leo 99

Lubitsch, Ernst 189

Lucian of Samosata, *The True History* 113

Lyotard, Jean-François 9, 11
The Postmodern Condition 130

McCaffery, Anne 113

McCarthyism 100
and science fiction 117–18, 146

McCartney, Paul 79

Macdonald, Dwight 11, 93, 104, 127
'A Theory of Mass Culture' 7–8, 62–4, 77, 78

McDonald, Peter 269, 270

McHugh, Vincent 99

McNamara, Kevin
  'Blade Runner's Post-Individual
    Worldspace and Philip K. Dick's Do
    Androids Dream of Electric Sheep?'
    125–6
  on female characters in Dick's fiction
    145

MacNeice, Louis 264

magazines, science fiction 113–14

magic realism, and Latin American authors
  189

Mailer, Norman, Armies of the Night 374

Malcolm X 125

male readers, of Rebecca 50

male sexuality, in Freud's 'Female Sexuality'
  27

Mandelstam, Osip, Tristia 282

Marcuse, Herbert 177
  Eros and Civilization 176
  One-Dimensional Man 176

marriage
  in Rebecca
    and class 31, 32–3
    Hitchcock film 43–4
    and Jane Eyre 39
    and Manderley 18–19
    and du Maurier 53
    and Mrs de Winter 45, 46
    and murder 24–6, 40–1
    and the nameless narrator 20–1
    and romance 39–41, 45
  in Rebecca's Tale 47–8

Marrus, Michael 234

Mars-Jones, Adam 356, 374

Marvel Science Stories 114

Marx, Karl
  Capital 136
  and Engels, Friedrich
    The Communist Manifesto 119–21
    The German Ideology 120, 121

Marxism
  and Dick's fiction 108, 117, 130

Do Androids Dream of Electric Sheep?
    119–29, 137
  and Freudianism 176
  and Kiss of the Spider Woman 171, 176,
    186
  and postmodernism 131
  and science fiction 116

Marxist critics, on popular literature 10

Maschler, Tom 295

masculine genres, and science fiction 6, 144

masculinity
  and The Ghost Road 370–1
  in Kiss of the Spider Woman 172, 174–5
  in O'Hara's poetry 76, 77
  see also gender

Maslen, Elizabeth 330–1

Mass Culture: The Popular Arts in America
  (Rosenberg and White) 62–4

mass culture
  and Do Androids Dream of Electric Sheep?
    127–9
  and Ginsberg's poetry 94
  Macdonald on 7–8, 11, 62–4, 77, 78,
    93, 104, 127
  and O'Hara's poetry 66, 104
    cinema and gay New York 72–9
    and high culture 57, 58, 62–4, 77–9

Matrix trilogy 111

Matthau, Walter 157

Mayakovksy, Vladimir 90

Melville, Herman 61, 146

Mendlesohn, Farah 109

Mercier, Vivian 218
  The Irish Comic Tradition 238

Merleau-Ponty, Maurice 244

Merrill, Judith 142, 143

Merrim, Stephanie, 'Through the Film
  Darkly' 179

metafictional novels 373

metanarratives, and postmodernism 130

Metropolis 89

Michelangelo 78

Miles, Barry 94, 98

Miller, Henry 189

Millett, Kate 177

Milton, John 5, 7, 91, 93
'Lycidas' 67
Paradise Lost 87, 113

Milton Manor, near Peterborough, and
Rebecca 17, 18

minority literature, and popular literature
8–9

Minority Report 147

Mistral, Gabriela 188, 211, 212

Mitchell, Margaret, *Gone with the Wind* 41,
45

Mo, Timothy 317

modernism
and Conrad's *Heart of Darkness* 319
and Latin American fiction 189
and novel-reading 347
and popular literature 8
and postcolonialism 338
and postmodernism 155, 156, 251–3
and *Waiting for Godot* 253

Modleski, Tania
on the film version of *Rebecca* 42
on Gothic romance 33–4

Moloch (Old Testament fire god of Canaa),
and Ginsberg's 'Howl' 87–9, 102, 103

Moloney, Alan 215

Moore, C.L. 113

Moorehead, Alan 324

Moravia, Alberto 189

More, Thomas, *Utopia* 113

Morrison, Blake 273–4

Mozart, Wolfgang, *The Magic Flute* 133

Murao, Shigeyashi 97, 98, 99

music
and the 'Beat Generation' 82

education/class origin and musical taste
204
and Ginsberg's poetry 86, 89
and O'Hara's poetry 60–1, 63
popular 6, 128

Naipaul, V.S. 302
'A Bend in the River' 319

Neilson, Donald 374

Neruda, Pablo 213

Net Book Agreement (NBA) 354, 355,
359–60

Neuberger, Julia 333

New Criticism 163
and O'Hara's poetry 64, 65, 72

New Journalism 374–5, 383

New Republic 81

New York
Museum of Modern Art 60, 63
and O'Hara's poetry 57, 58, 60–1
and the anti-pastoral 66, 67
cinema and gay New York in the
1950s 72–9
in 'The Day Lady Died' 66
and 'The Equestrian' statue in
Central Park 59

New York Times Book Review 79, 350

Ngugi wa Thiong'o 308
Weep Not, Child 309

Nietzsche, Friedrich 244

Niven, Alastair 299

Nobel Prize for Literature 199, 200, 204,
208
and African aesthetics 207
and Beckett 213–15, 263
Waiting for Godot 214, 254–6
and feminist aesthetics 206
and Heaney 265–71, 276, 289, 290
history 210–13

Northern Ireland, and Heaney's poetry 262,
265, 271–3, 280, 281–2, 284, 290

Northern Pursuit 75

Norton, André 113

novel-reading 344–50
   consumerist approach to 345
   first readings 349
   and reader-centred approaches 348–9
   rereading and judging literature 345–7

O'Brien, Conor Cruise 238, 281, 282

The Odd Couple 157

O'Donoghue, B. 273–4

Oedipus complex, in Freud's 'Female
   Sexuality' 27, 29

O'Hara, Frank 3, 5–6, 9, 60–79, 104,
   410–23
   'Ave Maria' 75, 76, 193, 417–18
   Collected Poems 60, 62, 421–3
   'The Day Lady Died' 57, 65–70,
     412–13
   death 73
   'Fantasy' 57, 75, 76, 77, 420–1
   'Five Poems' 416–17
   'For James Dean' 65–6
   friends and acquaintances 60
   'Getting Up Ahead of Someone (Sun)'
     57, 66–7, 421
   and Ginsberg 57–8, 60, 70, 77, 84, 103
   'Having a Coke with You' 78, 423
   and Heaney 265
   and high and mass culture 57, 58, 62–4,
     77–9, 104
   'In Memory of My Feelings' 68
   Lunch Poems 64, 72, 410–21
   'Meditations in Time of an Emergency'
     66
   'Music' 57, 58, 59, 61, 410–11
   and the 'New York School' 58
   'Personal Poem' 57, 61, 71, 74, 77,
     414–15
   'Personism: A Manifesto' 60, 70–2
   'Poem' ('Khruschev is coming on the
     right day!') 413–14
   'Poem' ('Lana Turner has collapsed!')
     57, 76–7, 419–20
   'Radio' 421–2
   'Rhapsody' 75, 415–16

and the Second World War 100
   'A Step Away from Them' 68, 411–12
   'Steps' 57, 74–5, 76, 77, 418–19
   'To the Film Industry in Crisis' 422–3
   'Walking' 66

Okigbo, Christopher 252, 304
   Labyrinths with Path of Thunder 200

Okri, Ben 302
   The Famished Road 299

Oldenburg, Claes 70

Olivier, Laurence 41

Olson, Charles 64

O'Meara, John J. 237

Ondaatje, Michael 302
   The English Patient 355

O'Neill, Terence 271

Onetti, Juan Carlos 188

Orange Prize 208, 255

Orlovsky, Lafcadio 82

Orlovsky, Peter 82

Orwell, George, *Nineteen Eighty-Four* 112

the Other, Levinas on the individual self and
   the Other 138–40, 141

Ovid 282

Owen, Wilfred
   in *The Ghost Road* 362–3, 376, 378–80,
     381, 384–5, 391
   in *Regeneration* 352

Padgett, Ron and Shapiro, David, *Anthology
   of New York Poets* 70

Pagetti, Carlo 127, 136

Pakenham, Thomas, *The Scramble for Africa*
   321, 322

The Panther Woman 160

Paradise (Gurnah) 199, 207, 294–340
   and African fiction 309–10, 319–20
   ambivalence in 319–20
   Arab imperialism in 310, 312–13, 314,
     315, 319, 323, 328

as *Bildungsroman* 311, 313, 337
and the Booker Prize 294, 295–310,
    333–8, 339
and colonialism 320–3, 335–6, 337
European imperialism in 310, 311–12,
    313, 314, 315, 316, 319, 323, 328,
    331–3
the Garden of Paradise in 318, 326–9,
    337
and *The Ghost Road* 344, 369
histories in 310, 313–14, 315, 316–17
languages spoken in 340
The Late Show discussion of 334–7
narrative strategies in 325–9
and postcolonialism 308, 310, 334, 336,
    337–8, 339–40
religious story of Yusef/Joseph 318, 319,
    325–6, 328, 337
representations of 'Africa' in 318,
    319–25, 337
slavery in 310, 314–15, 332
storytelling in 318, 328–33
    of Europeans 331–3
    tale of the magic jinn 329–30
trading in 314–15, 323
'The Walled Garden' 311–13
Parker, Charlie 89
Parker, Michael 262–3
Parks, Rosa 73, 125
Parmenides 108
parody, in Puig's fiction 155–6
Pasternak, Boris 211, 212
Patterson, Harriet, review of *The Ghost Road*
    356–9, 364, 382–3
Paulin, Tom 334, 335, 337
Pearse, Patrick 267
Penfield, Wilbur 109–10
Penguin Books
    and the Booker Prize shortlist 296
    and *The Ghost Road* 354
Perloff, Marjorie 60
Perón, Eva 156

Perón, Juan 156
Pfeil, Fred 144
Phillips, Caryl 317
philosophy
    and aesthetics 201–3, 205–6
    and *Do Androids Dream of Electric Sheep?*
        108–9
    and science fiction 112, 116
Pinter, Harold 249
Pirandello, Luigi, *Six Characters in Search of
    an Author* 218
Planet Stories 114
Plato 108, 244
    Crito 156
    The Republic 113
Podhoretz, Norman, 'A Howl of Protest in
    San Francisco' 81, 83
Poe, Edgar Allan 113
poetry
    and the 'Beat Generation' 57, 58,
        79–83, 86, 97
    Lehman on academic and antiacademic
        poetry 85
    and popular music 6
Pollock, Jackson 63
popular, definitions of 3, 4, 54
popular culture
    definition of 3–4
    and Ginsberg 104
    and literary judgements 200
    and O'Hara's poetry 57, 60, 61, 62, 104
        and high culture 57, 58, 62–4, 77–9
    and Puig's novels 174, 176
    and science fiction 146–7
popular literature
    definitions of 3, 5–6, 8
        and audiences 6, 8
        and categories of literature or
            culture 6
        and context 6
    and mass culture 6–8
    and minority literature 8–9

and modernism 8
and postmodernism 9
value attached to 9–11

popular music 6, 128

postcolonialism
and the Booker Prize 301, 302–10, 334,
336
Gurnah on 308–9
and historical fiction 369
and *Paradise* 308, 310, 334, 336, 337–8,
339–40

postmodernism
characteristics of 129–30, 138
definition of 155
and Dick's fiction 108, 147
Do Androids Dream of Electric Sheep?
129–36
and *The Ghost Road* 380
and historical fiction 370
and *Kiss of the Spider Woman* 155, 167,
185–6
and *Paradise* 340
and popular literature 9
postmodernist thinkers 130–2
and science fiction 108, 146
and *Waiting for Godot* 251–4

poststructuralism, and *Waiting for Godot*
250–1

Pound, Ezra 264

power relations, in *Kiss of the Spider Woman*
186–7

Powys, T.F. 7

Pratchett, Terry 109

Proust, Marcel 246

Prudhomme, Sully 210

psychoanalytic theory
and *Kiss of the Spider Woman* 172–3,
175–6, 177, 178–9
and *Rebecca* 26–30

Ptolemy 324

publishing industry, and the Booker Prize
296, 354

Puig, Manuel 5–6
background 153–4
Betrayed by Rita Hayworth 154, 157,
164, 173–4, 176, 183, 192
and the 'boom' in Latin American
fiction 187–91, 193
The Buenos Aires Affair 154–5, 157
Eternal Curse on the Reader of these Pages
163–4
on feminism 173–4
food in the novels of 176
Heartbreak Tango 154, 155, 164
and high and popular cultural forms
162–3, 182
and hybrid culture 154–5
multilingual writing 163–4
Sangre de amor corespondido 164
see also *Kiss of the Spider Woman* (Puig)

Pullman, Philip 109

Pynchon, Thomas 146

Quiller-Couch, Sir Arthur ('Q') 15

race
in Argentina 189–90
Dick's attitudes to 126–7
in *Do Androids Dream of Electric Sheep?*
124–7
and postmodernism 130
racial segregation in the USA 124–5
and *Waiting for Godot* 257

Radcliffe, Ann, *The Mysteries of Udolpho* 36,
112

Radway, Janice 9, 38, 180–1
A Feeling for Books 5

Rago, Henry 98

rational Gothic novels 112

reader-response criticism 349

realism
and non-fiction writing 372, 383
and science fiction 114

Rebecca (du Maurier) 3, 13–54, 200
class in 20, 30–3
and literary tourism 51, 52

middle-class female readership
38–9, 50
Cornwall in 14
and literary tourism 13, 51–4
costume ball scene 23, 36
as a cultural myth 51
domesticity in 26, 32–3, 40, 45
dreams in 13–14, 25–6
first draft of the epilogue 26
Hitchcock film of 13, 41–4, 47, 179
intertexts with
Mrs de Winter 13, 44–6, 47
*The Rebecca Notebook and Other
Memories* 19, 26, 47
Rebecca's Tale 13, 44, 45, 46–8, 53
and *Jane Eyre* 9, 13, 34–40, 403
as 'high text' and 'popular classic'
37–9
Hitchcock film 43, 44
and the Radio 4 Book Club 48
similarities between 34–6
and *Kiss of the Spider Woman* 165, 179,
180
Maxim's confession 24
and Menabilly/Manderley 14, 15–19,
52, 53–4
murder in 25, 26, 29, 40–1
Hitchcock film 43
and *Mrs de Winter* 45
and the Radio 4 Book Club 49, 50
narrator in
Hitchcock film 42–3
and literary tourism 52
and *Mrs de Winter* 45, 46
namelessness of 19–22
and reader identification 41, 48–50
opening chapter 13, 15–19
opening sentence 13
and personal reminiscence 14–15
as a popular classic 13, 37, 41, 49–50,
54–5
and the Radio 4 Book Club 48–51
Rebecca in 22–4, 25–6
Hitchcock film 42
and the Radio 4 Book Club 49
as romance fiction 6, 33, 39–41, 45
sales figures 41

sexuality in 22–3, 24–6
and class 30–1
Freudian theories of 26–30
Hitchcock film 42
and psychoanalytic theory 26–30
use of names and titles in 20–1
writing of a sequel to 45–6
reception theory 349, 395
religion
in Dick's fiction 119
Do Androids Dream of Electric Sheep?
140
and Ginsberg's poetry 91, 97
and O'Hara's poetry 68
in *Waiting for Godot* 237, 240–4
Remarque, Erich Maria, *All Quiet on the
Western Front* 367
Rendell, Ruth 356
Review of Contemporary Fiction 164
Rexroth, Kenneth 99
Rhys, Jean, *Wide Sargasso Sea* 37–8, 165
Richards, I.A. 163
Riefenstahl, Leni 158
Rimbaud, Arthur 82
Rivers, W.H.R.
in *The Ghost Road* 357, 358, 363–4, 370,
376, 377
and Freud 351, 370
Melanesian material 366–7, 377–8,
381–3, 386, 387–93
and 'The Primitive Conception of
Death' 386, 391–2
in *Regeneration* 351–2
Robbe-Grillet, Alain 189
Rodd, Candice, review of *The Ghost Road*
356–9, 370, 382
Rogers, Ginger, in O'Hara's poetry 75
the Rolling Stones 79
romance
defining 33
and *Kiss of the Spider Woman* 180–1

Rebecca as romance fiction 6, 33, 39–41, 45
    and the writing of a sequel 45
and *Rebecca's Tale* 46–8
women and popular romance 54

Romanticism
    and feminist aesthetics 205–6
    and Ginsberg's 'Howl' 90
    and literary creation 181, 203
    and taste 200

Ronan, Ilan 257

Rosenberg, Bernard and White, David, *Mass Culture: The Popular Arts in America* 62–4

Ross, Andrew 73, 77

Ross, Robert 352

Roszack, Theodore 175

Rowling, J.K. 109

Rushdie, Salman 189, 302, 306, 317, 359, 394
    Imaginary Homelands 317
    Midnight's Children 295, 299, 303, 355
    The Moor's Last Sigh 355
    The Satanic Verses 355
    Shame 355

Russ, Joanna 34, 113

Sachs, Nelly 213

Sackville-West, Vita 19

Sage, Lorna, 'Both Sides' (review of *The Ghost Road*) 360, 365–8, 373, 383–4, 385

Said, Edward, *Culture and Imperialism* 304

Sarmiento, Domingo, *Civilization and Barbarism* 190

Sartre, Jean-Paul
    and Beckett 213–14
    Being and Nothingness 245
    and existentialism 244, 245, 246, 248
    and the Nobel Prize for Literature 212–13, 214
    'A Plea for Intellectuals' 212–13

Sassoon, Siegfried
    in *The Eye in the Door* 353, 388
    in *The Ghost Road* 362, 365, 383
    in *Regeneration* 351, 372
    'Survivors' 365

Satie, Erik 63

Scanlan, Margaret 361, 362

Schechner, Richard 257

Schindler, Oskar 375, 383

Schorer, Mark 99

Schwitters, Kurt 90

science fiction 6
    definitions of 112–17
    fans 129, 145, 146
    and gender 112, 113, 144–5
    genre of 109–17
    historical timeframe of 113
    and McCarthyism 117–18
    magazines 113–14
    as popular or high culture 146–7

Science Fiction Studies 130

Science Wonder Stories 114

Scientific Detective Monthly 114

scientification, and Gernsback's *Amazing Stories* 113–14

Scott, Paul 350
    Staying On 297, 298, 302

Scott, Ridley 143

Scottish novels, and the Booker Prize 333

Second World War
    and France 233–6
    and the USA 100

Seferis, Giorgos 212

the self, Levinas on the individual self and the Other 138–40, 141

Selznick, Harry O. 42

sexuality
    and postmodernism 130
    and race 126
    see also female sexuality; homosexuality

Shaftesbury, Lord 200

Shakespeare, William 5, 7, 8, 201

Shapiro, David *see* Padgett, Ron and Shapiro, David

Shaw, George Bernard 238

Shelley, Mary, *Frankenstein* 111, 113

Shelley, Percy Bysshe 93, 265
    'Adonais' 90
    'Ode to the West Wind' 90
    'The Sensitive Plant' 379, 380

Shephard, Ben, *A War of Nerves* 370

Sheriff, Abdul 322

Shils, Edward 78

Sholokov, Mikhail 213

Shrader, Paul 158

Shklovsky, Viktor, concept of *ostranenie* (defamiliarization) 115

Simak, Clifford D. 147

Simmons, James 264

Singer, Alan and Dunn, Allen, *Literary Aesthetics* 201

Smart, Christopher, 'Jubilate Agno' 90–1

Smith, Grafton Elliot 351

Smith, Patti 79

Snow White 44

Sobel, Bernard 223

social inequalities, and Ginsberg's poetry 58, 59

Solomon, Carl, and Ginsberg's 'Howl' 87, 89–90

Sontag, Susan 256

Soviet Union, and wartime France 235

Soyinka, Wole 308

Spenser, Edmund
    The Faerie Queene 275
    and Heaney's poetry 275–6
    The Shepheard's Calendar 275
    'A View of the Present State of Ireland' 275, 276, 424

Spielberg, Steven 143–4

Spillane, Mickey, *One Lonely Night* 97

Stallworthy, Jon 385

Stanley, Henry Morton 319, 322

Star Trek 111, 129, 145

Star Wars 111

Stein, Kevin 64–5, 72

Sternberg, Joseph von 189

Stoker, Bram, *Dracula* 25

Stonewall riots (1969), and O'Hara's poetry 73

Storey, John, 'Mass Culture in America: The Post-War Debate' 77–8

Strangers in a Strange Land 317

Strindberg, August 210

Strongman, Luke, *The Booker Prize and the Legacy of Empire* 304

Sturgeon, Theodore 146, 147

supernatural Gothic novels 112

Suvin, Darko 142, 143
    'Cognition and Estrangement' 115–17

Swift, Graham 368

Swingtime 75

Sykes, Robert 288

Synge, J.M. 237

Tagore, Rabindranath 211–12

Talese, Gay 374

taste
    definition 200
    and novel-reading 347

Taylor, D.J. 303, 360

Taylor, Elizabeth 75

television
    and the Booker Prize 296, 334–7
    and science fiction 111

Tennyson, Alfred, 'In Memoriam' 67–8

Theatre of the Absurd, and *Waiting for Godot* 248–50

Thomas, Edward 385

Thompson, Denys, *Culture and Environment* 7

Thousand and One Nights 156–7

Times Literary Supplement 356

Tippu Tip 323, 324

Tiptree, James 113, 147

Tittler, Jonathan 178

Todd, Richard, *Consuming Fictions* 303–4

Tolkien, J.R.R. 109

Tolstoy, Leo 8, 168

Total Recall 147

Tourneur, Jacques 158, 159, 179

Tremain, Rose, *Restoration* 361–2

Triumph of the Will 158

Truman, Harry S. 100, 101

Turing, Alan 137

Turner, Lana, in O'Hara's poetry 74, 75, 76–7

Tynan, Kenneth 239–40

Uhlmann, Anthony 235

USA
    in the 1940s and 1950s 100–4
    American Civil War 126
    anti-communism and McCarthyism 81, 100, 101, 117–18, 146
    and 'non-fiction novels' 374
    Puig and US popular culture 186
    race relations 124–6
    see also cold war

Unknown 114

Unsworth, Barry
    Morality Play 355
    Sacred Hunger 355

utopian writings, as science fiction 113

Vargas Llosa, Mario 188

Vaughan, Paul 353, 369

Verlaine, Paul 66

Verne, Jules 113, 144

Vesalius, Andreas, *On the Fabric of the Human Body* 286–7

Vinci, Leonardo da 78

Virgil, and Heaney's poetry 285

visual arts, and O'Hara's poetry 63–4, 78

Waiting for Godot (Beckett) 199, 215–58
    action 229–33
    and the audience 217, 218–19, 225, 236
    Beckett's authorship of 216, 256–7
    critics on 239–40, 254–5
    dialogue 225–9, 250–1
    and ideas 239–54
        existentialism 240, 244–8
        postmodernism 251–4
        poststructuralism 250–1
        religion 237, 240–4
        the Theatre of the Absurd 248–50
    monologues 229
    and the Nobel Prize for Literature 214, 255–6
    overall structure 218–20
    performances
        Dublin (1988) 222
        English productions 215, 221, 239–40
        film version 215–16, 220, 237, 256
        French productions 215, 223, 239
        and gender 256–7
        Germany (Berlin, 1975) 215, 221, 256
        and racial and ethnic conflicts 257
    protagonists 224–5, 247–8
    setting 220–4
    social/political contexts 233–9
        Irish 236–9
        postwar France 235–6
    text
        English version 215, 216, 231–2, 233

French version 215, 216, 231, 232–3
German version 215, 216
as theatre about theatre 231, 239
uncertainties in 219, 235–6, 239–40, 253, 254
use of theatrical conventions 215, 216–18, 229–31

Walcott, Derek, 'The Muse of History' 339, 340

Walden, George 356, 359–60, 368, 395

Waldron, Mal 69, 70

Wallace, Edgar 7

Walsh, John 359

Walsh, J.S. 240

Walt Disney cartoons, Marxist critics on 10

war
in Ginsberg's poetry 101–2, 103–4
see also First World War; Second World War

Ward, Geoff 70, 72

Warhol, Andy 60, 70

Warren, Vincent 78

Warrick, Patricia, 'Mechanical Mirrors, the Double, and Do Androids Dream of Electric Sheep?' 134

Waugh, Patricia 373

Weldon, Fay 144, 147

Welles, Orson 41

Wells, H.G. 113, 114
'Scientific Romances' 111–12

Westfahl, Gary 113

White, David see Rosenberg, Bernard and White, David

Whitman, Walt 71, 146
and Ginsberg's poetry 92–3
Leaves of Grass 92
'Song of Myself' 92

Wilde, Oscar 238
Salome 352

'The Decay of Lying' 345, 346

Williams, Raymond, Keywords: A Vocabulary of Culture and Society 3–5

Williams, William Carlos 64, 71, 90
introduction to Ginsberg's Howl and Other Poems 96–7

Windeby Girl, and Heaney's poetry 277, 279, 280, 283–4

Winton, Tim, The Riders 355

Witt-Diamant, Ruth 98

Wolfe, Gary, Critical Terms for Science Fiction and Fantasy 112

Wolfe, Tom 374

Woman of the Port 159

women
actors in Waiting for Godot 256–7
in Barker's novels 367
and domesticity 32
English literature and writings by 5
judging women's literature 208
and Kiss of the Spider Woman 159–60, 193
Latin American women writers 188
and popular romance 54
and science fiction
female characters 112, 145
female writers of 113, 145
see also femininity; gender

Wood, James 337

Woolf, Virginia 7, 66, 252, 373
'How Should One Read a Book?' 345–6, 347
Mrs Dalloway 6
Orlando 19, 361
A Room of One's Own 38

Worlds of Tomorrow 119

Wright, James 64

Wuthering Heights, film version of 41

Yeats, W.B. 237
and Heaney 263, 267, 270–1, 289
'Meditations in Time of Civil War' 270, 276

and the Nobel Prize for Literature 284
'The Rose Tree' 267
'The Scholars' 289
'The Stare's Nest by My Window'
    270–1

Yugen 7 70

Zanzibar
    and *Paradise* 294, 314, 317
        hinterland of 320–2, 323–5
Zegel, Sylvian 239
Zinne, Howard 101
Zinnes, Harriet 60
Zinoman, Joy 257